# Black Defenders of America

# 1775-1973

## A Reference and Pictorial History

# BLACK DEFENDERS OF AMERICA

# 1775-1973

## Robert Ewell Greene

 Johnson Publishing Company Inc. Chicago: 1974

Printed in the United States of America
Type set in Sabon and in Helvetica display faces.
Design, typography and cover design by Norman L. Hunter

Library of Congress Cataloguing in Publication Data
Greene, Robert Ewell, 1931–
    Black Defenders of America, 1775–1973
    Bibliography, p.
        1. United States—Armed Forces—Negroes.
I. Title.              Oct. 3, 1974
E185.63.073      355.1      73–15607
ISBN 0–87485–053–3

*To my patient family*
*Joyce, Robert II and David*
*and to my parents*
*Ruth, Rose and Arthur*

## Photograph Credits

The majority of the pictures in this book are included through the courtesy of the Department of Defense, Public Affairs Office and the Pictorial Sections of the Information Offices of the Departments of the Navy, Army and Air Force and the Marine Corps and United States Coast Guard. Pictures not supplied by the Department of Defense have been copied from non-copyrighted sources located in the Library of Congress.

# CONTENTS

# FOREWORDS

**1.** One picture is worth a thousand words . . . *Black Defenders of America* is already a rare volume by its very nature. From close association with the development of this volume, I can attest to the extensive, meticulous research which has brought forth the wealth of rare documents and photographs presented herein by Major Greene.

This book essays to bring true color tones into American military history. It attempts to balance out the omissions which, by design or otherwise, have prevented accurate portrayals in study after study and volume after volume.

Fortunately, there is now a favorable tide demanding the truth and the whole truth. This pictorial history is most timely in helping to meet the demand for the full, accurate portrayal of historical fact. It brings forward witness after witness to assert, through military service and sacrifice, that all blood is red, and that "of one blood" we all live and move and have our being.

James C. Evans
*Counsellor, Office of the Secretary of Defense*
*The Pentagon*   July 4, 1970.

2. In broad perspective, *Black Defenders of America* is a comprehensive and serious contribution to the slowly growing scholarly position that the study of war involves more than a recital of campaigns and strategy by writers of narrow military background, defending a policy, or striving to use military history for didactic purposes in the military establishment. It appears to be the position of Major Greene that historiography must recognize that war is and has been too significant a cultural phenomenon to be ignored or minimized any longer by the professional historian. The major is to be commended for blending his professional military experience with his scholarly training as an historian to create a work which through the extensive use of photographs and biographies affords us an overview of a significant segment of the social history of the United States. But my many discussions with Major Greene have convinced me that his work, implicitly at least, is a document with wider implications. *Black Defenders of America* may be viewed as broadening the foundation for the thesis that much of the success in western territorial expansion (this includes the "winning of the West" as well as, for example, British conquest of India) was due to the capacity of western powers to mobilize indigenous manpower for military conquest of their own people. This is a thesis which requires major revisions in the interpretation of world history over the last five hundred years; this work will facilitate those revisions.

*Black Defenders of America* in a narrow, but just as fundamental perspective, addresses itself to the problem both of enriching the history of blacks in the military affairs of the United States and of filling gaps in the narrative of their role. I believe it was a wise choice to incorporate biographies from all of the military services, including the coast guard. Students of military history are aware of differing responses of the armed services to demands for black participation. For example, the marine corps excluded blacks in its original statutory authority and the attitudes of the various branches of the service in the 1940's to integration varied and often depended upon the personal views at cabinet level.

*Black Defenders of America* is also a contribution, I repeat, to the social history of the United States and thus avoids the temptation to become as partisan and as narrow as some of the works which Major Greene so effectively neutralizes.

Harold O. Lewis
*Professor of History    Howard University*
*Washington, D.C.*    July, 1973.

# AUTHOR'S PREFACE

There is in America a new awareness of the importance of Negro history. Every day, more material is becoming available to add to the sum of our knowledge of the role of the Negro in the military history of the United States. Information exists in contemporary volumes and in military and state archives, but the black defenders who have served their country with fidelity, bravery and distinction from its earliest days are largely overlooked in currently published histories.

This partial account of Negro military personnel in the armed forces from 1775 until 1973 is presented as a reference and guide for those who want to learn the truth about America's neglected black soldiers, sailors, marines and airmen. Using pictures and documented biographies, an attempt has been made to illustrate the black American's presence in past and present wars.

Throughout history, man has established governments, dynasties, kingdoms and empires. The security and defense of these establishments has depended on the men who bore arms. In pre-Colonial days, black men were to be seen in America, not as conquerors or colonizers, but as servants who fought only in defense of their masters. As the American colonies were settled, the need for laborers was met by using black slaves and when these colonies united in 1775 and decided to form an independent union, black men contributed blood as well as labor to their masters' cause and fought for freedom, even though their own shackles were still intact. Crispus Attucks, Salem Poor and Seymour Burr are now well-known, but in these pages some less familiar names are introduced.

In post-Revolutionary Louisiana, the Negro assisted in developing and defending the new territory. During the War of 1812, the records relate the gallant exploits of the black Corps D'Afrique. Historians have asserted that there is no record of black participation in the Mexican Wars, but in those years, 1846 to 1848, as can be seen from this volume, there were Negroes serving both on land and sea. From 1850 to 1860, black Americans served mainly in the navy, but in 1861, with the outbreak of the Civil War, blacks became not only the center of controversy but were a major factor in the armies of both the Union and Confederate forces. In the South, black labor made possible the construction of fortifications and bridges, the staffing of hospitals, and the construction of plantations left to the care of black overseers when their owners went to war. Negroes also accompanied their masters to the battlefield, serving as cooks and body servants. On the Union side, black soldiers were present at all the major battles and distinguished themselves with heroism on many occasions. Civil War veterans often continued their careers in the militia, or turned to politics in the brief flowering of the Reconstruction period. In South Carolina at least nine black men became general officers.

The western territories of the United States were not acquired without help from black soldiers, scouts, and guides. Many Negroes who had intermarried with Indian tribes, in particular the Seminole Negro Indians, rode the plains with the white troopers who subdued and subsequently defended America's expanding possessions.

The Spanish-American war, which started with the sinking of the *USS Maine,* saw the United States calling both black and white men to arms. The Negro National Guard of America was formed and a black colonel served in Cuba with a composite regiment. The first troops to occupy the famous San Juan Hill were black. Black military service was minimal from 1900 until World War I, although Negro soldiers served with Roosevelt and his Rough Riders and in the Philippines. National Guard units returned to inactive status, and the Ninth and Tenth Cavalry and the Twenty-Fourth Infantry regiments were the only Negro regular army units on active service. In 1917, when America entered World War I, black troops were recruited and distinguished themselves in France and in naval actions.

In World War II black soldiers, still serving in segregated units, earned distinguished records in Europe and the Pacific, although none were awarded the Medal of Honor. The Korean War, however, saw the beginning of desegregation in the armed forces; the first Medal of Honor in this conflict was awarded to a black soldier, PFC Thompson. The Twenty-Fourth Infantry Regiment's glorious career ended with integration but not before the regiment had achieved the honor of being the first to engage the enemy in combat.

In 1962, the United States was again involved in an Asian conflict and in the war in Vietnam black soldiers for the first time served on equal terms with their white comrades and the military offered a road to success to the career black officer. Today black soldiers can look back on a checkered history, where the hero of one day was the slave of the next. The situation today has its imperfections, but it can be said that the years of the black soldier's patriotism and devotion to his country's cause, so often thankless and unrewarded, have brought him status, equality and dignity in the armed services.

It is the intent of this book to present the history of this journey towards recognition and equality, to detail facts both glorious and inglorious that prove and illustrate the presence of black soldiers from the days of the earliest settlers in the United States of America.

Robert E. Greene
July, 1973

# ACKNOWLEDGMENTS

I will deviate from the normal procedure and acknowledge not a few but many persons. I wish to thank the following people for their contributions in making this manuscript possible.

Kenneth Allen
Sherry Alston
Dudley Ball
Albert U. Blair
Cornelius Boykin
Maxie M. Berry Jr.
John Calhoun
John Cole
William O. Davis
Martha B. Dellinger
Joseph Dinda
Ralph W. Donnelly
James C. Evans
Robert E. Feeney
John L. Ferguson
Virginia Fincik
Leo Flaherty
Norman J. Furth
Joseph Greco, Jr.
Anthony J. Leon Guerrero
Milt Harris
Mary Tarrah Herrick
Cleo A. Hughes
Pauline Irvine
Joseph Israeloff
Sara Dunlap Jackson
Phebe R. Jacobsen
Francis W. Jennings
Edward N. Johnson
Mary Johnson
Albert Kisho

Dorothy Latham
Edward Lewis
Raymond Lewis
William E. Lind
Morris J. MacGregor
Joanne Mattern
Delris Moore
Joseph K. Mosely
Elmer Omata
Elmer Parker
Larry D. Phillips
Dorothy B. Porter
Hubert E. Potter
Charlotte S. Price
Kenneth Rapp
Charlotte Ray
Charles F. Ramanus
Doris E. Saunders
Paul Scheips, Jr.
Aline Skinner
Robert Slocum
Major Smith
Bettie Sprigg
Isabelle J. Swartz
Jean Waggener
James D. Walker
George Washington
Wylma Wates
William West
Ralph Young

I am most grateful for the excellent assistance and support that I received from members of the staff of the following institutions and organizations consulted during the writing of this book.

National Archives, Washington, D.C.

Library of Congress, Washington, D.C.

South Carolina Department of Archives and History, Columbus, South Carolina

Historical Society of Delaware, Old Town Hall Wilmington, Delaware

Hall of Records, Annapolis, Maryland

Department of Archives and History Atlanta, Georgia

Tennessee State Library and Archives Nashville, Tennessee

U.S. Army Photographic Agency Pentagon, Washington, D.C.

Office of Chief of Military History Department of the Army Washington, D.C.

Patton Museum Fort Knox, Kentucky

Audio Visual Division Office of the Secretary of Defense Pentagon, Washington, D.C.

WAC Director's Office Pentagon, Washington, D.C.

Public Information Office Fort George C. Meade, Maryland

Manassas National Battlefield Park
  Manassas, Virginia

The Associated Publishers
  Washington, D.C.

The Association for the Study of Negro Life and
  History, Inc.

Public Libraries
  Washington, D.C.

Department of the Navy
  Office of Information
  Pentagon, Washington, D.C.

Technical Information Office
  Surgeon's Office
  Department of the Army
  Washington, D.C.

Office of Deputy Chief of Staff Intelligence
  U.S. Air Force

Magazine and Book Section
  Air Force University Library
  Maxwell Air Force Base
  Montgomery, Alabama

United States Marine Corps
  Equal Opportunity Branch
  Washington, D.C.

National Guard Bureau
  Pentagon, Washington, D.C.

National Guard Association
  Building Library
  Washington, D.C.

Public Library
  Fairfax, Virginia

Moorland Room, Founders Library
  Howard University, Washington, D.C.

Adjutant General's U.S. Army Library
  Pentagon, Washington, D.C.

State of Mississippi
  Department of Archives and History
  Jackson, Mississippi

The Airman, Official Magazine of the U.S. Air
  Force
  Bolling Air Force Base,
  Washington, D.C.

State of Alabama, Military Records Division
  Department of Archives and History
  Montgomery, Alabama

Texas State Library
  Texas Archives and Library Building
  Austin, Texas

Kentucky Historical Society
  Frankfort, Kentucky

State of Missouri
  Office of the Secretary of State
  Records and Management and Archives Service
  Jefferson City, Missouri

State of Florida, Department of State
  Division of Archives, History and Records Man-
    agement
  Tallahassee, Florida

Louisiana Landmarks Society, Inc.
  New Orleans, Louisiana

The Commonwealth of Massachusetts
  Archives Division
  Office of the Secretary, State House,
  Boston

The Historical Unit
  U.S. Army Medical Department
  Forrest Glen Section
  Walter Reed Army Medical Center
  Washington, D.C.

Archives, Department of the Army
  United States Military Academy

Headquarters, U.S. Army Field
  Artillery Center and Fort Sill, Oklahoma
  Information Office

Headquarters, Military District of Washington
  Public Information Office

Department of the Navy
  Headquarters, U.S. Marine Corps
  History Division Records
  Washington, D.C.

United States Coast Guard
  Public Information Office and Minority Section

Arkansas Historical Commission
  Old State House
  Little Rock, Arkansas

Commonwealth of Virginia
   Virginia State Library
   Richmond, Virginia

Virginia Polytechnic Institute
   Department of History
   Blacksburg, Virginia

State of North Carolina
   Department of Archives and History
   Raleigh, North Carolina

U.S. Army Reserve Magazine Office
   Pentagon, Washington, D.C.

*Army Digest Magazine*
   Office of Chief of Information
   Department of Army
   Washington, D.C.

Army Times Publishing Company
   Washington, D.C.

Air Force Audio Visual Service
   Still Picture Branch
   Arlington, Virginia

Georgetown University
   Reference Library
   Washington, D.C.

Military Division (War Records)
   Commonwealth of Massachusetts
   State House,
   Boston, Massachusetts

The University of Texas
   Institute of Texan Cultures
   San Antonio, Texas

I am most appreciative of the superb copying of non copyright photographs by photographer Brian D. McLarnon of Weymouth, Massachusetts.

I sincerely thank Walter S. Roach and those patient and efficient young ladies, Mary Duarte, Janice Jasmer, and Charlene Coleman, whose secretarial assistance has been invaluable.

My appreciation is also hereby expressed to those wonderful persons who have assisted me and may have been inadvertently excluded.

I wish to thank my wife, Joyce, for her understanding and unswerving support that have made this manuscript become a reality.

Last but not least I cordially thank my editor, Brenda M. Biram, for her untiring patience, understanding and scholarly expertise in the editing of this manuscript.

R.E.G.

# Chapter One

## The American Revolution, 1775-1783

In 1775 a nation was emerging. The citizens of the Massachusetts colony were setting a course for a war that would decide the fate of a nation. Among these concerned citizens was Crispus Attucks, a black man who gave his life for his beliefs. Once the colonies decided to rebel against the oppressive rule of England, many black men joined the militia. They appeared in the handsome uniform of the Colonial forces and their names were officially entered on the muster roles.

Attucks, Burr, Lew, Ranger, Poor, Forten, Armistead, Haynes, Tarrant, Whipple, Cromwell, Matthews, Flora, Salem, Charleston, and Robinson are a few of those revolutionary black heroes. Their names are recalled here and listed along with those of other black men who served as waiters, body servants, soldiers, sailors, drummers and fifers, but above all as loyal Americans.

The southern colonies—Virginia, North and South Carolina, Maryland and Georgia—were well represented by black soldiers. The eastern colonies had some integrated units and some all-black companies under white leadership.

During the American Revolution, General George Washington issued an order forbidding the recruiting of Negroes, but only a month later (in December, 1775) reversed the order, and black men continued to serve until the end of the war. There were black marines as well as black soldiers; and there were black men serving on privateers and warships. It was during the Revolutionary War that black men were introduced into the armed services, and here began their history of achievements and of heroism which has to a great extent been omitted from books of American history. However, the facts are to be found in the records, and are published here as a reminder that American blacks were a part of the glorious "spirit of 76."

## William Appleby

Recruit, Colonel Thomas Ewing's Battalion for the Flying Camp.

A document in the Maryland Hall of Records indicates that men enrolled by Captain James Bond, Lieutenant John Smith, Captain James Young and Ensign James Tool to compose one company in Colonel Thomas Ewing's battalion for the Flying Camp, August, 1776, included a William Appleby, with "black, curled hair, enlisted at age twenty-four, was from Baltimore County, and born in America.[1]

## Crispus Attucks

Patriot, Boston Massacre.

The name of Crispus Attucks has been immortalized as the first black American to die for his country in the days before the American Revolution. Some authors have spoken of Attucks as a soldier, but he was not a member of any militia or army. He was born about 1723 in the vicinity of Cocetuate Lake, Framingham, Massachusetts, probably of Negro and Indian parentage. He has been described as a well-proportioned mulatto with curly hair, and at the time of his death was about forty-seven. The following story relates the actual occurrences on March 7, 1770 which eventually caused the death of America's first known black patriot.

*Early on the evening of the fifth a quarrel took place between a barber's boy and a redcoat (British soldier) when the latter was accused by the former of not having paid his bill for a hair cut. The boy received a blow on the head for this taunt*

which made him cry out with pain. Following this event a number of soldiers came up, threatening to kill everyone in sight, and another boy was knocked down. By this time the excitement was so great that the alarm bell at the head of King street was rung. This, of course, brought out a number of people, both citizens and English troops. Partly through the interference of well-disposed officers and partly through the courage of Crispus Attucks, a mulatto, this affray was soon over.

The indignation of the populace was at a high pitch, however, and while some of the cooler heads were for going home, many others were for an immediate attack upon the quarters of the main guard, or the "Nest," as they called it, located on the green or common. So, bent on avenging their wrongs and "led" by Attucks, the wrathful townfolk pressed on, the crowd growing larger and larger each minute. Many boys and youths fell into line. Some, like the barber's boy, fomented their anger as they proceeded by the recital of personal affronts from the soldiers. Up what was then King street they went, crying out, "Let us drive out these ribalds. They have no business here." At the custom house the band, still led by the mulatto, assailed the sentinel with snowballs, pieces of ice or anything else that could be used as missiles. So furiously did they do this that their victims called for the guard, and the corporal and a few soldiers were sent to protect them. These were met by the patriots, who in warm language dared them to fire. As a result the noise and confusion were terrific. Men howled and swore, and bells rang. The soldiers awaited the order to fire, knowing full well that under existing circumstances it should come from a civil magistrate. It is impossible to tell whether Attucks and those with him knew this fact or not. At any rate he, with twelve of the men, began to strike upon the muskets of the soldiers with clubs and to taunt them with being afraid to fire and crying to the people behind them, "Be not afraid; they dare not fire. Why do you hesitate? Why do you not kill them? Why not crush them at once?" Whereupon Captain Preston came up and attempted to disperse the crowd. Attucks struck at the English officer's head, who warded off the blow with his hand. Just then a soldier's musket fell to the ground and Attucks seized it. A struggle followed between the two men for its possession, and the owner was either knocked down or else he fell to the ground. At this time voices in the crowd took up the cry, "Why don't you fire?" Upon hearing these words the soldier, struggling to his feet, fired as he arose and the brave Crispus, leaning upon a stick, received two balls in each breast. These caused his death. More firing occurred and three others were immediately killed. They were Caldwell, Maverick and Gray. Five persons were dangerously injured and several slightly hurt.

The dead men were regarded as heroes and a

*The death of Crispus Attucks
on March 7, 1770.*

public funeral was given them, the rites being celebrated in the most solemn manner as a manifesta-
tion of the sorrow and the regret felt by the people
for their death. The service for all three* of them
was held at the same hour in Faneuil Hall on the
8th of March, the bells of Roxbury, Boston and of
Charlestown being tolled meanwhile. The three
processions, made up of carriages in which rode
distinguished men and friends of the victims, met
at King street and wound their way to Middle

Burying Ground on Tremont street, a few steps
from the head of the Boston Common. Here the
bodies were interred in one tomb, located in the
extreme northeastern corner of the cemetery.

The spot on which Attucks fell, located on what
is now State street, somewhat to the east of the old
State House, is today marked by an arrow em-
bedded in the sidewalk. On the Boston Common
stands a monument of granite erected in honor of
the men who fell in the massacre.

Attucks always received due credit for his patriotism on these occasions, from even such men as
Hancock and Washington . . .[2]

* The body of one was claimed by friends and buried out of
Boston.

## William Balontino

Private, Second Rhode Island Regiment.

William Balontino was a resident of Anne Arundel County, Maryland. At the age of twenty-five he enlisted in the army for three years. The official record listed his description as "hair: black, complexion: mulatto." He served during the American Revolution in a unit from the state of Maryland.[3]

## Stephen Bond

Crew Member, schooner *Defence*.

The Revolutionary War service of Stephen Bond is documented in a record which is presently on file in the South Carolina archives. The record stated that "The Public of South Carolina" paid to Stephen Bond, a free Negro, the sum of £44.10 as wages for two months and five days on board the schooner *Defence* in 1776, at the rate of £21 a month.[4]

## Charles Bowles

Enlisted Soldier.

Charles Bowles, a black man, was born in Boston, Massachusetts, in 1761. His father was the son of Colonel Morgan, an officer in the American Army Rifle Corps. At the age of twelve he was placed in the family of a Tory, and at the age of fourteen he was serving in the Colonial army as waiter to an officer. Not appreciating this situation, Bowles enlisted in the American army and served for the entire war. After the war, with a pension for his services, he moved to New Hampshire and became a Baptist preacher. Bowles died on March 16, 1843, at the age of eighty-two.[5]

## Scipio Brown

Private, Drummer and Musician, Rhode Island Regiment.

Scipio Brown, a black, enlisted on May 1, 1778 in the Rhode Island Regiment commanded by Colonels Christopher Greene and Jeremiah Olney. He filed for a pension on April 8, 1818, while a resident of Scituate, Rhode Island. On February 16, 1834, he died at the age of about seventy-seven. Brown was one of numerous musicians who served during the Revolutionary War.[6]

## George Buley (also Bewley)

Private, Captain David Lynn's Company, Colonel Thomas Woolford's Maryland Regiment.

George Buley was born in 1761 in Prince George's County, Maryland. Records in the year 1855 state that he was a free colored man. On March 10, 1781, he enlisted in the Revolutionary Army. He was present at the siege of Yorktown and the surrender of Cornwallis. Later he was assigned the task of guarding prisoners to Fredericksburg, Virginia. Buley was discharged on December 3, 1781 and after the war moved to Dorchester County, Maryland. He received a pension from the government and the state of Maryland. He was married to Grace Cromwell on June 18, 1824, at Cambridge, Dorchester County, Maryland and died on August 15, 1836 or 1837, at Schoal Creek, Dorchester County.[7]

## Seymour Burr

Seventh Massachusetts Regiment.

Seymour Burr was born a slave and belonged to Colonel Aaron Burr. He served in the Seventh Massachusetts Regiment, commanded by Colonel Brooks, and was present at the siege of Fort Catskill and at Bunker Hill. After the war he moved to Canton, Massachusetts and married a Punkapog Indian. He received a pension from the government.[8]

## Isaac Carr

Private, Second Maryland Regiment.

Isaac Carr was born in Montgomery County, Maryland, and served in a Maryland unit. He enlisted, at the age of twenty, on March 6, 1782, for a term of three years. The official record described him as having black hair, being five foot seven inches tall, with a complexion "yellow molato" (mulatto).[9]

## Noel Carrière

Sub-Lieutenant, Bernardo de Galves' Troops.

Noel Carrière served under Colonel Bernardo de Galves of the New Orleans Permanent Regiment, who became governor of Louisiana in 1779. Carrière was freed in 1777 and married Marianne Thomas, a free Negro woman. They had several children, and one son, Noel, served as a commissioned officer in the Colored Militia. The elder Noel always signed his name with "Negro libre" (free Negro) or its abbreviation, N.L. He was awarded a medal by the Spanish royal house for his services to the crown, and was later promoted to captain.[10]

### Samuel Charlton

Private, Teamsters.

Samuel Charlton was born a slave in the state of New Jersey. He was sent to war at the age of sixteen to serve as a substitute for his master. He saw active service at Monmouth and participated in several other engagements in different parts of the state. Charlton was a great admirer of General Washington and was, at one time, attached to his baggage train when he received the general's commendation for devotion to duty. At the conclusion of the conflict Charlton returned to his master in New Jersey and continued to serve in bondage. Upon his master's death he received his freedom and moved to New York with his wife and son. Samuel Charlton was a member of the Dutch Reformed Church. He died at the age of eighty, in 1843.[11]

### Caesar Clark

Private, Captain Brown's Company, Colonel John Durham's Connecticut Regiment.

Caesar Clark was born in Africa and enlisted in the army in 1777 at Ashford, Connecticut. He was present at the battles of Mud Fort, Germantown and Monmouth. He served until June, 1783, and it has been stated that he was at Valley Forge in the winter of 1777–78. After the war, Mr. Clark moved to Montiville, Connecticut, and received a pension.[12]

### Jack (Coburn)

A microfilm copy of the state of Kentucky's Vital Statistics, Deaths, 1852–1861, Mason County, indicated that a male servant named Jack, of Germantown, Kentucky, died at the age of one hundred, of apoplexy, on December 27, 1852. The name of his parent or owner was given as Dr. John Coburn and under remarks was written: "In the Revolutionary War."[13]

### George Cooper

Crew member, schooner *Defence*.

The Revolutionary War service of George Cooper is documented in a record which is on file in the South Carolina Archives and states that "The Public of South Carolina" paid George Cooper, a free Negro for one month and six days on board the schooner *Defence* at £21 a month.[14]

### Richard Cozzens

Fifer, Second Company, First Battalion, Rhode Island Regiment.

Richard Cozzens was born in Africa. He enlisted in the regiment commanded by Colonel Christopher Greene for the duration of the war and served for five years under the command of Colonel Greene and of Colonel Jeremiah Olney. He was discharged at Saratoga, in the state of New York. The official muster roll of the Second Company of the First Battalion of Rhode Island forces in the service of the United States (Colonel Christopher Greene commanding), dated 1780, lists Richard Cozzens as a fifer.

The Veterans Administration files have the following information about Richard Cozzens, who died in the year 1829.

*Richard Cozzens, a man of colour, on the fifteenth day of March, 1778, enlisted for and during the war into the regiment commanded by Colonel Christopher Greene in the Rhode Island Line on the Continental establishment. That he served as fifer or musician in said regiment while commanded by Colonel Greene and afterwards by Colonel Jeremiah Olney from the time of his enlistment until the fifteenth day of June 1783, when he received a furlough granted in pursuance of a General Order issued by General Washington the second day of June 1783, which eventuated in a discharge from said regiment then commanded by said Jeremiah Olney at Saratoga in the state of New York. All of which appear by the Regimental Book of Occurrences now in my property.*

The entry is signed by Dexter State, Major of the Regiment, and dated Providence, March 10th, 1818.[15]

## Oliver Cromwell

Private, Captain Lowery's Company, Second New Jersey Regiment.

Oliver Cromwell was born on May 24, 1753, at Black Horse (now Columbus, Burlington County), New Jersey. He lived with the family of John Hutchin and was raised as a farmer. Cromwell had a light complexion and it is believed that he was never a slave. During the Revolutionary War he enlisted in a company commanded by Captain Lowery of the Second New Jersey Regiment, Colonel Israel Shreve commanding. Cromwell was present at the battles of Trenton, Princeton, Brandywine, Monmouth and Yorktown and at the memorable crossing of the Delaware on December 25, 1776. Upon his discharge from the army, he received an annual pension of ninety-six dollars. He had fourteen children and saw his grandchildren to the third generation. Cromwell died in Columbus on January 24, 1853, and was laid to rest in the churchyard of Broad Street Methodist church.[16]

## Austin Dabney

Artilleryman, Colonel Elijah Clark's Corps.

Austin Dabney's early life is vividly described in Gilmer's *Sketches of First Settlers of Upper Georgia:*

*Many years before the Revolutionary War, a Virginia gentleman resided upon his plantation near Richmond. He was a bachelor who indulged in card-playing, drinking, and horseracing. He had a large estate with many Negroes. No Caucasian lived with him except a little girl, whose parentage was unknown. When the bachelor left home, the little girl remained under the care of a Negro mammy. As the little girl matured, her acquaintances were the bachelor and the Negroes of the household. Suddenly and secretly, the old gentleman left his plantation taking the little girl with him. He went to North Carolina, where he remained some time with a man named Aycock. Later Aycock moved to Georgia along with the emigrants from North Carolina who first settled Wilks County carrying with him a Mulatto boy. Aycock not desiring to fight as a soldier during the Revolutionary War, he enrolled the Mulatto boy in Clark's Corps. The Mulatto boy was called Austin Dabney. Dab-*

*ney participated in the battle of Battle Creek, Georgia and was wounded on February 4, 1779 when a musket ball passed through his thigh. He was left on the battleground and later was found by a man named Harris. Harris took him to his home and cared for Dabney during his recovery. Austin Dabney worked for Harris and his children and served them more faithfully and efficiently than any slave ever served a master. He moved with the Harris family to Madison County, Georgia. When Harris sent his oldest son to school and afterwards to college, the finances were provided by the toils of Austin Dabney. He lived upon the poorest diet and wore old patched clothes in order to assist the young Harris. When the young Harris completed Franklin College, Dabney was responsible for him obtaining a job in the office of state legislator Stephen Upson. Upson was instrumental in persuading the Georgia assembly to pass an act for Dabney to receive a pension. [In 1821, the Act was passed and Dabney was awarded 112 acres of land in Walton County, Georgia.] Austin Dabney traveled once a year to Savannah, Georgia, to obtain his pension. On one occasion as he passed the house of General Jackson, then governor of the state, who was standing in the doorway, the governor recognized Dabney. He ran into the street, seized him by the hand, drew him from his horse and carried him into his house, where he greeted him as a guest.*

*It was very strange that Austin Dabney, who never knew his grandfather, should have inherited the taste of the Virginia gentleman for horseracing. He owned fine horses, attended the race course, entered the list for stake, and betted with all the finesse of a professional.*

*Austin Dabney's protégé, young Harris, moved away from Madison County and Dabney went with him and continued to give him the devoted personal services and his property as long as he lived. Dabney died in Zebulon, Georgia.*

The life of Austin Dabney characterizes the image of many blacks born of a white mother or father and passed from one master to another. Dabney successfully escaped a lifetime of servitude. His obedience and faithfulness to the Harris family was of his own volition. Dabney was a soldier, settler and above all a man of undaunted courage and fidelity to those who had befriended him in a time of need.[17]

### Charles Davis

Private, Maryland Second Regiment.

Charles Davis was born in Baltimore, Maryland. On April 23, 1782, at the age of nineteen, he enlisted in the army, for one year. The official record lists his description as "hair: black and complexion: Negro." He served during the Revolutionary War in a unit from the state of Maryland.[18]

### Joshua Dunbar

Private, Captain Joseph Cole's Company, Colonel John Jacob's Massachusetts Regiment.

Joshua Dunbar was born in May, 1763 near Bridgewater, Massachusetts. He was the son of Sampson Dunbar of Stoughton who was about one-half African. Joshua Dunbar enlisted on January 1, 1775, and served for one year as a private in the Massachusetts Regiment. It was also stated that Dunbar had served as a cook on a privateer. After the war, he moved to Seneca, Ontario County, New York. In 1787, he married Lydia (maiden name unknown) of Cummington. Their children were John, born January 2, 1788; Polly, born December 4, 1791; Noah, born June 15, 1795; Ephraim, born March 7, 1797; Jacob, born December 27, 1799; Lydia, born December 9, 1801; Joshua Jr., born October 1, 1803, and Stephen, born January 1, 1805.

Joshua Dunbar died in 1820 at Seneca, Ontario County, New York.[19]

### Samuel Dunbar

Private, various U.S. Army regiments.

Samuel Dunbar, a black man, was born on October 14, 1764, in Braintree, Massachusetts. He enlisted at Braintree, and his army service record was as follows: three months in Captain Stevens' Massachusetts Company; six weeks in Captain Baxter's Massachusetts Company when he was in General Sullivan's Rhode Island expedition; nine months, in 1779, in Captain Jacob Noles Company, Colonel Marshall's Massachusetts Regiment during which he served for about twenty days in Captain Cooper's Company, Colonel Thomas' Regiment and was in the engagement at White Plains, New York. Dunbar was discharged in April, 1780.

While living in Crotin Manor, New York, he enlisted in April or May, 1780, and served three months in Captain Stevens' New York Company. He was granted a pension on April 15, 1832.[20]

### Prince Easterbrooks

Prince Easterbrooks was wounded during a battle at Lexington. *The Salem Gazette* or *Newberry and Marblehead Advertiser* for April 21, 1775 gives the name of Prince Easterbrook "(Negro man)" as "wounded (Lexington)."[21]

### John Featherston

Crew member, schooner *Defence*.

The revolutionary war service of John Featherston is documented in the South Carolina Archives, where a record of "The Public of South Carolina" lists payment of £63 to John Federson, a free Negro, in 1776, for three months wages aboard the schooner *Defence* at £22 a month.[22]

### Cato Fisk (also Fiske)

Private, Captain William Powell's Company, Colonel George Reid's New Hampshire Regiment.

Cato Fisk, a black, enlisted in the army in 1777 and was discharged on June 7, 1783. It was stated in his records that he was a drummer in the army and a fiddler in civilian life. On March 7, 1783 he was married to Elsa or Else Huso or Huson in Brentwood, New Hampshire. Later the couple moved to Exeter, New Hampshire. Fisk was granted a pension on an application executed on April 6, 1818, and in 1837 his wife was also allowed a pension. A James Fiske stated in 1837 that he was the eldest child of Cato Fiske and that he was born in Exeter, New Hampshire. The names of Nancy Dale, a daughter, and a son, Ebenezer, were also mentioned in the records. Cato Fisk died on March 24, 1824 at Epsom, New Hampshire.[23]

### James Forten

Powder Boy, United States Navy.

James Forten was born in Philadelphia on September 2, 1766, the son of Thomas Forten, who died when James was seven years old. He left school at the age of nine and worked at home and in a grocery store. In 1780, he joined the vessel *Royal Louis,* commanded by Stephen Decatur. Forten was taken prisoner at sea, and was fortunate not to be shipped to the West Indies for a life of servitude. He was transferred to an English vessel, the *Amphylon,* commanded by a Captain Beaseley. James became friendly with the captain's son, and he was offered the opportunity to go and live in England. However, Forten wanted to remain an American and refused to be a traitor to his country. Later he was transferred to the ship *Old Jersey,* and after seven months was able to obtain his release and to make his way to Trenton, New Jersey, where he worked as apprentice to a sailmaker until 1798. In talking about his experiences at sea Forten often remarked that "On board the *Royal Louis* were twenty colored seamen and the *Alliance, Trumbull, South Carolina, Confederacy* and the *Randolph,* were all manned in part by colored men." After the war he resided in Philadelphia, Pennsylvania, and became a wealthy anti-slavery philanthropist, supporting the work of abolitionists. He participated in the first convention of Free Negroes in Philadelphia in 1817. In the year 1842, on March 15, James Forten, powder boy in the American Revolution, former prisoner of war of the British, a free Negro who donated his last years to the cause of Negro equality, died.[24]

### Artillo Freeman

Private, Third and Fourth United States Infantry Regiments.

Artillo Freeman enlisted at Roxbury, Massachusetts, and served faithfully until he was discharged at West Point. Freeman's pension records state that he had two children and four grandchildren and was commonly called a black man. The pension files also inform us "Artillo Freeman enlisted in the service . . . and that he first acted as body servant to Colonel Hull at the town of Boston in the third regiment of United States Infantry, and later was transferred to the fourth regiment."

Freeman participated in the battles of White Plains, Monmouth, the siege of Little Fork, Virginia and a number of minor engagements. The records further state that he had a wife, aged eighty-eight years, in 1820. He had no particular

trade but picked oakum and received aid from the county and individual contributions. He applied for a pension in 1818, at the age of ninety-seven. According to the pension papers, he was ninety-nine years old in July, 1820, and died on November 12, 1837 (possibly one hundred and sixteen years old).[25]

### Call Freeman

Private, Colonel Herman Swift's Regiment.

Call Freeman, a black man born in Sharon, Litchfield County, Connecticut, was enlisted in the army in 1777 by a Captain Luther Bardoly. Freeman served on the Connecticut line until 1783. He was married to a woman named Candis and they were the parents of five children: Lumans, Cyrus, Mary, Phome and Cynthia. Cynthia was a sick child and was supported by the town of Sharon.[26]

### Casar Freeman

Private, Captain Williams' Company, Colonel Webb's Regiment.

The military pension files indicate that Casar Freeman served on the Connecticut line during the American Revolutionary War and was honorably discharged. The records also refer to a "Casar Freeman, a black man worth fifteen dollars (property in estate) a cow worth twelve dollars and seven chickens." He was married to a woman named Lemen who was fifty years old in 1818, when he was sixty-one. They lived in Oneida County, New York.[27]

### Doss Freeman

Private, Captain Bancroft and Captain Wade's Company, Colonel Michael Jackson's Massachusetts Regiment.

Doss Freeman, a black, was born in Reading, Massachusetts. He enlisted on June 2, 1777 and was discharged on December 31, 1780. He married a Sarah Davis on November 14, 1788. Doss Freeman died on August 29, 1805, in South Reading, Massachusetts.[28]

### Fortune Freeman

Private, Captain Danford's Company, Colonel Nixon's Regiment.

Fortune Freeman, a black, enlisted in 1780 at Boston, Massachusetts. He was honorably discharged on December 31, 1783. Freeman participated in the battles of Brandywine and Monmouth, and was wounded in the thigh by a musket ball at Brandywine. He was also present at the capture of General Burgoyne's army at Saratoga, and was with the campaign when Lord Cornwallis was captured. Freeman was seventy-one years old on April 25, 1818, when he filed for a pension. He had one child, Mary, who was bound out to service.[29]

### Prince Freeman

Private, Captain Bulkey's Company, Colonel Samuel P. Webb's Connecticut Regiment.

Prince Freeman, a black man, enlisted in the army in May, 1777. He was discharged from the military on June 8, 1782. The records state that he had two children named Avis and Prince. On April 10, 1818, a pension application was executed in his name, at which time he was living in Grafton, Windom County, Vermont.[30]

### Peter Galloway

Private, Colonel Butler's Regiment.

Peter Galloway enlisted in the army in June, 1777, and was honorably discharged on June 7, 1783. He married a woman named Nancy in 1785. Galloway died July 20, 1848, and in 1851, at the age of eighty-three years, Nancy Galloway requested a widow's military pension. She was living in Woodbury, Connecticut. Her brother, Cyrus Homer, aged eighty-nine, wrote a statement that he knew of Galloway's service in the army. Homer was born in Milford, Connecticut, and his former master was a Colonel Edward Allen.[31]

### Tobias Gilmore

Private, Colonel George Williams' Regiment.

Tobias Gilmore was born an African prince with the name of Shilbogee Túrry-Werry. He was sold as a slave on an auction block at Newport to a Captain Gilmore of Taunton, Massachusetts. He enlisted as a private in 1776 and at one time served as one of General Washington's bodyguards. After the war he received a section of land and a cannon for his faithful service. Each Independence Day, Tobias Gilmore would take his cannon to Taunton Green and fire once for each of the thirteen original states, and once for Washington. This cannon was later presented to the Taunton Historical Society. As late as 1918, the Gilmore cannon was in the possession of the historical society.[32]

### Jude Hall

Private.

Jude Hall, a black, was a native of Exeter, New Hampshire. He joined the Colonial army during the American Revolution and served a total of eight years. He was known to have been at Bunker Hill, and was referred to as "Old Rock."[33]

### Primus Hall (also Primus Trask)

Private, Captain Joseph Butler's Company, Colonels John and Thomas Nixon's Massachusetts Regiment, Captain Samuel Flint's Company, Colonel Johnson's Massachusetts Regiment, and Captain Woodburg's Company of Massachusetts Troops.

Primus Hall was the son of Prince, a free man, and Delia, who was a servant in the family of a Mr. Walker. He was born February 29, 1756 on Beacon Street in Boston, Massachusetts. At the age of one month, he was given to Mr. Ezra Trask, resident of Beverly, Essex County, Massachusetts. At the age of fifteen, Primus was released from his apprenticeship to a shoemaker and in January, 1776 he enlisted in the army. He participated in the retreat from Governor's Island, and in skirmishes at Rattlesnake Hill, Harlem Heights, Mile Square and at the battles of White Plains, Trenton and Princeton. In the battle of Princeton, Hall captured British soldiers single-handed after chasing them over half a mile. He was discharged from the service after one year and six weeks of duty. In 1777, Hall enlisted in Captain Samuel Flint's Company, Colonel Johnson's Massachusetts Regiment. He was at the second battle of Stillwater, and was at his captain's side and caught him when he fell mortally wounded. Hall was also at the capture of General Burgoyne. It is believed that he served as a waiter to Captain Flint.

Primus Hall enlisted again in 1778 and served as a private in Captain Woodburg's Company of Massachusetts Troops. He marched to Rhode Island, where he assisted in building a fort. At one time he was detached for service with French sappers and miners.

During the years 1781 and 1782 he served twenty-two months as a servant to Colonel Timothy Pickering, Commissary General of the Army. He was with the colonel at the siege of Yorktown. He was discharged at Newburg, New York in December, 1782.

After the war, Hall became engaged in the coal boiler business. It is stated that he accumulated real estate and personal property worth over $6,000. On October 29, 1817, Hall married Anna or Ann Clark in Boston, Massachusetts. He was eventually allowed a pension by a Special Act of Congress, approved June 28, 1838. He died in 1855.[34]

### ———— Hanberry

A microfilm copy of Vital Statistics Deaths, 1852–1861, state of Kentucky, indicated that a ———— Hanberry died in Trigg County at the age of seventy-six in 1857. He is described as black, his birthplace is given as No. Ca. (probably North Carolina) and his parent's name as J. J. Hanberry. A notation under remarks says "Served Washington in 1776."[35]

### John Harris

Servant, Colonel Faulkner's Virginia Regiment, Captain Harris' Company, Colonel Wallace's Virginia Regiment, and Colonel William Davies' Virginia Troops.

John Harris, a black man, enlisted in the Revolutionary army in 1777 and was assigned to Colonel Faulkner's Virginia Regiment. Later he was transferred to Captain Harris' Company, Colonel Wallace's Virginia Regiment. During the war John Harris was assigned as servant to Major James Monroe, who later became President of the United States. He was with Major Monroe at the battle of Monmouth and was discharged in 1779. He later served six months in Colonel William Davies's Virginia Troops and was discharged October 15, 1780.

After the war he resided near Petersburg, Dinwiddie County, Virginia. John Harris died on March 11, 1838.[36]

### Job Hathaway

Private, Colonel Henry Jackson's Fourth Massachusetts Regiment.

Job Hathaway, a black, enlisted about the year 1777. A daughter, Jane Fisher, made application for his pension on March 15, 1833, in Bristol County, Massachusetts and for the bounty land due to her as one of the heirs. One hundred acres of bounty land was allowed on warrant no. 1931 on account of his services. In 1833, the following were the surviving heirs of Job Hathaway—daughters: Jane Fisher of Taunton, Massachusetts, and Amy Clark of Bristol, Rhode Island; grandchildren: Eleanor Hyde and Polly Williams of Dighton, Massachusetts; Isaac Hyde and Nancy Munroe of Bristol, Rhode Island; Joseph Hyde and Chloe Babbitt of Providence, Rhode Island, and Joseph Hyde and Nancy Dean, alias Williams, residence not known. Job Hathaway died around 1813, at Dighton, Bristol County, Massachusetts.[37]

### James Hawkins

Private, Captain Bohannan's Company.

James Hawkins enlisted in 1779 or 1780, in the state of Virginia, and was later assigned as waiter to a Major Croghan. After the war he lived in Fluvanna County, Virginia and was awarded a pension. James Hawkins died on January 21, 1824.[38]

### Lemuel Haynes

Private, Captain Lebbeus Ball's Company, Minute Men.

Lemuel Haynes was born on July 18, 1753 to a Caucasian woman and a Negro man in West Hartford, Connecticut. At the age of five months, he was given to a Deacon David Rose of Granville, Massachusetts and raised as a boy servant in an atmosphere of hard work with a strong Christian background. He joined a church in East Granville and began to demonstrate an interest in the ministry.

In 1774, Lemuel Haynes enlisted as a Minute Man. He participated in the weekly manual exercises and prepared himself for military readiness in case of an emergency. After the battle of Lexington, Haynes joined the American Army at Roxbury, Massachusetts and volunteered for the expedition to Ticonderoga to impede the advance of General Burgoyne's army. Haynes was a private assigned to Captain Lebbeus Ball's Company of

Minute Men. Ball's company marched on April 20, 1775 in response to the alarm of April 19, 1775. Haynes was discharged May 14, 1775 with active military service of twenty-four days. The official records list him as "Hanes" from Granville, Massachusetts.

After completing his military service, Haynes returned to Granville, Massachusetts and resumed his farming duties for the Rose family. On November 29, 1780, after taking an examination in languages, sciences, and gospel doctrines, he was recommended as qualified to preach the gospel. At the age of twenty-seven, he was invited by a congregational church in Middle Granville to accept a pastoral position. He served this church for several years.

Haynes was married to Elizabeth Babbitt, a former school teacher, in Granville. They became the parents of six girls and three boys.

On November 9, 1785, Haynes was ordained a minister of the gospel and accepted a pastoral position at Torrington, Connecticut. There was one man in Torrington who at first was concerned about the appointment of Haynes to the ministry. This man refused to attend church but finally he decided to do so. One day he appeared at church services and took a seat in the crowded assembly, and, with calculated disrespect, kept his hat on. Mr. Haynes gave out his text and began with his usual impassioned earnestness, apparently unconscious of anything amiss in the congregation. "The preacher had not proceeded far in his sermon," said the man, "before I thought him the whitest man I ever saw. My hat was instantly taken off and thrown under the seat, and I found myself listening with the most profound attention."

The biographer of Lemuel Haynes, Timothy M. Cooley, has mentioned several other instances of people's awareness of Haynes' African ancestry. A Daniel Judson wrote in a letter dated March 5, 1836, "I well recollect that Reverend Lemuel Haynes, the partially coloured preacher, did preach in this place, before the General Association of Connecticut as delegate from Vermont in 1814." The wife of a former congressman and governor of Vermont, Mr. Richard Skinner wrote in 1836 that Lemuel Haynes "held the station of a man without blemish, never appearing to repine that

God had not made without a stain upon his skin: nor was he often called upon to remember it, unless more than ordinary tenderness, manifested by others in their intercourse with him should have reminded him of it."

Haynes accepted a ministry in Rutland, Vermont and remained there for some thirty years. He died on September 28, 1833.[39]

### Edward Hector

Private, Captain Hercules Courtney's Company, Third Pennsylvania Artillery.

Edward Hector, a black, was mustered into the army on March 10, 1777. At the Battle of Brandywine, he was in charge of an ammunition wagon attached to a Colonel Proctor's regiment when an order was given to abandon the wagon and retreat. Hector refused to leave his wagon; he gathered up some firearms that had been left on the field and safely took his wagon and horses out of the range of the advancing enemy.

After the war, some of his friends attempted to obtain a pension for Hector, but they were not successful. Later the legislature decided to make him a donation of forty dollars.[40]

### Francis Herd

Recruit, Colonel Thomas Ewing's Battalion for the Flying Camp.

Francis Herd is mentioned in a document in the Maryland Hall of Records which indicates that a list of men enrolled by Captain James Young, Lieutenant James Bond, Lieutenant John Smith and Ensign James Tool to form a company in Colonel Thomas Ewing's Battalion for the Flying Camp in August, 1776, included a black Fifer, Francis Herd (a servant), who enlisted in Hartford County on July 5, 1776, at the age of twenty, was American born, and had "short, curled hair."[41]

### Ebenezer Hills

Private.

Ebenezer Hills was born a slave in Stonington, Connecticut, and became a free man at twenty years of age. He served during the American Revolution at the battles of Saratoga and Stillwater, and was present at the surrender of General Burgoyne. Ebenezer Hills died in Vienna, New York,

in August, 1848, at the reputed age of one hundred and ten.[42]

### Thomas Hollen

Private, Colonel Charles Gouldsbury's Regiment.

Thomas Hollen, a black, was a native of Dorset County, Maryland. He was wounded in the Revolutionary War by a musket ball in the calf of his leg. He died in 1816 at the age of seventy-two in the town of Blackwood, New Jersey, and was buried in the Snowhill churchyard, east of Woodbury.[43]

### Agrippa Hull

Body servant to General Kosciuszko.

Agrippa Hull, a native of Stockbridge, Massachusetts, served four years during the American Revolution as a body servant to the Polish-American General Kosciuszko. A photograph of a portrait of Hull has been on display in the old Historical Corner House in Stockbridge, Massachusetts. The painter of the original portrait is unknown, but the photograph was by Clemens Kalischer (1874). A great-grandson of Agrippa Hull, Mr. David Gunn, recently resided in Stockbridge, Massachusetts.[44]

### Peter Jennings

Private, Captain Vener April's Company, Colonel Edward Oneys' Fifth Regiment of Artillery of Blacks; Captain James Sterling's Company, Colonel Clifford's Regiment.

Peter Jennings was born at Pequanock, three miles east of Fairfield, Connecticut. He enlisted in the army in Providence, Rhode Island, in 1776, and served as a private in Captain Vener April's Company, Colonel Edward Oneys' Fifth Regiment of Artillery of Blacks. He was later transferred to Captain James Starling's Company, Colonel Clifford's Regiment. He was in the battles of Trenton, Princeton, Brandywine and Germantown. Jennings' records also state that he served under Captain Edgar, Major Tallmadge and Colonel Brewster. He was allowed pension on his application executed August 23, 1832, at which time he was eighty years old. He lived in Murfreesboro, Rutherford County, Tennessee. He died on January 22, 1842.[45]

### Joseph Johnson

Private, Major James Rosencrans's and Captain Henry Dubois's Company, Colonel Lewis Dubois's New York Regiment.

Joseph Johnson was born at Fishkell, New York. He stated in a pension application dated September 1, 1832, that he enlisted in the army in 1778. He was in General Sullivan's Indian expedition and at the battle of Newtown. Johnson also served as waiter to Major Rosencrans and lived with the Rosencrans family. His pension claim was not allowed, as the records indicated that a private of the name of Joseph Johnson enlisted in the Rosencrans Company on May 19, 1778 and deserted on January 15, 1780. After the war, Johnson lived in Fishkell, New York, Litchfield County, Connecticut, and Bethlehem, Connecticut.[46]

### Jabez Jolly

Private, Captain John Russell's Company, Fourteenth Massachusetts Regiment.

Jabez Jolly, a black, enlisted in the army on May 15, 1777, for a three-year period. He was assigned to Captain John Russell's Company, Fourteenth Massachusetts Regiment, Colonel Gamaliel Bradford commanding. In June, 1780, Jolly was wounded.[47]

### Jeremy Jonah

Private, Seventh Massachusetts Regiment.

Jeremy Jonah, a black, served in the Seventh Massachusetts Regiment, under the command of Colonel Brooks, along with Samuel Burr. According to William C. Nell, the two veterans would tell tales of their military adventures, especially the drill on one occasion when Jonah stumbled over a heap of stones and was severely reprimanded by the colonel. He was awarded a pension for his services during the American Revolution.[48]

### Prince (or Primus) Lane

Private, Captain Harris's Company, Colonel Nathan Hale and Colonel George Reid's New Hampshire Regiment.

Prince Lane (whose name also appears on the records as Primo Coffin) enlisted in the army in 1777 and served until 1783. During part of his service, he worked as a waiter to Ensign Daniel Gookin. After the war he lived in Deerfield, Rockingham County, New Hampshire and was allowed a pension on an application executed on September 28, 1819. Later he moved to Meredith, Stafford County, New Hampshire.[49]

## Barzillai Lew

Private, Captain Ford's Company, Colonel Bridges' Twenty-Seventh Massachusetts Regiment, and Captain Varnum's Company, Colonel Iona Reed's Regiment.

Barzillai Lew, a black, was born in Groton, Massachusetts on November 5, 1743. He married a Dinah Bowman and raised a large family as indicated on a document "The Family of Barzillai and Dinah Lew." The adjutant general's files state that he was on the muster rolls of the Twenty-Seventh Massachusetts Regiment as a fifer for eight months during the Revolutionary War. He enlisted on May 6, 1775, and was at Chelmsford and at Ticonderoga as a fifer in 1776. In 1777, Private Lew was listed on the roll of Captain Varnum's Infantry, Colonel Iona Reed's Regiment. He died on January 19, 1821.[50]

## Ambrose Lewis

Seaman and Private, Captain John Halliday's Company, Colonel George Stubblefield's Virginia Regiment.

Ambrose Lewis, a black, enlisted at Fredericksburg, Virginia on April 15, 1776 as a seaman and served under Captain Markham aboard the galley *Page*. On March 30, 1778 he joined the ship *Dragon I*, commanded by Captain Elisha Collender. Lewis was in battle with the enemy privateer *Lord Howe* and served until April 16, 1779. Lewis's service included participation in the battle of Camden on August 16, 1780 when he was severely wounded, receiving a ball through his thigh and bayonet thrusts in different parts of his limbs and body. He was taken prisoner and confined until the end of the war. After the war he was given a pension on account of the disability caused by his wounds. He lived for a time in Alexandria and moved in 1821 to Washington, D.C.[51]

## Job Lewis

Enlisted man.

Job Lewis was a former slave from Lancaster, Massachusetts. He enlisted for two terms of three years each, and a third time for the remainder of the Revolutionary War. Lewis died in November, 1797.[52]

## Titus Minor

Private, Colonel Nathan Stoddard's and Colonel Sanford's Company, Colonel Chandler and Colonel Sherman's Connecticut Regiment.

Titus Minor enlisted at Woodburg, Litchfield County, Connecticut in 1777 and was discharged in January, 1782. He was allowed a pension on April 6, 1818, while residing in Woodburg. Titus Minor, a black man, died on January 22, 1821.[53]

## Jeremiah Moho

Private, Colonel Henry Jackson's Fourth Massachusetts Regiment.

Jeremiah Moho, a black, enlisted in 1777 and was discharged at the end of the conflict. After the war, he accidentally drowned in New York Pond, Stoughton, Norfolk County, Massachusetts. The records state that he had no wife or children. However, on November 8, 1833, Mary Burr of Canton, Norfolk County, Massachusetts, applied on behalf of herself and Elizabeth Williams, cousins and only known heirs of Moho, for bounty land which was due Moho for his services. They were successful in their application.[54]

## Luke Nickelson (or Nickerson)

Private, Captain John Rod's Company, Colonel Alden and Colonel Brooks' Massachusetts Regiment.

Luke Nickelson enlisted at Harpswell, Massachusetts, in January, 1777. Nickelson was present at the surrender of General Burgoyne, where he was wounded in the thigh by a musket ball. He was discharged in January, 1780 and was awarded a pension on April 25, 1818. After the war he lived in Brunswick, Cumberland County, Massachusetts. He died on May 4, 1829, at the age of eighty-four.[55]

## Orang

Marine, Captain Robert Mullan's Company of Marines.

Orang enlisted in the Company of Marines on October 1, 1776, and was assigned number seventy on the payroll. The early records of the First Marine Company give the following references to Orang: Payroll of Captain Robert Mullan's Company of Marines, to December 1, 1776, No. 70 Orang, Negro; Date of Enlistment, October 1; months, 2. Payroll of Captain Robert Mullan's Company of Marines from December 1, 1776 to April 1, 1777, No. 43, Orang, Negro. A muster roll of the same company to April 1, 1777, list No. 54, Orang, Negro, time of enlistment October 1, months, 4, days, 10. The inclusion of Orang's name in these early records clarifies the question of whether blacks were enlisted in the Marine Corps prior to 1942.[56]

## Isaac Perkins

Private, Captain Silas Sears Stephensons' Company, Colonel Shepard's Tenth North Carolina Regiment and Captain Clement Hall's Company, Colonel Patten's Second North Carolina Regiment.

Isaac Perkins, a black native of North Carolina, enlisted in the army in May, 1777. He was taken prisoner at Charleston, South Carolina, but he successfully escaped and returned to North Carolina. He was discharged from the military after serving for three years; the records state that he served in the North Carolina Militia until an armistice was declared.

Perkins successfully applied for a pension on June 9, 1818, when he was living in Craven County, North Carolina. He mentioned his wife Deborah, but no reference was made to any children. Isaac Perkins died on May 23, 1830.[57]

## Pomp Peters

Private, Captain Smith's Company, Colonel Marshall and Colonel Tupper's Massachusetts Regiment.

Pomp Peters, a black, enlisted in June, 1778. He served at the battle of Monmouth, at the seizure of Cornwallis, and in a skirmish at King's Bridge. He was discharged from the army in June, 1783 and was allowed a pension on his application executed April 6, 1818, when he was fifty-eight years of age. He resided in New Boston, Hillsborough County, New Hampshire.[58]

## Samuel Philips (name appears as **Phillips**)

Private, Colonel Herman Swift's Connecticut Regiment.

Samuel Philips, a black, enlisted in the army on March 30, 1777. He served, according to his own account, under Captains Stone and Morgan of Colonel Herman Swift's Connecticut Regiment, although the captains' names could not be verified. Philips was discharged on March 31, 1780. After the war he lived in New Milford and on May 25, 1780 he married his wife Lydia, of Windham. She was granted a pension on her application executed September 11, 1837. Samuel Philips died on November 1, 1815.[59]

## Richard (Dick) Potter

Colonel Christopher Greene's Regiment.

The military pension record states that "Richard Potter, a man of colour, served for three years on the Rhode Island line." Richard Potter was fifty-nine years of age when he applied, on November 8, 1819, for a military pension. He was living in Charlestown, Rhode Island.[60]

## Christopher Poynos

Private, Second Maryland Regiment.

Christopher Poynos was born in Ireland but was living in Maryland when, at the age of thirty-five, on May 9, 1772, he enlisted in the army for three years. The official record lists his description as hair: black and complexion: black. He served in a unit from the state of Maryland.[61]

## Cato Prince

Private, Captain Smith's Company, Colonel Jackson's Regiment.

Cato Prince, a black, was enlisted in the army by an Ensign Hedrick, who marched him to New York from Marblehead, Massachusetts. Prince was honorably discharged from the continental establishment after serving three years. He received a monthly pension of eight dollars and on April 18, 1818, at sixty years of age, he signed for it with an X mark.[62]

### Toney Proctor

Body servant to an English officer.

Toney Proctor was born on the island of Jamaica around the year 1743. At the age of sixteen, he became a body servant to an English officer. He was at the battle of Quebec with his master, on September 13, 1759. During the Revolutionary War he served as body servant to another officer and was present at Lexington. Later he moved to St. Augustine, Florida, where he purchased his freedom and reared a large family. During the campaigns and military exploits of General Jackson and General Harney, Proctor offered his services as an Indian interpreter. He died on June 15, 1855, at the reputed age of one hundred and twelve. *The Tallahassee Sentinel* published a notice of his death in 1855.

This brief sketch of Toney Proctor illustrates the early advent of the Negro as a body servant during military campaigns. In many cases, the extent of their combat participation is not known, but their constant presence at their masters' sides in battle leaves no doubt that they faced the dangers of war.[63]

### Arly (or Aly) Randale

Private, Maryland Second Regiment.

Arly Randale was a resident of Virginia. He enlisted in the army on April 22, 1782 for one year, at the age of twenty-four. The official record lists his hair as black and his complexion, Negro. He served during the Revolutionary War in a unit from Maryland.[64]

### Joseph Ranger

Seaman, U.S. Navy.

Joseph Ranger was a free black man. He enlisted in the navy from North Cumberland in 1776, and continued in service until the Commonwealth of Virginia disposed of its last vessel in 1787. Ranger served on the vessels *Hero, Dragon, Jefferson* and *Patriot.* He was aboard the *Jefferson* when it was blown up by the British on the James River, and was taken prisoner in October, 1781. He was discharged from the navy in 1787 and official records indicate that he received a pension and a land grant of one hundred acres from the Common-wealth of Virginia, and later a pension of ninety-six dollars a year from the federal government.[65]

### Abram Read

Private, Captain Cole's Company.

Abram Read was born around 1763 in Nansemond County, Virginia. His pension files state: "In Nansemond County court 13 May 1833 . . . personally appeared in open court . . . Abram Read, a free man of colour by birth, a resident of Nansemond County and State of Virginia, age 69 years . . ."

Read said in his sworn declaration that he entered the service in 1779 and served until near the end of the American Revolution. He first enlisted under the command of Captain John Cole and served for six months at Portsmouth, Norfolk County, Surrey County, and in the area of Smithfield, Virginia. He was discharged at Babbs field, Isle of Wight County.

A William Boothe of Wight County asked Read to enter military service as a substitute for him. Abram Read agreed and served under a Captain Roberts or Robertson, in the region north of the James River. He was discharged after three month's service as Boothe's substitute, returned home and was asked to volunteer his services at Portsmouth. He went to Portsmouth and dug embankments. Read was awarded a pension in 1831.[66]

### Pomp Reeves

Private, Colonel Christopher Greene and Colonel Jeremiah Olney's Rhode Island Regiment.

Pomp Reeves, a black, enlisted and served in the Rhode Island Regiment. He was married on April 15, 1777, in Smithfield, Providence County, Rhode Island, to a wife whose first name was Thankful. After the war he moved to Pawtucket, Rhode Island and in 1785, he died in New York. His widow remarried a Jonathan Corlis or Coles on August 31, 1834, but was again a widow when he died in September, 1836. She applied for a pension on the grounds of Reeves' service in the Revolutionary War and the pension was executed on February 5, 1840, at which time she was living in Providence, Rhode Island.[67]

### Job Ripley

Private, Captain Abraham Watson's Company, Colonel Greaton's Third Massachusetts Regiment.

Job Ripley was present at the capture of General Burgoyne and at numerous battles and skirmishes. He was discharged in June, 1783. After the war Ripley was given a pension and lived in Hudson, Columbia County, New York. He was married to a Sarah Fuller and died in 1848.[68]

### Cuff (or Cuffee) Roberts

Private, Captain Peckham's Company, Colonel Christopher Greene's and Jeremiah Olney's Rhode Island Regiment.

Cuff Roberts, a black, enlisted in the army on March 15, 1778. He was discharged on June 15, 1783 and in 1818 was allowed a pension.[69]

### Esek Roberts

Private, Captain Hoppins Company, Colonel John Topham's Rhode Island Regiment.

Esek Roberts, a black man, was born in Coventry, Rhode Island on October 5, 1761. He enlisted in June, 1777, and served nine months with General Cornell's Brigade. He was also with General Sullivan's Rhode Island expedition.

Roberts lived in West Greenwich and in September, 1818, was married by a Reverend Henry Tatum to Delana Profit. They had a son, Benjamin, who was living in Cranston, Rhode Island in 1853. Esek Roberts died on September 9, 1844.[70]

### James Robinson

Soldier.

James Robinson was born a slave in Maryland on March 21, 1753. He served at the battle of Brandywine, and was decorated with a gold medal by General Lafayette for acts of military valor at the battle of Yorktown. After the war he did not receive his freedom and was deported to Louisiana. With the start of the War of 1812, he offered his services, but did not become a free man until the Civil War. Once freed, he moved to Detroit where he resided until March, 1868. He died at the reputed age of one hundred and fifteen.[71]

*Peter Salem
at the Battle
of Bunker
Hill, June
17, 1775*

### Philip Rodman

Private, Captain James Tew's Company, Colonel Christopher Lippitt's Rhode Island Regiment.

Philip Rodman, a black, enlisted at South Kingston, Rhode Island, in October, 1776. He was in the battles of White Plains, Trenton, and Princeton. He was discharged in November, 1777, and after the war lived in Providence, Rhode Island. In 1823 he moved to the state of Connecticut.[72]

### Jack Rowland (also Jack Freeman)

Private, Captain Ezekiel Sandford's Company, Colonel Philip B. Bradley's Connecticut Regiment.

Jack Rowland, a black, enlisted in the army in the spring of 1777 and served on the Connecticut line. At times he was called "Jack Freeman." He served under Colonel Bradley and was present at the battles of Germantown and Valley Forge.[73]

### Peter Salem (alias Salem Middleux)

Private, Captain John Nixon's and Captain Simon Edgell's Companies.

Peter Salem was born in Framingham, Massachusetts. He was a slave owned originally by a Captain Jeremiah Belknap of Framingham. Later he was sold to a Major Lawson of Buckminster. When Salem enlisted in the army he was given his freedom. In 1783 he was married to Katie Benson. After the war he moved to Leicester, Massachusetts.

During the American Revolutionary War, Peter Salem exhibited unusual heroism in shooting down Major Pitcairn at the Battle of Bunker Hill. Pitcairn was hit by Salem's bullet as he was mounting the redoubt, shouting, "The day is ours!" Salem served for seven years and was also present at Concord and Saratoga. He died on August 16, 1816.

In 1882, a monument was erected in Boston in honor of Peter Salem. The Freedmen's Bank of Boston for many years commemorated Salem's deeds by printing his picture on their bank notes. Peter Salem is pictured in John Turnbull's historic painting of the battle of Bunker Hill which is in the rotunda of the nation's capitol. The Daughters of the American Revolution also honored Salem when they acquired his home in 1909 and beautified the area.[74]

### Edward Sands

Private, Captain Miller's Company of Blacks, Colonel Joseph Voss' First Massachusetts Regiment.

Edward Sands, a black man, enlisted in the army in February, 1781 for three years and was honorably discharged at West Point at the end of the war. He served in the battle at Kings Bridge and in several skirmishes. During part of his enlistment he was a waiter to Colonel Voss. In 1820, Sands applied for a government pension.[75]

### Caesar Sankee

Private, Colonel Dearborn's New Hampshire Regiment.

Caesar Sankee enlisted in the Revolutionary Army in March, 1781, at Dover, New Hampshire. He served faithfully in Colonel Dearborn's regiment during the war period, and was later granted a pension. After the war, Sankee lived in Pomfret, Windsor County, Vermont.[76]

### Pomp Sherburne

Private, Captain Rowell's Company, Colonel George Reid's New Hampshire Regiment.

Pomp Sherburne, a black, served as a cook and waiter to Colonel Reid. He enlisted in the army in 1781, having married a Flora or Floriana Taggart of Londonderry, New Hampshire, in 1779 or 1780. On October 7, 1844, Jesse D. Sherburne of Reading, Windsor District, Vermont, who was born October 19, 1791, made application for the pension that was due his mother. He stated on the application that he was the fifth and only surviving child of Pomp and Flora Sherburne, and the claim was allowed. Pomp Sherburne died around 1795 in Londonderry.[77]

### Jack Sisson

Private, Rhode Island Militia.

Jack Sisson, a black man, was instrumental in the capture of Major General Richard Prescott, Commander in Chief of the British Forces in Rhode Island. On the night of July 9, 1777, six officers and thirty-eight men, under the command of Lieutenant Colonel William Barton, set out to capture the British general. Disembarking from their boat at about midnight, Colonel Barton, taking Sisson and another soldier with him, ordered the rest of the company to follow at a distance. Colonel Barton and Sisson together attacked the sentry at Prescott's door and Sisson broke down the door and entered the general's bedroom. Prescott surrendered and the Americans slipped him out of the camp without being observed or halted.[78]

### Cato Stedman

Private, various companies, First and Third Connecticut Regiments.

Cato Stedman, a black, served in Captain Daniel Allen's Company in the Connecticut Regiment commanded by Captain Samuel Wyllys. Company muster rolls from June to July 21, 1778, show that Stedman was assigned to a Captain Elias Stilwell's Company, Third Battalion of Connecticut Regiment, commanded by Colonel John Durkee, in March, 1782. Stedman also served under Zebulon Butler, Second Company, First Connecticut Regiment. On November 15, 1791, he received bounty land of one hundred acres.[79]

### William Stewart

Private, Captain Robert Fenner's Company, Colonel John Patlen's North Carolina Regiment.

William Stewart, a black man, was born in Brunswick County, Virginia. During his Revolutionary War service he was at the battle of Monmouth. He was discharged in June, 1780 and, in 1835 at the age of seventy-seven, applied for a pension. His pension claim was denied because the records indicated that he deserted in January, 1780. After the war, he moved to the state of Pennsylvania with his family.[80]

### Joel Taburn (also Taborn)

Private, Captain Tanant's and Captain Thomas Donoho's companies, Colonel Archibald Lytle's and Hardy Murfree's North Carolina Regiments.

Joel Taburn, a black, was born in March, 1761. He enlisted in the army at Nash County, North Carolina, in the spring of 1776. Taburn was present at the siege of Charleston, and at the battle of Eutaw Springs. He was discharged in 1783. In 1797, Taburn was a resident of Northhampton County, North Carolina. When he was granted a pension on his application executed December 1, 1820, he was living in Granville County, North Carolina, and in 1821 he moved to Nash County, in the same state.[81]

### William Taylor

Private, Fifth Maryland Regiment.

William Taylor was a native of Montgomery County, Maryland. On April 2, 1782, at the age of twenty-nine, he enlisted in the army for one year. The official records lists his description as "hair: short dark, complexion: yellow mulatto." He served during the American Revolution in a unit from the state of Maryland.[82]

### William Thomas

Private, Colonel Richard Parker's Virginia Regiment and Captain Joseph Scott's Virginia Company.

William Thomas, a black, enlisted in the army in 1777 at Charles City Court House, Charles City County, Virginia. He was at the battle of Monmouth and was later taken into the family of General Muhlenberg and was at the siege of Yorktown. He was discharged in December, 1751 and was allowed a pension on his application of May 21, 1818. He died on July 25, 1824.[83]

### Prince Vaughn

Private, Captain Peckham's Company, Colonel Christopher Greene's and Colonel Jeremiah Olney's Rhode Island Regiment.

The military pension files of Cuff or Cuffee Roberts (q.v.) include a letter from a Prince Vaughn stating that he had served in the same company and regiment with Cuff or Cuffee Roberts during the American Revolutionary War. Prince Vaughn wrote:

I, *Prince Vaughn a man of colour of Providence in the County of Rhode Island being now in the ninety-sixth year of my age on oath declare and say that I am personally acquainted with Cuffe Roberts, a man of colour who is now present . . . and formerly a soldier in the Revolutionary War. We served in the same company of the regiment more than five years. We were together in a number of battles and during all our service said Cuffee was a brave and faithful soldier. Signed: Primus (Prince) Vaughn.*[84]

### Isaac Walker

Marine, Captain Robert Mullan's Company of Marines.

Isaac Robert Walker enlisted in the company of marines on August 27, 1776, and was assigned No. 69 on the payroll. The early records of the First Marine Company show the following mentions of Walker: Payroll of Captain Robert Mullan's Company of Marines to December 1, 1776, "No. 69, Isaac Walker (Negro), Date of Enlistment, August 27, Mo.–3, days–4, pay 5–6–8." A payroll of Captain Robert Mullan's from December 1, 1776 to April, 1777 mentions "No. 53, Isaac Negro, time of enlistment, August 27, months and days, 4, 10." The inclusion of Walker's name on the early records of the First Marine Company is further evidence in the controversy about whether blacks were enlisted in the Marine Corps prior to 1942 (see also Orang).[85]

### Caesar Wallace

Private, Captain Caleb Robinson's Company, Colonel George Reid's New Hampshire Regiment.

Caesar Wallace, a black man, enlisted at Newbury, Massachusetts, around 1777 and was present at the battles of Monmouth, Horse Neck and Newton. He was discharged June 7, 1783. Wallace was allowed a pension on his application executed April 23, 1818, when he was eighty years old and living in Meredith, Stratford County, New Hampshire. In 1820 he stated that his family consisted of his wife Valy, aged seventy-two, and one daughter, Lucy, aged twenty-seven.[86]

### Sipeo (also Sip and Zip) Watson

Private, Captain Christopher Ely's Company, Colonel Samuel Prentice's Connecticut Regiment.

Sipeo Watson, a black native of Plainfield, Windham County, Connecticut, enlisted early in May, 1777, and served until the end of the conflict. He was married to a Juda or Judah Wheeler, who was allowed a pension on her application executed February 27, 1839. The names of two children are recorded: Dinah and Joseph, both deceased by the time of the application. Sipeo Watson died on March 4, 1815, at Griswold, Connecticut.[87]

### Thomas Watson

Private, Captain Richard Sill's Company, Colonel Isaac Sherman's Connecticut Regiment and Captain Starr's Company, Colonel Butler's Connecticut Regiment.

Thomas Watson, a black native of Stonington, served for three years during the American Revolution and was discharged in May, 1783. He executed an application and was awarded a pension on December 23, 1819, when he was living at South Kingston, Washington County, Rhode Island. He was married, at Charleston, Rhode Island, in April, 1792 and his widow, Sarah, was allowed a pension on her application executed on September 10, 1838. It is stated in the records that thirteen children were born. Thomas Watson died in September, 1822, at South Kingston, Rhode Island.[88]

### Cuff Wells (also Saunders)

Private, Captain Benjamin Throop's Company, Colonel John Durkee's and Colonel Zebulon Butler's Connecticut Regiment.

Cuff Wells was born in Guiana. He came to America as a child and was owned by Deacon Israel Wells of Colchester, Connecticut, and later by a doctor of Hartford, Connecticut. The doctor had a pharmacy or apothecary shop and he taught his assistant, who came to be known as "Dr. Cuff" how to compound medicines. Wells enlisted in the army in 1777 or 1778 and because of his knowledge of pharmaceuticals was detached to serve as a waiter to the surgeons in the hospital in Danbury. Wells was discharged in 1783 and in the same year he married Phillis, the servant of Charles and Elizabeth Hinckley. Cuff Wells died in December, 1788, of influenza. He had a son, named Prince Saunders, who was born February, 1785, was educated at Dartmouth College and later taught at the colored school at Colchester Academy. Prince Saunders went to Haiti and was made bishop and later attorney-general. He died in Haiti in February, 1839.[89]

### John Wheeler

Private, Captain Luke Day's Company, Colonel Ichabod Alden's and Colonel John Brooks's Seventh Massachusetts Regiment.

John Wheeler, a black, enlisted in the army in May, 1777, at Belchertown, Massachusetts. He served at the battle of Bemus Heights, the siege of Burgoyne and at Cherry Valley, where Colonel Alden was killed. Wheeler was also in battle with the Indians on the Tioga River in 1779. He married Ruth Thayer on January 8, 1789, at Greenwich, Massachusetts, and they had four children: Levila, Mary, Electra and Enos. John Wheeler died July 20, 1845, at Ware, Massachusetts.[90]

### Prince Whipple
Servant to General Whipple.

Prince Whipple was born in Amabou, Africa, and at the age of ten was sent to America to be educated. The ship's captain who transported him to America carried him to Baltimore and sold him as a slave. Later he became the property of General Whipple, though he was emancipated during the war. In the engravings of Washington crossing the Delaware on the evening before the battle of Trenton, December 25, 1779, a colored soldier on horseback can be seen near the commander-in-chief. The same figure is seen, in other sketches, pulling the stroke oar. This colored soldier was Prince Whipple, bodyguard to General Whipple of New Hampshire, who was an aide to General Washington. Prince Whipple later settled in Portsmouth, New Hampshire, and died at the age of thirty-two, leaving a wife and children.[91]

### Archelaus White
Private, Captain Jeremiah Gilman's Company, Colonel John Nixon's Massachusetts Regiment.

Archelaus White, a black, was a native of Plaistow, New Hampshire. He enlisted in the army in 1776 and served for eight months in a Captain Jeremiah Gilman's company. Immediately after the termination of his service, he re-enlisted and served for one year in Gilman's company, which was part of Colonel John Nixon's Massachusetts Regiment. The records state that White served at one time in Captain Page's company and was present at the seizure of General Burgoyne. White died on July 29, 1826.[92]

### Cuff Whitemore
Private, Captain Benjamin Locke's Company, Colonel William Pond's Massachusetts Regiment.

Cuff Whitemore also served in Captain Daniel Egery's Company, Colonel William Bond's Massachusetts Regiment, and in Colonel Shepard's Fourth Massachusetts Regiment. He was discharged at the end of the war. Whitemore was a prisoner at the time of General Burgoyne's surrender, and was ordered to take care of his chargers for a few moments. Seizing his opportunity, he mounted one of the horses and made his escape.[93]

### Cato Wood
Private, Major Nathaniel Winslow's Company, Colonel Thomas Marshall's Tenth Battalion of Massachusetts Forces.

Cato Wood, a black, was entered on the muster roll of Major Nathaniel Wood's Company from March, 1779 to April 8, 1779. He enlisted in the army on June 14, 1778, for three years, but was discharged in 1779, as a casualty, from the Pillsburg Company of Colonel Edward Wigglesworth's Thirteenth Massachusetts Regiment.[94]

### Jesse Wood
Private, various companies, Colonel Davis's Virginia Regiment.

Jesse Wood, a native of King William County, Virginia, a free black man, enlisted in the army in the summer of 1778. He served in a Captain I. or J. Hickman's Company, Colonel Davis's Virginia Regiment, and he was also assigned at various times to Captain Hastings', Captain Marks' and Captain John Peyton's Virginia companies. Wood was discharged from the service after the surrender of Cornwallis. In 1782, he moved to Fluvanna County, Virginia, and on November 26, 1832, he executed an application for a pension, in which he was successful.[95]

## Notes to Chapter One

1. Archives of Maryland and Official Records of Services of Maryland Troops in the American Revolution 1775–1783, Baltimore Historical Society, 1900, p. 54, Maryland Hall of Records, Annapolis, Maryland.

2. Laura E. Wilkes, *Missing Pages in American Mili-*

*tary History 1641–1815* (Washington, D.C., 1919).

3. Revolutionary War Rolls, 1775–1783, Roll 34, Maryland Jacket Numbers 18–1–35–3 (35–3 Maryland Organization, Miscellaneous Records), Microcopy 246, National Archives, Washington, D.C.

4. Record of Revolutionary War Service of Stephen Bond, Folder AA 2547, South Carolina Department of Archives and History, Columbus, S.C.

5. William C. Nell, *The Colored Patriots of the American Revolution* (Boston: Robert F. Wallcut, 1855), pp. 28-29.

6. Military Pension File of Scipio Brown, RG 15, Records of the Adjutant General's Office, National Archives, Washington, D.C.

7. Military Pension File of George Buley, *loc. cit.*

8. Nell, *The Colored Patriots,* pp. 21–22.

9. Revolutionary War Rolls, 1775–1783, *loc. cit.*

10. Roland C. McConnell, *Negro Troops of Antebellum Louisiana, A History of the Battalion of Free Men of Color* (Baton Rouge: Louisiana State University Press, 1969) pp. 11, 18–19.

11. Nell, *The Colored Patriots,* pp. 162–163.

12. Military Pension File of Caesar Clarke, *loc. cit.*

13. Vital Statistics Records (Microfilm), 1852–1861, Kentucky Historical Society, Frankfort, Kentucky.

14. Record of Revolutionary War Service of George Cooper, Folder AA 257, South Carolina Department of Archives and History, Columbus, S.C.

15. Military Pension File of Richard Cozzens, *loc. cit.*

16. Nell, *The Colored Patriots,* pp. 160–162.

17. George R. Gilmer, *Sketches of Some of the First Settlers of Upper Georgia,* Baltimore: Baltimore Genealogical Publishing Co., 1965). [Courtesy of Georgia Department of Archives and History, Atlanta, Ga.]

18. Revolutionary War Rolls, 1775–1783, Roll 34, Maryland Jacket Numbers 18–1–35–3 (35–2 Maryland Organizations, Miscellaneous Records), Microcopy 24, National Archives.

19. Military Pension File of Joshua Dunbar, *loc. cit.*

20. Military Pension File of Samuel Dunbar, *loc. cit.*

21. Russel's *Salem Gazette,* April 21, 1775 (located Rare Book Room, Library of Congress, Washington, D.C.).

22. Record of Revolutionary War Service of John Featherston, Folder AA 2567, South Carolina Department of Archives and History, Columbus, S.C.

23. Military Pension File of Cato Fisk, *loc. cit.*

24. Nell, *The Colored Patriots,* 166–181.

25. Military Pension File of Artillo Freeman, *loc. cit.*

26. Military Pension File of Call Freeman, *loc. cit.*

27. Military Pension File of Casar Freeman, *loc. cit.*

28. Military Pension File of Doss Freeman, *loc. cit.*

29. Military Pension File of Fortune Freeman, *loc. cit.*

30. Military Pension File of Prince Freeman, *loc. cit.*

31. Wilkes, *Missing Pages in American History,* p. 16.

32. Military Pension File of Peter Galloway, *loc. cit.*

33. Wilkes, *Missing Pages in American History,* pp. 32–33.

34. Military Pension File of Primus Hall, *loc. cit.*

35. Vital Statistics Records (Microfilm), 1852–1861.

36. Military Pension File of John Harris, *loc. cit.*

37. Military Pension File of Job Hathaway, *loc. cit.*

38. Military Pension File of James Hawkins, *loc. cit.*

39. Timothy M. Cooley, *Sketches of the Life and Character of the Rev. Lemuel Haynes* (New York: John S. Taylor, 1839), pp. 46, 83–86.
Secretary of the Commonwealth, *Massachusetts Soldiers and Sailors of the Revolutionary War,* vol. 7 (Boston: Wright & Potter) p. 227.

40. National Association for the Advancement of Colored People (NAACP), *Black Heroes of the American Revolution 1775–1783* (New York: NAACP, n.d.).

41. Archives of Maryland and Official Records of Services of Maryland Troops in the American Revolution 1775–1783, Baltimore Historical Society, 1900, p. 54, Maryland Hall of Records.

42. Nell, *The Colored Patriots,* p. 136.

43. *Ibid.,* p. 203.

44. Stockbridge Library Association, *1969 Annual Report* (Stockbridge, Mass.: Stockbridge Library Association, 1939).

45 Military Pension File of Peter Jennings, *loc. cit.*

46. Military Pension File of Joseph Johnson, *loc. cit.*

47. Military Pension File of Jabez Jolly, *loc. cit.*

48. Nell, *The Colored Patriots,* pp. 22–23.

49. Military Pension File of Prince Lane, *loc. cit.*

50. Military Pension File of Barzillai Lew, *loc. cit.*

51. Military Pension File of Ambrose Lewis, *loc. cit.*

52. Nell, *The Colored Patriots,* p. 35.

53. Military Pension File of Titus Minor, *loc. cit.*

54. Military Pension File of Jeremiah Moho, *loc. cit.*

55. Military Pension File of Luke Nickelson, *loc. cit.*

56. Early Records of the First Marine Company. The Historical Society of Pennsylvania (Courtesy of Marine Corps Library (vol. 23 PH), Department of the Navy, Headquarters U. S. Marine Corps, Washington, D.C.).

57. Military Pension File of Isaac Perkins, *loc. cit.*

58. Military Pension File of Pomp Peters, *loc. cit.*

59. Military Pension File of Samuel Philips, *loc. cit.*

60. Military Pension File of Richard Potter, *loc. cit.*

61. Revolutionary War Rolls, 1775–1783 (35–2 Maryland Organizations, Miscellaneous Records), Microcopy 246, National Archives, Washington, D.C.
62. Military Pension File of Cato Prince, *loc. cit.*
63. Nell, *The Colored Patriots,* pp. 307–309.
64. Revolutionary War Rolls, 1775–1783.
65. NAACP, *Black Heroes of the American Revolution.*
66. Military Pension File of Abram Read, *loc. cit.*
67. Military Pension File of Pomp Reeves, *loc. cit.*
68. Military Pension File of Job Ripley, *loc. cit.*
69. Military Pension File of Cuff or Cuffee Roberts, *loc. cit.*
70. Military Pension File of Esek Roberts, *loc. cit.*
71. NAACP, *Black Heroes of the American Revolution.*
72. Military Pension File of Philip Rodman, *loc. cit.*
73. Military Pension File of Jack Rowland, *loc. cit.*
74. Joseph T. Wilson, *The Black Phalanx* (Hartford, Conn.: Hartford Publishing Co., 1890).
75. Military Pension File of Edward Sands, *loc. cit.*
76. Military Pension File of Caesar Sankee, *loc. cit.*
77. Military Pension File of Pomp Sherburne, *loc. cit.*
78. NAACP, *Black Heroes of the American Revolution.*
79. Military Pension File of Cato Stedman, *loc. cit.*
80. Military Pension File of William Stewart, *loc. cit.*
81. Military Pension File of Joel Taburn, *loc. cit.*
82. Revolutionary War Rolls, 1775–1783.
83. Military Pension File of William Thomas, *loc. cit.*
84. Military Pension File of Cuff or Cuffee Roberts, *loc. cit.* (Prince Vaughn letter).
85. Early Records of the First Marine Company.
86. Military Pension File of Caesar Wallace, *loc. cit.*
87. Military Pension File of Sipeo Watson, *loc. cit.*
88. Military Pension File of Thomas Watson, *loc. cit.*
89. Military Pension File of Cuff Wells, *loc. cit.*
90. Military Pension File of John Wheeler, *loc. cit.*
91. Nell, *The Colored Patriots,* p. 198–199.
92. Military Pension File of Archelaus White, *loc. cit.*
93. Military Pension File of Cuff Whitemore, *loc. cit.*
94. Military Pension File of Cato Wood, *loc. cit.*
95. Military Pension File of Jesse Wood, *loc. cit.*

# Chapter Two

## The War of 1812, 1812-1815

After the signing of the Treaty of 1783, Great Britain appeared reluctant to recognize America's independence. She gave instructions to her naval captains to halt American merchant vessels anywhere on the high seas and search them for any British subjects serving in America's military or marine service. In 1806, the American frigate *Chesapeake* was captured by the British man of war *Leopard*. Three of the four men taken from the *Chesapeake* were Negroes.

The captives were carried to Nova Scotia and later (1811) all except the one Englishman were released. This affair and other international complications gradually led America into war in June, 1812.

The battles of the various campaigns of the War of 1812 were fought on sea and land, and many Negroes served aboard naval vessels as well as in the army.

During this period, blacks were enlisted in regular army units and in some cases they were in actual battles, where some were taken prisoner. The records indicate that a Captain William Bezean of the Twenty-sixth U.S. Infantry Regiment enlisted 247 colored recruits at Philadelphia, Pennsylvania from August 30, 1814 to February 15, 1815, some for five years and others for the duration of the war. No specific authority for this was discovered, although he was at the same time enlisting white men. Some archival records state that Bezean's colored recruits do not appear to have been assigned to active service. In the spring of 1815, they were discharged with the remarks: "Discharged under an order of War Department directing that soldiers of color be discharged." The register of discharges of military district number 1, (Boston) bears the following remarks: "Being a Negro is deemed unfit to associate with the American and on account of being a Negro . . . not fit to accompany American soldiers."

Although Captain Bezean's recruits may not have experienced active service, the register of enlistments of the U.S. Army 1789–1914 (1812–1815 period) indicates that men of color were enlisted, in some cases served until 1817, and in some were taken prisoner. Black military men were present at the battles of Lake Erie and New Orleans.

During the War of 1812, American Negroes provided civilian manual labor and served as seamen aboard the war vessels at sea; on land the black soldiers fought in some famous battles. Though small in number blacks again contributed to America's defense.

## John Alfred
Private, 30th U. S. Infantry Regiment.

John Alfred was born in Vermont, where he was a farmer. He was enlisted in the army on March 24, 1814, by a Captain Wright. The official records list his description as eyes: black, hair: black, and complexion: black. He was discharged on June 17, 1815, when his term of enlistment expired.[1]

## George Barnwell
Private, Twenty-Third U.S. Infantry Regiment.

George Barnwell was born in New Orleans, Louisiana. He was enlisted in the army by a Lieutenant Wetmore in 1814. His occupation was given as sailor or farmer. Barnwell's name appeared as "present" on the duty rolls of Captain Peter Mills, dated September, 1814. He was also assigned to Captain A. W. Odell and Captain P. B. Van Buren. The official records gave his description as eyes: black; hair: black, and complexion: black.[2]

## George Bolton Jr.
Private, Thirty-Fourth U.S. Infantry Regiment.

George Bolton was born in Augusta, Massachusetts. A farmer, he was enlisted in the army in Portland, at the age of twenty-seven, on March 26, 1814, by a Lieutenant W. A. Springer. The official records state that he deserted at Plattsburgh in September, 1814. His description was given as eyes: grey; hair: black, and complexion; black.[3]

## John Bowen
Private, U.S. Artillery Regiment.

John Bowen was born in North Hampton, Massachusetts. He was a farmer. He was enlisted in the army at twenty-seven years of age, at Boston, on October 6, 1814, by a Captain Campbell, and was discharged on March 31, 1815, at the expiration of his term of service. The official records list his description as eyes: black; hair: black, and complexion: black.[4]

## Francis (Frances) Brown
Private, U.S. Eighth Artillery Regiment.

Francis Brown was born in Providence, Rhode Island. He was enlisted in the army by a Captain Campbell on August 22, 1814. His description was given as eyes: black; hair: black, and complexion: black.[5]

## John Brown
Private, U.S. Marine Corps.

John Brown was born in Huntington, New York. At the age of twenty-two he was enlisted in the marine corps, on June 8, 1815, at New York by a Captain Sterne. His civilian occupation was that of a blacksmith. The official size roll listed his description as, eyes: blue; hair: brown, and complexion: black.[6]

## John Davis
Corporal, Fifth Infantry Regiment.

John Davis was born in Orange County, New York. He gave his occupation as "soldier" and enlisted in the army at Chicago, Illinois for five years on September 5, 1838, at the age of thirty. The muster and description roll listed his description as height: five feet, eleven inches; eyes: black; hair: black, and complexion: black.[7]

## John DeCass
Private, Lieutenant George Morris's Company, U.S. Artillery.

John DeCass was born in St. Croix, and was a seaman. He enlisted in the army at Boston, on August 4, 1814, at the age of twenty-two. He was enlisted by Captain Washburn. He was present on the duty rosters in October, 1814, but later deserted. His description was given as eyes: black; hair: curly, and complexion: black.[8]

## Joshua Derwood
Private, Twenty-Sixth U.S. Infantry Regiment.

Joshua Derwood was born in New Jersey and was a farmer. He was enlisted in the army at the age of twenty-seven on February 1, 1815 at Philadelphia, Pennsylvania, by Captain Bezean. The duty roster of colored men listed him as present in April, 1815. The official records give his description as eyes: black; hair: curly; complexion: black.[9]

## Jacob Dexter
Private, Captain D. Ketcham's Twenty-Fifth Infantry Company, Colonel G. McFeely, Regimental Commander.

Jacob Dexter was enlisted in the army on March 18, 1814, by a Lieutenant Shaylor. He was a farmer. The company book showed Dexter present for duty on February 28, 1815, and on March 19, 1815 his name was on the duty roster. However, a duty roster dated January 24, 1815, stated that he had deserted at Sacketts Harbor, New York. He was wounded in the battle of Chippewa, July 5, 1814, and was discharged March 28, 1815. The official records describe him as a colored man, eyes: black; hair: black, and complexion: black.[10]

### Harry Dickinson

Private, Thirtieth U.S. Infantry Regiment.

Harry Dickinson was born in Philadelphia City, Pennsylvania, and was a cord weaver. He enlisted in the army on April 14, 1815, at the age of twenty-one, at Burlington. His enlistment officer was a Lieutenant Barney. The duty roster for February 28, 1815, lists him as present and to be transferred to the U.S. Artillery on June 17, 1815. The official records give Dickinson's description as hair: curly; eyes: black, and complexion: black.[11]

### Jean Louis Dolliole

Private, Captain Charles Porees' Company, First Battalion, Louisiana Militia.

Jean Louis Dolliole served as a private in the First Battalion of Colored Men in the Louisiana Militia. His name appears on the company muster rolls for December 16, 1814 to March 25, 1815, dated in New Orleans. His date of appointment was December 16, 1814 and the company pay roll showed his pay as "three months, nine days, eight [dollars] per month. Total, twenty-six dollars and thirty-four cents."[12]

### Samuel Draper

Private, Twenty-Sixth U.S. Infantry Regiment.

Samuel Draper was enlisted in October, 1814, by Lieutenant William Bezean at Philadelphia. He was born in Maryland and he worked as a laborer. He was nineteen years old when he enlisted, and was discharged in 1815 because he was a minor. His description was given as hair: black; eyes: black, and complexion: black.[13]

### Edward Duffin

Recruit, Captain Bezean's Company, Twenty-Sixth U.S. Infantry Regiment.

Edward Duffin was born in Pennsylvania, where he worked as a laborer. He enlisted in the army at the age of twenty-six, on January 3, 1815, at Philadelphia. He was listed as present on the duty roster of a detachment of recruits of colored men. His description was given as eyes: black; hair: curly, and complexion: black.[14]

### Simon Duke

Private, Twenty-Sixth U.S. Infantry Regiment.

Simon Duke was born in Pennsylvania. He was a laborer, but enlisted in the army at twenty-one years of age on February 3, 1815, at Philadelphia. He was enlisted by Captain Bezean. The duty roster of colored men dated April 1, 1815, states that he was present. The official records list his description as eyes: black; hair: curly, and complexion: black.[15]

### Alexander Durker

Rercruit, Captain William Bezean's Company, Twenty-Sixth U.S. Infantry Regiment.

Alexander Durker was enlisted in the army at the age of twenty-six by Captain Bezean on January 1, 1815, at Philadelphia. He was a farmer and was born in New York. The duty roster of colored men showed that he was present on April 1, 1815. He deserted later. His description was given as eyes: black; hair: curly, and complexion: brown.[16]

### Joseph Dury

Private, Twenty-Sixth U.S. Infantry Regiment.

Joseph Dury was enlisted in the army by Captain Bezean at the age of twenty-seven on February 1, 1815, at Philadelphia. He was born in New York. He deserted his unit on February 6, 1815. The official records state that his eyes were black, his hair black, and his complexion black.[17]

### John Eames

Private, J. R. Bell's Company. U.S. Light Artillery Unit.

John Eames was born in New Jersey and was a farmer. At the age of twenty-four, on November 4, 1814, he was enlisted in the army by a Captain Campbell. The records state that his hair was black, his eyes black, and his complexion black. The duty roster for February 16, 1815 at Fort Independence, listed him as present. He was discharged in April, 1815.[18]

## Joshua Edmund

Private, Captain William Bezean's Company, Twenty-Sixth U.S. Infantry Regiment.

Joshua Edmund was a farmer, born in Pennsylvania. He was enlisted by Captain Bezean at the age of twenty-eight on January 16, 1815, at Philadelphia. The duty roster of colored men shows that he was present on April 1, 1815. His description was given as eyes: black; hair: curly, and complexion: black.[19]

## Charles Ellsberry

Private, Lieutenant George N. Morris's Company, U.S. Artillery Regiment.

Charles Ellsberry was born in Dover, Delaware. His civilian occupation was that of a mariner. He was enlisted in the army for five years by a Captain W. Campbell, at the age of thirty-five, on October 5, 1814, at Boston. The duty roster of J. R. Bell's Company listed him as present on February 28, 1815, at Fort Independence. He was discharged on March 31, 1815, because he was a Negro and "unfit to accompany American soldiers." His description was listed as eyes: black; hair: black, and complexion: black.[20]

## Peter Embar

Private, Twenty-Sixth U.S. Regiment.

Peter Embar was born in Pennsylvania and he was a farmer. On January 10, 1815, he was enlisted in the army at Philadelphia by Captain Bezean. He was present on April 1, 1819, according to the duty roster of colored men. His description was: hair: black; eyes: black, and complexion: black.[21]

## Cuff Farmer

Recruit, Twenty-Sixth U.S. Infantry.

Cuff Farmer was born in New Jersey and worked as a farmer. At the age of thirty-six, he was enlisted in the army on November 28, 1814, at Philadelphia, by Lieutenant Bezean. The official records state that his eyes, hair, and complexion were black. Farmer was discharged on March 30, 1815.[22]

## William Flora

Private, Colonel William Woodford's Second Virginia Regiment.

William Flora served his country in both the American Revolutionary War and the War of 1812. During the American Revolution he exhibited bravery in action when a British force of two hundred stormed a bridge and were met by the sentinels. Flora continued to fire at the enemy after his comrades had retired into the fortifications.

In the War of 1812, William Flora served briefly as a marine on a gunboat. After the war he returned to Virginia and established himself as a successful businessman. He owned property in Portsmouth, Virginia, and operated a livery stable. He received a bounty allotment of one hundred acres for his military services. William Flora died in 1820.[23]

## Ezekieh Folden

Private, Twenty-Sixth U.S. Infantry.

Ezekieh Folden was born in Pennsylvania. He was a farmer, but at the age of thirty-four, on February 8, 1815, he joined the army at Philadelphia, Pennsylvania. He was enlisted by Captain Bezean. The duty roster of colored men dated April, 1815, listed him as present. He was described as having curly hair, black eyes and complexion.[24]

## Charles Forneret

Captain, DeClouet's Regiment, Louisiana Militia.

Charles Forneret commanded a company that was recruited at Fort St. Leon on December 23, 1814. The company consisted of forty-one men, and while performing garrison duty it was under the command of General David Morgan at Fort St. Leon. The official records mention Captain Forneret as follows: "Charles Forneret, Captain, Company of People of Color, Louisiana Militia." His name appeared on the company muster roll from December 23, 1834, to March 11, 1815. The roll was dated March 11, 1815, Fort St. Leon. His date of appointment was December 23, 1814.[25]

## Charles Forrest

Private, Twenty-Sixth Infantry Regiment.

Charles Forrest was born in Pennsylvania. At the age of thirty-four he was enlisted in the army at Philadelphia on February 11, 1815, by Captain Bezean. Forrest had worked as a laborer. The duty roster of colored men dated April, 1815, showed him as present. He was described as having curly hair, black eyes and complexion.[26]

### Joseph Francis

Private, U.S. Artillery Regiment.

Joseph Francis was born in San Salvador, West Indies. At the age of twenty-three, he was enlisted in the army for the duration of the war by a Lieutenant Washburn on July 18, 1814, at Boston. He was discharged at Pittsburgh on May 13, 1815, when his term expired. The official records described his hair, eyes and complexion as black.[27]

### John Frank

Private, Captain G. W. Banker's Company, Colonel William N. Irvine's Forty-Second Infantry Regiment.

John Frank was born in Germany. At the age of thirty-three, he was enlisted by a Captain J. J. Robinson, on September 17, 1814, at Philadelphia. He was assigned to Captain G. W. Banker's Company, Colonel William N. Irvine's Regiment. The duty roster for February 16, 1815, states that he was present. Official records describe him as having brown eyes, black hair and complexion.[28]

### Jacob Franklin

Private, Twenty-Sixth U.S. Infantry Regiment.

Jacob Franklin was born in Pennsylvania and was a farmer. He was enlisted in the army by Captain Bezean on January 27, 1815, at the age of thirty-five. The duty roster of colored men for April 1 indicated that he was present. He was described as having black eyes, curly hair, and a brown complexion.[29]

### Jacob Freeny

Recruit, Twenty-Sixth U.S. Infantry Regiment.

Jacob Freeny was born in Delaware. At the age of twenty he was enlisted into the army by Lieutenant William Bezean on December 28, 1814. The duty roster indicate that he was present on March 30, 1815. His description was: hair: curly; eyes: black, and complexion: black.[30]

### Michael Frey

Private, Captain George F. Goodman's Company, Thirty-Second U.S. Infantry Regiment.

Michael Frey was born in Pennsylvania and his occupation was farming. At the age of twenty-four, he enlisted in the army, on either January 17 or February 16, 1814, at Easton, Pennsylvania. He was discharged in May, 1815, because of time expiration, at Governor's Island. The official records describe him as being six feet and three-fourths of an inch tall, with black hair, eyes, and complexion.[31]

### Quamenaugh Fuller

Private, U.S. Artillery Regiment.

Quamenaugh Fuller was born in Hartford or Lynn, Connecticut. On August 13, 1814, he joined the army, at the age of twenty-seven, his occupation having been that of a laborer. He was enlisted at Providence or Dedham by a Captain Campbell. The rosters indicate that he was present for duty at Boston, Massachusetts, and was discharged on March 31, 1815, when his term expired. His description was: eyes: black; hair: black, and complexion: black.[32]

### William Gansey

Private, Twenty-Sixth U.S. Infantry Regiment.

William Gansey was born in Africa. Captain Bezean enlisted him in the army at the age of thirty at Philadelphia in December, 1814. His occupation was that of a laborer. The duty rolls list him as present on December 31, 1814 and he was discharged at Philadelphia on March 20, 1815, when his term of service expired. He was described as having black eyes, curly hair, and a chestnut complexion.[33]

### Edward Gardener

Recruit, 26th U.S. Infantry Regiment.

Edward Gardener was born in New York. He was enlisted in the army by Lieutenant Bezean at the age of twenty-nine on September 21, 1814. The duty roster states that he was present on December 3, 1815, at Lazaretta. Gardener was discharged on May 23, 1815. He was officially described as having black eyes, curly hair, and a black complexion.[34]

### William Gardner

Private, U.S. Artillery Regiment.

William Gardner was born in Massachusetts,

and was a laborer or chimney sweeper. He was enlisted at the age of nineteen on July 29, 1814, in Boston by Lieutenant Washburn. His name appears as present on the duty rolls, and he was discharged on March 31, 1815, when his term of service expired. His official description lists his eyes, hair, and complexion as black.[35]

## William Garland

Private, Twenty-Sixth U.S. Infantry Regiment.

William Garland was born in Pennsylvania, and worked as a laborer. He was enlisted in the army by Captain Bezean and appeared as present on the duty rolls. Garland was described as having black eyes, curly hair, and a chestnut complexion.[36]

## William George

Recruit, Twenty-Sixth U. S. Infantry Regiment.

William George was born in Virginia, and was enlisted on the army on October 7, 1814, by Lieutenant Bezean. The official duty rosters show him present on December 31, 1814 and on March 30, 1815. He was discharged in 1815 when his term expired. The records also describe him as having a black complexion, eyes, and hair. He was twenty-two years of age when he enlisted and he had worked as a blacksmith.[37]

## Nathan Gilbert

Private, Thirty-First U.S. Infantry Regiment.

Nathan Gilbert was born in Boston, Massachusetts, and was enlisted in the army on April 3, 1814 by a Lieutenant Brown. He was discharged at Plattsburgh on June 4, 1815, when his term of service expired. His description on official records read eyes: black; hair: black, and complexion; black.[38]

## Daniel Goforth

Private, Captain William Sheehan's Company, Twenty-Sixth U. S. Infantry Regiment.

Daniel Goforth was born in Pennsylvania. He enlisted, at the age of twenty-eight, at Philadelphia, Pennsylvania, on January 1, 1815. The enlisting officer was Captain Bezean. The duty rosters of colored men dated March 25 and April 1, 1815 showed him as present. He was discharged at Philadelphia on May 1, 1815. He is described as having black eyes, curly hair and chestnut complexion.[39]

## James Gomaus

Private, Captain S. H. Holley's Company, Eleventh U.S. Infantry Regiment.

James Gomaus enlisted in the army for five years in June, 1812, having worked in civilian life as a baker. The records describe him as having black hair, eyes and complexion. The duty roster indicated that he died on February 19, 1813.[40]

## Abraham Gossard

Private, Captain William Bezean's Company, Twenty-Sixth U.S. Infantry Regiment.

Abraham Gossard was born in New York and his occupation was listed as "seaman." He enlisted in the army in New York and was described as having blue eyes, curly hair, and a black complexion.[41]

## John Gray

Recruit, Lieutenant William Bezean's Regiment, Twenty-Sixth U.S. Infantry Regiment.

John Gray, a native of Delaware, was enlisted in the army at Philadelphia by Lieutenant Bezean on November 6, 1814, at the age of twenty-seven. He was described as having black eyes, brown or black hair and complexion. The word "col'd" was written beside his name. Gray was discharged on March 30, 1815, because of a disability.[42]

## Martin Grinton

Private, Tenth U.S. Infantry Regiment.

Martin Grinton was born in Wilks, North Carolina, where he worked as a farmer. He was enlisted in the army at Wilks, by Lieutenant Gordon on April 23 or 24, 1813, at the age of twenty-two. The duty roster records him as present in Captain Robert Mitchell's Company on February 16 and February 28, and on April 30, 1815; with Captain F. J. Leigh's Company on February 16, 1815, and with Captain H. H. Willard's detachment in Washington on July 31, 1815. He was present in confinement, having deserted at July 22, 1815. He was discharged at Elkton on August 22 of the same year. His eyes, hair and complexion were described as black.[43]

## William Hunter

Private, Twenty-Sixth U.S. Infantry Regiment.

William Hunter was born in Delaware and at the age of thirty-four was enlisted in the army by Captain Bezean on February 12, 1815, at Philadelphia. His occupation was that of a seaman. The duty roster of colored men listed him as present on April 1, 1815, and the official records described him as having black eyes and complexion, and curly hair.[44]

## John Johnson

Private, U.S. Light Infantry Regiment.

John Johnson was born in Danbury, Connecticut. He worked as a laborer until, at twenty-two years of age, he was enlisted by a Captain Campbell for the duration of the war, at Dedham, Massachusetts, on September 22, 1814. The official records of men enlisted in the U.S. Army prior to the Peace Establishment on May 17, 1815, gave the following information about John Johnson: Company Book 1814: present on October 16 and October 30, 1814. Present on the duty roster of Captain J. R. Bell's Company on February 16, and February 28, 1815. Company Book 569 lists him as discharged, March 31, 1815, "on account of being a Negro and unfit to accompany American soldiers."[45]

## Noah Ladine

Private, Twenty-Sixth U.S. Infantry Regiment.

Noah Ladine was born in Delaware and was enlisted in the army by Captain William Bezean on October 7, 1814, at the age of twenty-eight, at Philadelphia, Pennsylvania. The official records described him as having black eyes, hair and complexion. The duty roster for March 30, 1815, lists him as present.[46]

## Peter Lawrence

Private, U.S. Artillery Regiment.

Peter Lawrence was born at Petersburg, Virginia. At the age of twenty-three, on October 7, 1814, he was enlisted in the army by a Captain Campbell in Boston, Massachusetts. He had been a mariner in civilian life. Duty rosters and company books show that Lawrence was present for duty until March 11, 1815, when his term of enlistment expired. The official records describe him as follows: eyes; black; hair: black, and complexion: black.[47]

## Frederick Lewis

Recruit, U.S. Army Light Artillery Unit.

Frederick Lewis, a native of Baltimore, Maryland, was enlisted in the army by Lieutenant Washburn on July 14, 1814, at Boston, Massachusetts. The official records list his description as: hair: black; eyes: black, and complexion: black. The duty roster of Captain J. R. McIntosh's Company shows him present on February 16, 1815. He was discharged at Plattsburgh on May 21, 1815, at the expiration of his term of service.[48]

## Samuel Looks

Musician, Captain Harrison's and Captain Deshas' Company, Second U.S. Rifles.

Samuel Looks was born in Quebec, Canada. He was enlisted into the army by a Captain Morrison, at Chillicothe, Ohio, on July 4, 1814, for a term of five years. At that time he was twenty years old. Looks was assigned to Captain Harrison's and Captain Deshas' Company, and was listed as present for duty on April 30, 1815. On the official records his eyes, hair and complexion are described as black.[49]

## John Moore

Recruit, Thirty-First U.S. Infantry Regiment.

John Moore was born in Londondery, New Hampshire and worked as a barber. At the age of twenty-one he was enlisted in the army by a Lieutenant Brown, for the duration of the war. The official records describe him as having black hair, eyes and complexion. It is believed that he served until March 31, 1815.[50]

## Samuel Moore

Private, Captain J. McIntosh's Company, First U.S. Light Artillery.

Samuel Moore was born in Swisborough, Massachusetts. On July 15, 1814, he was enlisted at Boston by a Lieutenant Washburn for the duration of the war. Samuel Moore's name appeared on the recruit roll dated July, 1814, Book 567, as having entered the hospital on September 9 and having been discharged on September 30, 1814. He was listed as absent in the duty roster of Captain J. McIntosh's Company on February 16, 1815, having left Plattsburgh. He is described in the records as being five feet six inches in height, with black hair, eyes and complexion.[51]

### Silas Moore

Private, Fourth U.S. Infantry Regiment.

Silas Moore was born in Dumbarton, New Hampshire and was enlisted in the army at the age of twenty-six by a Lieutenant Sow at Hillsborough on October 4, 1814. The duty roll of Captain E. Ways' Company showed him as present on February 16, 1815. Moore was discharged at Portsmouth, New Hampshire on April 1, 1815, at the expiration of his term of service. The official records describe him as having black eyes, hair and complexion.[52]

### Jacob Palmer

Private, Thirty-First U. S. Infantry Regiment.

Jacob Palmer was a farmer, born at Stonington, New London, Connecticut. He was enlisted in the army by a Captain Burnaps on February 22, 1814, at Plattsburgh, New York. The official records describe his eyes, hair and complexion as black. He deserted from his unit on July 9, 1814.[53]

### Isaac Parcells

Private, U.S. Artillery Regiment.

Isaac Parcells enlisted in the army at New York on December 4, 1812, and served until the expiration of his term on December 4, 1817. The official records describe him as having black eyes, hair and complexion.[54]

### John Paskal

Recruit, Twenty-Sixth U.S. Regiment.

John Paskal was born in Delaware, and was enlisted in the army on November 2, 1814, at Philadelphia, by Lieutenant William Bezean. His description listed his eyes, hair and complexion as black.[55]

### John Paul

Private, U.S. Artillery Regiment.

John Paul was born in New Orleans, and was enlisted in the army at Boston, Massachusetts on July 15, 1814, by a Lieutenant Washburn. Paul served in the war until he was reported missing. The records describe his eyes, hair and complexion as black.[56]

### James Perry

Recruit, U.S. Artillery Regiment.

James Perry enlisted in the army in November, 1814 and was discharged, according to the records, on March 2, 1815, being "a Negro and not fit companion for the American soldier." His description was: eyes: black; hair: black, and complexion: black.[57]

### John Peters

Recruit, Twenty-Sixth U.S. Infantry Regiment.

John Peters was enlisted in the army at Philadelphia on November 23, 1814, by Lieutenant William Bezean. He was officially described as having black eyes, hair and complexion.[58]

### George Philip

Private, Twenty-Sixth Infantry Regiment.

George Philip was born in Pennsylvania, and at thirty years of age enlisted in the army on October 31, 1814, in Boston, Massachusetts. He was listed as a "Colored Man" and described as having black eyes, hair and complexion. Philip was discharged on May 1, 1815.[59]

### Bartholemy Populus

Lieutenant, First Battalion of Free Men of Color (Fortiers), Louisiana Militia.

Bartholemy Populus became the second Negro officer in the battalion when he was appointed adjutant on December 15, 1814. The company muster roll for December 16, 1814 to March 25, 1815, roll dated New Orleans March 25, 1815, shows the name Populus, Bartholemy, Lieutenant. His date of appointment was December 16, 1814.[60]

### Vincent Populus

Second Major, First Battalion of Free Men of Color (Locoste's), Louisiana Militia.

Vincent Populus was the ranking Negro officer of the battalion. According to historian Roland C. McConnell, this was the first recognition by the

United States of a colored officer of field grade status. Populus appears with the rank of major on a muster roll of the Field Staff Officers and Band, First Battalion of Free Men of Color, Louisiana Militia, for December 16, 1814 to March 25, 1815. A roll dated New Orleans, March 25, 1815, indicates that Major Populus was present.[61]

### Belton Savarie (Savary)

Sergeant, Second Battalion (D'Aquin's), Free Men of Color, Louisiana Militia.

Belton Savarie served in combat operations in the War of 1812. The official records state that Sergeant Savarie was a member of Captain Marcelin Gilot's Company of militia of volunteers of San Domingo and of the battalion commanded by Major D'Aquin. His name appears on the company muster roll for December 19, 1814 to March 20, 1815, dated New Orleans, March 20, 1815. His date of appointment was December 19, 1814. Sergeant Savarie was mortally wounded and died on January 10, 1815.[62]

### Joseph Savory

Major, Second Battalion (D'Aquin's) Free Men of Color, Louisiana Militia.

Joseph Savory was a free man of color who came to Louisiana from Santo Domingo and was instrumental in organizing the Second Battalion. He served at the battle of New Orleans and his leadership and performance of duty were commendable. Major Joseph Savory's name appears on a muster roll of the field and staff and noncommissioned officers, Battalion of Free Men of Color, Militia, state of Louisiana, commanded by Major D'Aquin. His date of appointment was December 19, 1814, commencement of service December 19, 1814, and expiration of service March 20, 1815, presented by order of General Johnson.[63]

### John Scott

Private, Captain Shelton's Company, Tenth Virginia Regiment.

John Scott was a free man who served until the end of the War of 1812. He was allowed a pension on his application executed August 13, 1829, when he was living in Hamilton Township, Warren County, Ohio.[64]

### Solomon Sharp (or Sharpe)

Private, Eleventh U.S. Infantry Regiment.

Solomon Sharp, a black, was a farmer, born in Conway, Massachusetts. At the age of twenty-nine, he was enlisted in the army by a Lieutenant Smead. The duty roll shows him as absent at Plattsburgh on April 15, 1814. He was later exchanged as an American prisoner of war and received at Chazy on May 11, 1814. He was discharged on February 2, 1818.[65]

### William Sherbourne

Recruit, U.S. Artillery Regiment.

William Sherbourne was born in Londonderry, New Hampshire and was a mariner in civilian life. He was enlisted in the army by Lieutenant Smead, at the age of twenty-nine. His eyes, hair and complexion were listed as black.[66]

### Peter Simpson

Private, Twenty-Third U.S. Infantry Regiment.

Peter Simpson was born in Brookfield, Connecticut, and worked as a shoemaker. He enlisted in the army on January 7, 1814. The duty roll shows that he was present on September 30, 1814, and was at Buffalo General Hospital, wounded. His description is "mulatto."[67]

### Samuel Stanley

Private, Eleventh U.S. Infantry Regiment.

Samuel Stanley was born in Oxford, Massachusetts and was a farmer. He was enlisted in the army on February 16, 1813, at Pottersfield, for a period of eighteen months, by a Captain J. Stark. Company Book 285 shows that he was discharged on August 10, 1814, at the expiration of his term of service. His eyes, hair and complexion were officially listed as black.[68]

### William Thatcher

Private, First U.S. Infantry Regiment.

William Thatcher was born in New Jersey and was a farmer. He was enlisted in the army on September 21, 1840 at Easton by a Major Graham when he was twenty-seven years old. The records state that he died on October 5, 1841, at Fort Winnebago, New Jersey. He is described as having hazel eyes, black hair and black complexion.[69]

**Francis Thompson**

Private, Eleventh U.S. Infantry Regiment.

Francis Thompson was a native of Bethlehem, Rensselaer County, New York. He was a farmer and enlisted in the army in March, 1813, at the age of twenty-one. His name appears on the roster of Lieutenant Isaac Clark's Company. Thompson was wounded and became a prisoner of war. He is described as having black eyes, hair and complexion.[70]

**John Bathan Vashon**

Common Seaman, *USS Revenge,* U.S. Navy.

John B. Vashon was born in 1792 in Norfolk, Virginia. His mother was a mulatto and his father was Captain George Vashon, a Caucasian of French ancestry who had served as an Indian agent under General Washington and President Van Buren.

In 1812, at the age of twenty, Vashon went to sea on board the *USS Revenge,* as a seaman. He was taken prisoner by the English, with other crew members, in an engagement off the coast of Brazil. Later the prisoners were released in an exchange and John Vashon returned to live in his native Virginia, first at Fredericksburg and later at Dumfries and Leesburg. He was proprietor of a public saloon in Carlisle, Pennsylvania, for seven years, but in 1829 he moved his family to Pittsburgh, Pennsylvania and became active in the anti-slavery movement. Vashon was associated with the abolitionist William Lloyd Garrison and was also a member of Temperance and Moral Reform societies. He was one of the vice presidents of the National Convention of Colored Men, held at Rochester, New York, in July, 1853.

On January 8, 1854, John Vashon died while attending a national convention of old soldiers of 1812 in Philadelphia. He was a man of courage, and of untiring fidelity to his country and the cause of Negro emancipation.[71]

**Joseph Wendall (or Wendell)**

Private, First U.S. Artillery Regiment.

Joseph Wendall was born in Boston, Massachusetts and was a ropemaker. He was enlisted in the army by Lieutenant Washburn on July 15, 1814. Wendall was reported as sick at Brownsville, and was discharged on May 31, 1815 at the expiration of his term of service. His eyes, hair and complexion were listed as black.[72]

**Charles White**

Private, Twenty-Sixth U.S. Infantry Regiment.

Charles White was a laborer, born in the state of Delaware. At the age of twenty-one he was enlisted in the army, at Philadelphia, on February 4, 1815, by Captain William Bezean. The duty rolls of colored men dated April, 1815, showed him as present. His description was: eyes: black; hair: curly, and complexion: black.[73]

**James White**

Private, Twenty-Sixth U.S. Infantry Regiment.

James White was a black farmer and was born in Pennsylvania. He was enlisted in the army at Philadelphia on October 25, 1814 by Lieutenant Bezean. White was discharged in May, 1815.[74]

**John White**

Private, U.S. Marine Corps.

John White was born in Camden, North Carolina and worked as a laborer. He was enlisted by a Captain Henderson in the Marine Corps on May 16, 1813 at Charlestown, for a term of five years. The official size roll describes him as having dark eyes, brown hair and a black complexion.[75]

**Cato Williams**

Private, Eleventh U.S. Infantry Regiment.

Cato Williams was born in Lanesborough, Massachusetts. He worked as a farmer, but was enlisted in the army on May 24, 1812 by a Captain Holly. He was listed as present on the duty roster of Captain John Bliss's Company on November 30, 1813; as absent and left sick at Burlington on May 31, 1813, and as transferred to Lieutenant Green's Company on December 20, 1813. On April 30, 1814, he was reported absent in the navy on Lake Champlain. Williams was described as having black hair, eyes and complexion.[76]

**Henry Williams**

Private, U.S. Artillery Regiment.

Henry Williams was born in St. Croix. His

civilian occupation was as a laborer and he was enlisted in the army on October 3, 1814, by a Lieutenant George Morris. His description was listed as: eyes: black; hair: black, and complexion: black.[77]

## Henry Willis

Private, Twenty-Ninth U.S. Infantry Regiment.

Henry Willis was a laborer, born in Stockbridge, Massachusetts. He was enlisted in the army on July 6, 1814, at Troy, New York, by Lieutenant Dumbleton. Willis was assigned to Captain John C. Rochester's Company, and the records state that he deserted in April, 1816, from Halfmoon, New York. He was described as having black hair, eyes and complexion.[78]

## George Wilton

Private, Twenty-Sixth U.S. Infantry Regiment.

George Wilton was a farmer, born in Delaware. He was enlisted in the army by Captain Bezean on February 4, 1815, at Philadelphia. The duty or drill roster for May 1, 1815, listed him as present. His eyes were described as black, his hair as curly, and his complexion, black.[79]

## Abraham Winters

Private, Twenty-Sixth U.S. Infantry Regiment.

Abraham Winters was born in Pennsylvania and was a farmer. At the age of twenty-two, he was enlisted in the army at Philadelphia by Captain Bezean, on January 8, 1815. His eyes were described as black, his hair, curly, and his complexion, brown.[80]

# Notes to Chapter Two

1. Register of Enlistments in the United States Army 1797–1814, John Alfred, May, 1815, Microcopy 233, National Archives, Washington, D.C.
2. Register of Enlistments, George Barnwell, May, 1815, *loc. cit.*
3. Register of Enlistments, George Bolton Jr., May, 1815, *loc. cit.*
4. Register of Enlistments, John Bowen, May, 1815, *loc. cit.*
5. Register of Enlistments, Frances Brown, May, 1815, *loc. cit.*
6. Size Roll of the Marines Commanded by Lieutenant Colonel Franklin Wharton enlisted in the service of the United States, January 1, 1806 to December 31, 1821, Record Group 27, Entry, 31, National Archives, Washington, D.C.
7. Muster and Description Roll of a Detachment of U.S. Recruits by the General Superintendent for the Companies of the Fifth Regiment of Infantry Stationed at Fort Howard Green Bay Pursuant to Order No. 3, dated October 12, 1838, at Fort Dearborn, Chicago, RG 94, National Archives.
8. Register of Enlistments, John DeCass, May, 1815, *loc. cit.*
9. Register of Enlistments, Joshua Derwood, May, 1815, *loc. cit.*
10. Register of Enlistments, Jacob Dexter, May, 1815, *loc. cit.*
11. Register of Enlistments, Harry Dickinson, June, 1815, *loc. cit.*
12. Register of Enlistments, Jean Louis Dolliole, December, 1814, *loc. cit.*
13. Register of Enlistments, Samuel Draper, 1815, *loc. cit.*
14. Register of Enlistments, Edward Duffin, 1815, *loc. cit.*
15. Register of Enlistments, Simon Duke, 1815, *loc. cit.*
16. Register of Enlistments, Alexander Durker, 1815, *loc. cit.*
17. Register of Enlistments, Joseph Dury, 1815, *loc. cit.*
18. Register of Enlistments, John Eames, 1815, *loc. cit.*
19. Register of Enlistments, Joshua Edmund, 1815, *loc. cit.*
20. Register of Enlistments, Charles Ellsberry, 1815, *loc. cit.*
21. Register of Enlistments, Peter Embar, 1815, *loc. cit.*
22. Register of Enlistments, Cuff Farmer, May, 1815, *loc. cit.*
23. NAACP, *Black Heroes of the American Revolution 1775–1783* (New York: NAACP, n.d.).
24. Register of Enlistments, Ezekiel Folden, 1815, *loc. cit.*
25. Muster Roll of Captain Forneret, RG 15, Record of the Adjutant General's Office, National Archives.
26. Register of Enlistments, Charles Forrest, 1815, *loc. cit.*
27. Register of Enlistments, Joseph Francis, 1815, *loc. cit.*
28. Register of Enlistments, John Frank, 1815, *loc. cit.*

29. Register of Enlistments, Jacob Franklin, 1815, *loc. cit.*

30. Register of Enlistments, Jacob Freeney, 1815, *loc. cit.*

31. Register of Enlistments, Michael Frey, 1815, *loc. cit.*

32. Register of Enlistments, Quamenaugh Fuller, 1815, *loc. cit.*

33. Register of Enlistments, William Gansey, May, 1815, *loc. cit.*

34. Register of Enlistments, Edward Gardener, 1815, *loc. cit.*

35. Register of Enlistments, William Gardner, May, 1815, *loc. cit.*

36. Register of Enlistments, William Garland, May, 1815, *loc. cit.*

37. Register of Enlistments, William George, 1815, *loc. cit.*

38. Register of Enlistments, Nathan Gilbert, May, 1815, *loc. cit.*

39. Register of Enlistments, Daniel Goforth, 1815, *loc. cit.*

40. Register of Enlistments, James Gomaus, 1812, *loc. cit.*

41. Register of Enlistments, Abraham Gossand, 1815, *loc. cit.*

42. Register of Enlistments, John Gray, 1814, *loc. cit.*

43. Register of Enlistments, Martin Grinton, 1813, *loc. cit.*

44. Register of Enlistments, William Hunter, May, 1815, *loc. cit.*

45. Register of Enlistments, John Johnson, 1815, *loc. cit.*

46. Register of Enlistments, Noah Ladine, 1815, *loc. cit.*

47. Register of Enlistments, Peter Lawrence, 1815, *loc. cit.*

48. Register of Enlistments, Frederick Lewis, May, 1815, *loc. cit.*

49. Register of Enlistments, Samuel Looks, 1815, *loc. cit.*

50. Register of Enlistments, John Moore, 1815, *loc. cit.*

51. Register of Enlistments, Samuel Moore, 1815, *loc. cit.*

52. Register of Enlistments, Silas Moore, 1815, *loc. cit.*

53. Register of Enlistments, Jacob Palmer, 1815, *loc. cit.*

54. Register of Enlistments, Isaac Parcells, May, 1815, *loc. cit.*

55. Register of Enlistments, John Paskal, May, 1815, *loc. cit.*

56. Register of Enlistments, John Paul, May, 1815, *loc. cit.*

57. Register of Enlistments, James Perry, May, 1815, *loc. cit.*

58. Register of Enlistments, John Peters, May, 1815, *loc. cit.*

59. Register of Enlistments, George Philip, May, 1815, *loc. cit.*

60. Military Pension Files of Bartholemy Populus, RG 15, Records of the Adjutant General's Office, National Archives, Washington, D.C.

61. Muster Roll, First Battalion of Free Men of Color, Louisiana Militia, RG 94, National Archives, Washington, D.C.
McConnell, Roland C., *Negro Troops of Antebellum Louisiana* (Baton Rouge: Louisiana State University Press, 1968), p. 68.

62. Military Pension File of Belton Savarie (Savary), *loc. cit.*

63. Military Pension File of Joseph Savory, *loc. cit.*

64. Military Pension File of John Scott, *loc. cit.*

65. Register of Enlistments, Solomon Sharpe or Sharpe, May, 1815, *loc. cit.*

66. Register of Enlistments, William Sherbourne, May, 1815, *loc. cit.*

67. Register of Enlistments, Peter Simpson, May, 1815, *loc. cit.*

68. Register of Enlistments, Samuel Stanley, May, 1815, *loc. cit.*

69. Register of Enlistments, William Thatcher, May, 1851, *loc. cit.*

70. Register of Enlistments, Francis Thompson, May, 1815, *loc. cit.*

71. Nell, William C., *Colored Patriots of the American Revolution* (Boston: Robert Wallcut, 1855), pp. 181–188.

72. Register of Enlistments, Joseph Wendall, or Wendell, May, 1815, *loc. cit.*

73. Register of Enlistments, Charles White, May, 1815, *loc. cit.*

74. Register of Enlistments, James White, May, 1815, *loc. cit.*

75. Size Roll of Marines Commanded by Lieutenant Colonel Franklin Wharton.

76. Register of Enlistments, Cato Williams, May, 1815, *loc. cit.*

77. Register of Enlistments, Henry Williams, May, 1815, *loc. cit.*

78. Register of Enlistments, Henry Willis, May, 1815, *loc. cit.*

79. Register of Enlistments, George Wilton, May, 1815, *loc. cit.*

80. Register of Enlistments, Abraham Winters, May, 1815, *loc. cit.*

# Chapter Three

## The Mexican War, 1846-1848

The United States in 1845 claimed that it had a legitimate right to controversial land beyond the Nueces and Rio Grande on the Mexican side. This dispute developed into a conflict that lasted from 1846 until 1848. The Congress authorized an enlistment of fifty thousand volunteers and black men were among those who answered their country's call.

The Negro's participation was mainly in the navy, with an estimated one thousand blacks in naval service during the Mexican War. A review of the Register of Enlistments of the United States Army, 1798–1914, reveals that Negroes also served in the army in regular and volunteer units.

Blacks served in the First Regiment of Volunteers, New York; the Fourth Artillery Regiment, the Ninth, Tenth, Eleventh and Thirteenth Infantry regiments, and other units. Negroes served as infantrymen and as musicians, the most notable being the black musician Jordan B. Noble, a veteran of New Orleans in the War of 1812.

## Peter Allen

Musician, Captain Wyatt's Company.

Among those Texas soldiers who were massacred with Colonel James Fannin at Goliad in 1836 was Peter Allen, a free Negro from Pennsylvania, who operated a blacksmith shop at Huntsville. Allen volunteered for Captain Wyatt's Company at Huntsville in 1835, and was designated the company musician because he played both flute and banjo. He was among three hundred soldiers who were slaughtered on Palm Sunday.[1]

## Hendricks Arnold

Guide.

One of the first Negro freedmen in Texas was Hendricks Arnold, whose father was a member of Austin's "Old 300" (the original colonists). Hendricks Arnold was a hunting companion and close friend of the famed scouts, Erasmus (Deaf) Smith and Henry Wax Karnes. He was so essential as a guide for the Texans when they attacked Bexar in 1835 that the attack was delayed for a day, waiting for him to return from a hunt. Arnold was cited in the Texas report of the capture of San Antonio for distinguished service. He served with Smith and Karnes in the Texas spy company at San Jacinto, and later married Smith's step-daughter. Given a tract of land for his services in the Revolution, Arnold settled in San Antonio and operated a grist mill. A portion of his mill stands today near Mission San Juan Capistrano. The site of his home was marked for years as a historical monument. His grave, located in a small plot beside the Medina River, on land which once was part of his bounty as a hero of the Republic, bears a state monument.[2]

## John Bechtel

Private, Company B, First Regiment of Volunteers, New York.

John Bechtel was a native of Berwange, Germany, and worked as a laborer. On December 5, 1846, at the age of twenty-four, he was enlisted into the army at New York by a G. Bongard. The official records describe him as being five feet, ten inches tall, with brown hair and eyes and a "colored" complexion.[3]

### David Black

Private, Second Dragoon Company.

David Black was born in Poeble County, Ohio. At the age of twenty-one, on August 12, 1847, he was enlisted in the army at Fort Wayne by Captain Armstrong. The official records give the following description: eyes: dark; hair: grey, and complexion: black. David Black was discharged from the army on July 10, 1848, at Jefferson Barracks. His civilian occupation was farming.[4]

### James Bose

Private, New York Company B, First Regiment of Volunteers.

James Bose, a native of Ireland and a baker by trade, was enlisted in the army on December 10, 1846 by N Decroft. He was twenty-two years old. The official records give his height as five feet, five inches, his complexion as colored; his eyes, grey, and hair, brown.[5]

### Thomas B. Brashear

Corporal, Rifle G Company.

Thomas Brashear was born in Lafayette, Louisiana. While working as a clerk he decided to join the army and was enlisted on April 19, 1847, at New Orleans, by a Captain Barker. He was discharged on July 31, 1848, at Jefferson Barracks. He is described as having hazel eyes, black hair and complexion.[6]

### Barbee G. Collins (or Collon)

Private, Company B, Tenth Infantry Regiment.

Barbee Collins, a native of Tennessee, was a farmer. He was enlisted in the army, at the age of twenty, by a Captain Clay, on May 1, 1847. The official records describe him as having blue eyes, black hair and complexion. Collins was discharged from the army at the expiration of his term of service at Mobile, Alabama.[7]

### John Conter

Fifer, Thirteenth Infantry, Fourth Regiment.

John Conter, a black native of De Kalb, Georgia, was enlisted in the army in April, 1847, at Atlanta, Georgia, by F. Kirkpatrick, and was discharged on January 9, 1848 at Suole Natural, Mexico. He worked as a carpenter in civilian life.[8]

### Michael Curran

Private, Second, Third, Fourth and Fifth Regiments of Infantry Recruits.

Michael Curran was enlisted in the army at the age of thirty, by a Lieutenant Grafton at Boston, Massachusetts on August 14, 1848. The official records describe him as having hazel eyes and black hair and complexion.[9]

### Daniel Cutler

Private, Ninth Regiment.

Daniel Cutler was born at Montpelier, Vermont, and worked as a farmer. He was enlisted in the army at the age of twenty-five, on April 21, 1847, by a Lieutenant Newman at Montpelier. Official records give his description as: eyes: blue; hair: black, and complexion: black. Cutler was discharged on April 12, 1848, at Pachuico, Mexico.[10]

### Josephus Daines

Private, Fourth Artillery.

Josephus Daines was born in Milo, New York, and worked as a mason. At the age of thirty-five he decided to join the army, and was enlisted on February 5, 1847, at Fort Polk by a Captain Bainbridge. The official records describe his eyes as hazel, his hair, dark, and his complexion, black. He died on July 17, 1847, of chronic diarrhea, at Puebla, Mexico.[11]

### George Daric (or Daril)

Private, Company B, First Regiment Volunteers, New York.

George Daric, a native of Baldin, Germany, and a laborer by trade, was enlisted in the army at twenty years of age on December 4, 1846, at New York, by G. Reichardt. Official records give his height as five feet, five inches, his complexion, colored, hair, brown and eyes, blue (or bleu).[12]

### Charles Debeque

Private, First Regiment Volunteers, New York.

Charles Debeque was born in Rouen, France and worked as a clerk. He was enlisted in the army by G. deBargard on December 26, 1846, at Fort Hamilton. His official description lists his age at twenty-three, his height as five feet, six inches; his complexion, colored; his eyes, blue, and his hair, brown. The records state that he died at Puebla on June 11, 1847.[13]

### Dick the Drummer

Several Negroes participated in the Battle of San Jacinto, in various capacities. Their patriotic spirit exemplified by a gray-haired freedman known as "Dick the Drummer." *The Texas Gazette,* describing a banquet attended by Dick and other veterans of the Battle of San Jacinto in 1850, used these words:

*By the effective beating of his drum, this gray-haired descendent of Ham carried consternation into the ranks of Santa Anna's myrmidons.*

None of the accounts give Dick's last name.[14]

### Alexander C. Elliot

Private, Captain Duncan's Company, Volunteer Regiment.

Alexander Elliot was enlisted in the army at the age of twenty-four by J. Duncan in Ohio on May 4, 1847. Eliot was born in Newark, near Columbus, Ohio, and worked as a farmer. His official description is: eyes: gray; hair: black; complexion: black, and height: five feet, eleven and one-half inches.[15]

### Joseph Garrison

Private, Rifle K

Joseph Garrison was born in Baltimore, Maryland and was a sailor before joining the army. He was enlisted on February 9, 1847, at Baltimore, Maryland, by a Lieutenant Walker. The records describe him as having blue eyes, dark hair and a black complexion. Garrison died on January 13, 1848 at Mexico City.[16]

### William Goyens

The Texas Congress awarded a tract of land to William Goyens for his service in the Army of Texas in 1836. Goyens was already a wealthy man who operated a blacksmith shop and bought and sold land and racehorses at Nacogdoches.

The first recorded mention of Goyens was in 1832, when a visitor to Texas, named Benjamin Lundy, wrote that Goyens' two white brothers-in-law from Georgia had come to visit him and their

sister. General Sam Houston appointed Goyens as agent to deal with the Cherokee Indians and a successful treaty was negotiated. Goyens spoke Spanish and several Indian dialects, as well as English. He had freed himself, having run away from a life of slavery in South Carolina in 1821. He came to Texas via Galveston Island and operated a sawmill on a two thousand-acre tract west of Nacogdoches on what is still known as "Goyens' Hill" and also raised cattle and horses. Historical records show that in 1841 he owned 4,160 acres of improved land worth $20,600, two town lots, fifty head of cattle, two work horses and other property. A state Centennial marker at the Goyens cemetery near Nacogdoches reads as follows:

*William (Bill) Goyens, born a slave in South Carolina, 1794. Escaped to Texas in 1821. Rendered valuable assistance to the Army of Texas, 1836. Acquired wealth and was noted for his charity. Died at his home on Goyens Hill, 1856. His skin was black, his heart, true blue.*[17]

### Dominick Griffaton

Private, B Company, Eleventh Infantry Regiment.

Dominick Griffaton was born in France. He decided to enlist in the army while working as a laborer, and on March 16, 1847, he was enlisted by a Lieutenant Woods. He was discharged at Jefferson Barracks on July 31, 1848. Griffaton was described as having dark eyes and hair and a black complexion.[18]

### Moses Johnson

Private, Second Artillery Regiment.

Moses Johnson, a native of Mohawk, New York, was enlisted in the army on April 11, 1848, at Buffalo, New York, by a Captain Maclay. He deserted on March 3, 1848. His description was: eyes: hazel; hair: brown; complexion: black, and height: five feet, nine inches.[19]

### John Leudwich (or Ludwich)

Private, First Regiment Volunteers, New York, First Infantry.

John Leudwich was born in Barbuck, Germany. He worked as a farmer, but at twenty-one years of age was enlisted in the army by N. DeCroft at Syracuse, New York, on December 20, 1846. The official roster describes him as being five feet, nine inches in height, with grai (or gray) eyes, light brown hair and a colored complexion.[20]

### Greenberry Logan

Greenberry Logan, a Negro blacksmith who had been set free in Kentucky, came to Texas in 1831, and was one of the "free men of color" who fought for Texas' independence. He was a soldier under Fannin at the Battle of Concepción, and accompanied Ben Milam into San Antonio in December, 1835, when the Texan army defeated General Cos. Logan was wounded during the fighting in the vicinity of Main Plaza in the heart of San Antonio, when a ball passed through his right arm, permanently disabling him. He obtained some land from Stephen F. Austin on Chocolate Bayou, in Brazoria County. His wound made it impossible for him to continue in the blacksmith's trade, and he opened a boarding house at Brazoria.[21]

### Samuel McCullough Jr.

Private, Captain James Collingsworth's Company.

Samuel McCullough was one of the first soldiers to shed his blood in Texas' struggle for independence from Mexico. A free Negro from Jackson County who enlisted in Captain James Collingsworth's Company at Matagorda in October, 1835, McCullough was wounded in the right shoulder when the company captured Goliad, and the injury left him crippled for life. He was the only Texan wounded in the battle, during which one Mexican soldier was killed and three wounded. McCullough married Mary Lorena Vess, the daughter of Jonathan Vess, in 1837, and they had three children during the next ten years. In 1840, a law was passed ordering free Negroes to leave Texas. McCullough filed a petition with the Congress of the Republic of Texas, reminding them of his military service and asking permission to remain. The Texas Congress passed a law which granted him this permission.[22]

### Charles McGee

Private, Company B, Fifth Infantry Dragoon Regiment.

Charles McGee, a native of Ireland, was enlisted in the army at the age of thirty, on August 19,

1847, by F. Whitsall. He was described as having grey eyes, black hair and complexion, and being five feet, five and one-half inches in height.[23]

### Martin Mastley

Private, First Regiment Volunteers, New York, First Infantry.

Martin Mastley was a native of Franken, Germany. He worked in the United States as a gardener and was enlisted in the army at New York on December 16, 1846, by G. Bongard. He was twenty-two years old at the time. The records state that Mastley deserted on March 23, 1847, with full arms and equipment. The official roster listed his description as height: five feet ten inches; complexion: colored; eyes: krocked; hair: brown. (There could have been an error in the original record: eyes: brown and hair krocked or crocked may be correct.[24]

### Conday Monison

Private, Company A, Tenth Infantry Regiment.

Conday Monison was born in Albany, New York and worked as a shoemaker. He was enlisted in the army by a Lieutenant Howard on April 15, 1847, at Albany and was discharged on August 20, 1848, at Fort Hamilton, New York. His description was: eyes: dark; hair: gray, and complexion: black.[25]

### Jordan B. Noble

Drummer Boy, Seventh Regiment and Principal Musician, First Regiment, Louisiana Volunteers.

Jordan B. Noble was born around 1800, in Georgia. Later he moved to Louisiana and, at the age of thirteen, was serving with the Seventh Regiment of General Andrew Jackson's force during the War of 1812. He beat his drums at many famous battles and other events, and on January 8, 1815, played the drums at reveille and before an important engagement. It has also been stated that he served in the Seminole War in Florida in 1836.

Noble served as a principal musician during the Mexican War (one of the few Negroes known to have served in this war) with the First Regiment, Louisiana Volunteers, Colonel Walton commanding. His name appears in the military service records as follows:

*Drummer Boy*
*Jordan B. Noble*

*Noble, J. B., Company Field and Staff, First Louisiana Military Volunteers (Mexican War) Principal Musician. Enrolled May 9, 1846 at New Orleans, Louisiana, for six months. On roll dated August 1846. Book Mark 970 B 1884. Mexican War.*

He was paid a bounty for his services in the Mexican War.

After the War of 1812, Noble remained in New Orleans and associated with "free people of color." In 1860, he was honored at the St. Charles Hotel in New Orleans and was presented with a medal.

Jordan Noble started his military career when he was still a child and even in old age he relived his years of martial glory. Three wars, The War of 1812, The Mexican War and the Civil War made up a soldier's career in which his contributions as a musician had been outstanding. As a citizen he had been highly respected. He was a remarkable soldier, who should be remembered for the part he played in the early days of America's quest for freedom and democracy.[26]

### William Paxton

Private, Third Regiment.

William Paxton, a native of Mickleberg, was enlisted in the army at the age of twenty-five on April 5, 1847, at Charlotte, by an officer named Catwell. He was discharged on July 31, 1848, at Jefferson Barracks, Missouri. His description was: eyes: blue; hair: black, and complexion: black. He was five feet six inches tall.[27]

### John Rouse

Drummer Boy.

John Rouse was in charge of the main door of the House of Representatives at Washington for thirty years. He was the youngest veteran of the Mexican War on the House list and was a drummer boy at Vera Cruz, where he lost part of his left arm.[28]

### Thomas Savoy

Vagabond Soldier.

Thomas Savoy was a native of the state of Maryland. He also lived in Washington, D.C. and Mississippi, and later moved to Texas with a company of Mississippi volunteers which joined General Houston shortly after the battle of San Jacinto. Savoy, also known as "Black Tom," joined an expedition under Jordan. He was with General Wall when he invaded Texas with a Mexican Army and was defeated at Salado. Tom was wounded in the fighting.

Later Black Tom participated in Indian conflicts and followed his comrades under Taylor's banner at the battles of Monterey and Buena Vista. He returned to Texas with the Kentucky volunteers and made San Antonio his home until July 15, 1853, when his body was found two miles west of the city. (The foregoing narrative is paraphrased from a correspondent's article in the *New Orleans Picayune* during that period.)

Thomas Savoy was a black man whose courage and desire to fight prevailed, even though he was not attached to a regular military unit. Many other such stories remain untold.[29]

### James Shaw

Private, Second Dragoon Regiment.

James Shaw was born in Pittsburgh, Pennsylvania. He was enlisted in the army on September 21, 1840, by a Major Ashby, at Fort Shannon. He was discharged on July 23, 1845 at Fort Jessup, Louisiana, at the expiration of his term of service. He was described as having black eyes, brown hair and a black complexion.[30]

### Andrew Smith

Private, Rifle H.

Andrew Smith was born in Tyrone, Ireland, and was enlisted in the army by a Captain Walker on April 1, 1847, at New Orleans, when he was twenty-nine years of age. He was a clerk in civil life. Smith was described as having gray eyes and black hair and complexion. He was killed in action at Puebla, Mexico, in 1847.[31]

### Robert Spottswood

Private, Eighth Infantry Regiment.

Robert Spottswood was born in Adams, Pennsylvania. He was enlisted in the army at the age of eighteen in Reading, Pennsylvania, by a Lieutenant Prince. He had worked as a tailor. Spottswood deserted from the army on March 5, 1847. He was described as being five feet, eight inches tall, with gray eyes and black hair and complexion.[32]

### Henry C. Sprague

Recruit, U.S. Army.

Henry C. Sprague was a native of Brandywine, Ohio, who worked as a laborer. He was enlisted in the army on April 19, 1847, at New Orleans, by a Captain Lynde. He was discharged at the expiration of his term of service at Newport Barracks on June 20, 1848. Sprague was described as five feet, three inches tall, with black eyes, brown hair and a black complexion.[33]

### Joe Travis

Servant to Colonel William Travis.

When the Mexican Army captured the Alamo and killed Colonel William Travis and all of his soldiers, they spared his Negro servant, Joe, who was not considered a combatant. Joe went to Washington-on-the-Brazos and gave one of the first eye-witness accounts of the fall of the Alamo to members of the Provisional Government. Joe described the deaths of Crockett, Bowie and Travis and said that he was taken to General Santa Anna, who questioned him about the Texas Army. Joe said he was detained in San Antonio long enough to watch a review of the Mexican troops and was told that they numbered eight thousand. He was then permitted to go.[34]

### Carel Wentzel

Private, First Regiment Volunteers, New York, First Infantry.

Carel Wentzel was a native of Fredeburgh, Germany. He was enlisted in the army at New York on December 16, 1846, by a Colonel Burnott, having been a merchant in civilian life. Official records state that he was transferred to Company H on January 1, 1847 and that at the age of twenty-six he was five feet, nine inches in height, with bleu or blue eyes, brown hair and a colored complexion.[35]

## Notes to Chapter Three

1. The University of Texas Institute of Texan Cultures, Record of Peter Allen, San Antonio, Texas.
2. Institute of Texan Cultures, Record of Hendricks Arnold.
3. Description Book Companies A, B, D, E, F, G, I, First Infantry Regiment Volunteers, New York R & P Offices, p. 4, No. 14, Mexican War, RG 94, National Archives, Washington, D.C.
4. Register of Enlistments in the U.S. Army 1798–1914, David Black, 1848, Microcopy 233, National Archives.
5. Description Book, Companies A, B, D, E, F, G, I.
6. Register of Enlistments Thomas B. Brashear, 1848, *loc. cit.*
7. Register of Enlistments, Barbee G. Collins or Collon, 1848, *loc. cit.*
8. Register of Enlistments, John E. Conter, July, 1840 to May, 1848, *loc. cit.*
9. Muster Rolls, Return of Regimental Papers, Michael Curran, 1848, Office of the Adjutant General, National Archives.
10. Register of Enlistments, Daniel Cutler, 1848, *loc. cit.*
11. Register of Enlistments, Josephus Daines, 1848, *loc. cit.*
12. Description Book, Companies A, B, D, E, F, G, I.
13. *Ibid.*
14. Institute of Texan Cultures, Record of Dick the Drummer.
15. Description Book, Independent Company, Captain Duncan's Company, MTD Volunteers.
16. Register of Enlistments, Joseph Garrison, 1848, *loc. cit.*
17. Institute of Texan Cultures, Record of William Goyens, *loc. cit.*
18. Register of Enlistments, Dominick Griffaton, 1848, *loc. cit.*
19. Register of Enlistments, Moses Johnson, 1848, *loc. cit.*
20. Description Book, Companies A, B, D, E, F, G, I.
21. Institute of Texan Cultures, Record of Greenberry Logan.
22. Institute of Texan Cultures, Samuel McCullough Jr.
23. Register of Enlistments, Charles McGee, 1847, *loc. cit.*
24. Description Book, Companies A, B, D, E, F, G, I.
25. Register of Enlistments, Conday Monison, 1848, *loc. cit.*
26. Military Pension File of Jordan E. Noble, RG 15,

Record of the Adjutant General's Office, National Archives.

27. Register of Enlistments, William Paxton, 1847.
28. *Alexander's Magazine,* May 2, 1906.
29. Nell, William C., *The Colored Patriots of the American Revolution,* pp. 201–202 (Boston: Robert F. Wallcut, 1855).
30. Register of Enlistments, James Shaw, 1845, *loc. cit.*
31. Register of Enlistments, Andrew Smith, 1847, *loc. cit.*
32. Register of Enlistments, Robert Spottswood, 1847, *loc. cit.*
33. Register of Enlistments, Henry C. Sprague, 1847, *loc. cit.*
34. Institute of Texan Culture, Record of Joe Travis.
35. Description Book, Companies A, B, D, E, F, G, I.

# Chapter Four

## The Civil War, 1861-1865

When a divided nation sounded the call to arms in 1861, black Americans responded. They were seen on the battlefield in Union blue and Confederate gray; they worked as manual laborers, as body servants and cooks, and followed their masters to battle.

At the beginning of the war Negroes tried to enlist in both the Union and Confederate armies. Their services were refused. In 1862, the Union Army decided to enlist the services of slaves and free Negroes. Under outstanding Caucasian military leaders, a nucleus of superior soldiers was eventually organized. This was the beginning of America's first official recognition of a Negro regiment, the United States Colored Troops. A few Negro officers were commissioned near the end of the war, but very few therefore had leadership experience as officers.

Unfortunately, the accomplishments of these brave men have been excluded from the history texts used in America's public schools, though their deeds were many and in some cases notable. This chapter recounts the heroism, tribulations and accomplishments of black Americans of Civil War days.

The number (twenty-four) of Congressional Medals of Honor awarded to black men during the Civil War is outstanding; the many battlefields of the Civil War stand as a memorial to the veterans, black as well as white, of the conflict between the states.

### Ruff Abernathy

Cook, Third Tennessee Infantry Regiment, Confederate Army.

Ruff Abernathy applied for a pension on June 15, 1921, when he was seventy-six years old and living in Aspen Hill, Giles County, Tennessee. His master had been a Tom Abernathy. He stated on his application that he had been a cook for a Captain Barber, Third Tennessee Infantry Regiment, and that when Captain Barber was killed at the Battle of Resaca, Georgia, he was assigned to work as a servant in the Distributing Hospital in Atlanta. Abernathy was later transferred to a hospital at Alisonia, Alabama. He was released from the Confederate Army in 1865.[1]

### Aaron Anderson

Landsman, U.S. Navy.

Aaron Anderson, a black, was born on a farm in Plymouth, North Carolina. He enlisted in the navy on April 17, 1863. On March 17, 1865, while serving on board the USS Wyandank, he participated with a boat crew in the clearing of Mattox Creek. Anderson carried out his duties courageously in the face of opposing fire which cut away half the oars, pierced the launch in many places, and cut the barrel off a musket being fired at the enemy. He was awarded the Medal of Honor.[2]

### Joe Anderson

Musician, Company G, 109th Regiment, United States Colored Troops, Union Army.

Joe Anderson enlisted at Greensburg, Kentucky, on June 4, 1864, and served until February, 1865.[3]

*Lieutenant Colonel Alexander T. Augusta*

### Alexander T. Augusta

Lieutenant Colonel, Union Army.

Alexander Augusta was born a free man on March 8, 1825 in Norfolk, Virginia. He studied medicine under private tutors in Baltimore, Maryland. Later he studied in Philadelphia, California and Canada. In 1856, he graduated from Trinity Medical College, Toronto, Canada with the degree of bachelor of medicine. He then practiced medicine in Toronto, Canada and in the West Indies.

In 1862, Augusta moved to Washington, D.C. On October 2, 1863, he was appointed surgeon of the Seventh U.S. Colored Troops which were part of the expedition sent to Beaufort, South Carolina. Later he was in charge of a hospital at Savannah, Georgia. On March 13, 1865, he was brevetted a lieutenant colonel, U.S. Volunteers, for meritorious and faithful service, one of the few black field grade officers in the Civil War. He was mustered out of the service on October 13, 1866, and resumed the practice of medicine. He married Mary O. Burgoin of Baltimore, Maryland, who was of Hugenot descent.

Augusta was one of the first Negro faculty members in the Department of Medicine at Howard University. He was on the faculty at Howard until 1877 and practiced medicine in the District of Columbia until his death on December 21, 1890. He is buried in Arlington National Cemetery.[4]

### Jasper Banks

Cook, Confederate Military Service.

A Jasper Banks served as a cook for the Confederate military service from 1861 to 1865. His pension application stated that he was attached to a General Charles Jones.

Banks was residing in Buckingham County, Virginia and claimed to be one hundred and five years old when he applied for a pension on January 30, 1925.[5]

### William H. Barnes

Private, Company C, Thirty-Eighth U.S. Colored Troops, Union Army.

William Barnes, a black, was born in St. Mary's County, Maryland. On September 1, 1864, Barnes was the first man to enter the enemy's works. Although wounded, he heroically continued to perform his duties. He was awarded the Medal of Honor on April 6, 1865.[6]

## Powhatan Beaty

First Sergeant, Company G, Fifth U.S. Colored Troops, Union Army.

Powhatan Beaty was born in Richmond, Virginia. At Chapin's Farm, Virginia, on September 29, 1864, Beaty assumed command of his company when all the officers had been either killed or wounded. He was awarded the Medal of Honor for his gallant leadership on April 6, 1865.[7]

## William Bell

Private, Company H, Fourteenth Rhode Island Regiment, Heavy Artillery, Union Army.

William Bell, a black, enlisted at Providence, Rhode Island, on November 6, 1863, and served until 1865. His signature on the official records was indicated by a mark.[8]

## Charles Bentley

Private, Company A, Twenty-Ninth Connecticut Infantry Regiment, United States Colored Troops, Union Army.

Charles Bentley, a black, enlisted at New Haven, Connecticut, on December 9, 1863. He was killed in the battle of Kill House, Virginia, on October 27, 1864.[9]

## William Bibb

Body Servant, Company G, Twelfth Alabama Volunteer Infantry, Confederate Army.

William Bibb, a black, was born in Lowndes County, Columbus, Mississippi in 1840.

A sworn statement by a Kate Lytle, daughter of Algernon Bibb (William Bibb's master) revealed the following:

Prior to the Civil War, William Bibb was a carriage driver and waiter for the Algernon Bibb household. In 1861, Algernon Bibb organized a company of Confederate soldiers in Jackson County, Alabama, and when the company entered Confederate military service, William Bibb was taken along as a body servant.

Mrs. Sarah Bibb aged eighty-one years (in 1921) said in a sworn statment that:

*When the war begun and my husband joined the Confederate service, said William Bibb went with him into the service and was his body servant and he was faithful and devoted to his master during the war and he on one occasion screened his master from being captured by the Federals by joining with them and riding his master's horse for several hours and then made his escape back to Captain Bibb, riding a horse which had been presented his master by General Walker.*

Bibb's application for a pension, on December 31, 1921, was approved.[10]

## Nicholas Biddle

Artillerist, Washington Artillerists, Union Army.

Nicholas Biddle was a native of Pottsville, Pennsylvania. On April 17, 1861 the Washington Artillerists and the National Light Infantry departed Harrisburg for Washington, D.C. and Nicholas Biddle was among the troops. On April 18, 1861, the troops arrived in Baltimore, Maryland. As the soldiers were marching from one train station to another, a mob attacked some of them. Biddle was struck in the face with an object hurled from the crowd and was injured so severely as to expose the bone. The troops continued to Washington. While Biddle was resting on the Capitol floor, he was visited by President Abraham Lincoln who arrived to greet the soldiers assigned to sentry duty around the Capitol area. Biddle continued to serve faithfully during the war. The people of Pottsville didn't forget their own Negro soldier. His grave was marked with the following inscription:

*In Memory of Nicholas Biddle*
*His was the proud distinction of shedding the first blood in the late war for the union, being wounded while marching through Baltimore with the First Volunteers from Schuylvill County.*[11]
*18 April, 1861*

## William Blackwell

Slave-Servant, Company C, Fourth Kentucky Infantry Regiment, Confederate Army.

William Blackwell was a slave of the Blackwell family in Union County, Kentucky, and accompanied his master, Lieutenant Thomas C. Blackwell, of Company C, Fourth Kentucky Infantry, to the Confederate service in 1861, staying with him almost four years. Blackwell was one of the many Negro servants who displayed an earnest obedience to their masters even in the period of the Civil War. He never showed any desire to escape to the North and at the conclusion of the war preferred to remain with his master.[12]

### Robert Blake

Contraband, U.S. Navy.

Robert Blake, a black man, enlisted in the navy after escaping from a Virginia plantation. While on board the U.S. steam gunboat *Marblehead* off Legareville, Stone River, on December 25, 1863, Blake displayed heroism in an engagement with the enemy on John's Island. Manning the rifle gun, he carried out his duties bravely throughout the engagement, which resulted in the enemy's abandonment of munitions, leaving a caisson and one gun. On April 16, 1864, Robert Blake was awarded the Medal of Honor.[13]

### John R. Bowles

Chaplain, Fifty-Fifth Massachusetts Volunteer Infantry Regiment, Union Army.

John Bowles, a black, was born in Lynchburg, Virginia on June 13, 1826, and was married and living in Chillicothe, Ohio, when commissioned. He was assigned as chaplain of the Fifty-Fifth Regiment on March 27, 1864, and resigned in June, 1865. He went back to Ohio and lived in Albany, Athens County.[14]

### Richard Henry Boyd

Slave-Servant, Confederate Army.

Many Negro slaves, accustomed to the relative security of the plantation, found it difficult to adjust to the outside world. But a number of former slaves exhibited amazing qualities of leadership immediately upon being freed. Among these was Richard Henry Boyd, who had accompanied his master through the battles of the Civil War on the Confederate side. After his master was killed, Boyd returned to Texas and managed the plantation until the end of the war. Then he educated himself, became a Baptist minister and rose to a position of leadership in the Texas Baptist Convention. In

*William Blackwell*

1897 he organized the National Baptist Publishing Board. This enterprise is still active and has published many important books and pamphlets over the years.[15]

### John Bradshaw

Fifer, Company D, Tenth Regiment of Colored Troops, Union Army.

John Bradshaw enlisted in the Union Army at Lexington, Kentucky, on May 27, 1864, and served until November, 1865. He was one of several Negro fifers in the Civil War.[16]

### James Bright

Musician, First (McCreary's), South Carolina Infantry Regiment (First S.C., Infantry Provincial Army), Confederate Army.

James Bright was enlisted as a musician in a Confederate unit at Suffolk, Virginia, by Captain T. P. Alston for the duration of the war. The field and staff muster roll indicated that "Bright, colored man free," was discharged 26 May, 1861, on account of blindness.[17]

### William H. Brocidy

Hostler, Confederate Military Service.

William Brocidy entered the Confederate military service on August 2, 1864. He was with Confederate units at Columbia, South Carolina; Greensboro, North Carolina, and Lynchburg, Virginia. Brocidy applied for a pension on June 10, 1925, when he was seventy-eight years old, and living at Amherst, Virginia. His master was a Charles P. Claiborn.[18]

### James H. Bronson

First Sergeant, Company D, Fifth U.S. Colored Troops, Union Army.

James Bronson was born in Indiana County, Pennsylvania. He assumed command and gallantly led his company on September 29, 1864, at Chapin's Farm, Virginia, when all the officers had been either killed or wounded. He was awarded the Medal of Honor on April 6, 1865.[19]

### William Bronson

First Sergeant, Company A, First South Carolina Volunteer Regiment, Union Army.

*William Bronson*

William Bronson was one of the few members of his unit who could read and write. Company A seems to have been the first company of Negro troops to engage in actual fighting. When at St. Helena island, from November 3 to 10, 1862, they participated in an expedition along the coast of Georgia and Florida under Lieutenant Colonel Beard of the Forty-Eighth New York Infantry.[20]

### William Brooks

Body Servant, Seventh Virginia Infantry Regiment, Confederate Army.

William Brooks, a black man, entered the Confederate military service as a body servant to John J. Winn. He applied for a pension at the age of eighty when living in Albemarle County, Virginia.[21]

### Alfred Brown

Body Servant, Confederate Army.

Alfred Brown, black, was born in 1844 in Anderson District, South Carolina. His masters were Dr. George Brown and Dr. James Brown. When he was thirteen years old, Alfred Brown accompanied Dr. James Brown when he joined the army, and in 1861 himself entered the Confederate military service. Dr. Brown served as a physician and surgeon in the Confederate Army and Alfred Brown assisted him as a servant, courier, and as a nurse to the wounded soldiers. He was wounded at the battle of Chickamauga.

Alfred Brown was living in Cleveland, Georgia in 1927. At the age of eighty-three, he applied, successfully, for a pension. The application stated:

*James Brown had his office in the rear of the battlefield, but close enough to the line of battle that bullets and shells could reach him (emphasis added) and in this way Alfred Brown, the colored servant, was wounded twice in one day. A . . . ball was shot through his left thigh and he was wounded in the right leg by a piece of bomb shell.*[22]

### Goodman Brown

Enlistee, Union Army.

Goodman was born in Surrey, Virginia, in 1841, a third generation free man. His father, Herbert Brown, owned fifty acres of land. During the civil war, Goodman Brown enlisted in the Union Army, and when the war was over he taught school. He was elected a member of the Virginia House of Delegates from Prince George and Surrey, Virginia and served from 1887–1888. He died in 1928.[23]

### Henry C. Brown

Private, Third Regiment Missouri Volunteers of African Descent, Union Army.

Henry Brown joined the Missouri Volunteers at Columbia, Missouri, and was reported as present for duty on February 10, 1874.[24]

### Jefferson Brown

Private, F Company, Second Mississippi Heavy Artillery Regiment, Union Army.

Jefferson Brown entered the service at Natchez, Mississippi on October 23, 1863, and served until March, 1864.[25]

### William H. Brown

Landsman, U.S. Navy.

William Brown, a black, was born in 1836 in Baltimore, Maryland. He was awarded the Medal of Honor for gallantry while serving on the *USS Brooklyn* during an attack on rebel gunboats. His citation reads as follows:

*On board the* USS Brooklyn *during successful attacks against Fort Morgan rebel gunboats, and the ram* Tennessee *in Mobile Bay on 5 August, 1864. Stationed in the immediate vicinity of the three ships which were twice cleared of men by bursting shells, Brown remained steadfast at his post and performed his duties in the Powder Division throughout the furious action which resulted in the surrender of the huge rebel ram* Tennessee *and in the damaging destruction of batteries at Fort Morgan.*[26]

### Wilson Brown

Boy, Sloop of War Flagship, *USS Hartford,* U.S. Navy.

Wilson Brown was born in 1841 in Natchez, Mississippi. He enlisted in the navy on March 18, 1863 and was sent to the *USS North Carolina.* The complete list or muster roll of the crew of the U.S. Sloop of War *Hartford* for March, 1863, indicated the following: Ship Number 351, Brown, Wilson, Contraband." The complete description lists or muster rolls for the *Hartford* from January 1, 1864, to March 31, 1864, July 1, 1864 and September 30, 1864, give us the following information about Brown: Rating—Boy; Date of Enlistment—March 18, 1863; place enlisted—North Carolina; place or vessel received—North Carolina; where born—Mississippi; age—twenty-two; Contraband; complexion—Negro.

On August 5, 1864, the *USS Hartford* was engaged in successful attacks against Fort Morgan, rebel gunboats and the ram *Tennessee* in Mobile Bay. During the attacks, Brown was knocked unconscious into the ship's hold when an enemy shell burst, fatally wounding a man on the ladder above him. As soon as he regained consciousness, Brown returned to the ship's deck and zealously continued to perform his duties, although four of the men at this station had been either killed or wounded by enemy fire. Wilson Brown was awarded the Medal of Honor on December 31, 1864, for his courageous performance of duty.[27]

### George W. Burrows

Private, Fifth Massachusetts Cavalry Regiment, Union Army.

George Burrows, a black, entered military service in Boston, Massachusetts, and was mustered out on December 21, 1865.[28]

### Frank Cage

Private, Company B, Sixth Mississippi Regiment of Volunteers of African Descent, Union Army.

Frank Cage enlisted in the army at Natchez, Mississippi, on August 16, 1863, and served until 1865.[29]

### Andre Cailloux

Captain, First Louisiana Native Guards Regiment, Union Army.

Andre Cailloux was born a freeman and was wealthy. He commanded Company E, color company of the First Louisiana Native Guards, which he had raised by his own efforts. On May 27, 1863, the two colored regiments of the Louisiana Native Guards were ordered to attack Port Hudson, an important Confederate facility. As Cailloux was leading his men into battle he injured his arm, but refusing to leave the field, he gallantly led his troops forward, in the face of offensive fire power. A shell hit him, and he died only fifty yards from the objective. Captain Cailloux was given a hero's burial in his native city, New Orleans, Louisiana.[30]

### Daniel Campbell

Private, First Kansas Colored Infantry Regiment, Union Army.

Daniel Campbell, a native of Wyandotte, Kansas, entered the service on September 14, 1862 and served until August 15, 1865.[31]

### William H. Carney

Sergeant, Company C, Fifty-Fourth Massachusetts Colored Infantry Regiment, Union Army.

William Carney was born at New Bedford, Massachusetts. On July 18, 1863, while engaged in a conflict at Fort Wagner, South Carolina, Carney displayed unusual bravery. His citation stated that when the color sergeant was shot down, Carney grasped the flag, led the way to the parapet, and planted the colors therein. When the troops

*Sergeant William H. Carney*

fell back, he brought off the flag under a fierce fire in which he was twice severely wounded. Sergeant Carney was awarded the Medal of Honor for outstanding devotion to duty on May 23, 1900.[32]

### George Carnish

Private, Company F, Seventh U.S. Colored Infantry Regiment, Union Army.

George Carnish enlisted in the army at Dorchester, Maryland, and served until 1866.[33]

### Edward C. Carroll

Private, Twenty-Ninth Connecticut Volunteer Regiment, U.S. Colored Troops, Union Army.

Edward Carroll enlisted in the army on December 22, 1863, at Norwich, Connecticut.[34]

### John H. Chambers

Private, First Iowa Volunteer Regiment of African Descent, Union Army.

John Chambers entered the service at St. Louis, and was present for duty at Fort Snelling, Minnesota. He was discharged on June 13, 1865, by order of Major General J. J. Reynolds.[35]

### T. Morris Chester

Brigadier General, Fourth Brigade, First Division Louisiana State National Guard.

T. Morris Chester was born on May 11, 1834 in Harrisburg, Pennsylvania. He was the son of George and Jane Maria Chester. Chester received his elementary and secondary education at Avery Institute, Allegheny City, Pennsylvania and Alexander High School, Monrovia, Liberia. He returned to the United States in 1854 after spending some years in Liberia. Chester entered the Thetford Academy in Vermont, graduated in 1856, and returned to Liberia as a teacher. In 1861, he returned to the United States and assisted in the enlistment of black soldiers for the Fifty-Fourth and Fifty-Fifth Massachusetts Regiments.

Chester displayed ability in writing and was selected to report the proceedings of the General Conference of the African Methodist Episcopal Church in the city of Philadelphia, in 1864 for the Philadelphia *Daily Press*. He was also selected to serve as a special war correspondent for the *Daily Press* and covered the Army of the James and Potomac. In 1866 Chester traveled to Europe, visiting England, Paris, Brussels, Berlin and Moscow. He was received by the Russian court as Captain Chester, a title given him in recognition of his commanding a company of civilians to protect the capital at Harrisburg, Pennsylvania against Confederate forces during the Civil War. He was received by Emperor Alexander and also at the courts of Denmark, Sweden, Saxony and England.

After living four years in Europe he returned to the United States in 1871 with a law degree from Middle Temple Inn, London. He returned to Louisiana and practiced law in the civil and criminal courts and before the supreme court.

In June, 1870, Negro troops were first organized by Louisiana Governor Henry C. Warmoth and placed under the command of General James Longstreet. During the period 1870–1877 Negro troops were used on various occasions. The list of commissions issued in 1873 shows that T. M. Chester was commissioned as a brigadier general on May 27, 1873. A register of military force for 1874 lists him in command of the First Division, Fourth Brigade.

T. Morris Chester was one of the blacks appointed by white governors to general rank in state militias or national guards during the Reconstruction period, 1870–1874. The real exploits or accomplishments of men like Chester in state national guards are still unknown today to many Americans.[36]

### Richard H. Chew

Private, Sixth Infantry Regiment, U.S. Colored Troops, Union Army.

Richard Chew was present for duty on August 15, 1861. He entered the service at West Chester, Pennsylvania.[37]

### Wade Childs (or Chiles)

Sergeant, Confederate Army.

Wade Childs entered the service in 1862 and served until 1866. He was a servant to Captain Cothran, and affidavits in his service file stated that when the captain was wounded at the Second Manassas, Childs carried him back to the rear. The affidavit also stated that Childs did not know that

Captain Cothran had made this statement about him, and that he was a faithful dependable Negro, humble to white people and always willing to serve them. He applied for a pension on April 6, 1923, when he was living in Anderson, Anderson County, South Carolina. The pension application was approved on April 12, 1923.[38]

### Henry Church
Body Servant, Forty-Eighth Tennessee Regiment, Confederate Army.

Henry Church was born in Moury County, Tennessee on June 1, 1845. He entered the Confederate military service in 1861 as a body servant to Captain J. P. Church. He was present at the battles of Vicksburg and Nashville, and served with the Forty-Eighth Tennessee Regiment until the surrender. The Tennessee legislature rewarded Church for his services to the Confederacy by giving him a job as a porter in the legislature. He made an application for a pension, which was approved.[39]

### James Clark
Fifer, Company K, Twenty-Eighth Georgia Regiment, Confederate Army.

James Clark, a free Negro, was born in Burke County, Georgia in 1804. In 1904, at the age of *one hundred years,* Clark applied for an indigent pension. At this time he was living in Emanuel County, Georgia. Clark stated on his application that he was a free Negro, and joined the Twenty-Eighth Georgia Regiment, Company K, in 1861 and served as a fifer until discharged. He had farmed a little, but was destitute in 1904. John E. Youmans, Ordinary, Emanuel County, Georgia stated that he had talked with several members of the company to which Clark stated that he had been assigned. These men told Youmans that he was not mustered in the service, but came in on his own account and was paid by the company for his *services as fifer.*

The Georgia Pension Board disapproved James Clark's pension.[40]

### William Clark
Musician, Company H, Eighty-Eighth Infantry Regiment, United States Colored Troops, Union Army.

William Clark enlisted in the army and served until April, 1865.[41]

### Charles Cleopor
Private, Confederate States Naval Brigade.

Charles Cleopor is mentioned in records relating to Confederate Naval and Marine personnel as follows: "Chas. Cleoper, Private (col'd)." Cleopor was one of the few Negroes whose names have been actually identified on official Confederate Naval records.[42]

### Holt Collier
Servant to Lieutenant Tom Hinds, Major Burns' Artillery and Captain Perry Evans' Company, Ninth Texas Regiment, Confederate Army.

Holt Collier, according to correspondence of Headquarters Third Brigade, Mississippi Division, United Confederate Veterans, Greenville, Mississippi, dated April 5, 1906, was the only Negro ever enrolled in the Mississippi contingent of the Confederate Army. This letter also stated that Collier was loyal to the cause, and that he was selected to be a bodyguard for President Roosevelt on a hunting trip when he was visiting Mississippi. A pension application dated July 29, 1916, gives us the following information about Holt Collier: "Lifetime resident of Mississippi, resided in Washington County, post office Greenville, Mississippi, served during the entire war, at the close of the war was at Vicksburg and was wounded in the ankle." He was one of the very few blacks who were recognized by the Mississippi Confederate forces as having served the Confederacy.[43]

### Sam Collier
Body Servant to Colonel William Edwards, Confederate Military Service.

Sam Collier was born in Madison County, Tennessee, in 1839. His master was William R. Collier and he served in the Confederate military service as a body servant to Colonel William Edwards, a nephew of William R. Collier. Sam Collier looked after the horses and also nursed his master when he was ill.

In 1931, when he was living at 717 Madison Street, Jackson, Tennessee, Collier, then aged ninety-two years, applied for and was granted a pension. He made the following statement in his application:

*Colonel Edwards was shot at Belmont and they sent him home and I had to nurse him and take care of him. . . . When the Yankees came into Madison County, I hid Colonel Edwards' uniforms up in the attic. When they came to our house that night, and Colonel Edwards told me to burn it up, so I slipped it out early the next morning before daylight and burned it up, so the Yankees could not see it, and find out that he had been in the Confederate Army. Captain McCutcheon and other Confederate leaders in Madison County carried me to the first Confederate reunion at Louisville, Kentucky, and I have also been to Memphis and other places to reunion.*

Sam Collier died in March, 1932.[44]

### Hiram Conaway

Body Servant to Major Cyrus H. Harding, Confederate Army.

Hiram Conaway was born in Virginia in August, 1839. He entered the Confederate Army in 1861, and served as a cook and bodyguard to Major Cyrus H. Harding. He applied for a pension, at the age of ninety-two, on July 7, 1932, when he was living in Westmoreland County, Virginia. His application stated that he "was captured and held prisoner near Winchester till the end of war."[45]

### James Henry Conyers

Cadet Midshipman, U.S. Naval Academy.

James Conyers was born on October 24, 1855, at Columbia, Richland County, South Carolina. He was the first Negro known to be appointed as a cadet midshipman in the U.S. Naval Academy in Annapolis, Maryland. The appointment was made by the Honorable Robert E. Elliot, the Third Congressional District of South Carolina, on September 24, 1872 (Elliott was also a major general in the South Carolina Militia). However, Conyers was not successful in his studies at the Academy. In June, 1873, it was recommended that he be dropped because of deficient studies, though he was allowed to be re-examined in October, 1873. He was again deficient and again recommended to be dropped. Conyers decided to submit his resig-

nation on November 10, 1873, and it was accepted. The Honorable George M. Robeson was then the Secretary of the Navy and John L. Warden Superintendent of the Academy.[46]

### Taylor Cromwell

Seaman, *USS Black Hawk*, U.S. Navy.

Taylor Cromwell was one of many black Americans who served faithfully in the Union Navy during the Civil War. He served on board the *USS Black Hawk*.[47]

### Sam Cullom

Body Servant, Company F, Eighth Tennessee Infantry Regiment, Confederate Army.

Sam Cullom, a black man, stated in a pension application made in June, 1921, that he was born in the state of Maryland and came to Tennessee when he was about nine years old. He thought he was eighty-six or more when he made the application, which was successful.

Cullom served as a servant for Jim and Rus Cullom, with Company D and F of the Eighth Tennessee Infantry. When his master, Jim Cullom, was killed at Atlanta, Sam Cullom buried him before returning to Tennessee.[48]

### Joseph Cuney

Private, Sixty-Third Pennsylvania Volunteer Regiment, Union Army.

An acquaintance of Joseph Cuney remembered him as "a quiet man who spent a great deal of his time reading." Reserved though he may have been, Cuney was a man of strong convictions. The older brother of Norris Wright Cuney, he was born at Sunnyside Plantation, in Waller County, in 1840. Joseph was set free and sent to a private school in Pittsburgh preparatory to entering an eastern college. He was attending this school in Pittsburgh when the Civil War started, and he immediately joined the Sixty-Third Pennsylvania Volunteers in 1861 and fought as a Union soldier during the entire war. His mother, learning that he was stationed in Virginia, wrote and asked him to go and see her mother, Hester Neale Stuart of Centreville, Virginia. Joseph found and "liberated" his grandmother in Virginia in the closing days of the war. His mother, who had not seen her mother for forty years, was overjoyed to find her again. Joseph's grandmother lived to be one hundred years old. After the war, Joseph joined his brother, Wright, in Galveston and in 1881 opened a law office there. He is believed to be the first native Texan Negro attorney to practice law in the state. He and his brother, Wright, also operated a print shop.[49]

### William Dabney

Body Servant to Captain Tom Hage, Confederate Army.

William Dabney, a black man, served as a body servant to Captain Tom Hage from 1861 to 1865, and was present at the battles of Manassas and Yorktown. His owner was Dr. Elliot Hamer.

Dabney applied for a pension on July 2, 1930, when he was ninety-one years of age. He was living in King William County, Virginia and had been a sexton at the West Presbyterian Church, Richmond, Virginia.[50]

### Ben Davis

Body Servant, General Forrest's Headquarters, Confederate Army.

Ben Davis was born on March 4, 1836, at Fayette, Tennessee. His owner was Hugh Davis, of La Grange, Tennessee. In 1861, Ben Davis entered the Confederate military service as personal body servant to General Forrest. After the war he lived at 608 Railroad Avenue, Memphis, Tennessee, wih his wife Mary, and in 1921 was awarded a pension. The pension application stated that "Ben Davis was given to General Forrest as a personal body servant by Hugh Davis and he acted as such throughout the war.[51]

### Benjamin Davis

Musician, Eighty-Ninth Infantry Regiment, United States Colored Troops, Union Army.

Benjamin Davis enlisted at Port Hudson on September 2, 1863, and was assigned as a musician.[52]

### Isham Davis

Servant, Confederate Army.

Isham Davis, a black man, said on a pension application of April 24, 1923, that he served as a servant under Lieutenant John Bankston Davis, who was in Captain Buck Bishop's Company I, Holcomb Legion. He entered the service around January, 1861 and served until the fall of the same year. Davis was living at Campobello in Spartanburg County, South Carolina, at the time of his pension application.[53]

### Tobias Dawson

Musician, Company K, First (McCreary's) South Carolina Infantry Regiment (First S.C. Inf. Prov'l Army), Confederate Army.

Tobias Dawson was enlisted in a Confederate unit on October 1, 1861, by Captain McCrady. He was listed as a musician on the company muster roll for November and December, 1861; and as absent without leave on the field and staff muster roll for January and February, 1863. The March and April, 1863, roll shows that he deserted from camp near Fredericksburg. He is described as "colored man (free)."[54]

### Clement Dees

Seaman, *USS Pontoosuc*, U.S. Navy.

Clement Dees was awarded the Medal of Honor on the recommendation of Commander William G. Temple, *USS Pontoosuc*, James River, Virginia, for gallantry and coolness in action during operations in and about Cape Fear River, December 24, 1864 to February 22, 1865, which resulted in the capture of Fort Fisher and Wilmington. U.S. Navy Department General Order No. 59, dated June 22, 1865, stated: "Awarded Medal of Honor to: Clement Dee, Seaman (colored), Pontoosuc." An asterisk indicated that the medal was forfeited by his desertion.

Three other persons also forfeited their medals through desertion. Samuel Dees and the other deserters may never have realized that in 1865 they had been awarded the nation's highest military medal for heroism.[55]

### Martin R. Delaney

Major, Medical Officer, United States Colored Troops, Union Army.

Martin R. Delaney was born in Charlestown, Virginia. His family was freed and moved to Western Pennsylvania, and Delaney was able to study medicine at Harvard Medical School. He served as a medical officer during the Civil War, and was an important political figure in South Carolina in the Reconstruction years. Delaney served in the Freedmen's Bureau for three years, and later as a customs house inspector and trial judge in Charleston. He was an unsuccessful Republican candidate for lieutenant governor of South Carolina. He edited a weekly newspaper, *The Mystery,* from 1843–1847 and his writings include *The Condition, Elevation, Emigration and Destiny of the Colored People of the United States Politically Considered* (1852). In 1861 he wrote the official Report of the Niger Valley Exploring Party, which he had led in 1859. He died in Xenia, Ohio, on January 24, 1885.[56]

### Eli Dempsy

Private, Company G, First North Carolina Army (Tenth State Troops), Confederate Army.

Eli Dempsy was assigned to a Confederate unit from the state of North Carolina. A roll of prisoners of war shows that Dempsy was captured at Plymouth, North Carolina, on October 31, 1864, and was confined as a prisoner at Military Prison Camp, Hamilton, Virginia, on November 16, 1864. The record describes him as "Dempsy, Eli (Col'd)."[57]

### Thomas Sanford Dixon

Captain's Steward, U.S. Navy.

Thomas Dixon was born on February 10, 1847, at Buckler Bluff, St. John River, Florida. He was the son of April and Mary Dixon. His father was a slave belonging to Planter Plumer, or Plummer, and his mother was free. Dixon went to sea at the age of eight and at the beginning of the Civil War enlisted in the U.S. Navy and served aboard the *USS Constitution.* He later re-enlisted and served on the *USS Uncan, USS Paul Jones* and *USS Isaac Smith* as a ward room and captain's steward. In 1864 he was transferred to a naval battery on Morris Island. After the evacuation of Charleston, South Carolina, he was transferred to Delaware and assisted in the raising of the Confederate ram, *Columbia,* from Charleston harbor. Dixon was assigned to the old *Constitution* in 1865. After the war he returned to civilian life and settled in Bethlehem, Pennsylvania, where he opened a restaurant and saloon.[58]

*Major Martin R. Delaney*

*Steward Thomas S. Dixon*

### Decatur Dorsey

Sergeant, Company B, Thirty-Ninth Regiment, U.S. Colored Troops, Union Army.

Decatur Dorsey was born in Howard County, Maryland, and entered the service in Baltimore County. On July 30, 1864, Dorsey planted his unit's colors on the Confederate works at Petersburg, Virginia, in advance of his regiment. When they were driven back to the Union works, he carried the colors and bravely rallied the men. He was awarded the Medal of Honor for his heroic deeds on November 8, 1865.[59]

### George W. Douglas

First Sergeant, Eighty-Eighth Infantry Regiment, U.S. Colored Troops, Union Army.

George Douglas enlisted in the army on August 13, 1864, at Huntsville, Alabama, and served until December 31, 1865.[60]

### Lewis H. Douglass

Sergeant Major, Fifty-Fourth Massachusetts Volunteer Infantry Regiment, Union Army.

Lewis Douglass was a native of Washington, D.C., the son of the distinguished abolitionist, Frederick Douglass. He enlisted in the Fifty-Fourth Massachusetts Regiment on March 25, 1863 and was discharged on May 10, 1864. He was the original sergeant-major of the regiment.[61]

### William H. Dove

Cook, Company R, Fifth North Carolina Cavalry (Sixty-Third State Troops), Confederate Forces.

William Dove served as a cook, and was officially listed on the company muster roll for November and December, 1863. The records show that he was enlisted on December 22, 1862 at Kenansville by a Captain Harris, as a cook—"a free Negro, has no home."[62]

### William Dupree

Second Lieutenant, Fifty-Fifth Massachusetts Volunteer Infantry Regiment, Union Army.

William Dupree was born in Petersburg, Virginia on March 13, 1838. He was a plasterer and was single prior to his enlistment in the army in Chillicothe, Ohio, on June 5, 1863, as a private in Company H, Fifty-Fifth Regiment. He was promoted to first sergeant on June 25, 1863 (reference gives June 5 and June 25, 1865, but should read 1863), and was commissioned a second lieutenant on May 30, 1864, but not mustered until July 1, 1865. Dupree mustered out of the regiment on August 29, 1865, and after the war was employed at the Boston post office.[63]

### Peno Edwards

Private, Company B, Third South Carolina Infantry Regiment, Union Army.

Peno Edwards entered the military in South Carolina and was present for duty at Hilton Head, South Carolina, on April 27, 1863.[64]

### Robert B. Elliott

Major General, National Guard of the State of South Carolina.

Robert B. Elliott was born in Boston, Massachusetts, on August 11, 1842. He attended High Holborn Academy in London and graduated from Eton College in 1859. He studied law, was admitted to the bar, and commenced to practice law in Columbia, South Carolina. Elliott was a member of the state House of Representatives from July 6, 1868 to October 23, 1870. The official records of the state of South Carolina for 1870 and 1873 show that on August 1, 1870, Robert B. Elliott was commissioned as major general, commanding, National Guard of the State of South Carolina (NGSSC). A register of letters received in the adjutant general's office indicates that letters were received from "Elliot, R. B., Major General Commanding," as follows:

January 29, 1872—requesting that certain gentleman be commissioned with a view of being appointed on his staff.

January 31, 1872—requesting that H. W. Purvis be commissioned brigadier general with a view of appointing him his chief of staff.

February 3, 1872—recommending that certain gentlemen be commissioned with a view of appointing them on his staff.

March 29, 1872—requesting that Colonel P. R. Rivers be commissioned brigadier general, third Brigade, Second Division, NGSSC.

Elliott was elected Republican representative to the Forty-Second and Forty-Third Congresses and

*Major General Robert B. Elliott*

*Sergeant Major Christian A. Fleetwood*

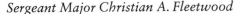

served from March 4, 1871 until his resignation in 1874. He was elected again as a member of the state House of Representatives in 1874–1876, and was an unsuccessful candidate for attorney general of South Carolina in 1876. Later, he moved to New Orleans and practiced law there until his death on August 9, 1884.

Major General Elliott attained a notable position in the state militia of South Carolina in 1870. This was a monumental achievement in view of the fact that it was not until World War II, that a Negro officer attained general officer's rank in the active U.S. regular army.[65]

## William Emory

Musician, Company I, First (McCreary's) South Carolina Infantry Regiment (First S.C. Inf. Prov'l Army), Confederate Army.

William Emory was enlisted as a musician on October 1, 1861, at Richmond, Virginia by Thomas Grayson. His name appeared on the company muster roll in November and December, 1861, and on the field and staff muster roll. He was listed as "colored man (free)."[66]

## Emmanuel Evans

Musician, Company H, One Hundredth Regiment, United States Colored Troops, Union Army.

Emanuel Evans enlisted in the Union Army at Nashville, Tennessee, on December 12, 1864. He served as a musician until November 10, 1865.[67]

## Christian A. Fleetwood

Sergeant Major, Fourth United States Colored Troops, Union Army, and Major, National Guard, District of Columbia.

Christian A. Fleetwood was born in Baltimore, Maryland. He enlisted in the Union Army at Baltimore, Maryland in July, 1863 and served with the Fourth U.S. Colored Troops. He was promoted to Sergeant Major on July 11, 1863 and served continuously in that rank until mustered out of service on May 9, 1866. During his period of enlistment, he performed duties at regimental headquarters consisting of maintenance of rosters, books, returns and reports. During the period June to December, 1864, he experienced combat action at

Fort Harrison and Chapin's Farm, New Market Heights. He also accompanied the Butler expedition to Fort Fisher in December, 1864, and the Terry Expedition in January, 1865. He was at the capture of Fort Fisher, of Sugar Loaf and of Wilmington, North Carolina, and at General Johnson's surrender of Goldsboro, North Carolina, in April, 1865. He performed provost duty at New Berne, North Carolina from June to October, 1865 and garrison duty and defenses of Washington, D.C. from October, 1865 to May, 1866.

After being discharged from the army, Christian Fleetwood did not entirely sever his military relations, but became active in the public schools, student military cadet program. He was also a member of the District of Columbia's National Guard and was Captain, Independent Company, from December, 1880 to July, 1887. During the period July, 1887 to June, 1892, he was a major in the District of Columbia National Guard. He resigned in 1892. Christian Fleetwood was employed in the War Department from 1881–1892, assuming positions in the Surgeon General's Office, Adjutant General's Office and Record and Pension Office.

He was awarded the Medal of Honor on April 6, 1865, for his courageous and brave conduct at Chapin's Farm, Virginia. His official citation read as follows: "Chapin's Farm, Virginia, 29 September 1864, he seized the colors after two color bearers had been shot down and bore them nobly through the fight."

Sergeant Major (Major DCNG) Christian A. Fleetwood was one of the more educated black Medal of Honor recipients during the Civil War. As a military man his record was commendable and his accomplishments meritorious. Upon assuming the status of a civilian, he continued to display his leadership abilities and became active in military cadet programs and national guard organizations, and was often invited to speak to community groups.[68]

## R. B. Forten

Sergeant Major, Forty-Third Regiment, Company C, U.S. Colored Troops, Union Army.

R. B. Forten enlisted in the army as a private and was assigned to the Forty-Third Regiment,

USCT. He had a liberal education and was well prepared to assume a position of responsibility. On April 8, 1864, he was appointed sergeant major. The regiment's history records that he died in June, 1864.[69]

### Willis Fountain

Body Servant, Confederate Army.

Willis Fountain, a black man, was born on August 12, 1836, in Georgia. He entered the Confederate military service in 1861 as a body servant to his master John W. Stephens. When Stephens died during the war, Willis Fountain served Colonel Lowrey (commanding officer) and Chaplain Hitt. After the surrender, Fountain returned to his mistress' home and lived with her family until around 1872. He later lived in Virginia and Tennessee.

In 1926, a daughter of Fountain's was living at 352 East Second Street, Erie, Pennsylvania, and a son at Tiptonville, Tennessee, according to a letter dated September 15, 1926 from Ewell T. Weakley, attorney at law, Dyersbury, Penn., to the Pension Board, Nashville, Tennessee.[70]

*Private Frederick Fowler*

### Frederick Fowler

Private, Company E, Twenty-Ninth Regiment, Connecticut Volunteer Infantry State Troops, Union Army.

Frederick Fowler was born a slave on January 1, 1833, at Frederick County, Maryland, and was the property of Michael Reel until 1847, when he was sold to a Dr. Lewis W. Willis for one thousand dollars. In 1858, he escaped to freedom by way of the underground railroad. On finding that Fowler had fled, Dr. Willis posted the following notice:

*$200 REWARD!*
*Ranaway from the subscriber, living at New Market, Frederick Co., Md. On Saturday night, the 8th of May inst., a Negro man named Fred Fowler, aged about twenty-six years, five feet ten or eleven inches high, stout made, dark copper color, round full eye, upper teeth full and even, has a down look when spoken to, lisps slightly in his speech, and has small hands; no other marks recollected. Had on, when he left, a glazed cap, dark pants and coat and light made shoes.*
*The above reward will be given for the arrest of said Negro, if taken out of the state of Maryland, and his delivery to the subscriber; or one hundred dollars, if taken in the state, and secured in jail.*
*Dr. W. L. Willis*
*New Market, Md., May 10, 1858.*

Fowler left Maryland on May 10, 1858, and arrived on August 1 in Bradford, Ontario, where he obtained work and his first education. From Bradford he went to Niagara Falls, on the Canadian side, and was employed as a waiter at the Clifton House.

In August, 1863, he returned to the United States and enlisted in the army at Lockport, Niagara County, New York. On August 18, 1863, he was assigned to Company E, commanded by Captain Henry C. Ward, Twenty-Ninth Connecticut Volunteer Infantry State Troops, as a private, for a period of three years or the duration of the war.

The regiment was stationed at Fair Haven, Connecticut during its organization and on March 8, 1864, was formerly mustered into the service. Fowler was with the regiment at Hilton Head and

Beaufort, South Carolina; at Bermuda Hundred and Petersburg, Virginia, and at Point Lookout, Maryland. He was honorably discharged at Brownsville, Texas, on October 24, 1865.

Fowler returned to Frederick County, Maryland and moved to Washington, D.C., in 1876, where he served for a few months as a waiter at the Capitol and was later appointed by Librarian Spofford as a messenger in the Mail Division of the Library of Congress. He later became doorkeeper of the Library of Congress Reading Room. He was a member of the Ebenezer African Methodist Church.[71]

*Private Benjamin Franklin*

## Benjamin Franklin

Private, Company B, U.S. Colored Infantry Regiment, Union Army.

Benjamin Franklin was born in Lexington, Kentucky on May 18, 1849. He enlisted in the Union Army on February 11, 1865, and was mustered out on April 27, 1866 as a free man. On returning to Kentucky, Franklin worked for his former master for a few years. Then he went to England and returned to the trade of steam boating as a second engineer. In 1871, he decided to become a barber.[72]

## John Fry

Private, Company E, Twenty-Ninth Connecticut Volunteer Regiment, Union Army.

John Fry entered the military service at Bridgeport, Connecticut, on December 23, 1863.[73]

## James Gardiner

Private, Company I, Thirty-Sixth U.S. Colored Troops, Union Army.

James Gardiner, a black, was a native of Gloucester, Virginia. He was engaged in battle at Chapin's Farm, Virginia, where he displayed courage that brought him the Medal of Honor on April 6, 1865. The citation read as follows: "On September 29, 1864, at Chapin's Farm, Virginia, he rushed in advance of his brigade, shot a rebel officer who was on the parapet rallying his men, and then ran him through with his bayonet."[74]

## Seymour Gardiner

Musician, Company H (McCreary's), South Carolina Infantry Regiment (First SC Inf. Prov'l Army), Confederate Army.

Seymour Gardiner was enlisted as a musician in a Confederate unit on October 1, 1861 by a Captain Haskell at Charleston, South Carolina. The official field and staff muster roll listed him as a "colored man (free)." It is stated that he deserted the unit some time in 1861.[75]

## Peter Geter

Body Servant, to Major R. G. Hay, Eleventh Regiment, Confederate Army.

Peter Geter entered the service in September, 1862 and served until February, 1865. In April, 1923, when living at Lyndhurst in Barnwell County, South Carolina, he applied for a pension and stated that he had been a body servant under Major R. G. Hay who was in Magood's Brigade, Eleventh Regiment. His request was approved on April 13, 1923.[76]

## Horace Gibson

Drummer, Company B, One Hundred and First Infantry Regiment, U.S. Colored Troops, Union Army.

Horace Gibson enlisted at Nashville, Tennessee, and was discharged on December 12, 1865.[77]

*Private Michael Gomes*

### James Gordon

Body Servant, Confederate Army.

James Gordon entered the Confederate military service in 1862, at Lafayette County, Mississippi, as a servant to John H. Marion. He remained in the service as a body servant until the surrender, and was eventually awarded a pension by the state of Mississippi.[78]

### John Graves

Musician, Company F (McCreary's), South Carolina Infantry (First S.C. Infantry Prov'l Army), Confederate Army.

John Graves, a black man, enlisted as a musician in a Confederate unit on January 15, 1862, for the period of the war. The company muster roll shows that he was absent without leave from August 31 to December 31, 1862, and was listed as a deserter in December, 1862.[79]

### Fish Green

First Sergeant, Company E, One Hundredth Infantry Regiment, U.S. Colored Troops.

Fish Green enlisted in the Union Army at London, Kentucky.[80]

### Gloster Green

First Sergeant, Company D, Eighty-Eighth Infantry Regiment, U.S. Colored Troops, Union Army.

Gloster Green enlisted at Memphis, Tennessee and was discharged on October 25, 1865.[81]

### Henry Grimes

Sergeant, Company H, First Regiment of Tennessee Infantry of African Descent, Union Army.

Henry Grimes enlisted in the army on October 17, 1863 at Corinth, Mississippi. The record states that he was of African descent.[82]

### Henry Harris

Private, Company G, Sixth Regiment of Mississippi Volunteers of African Descent, Union Army.

Henry Harris enlisted in the army at Natchez, Mississippi, on September 17, 1863.[83]

### James H. Harris

Sergeant, Company B, Thirty-Eighth Regiment, U.S. Colored Troops, Union Army.

James Harris, a native of St. Mary's County, Maryland, performed heroically during an assault at New Market Heights, Virginia, on September 29, 1864. He was awarded the Medal of Honor for gallantry in the assault, on February 18, 1874.[84]

### Arbaugh Harrison

First Sergeant, One Hundred and Thirteenth Regiment, U.S. Colored Troops, Union Army.

Arbaugh Harrison enlisted at Fort Smith, Arkansas, in October, 1863, and served until December 18, 1865.[85]

### Thomas Hawkins

Sergeant Major, Sixth Regiment, U.S. Colored Troops, Union Army.

Thomas Hawkins, a native of Cincinnati, Ohio, entered the service at Philadelphia, Pennsylvania. He was awarded the Medal of Honor on February 8, 1870, for retrieving the regimental colors at Deep Bottom, Virginia, on July 21, 1864.[86]

### Everett Hayes

Private, Company F, First North Carolina Artillery Regiment (Tenth State Troops), Confederate Army.

Everett Hayes enlisted in the Confederate Army in September, 1862, at Wilmington. The unit's muster roll indicated that "Hayes, Colored" enlisted on September 1, 1862 and served until June 30, 1864. He was listed on the muster roll of a Captain Andrews as a company cook, extra duty.[87]

### George W. Hays

Private, Union Army.

George W. Hays was born a slave in the state of Louisiana and was taken to Kentucky at the age of seven. With the outbreak of the Civil War, when he was about fourteen years old, he ran away to avoid the possibility of having to join the Confederate forces as a servant, and joined the Union army. After the war, he lived in Cincinnati, Ohio. He was appointed court crier in 1871, and served in the U.S. District Court in the Southern District of Ohio.

Hays is an example of a man born a slave who sought the Union side to continue the fight for his freedom. He became a respected citizen and member of his community.[88]

*Captain Samuel Harrison*

**Jas. Hicks**

Private, Confederate States Naval Brigade.

Jas. Hicks was one of the few Negroes whose names have been identified on official Confederate Naval records. "Records Relating to Confederate Naval and Marine Personnel" in the National Archives have the following listing: "Jas. Hicks (Col'd) Private."[89]

**Alfred B. Hilton**

Sergeant Major, Company H, Fourth Regiment, U.S. Colored Troops, Union Army.

Alfred Hilton, a black man, was born in Hartford County, Maryland. On April 6, 1865, he was awarded the Medal of Honor for bravery at Chapin's Farm, Virginia, on September 29, 1864. The citation read: "When the regimental colors bearer fell, this soldier seized the colors and carried it forward, together with the National standard, until disabled at the enemy's inner line."[90]

**Milton M. Holland**

Sergeant Major, Fifth Regiment, U.S. Colored Troops, Union Army.

Milton Holland, a black, was born in Austin, Texas, and entered the service at Athens, Ohio. Holland was awarded the Medal of Honor on April 6, 1865 for initiative and courage at Chapin's Farm, Virginia, on September 29, 1864. The citation read: "Took command of Company C, after all the officers had been killed or wounded, and gallantly led it."[91]

**Wesley Jackson**

Sergeant Major, Company C, Forty-Third Regiment, U.S. Colored Troops, Union Army.

Wesley Jackson was promoted to the rank of sergeant major for distinguished bravery on July 1, 1865. He was one of the few senior Negro non-commissioned officers assigned to the Forty-Third Regiment.[92]

**William Jackson**

Chaplain, Fifty-Fifth Regiment, Massachusetts Volunteer Infantry, Union Army.

William Jackson, a black man, was born in Norfolk, Virginia on August 16, 1818. His father was a pilot on the Norfolk port and was employed there during the War of 1812 in engaging the British blockading fleet. After the Nat Turner insurrection in 1831, his family moved to Philadalphia. Jackson served in the navy on board the sloop *Vandalia* from 1834 to 1835. In 1837 he joined the Baptist Church and on September 16, 1842, was ordained as pastor of the Oak Street Baptist Church in Philadelphia. Later he moved to Newburg, New York; Wilmington, Delaware; Philadelphia, and finally New Bedford, Massachusetts. He was appointed post chaplain at Readville, Massachusetts on March 10, 1863.

On July 14, 1863, he was appointed chaplain of the Fifty-Fifth Massachusetts Infantry Regiment. He resigned on January 14, 1864. Later he was pastor of the Salem Baptist church, New Bedford, Massachusetts.[93]

**Elijah M. Johnson**

Drummer, Company D, First Michigan Regiment of Colored Volunteers, One Hundred and Second Infantry Regiment, Union Army.

Elijah M. Johnson was reported present for duty on September 29, 1863. He entered the service at Kalamazoo, Michigan.[94]

**Henry Johnson**

Musician, Company K, Eighty-Eighth Infantry Regiment, U.S. Colored Troops, Union Army.

Henry Johnson enlisted in the army at Clarksville, Alabama, on September 17, 1864.[95]

**Joe Johnson**

Private, Confederate Service, Naval Brigade.

Joe Johnson's name appears in Records Relating to Confederate and Naval Personnel, as follows: "Joe Johnson (col'd) Private." Johnson was one of the few Negroes whose name has been identified on official Confederate naval records.[96]

**William Henry Johnson**

Volunteer soldier, Union forces.

William Johnson was born in Alexandria, Virginia, on March 4, 1833, of free parents. When he was twelve, with only a Sunday school education, he left home, and in May, 1850, went to Philadelphia where he learned to work as a hairdresser. He became interested in helping fugitive slaves and in 1851 went to Albany, New York, and became engaged in underground railroad activities. He returned to Philadelphia in 1855 and in 1857 he became a member of the Banneker Literary Institute. Eventually, Johnson was forced to leave Philadelphia, because of his assistance to fugitive slaves, and moved to Norwich, Connecticut.

Johnson was living in Connecticut when the Civil War began, and when he was not allowed to enlist because of his color, he joined a Connecticut regiment as an independent soldier and participated in the battles of Bull Run, Roanoke, and Newbern. Ill health compelled him to return to Albany, New York, where he became a recruiting agent for the Fourteenth Congressional District. Later he was a delegate to the National Convention. In 1864, he formulated the constitution for the New York State Equal Rights Commission, and in 1872 an amendment which he had drafted, striking out the word white, was made to the military code. He drafted a civil rights bill in 1873.

Before the Union Army accepted black volunteers, a number of black patriots, like Johnson, served as independent volunteer soldiers.[97]

## Leroy Jones

Body Servant, Company I, Fourth Tennessee Regiment, Confederate Army.

Leroy Jones was born in Shelby County, Tennessee, on March 9, 1838. He entered the military service with his master, Walis or Wallis Jones at Germantown, Tennessee, and stayed with him until he tied of typhoid fever in 1862 in Panola County, Mississippi. At this time Leroy Jones slipped through the federal lines and returned to his master's home, where he remained until he was given his freedom.

In September, 1921, when he was living in Covington, Tipton County, Tennessee, he applied for a pension and was successful.

In 1921, there were many concerned and honest Southerners who were sincere in helping blacks who had faithfully served the Confederacy to obtain pensions. Even though they used the manner and prevailing sentiments of the period, they did write letters and contact influential individuals to assist these forgotten body servants.

C. P. Simonton, clerk, County Court Tipton County, Covington, Tennessee, expressed his views in a letter, dated October 1, 1921, to the Secretary, Pension Board, Nashville, Tennessee. He wrote:

*It is a particular hardship on Negroes who saw some service in the Confederate army and refused to join the Federals, not to be given some assistance in their old age, when they are penniless and know of many Negroes who deserted their masters and joined the Federal army and are receiving a large pension. There are not many of these old faithful Negroes left and you of course realize it is hard for them to prove their service since so many of the confederates have crossed the river. Give the old Negroes, where they are worthy, the benefit of the doubt.*

R. H. Green, Covington, Tennessee wrote the Secretary of Pension Board, Nashville, Tennessee the following:

*In the fall of 1865, Leroy married one of Dr. John A. Greene's Negro girls. Rev. David H. Cummins, pastor of the First Presbyterian Church of Covington, performed the ceremony. From this time he lived with my grandfather and afterward my father for many years . He was what was known as a* white man's Negro [emphasis added], *and voted with us in every election thus incurring the enmity of the leading Negroes, but old Leroy always told them he was going to stick to his white folks. . . . He has been loyal to his white people ever since the war regardless of his freedom.*[98]

## Monroe Jones

Servant to James McAlpine, Company A, First Mississippi Light Artillery Regiment, Confederate Army.

Monroe Jones, a black man, was born in 1847 in Warren County, Mississippi, and later lived in Memphis, Shelby County, Tennessee. A pension application shows that he served with the First Mississippi Light Artillery for eight months in 1862. Around May 1 of that year he lost both of his legs when a shell exploded at Snyder's Bluff near Vicksburg, Mississippi. Jones was one of many blacks serving as cooks or servants in the Confederacy who were exposed to the dangers of combat.[99]

*Thomas Law (inset) messenger to*
*General Sheridan*

*The Shaw Memorial*
*Monument on Beacon*
*Street in Boston*
*represents Colonel*
*Robert Gould Shaw*
*and the Fifty-Fourth*
*Massachusetts*
*Volunteer Regiment*

### Preston Kearce

Servant, Confederate Army.

Preston Kearce, a black, applied for a pension on May 26, 1923, when he was living near Olar, Bamberg County, South Carolina. He stated on his application that he helped to build fortifications. He did not know the name of the company or regiment he served, but went into service in June, 1864 and served until February, 1865.

Oddly enough, his application was approved by a J. B. Kearce, Chairman, Board of Honor, Bamberg; it was sworn to and subscribed before a J. Carl Kearce, Notary Public for South Carolina, and an H. A. Kearce was a witness.[100]

### Alexander Kelly

First Sergeant, Company F, Sixth Regiment, U.S. Colored Troops, Union Army.

Alexander Kelly, a black man, was born in the state of Pennsylvania. He was awarded the Medal of Honor on April 6, 1865 for gallantry in action at Chapin's Farm, Virginia, on September 29, 1864. His citation read: "He seized the colors, which had fallen near the enemy's lines of abatis, raised them and rallied the men at a time of confusion and in a place of the greatest danger."[101]

### Taylor Kennard

Body Servant, Company K, Fifty-Fourth Tennessee Regiment, Confederate Army.

Taylor Kennard was born in Bedford County, Tennessee, in 1840. At the age of ninety, on March 25, 1930, he applied for a pension, stating that he was the first person to reach his master, Lieutenant William Yarbrough, after he was shot. Kennard remained with his master until he died, and was himself wounded in the left arm during the Civil War. His application for a pension was approved by the state of Tennessee. On April 6, 1933, he died, at the age of ninety-three.[102]

### Lewis Howard Latimer

Crew Member, USS Massasoit, U.S. Navy.

Lewis Latimer wah born in 1848, in the city of Boston, Massachusetts. As a small boy he sold copies of a newspaper called the Liberator, published and edited by abolitionist William Lloyd Garrison. At the age of sixteen, Latimer joined the navy and served aboard the USS Massasoit during the Civil War. After receiving an honorable discharge in 1865, he returned to Boston and worked as an office boy in a patent office. He later became interested in drafting and engineering, and studied electrical engineering. Eventually his skills were recognized by the inventors Alexander Graham Bell and Thomas Edison. Latimer was hired by the United States Electric Light Company in Bridgeport, Connecticut, and while employed there invented a method of making carbon filaments for incandescent lamps. Later he supervised the building of light manufacturing plants in New York, Philadelphia and Canada.

In 1884, he was appointed one of the first assistants to Edison when he joined the engineering staff of the Edison Electric Light Company. Latimer wrote a book explaining the workings of electric lamps and became involved in engineering and drafting. He retired as a member of the Edison Pioneers, a group of inventors who had worked with Edison.[103]

### John Lawson

Landsman, USS Hartford, U.S. Navy.

*Landsman John Lawson*

John Lawson was born in 1837 in the state of Pennsylvania. During the Civil War he served aboard the *USS Hartford*. On August 5, 1864, Lawson displayed outstanding valor and was awarded the Medal of Honor on December 31, 1864. His citation read as follows: "On board the flagship *USS Hartford* during successful attacks against Fort Morgan, rebel gun points and the raid on Mobile Bay, Tennessee on August 5, 1864. Wounded in the leg and thrown violently against the side of the ship when an enemy shell hit the deck. Lawson upon regaining his composure promptly returned to his station and although urged to go below for treatment, continued his duties throughout the remainder of the action."[104]

### Frank Lecke

First Sergeant, Company C, One Hundred and Sixth Regiment, U.S. Colored Troops, Union Army.

Frank Lecke, a black man, enlisted at Decatur, Alabama, on March 18, 1864 and served until October 30, 1865.[105]

### Clark Lee

Body Servant, First Georgia Infantry Regiment, Confederate Army.

Clark Lee, a black man, was born in Walker County, Georgia. He joined a Colonel Gordon's First Confederate Georgia Regiment with his master, Jim Lee, before the battle of Chickamauga. He applied for a pension in August, 1921, and needed support from several people before the application was approved. A letter was sent to the Pension Board in Nashville, Tennessee, by Major General John N. Johnson, formerly of the First Division, Forrest's Cavalry Troops.[106]

### Frank Lee

Body Servant, Company F, Ninth Virginia Cavalry, Confederate Army.

Frank Lee was born around 1856 in Lloyds Essex County, Virginia. He entered the Confederate military service as a body servant to Lieutenant Waring Lewis. His pension application, dated April 20, 1925, stated: "Served for Lieutenant Waring Lewis, Company F, Ninth Virginia Regiment,

*Company Sergeant Major Arthur B. Lee*

*Private Harrison Lee*

cooking, tending horses and *following him into battles*" [emphasis added].[107]

### Samuel J. Lee

Brigadier General, Chief-of-Staff, National Guard of the State of South Carolina.

Samuel J. Lee, a black man, was born in South Carolina and worked as a farmer, as a laborer and in a lumber mill. He educated himself to become a lawyer and was speaker of the South Carolina House of Representatives from 1872 to 1874. The official records of the state of South Carolina for 1873 show that Samuel J. Lee was commissioned brigadier general in the state militia on December 1, 1872. He was quite active in South Carolina politics in the Reconstruction period.[108]

### The Reverend William Mack Lee

Body Servant and Cook to General Robert E. Lee, Confederate Army.

William Mack Lee was born on June 12, 1835 at Westmoreland County, Virginia. He was raised at Arlington Heights, the home of his master, General Robert E. Lee. William Lee was with the general during the Civil War at the first and second battles of Manassas, the first battle of Bull Run and, on Sunday, April 9, 1865, at 9 A.M., was at Appomattox when the last gun was fired for the salute of the Confederate Surrender. Lee boasted of feeding his master's co-generals at the head-quarters in Petersburg, the battles of Decatur, Seven Pines, the Wilderness, on the Plank road between Fredericksburg and Orange County Court House, at Chancellorsville, the old yellow Tavern, Five Forks, Cold Harbor, Sharpsburg, Bonneville, Gettysburg, New Market, Mine Run, Cedar Mountain, Civilian, Louisa Court House, Winchester and Shenandoah Valley. At the close of the war, William Mack Lee, although free, decided to remain with his master until his death. William Lee often related to his friends stories concerning the war and his experiences with General Lee.

*I have even seen him cry. I never seed him sadder dan dat gloomy mawnin when he tol' me bout how General Stonewall Jackson had been shot by his own men. William he says to me, William I have lost my right arm—I'm bleeding at the heart*

*Rev. William Mack Lee*

*William he says, and I stepped out'n de tent cause he looked like he wanted to be by himself. A little later I came back and he told me that General Jackson had been shot by one of his own men. The general had told him to shoot anybody going or coming across the line and the general himself put on a federal uniform and scouted across the line, when he came back one of his soldiers raised his gun. Don't shoot, I'm your general, Marse Jackson yelled. They said the sentry was hard of hearing, anyway he shot the general and killed him. "I'm bleeding at the heart William, Marse Robert kept saying.*

William Mack Lee began preaching after the war and he became very active in religious matters. He traveled many miles to raise money for his benevolent projects. He pastored throughout the area and lived a very active Christian life. He received considerable support from white citizens and church groups. He stated that he organized the State Benevolent Association of Virginia for Colored People at Charlottesville in 1887, and in 1888 organized at Washington, D.C. the Supreme Grand Lodge United States Benevolent Association of the District of Columbia. He was ordained in Washington, D.C. July 12, 1881, as a Missionary Baptist preacher.

Lee's wife died in 1910. He was the father of eight daughters and had twenty-one grandchildren and eight great-grandchildren. William Mack Lee had a great respect for his master, General Robert E. Lee. He said that he was raised by one of the greatest men in the world and that there was never one born of woman greater than General Robert E. Lee. While collecting funds for his church, William Mack Lee sold for fifty cents a copy of the history of his life which clearly defined the devoted, faithful and unswerving loyalty of servant to master that he possessed. The cover of the pamphlet stated that he was still living under the protection of the Southern states.[109]

### James Lewis

Captain, First Regiment, Louisiana Native Guards, Confederate Army.

James Lewis was born in 1832 at Woodville, Mississippi. His father was Caucasian and his mother a mulatto woman. At an early age he went to Bayou Sara, Louisiana, and served as a waiter on a steamboat. In 1862, during the Civil War, he was a steward on a Confederate transport. He abandoned the vessel and went to New Orleans and joined the First Regiment, Louisiana Native Guards. After the war Lewis was a traveling agent for the education department of the Freedmen's Bureau. In 1867 he was appointed Louisiana State Customs Inspector and two years later became a sergeant on the Metropolitan Police Force. Later he was promoted to police captain. In 1870, Lewis served as a colonel in the state militia of Louisiana. Later he was made administrator of police and in 1872, was appointed administrator of public improvements. He was also naval officer of the Port of New Orleans, a position he occupied until 1880.

James Lewis was Louisiana delegate to the Republican National Convention in Chicago. He was also Superintendent of U.S. Bonded Warehouses. In 1884 he was confirmed by the U.S. Senate as Surveyor General of the State of Louisiana. Lewis died on July 11, 1914, at the age of eighty.[110]

### W. S. Lewis

Servant, Marine Corps, Confederate Forces.

W. S. Lewis applied for a pension in the state of South Carolina on April 5, 1923, when he was living in Charleston, South Carolina. Lewis stated on his application that he had served the state in the Civil War as a servant under James Thurston, who was in the Marine Corps in *CS Atlantis,* then with Edward N. Thurston until the close of the war. The application also stated that he remained faithful to the Confederacy during the war. His request was approved on April 14, 1923.[111]

### Owens Littleton

Enlistee, Union Army.

Owens Littleton, a black man, was born in Princess Anne County, Virginia, the son of John W. Metreatable and Cuffie Owens. He was a farmer, owning some acres of land in the Kempsville district and connected with one of the eight Owens families that had been free in Princess Anne County since the eighteenth century. Owens served

three years in the Civil War and represented Princess Anne County in the Virginia House of Delegates during the period 1879–1882.[112]

### Miles Loadholt

Cook, Captain Smart's Company, Third Regiment, Confederate Army.

Miles Loadholt, a black, entered the service as a cook under D. Loadholt in 1862, and served continuously until 1865. His request for a pension, made on October 2, 1923 when he was living in Allendale County, South Carolina, was approved.[113]

### Hutson Longstreet

Body Servant, Confederate Army.

Hutson Longstreet, a black man, served four years during the Civil War, attending his master, Gilbert Longstreet. When he was eighty years old, and living in Taylor, Mississippi, he applied for a pension, which was allowed by the state of Mississippi. The application stated that he was at Richmond, Virginia, at the end of the war and had received a bullet in the neck at Grenada, Mississippi.[114]

### William Lynch

Cook, Company E, Fifth North Carolina Cavalry (Sixty-Third State Troops), Confederate Army.

William Lynch enlisted in the Confederate unit on January 12, 1862. The official record stated that he was a "free Negro has no home, absent without leave at one time, Col'd Cook."

Lynch is one of the many Negroes who may have been officially enlisted on Confederate muster rolls as other than body servants.[115]

### John McConaha

Fifer, H Company, One Hundredth Infantry Regiment, U.S. Colored Troops, Union Army.

John McConaha enlisted in the Union Army on June 3, 1864, at Lexington, Kentucky, and served until November, 1865. He was one of several black fifers who served in the Civil War.[116]

### William J. Mason

Private, B Company, Twelfth Kentucky Heavy Artillery Regiment, U.S. Colored Troops, Union Army.

William Mason joined the Union Army from Colesburg, Kentucky, on December 7, 1864, and served until January, 1866.[117]

### Andrew Mathews

Body Servant, Company G, Second Alabama and Mississippi Regiment, Colonel Bill Wade commanding, Confederate Army.

Andrew Mathews, a black, applied for a pension at the age of seventy-five, when he was living in Thasher, Prentiss County, Mississippi. He entered the Confederate military service in 1861 and served for four years as a body servant to his master, Captain Beverly Mathews. His application for a pension was granted by the state of Mississippi.[118]

### Marshall Mattison

Cook, Confederate Army.

Marshall Mattison, a black man, entered the Confederate Army in March or April, 1864, and served until December, 1864. He stated on a pension application dated April 16, 1923 that he served as a cook under Wyatt Mattison in the Columbia, South Carolina Regiment under Captain R. D. Linn. The application was made when he was living at Belton, Anderson County, South Carolina.[119]

### Peter Mazyck

Musician, Company H (McCreary's), South Carolina Infantry Regiment (First S.C. Infantry Prov'l Army), Confederate Forces.

Peter Mazyck was enlisted on October, 1861, at Columbus, South Carolina, by Captain William T. Haskell's Company, First Regiment of South Carolina Volunteers, and served the Confederate unit as a musician. The field and muster roll of the regiment for November and December, 1861, states in the remarks column: "Col'd man (free)," and the company muster roll for January and February, 1862 indicated that Mazyck was last paid by a Major Carr. In December, 1862, records show him as absent without leave and in March and April, 1863, he was listed as having deserted.[120]

### James Mifflin

Engineer's Cook, USS Brooklyn, U.S. Navy.

James Mifflin was born in 1839 in Richmond, Virginia. He showed unusual heroism and devotion to duty while serving aboard the USS Brooklyn. His Medal of Honor citation read:

*On board the* USS Brooklyn *during successful attacks against Fort Morgan, rebel gunboats, and the ram* Tennessee *in Mobile Bay in August, 1864. Stationed in the immediate vicinity of the shell ships, which were twice cleared of men by bursting shells, Mifflin remained steadfast at his post and performed his duties in the Powder Division, throughout the furious action which resulted in the surrender of the prize rebel* Tennessee, *and in the damaging and destruction of batteries at Fort Morgan.*[121]

### James Miles

Corporal, Company B, Thirty-Sixth Regiment, U.S. Colored Troops, Union Army.

James Miles was born in Princess Anne County, Virginia, and joined the Union Army on September 30, 1844, at Norfolk, Virginia. Miles was awarded the Medal of Honor for his outstanding stamina and courage in continuing to perform his duties, though seriously wounded, on April 6, 1865. His citation stated that having had his arm mutilated, making immediate amputation necessary, he loaded and discharged his piece with one hand, and urged his men forward. This was within thirty yards of the enemy's works.[122]

### George Mills

Body Servant to Captain Walter Bryson, Judge William Shipp's Company, Hendersonville, North Carolina, and Ransome's Brigade of Lee's Army, Confederate Forces.

George Mills was born a slave in April, 1844, on Green River in Polk County, North Carolina. The following account is taken from the Hendersonville Times-News (N.C.) of May 7, 1960.

*He was the son of a slave named Mariah. His mother was the slave of Ambrose Mills, the first known white settler in present day Henderson County. Mills was transferred from owner to owner and at the age of thirteen he became the property of a Mr. William Bryson, a businessman in Hendersonville. George Mills was the valet and personal servant of Mr. Bryson's son, William. In 1861, the son was called to Confederate service and was enlisted in the company of Judge William Shipp. He had his faithful servant, George Mills to accompany him to war. George Mills followed his young master to the battlefields of Big Bethel, Manassas, Seven Pines, Fair Oaks, Malvern and Antietam Creek.*

*On September 17, 1862, Captain Bryson informed his servant that he wanted him to keep four hundred dollars and a valuable gold watch and to take care of them and take them to his mother if he did not come back. Captain Bryson left orders for his breakfast of corn bread, fat bacon and coffee and then departed for the battle area. After taking a stand on the right wing of the army, he was hit by a bullet which caused his death. Mills was given the body of his master, after insisting that he be allowed to escort his master's body home to Hendersonville, North Carolina. A rough pine coffin and an army wagon was provided by some of Captain Bryson's fellow officers. George Mills started the long journey home with his master's body. Upon reaching Fredericksburg, Virginia, he used one hundred dollars of the money given to him by his master to purchase a metal casket to which the body was transferred. He then shipped the remains by rail to Greenville, Tennessee. At Greenville, George hired a wagon and white driver for five dollars a day and finally he reached the old muster ground at Calvary Church, Fletcher, where he was met by the elder William Bryson.*

*George Mills joined the Home Guard along with his elder master until the end of the war.*

*In 1917, the casket of Captain Walter Bryson was moved from the old Methodist Cemetery to a new cemetery. At this time, George Mills, assisted in opening the grave and accompanied the remains to the new location. George Mills lived near the town of Hendersonville and was present at each reunion and gathering of "Old Soldiers." He often related his experiences in the army and his observing Confederate President Jefferson Davis at Richmond and Generals Lee and Jackson visiting the troops. He died in 1926.*

*On Tuesday, May 10, 1960, the Margaret Davis Hayes Chapter, United Daughters of the Confederacy, paid a special tribute to the memory of Body Servant George Mills. A head stone was unveiled*

*and dedicated at the desolate and barren grave site of the devoted former slave.*[123]

### Arthur Mitchell

Musician, Company K, First (McCreary's) South Carolina Infantry (First S.C. Inf. Prov'l Army), Confederate Forces.

Arthur Mitchell was enlisted in a Confederate unit on October 1, 1861, at Suffolk, by a Lieutenant Colonel Hamilton, and served as a musician until 1863, when he deserted, leaving camp near Bunkerhill, now Charleston, South Carolina. The remarks column of his service column read "colored man (free)." [124]

### Charles L. Mitchell

Captain, Fifty-Fifth Massachusetts Infantry Regiment, Union Army.

Charles Mitchell was born in Hartford, Connecticut. His father, William M. Mitchell was a deacon in the church. At the age of seventeen, Mitchell became an apprentice and worked in various offices including Garrison's Liberator Press. On July 1, 1863, he enlisted as a private in the Fifty-Fifth Massachusetts Infantry Regiment. He was later promoted to corporal and, on June 20, 1864, sergeant. In 1864, he was detailed for duty as a post printer at the headquarters of General Hatch, Morris Island, South Carolina. Learning that Union forces were preparing for immediate employment, he requested permission to rejoin his company. It was in the Battle of Honey Hill, that Sergeant Mitchell, while charging a battery in aiding General Sherman in cutting through a railroad, received the cannon shot which severed his right foot. He displayed unusual fortitude as they were carrying him past his superior officer on a stretcher in rising up, saluting and cheering a passing regiment making a new charge. During the war Mitchell also served in the seige of Charleston, South Carolina. In the battle of James Island he assisted in capturing two Napoleon guns and turning them upon the fleeing enemy with their own ammunition. He was placed in command of the detachments to serve these guns. Mitchell received an honorable discharge on October 20, 1865.

After the war, he returned to Boston, entered politics and was elected in 1866 as a representative to the Massachusetts legislature from Ward 6, Boston.

During the year 1898, Mitchell displayed unusual dedication to the national cause when he volunteered to assist in raising money and troops for Company L of the Sixth Massachusetts Infantry. In 1898, he had to return to the hospital because of his leg injury. While recuperating from an operation he received a letter from the former assistant adjutant general, U.S. Volunteers. The letter displayed humility, respect and a memorable recollection of a comrade's thoughts of his soldier days. The letter read as follows:

*Buffalo, New York, June 15, 1898*
*Lieut. Chas. L. Mitchell,*
*Mass. General Hospital, Boston, Mass.*

*My Dear Comrade, I am sorry to learn that the wound of your amputated limb is again giving you trouble, and that reamputation is thought to be a necessity.*

*I remember distinctly the main facts attending your detail for duty as printer at the headquarters of Gen. Jno. P. Hatch, on Morris Island, S.C., in 1864. In setting up the various orders issued, you of course knew we were on the eve of a movement that would mean active work in the field, when you made the request to rejoin your company in the 55th Mass., for the expedition up the Broad River that led up to the Battle of Honey Hill. I remember going to General Hatch with your request to be returned to your command, and of his reply, "That, while he would be glad to have the services of such a soldier with his company, he thought you would be needed at headquarters." [I said] that I would arrange for your return to us after we settled down again, if nothing happened to you. The general replied, that it was the liability of something happening that made him hesitate; and added "Do as you please in this matter, but if you lose a valuable man by it, do not find fault if you cannot fill his place at headquarters." I then informed you, that in compliance with your request, you had permission to rejoin your company on the eve of the departure of your regiment for Hilton Head.*

*The next time I remember to have seen you was during the Battle of Honey Hill as you were carried*

*Captain Charles L. Mitchell*

*by General Hatch on a stretcher, with your right foot shot off. The general noticed you and said to me the next morning, "The something did happen to Mitchell and you will be obliged to get another man to take charge of the printing press."*

*I am only too glad to serve one so heroic and worthy as you proved yourself to be, and hope that whatever is done for you at the hospital will give you permanent relief, and that you may have many years of comfort before you.*

*I remain yours fraternally, Leonard B. Perry, Late Assistant Adjutant General, U.S. Vol.*

Captain Charles L. Mitchell was one of many black soldiers who served during the War of the Rebellion, returned to their homes and found a position of respect and success in their community. The loyalty of Mitchell was evident when he volunteered again although suffering from a previous wound. His assistance in raising money and troops for the Spanish-American War again illustrates the

Negro's constant and devoted loyalty to his nation regardless of past and present oppression.[125]

### John Mitchell

Private, Company I (McCreary's), South Carolina Infantry Regiment (First S.C. Infantry Prov'l Army), Confederate Forces.

John Mitchell was enlisted in a Confederate unit on October 1, 1861, at Charleston, South Carolina, by a Captain Boag. The field and staff muster roll for November and December, 1861, note that Mitchell was a "colored man (free)." The company muster roll for January and February, 1862, indicate that he was re-enlisted in 1862, at Richmond, by a Thomas T. Grayson, for the period of the war.[126]

### Charles Moore

Sergeant, Company K, Fifty-Fifth Massachusetts Infantry Regiment (Col'd), Union Army.

Charles Moore was born a slave in Columbus, Georgia, but received his freedom on or before April 19, 1861. He was the son of Mrs. Elizabeth Moore of Fayetteville, Lincoln, Tennessee. Moore enlisted at the age of nineteen on June 22, 1863, and his name appears on the company muster rolls on June 22, 1863, at Readsville, Mass., and in March, April, May and June, 1864. He is described as having light complexion, and black eyes and hair. His civilian occupation is given as "painter." He was discharged on July 14, 1865, by General Order No. 50.

In July, 1970, it was learned that a widow, Mrs. Charles Moore, was living in Newton, Massachusetts, and that her husband had served in the Civil War. An inquiry was made to the National Archives and the service record of Charles Moore gave credence to previous suppositions that the lady living in Newton is the widow of Sergeant Charles Moore. His pension application file is still with the Veterans Administration, where files that are still active, with monthly pensions being paid, are located.[127]

### Henry Myers

Musician, Eighty-Eighth Infantry Regiment, U.S. Colored Troops, Union Army.

Henry Myers entered the Union Army at Memphis and served until April, 1865.[128]

*Musician Miles Moore*

### Charles Edmund Nash

Sergeant Major, Eighty-Second Regiment of Volunteers, U.S. Colored Troops, Union Army.

Charles Nash was born in Opelousas, Saint Landry parish, Louisiana, on May 23, 1844. He attended common schools and was a bricklayer by trade. During the Civil War, he enlisted as a private in the Eighty-Second U.S. Volunteer Regiment (USCT) and was later promoted to the rank of sergeant major. He lost a leg at Fort Blakely. After his discharge from the army, he was appointed night inspector of customs in Louisiana. He was elected representative to the Forty-Fourth Congress on March 4, 1875 and served until March 3, 1877. He was an unsuccessful candidate for re-election in 1876. Charles Nash died on June 21, 1913, in New Orleans. He was buried in St. Louis, Cemetery No. 3.[129]

### William Beverly Nash

Brevet Brigadier General, National Guard of the State of South Carolina.

William Nash was born of slave parents in 1822. He worked as a hotel porter and was also in the brick manufacturing business. Nash became active in politics in 1868, and was appointed magistrate in Columbia, South Carolina. He was elected to the state senate and served on various committees and as chairman of the State Finance Committee. He was a member of the Penitentiary and State Orphan Homes boards, and President of the Board of Regents of Lunatic Asylums. In 1874, he was appointed School Book Commissioner. While a member of the state senate he proposed ninety-three bills, of which thirty were approved.

William Nash was a colonel in the second regiment of the state militia in 1870. The official records of the state of South Carolina for 1873 indicate that he received a commission of brevet brigadier general, First Brigade, Third Division, National Guard of the State of South Carolina (NGSCC) on July 1, 1873. Nash was a member of the South Carolina State Militia during the Reconstruction period, when Negroes were able to command various state positions. He died on January 19, 1888, and was buried in Randolph Cemetery, Columbus, South Carolina.[180]

### Henry Nelson

Body Servant, Nineteenth and Twentieth Tennessee Regiments, Confederate Army.

Henry Nelson, a black man, was born in Murfreesboro, Rutherford County, Tennessee, in 1848. His master was George F. Nelson. He entered Confederate military service on September 1, 1863.

On June 20, 1921, Nelson applied for a pension. At the time he was destitute, his personal estate consisting only of some kitchen furniture. In 1920, his wife had made twenty-five to thirty dollars from chopping cotton and he made five dollars begging. A Causasian citizen of the town wrote a letter for him to the pension board, explaining his service and loyalty to the Confederacy. The following excerpts are typical of the experiences of former slaves loyal to the Confederate cause:

*I come from Olkhomas Mississippi. I made a crop. My master was in the army. I came home to make a crop for my mistress. While I was at home my master came home and went back to the army and taken sick and the yankies came while he was at home and ask me was it any soldier any where at round there. I told them a lie. I told them that it was not any soldiers around there. At the same time my master was there walking around. . . . I could have turn him up if I had been mean enough to turn him up, that show you that I was not a enemy to my mistress and master. I hid my master's horses in the thicket to keep the yankees from getting them. That shows you that I was a friend to the Southern army. I hid the meat from the yankees to keep them from taking everything we had.*

Henry Nelson was awarded a pension.[181]

### Sam Newsom

Body Servant, Confederate Military Service.

Sam Newsom, a black, was born on December 9, 1838, at Newsom Station in Hickman County, Tennessee. He was married to a Margaret Newsom, and a pension application made in 1932, when he was ninety-three years old, indicated that he had no property. At that time he was living at 900 Hawkins Street and Tenth Avenue, Nashville, Tennessee. The Tennessee Senate Bill No. 1342 which provided pensions for blacks who served as servants and cooks in the Confederate Army was passed on April 9, 1921. Newsom's application, made eleven years after the bill was passed, claimed that he was at the battle of Chickamauga.

Newsom was typical of the blacks who were still loyal to the Southern cause. He was a living reminder of better days to Southerners who continued to espouse white superiority and separatist doctrines. The *Tennessee Banner* newspaper published an article about Newsom in 1938. The headlines read: "Memories of Old South Still Linger With Former Slave. *Uncle Sam Newsom*" [emphasis added]. The article described how Sam Newsom brought his master's body home:

*We was sort of brought up together, master Will and I was, and maybe that's why everybody seemed to sort of trust him to me. I used to rock him to sleep. He got to be a fine and reckless sort of gentleman. Then the war came. I went with master Will. Nothing could stop him and I knew he would need me. He got to be a first lieutenant in the cavalry. I slept in the same tent. When he was fighting I stayed with the ambulances . . . I got wounded once at the battle of Sullivan's Creek . . . Master Will was killed at Chickamauga. I brought his body home. I smuggled him by the pickets, hired a wagon and got him to Chattanooga. From there I brought him on home.*[132]

### Samuel Page

Cook, Company A, Twentieth Battery, Virginia Heavy Artillery, Confederate Army.

Samuel Page was born free, of a free mother, although his father was a slave. He served in the Confederate military service as a cook, and was present at the battle of Manassas. Page applied for pension at the age of seventy-eight, while living in Appomattox County, Virginia. The following was written concerning him:

*I hereby certify that Samuel Page (a colored man) served in Company A, 20th Bat. Va. Hvy. Artillery for nearly 2 years as cook and I believe he would have taken his place in the ranks with his gun if told to do so. [emphasis added]. With great pleasure. E. F. Collins.*[133]

### Joachim Pease

Seaman, *USS Kearsarge*, U.S. Navy.

Joachim Pease, a black man, was born in Long Island, New York. He was awarded the Medal of Honor for gallantry under fire while serving aboard the *USS Kearsarge* on December 31, 1864. His citation read as follows: "Served as seaman on board the *USS Kearsarge* when she destroyed the *Alabama* off Cherbourg, France, 19 June, 1864. Acting as loader on the No. 2 gun during the bitter engagement, Pease exhibited marked coolness and good conduct and was highly recommended by his divisional officer for gallantry under fire."[134]

### Thomas S. M. Pierson

Member of Captain N. E. Elfining's Forty-Eighth New York Volunteers, Union Army.

Thomas Pierson, a black man, was born in Charleston, South Carolina, in 1846. In 1861 he enlisted in the army, and was assigned to the Forty-Eighth New York Volunteers. He was at the siege of Fort Pulaski, South Carolina; the storming of Fort Wagner, North Carolina, and in other engagements during the Civil War.

In 1863, Pierson was working as an office boy to a Dr. Daniel Tewksbury of Portland, Maine. Dr. Tewksbury arranged for him to go to public school during the day and to attend Bryant and Stratton's business college at night. He studied

*Thomas S. M. Pierson*

medicine with the physician and attended lectures at the Portland School of Medicine. From 1871 to 1874, he attended Howard University Medical College sessions and graduated from the college in 1874 when he became affiliated with Freedmen's Hospital, in Washington, D.C. He married Amanda Cooker of Augusta, Pennsylvania, in 1879.

Thomas Pierson practiced medicine in New York, and was a member of the New York County Medical Society. Among his achievements was the securing of a charter for the McDonough Memorial Hospital and Dispensary in New York City; he was a chief medical director of the Metropolitan Life Insurance of America.[135]

### Pinckney Benton Stewart Pinchback

Captain, Second Regiment, Louisiana Native Guards.

P. B. S. Pinchback, a black, was born on May 19, 1837, in Macon, Georgia, the son of a slave mother and a white Mississippi planter, William Pinchback, who subsequently manumitted the mother to her children. From 1848 to 1861 he earned a living as a steamboater on the Ohio, Missouri and Red rivers and in 1860, he married Nina Emily Hawthorne. In 1862, Pinchback recruited a company of black soldiers (Corps D'Afrique) in response to a call from Major General Benjamin J. Butler, but resigned his commission in 1863 because of lack of promotion. His military tenure was brief, but not without significance in that he was one of the few blacks to attain the rank of captain during the Civil War.

After the war Pinchback entered politics, organizing a Republican Club in 1862 and being elected a member of the Republican state committee in 1868. In 1870 he started the publication of a semi-weekly Louisiana paper. He was lieutenant governor of Louisiana from 1871–72 (succeeding Oscar J. Dunn, another black man and a former slave); governor for thirty-six days, 1872–73; and had the unusual distinction of going to Washington in 1873 as both congressman-elect and senator-elect from Louisiana. Pinchback's brief term as governor followed the impeachment of Governor Warmoth, and he held office until the Republican governor-elect, W. P. Kellog, was

*Captain P. B. S. Pinchback*

inaugurated on January 13, 1872. During that time he performed sterling service in restoring order and in preserving the machinery of government. A grateful Republican legislature elected him to the U.S. Senate which for three years debated his eligibility for office before finally refusing to seat him.

Pinchback served in various capacities from 1875–86: state delegate representative, state senator, internal revenue agent, National Republican Committee delegate, member of the Board of Trustees, Southern University and delegate to the Republican Committee in 1884. In 1885 he graduated in law from Straight University, New Orleans, and was admitted to the bar of federal and state courts in Louisiana in 1886. He died on December 21, 1921.[136]

### Robert Pinn

First Sergeant, Company I, Fifth Regiment, U. S. Colored Troops, Union Army.

Robert Pinn was born in Stark County, Ohio, and entered the military service at Massillon, Ohio. He was awarded the Medal of Honor on April 6, 1865 for bravery in action at Chapin's Farm, Virginia on September 29, 1864. His citation stated that he took command of his company after all the officers had been killed or wounded and gallantly led the men into battle.[137]

### Demps Whipper Powell

Recruit, Thirty-Third Regiment, Union Army.

Demps Powell was born in Louisville, Georgia on March 15, 1851. The following is an account of his life in his own words:

*During the Civil War, 1864, when General Sherman made his memorable march through Georgia, from "Atlanta to the Sea," I was then thirteen years of age, I left home with the Army and remained with them until they reached Washington, D.C. After receiving free transportation, I started for the South, upon reaching the city of Augusta, Georgia, I joined the Thirty-Third Regiment, Union Army. When the regiment moved to Charleston, South Carolina, Fort Sumter and adjacent islands, I accompanied the regiment. There the regiment was released from active service. The city of Charleston, South Carolina, was now under*

*martial law, a Provost court was established. It was at this court that I first saw lawyer W. J. Whipper, who later was to befriend me and become my adopted paternal parent. I became a part of his family and was fortunate to receive an education from Claflin College, Orangeburg, South Carolina, in 1873. I was taught the printing trade and received law experience by studying in my father's office. I was admitted to the bar in Beaufort, South Carolina, in 1877, appointed postmaster [for] Beaufort County, S.C. I was twice appointed census enumerator, 1890 and 1900.*

Demps Powell's achievements were notable, and are documented proof that a better position in life may be achieved by those who have been oppressed.[138]

### H. W. Purvis

Brigadier General, National Guard of the State of South Carolina.

H. W. Purvis was one of the black state politicians appointed to general officer's rank during the Reconstruction era in South Carolina. The official state records of South Carolina for 1873 list the name of H. W. Purvis as "Adjutant and Inspector General, with rank Brigadier General, from Columbus, South Carolina.[139]

### Joseph Hayne Rainey

Brigadier General, National Guard of the State of South Carolina.

Joseph Rainey, a black, was born on June 21, 1832, in Georgetown, Georgetown County, South Carolina. He had a limited education and worked as a barber until 1862, when he was forced to work on Confederate fortifications in Charleston, South Carolina. He escaped to the West Indies and remained there until the end of the Civil War.

On his return to South Carolina, Rainey became active in local politics and was a delegate to the State Constitutional Convention in 1868. He was a member of the state senate in 1870, but resigned and was elected as a Republican representative to the Forty-First Congress, the first black congressman. He filled a vacancy caused by the House of Representatives' action in declaring the seat of B. Franklin Whittemore vacant. Rainey was re-elected to the three succeeding Congresses, serving

*Brigadier General Joseph Hayne Rainey*

from December 12, 1870 to March 3, 1879. On May 22, 1879, he was appointed an internal revenue agent, and served until July 15, 1881. The state of South Carolina official records for 1873 show that Joseph Hayne Rainey was appointed and received a commission as judge advocate general with the rank of brigadier general of the state of South Carolina (NGSCC) for that year. General Rainey served during the Reconstruction period when the South Carolina National Guard was considered the Negro militia because of the predominance of Negro personnel. Rainey died on August 2, 1887, in Georgetown, South Carolina.[140]

### George Rapier

Private, Company E, One Hundredth Infantry Regiment, U.S. Colored Troops, Union Army.

George Rapier enlisted at Owensboro, Kentucky and served from May 31 to November, 1865.[141]

### Edward Ratcliff

First Sergeant, Company C, Thirty-Eighth U.S. Colored Troops, Union Army.

Edward Ratcliff, a black man, was born in James County, Virginia. He was awarded the Medal of Honor for unusual valor at Chapin's Farm, Virginia. His citation read as follows: "Commanded and gallantly led his company after the commanding officer had been killed; was the first enlisted man to enter the enemy's works."[142]

### William N. Reed

Lieutenant Colonel, First North Carolina Regiment, Union Army.

William Reed, who had studied in Germany, was one of the Negro officers commissioned in the North Carolina Regiment during the Civil War. He led his unit an a gallant charge at the battle of Olustee, Florida, where he was mortally wounded.[143]

### Prince R. Rivers

Major General commanding, Third Division, National Guard of the State of South Carolina.

Prince Rivers, a black man, was active in South Carolina politics in the Reconstruction period. The official records show that he was commissioned as a major general commanding the Third Division of the South Carolina National Guard on July 14, 1873. The Adjutant Inspector General's Office for the state of South Carolina records receiving letters from Major General Rivers on July 28, July 29 and August 29, 1873 on matters including the transmittal of his oath of office as major general, and recommendations about the appointment of his staff.[144]

## William Rudd

Cook, Company E, Fifth North Carolina Cavalry (Sixty-Third State Troops), Confederate Forces.

William Rudd enlisted in the Confederate Army on December 4, 1862. The official records state that he had no home and was "a col'd cook."[145]

## James Sayles

Private, Company F, Fifty-Ninth Infantry, U.S. Colored Troops, Union Army.

James Sayles, a black, enlisted in the Union Army at Memphis, Tennessee, on May 1, 1864. He was discharged on October 12, 1865.[146]

## William T. Scruggs

Cook, Confederate Military Service.

William Scruggs, a free black, entered the Confederate military service in 1864 as a cook for a Captain Smith. He applied for a pension at the age of seventy-six on September 16, 1924, when he was living in Cumberland County, Virginia.[147]

## Abram W. Shadd

Second Lieutenant, Fifty-Fifth Regiment of Massachusetts Volunteer Infantry, Union Army.

Abram Shadd was born in West Chester, Pennsylvania, on February 25, 1844. He was married and a teacher. He enlisted as a private in Company B, Fifty-Fifth Regiment, on May 16, 1863 and was appointed quartermaster sergeant on June 24, 1863. He returned to the company in consequence of a change in the quartermaster's department on November 19, 1863 and was promoted sergeant major on July 1, 1865. Shadd was commissioned a second lieutenant, but never mustered as the regiment was mustered out on August 29, 1865. After the war, he started a photographic gallery and studied law at Saginaw, Michigan.[148]

## John Freeman Shorter

Lieutenant, Fifty-Fifth Regiment of Massachusetts Volunteer Infantry, Union Army.

John Shorter was born in Washington, D.C., in 1842. His father was a messenger in the U.S. Senate for many years. Shorter acquired a fairly good education and before his enlistment worked as a mechanic in Delaware, Ohio. In the spring of 1863, he joined the Fifty-Fifth Regiment and was later appointed first sergeant of Company D. He continued to advance through the ranks and was selected for promotion, being commissioned second lieutenant by Governor Andrew on March 24, 1864. However Brigadier General John P. Hatch, the department commander, refused him a discharge as private and muster as lieutenant because men of African descent could not be commissioned in the U.S. Volunteers. Shorter was wounded in the foot on November 30, 1864, at Honey Hill, South Carolina, and was hospitalized. He continued on active duty with the regiment and when the secretary of war agreed to recognize colored line officers, a special order was issued to authorize his remuster. He was mustered as second lieutenant on July 1, 1865. He returned to Massachusetts with the regiment and was discharged with his company on August 29, 1865. Shorter then left for Delaware, where he had planned to be married. Unfortunately, he had been exposed to smallpox and soon after arriving at his destination, he died.[149]

## Jeremiah Sills

Landsman, USS Water Witch, U.S. Navy.

Jeremiah Sills was a member of the crew of the USS Water Witch during the Civil War. He fought most courageously, and was killed in battle.[150]

## Thomas Simms

Fifer, Company E, One Hundredth Infantry Regiment, U.S. Colored Troops, Union Army.

Thomas Simms, a black man, enlisted in the army at Owensboro, Kentucky, and served from May 28, 1864 to August, 1865.[151]

## Benjamin Singleton

Servant to Captain John H. Thompson, Company E, First South Carolina Infantry Regiment, Confederate Army.

Benjamin Singleton made an application for a pension on December 24, 1923, when he was living at Beaufort, South Carolina. He stated on the application that he had served as a servant to Captain John H. Thompson of the First South Carolina Infantry Regiment from May 1, 1861 until 1865. The request for a pension was approved.[152]

### Robert Smalls

Ships' Master, *The Planter* and Major General, South Carolina State Militia.

Robert Smalls was born in Beaufort County, South Carolina, in 1839, the son of a Jewish father and a Negro mother. His father was a sailmaker and rigger of schooners, sloops and other ships and Smalls learned the sailmaker's trade at an early age and later became a master rigger. He helped his father in delivering boats to their owners on plantations and in towns and large cities, and from this experience gained valuable knowledge of the shoals and currents of the waters in the Charleston area. Otherwise, his education came from the wharves and warehouses of Charleston.

When Fort Sumter was fired on in April, 1861, Smalls was pressed into the Confederate service and installed as pilot on the Confederate transport, *The Planter*, with a Negro crew under him and one or two white officers as his superiors. He successfully persuaded the Negro crew, including the engineer and all other essential assistants on the transport, to flee with the hope of throwing off the yoke of slavery and becoming free men and women. There were eight men, five women, and two children in the cargo of slaves who were taken to the Union fleet by Robert Smalls in May, 1862. At the time the *Planter* was heavily laden with munitions of war, food, and other supplies—a very valuable cargo worth $7,000,000.

On the night of May 12, 1862, the white officers in control of the *Planter* spent the night in the city of Charleston, as was their habit once or twice a week, for recreation. Shortly after the white officers had departed, Smalls and his crew hustled their families with their belongings on the boat. The next morning, May 13, Smalls started upon his perilous journey.

After taking the boat out of the harbor, he was hired as a pilot for the Union. He and his crew

*Ship's Master Robert Snalls*

remained in possession of the *Planter*. Smalls was ordered by the U.S. Navy to take the steamer to Philadelphia, Pennsylvania. On one of the trips of the boat through the mouth of the Stono River to Kiawah River that separates Johns Island from Kiawah Island, in securing slaughtered beeves, sheep, and hogs, the Confederates attempted to capture the steamer *Planter* by placing three jackass batteries along the Kiawah River on Johns Island. The stream adjacent to where the batteries were placed is not more than three hundred feet wide. The batteries were on a high bluff, which made it almost impossible for the shells to strike the *Planter* below the water line, though a part of the smoke stack, the lookout tower, and the roof of the wheel house were destroyed by shells. The roof of the wheel house in which Smalls sat at the wheel, was shot away. There was but one white naval officer on board at the time, Captain Nicholson. When he saw that there was little or no chance of escape, he ordered Smalls to beach the boat and surrender to the file of Confederate soldiers. Smalls answered, "Not by a damned sight will I beach this boat for you. A white man is regarded by the Confederate soldiers, but all of this crew are runaway slaves. No quarter will be shown us; hence, I will die at the wheel. I will sacrifice my own life, the life of the crew and the transport, but never, no never, will I beach this boat."

As the *Planter* proceeded, the batteries were opened upon her and she was struck several times. The white officer was panicstricken. He ran and hid himself in the steel coal bunker. As soon as Smalls had rushed the craft beyond the pale of eminent danger, he called an assistant to the wheel and made fast the lid to the coal bunker containing the white officer. For saving the boat and showing the condition of the panicstricken white officer, he was greatly praised and commended by the officers of the fleet; but, thereafter, most of the petty officers hated him and succeeded in getting an order from the commander of the fleet for Smalls to take the transport from Hilton Head, South Carolina to Philadelphia. The boast of the petty officers after they had secured the orders to go to Philadelphia was that they would run him out of the service, it being well known that he had never seen a written chart of the Atlantic coast line, knew nothing about Cape Hatteras, Hampton Roads, the Chesapeake Bay, or the Delaware Bay, which he had to enter to go to Philadelphia. They hoped to make a coward of him on account of his great ignorance of the Atlantic coastline and drive him out of the service or drown him. They said his frail craft, even in the hands of an educated pilot, would never get to Philadelphia. He received the order with buoyancy, and asked for three weeks shore leave, which, when granted him, he used well. He buried himself in the city and with the assistance of a former English sea captain, made a chart of the Atlantic Ocean coastline with his own insignia and hieroglyphics that enabled him to take the frail wooden craft that drew only five feet of water when laden around Cape Hatteras, past Hampton Roads and the mouth of the Chesapeake Bay. It is reported that he entered the Delaware Bay after 10 o'clock at night, and the transport was tied at the wharf in Philadelphia by noon the next day. He remained in Philadelphia nine months and became a student of Mr. Bassett and Mr. Catom, one teacher by day and the other by night.

The Battle of the *Keokuk* was fought in the harbor at Charleston on April 7, 1863 about a year after Smalls had escaped to freedom. The *Keokuk* was struck ninety-five times and sank to the bottom of the sea. During the battle, Smalls enjoyed a distinction that had never been bestowed upon any Negro in America—that of being one of the pilots during the fight. He remained at this post during the battle until the ship went down.

When his nine months in Philadelphia expired, Smalls had, under his two teachers, mastered the three R's. He remained thereafter a steady student of letters; hence, when the Constitutional Convention met in 1868 in South Carolina, he was as well equipped for membership as any of the delegates. To his book knowledge was added his practical experience, his education through years of contact in the business section of Charleston.

He was elected a member of the Constitutional Convention of South Carolina in 1868, to the lower house of the legislature in 1868 and 1870, to the state senate in 1872, and to the Congress of the United States in 1876, 1878, 1880 and 1882. He served longer in the Congress of the United States than any other Negro member. He was a member of the state militia from 1869 until he became a major general.

He enjoyed the distinction—one that comes to very few statesmen—of being a member of two Constitutional Conventions—one in 1868 and the other in 1895.

A search of official records does not reveal any evidence of Robert Smalls actually being enlisted or commissioned in the U.S. Navy. Records do indicate that he signed a contract for victualling and manning the U.S. steamer *Planter* for the United States as its master during the period of February–July, 1865. A copy of this contract may be seen in Appendix III. Official records of the South Carolina Archives indicate that a correspondence existed between Major General Robert Smalls, National Guard of the State of Carolina, and other correspondents.[153]

### Alfred Smith

Drummer, D Company, One Hundredth Regiment, U.S. Colored Troops, Union Army.

Alfred Smith enlisted in the Union Army at Nashville, Tennessee, on July 11, 1864, and served as a drummer until May, 1865.[154]

### James Spriggs

Private, Company A, Twenty-Ninth Infantry Regiment, U.S. Colored Troops, Union Army.

Private Spriggs enlisted at New Haven, Connecticut, on November 25, 1863. He was killed in the battle of Kill House, Virginia, on October 2, 1864.[155]

### Samuel Steed

Musician, Company C (McCreary's), South Carolina Infantry Regiment (First S.C. Infantry Prov'l Army), Confederate Forces.

Samuel Steed served from October 1, 1861, when he was enlisted in Columbus, South Carolina, by Captain Cordens. The field and staff muster roll remarks column describes him as "colored man (free)." The company muster rolls list him as deserted in January, 1863.[156]

### John Stinson

Sergeant, B Battery, Ninth Regiment, U.S. Colored Artillery (Heavy) Troops, Union Army.

John Stinson, a black man, entered the Union Army in Pomeroy, Ohio, on August 3, 1864, and served until 1865. His signature on the official record was a mark.[157]

*First Lieutenant Stephen A. Swails*

### Stephen Atkin Swails

First Lieutenant, Fifty-Fourth Massachusetts Volunteer Infantry Regiment, Union Army and Major General, Commanding, First Division, National Guard of the State of South Carolina.

Stephen Swails, a black man, was born on February 23, 1832, in Columbia, Pennsylvania, and in civilian life worked as a boatman. He entered the service at Elmira, New York, and was assigned to Company F of the Fifty-Fourth Regiment. He was promoted to first sergeant on April 23, 1862; commissioned a second lieutenant on March 11, 1864 and mustered January 17, 1865; and commissioned a first lieutenant on April 28, 1865, mustered June 3, 1865. On February 20, 1864, Swails was wounded at Olustee, Florida, and again on April 11, 1865, near Camden, South Carolina. He was discharged from active duty on August 20, 1865, at the expiration of his term of service.

After the Civil War, Swails moved to South Carolina, where he became quite active in state politics. He was elected Republican state senator in 1867 and attended the National Republican Convention in 1872. He edited a Republican newspaper in Kingstree, South Carolina. The official records of the state of South Carolina for the year 1873 state that Swails was appointed and received a commission as major general, commanding First Division (NGSSC) on July 14, 1873.[158]

### James T. S. Taylor

Enlistee, Union Army.

James Taylor was born free in 1840 at Berryville in Clark County, Virginia. He was the son of Fairfax and Ellen S. Taylor. His father was once a slave and had bought his freedom and later moved to Charlottesville. Taylor had been given the fundamentals of education by a white tutor hired by his father, and worked as a shoemaker. He enlisted in the army and returned home after the Civil War with a saving of one thousand dollars, with which he purchased real estate. He represented the community of Albemarle at the Constitutional Convention in 1867–1868. Taylor died in 1918.[159]

### Nat Tompkins

Servant, Company B, Hampton Legion, Confederate Army.

Nat Tompkins served from the beginning of the Civil War until the end. He stated on a pension application dated April 13, 1923, that he was a servant under Bab and Gus Tompkins, who were in Company B, Captain Gus Tompkins' Hampton Legion. He was living in McCormick County, South Carolina, when he made his request, which was approved on April 15, 1923.[160]

### Mathew James Townsend

Private, Company I, Fifty-Fourth Massachusetts Volunteer Infantry Regiment, Union Army.

*Lieutenant Harvey A. Thompson*

James Townsend, a black, was born in Gallipolis, Ohio, on August 18, 1841, the son of William
and Mary Ann Townsend. He attended public
schools in Ohio, and enlisted in the army on April
29, 1863, at Oxford, Ohio. At the time he was un-
married and working as a farmer. He was discharged from the army on August 20, 1865, and
received a state bounty of fifty dollars.

After the war, Townsend enrolled at Oberlin
College in Ohio and studied for two years. Later
he taught school at Evansville. In 1871, he was
ordained a deacon and pastor in Terre Haute,
Indiana. In 1883, Wilberforce University conferred on him an honorary doctor of divinity degree. Townsend represented Wayne County in the
Indiana legislature in 1885, the first Negro to serve
on that state's legislature. He died in Richmond,
Indiana, in 1913.[161]

### James Monroe Trotter

Second Lieutenant, Fifty-Fifth Regiment of Massachusetts Volunteer Infantry, Union Army.

James Monroe Trotter was born in Grand Gulf,
Mississippi, on February 7, 1842. He was a teacher,
living in Cincinnati, Ohio, when he enlisted as a
private in Company K of the Fifty-Fifth Regiment.
On June 11, 1863, he was promoted to first sergeant and on November 19, 1863, to sergeant
major. Trotter was slightly wounded at Henry
Hill, South Carolina, on November 30, 1864. He
was recommended for promotion to second lieutenant, but was not mustered as a lieutenant until
July 1, 1863. He mustered out of the regiment on
August 29, 1865.[162]

### Henry McNeal Turner

Chaplain, First U.S. Colored Troops, Union Army.

Henry McNeal Turner was born a free man in
Newberry, South Carolina on February 1, 1831.
His mother claimed descent from an African
prince. Turner was a carpenter and blacksmith
by trade in early life, when he also became very
interested in religion and the church. He was or-
dained to preach at an early age. When the Civil
War commenced, he was appointed by President
Lincoln as a chaplain, United States Army, Union
Forces. He was reappointed by President Andrew
Johnson. In 1865, Turner was mustered out of

*Chaplain Henry McNeal Turner*

the service and devoted his remaining days to the church. During his military tenure, he was successful in bringing converts and followers to his religious circle. He was also an inspiration to the men of his unit.

Chaplain Turner received honorary degrees from Pennsylvania University and Wilberforce University. He was later ordained a bishop in the African Methodist Episcopal Church (AME). He served the church faithfully for more than thirty-five years—in the dioceses of Georgia for twelve years and for several years in the Fifteenth Episcopal District (Michigan and Canada). Bishop Turner's travels included a visit to Africa when he received a degree from the Liberian College of the Republic of Liberia. Turner was also Chancellor of the University's Main Building and Theological Department, Morris Brown University, Georgia. On May 8, 1915, at the age of eighty-four, Bishop Turner died in Ontario, Canada.[163]

### Alfred Tyson

Body Servant, Company B, Twelfth Kentucky Regiment, Confederate Army.

Alfred Tyson was born in Haywood County, Tennessee, in 1845. In March, 1864, he entered the Confederate military service with the sons of his master, Benjamin Tyson. After one brother was wounded, Alfred Tyson continued to serve G. G. Tyson and was with him at the battles of Franklin and Nashville. Alfred Tyson was successful in a pension application made in September, 1921.[164]

### Charles C. Vaughn

Orderly Sergeant, Company F and later Company A, Thirteenth U.S. Colored Heavy Artillery Regiment, Union Army.

Charles Vaughn was born in Virginia on December 27, 1846, of slave parents, and was liberated by his master in 1852. He moved to Hamilton, Ohio, where he learned the alphabet, and at an early age he enlisted in the Union Army for three years. After leaving the army he continued his education, passed some qualifying examinations, and became a schoolteacher in Sidney, Ohio. Later he became a school principal.[165]

*Sergeant Charles C. Vaughn*

**Charles Veal**

Private, Company D, Fourth Regiment, U.S. Colored Troops, Union Army.

Charles Veal, a black man, was awarded a Medal of Honor for a heroic deed at Chapin's Farm, Virginia, on September 29, 1864. His citation stated that he seized the national colors after two color bearers had been shot down close to the enemy's works, and bore them throughout the remainder of the battle.[166]

*First Lieutenant Peter Vogelsang*

Peter Vogelsang

First Lieutenant, Company H, Fifty-Fourth Massachusetts Volunteer Infantry Regiment, Union Army.

Peter Vogelsang was born on August 21, 1815, in New York. He was married and in civilian life worked as a clerk. He entered the service in Brooklyn, New York, and was assigned to Company H. Vogelsang was promoted to sergeant and then to

quartermaster sergeant on April 17, 1863. He was commissioned a second lieutenant on April 28, 1865 and he mustered on June 3. On June 20, 1865, he was promoted to first lieutenant, and mustered on July 18, 1865. Vogelsang was wounded on July 18, at James Island, South Carolina, and discharged from the army on August 20, 1865, at the expiration of his term of service. He was one of the three black men in the Fifty-Fourth Massachusetts Regiment to be commissioned as officers. He died on April 4, 1887.[167]

**Samuel Walker**

Sergeant, Company F, Sixth U.S. Colored Cavalry, Kentucky, Union Army.

Samuel Walker entered the Union Army at Bowling Green, Kentucky, on September 3, 1864, and served until February 28, 1866. He indicated his signature by making a mark.[168]

**William Walker**

Body Servant, Third Regiment, FitzHugh Lee Cavalry, Confederate Army.

William Walker, a black man, was a body servant in the Confederate military service from July, 1861, to 1865. He applied for a pension on January 30, 1924, at the age of eighty, when he was living in Dinwiddie County, Virginia.[169]

**O. S. B. Wall**

Captain, One Hundred and Fourth U.S. Colored Troops, Union Army.

O. S. B. Wall was one of the few black officers commissioned during the Civil War. He served at one time with the One Hundred and Fourth USCT. The following is a copy of a letter which shows that Wall had been appointed for the purpose of recruiting and organizing Negro troops:

*War Department A.G.O., Washington, D.C., March 3, 1865*

*Brevet Major General R. Saxton, Sup't Recruiting and Orgn. of Col'd Troops, Department of the South, Beaufort, S.C.*

*General: I am directed by the secretary of war to inform you that the bearer, Captain O. S. B. Wall, U.S. Colored Troops, has been appointed for the purpose of aiding and assisting you in recruiting* and organizing colored troops, and you will assign him to duty at such place or places as you may think for the good of the service. You will observe that the regiment to which Capt. Wall is appointed is not designated although he has been mustered into service. You will cause Capt. Wall to be assigned to, and his name placed upon the rolls of, the first regiment of colored troops you may organize with his proper rank, not however with a view to his doing duty with such regiment.

Very respectfully, Your obedt. servant, C. W. Foster, A.A.G. Vols.[170]

## Lawrence Ward

Private, Company D, First North Carolina Artillery Regiment (Tenth State Troops), Confederate Army.

Lawrence Ward's name appears on a Roll of Prisoners of War at Plymouth, North Carolina. The roll, dated November 8, 1864, Headquarters, Sub-District of Albemarle, Roanoke Island, stated that Ward was captured at Plymouth on October 31, 1864. He was listed as a cook and a colored man.[171]

*Sergeant Frank T. Ware*

## Frank T. Ware

Orderly Sergeant, Union Army.

Frank Ware was born a slave on May 15, 1843, in Staunton, Virginia. His master hired him out until 1860, when he sold him to Negro slave traders who took him to Vicksburg, Mississippi. He was a dining car waiter until the Civil War, when he was taken as a body servant in the Confederate Army. After being captured by Federal troops, he joined the Union Army, and served until the end of the war, being promoted to the rank of orderly sergeant.

Frank Ware opened a hardware business in Staunton, Virginia, around 1865 and became a prominent businessman in his community. He was a delegate to the Republican Convention in 1880 and was a member of the Methodist Episcopal Church. He was one of many former slaves who joined the Union forces and served until the war ended.[172]

## Frank Watkins

Body Servant, Confederate Military Service.

Frank Watkins, a black, entered the Confederate military service in 1861 at Petersburg, Virginia and served as a body servant to Captain Ballard Bruce and to C. Overbey. His master was a John Terrell. At the age of eighty-four, on December 17, 1931, he applied for a pension and on the application stated: "I came home with the body of my young master who was killed at Fredericksburg, Virginia." Watkins lived in Mecklenburg County, Virginia.[173]

## Wade Watkins

Body Servant, Forty-Eighth Tennessee Cavalry, Confederate Army.

Wade Watkins, a black, stated on a pension application made in April, 1932, that he entered the Confederate military service when he was about twelve years old. He did not remember his birth date, but thought that in 1932 he was probably eighty-five years old. His master was a Dr. Willie Miller, the son of Bill Miller of Dancyville, Haywood County, Tennessee. Watkins was with his master when he was shot and killed by Union soldiers, and was himself shot *at the same time in the right leg* [emphasis added]. He continued in the

Confederate military service, working for a Colonel Bat Watkins, until the end of the war. Watkins' pension application was approved.[174]

### Frank Mark Welch

First Lieutenant, Company F, Fifty-Fourth Massachusetts Volunteer Infantry Regiment, Union Army.

Frank Welch, a black, was born on October 22, 1841, in Philadelphia, Pennsylvania. He was a single man, and enlisted in the service at West Meriden, Connecticut. He was assigned to Company F and promoted to sergeant and then to first sergeant on May 12, 1863. Welch was commissioned a second lieutenant on April 28, 1865 and mustered on June 3; first lieutenant on June 20, 1865 and mustered July 22. He was wounded at Fort Wagner on July 18, 1863. Welch was discharged on August 20, 1865, at the expiration of his term of service.[175]

*First Lieutenant Frank M. Welch*

### Alex Wharton (Big Alex)

Body Servant, Company I, One Hundred and Fifty-Fourth Tennessee Infantry Regiment, Confederate Army.

Alex Wharton, a black man, was born in Macknary County, Tennessee, in 1851. During the Civil War, he served as a body servant to Captain C. R. Wharton. A sworn statement signed by Richard J. P. Wharton reads: "Alex Wharton (Big Alex) . . . was a servant in the Confederate Army three years. He served me and my brother, Captain C. R. Wharton until 29 July 1864, at Atlanta, Georgia, when both of us were wounded. . . . At Chickamauga, Mission Ridge, and through the Georgia campaign, he helped care for the wounded in battlefields."[176]

### William J. Whipper

Brigadier General, Second Division, State of South Carolina National Guard.

William Whipper, a black man, was born on January 22, 1834, in Morristown, Pennsylvania. In 1866, he moved to Charleston, South Carolina, with his wife and child and opened a law office in the provost court. In 1867, he moved to Beaufort, South Carolina, and became active in the Reconstruction politics of the Republican party. He held several offices, including judge of the first judicial court of South Carolina. He served in the state House of Representatives from 1868–1872 and 1875–1876. His first wife, Mary Elizabeth, died in 1867 and in 1868 he married Frances Anne Rolleu. Five children were born of this union.

During the Civil War, Whipper joined a regiment of volunteers, but the highlight of his military service to the state came when the governor appointed him to the rank of general in the state militia during the Reconstruction period. The following letter commissioning William Whipper brigadier general is preserved in the Christian Fleetwood papers in the Library of Congress.

*The People of the State of South Carolina*
*By the Grace of God Free and Independent*
*National Guard S.S.C.*

*To William J. Whipper Greetings: We reposing special trust and confidence as well in your pa-*

*triotism, conduct, and loyalty as in your integrity and readiness to do us good and faithful service, have appointed and constituted and by these presents do appoint and constitute you the said William J. Whipper Brigadier General 2nd Division National Guard State of South Carolina with rank from July 14, 1873.*

*You are therefore to observe and follow orders and directions as you shall from time to time receive from our Commander-in-Chief of the military forces of our said state or any other, your Superior Officer according to the Rules and Discipline of War, and hold the said office in the manner specified in and by the Constitution and Laws of our said state in pursuance of the trust reposed in you, and for so doing, this shall be your commission. IN TESTIMONY WHEREOF, WE HAVE CAUSED OUR SEAL FOR MILITARY COMMISSION TO BE HEREUNTO AFFIXED.*

*WITNESS FRANKLIN J. MOSES JR. GOVERNOR OF OUR STATE, COMMANDER-IN-CHIEF OF THE MILITARY AND NAVAL FORCE OF THE SAME, AT OUR CITY OF COLUMBIA THIS FOURTEENTH DAY OF JULY ONE THOUSAND EIGHT HUNDRED AND SEVENTY-THREE.*[177]

### Nim Wilkes

Personal Servant and Wagoner to General Forrest, Tennessee Headquarters, Confederate Army.

Nim Wilkes was born in Maury County, Tennessee. On a pension application he was listed as "Nim Wilkes 'colored,' former personal servant and wagoner for General Forrest." Wilkes stated on the application that General Forrest pressed him into the service, with some others, at Columbus, Tennessee. He said that he was in every battle which General Forrest fought until his surrender, generally driving an ordnance wagon, and was never wounded. His was one of the few applications filed on a "Soldier's Application for Pension" which stated that the applicant was a soldier from the state of Tennessee in the war between the United States and the Confederate States; other pensions stated "colored man's application for pension" and the description was "servant" not "soldier."[178]

### Charles Wilkinson

Private, First Kentucky Company C, Eighth U.S. Colored Troops Heavy Artillery, Union Army.

Charles Wilkinson joined the army at Mayfield, Kentucky on February 23, 1864 and served until 1866. He indicated his signature by making a mark.[179]

*Sergeant Major George W. Williams*

### George Washington Williams

Sergeant Major, U.S. Volunteer Army, Union Forces.

George Williams was born on October 16, 1849, at Bedford Springs, Pennsylvania. His mother was of black and German parentage, and his father of black and Welsh descent. Williams received his elementary education in Pennsylvania and attended secondary school in Massachusetts. After four years at Newton Center, Massachusetts, he was enlisted in the Union Army by Major George L. Sterns.

Williams ran away from home at the age of fourteen and, using the name of a relative, he was accepted for enlistment. He was promoted rapidly from private to sergeant major. He was severely wounded and discharged from the service, but re-enlisted and was detailed to the staff of General Jackson in 1863 and accompanied him to Texas. While in Texas he was mustered out of the service, when he immediately enlisted in the Mexican Army. He was given the rank of orderly sergeant, First Battery, State of Tampico. A week later he was appointed to the rank of lieutenant colonel and given the position of assistant inspector general, artillery. After the capture and death of Emperor Maximilian in 1867 he returned to the United States and entered the calvary service of the regular army, serving in the Comanche campaign of 1867 with conspicuous gallantry.

In 1868, George Williams decided to leave the army and study for the ministry and on June 1, 1874 he was ordained a minister at Watertown, Massachusetts. Later he became the pastor of the Twelfth Street Baptist church in Boston.

Williams served briefly as a representative to the state legislature from Hamilton County, Ohio. He was also in the Grand Army of the Republic. He was the author of several books including *The History of the Negro Race in America from 1819 to 1880*; *Negroes as Slaves, as Soldiers and as Citizens* and *An Historical Sketch of Africa and an Account of the Negro Government of Sierra Leone, Africa*.[180]

### James Williamson

Company F, First (McCreary's) South Carolina Infantry Regiment (First S.C. Inf. Prov'l Army), Confederate Forces.

James Williamson was enlisted on October 1, 1861, in Suffolk, Virginia, by a Captain T. P. Alston, for the period of the war. The first muster mentioning Williamson stated that he was assigned to Captain T. P. Alston's Company, First Regiment South Carolina Volunteer Confederate. He appears on the muster roll for November

*Sergeant Major John H. Wilson*

and December, 1861, assigned as a musician. His name also appeared on an 1861 muster roll with the remarks column indicating that he was a "colored man—free." He was discharged on March 20, 1862, due to blindness.[181]

*Second Lieutenant Joseph T. Wilson*

## Joseph T. Wilson

Second Lieutenant, Louisiana Native Guards and Private, Company C, Fifty-Fourth Massachusetts Regiment, Union Army.

Joseph Wilson was born in 1836 at Norfolk, Virginia, but moved later to New Bedford, Massachusetts. As a young man he was a seaman, and travelled extensively in South America and the Caribbean. In 1862 he went to New Orleans and was enlisted in the Second Regiment, Louisiana Native Guards. Later he joined Company C, Fifty-Fourth Massachusetts Regiment. He was wounded at Olustee, Florida, on February 20, 1864, and was discharged from the Union service on May 8, 1864, at Boston.

After the war, Wilson became interested in civic affairs, and in writing books and articles on black history. One of his books, *Black Phalanx,* is a well-prepared documentary study of Negro progress and accomplishments in the military service before and during the Civil War; it was first published in 1890 by the Hartford (Conn.) Publishing Company. He was also the author of *Emancipation: Its Course* (1881), *Voices of a New Race* (1882) and *Twenty-Two Years of Freedom* (1882).

Wilson was a representative from Portsmouth, Virginia, to the First Republican State Convention in Richmond in April, 1867. He was appointed colonel (honorary) and aide de camp, Grand Army of the Republic, and historian of the *Negro Union Soldier.* He died on September 25, 1891, at Norfolk, Virginia, and is buried at the Hampton National Cemetery.[182]

*Crew Member James T. Wolff*

### James H. Wolff
Crew Member, *USS Minnesota,* U.S Navy.

James Wolff was·born on August 4, 1847, near Holderness, New Hampshire. He attended district schools of Holderness and Compton, and in 1860 went to Mayhew school in Boston, Massachusetts. In 1861, he decided to enlist in the U.S. Navy and had served three years, four months and four days when he was discharged in 1865. Wolff was attached to the *USS Minnesota* when the ship was engaged in battles on the Mississippi River and in Mobile Bay, and was present at the battle at Hampton Roads, Virginia. On leaving the service, he entered the first class of the New Hampshire College of Agriculture and Mechanic Arts in September, 1868. He taught school in Darien, Georgia, in 1871, but decided to study law and worked for three years in the law office of Daniel W. Gooch, and attended Harvard Law School for two years. He was called to the bar in April, 1875. A highlight of Wolff's career was his appointment as vice commander of the Department of Massachusetts Grand Army of the Republic.[183]

### Bill Yopp
Servant to Captain P. M. Yopp, Company H, Fourteenth Georgia Regiment, Confederate Army.

Bill Yopp was born in Laurens County, Georgia, around 1849, becoming the personal servant of P. M. Yopp at the age of seven. In 1861, Yopp accompanied his master to war, remaining with him throughout the four years of the conflict. It was reported that he had twice nursed his master back to health when he had been wounded in battle. Bill Yopp was given the nickname "Ten Cent" Bill for his practice of charging a fee of ten cents for any task assigned him, large or small. After the war, he received his freedom, secured a sharecropper's farm and worked it. He kept only enough food to live on and distributed the remainder to needy white families who had been impoverished by the war. It has also been claimed that he lobbied for the passage of a "spending money" pension for the Georgia Confederate Veterans.

Yopp was known to have used some of his own money to provide Christmas presents for residents of the Georgia Confederate Soldiers' Home. In recognition of his devotion and generosity, he was presented with a gold medal by the Confederate Veterans in 1920; in the same year the trustees of the Soldiers Home awarded him a lifetime home there. On June 2, 1936, Bill Yopp, a faithful, loyal and dedicated supporter of the Confederacy died at the Georgia Confederate Soldiers' Home at the reputed age of eighty-seven. He was paid final tribute with a full military funeral, soldiers in Confederate gray serving as honorary pallbearers. A firing squad from Fort McPherson was in attendance and a bugler sounded taps over his grave in the Marietta Confederate Cemetery. Rev. R. C. Huston, pastor of the Central Baptist Church, officiated.[184]

## Notes to Chapter Four

1. State of Tennessee, Colored Man's Application for Pension, Ruff Abernathy, No. 14, Tennessee State Library and Archives, Nashville, Tennessee.
2. *Medal of Honor Recipients 1863–1963,* 88th Congress, 2nd session, Committee Print, U.S. Government Printing Office, Washington, D.C.
3. United States Colored Troops (USCT) Clothing Book, Company G, 109th Infantry Regiment, AGO, Founders Library, Howard University, Washington, D.C.
4. Daniel Lamb, *Howard University Medical Department* (Washington, D.C.: Beresford, 1900). Rayford W. Logan, *Howard University, 1867–* 1967 (New York: New York University Press, 1969) p. 41.
5. State of Virginia, Confederate Pension Application, Servants Box 151, Archives Division, Virginia State Library, Richmond, Virginia.
6. *Medal of Honor Recipients, 1863–1963.*
7. *Ibid.*
8. USCT Clothing Book, Company H, 14th Regiment Rhode Island, Heavy Artillery, AGO, Founders Library.
9. USCT Clothing Book, Company A-B-C, 29th Infantry Regiment, Connecticut, AGO, Founders Library.

10. State of Tennessee, Colored Man's Application for Pension, William Bibb, No. 136.
11. James M. Guthrie, *Camp Fires of the Afro-American* (Philadelphia: Afro-American Publishing Co., 1899).
12. W. J. Pipkin, *The Negro in Revelation in History and in Citizenship* (St. Louis: 1902).
13. *Medal of Honor Recipients, 1863–1963.*
14. *Record of the Service of the Fifty-Fifth Regiment of Massachusetts Volunteer Infantry,* printed for Regimental Association (Cambridge: John Wilson & Son, 1868).
15. The University of Texas, Institute of Texan Cultures, Record of Henry Boyd, San Antonio, Texas.
16. USCT Clothing Book, Company D, 100th Infantry Regiment, AGO, Founders Library.
17. Compiled Service Records of Confederate Soldiers who Served in Organizations from the State of South Carolina, Microcopy No. 267, National Archives, Washington, D.C.
18. State of Virginia Confederate Pension Application, Servants Box 151, Archives Division, Virginia State Library, Richmond, Virginia.
19. *Medal of Honor Recipients, 1863–1963.*
20. Christian A. Fleetwood, *The Negro as a Soldier* (Washington: Howard University Press, 1895).
21. State of Virginia Confederate Pension Application, Servants Box 151.
22. State of Tennessee, Colored Man's Application for Pension, Alfred Brown, No. 233.
23. Luther Porter Jackson, *Negro Office Holders in Virginia 1865–1895* (Norfolk, Virginia: Guide Quality Press, n.d.).
24. 3rd Regiment Missouri Volunteers of African Descent, Records AGO, Founders Library.
25. USCT Clothing Book, Company F, 2nd Mississippi Heavy Artillery, AGO, Founders Library.
26. *Medal of Honor Recipients, 1863–1963.*
27. *Ibid.*
    Complete Descriptive Lists of Muster Rolls, Crew of *USS Hartford,* March 31, 1864, July 1, 1864 (3), September 30, 1864.
28. 5th Massachusetts Cavalry, Clothing Book, AGO, Founders Library.
29. USCT Clothing Book, Company H, 58th Infantry Regiment, AGO, Founders Library.
30. T. G. Steward, *The Colored Regulars in the United States Army* (Philadelphia: A. M. E. Book Concern, 1904), pp. 315–316.
31. 1st Kansas Colored Regiment Infantry, Clothing Book, AGO, Founders Library.
32. *Medal of Honor Recipients, 1863–1963.*
33. USCT Clothing Book, Company F, 7th Infantry Regiment, AGO, Founders Library.
34. USCT Clothing Book, Company —, 29th Connecticut Volunteers, AGO, Founders Library.
35. 1st Iowa Volunteers of African Descent, AGO Records, Founders Library.
36. State of Louisiana Military Dept, List of Commissions, 1873, and Annual Report of Adjutant General, 1873, Jackson Barracks, New Orleans, La. William J. Simmons, *Men of Mark* (George M. Rewell & Co.: 1887), pp. 463–465.
37. USCT Clothing Book, 6th Infantry Regiment, AGO, Founders Library.
38. State of South Carolina, Confederate Pension Application, Anderson County (Wade Childs), Department of Archives and History, Columbus, S.C.
39. State of Tennessee, Colored Man's Application for Pension, Henry Church, No. 19.
40. State of Georgia, Indigent Pension, James Clark, Department of Archives and History, Atlanta, Ga.
41. USCT, Clothing Book, Company H, 88th Infantry Regiment, AGO, Founders Library.
42. Records Relating to Confederate Naval and Marine Personnel, Microcopy 260, 1958, National Archives.
43. State of Mississippi Application for Pension, Form No. 5, Holt Collier, Department of Archives and History, Jackson, Miss.
44. State of Tennessee Colored Man's Application for Pension, Sam Collier, No. 257.
45. State of Virginia, Confederate Pension Application, Servants Box 151.
46. Personal Research Notes of Mr. J. B. Ross (Register 2202), National Archives.
47. *Journal of Negro History,* 32 (1947), p. 190.
48. State of Tennessee, Colored Man's Application for Pension, Sam Cullom, No. 136.
49. Institute of Texan Cultures, Record of Joseph Cuney.
50. State of Virginia, Confederate Pension Application, Servants Box 151.
51. State of Tennessee, Colored Man's Application for Pension, Ben Davis, No. 39.
52. USCT Clothing Book, Company —, 89th Infantry Regiment, AGO, Founders Library.
53. State of South Carolina Confederate Pension Application, Spartanburg County (Isham Davis).
54. Military Pension Files of Tobias Dawson, RG 15, Record of the AGO, National Archives.
55. *Official Records of the Union and Confederate Navies in the War of the Rebellion* 2, ser.1, p. 488.

M. S. Thompson (compiler), General Orders and Circulars Issued by the Navy Department From 1863–1887 (Washington, D.C.: U.S. Government Printing Office, 1887).

56. Sterling A. Brown et al. (eds.), The Negro Caravan (New York: Arno Press, 1941), pp. 633–634.

57. Military Pension Files of Eli Dempsy, RG 15.

58. The Colored American Magazine 6 (November, 1902), p. 48.

59. Medal of Honor Recipients, 1863–1963.

60. USCT Clothing Book, Company —, 88th Infantry Regiment.

61. Luis F. Emilio, History of the Fifty-Fourth Regiment of Massachusetts Volunteer Infantry, 1863–1865 (Boston: Boston Book Co., 1894).

62. State of North Carolina Confederate Pension Service Records, William H. Dove, Microcopy 267, National Archives.

63. Record of the Service of the Fifty-Fifth Regiment of Massachusetts Volunteer Infantry.

64. Third South Carolina Infantry, Company B, AGO Records, Founders Library.

65. Biographical Directory of the American Congress, 1774–1949 (Washington. U.S. Government Printing Office, 1950).
Register of Letters Received, Adjutant Inspector General's Office, South Carolina, 1872.
Report of the Adjutant and Inspector General of the State of South Carolina to the General Assembly for Fiscal Year Ending Oct. 31, 1873.
Reports and Resolutions 1873, Collection South Carolina Department of Archives and History, Columbus, S.C.

66. Military Pension Files of William Emory, RG 15.

67. USCT Clothing Book, Company H, 100th Infantry Regiment, AGO, Founders Library.

68. Medal of Honor Recipients, 1863–1963.

69. The Forty-Third Regiment, U.S. Colored Troops (Gettysburg: J. E. Wible, 1866).

70. State of Tennessee, Colored Man's Application for Pension, No. 184, Willis Fountain.

71. Colored American Magazine, n.d. Library of Congress.

72. D. D. Johnson, Biographical Sketches of Prominent Negro Men and Women of Kentucky (Lexington: 1897).

73. USCT Clothing Book, Company E, 29th Connecticut Volunteers, AGO, Founders Library.

74. Medal of Honor Recipients, 1863–1963.

75. Completed Service Records of Confederate Soldiers Who Served in Organizations from the State of South Carolina.

76. State of South Carolina, Confederate Pension Applications, Barnwell County, Peter Geter.

77. USCT Clothing Book, 101st Infantry Regiment, Company B, AGO, Founders Library.

78. State of Mississsippi, Application for Pension Form No. 3, Servant James Gordon.

79. Compiled Service Records of Confederate Soldiers . . . State of South Carolina.

80. USCT Clothing Book, Company D, 88th Infantry Regiment, AGO, Founders Library.

81. USCT Clothing Book, Company D, 88th Infantry Regiment, AGO, Founders Library.

82. USCT Clothing Book, Company H, 1st Infantry Regiment, AGO, Founders Library.

83. USCT Clothing Book, Company G, 58th Infantry Regiment, AGO, Founders Library.

84. Medal of Honor Recipients, 1863–1963.

85. USCT Clothing Book, Company —, 113th Infantry Regiment, AGO, Founders Library.

86. Medal of Honor Recipients, 1863–1963.

87. Completed Service Records of Confederate Soldiers . . . from the State of North Carolina, Microcopy 267, National Archives.

88. Crisis Magazine 10 (September, 1915), pp. 222–23.

89. Records Relating to Confederate Naval and Marine Personnel, Microcopy 260, 1958, National Archives.

90. Medal of Honor Recipients, 1863–1963.

91. Ibid.

92. The Forty-Third Regiment, U.S. Colored Troops.

93. Record of the Service of the Fifty-Fifth Regiment of Massachusetts Infantry.

94. First Michigan Regiment of Colored Volunteers, 102nd Infantry Records, AGO, Founders Library.

95. USCT Clothing Book, Company K, 88th Infantry Regiment, AGO, Founders Library.

96. Records Relating to Confederate Naval and Marine Personnel, Microcopy 260, 1958, National Archives.

97. Notes from Personal Papers of Daniel Murray (Former Special Collection, Negro Authors, Daniel Murray Bequest), Library of Congress, Washington, D.C.

98. State of Tennessee, Colored Man's Application for Pension, Leroy Jones, No. 120.

99. State of Tennessee Colored Man's Application for Pension, Monroe Jones.

100. State of South Carolina, Confederate Pension Applications, Bamberg County, Preston Kearce.

101. Medal of Honor Recipients, 1863–1963.

102. State of Tennessee, Colored Man's Application for Pension, Taylor Kennard, No. 227.

103. *Legacy for All: A Record of Achievements by Black American Scientists* (Western Electric Company pamphlet).

104. *Medal of Honor Recipients, 1863–1963.*

105. USCT Clothing Book, Company C, 106th Infantry Regiment, AGO, Founders Library.

106. State of Tennessee Colored Man's Application for Pension, Clark Lee, No. 107.

107. State of Virginia, Confederate Pension Application, Servants Box 151.

108. W. E. B. Du Bois, *Black Reconstruction* (New York: Harcourt, Brace & Co., 1935).
Report of the Adjutant and Inspector General of the State of South Carolina . . . October 31, 1873.
Reports and Resolutions 1873, South Carolina Department of Archives and History.

109. *History of the Life of Reverend William Mack Lee, Body Servant to General Robert E. Lee* (Norfolk: The Smith Printing Co., 1916).

110. Marcus B. Christian, "James Lewis" *The Negro Bulletin* 3 (March, 1942).

111. State of South Carolina, Confederate Pension Application, Charleston County, W. S. Lewis.

112. Luther Porter Jackson, *Negro Office Holders* . . .

113. State of South Carolina, Confederate Pension Application, Allendale County, Miles Loadholt.

114. State of Mississippi, Application for Pension, Form No. 5, Hutson Longstreet.

115. Compiled Service Records of Confederate Soldiers . . . North Carolina, Microcopy 267, National Archives.

116. USCT Clothing Book, Company H, 100th Infantry Regiment, AGO, Founders Library.

117. USCT, Heavy Artillery, AGO, Founders Library.

118. State of Mississippi, Application for Pension, Form No. 3, Andrew Mathews.

119. State of South Carolina, Confederate Pension Applications, Spartanburg County, Marshall Mattison.

120. Compiled Service Records of Confederate Soldiers . . . South Carolina, Microcopy 267, National Archives.

121. *Medal of Honor Recipients, 1863–1963.*

122. *Ibid.*

123. *The Times-News,* Hendersonville, N.C. (May 7, 1960).

124. Compiled Service Records of Confederate Soldiers . . . South Carolina, Microcopy 267, National Archives.

125. "Sketches of Mitchell's Life," *Dorchester Beacon,* July 23, 1889 (Extract copy, Manuscript Division, Carter G. Woodson Collection), Library of Congress, Washington, D.C.

126. Compiled Service Records of Confederate Soldiers . . . South Carolina, Microcopy 267, National Archives.

127. Military Service Record of Charles Moore, RG 93, AGO Records, National Archives.

128. USCT Clothing Book, Company —, 88th Infantry Regiment, AGO, Founders Library.

129. *Biographical Directory of the American Congress, 1774–1949.*

130. Lawrence C. Bryant (ed.), *Negro Senators and Representatives in the South Carolina Legislature, 1868–1902* (1968).
Report of the Adjutant and Inspector General of the State of South Carolina . . . October 31, 1873.
Reports and Resolutions, 1873 Collection, South Carolina.

131. State of Tennessee, Colored Man's Application for Pension, Henry Nelson, No. 23.

132. *The Tennessee Banner,* 1938.
State of Tennessee, Colored Man's Application for Pension, Sam Newsom, No. 270.

133. State of Virginia, Confederate Pension Applications, Servants Box 151.

134. *Medal of Honor Recipients, 1863–1963.*

135. Daniel Smith Lamb, Howard University Medical Department, Washington, D.C.

136. P.B.S. Pinchback Papers, Moorland Room, Founders Library.

137. *Medal of Honor Recipients, 1863–1963.*

138. Leigh Whipper Manuscript Collection, Moorland Room, Founders Library.

139. Report of the Adjutant and Inspector General of the State of South Carolina . . . October 31, 1873.
Reports and Resolutions 1873, South Carolina Collection.

140. Bryant, *Negro Senators and Representatives in the South Carolina eLgislature, 1868–1902.*
Report of the Adjutant and Inspector General of the State of South Carolina.
Reports and Resolutions 1873, South Carolina collection.
*Biographical Directory of the American Congress, 1774–1949.*

141. USCT Clothing Book, Company E, 100th Infantry Regiment, AGO, Founders Library.

142. *Medal of Honor Recipients, 1863–1963.*

143. Carter G. Woodson and Charles H. Wesley, *The Negro in Our History* (Washington: Associated Publishers, 1966), p. 374.

144. Register of Letters Received, Adjutant and Inspector General's Office, South Carolina, 1873. Report of the Adjutant and Inspector General of the State of South Carolina . . . October 31, 1873. Reports and Resolutions 1873, South Carolina Collection.

145. Compiled Service Records of Confederate Soldiers . . . North Carolina, Microcopy 267, National Archives.

146. USCT Clothing Book, Company F, 59th Infantry Regiment, AGO, Founders Library.

147. State of Virginia, Confederate Pension Application, Servants Box 151.

148. *Record of the Service of the Fifty-Fifth Regiment of Massachusetts Volunteer Infantry.*

149. *Ibid.*

150. *Journal of Negro History* 32 (1947) pp. 10–190.

151. USCT Clothing Book, Company E, 100th Infantry Regiment, AGO, Founders Library.

152. State of South Carolina Pension Applications, Beaufort County, Benjamin Singleton.

153. Miscellaneous Papers Related to Robert Smalls, Carter G. Woodson Papers, Manuscript Division, Library of Congress.
Navy Records, RG 45, National Archives.
Letter Received: Robert Smalls, dated 31 July, 1873, S.C. Department of Archives and History.

154. USCT Clothing Book, Company D, 100th Infantry Regiment, AGO, Founders Library.

155. USCT Clothing Book, Companies A-B-C, 29th Infantry Regiment (Connecticut), AGO, Founders Library.

156. Compiled Service Records of Confederate Soldiers . . . South Carolina, Microcopy 267, National Archives.

157. USCT Clothing Book, Battery B, 9th Regiment, U.S. Colored Artillery (Heavy) Troops, AGO, Founders Library.

158. Luis F. Emilio, *History of the Fifty-Fourth Regiment . . .*
Lawrence F. Bryant (ed.), *Negro Senators and Representatives.*
Report of the Adjutant and Inspector General . . . October 31, 1873.
Reports and Resolutions, 1873, South Carolina Collection.

159. Luther Porter Jackson, *Negro Office Holders.*

160. State of South Carolina, Confederate Pension Application, McCormick County, Mat Tompkins.

161. *Negro History Bulletin* 5, (1942), p. 178.

162. *Record of the Service of the Fifty-Fifth Regiment.*

163. Henry McNeal Turner Collection, Moorland Room, Founders Library.

164. State of Tennessee, Colored Man's Application for a Pension, Alfred Tyson, No. 119.

165. J. D. Johnson, *Biographical Sketches of Prominent Negro Men and Women of Kentucky.*

166. *Medal of Honor Recipients, 1863–1963.*

167. Luis F. Emilio, *History of the Fifty-Fourth Regiment.*

168. USCT Clothing Book, Company F, 6th U.S. Colored Cavalry, Kentucky, AGO, Founders Library.

169. State of Virginia, Confederate Pension Application, Servants Box 151.

170. *The Negro in the Military Service of the United States 1639–1886.* Microcopy No. T-823, National Archives.

171. Compiled Service Records of Confederate Soldiers . . . North Carolina, Microcopy 267, National Archives.

172. *Colored American Magazine* 5, (April, 1901), p. 471.

173. State of Virginia, Confederate Pension Application, Servants, Box 151.

174. State of Tennessee, Colored Man's Application for Pension, Wade Watkins, No. 269.

175. Luis F. Emilio, *History of the Fifty-Fourth Regiment.*

176. State of Tennessee, Colored Man's Application for Pension, Alex Wharton, No. 171.

177. George Brown Tindall, *Negro Senators and Representatives in the South Carolina Legislature, 1868–1902, 1877–1900* (Columbus: University of South Carolina Press, 1953).
Christian Fleetwood Papers, Manuscript Division, Library of Congress.
Leigh Whipper Collection, Founders Library.

178. State of Tennessee Colored Man's Application for Pension, Nim Wilkes, No. 136.

179. USCT Clothing Book, Company C, 8th U.S. Colored Troops, Heavy Artillery, AGO, Founders Library.

180. William J. Simmons, *Men of Mark.*

181. Compiled Service Records of Confederate Soldiers . . . South Carolina, Microcopy 267, National Archives.

182. Joseph T. Wilson, *The Black Phalanx* (Hartford: 1890).

183. *Colored American Magazine* 5, (March, 1902).

184. *Atlanta Constitution* or *Atlanta Journal* (June, 1936), Georgia State Archives and History Department, Atlanta, Ga.

# Chapter Five

## The Indian Campaigns, 1866-1890

The Indian Campaigns were a series of skirmishes fought in the western and southwestern United States between 1866 and 1890. Regular soldiers and scouts were involved and Negroes participated in both capacities. The aim of these campaigns was to protect the interests of (mainly white) settlers who had moved into Indian territory.

In 1866, the Ninth and Tenth Cavalry Regiments were organized and in 1868–69, the Twenty-Fourth and Twenty-Fifth regiments of infantry established. These regiments were the permanent Negro regiments and were staffed mainly with white officers, although in several cases Negro officers were assigned to the units.

History books have recorded the days of the plains, the soldiers and the Indian fighters, but without mentioning the Negro units in the Indian skirmishes. The Ninth and Tenth Cavalry patrolled the plains from Arizona to the Dakotas. The Twenty-Fourth and Twenty-Fifth Infantry regiments performed garrison duty at various western posts and also patrolled the area.

These Negro units were present in campaigns against the Apaches, Kiowas, Cheyennes, Comanches, and Arapahoes. They escorted railroad surveyors and protected mail and stage routes between San Antonio and El Paso, Texas. The famous Tenth Cavalry was active in the Victoria War (Chief Victoria led some three hundred Indian warriors from the Warm Springs and Chiricachua tribes on September 2, 1877 on a raid from the San Carlos Reservation and were immediately pursued by black troops) and fought at the battle of Saint Angela (or Angelo).

During the Indian Campaigns, Indian scouts were used by the military. Some were recruited and assigned as a detachment of Indian scouts. Among the Indian scouts were the Seminole-Negro-Indian scouts who performed outstanding service in Texas and along the Mexican Border. Four of these scouts were awarded the Medal of Honor.

This chapter contains sketches of some of the heroes and ordinary soldiers of these pioneer days on the plains. This era saw Negroes attempting to pursue a military education at the academies of West Point and Annapolis and witnessed the gradual development of Negro soldiers, both as leaders and as well-disciplined troops.

### John Hanks Alexander

Lieutenant, Ninth U.S. Cavalry Regiment.

John Alexander was born on January 6, 1864, in Arkansas, the son of slave parents. He studied at Oberlin but left in 1883, in his freshman year, to attend the U.S. Military Academy. He was graduated in 1887, number thirty-two in a class of sixty-four, and in 1894 was assigned to Wilberforce University as professor of military science and tactics. His stay at Wilberforce was brief since on March 26, 1894, on a visit to Springfield, Ohio, he died suddenly of a ruptured blood vessel while sitting in a barber's chair.

Professor William Sanders Scarborough, the late distinguished professor at Wilberforce, told how

*Cadet John H. Alexander*

the unfortunate death of Lieutenant Alexander was received.

*The President, the Secretary, Mr. Wallace Clark and I at once left for that city [Springfield, Ohio] and made arrangements for his body to be brought back to the university. The esteem in which he was held showed itself at once by the offer of the Springfield white military guard to accompany the remains back to the University. Our own Arnett Guards met the body at the city limits and took up the escort to the university where the funeral services were held.*[1]

### Henry E. Baker

Cadet Midshipman, U.S. Naval Academy.

Henry Baker was born on September 18, 1857, in Columbus, Lowndes County, Mississippi. He was the third known Negro to be appointed as a cadet midshipman to the U.S. Naval Academy at Annapolis, Maryland. Prior to his appointment, he had attended the Union Academy, Columbus, Mississippi, In 1874. Baker was appointed to the academy by the Honorable H. W. Barry, Representative of the Third Congressional District of Mississippi, on September 24, 1874. While attend-

ing the academy, Baker had several experiences which accelerated his departure. An item in the *Army and Navy Journal* dated March 6, 1875 read as follows:

*The summary dismissal of two cadet midshipmen at the academy from the Southern states for maltreating the colored Cadet Baker, ought to have a beneficial effect. It is difficult to get these young men to appreciate the fact that the Department and the Superintendent of the Academy are determined, as long as the law authorizes the appointment of Colored Cadets, and they are sent to the institution, to protect them in their rights as much so as if they were white. The assault made upon the Cadet Baker, might have been made on any other one, but those engaged in it admitted that they had long wanted an opportunity to give him "fits," gloried in their success and acknowledged they would repeat the act on a similar pretense.*

On November 14, 1875, Baker was dismissed or resigned from the naval academy and returned to Columbus, Mississippi, where he became a superintendent of public education. Later he moved to Washington, D.C. where he resided at 738, Gresham Place N.W. He worked as an assistant examiner in the U.S. Patent Office and was the

*Cadet Henry E. Baker*

*Charles Daniels, Indian Scout,*
*with his family*

author of a book, *The Colored Inventor: A Record Of Fifty Years.* Henry Baker died on April 27, 1928.[2]

### Thomas Boyne

Sergeant, Company C, Ninth U.S. Cavalry Regiment.

Thomas Boyne was leading a detachment through the Nimbres Mountains, New Mexico, on May 29, 1879, and encountered some Indian warriors. As the detachment scattered, Boyne flanked the Indians and charged them, firing with precision, and eventually drove them away. Later, on September 27, 1879, at Cuchillo, New Mexico, the Ninth Cavalry confronted Indian warriors near Ojo Caliente. For two days the Indians and cavalrymen fought a running battle. Boyne, though wounded, killed one of three warriors and single-handedly captured a considerable number of the sixty horses and mules that were taken. His gallantry in action was rewarded by a Medal of Honor on January 6, 1882.[3]

*Scout J. Daniels (above) and Landsman J. Clinton de Villis (right)*

### Benjamin Brown

Sergeant, Company C, Twenty-Fourth U.S. Infantry Regiment.

Benjamin Brown was born in Spotsylvania County, Virginia. On May 11, 1889, between Cedar Springs and Fort Thomas, Arizona, a Twenty-Fourth Infantry Regiment payroll escort detail were challenged by robbers. Although shot in the abdomen, Sergeant Brown did not leave the scene until again wounded in both arms. He was awarded the Medal of Honor for his heroic action on February 19, 1890.[4]

### John Denny

Sergeant, Troop B, Ninth U.S. Cavalry Regiment.

John Denny was born at Big Flats, New York and entered the service at Elmira, New York. On September 18, 1879, at Las Animas Canyon, New Mexico, Denny showed unusual heroism in carrying back a wounded comrade, under fire, to a place of safety. He was awarded the Medal of Honor on November 27, 1894, for this gallant feat.[5]

### J. Clinton De Villis

Landsman, U.S. Navy.

Clinton De Villis was a native of Brooklyn, New

York. He was a painter and enlisted in the U.S. Navy in the hope of increasing his exposure to art and to historical paintings and sculptures. For most of his period of service he was stationed in European and Asian waters. When on shore leave he would study masterpieces in European museums, and at sea he made sketches in his free time. He was interested in painting landscapes and the human figure. As a civilian, De Villis was employed as a bookkeeper-salesman at the Rohlf Art Gallery in Brooklyn. He received his training at Adelphi College. Many blacks have enlisted in the service in order to further their chosen careers through travel or by earning money for future expenses. Military service in many cases was the means by which their dreams were translated into reality.[6]

### Pompey Factor

Private, Detachment Seminole Indian Scouts, U.S. Army.

Pompey Factor was born in Arkansas and on August 16, 1870 he enlisted in the Seminole Indian Scouts Detachment at Fort Duncan, Texas. He was later discharged but reenlisted during the period 1871–1879. Official records show that Factor served with forces mobilized for operations against hostile Indians in Texas in 1871, 1872, and 1875. He was with a detachment of scouts in an engagement with Comanche Indians on April 25, 1875, at the mouth of the Pecos River, in Texas. During the engagement, Factor assisted his comrades Isaac Payne and John Ward in rescuing a Lieutenant Bullis from a group of advancing Indians. He was awarded a Medal of Honor for his part in this rescue. His description on official records was: height: five feet, six inches; complexion: black; hair: black, and eyes: black.[7]

### Henry Ossian Flipper

Second Lieutenant, Tenth U.S. Cavalry Regiment.

Henry Flipper was born in Thomasville, Thomas County, Georgia, on March 21, 1856. His mother was the property of the Reverend Reuben E. Lucky, a Methodist minister, and his father, Festus Flipper, was owned by Ephraim G. Ponder, a slave dealer. In 1859, after receiving permission to buy his wife and child's freedom, Festus Flipper moved to Atlanta.

*Second Lieutenant Henry O. Flipper*

After the Civil War, Henry Flipper was appointed to the U.S. Military Academy by Congressman J. C. Freeman, Republican representative of the Sixth Congressional District of Georgia. At the academy, Flipper experienced his share of insults and hostility, but he faced both loneliness and intimidation with courage, and graduated fiftieth in a class of seventy-six on June 14, 1877. His first assignment was to Fort Sill (Indian territory), and he was later assigned to Forts Elliot, Texas, Concho, Davis, and Quitman, Texas.

In his short military career Flipper performed various duties, including surveyor and construction supervisor, as well as having combat experience against the Indian chief Victoria and his Apaches. He also served as post adjutant, acting assistant and post quartermaster, and commissary officer.

On August 13, 1881, a letter was sent by the commanding officer of Fort Davis, Colonel William Shafter, to the Adjutant General, Department of Texas, accusing Lieutenant Flipper of failing to mail $3,791.77 to the chief commissary. The colonel said that he had seen the lieutenant in town, on horseback with saddlebags, and he believed that Flipper was leaving the area. Lieutenant Flipper was arrested and, even though he had made good all the money for which he was responsible, was tried by a general court martial at Fort Davis on November 4, 1881.

Further investigation revealed that Flipper apparently had not sent the reports and checks to the chief commissary. A number of checks were found in his bunk. The verdict was not guilty on the charge of embezzlement, but he was found guilty on the charge of conduct unbecoming an officer and gentleman. His sentence of dismissal from the U.S. Army was confirmed by President Arthur and carried out on June 30, 1882. Efforts made by several Congressional leaders to have his sentence remitted were unsuccessful, and Flipper resumed civilian life.

It has been said that Flipper wondered if his enjoyment of horseback riding in the company of a white officer's wife at Fort Concho could have had some effect on the decision of the court martial.

After leaving the army Henry Flipper worked as a public surveyor and engineer for various mining companies. He was the author of several publications including *Negro Frontiersman. The Western Memoirs of Henry O. Flipper* edited by Theodore D. Harris; *Mexican Laws, Statutes,* etc. and a translation of *Venezuelan Laws, Statutes.* Flipper returned to Atlanta, Georgia, in 1930, and stayed there with his brother, Bishop Joseph Flipper of the African Methodist Church, until his death on May 3, 1940.

Flipper achieved many honors in his lifetime, but the most notable from a military viewpoint is the distinction of being the first American Negro to successfully complete the requirements of the U.S. Military Academy. Mrs. Sarah Jackson, a military historian and archivist, wrote the following concerning Flipper's civilian career:

*Had Henry Ossian Flipper remained in the army, he would probably have achieved far less. A man of vast strength and strong character, he confronted both prejudices and tradition, and carved out a constructive and productive life for himself.*

It is gratifying that today a man of color can look forward to achieving the kind of career that Lieutenant Flipper might have expected, without experiencing the same difficulties.[8]

*John Jefferson*

### Clinton Greaves

Corporal, Company C, Ninth U.S. Cavalry Regiment.

Clinton Greaves was born in Madison County, Virginia. He entered the military service at Prince George's County, Maryland. Greaves was awarded the Medal of Honor on June 26, 1879 for performing gallantly in a hand-to-hand fight with Indian warriors on June 24, 1877, at Florida Mountains, New Mexico.[9]

### Henry Johnson

Sergeant, Troop D, Ninth U.S. Cavalry Regiment.

Henry Johnson was a native of Boynton, Virginia. At Milk River, Colorado, during the period October 2–5, 1879, he displayed unusual valor for which he was awarded the Medal of Honor on September 22, 1890. The citation read: "Sergeant Johnson voluntarily left the fortified shelter and under heavy fire at close range made the rounds of the pits to instruct the guards; fought his way to the creek and back to bring water to the wounded."[10]

### George Jordan

Sergeant, Troop K, Ninth U.S. Cavalry Regiment.

George Jordan was born in Williamson County, Tennessee. He twice exhibited unusual heroism. On May 14, 1880, while commanding a detachment of twenty-five men at Tulersa, New Mexico, he repulsed a force of more than one hundred Indians at Carrizo Canyon. In the following year, on August 12, 1881, he stubbornly held his ground in an extremely exposed position and gallantly forced back a much superior number of the enemy, preventing them from surrounding the command. Sergeant Jordan was awarded the Medal of Honor on May 7, 1890.[11]

*Scout Billy July*

## William McBryar

Sergeant, Troop K, Tenth U.S. Cavalry Regiment.

William McBryar, a black, was born in Elizabethtown, North Carolina. He enlisted in the army in New York City. In Arizona, on March 7, 1890, Sergeant McBryar showed outstanding bravery in battle with Apache Indians. He was awarded the Medal of Honor on May 15, 1890.[12]

*Cadet Alonzo C. McClennan*

*Sergeant William McBryar*

## Alonzo Clifton McClennan

Cadet Midshipman, U.S. Naval Academy.

Alonzo McClennan was born on May 7, 1856, at Columbus, Richland County, South Carolina (one source states that his birth date was May 1, 1855). He attended public schools in Columbus, and was the second Negro known to be appointed to the Naval Academy. His appointment was made by the Honorable R. H. Cain, Congressman-at-Large from South Carolina, on September 24, 1873. According to some sources, he was deficient in his subjects in February, 1874, and submitted his resignation on March 14. His resignation was accepted and he left the Academy where, it has been reported, he resented the treatment of his fellow cadets to such an extent that he one night

fought all who came within his reach in the dining hall. Certain evidence was reported at a hearing, and he was advised to resign at the expiration of his sentence.

After leaving the Academy, McClennan attended school at Wilbraham, Massachusetts, and later enrolled at Howard University's School of Medicine, from which he graduated and started to practice medicine in Augusta, Georgia. In 1896, he established a hospital and training school for nurses. He died in 1912.[13]

## Isaiah Mays

Corporal, Company B, Twenty-Fourth U.S. Infantry Regiment.

Isaiah Mays, a black man, was born in Carters Bridge, Virginia, and entered the military service on May 11, 1889, in Arizona. He was awarded the Medal of Honor on February 19, 1890 for gallantry in a fight between Paymaster Wham's escort and a band of robbers.[14]

## Joseph E. Noil

Seaman, *USS Powhatan*, U.S. Navy.

Joseph Noil, a black, was born in 1841 in Nova Scotia. He was awarded the Medal of Honor for saving Boatswain J. C. Walton from drowning while serving on the *USS Powhatan* at Norfolk on December 26, 1872.[15]

### Adam Paine

Private, Detachment of Seminole Negro Indian Scouts, U.S. Army.

Adam Paine was born in Florida. He was awarded the Medal of Honor on October 13, 1875 for gallantry in action on September 20, 1874, at Staked Plains, Texas.[16]

### Isaac Payne

Private (Trumpeter), Detachment of Seminole Negro Indian Scouts, U.S. Army.

Isaac Payne was born in Mexico. He enlisted on October 7, 1871, at Fort Duncan, Texas and served until 1901, though he was discharged and reenlisted during this period. His gallantry at Pecos River on April 25, 1875 in helping Lieutenant Bullis to escape an approaching party of Indians earned him a Medal of Honor. He was discharged from the service on January 21, 1901, at Fort Ringold, Texas.[17]

*Cabin Boy John H. Paynter*

### John H. Paynter

Cabin Boy, U.S. Navy.

John Paynter, a black, was born in New Castle, Delaware, on February 15, 1862. Later his parents moved to Washington, D.C. and he enlisted at an early age as a cabin boy on a receiving ship, *USS Dale,* at Washington Navy Yard. He was discharged after five weeks of service.

Paynter enrolled at Lincoln University in Pennsylvania in 1879 and graduated in 1883. He then reenlisted in the navy as a landsman (the service designation at that time for a domestic) and served during a cruise of the *USS Ossipee.* He was later discharged.

While he was in the navy, Paynter benefited as much as he could from the opportunity to see other countries and places of historic interest. He wrote a book, *Joining the Navy* or *Abroad with Uncle Sam,* describing his experiences of naval service aboard the *USS Ossipee* and *USS Juniatu.*[18]

### William H. Penn

Sergeant, Third Squadron, Ninth U.S. Cavalry Regiment.

William Penn was born in 1863 at Baltimore, Maryland. He enlisted in the army before his seventeenth birthday and was assigned to the Ninth Cavalry. He served in the Indian Wars and in Cuba, the Philippines and Samoa Islands. It is believed that Penn's father and two uncles were killed in the Civil War. He retired from military service on February 14, 1908.[19]

### Thomas Shaw

Sergeant, Troop B, Ninth U.S. Cavalry Regiment.

Thomas Shaw enlisted in Company A of the Sixty-Fifth Colored Infantry on January 19, 1864 and served until October 7, 1866. On September 24, 1866 he enlisted in Troop B, 9th U.S. Cavalry and was honorably discharged at Fort Myer, Virginia, on March 3, 1894. While serving with the Ninth Cavalry he showed unusual heroism in action at Carrizo Canyon, New Mexico, on August 12, 1881, for which he was awarded the Medal of Honor. His citation stated that he forced the enemy back after stubbornly holding his ground in an extremely exposed position, and prevented the enemy's superior numbers from surrounding his command.

The official records describe Shaw as being five feet nine and one-half inches tall, with a brown complexion, iron gray hair and brown eyes. It should be noted that the Registers of Enlistment, U.S. Army, Microcopy 233, and the Military Pension file indicate that Shaw was assigned to the Ninth Cavalry. The Medal of Honor recipients book, however, dated 1968, lists a Thomas Shaw as being assigned to the Eighth Cavalry. The Eighth, however, was an all-Caucasian unit, while the Ninth was an all-Negro unit, except for its officers.[20]

### James Webster Smith

Cadet, U.S. Military Academy.

James Smith, a black, was born in South Carolina and graduated from a Hartford high school. In 1870, the Honorable S. L. Hoge appointed him to a cadetship at the U.S. Military Academy at West Point. Smith passed the physical and written examination and was received as a conditional cadet. He was the first Negro to be accepted at the academy.

Upon his arrival at West Point, white cadets at first accepted Smith except when the time came to assign him a table in the messhall. (He had been given a room to himself.) Cadets who found themselves seated next to Smith applied for transfers to other tables. Superintendent Thomas Pitcher placed two cadets under arrest for refusing to sit with Smith and told the others that he would not tolerate further disrespectful actions to the black cadet. While he was at West Point, Smith was given considerable press coverage and attempts were made by radical papers to have him denounce the academy. He labored through four years of study, being once turned back in class. At the end of his fourth class year, he was declared deficient in natural and experimental philosophy and he was dismissed from the academy on June 26, 1874.

After his dismissal, Smith tried for a time to refute various allegations against him by writing a series of letters to the *New National Era and Citizen*, a Negro political organ of that period.[21]

### Richard Smith

Private, Company E, Twenty-Fifth Infantry Regiment.

Richard Smith was born in Pulaski County, Virginia. He was twenty-six years old when he was enlisted in the army, on December 7, 1886 at Cincinnati, Ohio, by Lieutenant O'Connell. The official records describe him as having black eyes, hair and complexion. Richard Smith was discharged at the expiration of his term of service on December 6, 1891, at Fort Buford, North Dakota.[22]

### Howard Snowden

Private, Tenth U.S. Cavalry Regiment.

Howard Snowden was born in Howard County, Maryland. He was enlisted in the army at the age of twenty-three, on December 21, 1886, at Baltimore, Maryland, by a Captain Overton. He had worked as a laborer. The official records describe his eyes, hair and complexion black. Snowden was discharged on March 31, 1891, at Fort Apache because of disability.[23]

### Emanual Stance

Sergeant, Company F, Ninth U.S. Cavalry Regiment.

Emanuel Stance was born in Carroll County, Louisiana. He was awarded a Medal of Honor for gallantry displayed as an Indian scout on May 20, 1870 at Kickapoo Springs, Texas.[24]

### Jacob W. Stevens

Private, Company C, Tenth U.S. Cavalry Regiment.

Jacob Stevens was born in Franktown, Virginia, and was a sailor before joining the army at the age of twenty-two. He was enlisted at Baltimore, Maryland, on December 28, 1886, by Captain Overton. He served until the expiration of his term of service on December 27, 1891, at Fort Bayard, New Mexico. The records describe his eyes, hair, and complexion as black.[25]

### Charles Burrill Turner

Sergeant Major, Tenth U.S. Cavalry Regiment.

Charles Turner was born on June 25, 1859 at Mineral Point, Wisconsin. He received his formal education in Cincinnati, Ohio. On November 15, 1875, at sixteen years of age, he enlisted in the regular army at Indianapolis, Indiana. He was assigned to Troop E, Tenth U.S. Cavalry, in May, 1876, as a troop clerk, joining the unit at Pecos River, Texas. Turner was with the Tenth Cavalry in operations against the Indians from September, 1876 to June, 1879 and he served on the Mexican border at San Felipe. In 1880, Turner was present at the disarming of the Mescalaree Apache Indians in New Mexico, and in the same year he participated in the campaign against Victoria's band of renegades. Turner's combat campaigns also included operations against the Kiowas and Comanches in the Indian territory during July, 1881. He was with the regiment when it participated in chasing and capturing Geronimo. In January, 1888, Turner passed a board of officers for the

*Sergeant Major Charles B. Turner*

position of commissary sergeant. He was a delegate to the National Regular Army and Navy Union Convention at St. Louis, Missouri in 1893.

During the Spanish-American War, Turner was on regimental recruiting duty in the state of Kentucky. On November 6, 1898, he was appointed sergeant major of the Tenth United States Cavalry.[26]

### Augustus Walley

Private, Company I, Ninth U.S. Cavalry Regiment.

Augustus Walley was born at Reiserstown, Maryland. He displayed bravery in action with hostile Apache Indians on August 16, 1881, at Cuchillo Negro Mountains, New Mexico. He was awarded the Medal of Honor on October 1, 1890.[27]

### John Ward

Sergeant, Detachment of Seminole Negro Indian Scouts, U.S. Army.

John Ward was born in 1847 at Santa Rosa, Mexico. He enlisted in a detachment of Seminole Indian Scouts on August 16, 1870 and served during the period 1870–1894, receiving his final discharge on October 5, 1894, as a sergeant, at Fort Ringold. According to his official description he was five feet seven inches in height and had black hair, eyes and complexion.

On April 25, 1875, he displayed unusual gallantry in action with the Indians. He was with Lieutenant John L. Bullis of the Twenty-Fourth Infantry Regiment, Isaac Payne, and Trooper Pompey Factor when they struck a trail of about seventy-five horses and followed it to the Eagle's Nest crossing of the Pecos, coming upon the Indians as they were attempting to cross to the western side with the stolen herd. The party tethered their mounts and crept to within seventy-five yards before they opened fire, which they maintained for about forty-five minutes, killing three warriors, wounding a fourth, and twice forcing the raiders to retire from the herd. As the scouts reached their horses, mounted, and were preparing to leave, Sergeant Ward noticed that Lieutenant Bullis' mount, a wild and badly trained animal, had broken loose, leaving him without a horse among the Indians who were rapidly approaching. Sergeant Ward dashed back to the lieutenant's aid, followed by his comrades. The Indians opened fire on the rescue party and a bullet cut Ward's carbine sling. As he was helping the lieutenant to mount behind him, a ball shattered the stock. Factor and Payne had meanwhile been fighting off the Indians, and the three scouts and the lieutenant were able to make their escape, saved, as Lieutenant Bullis wrote, "by a hair." John Ward received the Medal of Honor for his bravery and devotion "beyond the call of duty" in this encounter.

John Ward died on March 24, 1911, in the Seminole Camp on a government reservation, and was buried on March 26, 1911, in the Seminole Negro Cemetery on Las Moras Creek, Kinney County. He was nearly sixty-four years old at the time of his death. He and his wife, Judy, had four children.[28]

### Johnson C. Whittaker

Cadet, U.S. Military Academy.

Johnson C. Whittaker, a native of South Carolina, entered the West Point Military Academy in 1876. His experiences at the academy were not calculated to help him graduate. When Henry O. Flipper was graduated in 1877, Whittaker was the only Negro cadet at the academy. He was found deficient in his subjects by the academic board in 1879, and his dismissal was proposed. However, Superintendent Schofield recommended that he be turned back a year and remain at the academy. On the morning of April 6, 1880, a tactical officer found Whittaker bound to his bed suffering from serious head injuries. Whittaker alleged that three masked men had attacked him. An official investigation reported that Whittaker had himself inflicted the blow, tied himself to the bed, and then invented a story to account for the incident. The investigating board suggested that his motive could have been to provide an excuse for not taking final examinations. This matter was debated at length and Whittaker constantly reiterated his innocence. He was finally dismissed because of deficiencies in his studies. Schofield stated that it was unreasonable to expect Negroes to compete with whites and that it was a mistake to make them try. This attitude on the part of the superintendent and other officials closed the doors of West Point to black youth for many years.[29]

### Moses Williams

First Sergeant, Company I, Ninth U.S. Cavalry Regiment.

Moses Williams, a black, was born in Carrol County Pennsylvania. He was awarded the Medal of Honor on November 12, 1896 for heroically rallying his detachment at the foothills of the Cuchillo Negro Mountains, New Mexico, on August 16, 1881. His citation read: "Rallied a detachment, skillfully conducted a running fight of three or four hours, and by his coolness, bravery, and unflinching devotion to duty in standing by his commanding officer in an exposed position under a heavy fire from a large party of Indians saved the lives of at least three of his comrades."[30]

*Scout Bill Williams and (right) the last mount of the Seminole Negro Indian Scouts*

### William O. Wilson

Corporal, Company I, Ninth U.S. Cavalry Regiment.

William Wilson, a black, was born in Hagerstown, Maryland. He entered the service at Dakota. He was cited for bravery during the Sioux campaign in 1890, and was awarded the Medal of Honor on September 17, 1891.[31]

### Brent Woods

Sergeant, Company B, Ninth U.S. Cavalry Regiment.

Brent Woods was born in Pulaski, Kentucky. He entered the service at Louisville, Kentucky, and was awarded the Medal of Honor on July 12, 1894, for outstanding bravery in saving the lives of his comrades on August 19, 1881, in New Mexico.[32]

# Notes to Chapter Five

1. Extract from the *Annual Pension, June 12, 1894.* (West Point: U.S. Military Academy, 1894). William Sanders Scarborough, "Autobiography," ed. Wilhelmina H. Robinson (unpublished mss, Central State University, Wilberforce, Ohio).

2. Personal Research Notes of Mr. J. B. Ross, Register 2492, National Archives, Washington, D.C. *The Army and Navy Journal,* March 6, 1875. Henry E. Baker, *The Colored Inventor. A Record of Fifty Years* (New York: 1917).

3. *Medal of Honor Recipients, 1863–1963,* 88th Congress, 2nd Session Committee Print (Washington, D.C.: U.S. Government Printing Office, 1964).

4. *Ibid.*

5. *Ibid.*

6. *The Voice of the Negro* (an illustrated monthly magazine) 2 (October, 1905).

7. *Medal of Honor Recipients, 1863–1963.* Military Pension File of Pompey Factor, RG 15, Record of the Adjutant General's Office, National Archives, Washington, D.C.

8. Henry Ossian Flipper, *The Colored Cadet at West Point. Autobiography of Lieutenant Henry Ossian Flipper,* U.S. (New York: Homer Lee & Co., 1878.) ———, *Mexican Laws, Statutes, etc.* (Nogales: A. T. Press of L. Squire, 1892). ———, *Venezuelan Laws, Statutes* (translation), (Caracas: Pontepac Petroleum Companies, 1925). Theodore D. Harris (Ed.), *Negro Frontiersman. The Western Memoirs of Henry O. Flipper.* (El Paso: Western College, 1963).

9. *Medal of Honor Recipients, 1863–1963.*

10. *Ibid.*

11. *Ibid.*

12. *Ibid.*

13. Personal Notes of Mr. J. B. Ross, register 2421, National Archives.

14. *Medal of Honor Recipients, 1863–1963.*

15. *Ibid.*

16. *Ibid.*

17. Military Pension File of Isaac Payne, *loc. cit.* *Medal of Honor Recipients, 1863–1963.*

18. John H. Paynter, *Joining the Navy* or *Abroad with Uncle Sam* (Hartford: American Publishing Co., 1895).

19. *Crisis Magazine* 25 (November, 1922), p. 126.

20. *Medal of Honor Recipients, 1863–1963.* Military Pension Files of Thomas Shaw, *loc. cit.*

21. Stephen Ambrose, *Duty, Honor, Country. A History of West Point* (Baltimore: Johns Hopkins Press, 1966). Flipper, *The Colored Cadet at West Point.*

22. Register of Enlistments in the U.S. Army 1798–1914, Richard Smith, Microcopy 233, National Archives, Washington, D.C.

23. Register of Enlistments, Howard Snowden, *loc. cit.*

24. *Medal of Honor Recipients, 1863–1963.*

25. Register of Enlistments, Jacob W. Stevens, *loc. cit.*

26. H. V. F. Cashin, Tennyson and Nealy, *Under Fire with the Tenth U.S. Cavalry* (New York: Alexander & Cashin, 1899).

27. *Medal of Honor Recipients, 1863–1963.*

28. *Ibid.* Military Pension Files of John Ward, *loc. cit.* Kenneth Wiggins Porter, "The Seminole Negro Indian Scouts, 1870–1881," *The Southwestern Historical Quarterly* 55 (July, 1951 to April, 1952), pp. 359–365.

29. Ambrose, *Duty, Honor, Country,* pp. 231–237.

30. *Medal of Honor Recipients, 1863–1963.*

31. *Ibid.*

32. *Ibid.*

# Chapter Six

## The Spanish-American War, 1898

The Spanish-American War saw the Negro officer take his place as a leader of his men. The national guard and state militias were a major part of the country's military force, and the Negro militia was represented. The famous Eighth Illinois Infantry Regiment was mustered into service under the command of a black colonel. Several other all-Negro volunteer units were commanded by Negro senior field grade officers.

During the war, Negro participation was evident. There were black sailors aboard the *USS Maine* when it was blown up on February 15, 1898, and black soldiers in Cuba at San Juan Hill and at El Caney, making history on the battlefields. Four regular Negro regiments were sent to Cuba in 1898—the Ninth and Tenth cavalry and the Twenty-Fourth and Twenty-Fifth infantry regiments. Numerous Negro volunteer units were called into service, although only three of them (the Eighth Illinois, Ninth U.S. Volunteers and Twenty-Third Kansas) went to Cuba. They were given garrison assignments and in some instances were used to suppress bandits.

Negro Americans found an opportunity in the Spanish-American War to organize volunteer state militias, to train additional commissioned and non-commissioned officers, and to demonstrate their abilities in command. Many black veterans of the Spanish-American War served in World War I, and provided excellent leadership in organizing newly activated black units. This chapter attempts to give the background of some of these black soldiers, some of whom received Medals of Honor and battlefield promotions. The war was fertile ground for the growth and development of a new Negro soldier, a commander and leader of black troops. However, in the period 1900 to 1941, this evolution was not encouraged and Negro officers in the regular army were not in evidence as they had been during the period of the Spanish-American War.

### John W. Alden

Lieutenant, Eighth Illinois Volunteer Infantry Regiment.

John Alden was born in Mound City, Illinois. He attended high school in Metropolis and was a student at Northwestern University. He was commissioned and served with the Eighth Illinois Regiment.[1]

### Allen Allensworth

Lieutenant Colonel, Twenty-Fourth Infantry Regiment, U.S. Army Chaplain, and Seaman, Petty Officer, U.S. Navy.

Allen Allensworth was born in Louisville, Kentucky, on April 3, 1843. His slave parents were Levi and Phyllis Allensworth. At the beginning of the Civil War, in 1861, Allensworth was sold in a slave market at New Orleans for one thousand dollars to ride race horses. In the summer of 1861, he was brought back to Louisville, Kentucky, by his new owner. He left Louisville in 1862 with Union soldiers and obtained his freedom in the winter of 1863. On April 3, 1863, he enlisted in the U.S. Navy and advanced in rank from seaman to petty officer. He was released from the navy on April 3, 1865.

*Lieutenant Colonel Allen Allensworth*

*Corporal George G. Anderson*

After the Civil War, Allensworth returned to Louisville and joined the Fifth Street Baptist Church. He became the janitor of the Ely Norman School in Louisville and later studied there. The Freedmen's Bureau selected him to be a teacher and school principal. He was determined to improve his education and enrolled in the Nashville Institute, later known as Roger Williams University. He pursued the normal and minister's course and then decided to leave the school. He became active with the General Association of Colored Baptists and also served as a pastor in churches at Franklin, Louisville and Bowling Green, Kentucky. Later he accepted a pastorate in Cincinnati, Ohio. The Roger Williams University subsequently conferred on him an honorary Master of Arts degree.

Allensworth was appointed by President Grover Cleveland as chaplain to the Twenty-Fourth U.S. Infantry and served courageously for many years.[2]

### John W. Allison

Lieutenant, Eighth Illinois Voluntary Infantry Regiment.

John Allison, a black man, was a native of Collierville, Tennessee. He was reported to be one of the best drill instructors in the regiment. He moved to Chicago in 1892.[3]

### George G. Anderson

Corporal, Eighth Illinois Volunteer Infantry Regiment and Company K, Twenty-Fifth Infantry Regiment.

George Anderson was a native of Paduca, Kentucky. He enlisted in the Eighth Illinois Volunteer Infantry Regiment and served six months in Cuba during the Spanish-American War. He reenlisted in the regular army on May 18, 1899, and was assigned to Company K, Twenty-Fifth Infantry Regiment. He also served for a time as headquarters clerk. Anderson was one of many black soldiers who served during the Spanish-American War and later decided to enlist in the regular army.[4]

### William H. Anderson

Chaplain, Tenth U.S. Cavalry Regiment.

William Anderson was born on August 20, 1859, at Saguin, Texas, and was a graduate of the Theological Department of Howard University, and

*Chaplain William H. Anderson*

of the Homeopathic College, Cleveland, Ohio. He was appointed chaplain of the Tenth U.S. Cavalry Regiment on August 16, 1897, and joined the regiment at Fort Assinniboine, Montana, on November 11, 1897. He was appointed post treasurer, librarian, and superintendent of the post school. He joined the regiment near Santiago, Cuba, on July 25, 1898.[5]

### Daniel Atkins

Ship's Cook First Class, *USS Cushing,* U.S. Navy.

Daniel Atkins, a black man, was born at Brunswick, Victoria. He was awarded the Medal of Honor for a display of gallantry on February 11, 1898, while serving on board the *USS Cushing.* The citation read: "Atkins attempted to save the life of the late Ensign Joseph C. Breckenridge, United States Navy, who fell overboard at sea from that vessel . . ."[6]

### Edward L. Baker Jr.

Sergeant Major (later commissioned Second Lieutenant), Tenth U.S. Cavalry Regiment.

Edward Baker, a black man, was born in Laramie County, Wyoming. He was awarded the Medal of Honor on July 3, 1902, for gallant action in Cuba. The citation read: "On July 1, 1898, at Santiago, Cuba, he left cover and under fire rescued a wounded comrade from drowning."[7]

### George T. Baker

First Lieutenant, Eighth Illinois Volunteer Infantry Regiment.

George Baker, a black, was born in New Orleans, Louisiana, on December 15, 1863. He spent his early years in Natchez, Mississippi, and in New Orleans, learning the trade of cracker baker. At the age of eighteen, he joined the Lynch Guards of Natchez and held a first lieutenant's commission. In 1888, he moved to Chicago, Illinois, and joined the Ninth Battalion where he was promoted first to corporal and then to first sergeant. In 1895 he was commissioned a lieutenant.[8]

### Dennis Bell

Private, Troop H, Tenth U.S. Cavalry Regiment.

*Sergeant Major Edward L. Baker*

Dennis Bell, a black man, was born in Washington, D.C., where he entered the army. He was awarded a Medal of Honor for heroic action in Cuba, the citation reading as follows: "Bell exhibited a heroic act when he voluntarily went ashore at Tayabacca, Cuba, 30 June 1898, in the face of the enemy and aided in the rescue of his wounded comrades; this after several previous attempts had been frustrated."[9]

### George Berry

Sergeant, Troop G, Tenth U.S. Cavalry Regiment.

George Berry served with his unit in Cuba, and was instrumental in the memorable occupation of San Juan Hill. He displayed courage and iniative when he carried the colors of the Third and Tenth up San Juan Hill. It was reported that he constantly shouted to his men, "Dress on the colors, boys. Dress on the colors." Berry retired from the army after thirty years of service.[10]

### Stewart D. Betts

Lieutenant, Eighth Illinois Volunteer Infantry Regiment.

Stewart Betts was born in 1875 in Kentucky and moved to Chicago at an early age. In 1886 he joined the Ninth Battalion and was promoted to first sergeant. His later commission as lieutenant was based on his merits.[11]

### Horace Wayman Bivins

Sergeant, Tenth U.S. Cavalry Regiment.

Horace Bivins was born in Pungoteague, Accomack County, Virginia, on May 8, 1862. He was raised on a farm and at the age of fifteen was given the responsibility of running an eight-horse farm one mile from Keller Station, Virginia. On June 13, 1885, Bivins enrolled at Hampton School where he received his first military training. On November 7, 1887, he enlisted in the army at Washington, D.C. He was sent to Jefferson Barracks, Missouri, and after training, on June 19, 1888, was assigned to Troop E, Tenth U.S. Cavalry, at Fort Grant, Arizona Territory. Bivins served with this troop on various missions around San Carlos, in the Arizona Territory and when the unit arrived at Fort Apache, Bivins was detailed as a clerk in the regimental adjutant's office. He held this position from

*Lieutenant Stewart D. Betts*

*Sergeant Horace W. Bivins*

November 10, 1889 until June 15, 1890. On April 14, 1898, his regiment was ordered to Chickamauga to prepare for participation in the Spanish-American War Cuban campaigns. Sergeant Bivins was a successful sharpshooter and at San Carlos participated in his first rifle competition. He gained second place in a troop of sixty men. In 1889 he was made a sharpshooter and represented his troop in 1892, 1893 and 1894, winning eight medals and badges in departmental competition. In 1894, Bivins won three gold medals representing the Department of the Dakotas at the army competition at Fort Sheridan.[12]

### D. J. Bowen

Captain, First Separate Company, First and Second Rhode Island Militia.

D. J. Bowen was a prominent businessman in Providence, Rhode Island. As a youth, he worked as an apprentice in a printing office in the main depot and was later employed in various large printing firms in the neighborhood of Providence, eventually owning his own business, the Excelsior Print Company.

In 1894, having risen from private to lieutenant in the First Separate Company, Rhode Island Militia, he was made captain in the Second Separate Company until the first and second companies were consolidated in 1895. He was the author of a military drama called *Fort Wagner,* which was produced in 1897.[13]

### Lewis Broadus

Sergeant, U.S. Army.

Lewis Broadus, a black, served in the army for more than twenty-six years, and was stationed in Cuba, Hawaii, and the Philippine Islands. In Cuba, Broadus distinguished himself recovering the horses of the mounted officers at great personal risk, and also saved the lives of four men of his unit. He received a certificate of merit from President Roosevelt in 1906 for saving the life of Sergeant J. M. Thompson of Fort Niobrara, Nebraska. Later in his career, Sergeant Broadus was assigned to the Connecticut State Armory at Hartford.[14]

*Captain D. J. Bowen*

*Lieutenant Arthur M. Brown*

*Second Lieutenant John Buck*

*First Lieutenant Pierre L. Carmouche*

*Seaman Nicholas H. Campbell*

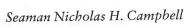

*Lieutenant William Carter*

*Chaplain Jordan Chavis*

### Horace G. Burke

Second Lieutenant, Eighth Illinois Volunteer Infantry Regiment.

Horace Burke, a black man, was born on July 4, 1872, at Houston, Texas. He later moved to Metropolis, Illinois, and enlisted in Company L, Eighth Battalion, as a first sergeant. While serving in Cuba during the Spanish-American War, he received a battlefield promotion to lieutenant.[15]

### T. C. Butler

Private, Company H, Twenty-Fifth Infantry, Spanish-American War.

T. C. Butler, a black, was the first man, according to eyewitnesses, to enter the blockhouse at El Caney, Cuba, and take possession of the Spanish flag for his regiment. An officer of the Twelfth Infantry came up while Butler was in the house and ordered him to give up the flag, which he was compelled to do, but not before he had torn a piece off the flag, which he used to substantiate a report of this injustice to his colonel.[16]

### Pierre Lacroix Carmouche

First Lieutenant, Company L, Ninth U.S. Volunteer Infantry Regiment.

Pierre Carmouche was born on November 20, 1862, in the town of Donaldsonville, Ascension

Parish, Louisiana. He was raised as a Roman Catholic and was active in the church. As a youth he was apprenticed to a barber and to a blacksmith, and later operated his own wheelwright blacksmith and farrier's shop. He was elected assessor for the town of Donaldsonville in the municipal elections of 1886, and succeeded himself in 1887.

It was reported that Carmouche was one of the first Afro-Americans to offer his services to President McKinley in the Spanish-American War, along with two hundred and fifty other colored men whom he had induced to join him. Later he served in Santiago, Cuba as first lieutenant of Company L in the Ninth U.S. Volunteer Infantry Regiment.[17]

### William Carter

Lieutenant, Eighth Illinois Volunteer Infantry Regiment.

William Carter, a black, was born in 1863 and later moved to Litchfield, Illinois, where he went into business. He enlisted in the Eighth Illinois Regiment and was commissioned a lieutenant.[18]

### Jordan Chavis

Chaplain, Eighth Illinois Volunteer Infantry Regiment.

*Lieutenant James W. Curtis*

*Captain Hilary Coston and family*

Jordan Chavis, a black man, was born in Massac County, Illinois, on February 16, 1856, and attended school in Metropolis, Illinois. In 1870, he moved to Mississippi and enrolled at Alcorn University, graduating from a normal course in 1876. He was then ordained a Baptist minister and pastored churches in the South, and in Chicago, Illinois.

Chavis assisted in organizing Company I from volunteers in Quincy, Illinois during the Spanish-American War and on August 1, 1898, he received an appointment from Illinois Governor Tanner as a commissioned chaplain, with the rank of captain, in the Eighth Illinois Regiment. He went with the regiment to Cuba, where he organized a congregation among the troops and baptized twelve soldiers in Cuban waters. It was believed that these baptisms were the first known Protestant baptisms in that province.[19]

### Hilary W. Coston

Captain, Ninth U.S. Volunteer Infantry Regiment.

Hilary Coston was born in Providence, Rhode Island. He attended Wilberforce University and graduated from Yale Divinity School, class of 1884. Coston joined the Ninth U.S. Volunteer Infantry and was chaplain on the commander's staff. He was the author of a book, *The Spanish-American War Volunteers,* a history of the Ninth Volunteers which was published in 1899.[20]

### James W. Curtis

Lieutenant, Eighth Illinois Volunteer Infantry Regiment.

James Curtis was born in Marion, Alabama, on July 29, 1856, the son of A. H. and Princess Curtis. His father was a state senator for six years. Curtis acquired his formal education in Alabama and later attended Lincoln University and Alabama State Normal School. In 1882, he was appointed as a clerk in the pension office in Washington and later served as a special agent for the pension office in Northwestern Illinois. Curtis next turned to the study of medicine and graduated from Howard University's Medical School in 1888. He practiced medicine in Chicago, Illinois, and in October, 1891, was appointed by Illinois Governor Tanner as assistant surgeon in the Eighth Illinois Volunteer Regiment. Curtis served as a medical officer in Cuba during the Spanish-American War.[21]

*Lieutenant William H. Dallas*

*Lieutenant Nathan Davis*

## Nathan Davis

Lieutenant, Eighth Illinois Volunteer Infantry Regiment.

Nathan Davis was born in Pittsylvania County, Virginia, in 1863. He moved to Cairo, Illinois, in 1887. Davis was commissioned a lieutenant in the Eighth Illinois Regiment.[22]

## James Elmer Dellinger

Major and Chief Surgeon, North Carolina Volunteer Regiment.

James Dellinger was born on November 3, 1862, at Lowesville, North Carolina, the son of James Monroe and Belgie Nance Dellinger. His foster parents were Cato and Delia Moore. Dellinger attended public schools in North Carolina, and studied at the State Normal School, then located at Salisbury, and at the medical department of Shaw University in Raleigh, North Carolina.

During the Spanish-American War, Dellinger was commissioned as a chief surgeon with the rank of major in the North Carolina Volunteer Regiment that was organized under the administration of Governor Russell. The regiment was distinctive in that its field grade officers were Negroes.

After the war, Dellinger resumed the practice of medicine and was quite active in civic affairs. He was married to Gertrude Camilla Farrer of Charlottesville, Virginia and, after her death, to Liggie P. Pentecost of Macon, Georgia.[23]

## Franklin A. Denison

Colonel, Eighth Illinois Volunteer Infantry Regiment and 370th U.S. Infantry Regiment (World War I).

Franklin Denison was born in 1862 in San Antonio, Texas. He was educated in Texas public schools. He graduated in 1888 from Lincoln University and in 1890 was valedictorian graduate from the Union College of Law in Chicago, where he was appointed assistant prosecuting attorney by Mayor Hempstead Washburn in 1891.

During the Spanish-American War, Denison served as a major with the Eighth Illinois Regiment in Cuba and was one of the judges of the Court of Claims at Santiago, Cuba. He was appointed by General Lawton to serve as president of a general court martial, the only Negro officer to be so appointed during the war.

*Colonel Franklin A. Denison*

*Captain Leon W. Denison*

On July 3, 1917, when the Eighth Illinois National Guard Regiment was called into active service and designated the Three Hundred and Seventieth Infantry, Colonel Denison became its commanding officer and the senior ranking Negro officer on active duty during World War I. To have attained the rank of colonel and the command of a regiment was a most significant achievement in the year 1917. Colonel Denison's career was both a personal triumph and strong evidence of the Negro's ability to serve in senior field grade position in both war and peace.[24]

### Leon W. Denison

Captain, Eighth Illinois Volunteer Infantry Regiment.

Leon Denison was born in San Antonio, Texas. He studied at the University of Michigan and at the Union College of Law in Chicago. He enlisted as a private in the Eighth Illinois Regiment and was later appointed to the rank of captain by the Governor of Illinois. Leon Denison was the brother of Franklin Denison who attained the rank of colonel in World War I.[25]

### Lee Fitz

Private, Troop M, Tenth U.S. Cavalry Regiment.

Lee Fitz, a black man, was born in Dinwiddie County, Virginia. He was awarded a Medal of Honor for bravery in action at Tayabaco, Cuba, on June 30, 1898, when he volunteered to go ashore in the face of the enemy and aided in the rescue of his wounded comrades, after several previous attempts had been frustrated.[26]

### George W. Ford

Major, Twenty-Third Kansas Volunteer Infantry Regiment.

George Ford was born in 1847 in the state of Virginia, but went to school in New York City. He enlisted in the Tenth U.S. Cavalry in 1867 and served as sergeant and regimental quartermaster sergeant. Ford was commended in general orders for acts of good judgment and gallantry in the Indian wars, and was honorably discharged in 1877.

During the Spanish-American War, in 1898, Ford was commissioned as a major in the National Guard and called to active duty with the Twenty-

Joseph E. Dibble

Second Lieutenant Saint Foster

Sergeant Major Frierson

Third Kansas Volunteer Infantry Regiment in Cuba, where he served for one year.

After the war, Ford worked as the superintendent of various government cemeteries, including the military cemeteries in Beaufort, South Carolina; Fort Scott, Kansas; Port Hudson, Louisiana, and Springfield, Illinois. He was also appointed treasurer of the Lincoln Exposition in Chicago, Illinois.[27]

### William H. Franklin

First Lieutenant, Ninth U.S. Volunteer Regiment.

William Franklin was born on March 25, 1857, in Gallafin, Sumner County, Tennessee. He enlisted in the Twenty-Fourth Infantry Regiment on April 16, 1876, and served successively as private, corporal, sergeant and first sergeant in companies J and E, until August 17, 1898. Franklin was appointed first lieutenant on August 16, 1898, at Siboney, Cuba. He participated in military engagements in Cuba during the Spanish-American War.[28]

### James Gilliard

Quartermaster Third Class, U.S. Navy.

James Gilliard was born on October 12, 1865, in Charleston, South Carolina, the son of Prince and Mary Gilliard. At the age of fourteen he enlisted as an apprentice in the U.S. Navy and was assigned to the *USS Kearsarge*, commanding officer W. R. Bridgman. He received his discharge on October 12, 1882, reenlisted on November 27 of the same year, and was assigned to the *USS Wyandotte* with a rating of ordinary seaman. His commanding officer was W. H. Webb. Gilliard was transferred to the *USS Speedwell*, D. McPritchett commanding, on November 28, 1882.

From 1884 to 1888 Gilliard served aboard the following ships as an ordinary seaman: *USS Franklin, USS Dale, USS Swatora, USS Wabash, USS Vermont, USS Santee, USS Constitution* and *USS Atlanta*. He was discharged on December 14, 1888, reenlisted, and was assigned to the *USS Dale* and *USS Franklin*. In the period 1889 to 1899 Gilliard served aboard the *USS Pensacola, USS Independence, USS Vermont, USS Dale, USS Dolphin, USS Newport, USS Lancaster* and *USS Celtic*. He was transferred to the *USS Newark* on April 19, 1901

*Second Lieutenant William H. Givens*

and to the *USS Wabash* on July 26, 1901. On August, 1901, Gilliard had completed over twenty-two years of naval service and was honorably discharged. He applied for an appointment with the U.S. Treasury Department on September 20, 1901. Charles A. Russell, a Congressman, wrote a personal letter on his behalf, on January 17, 1902, saying:

*He [Gilliard] has been in the navy some twenty years, including the time of the Spanish War and his last service was in the Phillipines. He has a good naval record and is represented to me as a faithful, honest man of good character.*

James Gilliard was not accepted for the post as ordnance man, but was given a job in the Navy Yard as a rigger. He was married to Adelaide Vincent on September 25, 1901, by a Reverend J. C. Dent at 154 Q Street SE, Washington, D.C. He applied for a job in the U.S. Navy Yard in Washington, a letter of reference was written to the Civil Service Commission by a navy commander, Stanford Moses, stating:

*James Gilliard served as a Seaman and as a Quartermaster in the Navy under my immediate supervision for about one year, 1900–1901. It was upon my recommendation that he was made a petty officer and the Captain of the ship allowed Gilliard to choose whether he should be rated Quartermaster or Gunner's Mate. He was qualified for either rating, being efficient, intelligent, and of good character, habits and deportment and possessing the required knowledge.*

James Gilliard died on June 12, 1942, at Walter Reed Hospital, Washington, D.C. He is buried at Arlington Cemetery.[29]

## Wade H. Hammond

Bandmaster, Ninth U.S. Cavalry Regiment.

Wade Hammond was born in the state of Alabama. He graduated from Alabama A. and M. College in 1895. When he joined the Ninth Cavalry he was assigned as bandmaster, and during his military career attended the Royal Military School of Music in London. He was also presented with a medal by the Mayor of Douglas, Arizona. The medal's citation read:

*Regimental Color Sergeant Abraham Hall*

*Bandmaster Wade H. Hammond*

*Musician Mitchell Harris*

*In the name of the Citizens*
*Presented to the Chief Musician, Ninth Cavalry Band, by the Citizens of Douglas, Arizona. September 14, 1914. Keep Step to the Music of the Union.*[30]

**Michael A. Healy**

Captain, U.S. Revenue Cutter Service.

Michael Healy was born near Clinton, Georgia, on September 22, 1839. He was the son of an Irishman, Michael Morris Healy, who had migrated to Georgia from Nova Scotia in 1812 and had settled in Clinton on February 26, 1818. His mother was a mulatto slave girl, born on a Clinton, Georgia plantation and probably the daughter of a local cotton magnate named Sam Griswald. Her date of birth was March 3, 1813. Michael Healy's parents owned many acres of land and some slaves; of their ten children three became Catholic priests: Father James Augustine, Father Patrick Frances, and Father Alexander Sherwood. Michael Healy, however, wanted to travel and look for adventure and had no desire to stay in school. His brother James became Bishop of Portland, Maine (the first Negro Catholic bishop), and Patrick was the only black president of Georgetown University in Washington, D.C., but Michael pursued his career at sea, eventually attaining the rank of captain in the U.S. Revenue Cutter Service.

Michael Healy was appointed to U.S.R.C.S. from the state of Maine on March 7, 1865. He was promoted to second lieutenant on June 6, 1866; to first lieutenant on July 20, 1870, and to captain on March 3, 1883. He commanded a number of cutters during his long career in the service, among them the *Chandler,* based at San Francisco, but working primarily in Alaska and the Arctic, and the *Bear,* which he commanded from 1886 until 1895. He made many trips to Alaska during this time serving as deputy marshall and was for many years the federal law in Alaska. Healy helped introduce reindeer to Alaska, bringing a dozen in from Siberia in 1879 (some eleven hundred animals were imported over a ten-year period).

Healy retired on September 22, 1903, at which time he was the third ranking captain in the U.S. Revenue Cutter Service. He died on August 30, 1904.[31]

*Lieutenant J. H. Hill*

*Captain Michael A. Healy*

*Captain William D. Hodge*

*Captain Charles L. Hunt*

*Lieutenant Walter J. Jackson*

**Charles L. Hunt**

Captain, Company B, Ninth Battalion, Eighth Illinois Volunteer Infantry Regiment.

Charles Hunt was born on June 22, 1862, in Chicago, Illinois, where he received his schooling. He joined the Hannibal Zouaves, and remained with them until they became Company A of the Sixteenth Battalion, National Guard. He joined Company B, Ninth Battalion on June 17, 1891, and was appointed first lieutenant on May 3, 1892.[32]

*Major Robert R. Jackson*

*Captain Wilt Jackson*

### W. T. Jefferson

Captain, Company B, Ninth Battalion, Eighth Illinois Volunteer Infantry Regiment.

W. T. Jefferson was born in Washington, D.C. on August 4, 1864. He later moved to Derby, Connecticut, where he went to public school. At the age of eighteen he was apprenticed to a local dentist, and worked there for eight years. In 1889, Jefferson enrolled at Howard University's College of Dentistry. He entered the American College of Dental Surgery in Chicago in 1890, graduating on March 24, 1891. On April 1, 1895, he joined Company B, Ninth Battalion, and on May 1, 1895, he was commissioned second lieutenant.[33]

### Joseph H. Johnson

Lieutenant Colonel, Eighth Illinois Volunteer Regiment.

Joseph Johnson was born in Washington, D.C. Before joining the army he worked on the railroad, but in 1880 he enlisted in the Ninth U.S. Cavalry, where his performance was outstanding. He won several medals for sharpshooting. In 1891, Johnson joined the National Guard as a private, was promoted to first sergeant and later, in 1892, adjutant. When the Eighth Illinois Regiment was

*Private Johnson*

*Lieutenant Joseph H. Johnson*

mustered into service in the Spanish-American War, Johnson was commissioned lieutenant colonel. He served with the regiment in Cuba where he held the distinctive position of senior grade field officer.[34]

*John Jordan*

*First Sergeant Noah H. Johnson*

### J. Leon Jones

Second Lieutenant, Ninth U.S. Volunteer Infantry Regiment.

J. Leon Jones was born on August 3, 1874, in Houston, Texas. He joined the Ninth U.S. Volunteer Infantry as first sergeant and was instrumental in organizing Company I. He was later commissioned a second lieutenant. Jones served faithfully in the Spanish-American War as a member of the regimental commander's personal staff, a rarity for Negro officers during this period.[35]

### John A. Logan

Sergeant Major, Ninth U.S. Cavalry Regiment.

John Logan enlisted in the army on August 21, 1892, at Chattanooga, Tennessee, and was assigned to Troop C, Ninth U.S. Cavalry. He served for five years with Troop C, and six with Troop L of the same regiment, and was promoted to sergeant major on August 29, 1904. In 1907 he was awarded the title of marksman for his prowess with weapons. Logan served for some time in the Philippines and fought at the battle of La Quasima, Cuba, July 1 to 11, 1898.[36]

### Frank W. Love

Squadron Sergeant Major, Company D, Twenty-Fifth U.S. Infantry Regiment.

Frank Love was born in Kansas City, Missouri, on November 20, 1877. He enlisted in the army on August 18, 1900, was assigned to the Twenty-Fifth Infantry Regiment, and served in the Philippine Islands from October 31, 1900 to July 8, 1902, and from May 31, 1907 to May 15, 1909. Love was assigned to the Ninth U.S. Cavalry Regiment in August, 1906. He was appointed squadron sergeant major on January 16, 1909.[37]

*First Lieutenant Howard Love*

*Captain Walter H. Loving*

## Howard Love

First Lieutenant, Eighth Illinois Volunteer Regiment.

Howard Love was born in Urbana, Ohio, and moved to Chicago in 1885. He joined the Ninth Battalion, Eighth Illinois, in 1891 and was promoted to sergeant. In 1897 he was commissioned a second lieutenant, and when the regiment mustered at Springfield he was promoted to first lieutenant and was assigned as ordnance officer.[38]

## Walter H. Loving

Captain, Bandmaster, Eighth Illinois Volunteers (Immunes).

Walter Loving was born in Washington, D.C., in 1872, and attended Dunbar High School (the old M Street school). He enlisted in the Twenty-Fourth U.S. Infantry Regiment, and in 1899 served as bandmaster of the Eighth Illinois Volunteers. (He completed a special course in band conducting at the New England Conservatory.) Loving was commissioned second lieutenant and also served with the Forty-Eighth U.S. Volunteers in the Philippines, where on February 13, 1902, he was assigned the task of organizing a band for the Philippine Constabulary Service. Captain Loving participated

in the St. Louis and Seattle expositions in 1906. His performance as a musician was commendable, a credit to the military and a testament to the Negro's progress during that period.[39]

## John Roy Lynch

Major (Paymaster), U.S. Volunteers and U.S. Army.

John R. Lynch was born in Vidalia, Louisiana, on September 10, 1847, the son of a white father and black slave mother. He remained a slave until the federal occupation, but then attended night school and became a photographer. He became active in politics, and was elected to the Mississippi legislature at the age of twenty-one. At twenty-four he became speaker of the Mississippi legislature and served from 1872 to 1873, when he was elected to the U.S. Congress as Representative from the Natchez district of Mississippi. He was a congressman from 1873 to 1877. In 1896, Lynch qualified for the Mississippi bar.

During the Spanish-American War, Lynch was appointed major and paymaster in the volunteer regiment and was later appointed paymaster in the regular army, with the rank of captain. He retired as a major in 1911. In 1913 his book, *The Facts of*

*Major John R. Lynch*

*Reconstruction,* was published. John R. Lynch died on September 2, 1939.[40]

**Joseph W. McAdoo**

Captain, Eighth Illinois Volunteer Infantry Regiment.

*Captain Joseph W. McAdoo*

Joseph McAdoo was born in 1898 at Gibson County, Kentucky. He lived in Cairo, Illinois. He received a commission in the Eighth Infantry Regiment and was promoted to the rank of captain.[41]

**Hugh McElroy**

Private, U.S. Army.

Hugh McElroy enlisted in Theodore Roosevelt's Rough Riders at fourteen, having lied about his age. He served in the Spanish-American War, and after that joined the Tenth U.S. Cavalry Regiment. He was with the troops who accompanied General Pershing into Mexico in 1916. During World War I, he served with the Three Hundred and Seventeenth Engineers, but was assigned temporarily to the French Seventh Army. While serving with the French he was awarded the Croix de Guerre for gallantry in action.[42]

*Lieutenant Alfred McKay*

### John R. Marshall

Colonel, Eighth Illinois Volunteer Infantry Regiment.

John Marshall was born in Alexandria, Virginia, on March 15, 1859. He attended public schools in Alexandria and in Washington, D.C. At the age of sixteen he was apprenticed to a bricklayer. Later he moved to Chicago, Illinois, where he was appointed deputy clerk in the county clerk's office.

Marshall joined the National Guard, where he was instrumental in organizing a battalion, in which he served as second lieutenant and as captain. In June, 1892, he was given a colonel's commission in the National Guard. During the Spanish-American War, Colonel Marshall assumed command of the Eighth Illinois Volunteers and performed his duties admirably with the unit in Cuba. He was the highest ranking Negro officer to serve in the Spanish-American War.[43]

*Colonel John R. Marshall*

### Edward Miller

First Lieutenant, Eighth Illinois Volunteer Infantry Regiment.

Edward Miller was born in Garrard County, Kentucky, on August 31, 1858, and attended public schools in Danville. In 1880 he moved to Meadville, Pennsylvania. He wanted to become a surgeon, and studied medicine in a doctor's office. He also studied at the Chicago Homeopathy Medical College and took graduate courses in 1897. Miller served with the Eighth Illinois Regiment in Cuba during the Spanish-American War.[44]

*First Lieutenant Edward Miller*

### James S. Nelson

Sergeant Major and Quartermaster, Eighth Illinois Volunteer Infantry Regiment.

James Nelson was born in Windsor, Canada. He later moved to the United States and in 1884 became a citizen. He studied law at the Chicago College of Law, and during the Spanish-American War served with the Eighth Illinois Regiment as sergeant major, and later quartermaster of the ninth battalion. In 1894 he married Dr. Ida Gray, at that time the only Negro female dentist in the United States.[45]

*Lieutenant John S. Nelson*

*G. S. Norman*

*Cabin Steward William C. Payne*

**William C. Payne**

Cabin Steward, *USS Dixie,* U.S. Navy.

William Payne served aboard the *USS Dixie* with personnel from the state of Maryland. After the war he wrote a book about his experiences during his time aboard the *Dixie* and these memoirs, *The Cruise of the USS Dixie, or On Board with the Maryland Boys in the Spanish-American War,* were published in 1899.[46]

# THINGS I NEED TO DO
## TODAY

Date _____

1. _____

2. _____

3. _____

4. _____

5. _____

6. _____

*Fireman First Class Robert Penn*

*Lieutenant Walter Pinchback*

## Robert Penn

Fireman First Class, *USS Iowa*, U.S. Navy.

Robert Penn was born on October 10, 1872, at City Point, Virginia. While serving aboard the *USS Iowa* at Santiago, Cuba, on July 20, 1898, he showed unusual devotion to duty in extremely dangerous conditions. A Medal of Honor was awarded to him on December 11, 1898, with the following citation: "Performing his duty at the risk of serious scalding at the time of the blowing out of the manhole gasket on board the vessel. Penn hauled the fire while standing on a board thrown across a coal bucket one foot above the boiling water which was still blowing from the boiler."[47]

## Walter Pinchback

Lieutenant, U.S. Army.

Walter Pinchback was born in Louisiana, the son of the noted statesman, senator, and one-time governor of Louisiana, P. B. S. Pinchback. He moved to Washington, D.C. in 1898, and served in the Spanish-American War as a lieutenant in the infantry. Walter Pinchback was a graduate of the Andover Academy and Howard University Law School; a member of the Executive Committee of the District of Columbia Suffrage Associa-

*Black sailors relax with music*

tion, and president of the Bloomington Civic Association. He died in Washington, D.C., in 1938 and was buried in Arlington National Cemetery.[48]

### George W. Prioleau

Chaplain, Ninth U.S. Cavalry Regiment.

George Prioleau was born in Charleston, South Carolina. He attended public school in Charleston, the Avery Institute and Claflin University. He taught in public schools for a time, and then entered the ministry. After graduating from the Theological School of Wilberforce University in 1884 he pastored several churches in Xenia, Ohio. In 1895, he was appointed chaplain of the Ninth U.S. Cavalry Regiment, with the rank of captain, and served until 1915, when he transferred to the Tenth and finally to the Twenty-Fifth Infantry Regiment.[49]

*Lieutenant John C. Proctor*

*Chaplain George W. Prioleau*

*Sergeant Frank W. Pullen*

*First Lieutenant William Whipper Purnell*

*Lieutenant Charles L. Reece*

### William Whipper Purnell

First Lieutenant and Assistant Surgeon, Forty-Eighth Volunteer Regiment.

William Purnell was born on January 25, 1869, in Philadelphia, Pennsylvania, the son of James W. and Julia A. Purnell. He attended Howard University Normal and Preparatory Department from 1880 to 1885; the Pharmaceutical College sessions 21 and 22 from 1888 to 1890, and the Medical College sessions 23, 24, and 25 in the period 1891 to 1893. Purnell practiced medicine in Washington for several years. He served during the Spanish-American War in the Philippines and in 1899 was appointed lieutenant and assistant surgeon in the Forty-Eighth Volunteers.[50]

### James M. Rawls

Lieutenant, Eighth Illinois Volunteer Infantry Regiment.

James Rawls, a black, served for five years with the regular army and was discharged with the rank of first sergeant. Later he joined the Eighth Illinois Volunteers and was commissioned a lieutenant. During the Spanish-American War, he was with the regiment in Cuba, on detached service at Palma Soriano.[51]

*Captain Richard P. Roots*

*Chaplain Osxae J. W. Scott*

### Richard P. Roots

Captain, Eighth Illinois Volunteer Infantry Regiment.

Richard Roots was born in Tuscaloosa, Alabama, in 1860, and attended school in Tennessee. He moved to Chicago in 1884 and was employed in the post office. He joined the Eighth Illinois Volunteers, was commissioned as a captain and served in Cuba in the Spanish-American War.[52]

### Oscar J. W. Scott

Chaplain, Twenty-Fifth U.S. Infantry Regiment.

Oscar Scott, a black, was born at Gallipolis, Ohio, on July 31, 1867, and was educated in the Ohio public schools. He attended Ohio Wesleyan University and Drew Theological Seminary. He was a minister in the African Methodist Episcopal Church and a former pastor of the Metropolitan Church in Washington, D.C. Scott was appointed chaplain in the U.S. Army on April 17, 1907. He served with the Twenty-Fifth Infantry Regiment in Texas, in the state of Washington, and overseas in the Philippines and Hawaii.[53]

### John W. Shreeves

Lieutenant, Eighth Illinois Volunteer Infantry Regiment.

John Shreeves was born in 1866 in New Bedford, Massachusetts, and was educated in the public schools there. He worked for a time at the Bureau of Engraving and Printing in Washington, D.C., but in 1890 moved to Chicago, Illinois. He joined the Ninth Battalion as a private in 1894 and was promoted to lieutenant in 1898. He served during the Spanish-American War at San Luis as Provost Marshal.[54]

*Lieutenant John W. Shreeves*

*First Lieutenant Jacob C. Smith*

### Jacob Clay Smith

First Lieutenant, Forty-Eighth U.S. Volunteer Infantry Regiment.

Jacob Smith was born in Spencer County, Kentucky, on June 25, 1857, the son of Daniel and Elnora Mason Maddox. His father died at an early age and Jacob assumed the last name of his stepfather. He attended school in Jeffersonville, Indiana and his first job was on a farm. He later worked in the rag and wool business at Rushville,

Indiana, for four years. On July 3, 1883, he married Mary Virginia Frances Vaughn from Texas.

Smith enlisted in the army on January 21, 1880, and served until February 17, 1908. He was in Cuba during the Spanish-American War, and was assigned to the Philippines for three years. He was commissioned a lieutenant in the Forty-Eighth U.S. Volunteer Infantry and saw duty with both infantry and cavalry units. He also acted as battalion sergeant major and quartermaster sergeant on the general staff. On his retirement from the service, Smith was employed by the Washington Park police for seven years. He was active in civic and fraternal organizations.[55]

### John Smith

Candidate, U.S. Naval Academy.

John Smith, a black man, was born in Chicago, Illinois, and in 1897 was appointed to the U.S. Naval Academy at Annapolis, Maryland, by Representative George E. White, Fifth Congressional District, Chicago, Illinois. The following is a newspaper account of Smith's arrival on May 14, 1897, at Annapolis.

*Another Negro at Annapolis, John Smith, a Negro candidate for admission to the Naval Academy, arrived here today. He was the object of interest at the academy, which he visited in the afternoon. He was accompanied to the academy by Dr. Bishop, a Negro physician at whose house he is staying. Candidate Smith was intensely interested in what he saw at the academy. He was appointed by Representative George E. White of the Fifth Congressional District of Illinois, which is part of Chicago, of which Smith is a resident. Smith will take the examination next Monday. He is about twenty years old, is tall, and of good form, and has a light yellow complexion. He converses well, is alert, and observant. In addition to Candidate Bundy, who is expected from Ohio in December, it is stated that the Negro Republican Representative from South Carolina intends to appoint a Negro Cadet. The sentiment at the academy is not one of joy over arrival of Candidate Smith.*

John Smith did not graduate from the Naval Academy; nor did Bundy.[56]

*Lieutenant Thaddeus Stepp*

### Thaddeus W. Stepp

Lieutenant, Eighth Illinois Volunteer Infantry Regiment.

Thaddeus Stepp was born in Springfield, Illinois, and was employed as Chief Custodian at a Plymouth Congregational Church. He was commissioned a lieutenant in the Eighth Illinois Volunteers and accompanied the unit to Cuba.[57]

*First Sergeant Frank Rudolph Stewart*

**Adolphus Thomas**

Captain, Eighth Illinois Volunteer Infantry Regiment.

Adolphus Thomas, a black, was born in Hancock County, Georgia, in 1872, and attended public schools in Atlanta. In 1882, he joined the Georgia National Guard and was later promoted to sergeant. In a National Competitive Drill in 1885 he had the honor of being the best drilled soldier on the field. He was later promoted to first lieutenant. After moving to Illinois, he joined the Eighth Illinois Regiment as a sergeant in Company B, Ninth Battalion. He was promoted to first lieutenant in 1892, and to captain in 1893. Thomas served with the regiment during the Spanish-American War.[58]

**Harvey A. Thomas**

Adjutant, Ninth U.S. Cavalry Regiment.

Harvey Thomas was born on July 24, 1863, in Columbus, Ohio. He attended public schools in Ohio and matriculated at Fisk University and Lemoyne College (known today as Lemoyne-Owen College), Memphis, Tennessee. In 1883 he enlisted in the Ninth U.S. Cavalry and served until 1888. After his discharge he studied at Meharry

*Sergeant William H. Tompkins*

Medical College in Nashville, Tennessee, for two years before moving to Chicago. He joined the Eighth Illinois Volunteer Infantry Regiment and served as the regimental adjutant during the Spanish-American War period.[59]

**William H. Tompkins**

Sergeant, Troop G, Tenth U.S. Cavalry Regiment.

William Tompkins was born at Paterson, New Jersey, and entered the service from there. During the Spanish-American War he was stationed at Toyabacoa, Cuba. He was awarded the Medal of Honor on June 23, 1899. His citation stated that on June 30, 1898 he voluntarily went ashore in the face of the enemy and aided in the rescue of his wounded comrades after several previous attempts had been frustrated.[60]

**John Henry Turpin**

Boatswain and Chief Gunner's Mate, *USS Maine*, U.S. Navy.

John Turpin enlisted in the U.S. Navy in 1883. At the beginning of the Spanish-American War he was aboard the *USS Maine*, and was one of the survivors of the vessel when it was blown up. Turpin was an excellent boatswain and a master driver. He left the naval service with the rank of chief gunner's mate.[61]

**Thomas Van Peet**

Captain, Eighth Illinois Volunteer Regiment.

Thomas Van Peet was born in Glen Falls, Warren County, New York, on September 29, 1857. He was educated in New York and later moved to Illinois, where he was one of the first men to enroll in the Ninth Battalion. He was appointed sergeant in October, 1891, and commissioned a lieutenant in 1894.[62]

**William A. Vrooman**

Quartermaster Sergeant, Ninth U.S. Cavalry Regiment.

William Vrooman enlisted in the army on June 18, 1886, at Buffalo, New York, and was assigned to Troop I, Ninth U.S. Cavalry. He was promoted to sergeant on January 22, 1887. Vrooman served in the Sioux Indian campaign in September, 1888, and participated in the engagement at Drexel Mission from December, 1890 to January, 1891. He was a superior marksman and was a competitor in the Tri-Department Rifle and Pistol Competition in 1892, winning second, third and fifth department rifle medals, and seventh department pistol medals.

Vrooman served in Cuba during the Spanish-American War, and in the Philippines from 1900–1902 and 1907–1908. He had over twenty-four years' service with the army, and in January, 1909 had attained the rank of regimental quartermaster sergeant.[63]

### George H. Wanton

Private, Troop M, Tenth U.S. Cavalry Regiment.

George Wanton was born in Paterson, New Jersey and entered the service from there. During the Spanish-American War, he was stationed at Toyabacoa, Cuba, and on June 30, 1889, exhibited unusual valor, for which he was awarded the Medal of Honor on June 23, 1899. His citation stated that he voluntarily went ashore in the face of the enemy and aided in the rescue of his wounded comrades, this after several previous attempts at rescue had been frustrated.[64]

### William Chapman Warmsley

Surgeon, Troop D, Ninth U.S. Cavalry Regiment, Twenty-Third Kansas Volunteer Regiment, Ninth Louisiana Infantry Regiment, Fifth U.S. Infantry Regiment and Tenth U.S. Cavalry Regiment.

William Warmsley was born on October 20, 1869, in Gloucester County, Virginia. In 1876, his father moved to Norwich, where William attended public schools and the free academy. On March 12, 1887, he enlisted in the Ninth U.S. Cavalry, and was assigned to Troop D. He served five years during which he was post teacher and post sergeant major. He attended sessions at the College of Medicine, Howard University, from which he graduated in 1898.

In the Spanish-American War, Warmsley served as a surgeon with the Twenty-Third Kansas Volunteers, acting assistant surgeon with the Ninth Louisiana Infantry, Fifth U.S. Infantry and Tenth U.S. Cavalry regiments. On September 9, 1899, he was appoinaed assistant surgeon in the Forty-Ninth U.S. Volunteers. He was confronted with problems of yellow fever in Cuba and dysentery and malaria in the Philippines. On April 24, 1900, he was stationed at Luzon in the Philippine Islands.[65]

*Surgeon William C. Warmsley*

*Lieutenant James Washington*

### James W. Washington

Lieutenant, Eighth Illinois Volunteer Regiment.

James Washington was born at La Grange, Missouri. After acquiring a basic education, he was ordained a minister. Washington was the editor and publisher of the *Douglas Optic,* the first colored paper published in Knox County, Illinois. He was commissioned lieutenant in the Eighth Illinois Regiment, and served with the unit.[66]

### Lincoln Washington

Second Lieutenant, Forty-Eighth U.S. Volunteer Infantry Regiment.

Lincoln Washington enlisted in the army on July 21, 1885 at Baltimore, Maryland. During his army career he served in the enlisted ranks as a squadron sergeant major and was later promoted to second lieutenant. He was in the Philippine Islands from January, 1900 to May, 1901 and from May 31, 1907 to May 15, 1909. He was an expert rifleman and one of the many Negro troopers whose performance gained them promotion from the ranks to commissioned status.[67]

### William Washington

First Lieutenant, Eighth U.S. Volunteer Regiment.

William Washington was born in New Orleans, Louisiana, on July 8, 1866. He enlisted in the army on September 11, 1888 at Baltimore, Maryland and was assigned to Troops E and F in the Eighth Volunteers. He was promoted from first sergeant to lieutenant on August 5, 1898—another Negro soldier whose ability gained him a commission.[68]

*First Lieutenant William Washington*

*Major William A. Wesley*

### Allen Alexander Wesley

Major, Eighth Illinois Volunteer Infantry Regiment.

Allen Wesley was born on September 25, 1856, in Dublin, Indiana, the son of Edward Edrington and Elizabeth Ava (Davis) Wesley. He was educated in Cincinnati public schools and Bryant and Stratton's Business College in Chicago, Illinois. He also graduated from Fisk University in 1884. In 1880 he started to study medicine under the tutorship of a Dr. William Mussey of Cincinnati. Later he completed a three-year course of study at Northwestern University Medical School and received a degree in medicine in 1887.

Wesley's professional career included the following positions: Practitioner in Chicago; Clinical Assistant to Walter Hay, Department of Mental and Nervous Diseases, Chicago Medical College; Clinical Assistant to Professor R. N. Isham, Department of Surgery; Physician for Cook County, Chicago, Illinois; Gynecologist at Provident Hospital. Wesley also lectured on surgical emergencies in the Provident Training School. He was one of the founders and was surgeon-in-charge at the Provident Hospital in Chicago.

In May, 1894, Wesley became a member of the Eighth Illinois Volunteer Regiment, Illinois National Guard. He was commissioned major and surgeon. On July 2, 1890, he went to Cuba and was assigned the responsibility of supervising a hospital at San Luis. Later he was chosen as one of a board of three physicians to examine all medical officers appearing before the board. He was the first Negro military physician to be a member of the examining board. Major Wesley was also responsible for the medical facilities available to the Twenty-Third Kansas Volunteers Signal and Pack Train units.

Major Wesley's brilliant career as a physician and his outstanding performance of duty as a military surgeon contributed greatly to the record of Negro achievements during the Spanish-American War period.[69]

*Captain Horace F. Wheaton*

*Color Sergeant William Wilcox*

*William Wilkes*

*Lieutenant Arthur Williams*

### Horace F. Wheaton

Captain, Company L, Sixth Massachusetts Infantry Regiment, U.S. Volunteers.

Horace Wheaton was born in Cleveland, Ohio, on January 17, 1870, and later moved to Boston. He was a member of the freshman class at Trefi's Medical College. On May 29, 1894, he enlisted in Company L, Sixth Massachusetts Infantry Regiment, Volunteer Militia. Company L was the first colored company mustered in the U.S. Volunteers. The unit participated in General Miles' expedition to Puerto Rico. Wheaton was assigned as an action hospital steward, Hospital Corps, and was commissioned an officer in the Volunteer Army on September 9, 1899, being later assigned to the Forty-Ninth Infantry Regiment, U.S. Volunteers, Jefferson Barracks, near St. Louis, Missouri. He was one of many Negroes from New England to serve in the Spanish-American War.[70]

*Major Richard R. Wright*

### 156

### Arthur Williams

Lieutenant, Eighth Illinois Volunteer Infantry Regiment.

Arthur Williams was born in 1870 at Athens, Georgia. He attended public schools until he was eighteen, and later moved to Atlanta, Georgia. He enlisted in the Ninth U.S. Cavalry and was stationed at Jefferson Barracks. He was promoted to sergeant and served as a drillmaster for eight years. In the 1890's he enlisted in the Volunteer Regiment and was commissioned a lieutenant.[71]

*Regimental Sergeant Major Walter B. Williams*

*Captain Julius Witherspoon*

### Julius Witherspoon

Captain, Eighth Illinois Volunteer Infantry Regiment.

Julius Witherspoon was born in 1859 at Arkadelphia, Arkansas, where he received his education. At the age of twenty-four, he moved to Bloomington, Illinois, and later joined the Eighth Illinois Regiment and served in the Spanish-American War.[72]

### Richard Robert Wright

Major and Paymaster, U.S. Army.

Richard Wright was born on May 16, 1855, in Dalton, Virginia, the son of Robert and Harriet Lynch Wright. His grandmother, Lucy Lynch, was a native of Africa and a member of the Mandingo tribe. He also had some Indian ancestry.

Wright was educated at Storrs School, Atlanta, and at Chicago and Harvard Universities. He earned A.B., A.M. and LL.D. degrees. In 1876, he was principal of Howard Normal School in Columbus, Georgia. During the Spanish-American War, he served as paymaster with the rank of major.

Wright was married to Lydia Elizabeth Howard of Columbus, Georgia. Several of their children made outstanding contributions in their chosen professions. Wright himself enjoyed an illustrious career in both civil and military life. His accomplishments have served as a model and an inspiration.[73]

*A gunner's mate*

*Mizzen Topmen on board the USS Galena (above left) and Officers of the Eighth Illinois Regiment*

**Charles A. Young**

Colonel, various regiments, U.S. Army.

Charles Young was born on March 12, 1864, in Mayslick, Kentucky, twelve miles from Maysville in Mason County. He was the son of two former slaves, Armintie Brown and Gabriel Young. His maternal grandparents were Cyrus Bruen and Julia Coleman Bruen, and his paternal grandparents Peter and Susan Young. His father enlisted on February 13, 1865, as a private in Captain James H. Johnson's Company F, Fifth Regiment of Colored Artillery (Heavy) Volunteers. He served for one year and was discharged on February 12, 1866 near Vicksburg, Mississippi. When he was fourteen months old, Charles Young's parents decided to move across the river to Ripley, Ohio, where his maternal grandmother assisted him in his school work. Charles Young attended grammar school in Ripley, Ohio and graduated with honors.

An advertisement appeared in a Ripley daily newspaper in 1883, stating that examinations for potential military academy cadets would be conducted at Hillsboro, Ohio. The announcement was made by U.S. Congressman Alphonso Hart, from the Twelfth District of Ohio.

Charles Young was teaching school under the supervision of J. T. Whitson, the principal of Ripley High School. Dr. Whitson discussed the newspaper announcement with him and urged him to compete for the West Point appointment. Young was successful, making the second highest score, and in September, 1883, he reported to the military academy as an alternate candidate. In December, 1883, preliminary examinations were given and Young passed twenty-second out of a hundred candidates.

Charles Young arrived at West Point in June, 1884, to formally commence the four-year course. He was turned back to the new fourth class in June, 1885 because of a deficiency in mathematics. He graduated from the military academy on August 31, 1889, number forty-nine in a class of forty-nine members. He was commissioned as a second lieutenant.

After he was appointed to the Tenth U.S. Cavalry Regiment in 1889, the War Department decided to transfer him to the Twenty-Fifth U.S. Colored Infantry Regiment. However, Young preferred an assignment to a cavalry regiment and on October 31, 1889, special orders were issued transferring him to the Ninth Cavalry Regiment, his first assignment, at Fort Robinson, Nebraska, on November 28, 1889.

On October 4, 1890 Young reported for duty at Fort Duchesne, Utah. Upon the sudden death of Lieutenant John Hanks Alexander, the second black graduate of West Point, on March 26, 1894, President S. T. Mitchell of Wilberforce University wrote letters to President Cleveland and senators requesting the appointment of Lieutenant Young as military professor at Wilberforce University. Charles Young arrived at Wilberforce University on May 21, 1894 to assume his new duties. A month later his father Gabriel Young died at the age of fifty-three.

On December 22, 1896, Lieutenant Young was promoted to the rank of first lieutenant and officially transferred to the Seventh Cavalry Regiment (an all-white regiment). The official records did not indicate any specific instances of Young actually serving in garrison with the Seventh Cavalry Regiment (December 22, 1896 to October 1, 1897).

During the Spanish-American War, in 1898, Young was granted a leave of absence from the regular U.S. Army to accept appointment in the Ninth Ohio Battalion National Guard as a field grade officer with the rank of major. The Ninth Battalion was assigned to the Second Army Corps, located at Camp Russell A. Alger, near Falls Church, Virginia. In August, 1898, the unit was transferred to Camp George G. Mead, near Middletown, Pennsylvania, and in November, 1898 to Summerville, South Carolina. Young did not see service in Cuba during the Spanish-American War. He experienced the following incident at Camp Algers, Virginia:

*A white regiment came in from South Carolina, the men began to call the raw recruits "fresh fish" and some of the new Southern recruits began hollering, "I am not going to be near no damn niggers." After a while a soldier of that regiment refused to salute Major Charles Young. The camp commandant found it out and one day called this fellow in and also Young. Major Young was told*

*to take his coat off and put it on the chair and then the (white) soldier was told to salute the chair with the coat. Then Young was instructed to put his coat on and the white soldier saluted Young.*

After the Spanish-American War, Young returned to his assignment at Wilberforce University. He rejoined his regiment on September 22, 1899, at Fort Duchesne, Utah. While stationed at Fort Duchesne, Charles Young and sixty men were detailed to proceed to the scene of an incident involving Indians and sheep herders to investigate the matter and maintain order. Young was successful in arranging a meeting between the sheepowners and Indians.

*The Colored American Magazine* of May, 1901 published an article concerning the career of then Lieutenant Benjamin O. Davis, Sr. (later brigadier general). The article mentioned the following concerning Young:

*At Fort Duchesne, Utah, where the Third Squadron of the Ninth Cavalry was stationed was Lieutenant Young, at that time the only colored officer in the regular establishment. He became very much interested in Sergeant Major Davis and encouraged him to study and take the examination for lieutenancy. Even the white officers encouraged him to do so and offered him every necessary aid and instruction. Under Lieutenant Young he applied himself at his severe task for nearly two years studying history, geography, surveying and drill regulations . . .*

In February 1901, Charles Young was assigned to the Philippines. He commanded troops at Samar, Blanca Aurora, Daraga, Tobaca, Rosana and San Joaquin from July, 1901 to October 6, 1902. He participated in numerous engagements against insurgents on the island of Samar.

On May 20, 1903, Charles Young was appointed acting superintendent of Sequoia and General Grant National Parks, California. He was responsible for the supervision of payroll accounts and also directed the activities of the Forest Rangers. Colonel Young was transferred on November 2, 1903 and assigned as a troop commander at the Presidio of San Francisco, California. The Visalia Board of Trade, California showed their apprecia-

tion of Young's performance of duty as the park's acting superintendent. He was given a citation. On February 12, 1904, a bill was introduced in the House of Representatives to provide for acquiring title to certain patented lands in the Sequoia and General Grant National Parks in the state of California. There was mention of Captain Charles Young in the bill.

*As recommended by Captain Young, acting superintendent of said parks, in his report to the Secretary of Interior, dated September twenty-eight, nineteen hundred and three.*

While stationed at the Presidio, San Francisco, Captain Young accepted an invitation to address a group of students at Stanford University, (according to the *Daily Palo Alto,* [Stanford, California] December 9, 1903.) Young reminded the audience that the famed Tuskegee educator, Booker T. Washington's system of race solution would not succeed because when the black man has conquered the industrial trades and is ready for employment, he then confronts the old remark that no Negroes need apply.

On May 13, 1904, Captain Young assumed his duties as military attaché to the United States Legation, Port au Prince, Haiti. He was accompanied by his wife, the former Ada Bar. While in Haiti, Young prepared a detailed monograph on the Republic of Haiti (consisting of 284 pages and a map). In July 1905, Young prepared a little handbook of Creole French as spoken in Haiti.

Later Captain Young was accused of sketching fortifications in the interior and gathering information about the Haitian government. Unfortunately matters did not improve for Young; in 1907 while he was absent on a trip to Cape Haitian, Port de Paix and northern areas some papers were stolen from his quarters. Charles Stephens, a clerk in his employ reputedly sold the papers to the Haitian government for six hundred dollars. The United States government became alarmed about the possible diplomatic complications and the Military Information Division decided on March 26, 1907 that it would be advisable for Captain Charles Young to be relieved of his military attaché duty at Port au Prince. Captain Young departed Haiti on April 28, 1907 and reported for duty with the

Second Division, General Staff, Washington, on May 7, 1907.

After a temporary assignment in the chief of staff's office, Young rejoined the Ninth Cavalry Regiment as a troop and squadron commander in the Philippine Islands. He assumed command of his troops on August 7, 1908.

In May 1909, Captain Young was assigned to Fort D. A. Russell, Wyoming where he participated in field training exercises and also commanded Troop I and the Third Squadron.

Captain Young reported for duty to the Office of Chief of Staff, United States Army on December 31, 1911. On November 18, 1911, Booker T. Washington wrote Young asking him if he were interested in a position as military attaché to Liberia. Young replied that he would be glad to accept the assignment.

On March 8, 1912, prior to his assignment to Liberia, Charles Young was elected as the second honorary member of the Omega Psi Phi fraternity. He also wrote a book, *Military Morale of Nations and Races* published in the same year.

Captain Charles Young arrived in Monrovia, Liberia, on May 2, 1912 to assume the duties of military attaché to the American Legation. President D. E. Howard of the Republic of Liberia wrote Major Charles Young a letter on November 23, 1912 requesting him to take an expedition to the relief of a Captain Browne who was surrounded by a group of hostile natives. Young was offered some one hundred men to accompany him on the mission and departed on November 25, 1912 in search of Captain Browne. Young returned to Monrovia on January 15, 1913. He prepared detailed recommendations for improved relations between the government and indigenous tribes for the Liberian government to consider.

In April, 1913, Major Charles Young suffered a very serious attack of malignant malaria (black water fever) and he was granted sick leave and returned to America on May 12, 1913. After recuperating from his illness, he left Ohio to resume his duties in Liberia. He arrived in Liberia for duty on August 11, 1913.

Major Charles Young was officially assigned to the Tenth Cavalry Regiment on September 9, 1915. He reported for duty to Fort Huachuca on

*General Pershing, General Bliss and Lieutenant Colonel Charles Young*

or about December 31, 1915. This was Young's first *active duty* assignment with the Tenth Cavalry. On February 22, 1916, Major Charles Young was awarded the Spingarn Medal for his outstanding performances of duty in Liberia. He also served in Mexico with the Tenth Cavalry Regiment as part of the Punitive Expedition. On June 29, 1916 an Army Examining Board found him physically fit and he was promoted lieutenant colonel on September 2, 1916. This promotion was monumental progress. However, there were difficulties ahead. While assigned to the two black cavalry regiments as a junior officer, Young had not experienced much opposition from the other officers who, being white and not directly under the command and supervision of Young, did not complain. However, as Young began to assume command of the regiment and squadron more often, racial prejudice became evident and some officers personally exercised their right to request transfers in order to avoid serving under the black officer.

There was one officer who initiated a campaign to avoid Young's command even before Young reported to the regiment. In May 1915, Lieutenant John Kennard wrote the adjutant general requesting transfer to the Fifteenth Cavalry Regiment, or to any white cavalry regiment serving on the border. A Walter D. Denigre of Manchester, Massachusetts wrote the following to the Secretary of War in December 1915.

"Desire transfer of John Kennard to some other regiment, because he does not wish to serve under Major Charles Young, Tenth Cavalry, who is colored." When John Kennard requested a transfer from the Tenth Cavalry Regiment in May 1915, Lieutenant Colonel Young was still stationed in Liberia. He was assigned to the Tenth Cavalry Regiment on September 9, 1915. However, he did not arrive at Fort Huachuca, Arizona until December, 1915. In August, 1916, John Kennard was transferred to the Seventh Cavalry Regiment. Colonel John Kennard died on December 9, 1959 at New Orleans, Louisiana at the age of seventy. He was eulogized with the following remarks:

*He was a man who was representative of the best in the South. In the tradition of the great Confederate Cavalry leaders, he had a wonderful physique, horsemanship, the quick reflexes of an athlete, determination to pursue to the end what he thought was right . . .*

After the Punitive Expedition, Young returned to Fort Huachuca and established a school for enlisted men at the fort. On May 23, 1917, he was directed to proceed to the Presidio of San Francisco, California and report in person to the commanding officer, Letterman General Hospital for observation and treatment. On June 25, 1917, President Woodrow Wilson wrote a personal and private letter to Secretary of War, Newton D. Baker, and stated that a Senator Sharpe Williams of Mississippi was concerned about a first lieutenant in the Tenth U.S. Cavalry, a Southerner who found it "not only distasteful but practically impossible to serve under a colored commander." President Wilson asked Secretary Baker if the lieutenant could be transferred and send someone in his place "who would not have equally intense prejudices."

Secretary Baker replied to the president on June 26, 1917 that he had received several letters from senators concerning officers in the Tenth Cavalry who desire not to serve under a black officer. Baker wrote: "The situation is of course, very embarrasing, but I am endeavoring to meet it by using Colonel Young in connection with the training of colored officers for the new army at Des Moines, Iowa. It seems likely that I will be able to tide over the difficulty in that way for at least a while." Secretary Baker also said, "There does not seem to be any present likelihood of his early return to the Tenth Cavalry so that the situation may not develop to which you refer." President Wilson wrote Senator John Sharp Williams of Mississippi that the "Lieutenant Colonel referred to [Young] will not in fact have command because he is in ill health and likely when he gets better himself to be transferred to some other service."

On June 30, 1917, Senator John Sharpe Williams wrote President Wilson that "You seem to have forgotten that it is a Negro regiment as well as a Negro colonel. I send both your letter to me and my letter to you by my secretary so that you can read them (letter) and destroy them, if you choose." President Wilson wrote Secretary Baker again on July 3, 1917 and told him "that Senator Williams said that there is some danger of trouble of a serious nature if this officer is not separated from his present command." On July 9, 1917, Wilson wrote, "I am sorry to bother you [Secretary Baker] about the case [white officer] . . . but the trouble it would seem is not now the fear . . . that he will be put under a Negro officer but that it has got on his nerves that he himself remains an officer in a Negro regiment, and I was wondering whether without violation of the best practices of the department some officer of Northern birth could be substituted for him."

On July 7, 1917, Secretary of War Baker wrote President Wilson: "Prior to your note to me Lieutenant Colonel Young was ordered before a retiring board on the report of the surgeons that he was incapacitated for duty by reason of Bright's disease. Meanwhile, the adjutant general of the State of Ohio has urgently requested his services with the colored command of that state. As soon as the proceedings of the retiring board have been completed and pending final action on them by the War Department, Colonel Young will be directed to report to the adjutant general of the state of Ohio for the above duty. This, I think, will remove the cause of trouble so far as I now understand it. The Colonel [of the white officer] is a white officer, as are also the other officers of the regiment." The War Department issued orders on July 10, 1917 assigning Colonel Young to the adjutant general of Ohio for duty. Colonel Young was later retired from active service and remained in the area of Wilberforce, Ohio.

On June 6, 1918, in an attempt to prove his physical fitness for active duty Colonel Young rode on horseback and walked one quarter of the way from Ohio to Washington, four hundred and ninety-seven miles and unattended. Young arrived in Washington on June 22, 1918 having rested only one day. The trip lasted sixteen days. Colonel Young was recalled to active service in 1918, though the war was near its end. He was assigned to Camp Grant, Illinois, and he returned to Monrovia, Liberia as Military Attache in 1919.

On November 15, 1921, Colonel Young departed on the Spanish steamer, *Catalina* for Fernando Po and Nigeria. Colonel Young was

*Lieutenant Colonel Charles Young*

admitted on December 25, 1921 to Gray's Hospital, Lagos, Nigeria suffering from nephritis, medically reported as "acute exacerbation of an old-standing complaint." He was attended daily by a European physician, Dr. Aitken. He died on January 8, 1922, was given a military funeral in Lagos, Nigeria and buried in an English cemetery. His body was brought to the United States in 1923 and on June 1, 1923, America's third black West Point graduate was given a hero's burial in Arlington National Cemetery.[74]

*A Spanish block house on San Juan Hill,
Santiago (top left); Sergeant William Chambers,
Sergeant Major A. A. Marrow and
Commissary Sergeant D. P. Green in the
Philippines (top right); Company L of the
Sixth Regiment, Massachusetts Volunteer
Infantry, on their return from Cuba (above)
and black scouts in the Philippines (below).*

Berthdecks Cooks, USS Atlanta (above)
and U.S. Army Chaplains (below)

Gunners Gang of the USS Maine,
"Uncle Sam's Navy"

*Officers of the Seventh U.S. Volunteer Infantry (above); Company F. Eighth Illinois (left), Barber shop, USS Brooklyn*

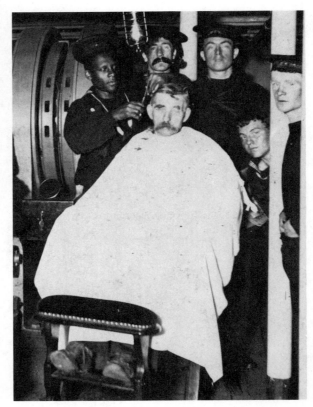

### James Hunter Young

Lieutenant Colonel, Thirty-Second North Carolina Volunteer Regiment.

James Young was born in 1860 at Henderson, North Carolina. He attended public schools in Henderson and Shaw University, North Carolina. In 1877, he accepted a position as a federal officer and for eight years was a deputy collector for the Internal Revenue Service. He was appointed Registrar of Deeds, Wake County, North Carolina, for three years in 1886. He also served for four years as special customs inspector, district of North Carolina, South Carolina and Georgia. He was a member of the state legislature in 1895, representing Wake County, and was appointed state inspector of agriculture in the same year. Young's outstanding background in state legislative positions was instrumental in his selection for field grade rank in the North Carolina Volunteers during the Spanish-American War.[75]

*Lieutenant Colonel James Hunter Young*

## Notes to Chapter Six

1. Harry Stanton, B. S. McCord and Henry Turnley, *History of the Eighth Illinois Volunteers Infantry Regiment* (Chicago: E. F. Harmon Co., 1899).
2. William J. Simmons, *Men of Mark* (George M. Rewell & Co., 1887), pp. 595–598.
3. Stanton *et al., History of the Eighth Illinois.*
4. *The Colored American Magazine* 4 (April, 1902).
5. H. V. F. Cashin *et al. Under Fire With the Tenth U.S. Cavalry* (New York: Alexander & Cashin, 1899), pp. 289–291.
6. *Medal of Honor Recipients, 1863–1963.* 88th Congress, 2nd Session, Committee Print (Washington, D.C.: U.S. Government Printing Office, 1964).
7. *Ibid.*
8. Stanton *et al., History of the Eighth Illinois.*
9. *Medal of Honor Recipients, 1863–1963.*
10. Cashen *et al. Under Fire with the Tenth U.S. Cavalry.*
11. Stanton *et al. History of the Eighth Illinois.*
12. Cashin *et al. Under Fire with the Tenth U.S. Cavalry,* pp. 57–62.
13. J. J. Pipkin, *The Negro in Revelation in History and in Citizenship* (St. Louis: N. D. Thompson Co., 1902).
14. *Crisis Magazine* 14 (June 2, 1917), p. 83.
15. Stanton *et al., History of the Eighth Illinois.*
16. Edward A. Johnson, *A History of Negro Soldiers in the Spanish-American War.*
17. J. J. Pipkin, *The Negro in Revelation.*
18. Stanton *et al., History of the Eighth Illinois.*
19. *Ibid.*
20. Hilary W. Coston, *The Spanish-American War Volunteers* (1899).
21. Stanton *et al., History of the Eighth Illinois.*
22. *Ibid.*
23. A. B. Caldwell, *History of the American Negro, North Carolina Edition.* (Atlanta: A. B. Caldwell Publishing Co., 1922).
24. Stanton *et al., History of the Eighth Illinois.*

25. *Ibid.*
26. *Medal of Honor Recipients, 1863–1963.*
27. *Crisis Magazine* (April, 1916), p. 291.
28. Coston, *The Spanish-American War Volunteers.*
29. Military Pension File of James Gilliard, RG 15, Record of the Adjutant General's Office, National Archives, Washington, D.C.
30. *Crisis Magazine* 2 (November, 1915).
31. U.S. Coast Guard Public Affairs Office, Washington, D.C., Official Register of Officers, U.S. Revenue Cutler Service, U.S. Coast Guard Public Information Division.
   Albert S. Foley, *God's Men of Color* (New York: Farrar, Strauss & Co., 1955).
   Josephine Kelly, *Dark Shepherd* (Paterson, N.J.: St. Anthony Guild Press, 1967).
   *Report of the Revenue Steamer Corwin in the Arctic Ocean,* Captain M. S. Healy U.S. Revenue Marine Commander (Washington, D.C., U.S. Government Printing Office, 1887).
32. Stanton *et al., History of the Eighth Illinois.*
33. *Ibid.*
34. *Ibid.*
35. Coston, *The Spanish-American War Volunteers.*
36. Medley and Jensen, *Illustrated Review, Ninth U.S. Cavalry* (Fort D. A. Russell, Wyoming, 1910).
37. Stanton *et al. History of the Eighth Illinois.*
38. *Ibid.*
39. *The New Business League Herald* 1, No. 2 (May 15, 1909).
40. Maurine Christopher, *America's Black Congressmen* (New York: Thomas Y. Crowell Cp., 1971).
41. Stanton *et al., History of the Eighth Illinois.*
42. The University of Texas, Institute of Texan Cultures, Record of Hugh Melray, San Antonio, Texas.
43. Stanton *et al., History of the Eighth Illinois.*
44. *Ibid.*
45. *Ibid.*
46. William C. Payne, *The Cruise of the USS Dixie or On Board with the Maryland Boys in the Spanish-American War* (Washington, D.C.: E. C. Jones, 1899).
47. *Medal of Honor Recipients, 1863–1963.*
48. *Washington Post,* July 13, 1938, Morland Room Founders Library, Howard University, Washington, D.C.
49. *Crisis Magazine* 16 (May, 1918).
50. Daniel Smith Lamb, *Howard University Medal Department* (Washington, D.C.: Beresford, 1900), p. 134.
51. Stanton *et al., History of the Eighth Illinois.*
52. *Ibid.*
53. *Crisis Magazine* 9 (December, 1914).
54. Stanton *et al., History of the Eighth Illinois.*
55. Caldwell, *History of the American Negro, Washington, D.C. Edition.*
56. *The Afro-American Beacon Light* (New York City) 2 (1897).
57. Stanton *et al., History of the Eighth Illinois.*
58. *Ibid.*
59. *Ibid.*
60. *Medal of Honor Recipients, 1863–1963.*
61. Dennis D. Nelson, *The Integration of the Negro in the United States Navy* (New York: Farrar, Straus, 1951).
62. Stanton *et al., History of the Eighth Illinois.*
63. Medley and Jenson, *Illustrated Review, Ninth U.S. Cavalry.*
64. *Medal of Honor Recipients, 1863–1963.*
65. Lamb, *Howard University Medical Department.*
66. Stanton *et al., History of the Eighth Illinois.*
67. Medley and Jenson, *Illustrated Review, Ninth U.S. Cavalry.*
68. *Ibid.*
69. Stanton *et al., History of the Eighth Illinois.*
70. *The Colored American Magazine* (n.d.), p. 460.
71. Stanton *et al., History of the Eighth Illinois.*
72. *Ibid.*
73. Caldwell, *History of the American Negro, Georgia Edition.*
74. Robert E. Greene, "Colonel Charles Young, Soldier and Diplomat" (unpublished manuscript).
   ———. "The Early Life of Colonel Charles Young 1864–1889," (1973) Department of History, Howard University.
75. *American Annual Cyclopedia* (New York: D. Appleton & Co., 1861–1902).

# Chapter Seven

## World War I, 1914-1918

During the period 1900–1917, the four regular Negro regiments and two volunteer units (forty-eighth and forty-ninth) were ordered to the Philippines, where they served during the insurrection. At the beginning of World War I, the black Americans were again summoned to service. Negro National Guard Units were the nucleus of the Ninety-Third Provisional Division, designated primarily for purposes of administration. A second division was organized, the Ninety-Second, which fought with the American armies while the Ninety-Third was brigaded with French troops. Units of the Ninety-Third were among the first American combat troops to arrive in France. The Three hundred and Sixty-Ninth, Three Hundred and Seventieth, Three Hundred and Seventy-First, and Three Hundred and Seventy-Second infantry regiments compiled an outstanding record while serving abroad. Some Negro units also served as supply troops during the war.

Negro troops participated in the battles of Argonne, Chateau Thierry, St. Mihiel, Champagne, Vosges, and Metz. Nearly four hundred thousand Negroes served during World War I according to Emmett Scott, former civilian aide to the Secretary of War, and their accomplishments were numerous. The Croix de Guerre was awarded to 171 Negro troops. There were two outstanding black heroes of the war, Henry Johnson of Albany, New York, and Needham Roberts of Trenton, New Jersey. Negro troops also served as pioneers in labor battalions, butchery companies and engineer service battalions.

Although the Negro draftees' overall training and educational background were quite low during World War I, black soldiers overcame many obstacles and their list of achievements and honors is further proof of their ability on the battlefield.

The following pages note some of the exploits and attainments of America's black veterans of World War I.

### Urbane F. Bass

Lieutenant, Three Hundred and Seventy-Second Infantry Regiment.

Urbane Bass, a native of Fredericksburg, Virginia, received his military training at Fort Des Moines, Iowa. He graduated from Shaw University in 1906 and practiced medicine in Fredericksburg until his army service. After being commissioned a lieutenant, Bass performed his duties as a medical officer in the Three Hundred and Seventy-Second Infantry Regiment in a dedicated and heroic manner. On October 7, while attending wounded soldiers on the firing line, he was struck by a shell which caused his legs to be severed at the thigh. Lieutenant Bass gave his life in the service of his country.[1]

*Lieutenant Robert C. Allen*

*William Henry Brooks*

*Lieutenant Robert S. Campbell*

**Robert S. Campbell**

Lieutenant, Three Hundred and Sixty-Eighth U.S. Infantry Regiment.

Robert Campbell was awarded the Distinguished Service Cross during World War I for bravery in combat operations in the Argonne Forest.[2]

**William Creigler**

Captain, Maryland National Guard, Separate Company.

William Creigler was born on August 26, 1884, in Baltimore, Maryland. He enlisted in the Separate Company of the Maryland National Guard on April 18, 1904, and served overseas during World War I as a first sergeant. His company, as Company I of the Three Hundred and Sixty-Seventh Infantry, was the first of the Maryland National Guard to leave for France after America entered the war. The company arrived in April, 1918, and was sent to the Argonne Forest area. During one of the battles in the Argonne, every officer was wounded and Creigler assumed command and led his men in an attack. He was later awarded the French Croix de Guerre and in August, 1921, when the company was reorganized, Creigler was promoted from sergeant to captain.[3]

**Arthur Leo Curtis**

First Lieutenant, Medical Corps, U.S. Army.

Arthur Curtis was born in Chicago, Illinois on July 26, 1889, the son of Dr. Austin M. Curtis and Namayoka Sockume Curtis who was of Delaware Indian ancestry. He went to school in Chicago and continued his education in Washington, D.C., where his family moved later. He attended Williston Academy, East Hampton, Massachusetts and graduated from Howard University's College of Medicine in 1912. He completed an internship at Freedman's Hospital and started a practice in Washington, D.C. in 1913.

Dr. Curtis volunteered for army service in 1918 and was commissioned a lieutenant in the Medical Corps. He was assigned to France and was one of the six Negro physicians at a field hospital at Dijon, France. After the war, Curtis returned to Washington, where he resumed the practice of medicine and was a member of the medical staff at Freedman's Hospital.[4]

*Major —— Dean*

*Lieutenant Colonel Otis B. Duncan*

## James Reese Europe

First Lieutenant, Three Hundred and Sixty-Ninth U.S. Infantry (Former Fifteenth New York National Guard).

James Europe was born in Mobile, Alabama, on February 20, 1884, the son of Henry Jefferson and Lorraine Saxon Europe. His father worked as a postal clerk in Mobile, Alabama and Washington, D.C. Europe attended grammar schools and the old "M" Street high school. As a young man he went to New York and began to travel as a violinist with Cole and Johnson, later becoming their musical director. He also founded the Clef Club. Europe was successful in organizing orchestras, and he did extensive business in supplying bands and players for society functions on the east coast. He was married to Mrs. Willie Starke on January 15, 1912.

During World War I, Europe was commissioned as a lieutenant and traveled in France as the conductor of the Fifteenth New York Infantry Band (Three Hundred and Sixty-Ninth U.S. Infantry).

James Reese Europe was often called the King of Jazz. For several years he led a band called Europe's Society Orchestra. During World War I, while serving in France, Europe participated in Paris in a contest of the five greatest bands of all the Allies, and his band won the prize. Later in the war, Europe was sent to the trenches and was put in charge of a machine gun company. He served a long period of combat and was gassed. After his recovery, he was reassigned to the band. Lieutenant Europe returned to the United States in January, 1919 and went on tour with his orchestra. While playing in Boston, he met an untimely death at the hands of a member of his band whose performance he had criticised.

His public funeral was held in New York City, New York, and it was said that he had one of the largest funerals that New York had seen since General Grant's death. Services were conducted in Washington, D.C. at Lincoln Temple Church. James Reese Europe was buried in Arlington National Cemetery with military honors. He was thirty-five years of age at the time of his death in 1919.[5]

*First Lieutenant James Reese Europe*

*Private Henry Johnson*

### Henry Johnson

Private, Three Hundred and Sixty-Ninth U.S. Infantry Regiment (former Fifteenth New York Regiment).

Henry Johnson was born in Albany, New York. During World War I, his unit was attached to French troops and had the responsibility of defending a long sector of front line trenches. One night in May, 1918, when Johnson was assigned to Company C, he was on double sentry duty. He was assaulted by a group of at least a dozen Germans, shot and wounded one of them and severely injured two others. Ignoring three wounds of his own, he ran to the assistance of a wounded comrade who was about to be carried away by the enemy. Johnson continued his resistance until the Germans retreated. Johnson was one of the first Americans to be awarded the French Croix de Guerre during World War I.[6]

### Thomas Edward Jones

Captain, Medical Corps.

Thomas Jones was born at Hill City, Lynchburg, Virginia, on May 26, 1880, the son of Campbell and Emma Glen Jones. He attended school in Lynchburg and graduated from Howard University College of Medicine in 1912. As a student, he worked as newsboy, waiter, watchman, messenger, and government laborer. After graduating he started medical practice in Washington, D.C. and during World War I was commissioned as an officer, attaining the rank of captain in the U.S. Army Medical Corps. He served in France for eight

*Captain Thomas E. Jones*

months in the Meuse-Argonne and Vosges defensive sector, and was awarded the Distinguished Service Cross for his courageous performance of duty. After the war he returned to Washington and was appointed to the staff of Freedmen's Hospital. He married Mrs. Leonie A. Sinkler of Charleston, South Carolina.[7]

*Captain Max C. King*

### Max C. King

Captain, Medical Corps, U.S. Army.

Max King was born on July 5, 1886 in Franklinton, North Carolina, the son of Guilford and Mary C. Cook King. He was educated at local schools and worked for some time on his parents' farm. Later he attended Franklin Christian College in Franklinton. In 1911, he obtained a bachelor's degree from Shaw University, and in 1915 he received an M.D. from Leonard Medical College. King volunteered for the army at the beginning of World War I and served as a first lieutenant from June, 1918 to February, 1919. On March 18, 1919 he was commissioned a captain, and in August of 1919 he was elected a member of the Association of Military Surgeons. He was one of many black surgeons to serve in the first world war.[8]

### Kenneth Lewis

Private, First Separate Battalion, District of Columbia National Guard.

Kenneth Lewis was a native of Washington, D.C., and volunteered for military service at the age of eighteen. He was killed in combat while serving in France. In recognition of his devotion, courage, and sacrifice, the French Army granted him the Medaille Militaire.[9]

### David Thomas Lynn

Sergeant, Company B, Forty-Eighth U.S. Engineers Regiment.

David Lynn was born on January 6, 1888, at Morrisville, North Carolina. He attended public schools in Morrisville and the Franklin Christian College in Franklinton, North Carolina, where he studied electrical engineering. Lynn joined the army at the beginning of the war and was assigned to the Forty-Eighth Engineers, Company B, reputedly a Caucasian unit. He went to France with this unit and after completing the necessary examinations he was transferred to another all-white unit, the Thirteenth Grand Division, and served as an electrician and mechanic. After the war, Sergeant Lynn returned to Norfolk and worked as an electrician and heating engineer. He was prominent in civic affairs in his community.[10]

### Iverson Othello Mitchell

First Lieutenant, Ninety-Second Division.

Iverson Mitchell was born in Washington, D.C., on June 6, 1893, the son of Paul and Margaret Richards Mitchell. He attended public schools in Washington, and studied at Howard University's College of Dentistry, from which he received the degree of doctor of dental surgery in 1915. He was commissioned a lieutenant in World War I, and served in France with the Ninety-Second Division. After the war, he returned to Washington, D.C., and resumed the practice of dentistry. Lieutenant Mitchell was one of the few commissioned Negro dental officers serving in World War I.[11]

### John H. Patton

Captain, Regimental Adjutant, Eighth Illinois Volunteer Regiment.

John Patton served as the regiment's adjutant

during the period June 26, 1916 to September, 1918. When the unit was called to active service during World War I and redesignated the Three Hundred and Seventieth Infantry, Captain Patton was assigned as commanding officer of the Second Battalion. He served in France and was at the Saint-Mihiel sector, Mont des Signes, and participated in the Oise-Aisne offensive. He was awarded the French Croix de Guerre for meritorious service.[12]

tenant on January 7, 1899, and provost marshal as an additional duty in 1901. According to Special Orders 41, Headquarters, 2nd District, Department of Northern Luzon, Apani, Philippines Island, dated February 19, 1901, "Second Lieutenant Perea, Forty-Ninth Infantry USV, was detailed additional duty as Provost Marshal at Pamplona, P.I." Lieutenant Perea died on April 3, 1915, and was the first known Negro officer to be buried with honors in the National Military Cem-

*Judge Advocate Major Adam Patterson*

*Sergeant William Payne*

### Beverly Perea

First Lieutenant, Seventh, Twenty-Fourth and Forty-Ninth Infantry Regiments.

Beverly Perea was born in Mecklenburg, Virginia. He and his wife, Missouri, had one daughter. Perea enlisted in the army on July 25, 1871, and was assigned at various times to companies A, I, E, B and M of the Twenty-Fourth Infantry Regiment. Perea served continuously for thirty-one years; he was two years, four months and sixteen days on foreign service in the Philippines and for two months and seven days in Cuba. He was cited as a first classman in marksmanship in 1897. Perea was appointed second lieutenant, Seventh U.S. Volunteers on September 16, 1898, first lieu-

etery at Arlington, which had been his dying wish.

Several newspapers carried the account of his death. A Boston paper published in April, 1915, read as follows:

*In response to an appeal of the widow of First Lieutenant Beverly Perea, U.S.A., retired, a colored citizen who died at the Cambridge Hospital Saturday, Mayor Curley has requested Secretary of War Lindley M. Garrison to give permission for the interment of the lieutenant's remains in the Arlington National Cemetery at Washington.*

Major Curley's personal appeal to Secretary Garrison was successful and Lieutenant Perea was buried at Arlington Cemetery on April 10, 1915.

His military records indicate that his service was honest and faithful and his character excellent.[13]

## Howard Donovan Queen

Colonel, Three Hundred and Sixty-Sixth U.S. Infantry Regiment.

Howard Queen was born on November 18, 1894 in Tee Bee, Maryland, the son of Richard Thomas and Rebecca Virginia Queen. He received a degree in engineering from Howard University and also attended various military schools before embarking on an outstanding military career.

Queen enlisted in the Washington, D.C., National Coast Guard in 1910, and served in the Tenth Cavalry from 1911 to 1917. In 1913 he was a corporal with his regiment in Winchester, Virginia, and was duly promoted until he reached the rank of colonel. In 1941 he became the commanding officer of the Three Hundred and Sixty-Sixth Infantry Regiment.

Colonel Queen's tactical experience included the battle at El Carrizal, Mexico, on June 21, 1916; the Punitive Expedition to Mexico with the Tenth Cavalry from 1916–1917; and service in France in the Vosges sector with the Three Hundred and Sixty-Eighth Infantry, the Meuse-Argonne offensive and the Metz sector from 1918–1919, and operations with the Three Hundred and Sixty-Sixth Infantry Regiment. His military lineage can be traced back to the American Revolution. His great-grandfather was present at the Battle of Boston Common; his grandfather and three uncles served with the Union troops during the Civil War, and his father served for fifteen years with the Twenty-Fourth Infantry Regiment and the Tenth U.S. Cavalry. His cousin lost his life aboard the *USS Maine* in the Spanish-American War, and a brother served as an officer with the Three Hundred and Sixty-Eighth Infantry in the Argonne offensive.[14]

## Samuel Alexander Reid

Captain, Three Hundred and Seventeenth Ammunition Train, Ninety-Second Division.

Samuel Reid was born on April 11, 1873, in Township No. 12, Cabarrus County, North Carolina, the son of James S. Reid, a farmer, and Mag-

gie Victoria (Boger) Reid. His father was born free and his mother born into slavery. Reid was educated in the public schools of Cabarrus County and in 1893 he enlisted as a private in the army at Chicago, Illinois. He served in Cuba during the Spanish-American War and was also in the Philippines for three years.

On October 15, 1917, Reid was commissioned a captain at Fort Des Moines, Iowa, and was assigned to the Three Hundred and Seventeenth Ammunition Train, Ninety-Second Division. He saw service in France and in 1918 retired from the army. Captain Reid was a member of the Presbyterian church and of the United Spanish War Veterans and the Military Order of the Serpent.[15]

## Needham Roberts

Private, Three Hundred and Sixty-Ninth U.S. Infantry Regiment (former Fifteenth New York National Guard Regiment).

Needham Roberts was born in Trenton, New Jersey. During World War I, his unit was attached to French troops, with the responsibility of defending a long sector of front line trenches. In May, 1918, Roberts was assigned to Company C. One night, when on double sentry duty, he was assaulted, receiving serious wounds in the leg, but continued to resist the advancing enemy, throwing hand grenades from a prone position until the enemy retreated. Following this action, Private Roberts was one of the first Americans to be awarded the French Croix de Guerre during World War I.[16]

*Private Needham Roberts*

*S.A.T.C. Cadets at Clark Hall, Howard University*

*366th Infantry Officers in France: Lieutenant Colonel Abbott, Captain Joseph Lewis, Lieutenant A. P. Fisher, Captain E. White*

*Black soldiers being decorated in World War I*

Fort Keogh barracks (top left), 370th Infantry
being decorated (top right), Bert Williams
with Colonel Hayward (left). Court martial
of 64 members of 24th Infantry for mutiny and
murder (below left), and a black soldier at
Howard University

*Color Guard of the 9th Cavalry Regiment*

*First Sergeant John C. Sanders*

### John C. Sanders

First Sergeant, Tenth U.S. Cavalry Regiment.

John Sanders served with the Tenth U.S. Cavalry Regiment for twenty-nine years, seven months, and fifteen days. At the time of his retirement on February 3, 1942, Sanders had accumulated the longest service record of any first sergeant in the army, having been promoted to that grade in 1916.[17]

*Emmett J. Scott author of* The Official History of the American Negro in the World War

*Sergeant A. W. Thompson*

### James E. Walker

Major, First Separate Battalion, District of Columbia National Guard.

James Walker was born on September 7, 1874, in the state of Virginia. He attended the "M" Street High School in Washington, D.C., and in 1894 studied at the Miner Normal School. He was affiliated with the District of Columbia for twenty-four years, serving in the position of teacher and supervising principal.

Walker enlisted in the D.C. National Guard and in 1896 was commissioned a first lieutenant. In 1909 he was promoted to the rank of captain and in 1912, through competitive examinations, to major. He was called to active duty in World War I. While his unit was performing guard duty in the White House area, Walker fell ill and was sent to a U.S. Hospital at Fort Bayard, New Mexico, for treatment. He died on April 4, 1918. Major Walker was one of the few Negro field grade officers in the National Guard unit at that time.[18]

### Joseph A. Ward

Major, Medical Corps.

Joseph Ward served as a Medical Corps officer during World War I. It is believed that Major Ward was the only Negro medical officer to attain field grade in this war.[19]

*Major Joseph A. Ward*

*Lieutenant William H. York*

### James Malachi Whittico

First Lieutenant, Medical Corps, U.S. Army.

James Whittico was born on September 22, 1887, in Henry County, Virginia, the son of Hezekiah J. and Letitia Pace Whittico. Whittico's family moved to Williamson, West Virginia. He studied at Martinsville and Mary Potter schools at Oxford, North Carolina. In 1912 he graduated from Meharry Medical College in Nashville, Tennessee and started a general practice in Williamson, West Virginia. Whittico went to Des Moines, Iowa, in 1917 for military training and was commissioned a first lieutenant. He served at Camp Meade and also with the American Expeditionary Forces in France. At the end of the war, he returned to his medical practice in West Virginia.[20]

### William H. York

Lieutenant, U.S. Army.

William York was born in Springfield, Illinois, in 1874. He graduated from Wilberforce University in 1912. While a student cadet in college, he served as a captain in the Student Battalion. He served in the Philippines in 1914, and was appointed a lieutenant in the force that went to Liberia under the command of Colonel Young.[21]

## Notes to Chapter Seven

1. *Crisis Magazine* 17 (February, 1919).
2. Emmett J. Scott, *Scott's Official History of the American Negro in the World War* (Emmett J. Scott, 1919).
3. *Chicago Defender* (December 7, 1944).
4. A. B. Caldwell, *History of the American Negro, Washington, D.C. Edition* (Atlanta: A. B. Caldwell Publishing Co., 1922), pp. 55–56.
5. *Ibid.*
6. Scott, *Scott's Official History*, pp. 256–258.
7. Caldwell, *History of the American Negro, Washington, D.C. Edition*, pp. 99–100.
8. ———, *History of the American Negro, North Carolina Edition*.
9. *Crisis Magazine* 17 (November, 1918).
10. Caldwell, *History of the American Negro, Virginia Edition*, pp. 547–549.
11. ———, *History of the American Negro, Washington, D.C. Edition*, p. 242.
12. *Crisis Magazine*, n.d.
13. Beverly Perea Papers, Manuscript Division, Library of Congress, Washington, D.C.
14. G. James Fleming and Christian E. Burckel (Eds.), *Who's Who in Colored America*, 7th Edition (Yonkers, N.Y.: Christian E. Burckel & Associates, 1950) p. 427.
    *Afro-American* (Baltimore), July 31, 1943.
15. Caldwell, *History of the American Negro, North Carolina Edition*.
16. Scott, *Scott's Official History*, pp. 256–259.
    *Crisis Magazine* (June 1918).
17. Public Information Office, Chief of Information, Department of the Army, Washington, D.C.
18. Scott, *Scott's Official History*.
19. *Ibid.*
20. Caldwell, *History of the American Negro, West Virginia Edition*, pp. 268–270.
21. *Crisis Magazine* 7 (January, 1914).

# Chapter Eight

## World War II, 1939-1945

The employment of black soldiers during World War II in combat operations and the establishment of Negro pilot training opened avenues towards advancement and eventual equality for the blacks in America's military services. Black men were drafted and in some cases volunteered at the beginning of the war. Those with minimal education were assigned to quartermaster, labor and engineer service battalions. Various branches of the three services excluded Negro participation, but due to the administrative and personal effort of civilian aides to the Secretary of War such as Judge William Hastie and Truman Gibson, blacks made great strides towards recognition and equality of assignments.

Black soldiers began to emerge from confinement to labor details and assignments to find opportunities as infantrymen, tankers, parachutists; as officers leading patrols on tactical missions; as pilots, nurses and doctors. The pattern of exclusion because of skin color was beginning to lose its uniformity and strength.

Although the war was nearing its end when combat forces were integrated, black soldiers no less than their white comrades proved themselves worthy of distinguished honors. Black soldiers served in Africa, and in the Pacific and European theaters of war. Although often used in menial and supply functions, their contributions to the overall tactical successes were praised by many senior commanders. When black Americans went into combat in Normandy, in the hills of Italy, and in the Pacific jungles, they established a record of pride and achievement.

Black officers and noncommissioned officers assumed greater responsibilities during World War II. Senior officers serving today received their rudimentary background and training on a wider basis than ever before as black men and women served on land, sea and in the air for the first time in America's history. For the first time the achievements of blacks in military endeavor were documented and accepted without debate or the desire to suppress unwelcome information.

The persons described in this chapter are only a few of the thousands of Negro Americans who served with distinction during World War II.

### Vernon J. Baker

First Lieutenant, Company C, First Battalion, Three Hundred and Seventieth U.S. Infantry Regiment, Ninety-Second Division.

From the following account of Lieutenant Baker's heroic conduct on April 5–6, 1945, he would appear to have deserved serious consideration for a Medal of Honor award. However, there were no such awards to black soldiers in World War II.

On April 5, 1845, the Ninety-Second Division was launching a diversionary attack prior to the Fifth Army's main attack toward Bologna, Italy. The immediate objective for the Ninety-Second's diversionary attack was Massa. The Three Hundred and Seventieth's lead company, C Company, had advanced toward the vicinity of its battal-

*First Lieutenant Vernon J. Baker*

ion objective, Castle Aghinolfi. Mortar and heavy rifle fire caused considerable casualties as the regiment continued its advance in the area of Castle Aghinolfi. The commanding officer of Company C decided that the company should withdraw to battalion lines. The lone Negro officer in the company, Lieutenant Baker, had personally destroyed an observation post, a well-camouflaged machine-gun position, and a dugout during the morning hours of April 5, 1945. Eight German occupants of the dugout were killed. Baker now volunteered to cover the withdrawal of the first group, containing most of the ambulatory wounded men, and to remain to help move the more severely wounded. Baker guarded the rear, leaving last after destroying equipment left by the killed and wounded. During the withdrawal, Baker's group encountered two machine-gun nests bypassed during an earlier attack. Lieutenant Baker, covered by his men, crawled up to the machine-gun positions and destroyed them with hand grenades. The following night, Baker led a battalion advance through heavy mine fields and heavy fire.

General Order 70, HQ Fifth Army, 10 June, 1945, awarded Lieutenant Vernon J. Baker the Distinguished Service Cross.[1]

## William Baldwin

Recruit, U.S. Navy.

William Baldwin was born in Washington, D.C., and it is believed that he was the first Negro recruit (apprentice seaman) inducted into the U.S. Naval Reserve during World War II. He received his oath of office from Navy Secretary Frank Knox.[2]

## Elvin Bell

Mess Attendant, Third Class, U.S. Navy.

Elvin Bell was a resident of Jamaica, New York. He was awarded the Navy and Marine Corps Medal for heroic action while serving on the *USS Lexington*. His citation read:

*For distinguished heroism while serving aboard the* USS Lexington *during the battle of the Coral Sea on May 8, 1942. Voluntarily joining a repair party fighting a fire in an area frequented by violent explosions of gasoline vapor and ammunition, Bell, although emerging in an exhausted condition, unhesitatingly entered the most dangerous section of the stricken carrier and assisted in removing injured personnel who had been trapped below decks. His courageous initiative and utter disregard for his own safety were in keeping with the highest traditions of the United States naval service.*[3]

## Versye O. Berry

Sergeant, Quartermaster Unit, U.S. Army.

Versye Berry had attended Rust College, Mississippi, and Philander Smith College in Arkansas. He was a sergeant in a quartermaster unit at Fort Ord, California. On June 13, 1942, Berry was awarded the Soldiers Medal, and was promoted from corporal to sergeant. The general order authorizing the Soldiers Medal award stated that he displayed heroism at San Bernardino, California. Seeing that a soldier was aiming a 45-calibre service automatic at another soldier with intent to kill, Berry without regard for his own safety succeeded in overpowering and disarming the soldier, thereby preventing the killing of the intended victim and possible injury to other soldiers.[4]

*Colonel Midan Bousefield*

*Lieutenant (JG) James R. Brown*

### John Walter Bowman

First Lieutenant, Chaplain Corps, U.S. Army.

John Bowman, S.V.D., of Lafayette, Louisiana, was the first known Negro Catholic chaplain appointed to the Chaplain Corps during World War II. He was a graduate of St. Augustine's Seminary, Bay St. Louis, Louisiana and parish pastor of the church of the Immaculate Heart of Mary, Lafayette, Louisiana.[5]

### Robert H. Brooks

Private, U.S. Army.

Robert Brooks was born in Tennessee. While serving in the Pacific Theater during World War II he was assigned to an armored unit, and was killed near Fort Stotsenburg, Philippine Islands on December 8, 1941. It is believed that Private Brooks was the first American soldier of the armored force to be killed in the Pacific Theater while engaging in combat operations. The main parade ground at the armor center at Fort Knox, Kentucky, has been named Brooks Field in his honor.[6]

### Edward A. Carter Jr.

Sergeant, Seventh Army Provisional Infantry Company 1, Fifty-Sixth Armored Infantry Battalion.

Edward Carter was awarded a Distinguished Service Cross, announced in HQ Seventh Army General Order 580, for bravery in action on May 23, 1945, when he was with a detachment of the Seventh Army Provisional Company riding on a tank near Speyer, Germany. The tank was confronted with heavy bazooka and small arms fire. Sergeant Carter voluntarily attempted to lead a three-man group across an open field. Within a short time, two of his men were killed and the third seriously wounded. Carter continued toward the enemy emplacement alone, was wounded five times and forced to take cover. When eight enemy riflemen attempted to capture him, Carter killed six of them and took two prisoner. He then returned across the field, using the two prisoners as a shield, and obtained from them valuable information about the disposition of enemy troops.[7]

### Kenneth W. Coleman

Lieutenant, Ninety-Second Division.

Kenneth Coleman was a native of Washington, D.C. He served in the Italian campaign with the Ninety-Second Division, and was awarded a posthumous Silver Star for bravery.[8]

**Joseph Cross**

Steward's Mate First Class, U.S.N.R., U.S. Navy.

Joseph Cross was born in New Orleans, Louisiana. He was awarded the Navy and Marine Corps Medal for unusual bravery in World War II. His citation read as follows:

*For heroic conduct during four submarine war patrols in enemy-controlled waters. Performing his duties with excellent judgment and conscientious skill, Cross contributed materially to the destruction by his ship of an important amount of Japanese shipping. His resolute courage was in keeping with the highest traditions of the United States naval service.*[9]

**Phyllis Daley**

Ensign, U.S. Navy Nurse Corps.

Phyllis Daley was the first Negro nurse to be commissioned in the Navy Nurse Corps during World War II. She was commissioned in New York City where she had served as a public health nurse for the New York City Department of Health and had almost two years of graduate nurse experience. During the early part of the war, there was considerable controversy about accepting Negro females as nurses in the armed forces. The selection of Miss Daley at that time was a milestone in the Negro female's progress in the navy's integration program.[10]

**Charles W. David**

Mess Attendant, U.S. Coast Guard.

Charles David was a resident of New York City. He and his wife Kathleen had a son, Neil Adrian. During World War II, he gave his life rescuing his executive officer and others from the icy waters of the Atlantic during rescue operations of torpedoed transport. The Navy and Marine Corps Medal was presented to his widow. The citation read:

*Quickly realizing that the benumbed and suffering men were too exhausted to climb aboard the rescue vessel because of heavy seas and intensely cold wind, David unhesitatingly volunteered to go over the side to assist them. Despite the rough near-freezing water and gale, he worked tirelessly with several comrades until ninety-six survivors had been rescued from certain death in the steadily mounting seas. His great courage and unselfish perseverance contributed to the saving of many lives and were in keeping with the highest traditions of the United States naval service.*[11]

*Lieutenant Lycurgus Connor*

*Mess Attendant Charles W. David*

*Brigadier General Benjamin O. Davis Sr.*

## Benjamin Oliver Davis Sr.

Brigadier General, U.S. Army.

Benjamin Davis Sr. was born on July 1, 1877 in Washington, D.C. He was the son of Louis P. H. and Henrietta Stewart Davis. He married Elnora Dickerson of Washington in 1902 (deceased 1916) and later married Sadie E. Overton of Mississippi, in 1919. He had three children, Olive Elnora (Mrs. George W. Streator), Lieutenant General Benjamin O. Davis Jr. (Ret.), Elnora Dickerson (Mrs. James A. McLendon). General Davis attended the Washington public schools and Howard University. He was commissioned a first lieutenant in the Eighth U.S. Volunteer Infantry and served from 1898–1899. He was mustered out, reenlisted as a private and became a squadron sergeant in the Ninth Cavalry, 1899–1901. On February 2, 1901 he was commissioned a second lieutenant in the Cavalry Regular Army. He was promoted periodically during the period 1901–1930 and attained the rank of general in 1940. He was commanding officer of the Three Hundred and Sixty-Ninth Infantry, New York National Guard, 1938–1940. He served with the Tenth Cavalry in Samar and Panay, Philippine Islands during the Insurrection of 1901–1902. General Davis was military attaché at the American Legation, Monrovia, Liberia from 1911–1912. He was in the Mexican Border Patrol from 1915–1917, and served as professor of military science at Wilberforce University and Tuskegee, Alabama. General Davis was the commanding general of the Fourth Cavalry Brigade from 1941–1944. During World War II he was a special advisor and coordinator to the theatre commander, European Theatre of Operations, 1944–1945. In 1945, he was appointed an assistant to the inspector general and later a special assistant to the secretary of the army. He was awarded a scroll by President Roosevelt for his fifty years service in the U.S. Army. General Davis retired from the army in 1948. He was appointed by the president as a special representative (with rank of ambassador extraordinary and plenipotentiary) to the First Centennial of Independence, Republic of Liberia.

General Davis' many decorations and awards have included Spanish-American War, Philippine Insurrection, Mexican Border, World War I, and World War II service medals: the Distinguished Service Cross, the Bronze Star medal and the French Croix de Guerre with Palm. He was the first Negro-American general in the United States military organization since the Reconstruction period, and was actually the first black general in the active regular army. During Reconstruction the Negro generals were in the state militia or national guard. General Davis died on November 26, 1970, at the Great Lakes Naval Hospital.[12]

*General Davis pins the Distinguished Flying Cross on his son, Colonel Benjamin O. Davis Jr.*

The 404th Army Services Band, recruited from members of the Women's Army Corps (top); Corporal Evelyn Rivers, teletype operator (below left) and apprentices Ruth C. Isaacs, Katherine Horton and Inez Patterson, the first black WAVES to enter the Hospital Corps

Black anti-aircraft gunners sight a Japanese
bomber (left); Representative Frances Bolton
meets Negro WAC officers at Fort Des Moines—
left to right are 2nd Officer Ruth Greeman,
1st Officer Charity Adams, 2nd Officer Sarah
Emmert and 2nd Officer Abbie N. Campbell
(below left); the first Negro WAVES
commissioned: Lt. (JG) Harriet Ida Parks and
Ensign Frances Wills (above), and Provost
Marshall George W. Webb inspects Negro Air
Corps cadets at the Basic and Advanced
Flying School at Tuskegee.

**Alonzo Douglas**

Sergeant, Twenty-Fourth Infantry Regiment.

Alonzo Douglas, a native of Chicago, Illinois, was assigned to the Twenty-Fourth Infantry during World War II. He saw front-line action with the regiment in the Solomon Islands (Bougainville) in 1944. According to newspaper accounts in the *Washington Post* and the *New York Times* of March 17, 1944, Sergeant Douglas was the first Negro infantryman to cause an enemy casualty in the Solomons. This was news because past military policies had excluded Negro troops from combat operations in the Pacific Theatre during World War II.

The Twenty-Fourth Infantry Regiment's First Battalion landed at Empress Augusta Bay, Bougainville, on January 30, 1944, as a support in the Fourteenth Corps Reserve. Four weeks later, on February 29, 1944, a decision was made to relieve the First Battalion of their service duties and attach them to the Thirty-Seventh Division to assist in the construction of regimental reserve line positions.[13]

**Joseph D. Elsberry**

Captain, Three Hundred and Thirty-Second Fighter Group, U.S. Army Air Force.

Joseph Elsberry received the Distinguished Flying Cross on September 10, 1944, while serving in Italy. His award was for extraordinary achievement in aerial flight against the enemy in the North African and Mediterranean Theatre of Operations. The citation read as follows:

*Throughout the extensive air offensive against the enemy in direct support of our ground troops and against targets of vital strategic importance deep within hostile territory, he through his aggressiveness and courage, has consistently aided in the success of combat operations. Against heavy and accurate enemy anti-aircraft fire, with his plane frequently seriously damaged by enemy fire, he had battled his way to his targets, defeating the enemy in the air and destroying his vital installations on the ground.*[14]

**Charles Sumner Finch**

Lieutenant Colonel, Medical Corps, U.S. Army.

Charles Finch graduated from the Michigan College of Medicine in 1934, and completed additional studies at the University of Pennsylvania's Graduate School. Before entering the military service, he was in private practice in Los Angeles. Finch, who is both a physician and psychiatrist, was commissioned a lieutenant in 1941, and during his military career has been assigned positions as assistant or chief of neuropsychiatry, psychology and mental hygiene sections at various installations in the United States and overseas. In 1959, Lieutenant Colonel Finch was appointed chief of the U.S. Disciplinary Barracks Mental Hygiene Department at Fort Leavenworth, Kansas. He has served over twenty years in the U.S. Army and has made an outstanding contribution in his field of endeavor. He and his wife are the parents of six children.[15]

**Royall B. Fleming**

Captain, Three Hundred and Sixty-Sixth Infantry Regiment.

Royall Fleming is a native of Kansas City, Missouri. During World War II, he served as a medical officer with the Three Hundred and Sixty-Sixth Infantry Regiment near Viareggio, Italy. Captain Fleming was cited for gallantry for his outstanding performance of duty as a medical officer.[16]

**Trueheart Fogg**

Private First Class, Ninety-Second Division.

Trueheart Fogg, a native of Newark, New Jersey, was assigned to the Ninety-Second Division in Italy during World War II. He killed a four-man enemy machine gun crew in action at Serchio Valley on December 26, 1944. He also halted a twenty-five-man German raiding party and single-handedly knocked out another enemy machine gun, thereby saving his platoon from probable annihilation. Fogg was awarded the Silver Star for this valorous action.[17]

**Wade Foggie**

Private, Company F, Second Battalion, Twenty-Fifth Infantry Regiment, Ninety-Third Division.

Wade Foggie was awarded his division's first Bronze Star in a General Order published on August 4, 1944 for valiant action in the Solomon Islands. When the Twenty-Fifth Regimental Combat Team arrived on Bougainville on March 29, 1944, the Second Battalion, One Hundred and Eighty-Second Infantry, was detached temporarily and assigned to a special task force, Thirty-Seventh Division. The task force was given a mission to pursue and destroy the enemy detachment withdrawing east and north along the Laruma River. The Second Battalion was ordered to ford the Laruma and proceed eastward, protecting lines of communication and securing a trail junction. On April 3, 1944, Private Foggie set up his rocket launcher while being subjected to heavy enemy fire and then fired eight rounds into three enemy pillboxes, destroying them and killing about ten of the hostile force.[18]

*Cadet James D. Fowler*

### Charles Jackson French

Mess Attendant Second Class, U.S. Navy.

Charles French, a resident of Foreman, Arkansas, was commended by Admiral William F. Halsey, U.S. Navy, Commander South Pacific Area and South Pacific Force, for heroism while serving on a destroyer in the Pacific area. His commendation, announced May 18, 1943, read as follows:

*For meritorious conduct in action while serving on board a destroyer transport which was badly damaged during the engagement with Japanese forces in the British Solomon Islands on September 5, 1942. After the engagement, a group of about fifteen men were adrift on a raft which was being deliberately shelled by Japanese naval forces. French tied a line to himself and swam for more than two hours without rest, thus attempting to tow the raft. His conduct was in keeping with the highest traditions of the naval service.[19]*

### Charles F. Gandy Jr.

Captain, Company F, Second Battalion, Three Hundred and Seventieth Regiment, Ninety-Second Division.

Charles Gandy was born in Washington, D.C. His performance of duty while assigned to the Ninety-Second Division was outstanding. On August 28, 1944, General Clark, the Army Commander, while visiting the Three Hundred and Seventieth Regimental Combat Team, promoted Gandy on the spot. He was recommended by his colonel as a qualified lieutenant long overdue for promotion. On October 12, 1944, Captain Gandy, though mortally wounded, led his company out of enemy fire into a safe area. His citation for the Silver Star medal read as follows.

*He personally led his company out in broad daylight and, through further reconnaissance and by personal example and leadership, succeeded in getting his entire company across a canal, with an abrupt twelve-foot wall. This was accomplished in rain and under extremely heavy enemy fire.*

*Halting the company at its intermediate objective, Captain Gandy went forward alone to reconnoiter the route of the next movement. While engaged in this activity, he was mortally wounded by enemy machine-gun fire. His outstanding gallantry and leadership in combat exemplify the heroic traditions of the U.S. Army.*[20]

**Clarence W. Griggs**

Captain (Chaplain), Five Hundred and Fourth Port Battalion.

Clarence Griggs was born in Temple, Texas, and before he entered military service in 1942 was the executive secretary of the Carver Welfare League at Schenectady, New York. He received his theological training at Union Theological Seminary, and was also a supply minister at an Indian Reservation. Chaplain Griggs was killed in action at Okinawa on April 12, 1945.[21]

reprinted. Haley returned to the United States on a service magazine assignment in 1944 and was reassigned to edit *Out Post,* the official Coast Guard publication. He won the Ships' Editorial Association award in 1945; was assistant to the public relations officer, Coast Guard District Headquarters from 1945 to 1949, and became the first chief journalist in the Coast Guard in 1949. He is the author of "They Drive You Crazy" in *This Week,* 1948, and many other articles.

In recent years he has been pursuing investigations into a study of his African heritage. His researches have taken him to Africa where he has traced his own ancestral line.[22]

*Chief Journalist Alexander P. Haley*

*Captain Charles Hall*

**Alexander Palmer Haley**

Chief Journalist, U.S. Coast Guard.

Alex Haley was born in Ithaca, New York on August 11, 1921, and attended State Teachers College, Elizabeth City, North Carolina, from 1937–1939. He enlisted in the U.S. Coast Guard as a mess attendant in 1939. He gained national attention as editor of the ship's paper aboard a Pacific supply vessel when one of his editorials was widely

*Colonel West A. Hamilton*

### West A. Hamilton

Colonel, U.S. Army.

Colonel Hamilton, a native of Washington, D.C., has had an illustrious career in the reserve and on active military service. In 1905 he enlisted as a private in the District of Columbia National Guard. In 1920, he was commissioned a captain in the reserve, following a tour in France during World War I. Colonel Hamilton was very interested in the reserve officer training program and his untiring efforts were beneficial in assisting many Negro men to obtain commissions. In 1926, 1928 and 1932, he was largely responsible for the presence of Negro officers at summer camps at Camp Devens, Camp Ritchie, and Fort Washington. In 1935, he was responsible for the formation of a training unit at Fort Howard, Maryland.

Colonel Hamilton's military experience has included participation in the Mexican border campaigns and the two world wars. He has also served as professor of military science at various colleges. He has held assignments with the office of the Chief of Staff, Eighth Service Command, Dallas, Texas, and as an administrative inspector and a member of the Discharge Review Boards.

The above is a brief resumé of the outstanding accomplishments of Colonel Hamilton. His contributions to the civilian community have been commendable, but his military exploits will always be regarded as a major contributing factor in the development of the Negro Reserve officer programs prior to World War II.[23]

### Leonard Roy Harmon

Mess Attendant First Class, U.S. Navy.

Leonard Harmon was a resident of Texas. During World War II, he distinguished himself heroically when he rendered valuable assistance to wounded personnel during a combat operation. He was awarded the Navy Cross posthumously. On June 8, 1943, the Secretary of the Navy, Frank Knox, asked Mrs. N. Harmon Carroll of Cuero, Texas to sponsor the destroyer escort *USS Harmon,* which was launched July 10, 1943 at Hingham, Massachusetts and was named in honor of Mrs. Carroll's son the late Leonard Roy Harmon. The citation for Harmon's Navy Cross award read as follows:

*For extraordinary heroism while serving aboard the* USS San Francisco *during action against enemy Japanese forces in the Solomon Islands area on November 12 and 13, 1942, with persistent disregard for his own personal safety, Harmon rendered invaluable assistance in caring for the wounded and evacuating them to a dressing station. In addition to displaying unusual loyalty in behalf of the injured executive officer, he deliberately exposed himself to hostile gunfire in order to protect a shipmate and as a result of this courageous deed, he was killed.*[24]

### Ivan Harrison

Captain, Seven Hundred and Sixty-First Tank Battalion.

Ivan Harrison was born in Detroit, Michigan. When he assumed command of the Seven-Hundred and Sixty-First Tank Battalion on November 3, 1945, he became the first Negro tank battalion commander. Before entering the service he worked in the post office in Cleveland, Ohio. Captain Harrison served courageously during World War II.[25]

**Eldern Holly**

Command Sergeant Major, Fourth Battalion (Hercules), First Artillery Regiment.

Eldern Holly entered military service in November, 1941, and in September, 1945, was promoted to first sergeant. He has completed over twenty-eight years of active service. During his career he has served overseas in the Southwest Pacific Islands, New Guinea, the Philippine Islands, France, Germany, Korea, and the Republic of South Vietnam. In the United States he has been stationed in Virginia, North Carolina, California, Kentucky, Kansas, Alaska, Massachusetts and Maryland. His decorations and awards include the Bronze Star (with one oak leaf cluster), Army Commendation medal (with two oak leaf clusters), Good Conduct medal (with six clasps), American Defense Service medal, American Campaign medal, Asiatic Pacific Campaign medal (with two Bronze Stars), National Defense Service medal, World War II Victory medal, and Philippine Defense Ribbon, Philippine Liberation Ribbon, Philippine Independence Ribbon, Republic of Vietnam Campaign Ribbon, Vietnam Cross of Gallantry (with palms), and the Air medal (with 4 oak leaf clusters). He has been assigned to artillery, transportation, ordnance and infantry units.[26]

**Jack D. Holsclaw**

First Lieutenant, Three Hundred and Thirty Second Fighter Group, U.S. Army Air Force.

Jack Holsclaw was awarded the Distinguished Flying Cross for action on July 18, 1944, when he led his flight as escort to heavy bombers attacking installations in Germany and despite severe weather conditions, brought it through to engage an enemy force of approximately three hundred army fighters. His citation read:

*In the ensuing engagement, despite the superiority in numbers of enemy aircraft, with complete disregard for his personal safety, Lieutenant Holsclaw, with an outstanding display of aggressiveness and combat proficiency, destroyed two enemy fighters and forced the remainder to break off their organized attack.*[27]

*Command Sergeant Major Eldern Holly (left) and Colonel Chaunsey Hooper (above)*

*Lieutenant Edward S. Hope*

### Edward Swain Hope

Lieutenant, Engineer Corps, U.S. Naval Reserve.

Edward Hope was the first Negro to obtain the rank of lieutenant in the U.S. Navy when he was commissioned, on May 15, 1944, in the Civil Engineer Corps of the U.S. Naval Reserve. Before his commission he was employed at Howard University, Washington, D.C. His primary assignment was at the U.S Naval Construction Training Center, Davisville, Rhode Island.[28]

### June Jefferson Jr.

Private First Class, Company A, Four Hundred and Fourteenth Infantry Regiment, One Hundred and Forty-Fourth Infantry Division.

June Jefferson was awarded the Silver Star during World War II while serving in the European Theater. His citation read as follows:

*When an enemy tank crashed through a road block and entered a recently captured town, Private Jefferson voluntarily and at great risk of his life crossed open, fire-swept terrain in the face of direct fire from the tank, made his way to the house where the tank was located, and dropped incendiary and fragmentation grenades into the open turret of the tank, causing it to catch fire.*

*As the crew emerged, he killed them with his rifle. He then returned to his position and quickly organized an assault of the enemy riflemen who were supporting the tank, killing, wounding, or capturing all of the enemy infantrymen.*[29]

### Ernest A. Jenkins

Private, Quartermaster Corps Unit.

Ernest Jenkins was a native of New York, and was assigned to the European Theater during World War II. He was awarded the Silver Star for action in France before its liberation. While driving a major through the town of Chateaudun, Jenkins and the officer located and destroyed an enemy gun position, killing three members of the crew and wounding others. After silencing the gun, Private Jenkins assisted the major in the capture of fifteen enemy soldiers found in a cave. Jenkins was credited with assisting in the capture of the city.[30]

### Joseph C. Jenkins

Ensign, U.S. Coast Guard.

Joseph Jenkins graduated from officers' training school on April 14, 1942. He was assigned as an engineering officer in Boston, Massachusetts, and it is believed that he commanded an integrated unit. Ensign Jenkins was one of the few Negro officers commissioned in the U.S. Coast Guard during World War II.[31]

### Philip T. Johnson

Major, Medical Corps.

Philip Johnson of Washington, D.C. was the chief of the Orthopedic and Physical Therapy Section, Hospital Number One, Fort Hauchuca, Arizona, during World War II. He was also an associate professor of Orthopedic Surgery at Freedmen's Hospital, Washington, D.C. Major Johnson was one of the few Negro medical personnel to attain prestigious positions in the medical services in the second world war period.[32]

### Ervin Lattimore

Sergeant, Seven Hundred and Sixty-First Tank Battalion, attached to the One Hundred and Third Division.

Ervin Lattimore was a tank commander during

Operation Task Force Rhine. On March 21, 1945, he was wounded while leading an attack against an enemy column on the road from Munchweiler, Germany. He refused to be evacuated and commanded his tank on into the town of Klingenmunster. Sergeant Lattimore was awarded the Silver Star for his gallant performance of duty.[83]

### Ulysses Lee

Major, U.S. Army.

Ulysses Lee was born in Washington, D.C. in 1913, and attended public schools there. He was a summa cum laude graduate of Howard University and was elected a Phi Beta Kappa. He was a Rosenwald Fellow at the University of Chicago and received his doctorate from that institution in 1942. Ulysses Lee was a teacher for nearly thirty years at Lincoln University, Missouri, at Morgan State College, and a visiting lecturer at the University of Pennsylvania. He has participated in seminars in Nigeria, Sierra Leone, and other West African countries, has made numerous contributions to historical journals and has served on the editorial boards of several publications.

Dr. Lee was a staff member at the office of the Chief of Military History from 1946–1952. He also served as an education officer in the field and at the headquarters of Army Service Forces. He was considered the leading authority on the history of Negroes in the army and his book, *The Employment of Negro Troops (World War II)*, was published in 1966. He was also co-editor of the Army Service Forces manual, *Leadership and the Negro Soldier*, published in 1944. Dr. Lee was co-editor (with Sterling Brown) of *The Negro Caravan*, an anthology of writings by black Americans, and was also associate editor of the *Midwest Journal* of the College Language Association and a member of the editorial board of the *Journal of Negro History*. He was instrumental in the writing of *Washington, City and Capital* and *The Negro in Virginia*, publications of the Federal Writers Project.

Dr. Lee will always be remembered as a modern pioneer in the research and documentation of the history of the Negro soldier. He died, a veteran of some years of military service, a renowned scholar and teacher, in 1960.[34]

*Major Ulysses Lee*

*Lieutenant Clarence D. Lester*

### Clarence D. Lester

Lieutenant, Three Hundred and Thirty-Second Fighter Group, U.S. Army Air Force and Colonel, U.S. Air Force.

Clarence Lester, when he was a lieutenant serving with the Three Hundred and Thirty-Second Fighter Group, participated in a mission on July 18, 1944 to escort heavy bombers attacking enemy installations in Germany. He was engaged with a large number of enemy fighters and despite severe and adverse weather conditions destroyed three enemy fighters. He was awarded the Distinguished Flying Cross, with the citation:

*With complete disregard of his personal safety, Lieutenant Lester destroyed three enemy fighters, thus materially aiding in preventing the enemy from making concentrated attacks on the bombers.*

Lieutenant Lester remained on active duty after the end of World War II, assumed various responsible assignments, and attained the rank of colonel before his retirement. His outstanding performance of duty in the U.S. Air Force made a significant contribution to the correction of traditional opinion of black military potential.[35]

### Theodore McClane

Lieutenant, Company A, Seven Hundred and Fifty-Eighth Tank Battalion (World War II) and Sixty-Fourth Tank Battalion (Korean War).

Theodore McClane was born in Boston, Massachusetts. He was awarded the Silver Star medal for gallantry at the Cinquale Canal crossing near Viareggio, Italy, during World War II. At that time he was executive officer of Company A, Seven Hundred and Fifty-Eighth Tank Battalion. Later, in the Korean War, McClane displayed his bravery while serving as a company commander in the Sixty-Fourth Tank Battalion, and was awarded an oak leaf cluster to the Silver Star medal.[36]

### Hazel P. McCree

Commander, U.S. Navy Nurse Corps.

Hazel McCree was a member of the Navy's Nurse Corps in World War II. Recently she attained the honor of being the first Negro woman appointed Commander in the Nurse Corps.[37]

### John M. Madison

First Lieutenant, Ninety-Second Infantry Division.

John Madison was posthumously awarded the Silver Star medal for gallantry in action while serving as a member of the Ninety-Second Division in Italy on February 8 and 10, 1945. The first action for which he was cited occurred after his company had taken its objective against light enemy resistance. Immediately afterwards the enemy subjected the position to terrific artillery and mortar fire which killed or wounded all the other officers. His citation stated:

*Extremely heavy casualties and the loss of lead-*

*ership disorganized the company and it sought to withdraw. First Lieutenant Madison quickly gathered the remaining fifteen men, and regardless of continuing enemy fire put them into positions to hold the hill. By sheer personal courage and disregard for his own life, First Lieutenant Madison inspired his men to repel three separate enemy counterattacks aimed exclusively at their position. He withdrew only upon orders. Two days later he captured seven enemy soldiers while leading his company in an attack routed through an extensive unmarked mine field.*

Lieutenant Madison was killed in action on April 5, 1945, in a combat operation with the Ninety-Second Division.[38]

### Woodall I. Marsh

Private, Ninety-Second Division.

Woodall Marsh, a native of Pittsburgh, Pennsylvania, was assigned to the Ninety-Second Division in Italy, and was awarded the Silver Star Medal for successfully transporting twelve wounded paratroopers from the front lines to safety, after being told he could not safely attempt the feat. His citation read:

*Under terrific enemy fire, he drove his truck through water up to the hubs of the wheels to get to the wounded men. On the return trip, he tried another route, but it turned out to be just as bad. He had to dig his truck out of the muck. For thirty minutes during the trip, the enemy was attempting to hit him and he was constantly under heavy mortar and artillery fire.*

It is believed that Marsh was the first Negro to earn the Silver Star in Italy during World War II.[39]

*Lieutenant Andrew D. Marshall, pilot in the Negro Fighter Corps of the Mediterranean Allied Forces*

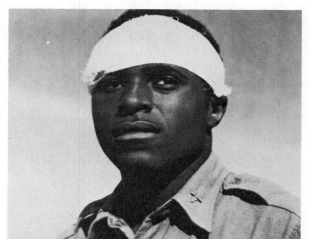

*Steward Dorie Miller is awarded the Navy Cross by Admiral Nimitz*

## Dorie Miller

Steward, *USS West Virginia*, U.S. Navy.

Dorie Miller served as a steward in the U.S. Navy prior to World War II. On December 7, 1941, he was one of the first Americans to display unusual heroism in action. While serving aboard the *USS West Virginia* which was docked at Pearl Harbor, Miller performed heroically when the vessel was attacked by Japanese aircraft. Miller first assisted his mortally wounded captain to cover and then manned a machine gun, which he was not accustomed to operate, and successfully destroyed two of the attacking aircraft. Miller was awarded the Navy Cross for this bravery by Admiral Nimitz. In 1943, he was a member of the crew of seven hundred men who were killed when a Japanese submarine torpedoed and sank the aircraft carrier *USS Liscombe Bay*.[40]

## Edward E. Mitchell

Lieutenant (Later Lieutenant Colonel), Three Hundred and Seventieth Infantry Regiment.

Edward Mitchell is a native of Cincinnati, Ohio. While serving as a platoon leader during World War II, he was awarded the Silver Star medal for bravery. He was later promoted to lieutenant colonel.[41]

## John Mitchell

Private, Ninety-Second Division.

John Mitchell, a native of Cincinnati, Ohio, was assigned to the Ninety-Second Division in Italy, where he served as a combat engineer attached to an infantry rifle company. On February 1, 1945, he was assigned the mission of blowing up enemy barbed wire entanglements impeding his company's advance. When additional sniper and machine-gun fire held up the advance by pinning down the company commander, Mitchell killed one enemy sniper, and wounded and captured another, clearing the way for his company to advance.[42]

## Henry T. Morgan

Captain (later promoted to Lieutenant-Colonel), Company A, Seven Hundred and Fifty-Eighth Tank Battalion.

Henry Morgan was serving as a captain when a display of unusual bravery at the Cinqualle Canal crossing north of Viareggio, Italy, caused him to be awarded the Silver Star medal.[43]

## Walter Morris

First Sergeant, Five Hundred and Fifty-Fifth Parachute Company.

Walter Morris was selected as the first enlisted member of the Five Hundred and Fifty-Fifth Parachute Company, which was the first Negro parachute organization put into service during World War II. The unit was activated at Fort Benning, Georgia.[44]

## Elbert H. Oliver

Steward's Mate First Class, U.S. Navy.

Elbert Oliver was a native of Little Rock, Arkansas. During World War II, he was cited for bravery while serving aboard a U.S. warship. The citation read as follows:

*For conspicuous gallantry and intrepidity while serving aboard a United States warship during a raid upon that vessel by approximately twenty-five Japanese torpedo planes in the vicinity of the Solomon Islands on June 30, 1943. When members of his 22-millimeter gun crew were severely wounded by a bursting projectile, Oliver quickly took over the station of the injured gunner and although he himself was bleeding profusely, maintained accurate fire against the attacking planes until eventually compelled to give way to a relief gunner. His aggressive fighting spirit and grim determination to carry on in the face of danger despite acute pain and waning strength were in keeping with the highest traditions of the United States naval service.*[45]

*Marine Recruit Howard D. Perry*

### Howard D. Perry

Recruit, U.S. Marine Corps.

Howard Perry was the first Negro to enlist in the Marine Corps in World War II. He was also a member of the first class of twelve hundred Negro volunteers who trained at Camp LeJeune, North Carolina.[47]

### William Cook Pinckney

Cook Third Class, *USS Enterprise*, U.S. Navy.

William Pinckney was the son of Mr. and Mrs. Renty Pinckney of Beaufort, South Carolina. He was awarded the Navy Cross for outstanding heroism in World War II. His citation stated:

*OC3/C.W. Pinkney receives Navy Cross*

*Master Sergeant Hansen Outley*

### Hansen Outley

Master Sergeant, U.S. Army.

Hansen Outley had completed twenty-five years of army service in 1941, when he was stationed at Fort Sill, Oklahoma. During his years of service, he was given leave to serve as chief of staff of the Liberian Army and in 1930 he was knighted by the President of the Republic of Liberia.[46]

*For extraordinary heroism while serving aboard the USS Enterprise during the engagement with enemy Japanese naval forces near Santa Cruz islands on October 26, 1942. When a heavy bomb exploded in the near vicinity Pinckney, standing at his battle station in the ammunition handling room, was knocked unconscious. With several compartments completely wrecked and four of five companions killed, Pinckney regaining consciousness groped his way through the burning and tangled wreckage to a point under an open hangar deck hatch. When the man fell unconscious, either from his wounds or from smoke and fumes, Pinckney, unmindful of his own danger, lifted his comrade through the hatch to safety before he himself battled his way out of the burning and smoke-filled compartment. By his dauntless courage in saving his comrade's life at great risk to his own, Pinckney upheld the highest traditions of the United States naval service.[48]*

*Colonel Anderson F. Pitts*

### Willis D. Polk

Major, Three Hundred and Sixty-Sixth Infantry Regiment.

Willis Polk was a native of Philadelphia, Pennsylvania. He was killed in action while serving as a battalion commander in the Three Hundred and Sixty-Sixth Infantry Regiment and was posthumously awarded the Silver Star medal for bravery.[49]

### William E. Porter

First Lieutenant, U.S. Army.

William Porter was a native of Indianapolis, Indiana. While serving in the European Theater he was awarded the Silver Star medal for gallantry in action. Lieutenant Porter had exposed himself to enemy machine-gun fire. With his unit pinned to the ground, he succeeded in eliminating the machine-gun nests, killing an enemy officer and forcing the gun crew to retire.[50]

*Captain Wendell O. Pruitt*

### Wendell O. Pruitt

Captain, Flight Instructor and Veteran Combat Pilot, Thirty-Second Fighter Squadron, U.S. Army Air Force.

Wendell Pruitt was born in St. Louis, Missouri, and was educated at Charles Sumner High School, Stowe Teachers College and Lincoln University of Missouri. He was commissioned in the army air force on December 13, 1942. Captain Pruitt was credited with destroying three enemy planes in the air, eight on the ground and sinking a German destroyer during World War II. He was awarded the Distinguished Flying Cross Air medal, with seven oak leaf clusters. He was one of the outstanding pilots commissioned at Tuskegee and was honored by the citizens of St. Louis for his bravery and heroic accomplishments on December 12, 1944. On April 15, 1945, while on a routine local flight near Tuskegee, Alabama, his plane crashed and he was killed.[51]

### Marcus Ray

Colonel, Ninety-Second Infantry Division and Civilian Aide, Secretary of War.

Marcus Ray was a graduate of the University of Illinois and the University of Chicago. He was director of the South Central Clinical Laboratory in Chicago before his military service, and was a member of the Eighth Illinois National Guard. During World War II, he served in the Mediterranean Theater of Operations and was commanding officer of an artillery battalion of the Ninety-Second Infantry Division. He has been awarded the Legion of Merit, Bronze Star, and Italian Cross of Merit. Colonel Ray was also appointed professor of military science at Wilberforce University. During his military career and civilian assistance to the Secretary of War he contributed greatly to the progress of racial understanding in the armed services.[52]

### Ruben Rivers

Sergeant, Seven Hundred and Sixty-First Tank Battalion, One Hundred and Fourth Infantry Regiment, Twenty-Sixth Infantry Division.

Ruben Rivers was awarded the Silver Star medal in General Order 2 HQ 26th December, 1944, Infantry Division, for alertness and intrepid deeds on November 7, 1944, in the area of Vic-sur-Seille, France. Sergeant Rivers was riding in a lead tank in Company A which ran into roadblock obstructing the tank column. He dismounted under small arms fire, attached a cable to the roadblock and moved it off the road. His heroic action allowed the infantry tank team to continue their mission.[53]

### John Noble Roberts

Steward's Mate Second Class, U.S. Coast Guard.

John Roberts was a native of Bermuda, Louisi-ana, and served during the Normandy invasion on a coast guard ship. He was helping to place soldiers and equipment ashore on the beachhead when a German 88 shell severed one leg and riddled the other with shrapnel. He was awarded the Purple Heart.[54]

*Lieutenant Clarence Samuels*

### Clarence Samuels

Lieutenant, U.S. Coast Guard.

Clarence Samuels was born in Bohio, Panama on June 11, 1903. In July, 1920, he enlisted as a seaman aboard the cutter *Earp* in the Canal Zone, and through the next decade served aboard the cutters *Shawnee, Mojave* and *Argus,* during which time he was promoted to quartermaster first class. In the early 1930's he was promoted to chief quartermaster and assigned to command the Coast Guard patrol boat AB-15 at Savannah, Georgia. Later he served at the Pea Island lifeboat station in North Carolina.

Samuels was transferred to Coast Guard Headquarters in Washington, D.C. in 1938, and later his rating was changed to chief photographer's mate. He was appointed warrant boatswain in the U.S. Coast Guard in September, 1942; and promoted to lieutenant (junior grade) in September,

1943, and on September 1, 1944 to full lieutenant. During World War II, Samuels served aboard the *USS Sea Cloud*, at the Manhattan Beach Training Station and at Coast Guard Headquarters. His first command was aboard the Lightship No. 115 which served on the Navy Local Defense Forces in the Canal Zone. Later, Lieutenant Samuels commanded the Lightship No. 91 in the Canal Zone, from which he was transferred to command of the cutter *Sweet Gum*, also in the Canal Zone. His last command during the war was aboard the cutter *Tulip* in the Philippines.

In 1948, Lieutenant Samuels retired and remained in the Philippine Islands, but a few years later returned to the United States to live in Colma, California. He was one of the senior Negro officers in the U.S. Coast Guard during World War II.[55]

### Isaac Sermon

Private, Company F, Twenty-Fifth Infantry Regiment, Ninety-Third Division (attached for control purposes to the American Division).

Isaac Sermon was awarded the Silver Star in General Order 131 of October 31, 1944, for a gallant display of heroism and devotion to duty. On April 8, 1944, while Company F was engaged in extensive patrolling in the Toro Kina Valley in the Bougainville area of the Pacific Theater, Sermon was wounded by a shot in the neck when his patrol was ambushed. He immediately returned fire with his Browning automatic rifle and killed at least three of the enemy. After using his one magazine of ammunition, Private Sermon started crawling back to the rest of his patrol; he was wounded three more times but kept moving and maintained his position in the rapidly moving patrol for more than six hundred yards. He then collapsed from exhaustion and loss of blood and was carried back to safety for medical attention.[56]

### Andrew Shaw

First Sergeant, Member Chemical Unit, U. S. Army.

Andrew Shaw was cited for bravery under fire on March 21, 1944, at a Fifth Army Review in the Pozilli area, Italy. It is interesting to note that Shaw also received the Croix de Guerre from General Alphonse Juin, commanding general of the French Expeditionary Force. Numerous black sol-diers were awarded this high French honor during World War II while serving with French troops on the German front.[57]

### Theodore D. Smith

Lieutenant, U.S. Army.

Theodore Smith was born in Washington, D.C., graduated from Dunbar High School, and received a B.A. degree from Howard University. He was a captain cadet in the Reserve Officers Training Corps.

In January, 1945, Lieutenant Smith was awarded the Silver Star medal for bravery in leading a small patrol on a mission that enabled some prisoners to be captured. The citation stated that Lieutenant Smith led his fourteen-man patrol two miles across a mined area, through enemy lines, to climb a mountain where the enemy was holding ground. Risking his life to lead the mission, he made it possible for the Americans to accomplish their objective and capture an important position on the Fifth Army front. Lieutenant Smith was killed in action in Italy on February 11, 1945, at twenty-four years of age.[58]

### Rutherford Stevenson

Major, U.S. Army.

Rutherford Stevenson was a graduate of Howard University, and had a fellowship at the Menninger Foundation School of Psychiatry in Topeka, Kansas. Major Stevenson was reputed to be the first Negro psychiatrist integrated into a previously segregated veterans' hospital during World War II.[59]

### Richard Tatum Jr.

Private First Class, Ninety-Second Division.

Richard Tatum, a native of Cunard, West Virginia, was assigned to the Ninety-Second Division in Italy. He was a rifleman, but on one occasion, when he was acting as a forward observer during a unit attack, Private Tatum spotted a group of the enemy in a house and directed fire toward the building. Although under heavy fire himself, he remained in his position and killed six enemy soldiers. He was credited with preventing a strong enemy attack on his mortar squad position and was awarded the Silver Star medal.[60]

### Edward Taylor

Private First Class, Forty-First Engineer Regiment.

Edward Taylor was born in Baltimore, Maryland. On June 17, 1942, the first American Negro troops landed in Africa. Their mission was to protect vital areas in the trans-African lifeline of the United Nations under an agreement between the governments of the United States and Liberia. The pact gave the United States the right to construct, control, operate and defend airports in the West African Republic. Private Taylor led ashore the first known American expeditionary force in Africa.[61]

*Chief Warrant Officer Robert B. Terefruille*

### Charles L. Thomas

Captain, Company C, Six Hundred and Fourteenth Tank Destroyer Battalion, attached One Hundred and Third Division.

Charles Thomas was awarded the Distinguished Service Cross for gallantry while serving as a lieutenant and tank commander with the Six Hundred and Fourteenth Tank Battalion in World War II. He was stationed near Climbach, France. On the morning of December 14, 1944, Lieutenant Thomas was commander of the Six Hundred and Fourteenth's Company C in the lead armored scout car of a task force. As his scout car was approaching Climbach, it was hit by a shell and a mine. Thomas, though wounded, dismounted from his wrecked car and helped his crew, including another wounded man, to extricate themselves. Leaving the protection of the vehicle, Thomas ordered and directed dispersal and displacement of two of his tank destroyers and continued to direct his men despite multiple wounds in his chest and left arm. Only when he was certain that his platoon commander was in full control of the situation did he permit himself to be evacuated.[62]

### Jack Thomas

Private First Class, Company E, Sixtieth Regiment, Ninth Infantry Division.

Jack Thomas was awarded the Distinguished Service Cross for bravery when, with his platoon, he played an important part in the capture of Lengenbach, Germany. Private Thomas was leading his squad on a mission to knock out an enemy tank that was providing heavy caliber support for a roadblock. He deployed his squad and advanced on the enemy position, hurled two hand grenades and wounded several of the enemy. When two of the men at a rocket launcher were wounded, Thomas assumed control of the weapon and launched a rocket at the enemy, preventing them from manning their tank. He then picked up one seriously wounded member of the rocket launching team and carried him to safety through small arms and automatic weapon fire.[63]

*Lieutenant (JG) Arthur L. Thompson*

**Arthur Lee Thompson**

Lieutenant (Junior Grade), U.S. Naval Reserve.

Arthur Thompson was born in Detroit, Michigan, and attended Fisk University and Meharry Medical College. On July 12, 1944, he was sworn in as the first Negro physician to be commissioned in the U.S. Naval Reserve.[64]

**Rothschild Webb**

Staff Sergeant, Ninety-Third Division, Cavalry Reconnaisance Troops.

Rothschild Webb was a member of the Ninety-Third Division's Cavalry Reconnaisance Troops that remained on Bougainville in the Pacific Theater until October 25, 1944, operating with Americal Division Forces. On May 16, 1944, Webb's patrol was ambushed while on a mapping mission. After engaging in an exchange of fire with the enemy, Webb's patrol leader, Lieutenant Charles Collins was wounded first in the leg and later three more times and was unable to continue with the rest of the patrol. Sergeant Webb helped his injured patrol leader into a nearby swamp, and

after three days in enemy territory, led him to safety. He was awarded the Silver Star for his courageous efforts to assist his patrol leader. The award was announced in General Order 1097, dated July 22, 1944, published by HQ USAFISPA.[65]

**Edgar E. Zeno**

Sergeant, Company G, Thirty-Ninth Infantry Division.

Edgar Zeno was awarded the Silver Star medal for gallantry in action. While stationed in the European Theater, his company met heavy enemy machine gun fire near Siedlinghausen, Germany. Sergeant Zeno worked his way across open terrain armed with a Browning automatic rifle, firing continuously. When he was within approximately twenty-five yards of the machine-gun position, he hurled a hand grenade and rushed the emplacement. His action, during which seven of the enemy were killed and three wounded, led to the capture of the machine-gun position and enabled his unit to capture sixty prisoners.[66]

Officers of the 372nd Infantry Colored Regiment at the Boston Armory (above); the first contingent of black members of the WAC assigned to overseas service (left) and WAC staff photographer Sergeant Emma Alice Downs (below).

# Notes to Chapter Eight

1. Ulysses Lee, *The Employment of Negro Troops (World War II)* (Washington: Office of the Chief of Military History, U.S. Government Printing Office, 1966), pp. 582–583.
2. *The Washington News,* June 3, 1942.
3. Helen G. Douglas, *The Negro Soldier,* Congressional Reprint (Washington: U.S. Government Printing Office, 1946).
4. *Chicago Defender,* newsclippings, Colonel Campbell C. Johnson Collection, Moorland Room, Founders Library, Howard University.
5. *Call & Post,* Colonel Campbell C. Johnson Collection, Founders Library.
6. Douglas, *The Negro Soldier.*
7. Lee. *The Employment of Negro Troops,* p. 700.
8. Office of the Assistant Secretary of Defense, Manpower, *Integration and the Negro Officer in the Armed Forces of the United States of America* (Washington: U.S. Government Printing Office, 1946).
9. Douglas, *The Negro Soldier.*
10. *Army Times* files, Washington, D.C.
11. Douglas, *The Negro Soldier.*
12. G. James Fleming and Christian E. Burckel (Eds.), *Who's Who in Colored America,* 7th Edition (Yonkers: Christian E. Burckel & Associates, 1950).
13. Ulysses Lee, *The Employment of Negro Troops,* p. 497.
14. Douglas, *The Negro Soldier.*
15. *Afro-American Newspaper* (Baltimore) magazine section, May 11, 1963.
16. *Integration and the Negro Officer.*
17. *Amsterdam Star News* (N.Y.), March 31, 1945.
18. Lee, *The Employment of Negro Troops,* p. 505.
19. Douglas, *The Negro Soldier.*
20. *Ibid.*
    Lee, *The Employment of Negro Troops,* pp. 539, 549.
21. *Amsterdam Star News* (N.Y.), May 20, 1945.
22. Fleming and Burckel, *Who's Who in Colored America,* p. 233.
23. *Army Times* files, *loc. cit.*
24. Douglas, *The Negro Soldier.*
25. *New York Age,* December 8, 1945.
26. Public Information Office, Edgewood Arsenal, Edgewood, Maryland, 1970.
27. Douglas, *The Negro Soldier.*
28. John D. Silvera, *The Negro in World War II* (Military Press, Inc., n.d.)
29. Douglas, *The Negro Soldier,*
30. Silvera, *The Negro in World War II.*
31. Dennis D. Nelson, *The Integration of the Negro in the U.S. Navy* (New York: Farrar, Straus, 1951).
32. *Afro-American* (Baltimore), October 30, 1943.
33. Lee, *The Employment of Negro Troops,* p. 674.
34. *Ibid.*
    Obituary Notes, Ulysses C. Lee (1913–1969), Courtesy of Dr. Paul Schieps, Office of the Chief of Military History, Washington, D.C.
35. Douglas, *The Negro Soldier.*
36. *Integration and the Negro Officer.*
37. Minority Affairs Division, Office of Information, Navy Department.
38. Douglas, *The Negro Soldier.*
39. *Ibid.*
40. Department of the Navy, Office of Information, Washington, D.C.
41. *Integration of the Negro Officer.*
42. *Amsterdam Star News* (N.Y.), March 31, 1945.
43. *Integration and the Negro Officer.*
44. *The Chicago Defender,* June 22, 1944.
45. Douglas, *The Negro Soldier.*
46. Public Information Division, Office of the Chief of Information, Department of the Army, Washington, D.C.
47. Silvera, *The Negro in World War II.*
48. Douglas, *The Negro Soldier.*
49. *Integration and the Negro Officer.*
50. Douglas, *The Negro Soldier.*
51. *St. Louis Argus,* April 20, 1945.
52. *Amsterdam Star News* (N.Y.), January 19, 1946.
53. Lee, *The Employment of Negro Troops,* p. 664.
54. *Journal and Guide* (Norfolk, Va.), September 2, 1944.
55. Public Information Office, Department of Transportation, U.S. Coast Guard, Washington, D.C.
56. Lee, *The Employment of Negro Troops,* pp. 509–510.
57. Silvera, *The Negro in World War II.*
58. Douglas, *The Negro Soldier.*
59. *Chicago Defender,* April 6, 1945.
60. *Amsterdam Star News* (N.Y.), March 31, 1945.
61. Douglas, *The Negro Soldier.*
62. *Integration and the Negro Officer.*
    Lee, *The Employment of Negro Troops,* pp. 669–670.
63. *Ibid.,* p. 697.
64. Silvera, *The Negro in World War II.*
65. Lee, *The Employment of Negro Troops,* p. 514.
66. Douglas, *The Negro Soldier.*

# Chapter Nine

## The Korean War, 1950-1953

On June 25, 1950, South Korea was attacked by North Korean troops along the Onjin peninsula northwest of Seoul, the South Korean capital. Seoul was taken on June 29, and on June 30, the first U.S. ground forces entered the conflict as part of a United Nations "police action" to force North Korean troops back to beyond the thirty-eighth parallel.

Black soldiers were a part of the war, first in the segregated regiments, among them the First, Second and Third Battalions of the Twenty-Fourth Infantry Regiment, Twenty-Fifth Infantry Division and, after October 1, 1951, when the U.S. Army started to implement President Truman's order to integrate the armed forces, distributed throughout the military in an attempt to integrate all units as quickly as possible.

Various accounts have been given of the performance of black soldiers during the Korean Conflict. Unfavorable reports have been magnified, and allowed to remain unmodified by more creditable actions. In this chapter an attempt is made to counterbalance the account of the poor performance of the Twenty-Fourth Infantry Regiment in combat with some reports of individual actions of which black people can be proud. The story of the Twenty-Fourth Infantry follows.

On July 22, 1950, the Second Battalion of the Twenty-Fourth, with elements of the Republic of Korea Seventeenth Regiment were advancing into mountains near Sangfu. One of the Twenty-Fourth's companies was fired on and some men began to disperse in a disorderly manner and to show signs of panic. On August 12, 1950, the Third Battalion of the Twenty-Fourth were unreliable in their performance and later, on August 15, when the Second Battalion was attempting to occupy the Obong-san mountain ridge west of Battle Mountain, the battalion broke contact with the

enemy and withdrew to Battle Mountain and the ridge west of Haman. Some men abandoned their positions. The area of Battle Mountain changed hands several times and in September, 1950, on meeting the enemy south of Haman, some members of the First Battalion were reported to have fled to the rear. The commanding general of the Twenty-Fourth Infantry recommended to the commanding general of the Eighth Army that the Twenty-Fourth Regiment be removed from combat because of their demonstrated inefficiency. However, the Eighth Army commanding general did not concur in this recommendation and the Twenty-Fourth Infantry continued to serve with the Eighth Army until the regiment was dispersed in the integration process which was initiated in 1951.

More favorable reports were made about the performance of Negro soldiers in the following combat operations: Task Force Jackson at Kyongju; Task Force Kean near Hamon (when Private William Thompson of the Heavy Weapons Company set up his machine gun and fired at the enemy until he was killed by grenades); Task Force Matthews which involved the Twenty-Fourth Infantry, and Dolvin's combat operations near Chonju and Kanggyong in September, 1950.

The reports about the Twenty-Fourth Infantry Regiment should not be given undue weight in assessing the performance of Negro soldiers in combat; their illustrious record in previous wars, the heroism displayed by many in the Korean conflict, and their record in Vietnam should more than discount this one episode.[1]

214

**William Benefield**

Second Lieutenant, Seventy-Fourth Combat Engineer Company, Twenty-Fifth Infantry Division.

William Benefield served with the Twenty-Fifth Infantry Division and was killed while attempting to clear a mine field at Sangjie, Korea, under enemy fire in July, 1950. He was awarded the Distinguished Service Cross.[2]

**Jesse L. Brown**

Ensign, U.S. Navy.

Jesse Brown was born in Mississippi and was the first Negro known to earn a naval aviator's

*Ensign Jesse L. Brown*

wings. He was killed in Korea while on a close combat mission in December, 1950, and was posthumously awarded the Distinguished Flying Cross and Air Medal for his bravery.

On March 18, 1972, the U.S. Navy further honored Ensign Brown when they launched a Knox class ocean escort ship at Avondale Shipyards, Westwego, Louisiana, in his honor. This was the first ship of the U.S. Navy to be named after a black naval officer. His widow, Mrs. Gilbert W. Thorne, was the sponsor of the ship during the ceremony.[3]

**Cornelius H. Charlton**

Sergeant, Company C, Twenty-Fourth Infantry Regiment, Twenty-Fifth Infantry Division.

Cornelius Charlton was born in East Gulf, West Virginia, and entered the army in New York. He distinguished himself on June 2, 1951, at Chipo-ri, Korea, by a heroic performance beyond the call of duty, for which he was awarded the Medal of Honor. His citation read as follows:

*Sergeant Cornelius H. Charlton, RA 12265495, Infantry, United States Army, a member of Company C, Twenty-Fourth Infantry Regiment, Twenty-Fifth Infantry Division, distinguished himself by conspicuous gallantry and intrepidity above and beyond the call of duty in action against the enemy near Chipo-ri, Korea, on 2 June, 1951. His platoon was attacking heavily defended hostile positions on commanding ground when the leader was wounded and evacuated. Sergeant Charlton assumed command, rallied the men, and spearheaded the assault against the hill. Personally eliminating two hostile positions and killing six of the enemy with his rifle fire and grenades, he continued up the slope until the unit suffered heavy casualties and became pinned down. Regrouping the men he led them forward only to be hurled back again by a shower of grenades. Despite a severe chest wound, Sergeant Charlton refused*

*Sergeant Cornelius H. Charlton*

*medical attention and led a third daring charge which carried to the crest of the ridge. Observing that the remaining emplacement which had retarded the advance was situated in the reverse slope, he charged it alone, was again hit by a grenade but rallied the position with a devastating fire which eliminated it and routed the defenders. The wounds received during his daring exploits resulted in his death, but his indomitable courage, superb leadership, and gallant self-sacrifice reflect the highest credit upon himself, the infantry and the military service.*[4]

### Ernest Craigwell Jr.

First Lieutenant (later promoted to higher rank), U.S. Air Force.

Ernest Craigwell was born in Brooklyn, New York. He flew wingman for the U.S. Fifth Air Force's famed "Flying Parson" in the Korean War and was awarded the Distinguished Flying Cross for his heroic performance of duty.[5]

### George Gray

Major, U.S. Air Force.

George Gray was a native of West Virginia, and was killed while flying a mission in the combat zone during the Korean conflict. He was awarded the Distinguished Flying Cross for his valor.[6]

### Levy V. Hollis

Master Sergeant, U.S. Army.

Levy Hollis is a native of Texas. He was assigned to Haman, Korea, during the war and was awarded the Distinguished Service Cross in August, 1950, for heroic performance of duty.[7]

### Chester J. Lenon

Lieutenant (later promoted to higher rank on active duty), Seventy-Seventh Combat Engineer Company, Twenty-Fifth Infantry Division.

Chester Lenon was born in Texas. He was awarded the Distinguished Service Cross for gallantry while serving in the Korean conflict in 1950.[8]

### Thomas A. Mac Calla

First Lieutenant, Second Battalion, Fifth Marines, Eighty-First Mortar, First Marine Division.

Thomas Mac Calla was born in Bridgeport, Connecticut, on July 2, 1929, the son of Reuben A. and Esther Conway Mac Calla. He went to school in Bridgeport and graduated from Fairfield University in 1951, attaining a master's degree in 1954. In 1964 he was awarded a doctorate degree in education by the University of California at Los Angeles. Mac Calla married Jacqueline E. Campbell, and they are the parents of three children.

Thomas Mac Calla enlisted in the U.S. Marine Corps in 1952, and was assigned to Quantico, Virginia, where he took the officers candidate course, and was assigned to Korea on completion of his training. He also attended the fourteenth special basic training course. It is believed that Lieutenant Mac Calla was the first black marine officer assigned to Korea to receive a command position as a platoon commander. He was also the first Negro marine officer to be assigned to a general staff position when he was assigned to Headquarters, First Marine Division, as historical officer. He was responsible for compiling and writing the history of the division and for recording information relating to prisoner of war exchanges. He wrote the official diary and assembled the pictorial section of the Marines War Exchange of Prisoners of War during the period July–August, 1953. In 1954, Lieutenant Mac Calla was discharged from the active marine corps. He was a member of the marine reserves for twelve years and attained the rank of captain. In civilian life he has worked with the Connecticut Welfare Department; as a teacher in the Santa Monica, California, high school; as chairman of the English department, Santa Monica City College, and as a college administrator and professor. In 1957 he was selected to assist in the production of an academy award documentary film, called "A Force and Readiness."

Thomas Mac Calla was probably the first Negro officer assigned to the famed Marine First Division.[9]

### Luther McManus

Lieutenant Colonel (Retired), U.S. Army.

Luther McManus was awarded the Distinguished Service Cross for gallantry in action, inspiring his troops with his personal fearlessness and calling them to fix their bayonets as he led

*Lieutenant Colonel (Ret.) Luther McManus*

*Lieutenant Colonel Dayton Ragland*

them in a determined charge against a hostile position near Wolbong-ni on October 18, 1951.[10]

### Vance H. Marchbanks

Colonel, U.S. Air Force Medical Corps.

Vance Marchbanks, a senior flight surgeon in the U.S. Air Force and a former commanding officer of the U.S. Air Force Hospital, Loraine Air Force Base, Maine, was assigned to a special staff project as a member of the tracking station staff in Africa.[11]

### Dayton Ragland

Lieutenant Colonel, U.S. Air Force.

Dayton Ragland was awarded the Distinguished Flying Cross for his bravery and commendable performance of duty while flying combat operations in Korea. Lieutenant Ragland was a former assistant professor of air science at Howard University.[12]

### Hugh Robinson

Colonel, Corps of Engineers.

Hugh Robinson was born in Washington, D.C., the son of a former army officer, Colonel (Ret.) James Robinson, who was the first Negro to serve as a U.S. president's military aide. An alumnus of

West Point Military Academy, Colonel Robinson chose the Corps of Engineers as his basic branch. He has served in Korea, and at the Engineer Combat Office in St. Louis. He has a master's degree from the Massachusetts Institute of Technology.[13]

*Colonel Hugh Robinson*

## William Thompson

Private First Class, Company M, Twenty-Fourth Infantry Regiment.

William Thompson was born in New York City and entered the service in the Bronx, New York. He displayed great bravery near Haman, Korea, where he was mortally wounded. Private Thompson was awarded the Medal of Honor posthumously for his courage and self-sacrifice. His citation read as follows:

*Private First Class William Thompson, 422 59324, Company M, Twenty-Fourth Infantry Regiment, distinguished himself by conspicuous gallantry and intrepidity above and beyond the call of duty in action against the enemy near Haman, Korea, on 6 August, 1950. While his platoon was reorganizing under cover of darkness, fanatical enemy forces in overwhelming strength launched a surprise attack on the unit. Private Thompson set up his machine gun in the path of the onslaught and swept the enemy with withering fire, pinning them down momentarily, thus permitting the remainder of his platoon to withdraw to a more tenable position. Although hit repeatedly by grenade fragments and small arms fire, he resisted all efforts of his comrades to induce him to withdraw, steadfastly remained at his machine gun and continued to deliver deadly, accurate fire until mortally wounded by an enemy grenade. Private Thompson's dauntless courage and gallant self-sacrifice reflect the highest credit on himself and uphold the esteemed tradition of military service.*[14]

## Ellison Wynn

First Lieutenant, Company B, Ninth Infantry Regiment.

Ellison Wynn was assigned to the Ninth Infantry Regiment during the Korean War, and on one occasion was engaged in a combat operation that displayed his heroic abilities, and for which he was awarded the Distinguished Service Cross. Lieutenant Wynn led his troops in an assault on an enemy position near Kuni-ri. During a counterattack, his machine gunner was killed. Lieutenant Wynn remained at his post throwing grenades until his men could rejoin him in defending his position. Although bleeding from wounds, he staunchly directed a withdrawal.[15]

*Private First Class William Thompson*

*Frederick C. Branch, the first black to be commissioned in the Marine Corps has his second lieutenant's bars pinned on by his wife.*

*"The Suicide Six" one of the fastest gun crews in the Second Infantry Division (above) and (right) Private Mangolia Ali and Private Esther L. Cannon, the first Negro WACs assigned to the Engineering School at Fort Belvoir since 1945.*

## Notes to Chapter Nine

1. Roy E. Appleman, *United States Army in the Korean War: South to the Nantong, North to the Yalu* (Washington, D.C.: Office of the Chief of Military History, U.S. Government Printing Office, 1961).

2. Carter G. Woodson and Charles H. Wesley, *The Negro in Our History* (Washington, D.C.: Associated Publishers, 1966), p. 641.

3. Department of the Navy, Office of Information, Washington, D.C.

4. *Medal of Honor Recipients, 1863–1963*, 88th Congress, 2nd Session, Committee Print (Washington, D.C.: .S. Government Printing Office, 1962).

5. Office of the Assistant Secretary of Defense Manpower, *Integration and The Negro Officer in the Armed Forces of the United States of America* (Washington, D.C.: U.S. Government Printing Office, 1962).

6. *Ibid.*

7. Irvin H. Lee, *Negro Medal of Honor Men* (New York: Dodd, Mead & Co., 1967), p. 13.

8. *Integration and the Negro Officer.*

9. *Who's Who in the West,* 10th Edition (Chicago: Who's Who Marquis Publications, 1970).
Personal interview with Dr. Thomas A. Mac Calla, May, 1970.

10. Woodson and Wesley, *The Negro in Our History.*

11. *Integration and the Negro Officer.*

12. *Ibid.*

13. "Bugle Call for Military Cadets," *Ebony,* June, 1966.

14. *Medal of Honor Recipients, 1863–1963.*

15. Irvin H. Lee, *Negro Medal of Honor Men.*

# Chapter Ten

## The Vietnam War, 1959-1973

Black Americans played an important role in the Revolutionary War, the War of 1812, the Mexican War, the Civil War, the Indian Campaigns, in World Wars I and II, and in the Korean War. From 1962 onwards, a new black soldier has been emerging—not a laborer or body servant, a part-time soldier or a rare hero, but an ordinary soldier, fighting and working on equal terms with whites in the military service of his country. Today, the Negro soldiers who fought on the battlefields of Southeast Asia are a monument to the fallen black heroes of history, who fought under the handicaps of unequal conditions, and emerged sometimes as heroes, and sometimes as slaves.

This chapter includes some of the accomplishments of Negro military personnel during the Vietnam War period in combat and other assignments. Many awards were won by black Americans during this time. There is no longer a need for blacks to prove their combat capability as black Americans, only to prove their fitness as American men or women.

Optimism about the future of black personnel in the military service can be based on numerous achievements of the Vietnam War period. It is still necessary to cite the progress of certain minority groups individually, and will be until America's racial attitudes have uniformly changed, but the advancement of black Americans in the military service today will be based on their qualifications and abilities, and not on their pigmentation.

Black and white Americans who now serve together in the armed forces all over the world exemplify the words of Major Martin R. Delaney, veteran of the Civil War:

Fleecy locks and black complexions cannot alter
  nature's claim
Skins may differ, but afflictions dwell in black and
  white the same.[1]

## Webster Anderson

Sergeant First Class, Battery A, Second Battalion, Three Hundred and Twentieth Artillery, One Hundred and First Airborne Division.

Webster Anderson was born on July 15, 1933, at Winnsboro, South Carolina, the son of Frizell Anderson. He and his wife Ida have two children. Sergeant Anderson joined the army at Columbia, South Carolina, on September 11, 1953, and has served at Camp Chaffie, Arkansas; Fort Bragg, North Carolina; Fort Campbell, Kentucky; the Dominican Republic; Vietnam, and Fort Gordon, Georgia. He has received the following awards: Medal of Honor, Purple Heart, Good Conduct medal—third award, Armed Forces Expeditionary medal, National Defense Service medal, Vietnam Service medal, Master Parachutist Badge, and Vietnam Campaign medal (Vietnamese). His citation for the Medal of Honor read as follows:

*Sergeant First Class Webster Anderson (then staff sergeant) distinguished himself by conspic-*

* The dates of American participation in the Vietnam War are approximately 1959, when two U.S. military "advisers" were killed, to the cease-fire and somewhat unstable peace agreement of 1973. U.S. forces in Vietnam were 4,000 in 1962, 15,000 in 1963; 23,000 in 1964, 125,000 in 1965; 358,-000 in 1966; 474,300 in 1967; 542,500 in 1969; 368,000 in 1970, 27,000 in 1971. In 1972 the basis for a cease-fire was announced and in 1973 all ground troops were withdrawn. No formal declaration of war was ever authorized by Congress.

uous gallantry and intrepidity in action while serving as chief of section in Battery A, Second Battalion, Three Hundred and Twentieth Artillery, One Hundred and First Airborne Infantry Division (Airmobile) against a hostile force near Tam Ky, Republic of Vietnam. During the early morning hours on October 15, 1967, Battery A's defensive position was attacked by a determined North Vietnamese Army Infantry unit supported by heavy mortar, recoilless rifle, rocket propelled grenade and automatic weapon fire. The initial enemy onslaught breached the battery's defensive perimeter. Sergeant Anderson, with complete disregard for his personal safety, mounted the exposed parapet of his howitzer position and became the mainstay of the defense of the battery position. Sergeant Anderson directed devastating direct howitzer fire on the assaulting enemy while providing rifle and grenade defensive fire against the enemy from his exposed position, attempting to overrun his gun section position, two enemy grenades exploded at his feet knocking him down and severely wounding him in the legs. Despite the excruciating pain and though not able to stand, Sergeant Anderson valorously propped himself on the parapet and continued to direct howitzer fire upon the closing enemy and to encourage his men to fight on. Seeing an enemy grenade land within the gun pit near a wounded member of his gun crew, Sergeant Anderson, heedless of his own safety, seized the grenade and attempted to throw it over the parapet to save his men. As the grenade was thrown from the position it exploded and Sergeant Anderson was again grievously wounded. Although only partially conscious and severely wounded, Sergeant Anderson refused medical evacuation and continued to encourage his men in the defense of the position. Sergeant Anderson by his inspirational leadership, professionalism, devotion to duty and complete disregard for his own welfare was able to maintain the defense of his section and to defeat a determined enemy attack. Sergeant Anderson's conspicuous gallantry and extraordinary heroism at the risk of his own life above and beyond the call of duty are in the highest traditions of the military service and reflect great credit upon himself, his unit and the United States Army.[2]

*Sergeant First Class Webster Anderson*

## Eugene Ashley Jr.

Sergeant First Class, Company C, Fifth Special Forces Group (Airborne), First Special Forces.

Eugene Ashley was born on October 12, 1931, in Wilmington, North Carolina. He and his wife Barbara have five children. Ashley attended Alexander Hamilton High School in Brooklyn, New York, and enlisted in the army on December 5, 1971, in New York City. He received special forces training at Fort Bragg, North Carolina, and during his military career was stationed at Fort Bragg; in the Federal Republic of Germany; Korea; Okinawa; the Dominican Republic, and Vietnam. He received the following military honors: Bronze Star medal, Purple Heart, Good Conduct medal Clasp (bronze) with three loops, Army of Occupation medal with one bronze oak leaf cluster, Korean Service medal, Armed Forces Expeditionary medal (Dominican Republic) Vietnam Service medal with one silver service star, Combat Infantry Badge, Master Parachutist Badge, and Vietnam Campaign medal (Vietnamese).

In February, 1968, while serving in Vietnam, Sergeant Ashley gave his life in an attempt to save

*Sergeant First Class Eugene Ashley Jr.*

the life of his comrades and commanding officer. He was posthumously awarded the Medal of Honor. His citation reads:

*Sergeant First Class Eugene Ashley Jr. distinguished himself by conspicuous gallantry and intrepidity while serving with Detachment A-101, Company C, Fifth Special Forces Group (Airborne), First Special Forces, near Lang Vei Special Forces Camp in the Republic of Vietnam. On 6 and 7 February, 1968, Sergeant Ashley was the Senior Special Forces Advisor of a hastily organized assault force whose mission was to rescue entrapped United States Special Forces Advisors at Camp Lang Vei. During the initial attack on the Special Forces camp by North Vietnamese Army forces, Sergeant Ashley supported the camp with high explosive and illumination mortar rounds. When communications were lost with the main camp, he assumed the additional responsibility of directing air strikes and artillery support. Sergeant Ashley organized and equipped a small assault force composed of local friendly personnel. During the ensuing battle, Sergeant Ashley led a total of five vigorous assaults against the enemy, continuously exposing himself to a voluminous hail of enemy grenades, machine gun and automatic weapons fire. Throughout these assaults, he was plagued by numerous booby-trapped satchel charges in all bunkers of his avenue of approach. During his fifth and final assault, he adjusted air strikes nearly on top of his assault element, forcing the enemy to withdraw and resulting in friendly control of the summit of the hill. While exposing himself to intense enemy fire, he was seriously wounded by machine gun fire but continued his mission without regard for his personal safety. After the fifth assault he lost consciousness and was carried from the summit by his comrades only to suffer a fatal wound when an enemy artillery round landed in the area. Sergeant Ashley displayed extraordinary heroism in risking his life in an attempt to save the lives of his entrapped comrades and commanding officer. His total disregard for his own personal safety while exposed to enemy observation and automatic weapons fire was an inspiration to all men committed to the assault. The resolute valor with which he led five gallant charges placed in the overpowering enemy forces and weapons positions through which the survivors of Camp Lang Vei eventually escaped to freedom. Sergeant Ashley's conspicuous gallantry at the cost of his own life was in the highest traditions of the military service, and reflects great credit upon himself, his unit and the United States Army.[3]*

*Private First Class Oscar P. Austin*

## Oscar P. Austin

Private First Class, Company E, Second Battalion, Seventh Marines, First Marine Division (reinforced).

Oscar Austin was born on January 15, 1948, in Nacogdoches, Texas, the son of Frank and Mildred Austin. He attended Booker T. Washington elementary school and Union high school in Phoenix, Arizona. On April 22, 1968, Austin was inducted into the Marine Corps, and in July, 1968, completed his recruit training at the Marine Corps Recruit Depot, San Diego, California. He completed additional training at Camp Pendleton, California, and on October 1, 1968, was assigned as a munitions specialist to Company E of the Second Battalion, Seventh Marines, First Marine Division (Reinforced) in the Republic of Vietnam. Private Austin received the following awards during his military career: Purple Heart, National Defense medal, Vietnam Service medal with two bronze stars, and the Republic of Vietnam Campaign medal. On February 26, 1969, Private Austin was killed in action, and was posthumously awarded the Medal of Honor for his courageous performance of duty. His citation read as follows:

*For conspicuous gallantry and intrepidity at the risk of his life above and beyond the call of duty while serving as an assistant machine gunner with Company E, Second Battalion, Seventh Marines, First Marine Division in connection with operations agains enemy forces in the Republic of Vietnam. During the early morning hours of 23 February, 1969, Private First Class Austin's observation post was subjected to a fierce ground attack by a large North Vietnamese Army force supported by a heavy volume of hand grenades, satchel charges and small arms fire. Observing that one of his wounded companions had fallen unconscious in a position dangerously exposed to the hostile fire, Private First Class Austin unhesitatingly left the relative security of his fighting hole and, with complete disregard for his own safety, raced across the fire-swept terrain to assist the marine to a covered location. As he neared the casualty he observed an enemy grenade laid nearby and reacting instantly, leaped between the injured marine and the lethal object, absorbing the effects of its detonation. As he ignored his painful injuries and turned to examine the wounded man, he saw a North Vietnamese Army soldier aiming a weapon at his unconscious companion. With full knowledge of the probable consequences and thinking only to protect the marine, Private First Class Austin resolutely threw himself between the casualty and the hostile soldier and, in so doing, was mortally wounded. Private First Class Austin's indomitable courage, inspiring initiative and selfless devotion to duty upheld the highest traditions of the Marine Corps and United States Naval Service. He gallantly gave his life for his country."[4]*

### Evangeline Geraldine Bailey

Musician Third Class (Petty Officer), U.S. Navy.

Evangeline Bailey was born in 1949, the daughter of Mr. and Mrs. William Bailey III, of Portsmouth, Virginia. Her father is a retired navy veteran with over twenty-two years of service. Miss Bailey has played the piano since the age of five, was a student at New York's Steinway Hall at nine, and has also studied at Norfolk State College, where she was a voice major with an interest in classical music. She appeared as Despina in the Norfolk State Opera Workshop production of *Cosi Fan Tutte*. She was a member of the Washington Ford Foundation, a gospel singing group, and of Collegium Musicum, a chorus that sang all types of music. She also appeared with a rock group called the Superlatives.

Petty Officer Bailey was assigned to the Bethesda Naval Medical Center as a Hospital Corps Third Class Musician when she made naval history. In May, 1972, Musician Third Class Evangeline Bailey was selected as the first female musician in naval history. She joined the rock group Port Authority, a unit of the United States Navy Band. The band toured U.S. military bases in Scotland, Italy, Sicily and Spain. Petty Officer Bailey is the navy's first female vocalist and also its first black female musician.[5]

*Musician Third Class Evangeline Bailey with members of the U.S. Navy Band*

**Margaret E. Bailey**

Colonel, U.S. Army Nurse Corps.

Margaret Bailey was born in Selma, Alabama, and graduated from Dunbar High School in Mobile. She studied at the Fraternal Hospital School of Nursing in Montgomery, and at San Francisco State College, where she received a degree.

Miss Bailey entered the army in June, 1944, and has been assigned to Fort Huachuca, Arizona; Station Hospital, Florence, Arizona; USAH, Camp Beale, California; Halloron General Hospital, Staten Island, New York; Tilton General Hospital, Fort Dix, New Jersey; Percy Jones General Hospital, Battle Creek, Michigan; Madigan General Hospital, Tacoma, Washington; Letterman General Hospital, San Francisco, California, and Fitzsimmons General Hospital, Denver, Colorado. Her overseas assignments include duty at the Ninety-Eighth General Hospital, Munich, Germany; Second General Hospital, Landstuhl, Germany; the USAH, Zama, Japan; One Hundred and Thirtieth General Hospital, Chinon, France, and the U.S. Army Element, Job Corps Health Office, Department of Labor, Washington, D.C.

Colonel Bailey attended a six months' course in psychiatric nursing at Fort Sam Houston, Texas, and subsequently saw extensive duty as a psychiatric nurse. She has served as a medical and surgical nurse on many assignments in her career.

At Fitzsimmons Hospital, Colonel Bailey was in charge of the Nightingale program which entailed visiting schools of nursing in the Denver area, speaking at meetings of local organizations, conducting tours of the hospital, and making television appearances with other nurses to stimulate recruiting. She was also active in the Colorado Nursing Association and the Colorado League of Nursing.

In 1964, Margaret Bailey became the first Negro nurse in the U.S. Army to attain the rank of lieutenant colonel. Upon her arrival at the One Hundred and Thirtieth General Hospital, she became the first Negro chief nurse in the U.S. Army since integration. On January 23, 1970, she became the first of her race to become a full colonel in the Army Nurse Corps.[6]

*Colonel Margaret E. Bailey*
*Master Sergeant Thomas N. Barnes*

*Brigadier General Julius Becton*

## Thomas N. Barnes

Chief Master Sergeant, the United States Air Force.

Thomas N. Barnes was born on November 16, 1930 in Chester, Pennsylvania. He attended elementary and secondary schools in Chester, Pennsylvania. In April, 1949, Barnes entered the United States Air Force and received his basic training at Lackland Air Force Base, Texas. He has been assigned to the following installations during his military career: Fourth Troop Carrier Squadron and Sixty-Second Troop Carrier Group, McChord AFB, Washington; Ashiya, Japan; Tachikawa, Japan; Thirtieth Air Transport Squadron, Westover AFB, Massachusetts; Seventeen Hundred and Eighth Ferry Group, Keely AFB, Texas; Loring AFB, Maine; Fairchild AFB, Washington; George AFB, California and Southeast Asia. His major job assignments have been: flight engineer and hydraulic specialist, crew chief/flight engineer, flight chief, senior controller and senior airman advisor.

Chief Master Sergeant Barnes is a graduate of the Eighth Air Force NCO Academy and the USAF Senior NCO Academy Pilot Class. His decorations include the Meritorious Service medal, Air medal, Air Force Commendation medal and Outstanding Airman medal. He is the top enlisted man in the United States Air Force. He will advise and assist the Secretary of the Air Force on all matters concerning enlisted members.[7]

## Julius Wesley Becton Jr.

Brigadier General, U.S. Army.

Julius Becton was born on June 29, 1926, at Bryn Mawr, Pennsylvania. He has a B.A. in mathematics from Prairie View A. and M. College and an M.A. in economics from the University of Maryland. He has also attended the Infantry School, U.S. Army Command, the General Staff College, Armed Forces Staff College and National War College. His major duty assignments have been: operations officer, plans officer and chief plans and operations, Office of the Assistant Chief of Staff G-3, Fourth Logistical Command, U.S. Army Europe; personnel staff officer, Reserve Affairs and Discipline Branch, Promotion and Retention Division, Office of the Deputy Chief of Staff for Personnel, U.S. Army, Washington; military analyst, Resources System Team, Force Planning Analysis Directorate, Office of the Assistant Vice Chief of Staff, U.S. Army, Washington; commanding officer, Second Squadron, Seventeenth Cavalry, One Hundred and First Airborne Division, Fort Campbell, Kentucky and later U.S. Army, Vietnam; deputy commander, Third Brigade, One Hundred and First Airborne Division, U.S. Army, Vietnam; member, Deputy Chief of Staff for Personnel, Special Review Board, and Department of the Army and Suitability Evaluation Board, Military District of Washington; commanding officer, Second Brigade, Second Armored Division, Fort Hood, Texas, and chief, Armor Branch, Officer Personnel Directorate, Office of Personnel Operations, U.S. Army, Washington.

General Becton has received the following medals and awards: Silver Star (with oak leaf cluster), Legion of Merit, Distinguished Flying Cross, Bronze Star medal (with oak leaf cluster), Air medal (with "V" device), Army Commendation medal (with oak leaf cluster), Combat Infantryman badge (second award) and Parachutist badge.

*Chief Boatswain Maxie H. Berry Sr. (above)*
*and a Coast Guard at the Pea Island station*

After the completion of over twenty-six years of military service, Julius Wesley Becton was promoted to brigadier general in 1972. His current assignment is deputy commanding general, U.S. Army Training Center, Infantry, Fort Dix, New Jersey.[8]

**Maxie H. Berry Sr.**

Chief Boatswain's Mate, U.S. Coast Guard.

Maxie Berry Sr. was born in North Carolina into a family with a rich heritage of service in the U.S. Coast Guard. His father served for more than thirty-two years as a surfman; his two sons are serving in the U.S. Coast Guard today, Maxie H. Berry Jr. as a lieutenant stationed at Coast Guard Headquarters in Washington, D.C. and Oscar D. Berry as a recruiter. Ironically, his father served in a segregated coast guard service and his son, Maxie Jr., has been assigned to work in the area of equal opportunity for minority groups. A cousin,

Lieutenant Herbert Collins, is also a member of the U.S. Coast Guard.

Maxie Berry Sr. served for twenty-seven and a half years, retiring in the rank of chief boatswain's mate. He spent the major part of his service at Pea Island Coast Guard Station, on the Atlantic Coast between Norfolk and Cape Hatteras. The story of Maxie Berry's Pea Island station, a homestead for him and his family, is a history in itself.

The Pea Island Coast Guard Station has been manned by an entire Negro crew since shortly after the Civil War. While all Negro Coast Guardsmen were serving in the Steward's branch prior to World War II, blacks were serving in positions of distinction in the USCG at Pea Island.

Many years ago, members of the Berry family and their close friends, all Negroes, took examinations to serve as Surfmen at the Coast Guard facility. They passed the examinations and were admitted to the Coast Guard. It is believed that at first, officials did not realize that these applicants

*Black U.S. Coast Guards (above) and the Pea Island Station near Cape Hatteras*

were of the Negro race; however, their efficiency as surfmen and life savers, was recognized by the Coast Guard and eventually the Pea Island Negro Coast Guard Station was officially established They had served for many years with the white personnel in crews at the station on Hatteras banks. A story is related that one day an all-white crew at one of the stations slept through the night with no one on watch. Unknown to the sleeping crew was a wreck in which the majority of the vessel's crew was lost. A few struggling survivors reached the beach to arouse the sleeping men. Later orders followed from Washington demoting the personnel in charge and assigning for the first time a Negro Captain of a Coast Guard Station, Chief Boatswain's Mate Ethridge.

Eventually, the entire station had a Negro crew.

This was the birth of Pea Island, the all-Negro Coast Guard Station which produced the legendary and dedicated Berry family. Other Negro captains in charge of the station have been Maxie Berry Sr., and Lieutenant Clarence Samuels.

Today, Pea Island is past history. However, the presence of members of the Berry Family on active duty with the U.S. Coast Guard is an indication that the Berry legend and tradition of service will remain.

The continuing progress and achievements of Negro personnel in the U.S. Coast Guard Service will stand as a memorial to the gallant performance of duty by Maxie Berry Sr., his father Joseph Berry, Chief Boatswain's Mate Ethridge, Lieutenant Clarence Samuels and those forgotten veterans of Pea Island Station, North Carolina.[9]

*Lieutenant Colonel Kenneth M. Berthoud Jr.*

## Kenneth M. Berthoud Jr.

Lieutenant Colonel, U.S. Marine Corps.

Kenneth Berthoud was born on December 28, 1928, the son of Mr. and Mrs. Kenneth H. Berthoud, in New York City. He attended grammar and high schools in New York, studied at Lincoln University in Pennsylvania for several years and graduated with an A.B. degree from Long Island University, New York, in 1952. He enlisted in the U.S. Marine Corps Reserve on August 11, 1952 and entered the Platoon Leaders Unit, Fifth Marine Corps Reserve and Recruitment District, Arlington, Virginia. He was commissioned a Marine

Corps Reserve second lieutenant after completing a course at the Basic School, Fourth Training Battalion, Marine Corps Schools, Quantico, Virginia, on December 13, 1952. Lieutenant Berthoud accepted a regular appointment in the Regular Marine Corps on July 13, 1953.

During his military career, Lieutenant Berthoud has been assigned as an instructor's assistant, Basic School, Quantico; company commander, First Provisional Casual Battalion, FMF, Pacific Troops; platoon commander, Two Hundred and Thirty-Fifth Company, Fourth Replacement Battalion, Staging Regiment, Marine Corps Base, Camp Pendleton, California; platoon leader, Company D, Third Battalion, Third Marine Division FMF; S-2 officer and company executive officer/company commander, Company A, First Tank Battalion, First Marine Division (Reinforced) FMF. He has also attended the Associate Armored Company Officers' Course, Armored School, Fort Knox, Kentucky, in September, 1955, and the Supply Officers' Course, Marine Corps Base, Lejeune, North Carolina. Other assignments have included assistant head (later head), Warehousing Branch, Material Division, Marine Corps Supply Activity, Philadelphia; officer in charge, Budget and Requirements Branch, Base Material Battalion, First Force Service Regiment; data processing planning officer, Marine Corps Supply Center, Barstow, California.

Lieutenant Colonel Berthoud served in the Republic of Vietnam with battalion operations, supply battalion, First Forces Service Regiment, Force Logistics Command. He was promoted to lieutenant colonel in October, 1967, and has earned the following decorations and awards: Navy Commendation medal with one bronze star, the Korean Service medal, the Vietnam Service medal with one bronze star, the United Nations service medal and the Republic of Vietnam Campaign medal. From 1967 to 1970, Lieutenant Colonel Berthoud was assigned as special advisor for Negro officer procurement, G-1 Division Headquarters, Marine Corps and Marine Corps Equal Opportunity Branch.

Lieutenant Colonel Berthoud is married to the former Joyce Elsie Hunt and they are the parents of three children.[10]

## Clotilde Dent Bowen

Colonel, U.S. Army Medical Corps.

Clotilde Bowen graduated from Ohio State University School of Medicine in 1947 and established a private practice in New York City, specializing in pulmonary diseases. She has also completed a residency in psychiatry at the Veterans Administration Hospital in Valley Forge, Pennsylvania. Colonel Bowen has held the position of chief of the Review Branch of the Army's Medicine Insurance Program (Civilian Health and Medical Program of the Uniformed Services) or CHAMPUS. She was the first Negro woman to attain the rank of full colonel in the United States military.[11]

*Colonel Clotilde D. Bowen*

## Herbert L. Brewer

Colonel, U.S. Marine Corps Reserve.

Herbert Brewer was born on December 1, 1924, in San Antonio, Texas, the son of Clifton L. and Marjorie E. Brewer. He attended public schools in San Antonio and enlisted in the Marine Corps in July, 1942, serving with the Fifty-First Defense Battalion at Camp Lejeune, North Carolina until January, 1944, when the unit deployed to the Pacific Theater of Operations. He attained the rank of sergeant as a fire control equipment technician and returned to the United States in August, 1944, to attend Purdue University under the Navy's V-12 program. In June, 1946, he was commissioned a Marine second lieutenant. After graduation from Purdue, Brewer was employed as an architect at the Philadelphia Naval Shipyard, and in October, 1948, he married Nellie M. Middleton of Philadelphia. He completed work on a master's degree in 1950, and in November of that year he was recalled to active duty and ordered to Quantico, Virginia. Later he was assigned to Camp Pendleton, California, where he served as Battery Officer of the First Anti-Aircraft Artillery Automatic Weapons Battalion until March, 1952, when he was released from active duty. In June, 1952, he was promoted to the rank of captain.

In 1953, Brewer took a civilian position as an engineer with the Philadelphia Water Department, and later joined the Army Corps of Engineers District Office. In 1957, he received his promotion to major. He continued to advance in civilian life as well as in the Military Reserve and in May, 1967, he became chief structural engineer for the Department of Architecture and Engineering of the School District of Philadelphia, having been promoted to lieutenant colonel on July 1, 1963. Colonel Brewer's medals and decorations include the American Campaign medal, the Marine Corps Reserve ribbon, the World War II Victory medal and the National Defense Service medal. He lives with his wife and five daughters in Philadelphia.

Colonel Brewer is the first Negro to attain the rank of marine colonel in active or reserve status.[12]

*Colonel Herbert L. Brewer*

## Harry W. Brooks Jr.

Brigadier General, U.S. Army.

Harry W. Brooks Jr. was born on May 17, 1928, in Indianapolis, Indiana. He received a B.S. degree in business administration from the University of Oklahoma. He has attended the Quartermaster School, Artillery and Guided Missile Schools, United States Army Command and General Staff College, and United States Army War College. His major duty assignments have been: advisor to U.S. Reserve Units, Northern New York Sector, II U.S. Army Corps, Syracuse, New York; advisor to U.S. Army Reserve Units Commanding Officer, U.S. Army Reserve Center, Northern Sector, II U.S. Army Corps, Syracuse, New York; commanding officer, Second Battalion, Fortieth Artillery, One Hundred and Ninety-Ninth Infantry Brigade, Fort Benning, Georgia, later U.S. Army, Vietnam; special assistant to deputy commanding officer, One Hundred and Ninety-Ninth Infantry Brigade, U.S. Army Vietnam; staff officer, Doctrine Branch, Doctrine and Concepts Division, Doctrine and Systems Directorate; officer, assistant chief of staff for force development, U.S. Army, Washington, D.C.; commanding officer, Seventy-Second Field Artillery Group, Europe, and chief, Equal Opportunities Division Office, deputy chief of staff for personnel, U.S. Army, Washington, D.C. Currently (1973) he is assistant division commander (ADC) 2d Infantry Division, Eight U.S. Army, Korea.

General Brooks has received the following awards: Legion of Merit (with oak leaf cluster), Bronze Star medal (with oak leaf cluster), Meritorious Service medal, Air medal (7th award) and Army Commendation medal.

In 1972, after completing twenty-four years of military service, Harry W. Brooks Jr. was promoted to the rank of brigadier general.[13]

*Brigadier General Harry W. Brooks Jr.*

**Wesley Anthony Brown**

Commander, U.S. Navy.

Wesley Brown was born in Baltimore, Maryland, on April 3, 1927, the son of Mr. and Mrs. William Brown. He was educated in Washington, D.C., and attended Howard University for one year as an army specialized training student, majoring in electrical engineering. He was appointed to the U.S. Naval Academy by Representative Adam Clayton Powell Jr., Twenty-Second New York Congressional district. Brown received his diploma from the naval academy on June 3, 1949, the first Negro to graduate from Annapolis.

After graduation, Brown was assigned duty for nine months in the Public Works Department, Naval Shipyard, Boston, Massachusetts. Later he completed a graduate course at Rensselaer Polytechnic Institute. In September, 1951, he was assigned as design and contract officer in the Public Works Department, Naval Supply Depot, Bayonne, New Jersey. He also served as senior company commander in a U.S. Mobile Construction Unit.[14]

*Brigadier General Cunningham C. Bryant*

**Cunningham C. Bryant**

Brigadier General, District of Columbia National Guard.

Cunningham Bryant was born in Clifton, Virginia, on August 8, 1921. After completing primary and secondary school, he attended Howard University and was enrolled in the advanced Reserve Officers Training Corps program by way of the Enlisted Reserve Corps in 1942. He was called to active service in 1943, and completed the Infantry Officer Candidate School at Fort Benning, Georgia. In April, 1944, Bryant was commissioned a second lieutenant and assigned as company commander, Three Hundred and Seventeenth Engineer (Combat) Battalion, Ninety-Second Infantry Division and served in Italy.

At the conclusion of World War II, having attained the rank of captain, he remained on active duty and served at Fort Benning, Georgia and Fort Belvoir, Virginia. He was promoted to major in 1949.

From 1950 to 1953, Major Bryant served in several USAR assagnments and in March, 1954, joined the District of Columbia National Guard as Operations and Training Officer, One Hundred and Fortieth Engineer Battalion. He was later assigned as battalion executive officer. Continuing to progress in the National Guard he was successively assistant operations and training officer in D.C. National Guard Headquarters, assistant commandant and commandant of D.C. National Guard Officer Candidate School. In 1962, he was promoted to lieutenant colonel and on January 1, 1968, he was promoted to colonel and became chief, Operations and Training Branch, Headquarters D.C. National Guard. On July 1, 1968, he was appointed to his present position: adjutant-general, and he served on active duty status until July 18, when he was finally recognized in the grade of brigadier general in the National Guard.

Brigadier General Bryant received his stars in an impressive Pentgon ceremony on July 29, 1971, becoming the first black general officer of the District of Columbia National Guard. His decorations include: Bronze Star medal, Purple Heart, Armed Forces Reserve medal, Army Commendation medal, Combat Infantryman badge, EAME Campaign medal with two battle stars. The general is married to the former Hyacinth F. Bowie and they have one son and two daughters.[15]

## William Maud Bryant

Sergeant First Class, Company A, Fifth Special Forces Group, First Special Forces.

William Bryant was born on February 16, 1933, in Cochran, Georgia, the son of Mr. and Mrs. Sebron Bryant. He attended Newark Vocational and Technical High School in Newark, New Jersey, and on March 16, 1953, he entered the U.S. Army at Detroit, Michigan.

Bryant attended various military schools during his career, including basic airborne course, Fort Benning, Georgia; basic heavy weapons course, Fort Campbell, Kentucky; jumpmaster course, Fort Bragg, North Carolina; advanced noncommissioned officer course, Fort Benning, Georgia; long range reconnaissance patrol school, Augsburg, Germany; explosive ordnance reconnaissance course, Hohenfels Training Area, Germany; counterinsurgency raider course, Fort Bragg, North Carolina; operations and intelligence course, Fort Bragg, North Carolina; special forces (airborne) course, Fort Bragg, North Carolina, and intelligence analyst special forces course, Fort Holabird, Maryland.

During the period March, 1953 to March, 1969, Bryant performed duty with the Eleventh Airborne Division Fort Benning, Georgia; Five Hundred and Fifth Airborne Infantry, Fort Bragg, North Carolina; the School Brigade, Fort Benning, Georgia; special forces training group (airborne) Fort Bragg, North Carolina; Seventh Special Forces Group (airborne) Fort Bragg, North Carolina, and Company A, Fifth Special Forces Group (airborne) First Special Forces, Vietnam. He also served in Germany and the Dominican Republic.

Sergeant Bryant's dedication to duty and past outstanding performances earned him the Bronze Star medal, Purple Heart, Good Conduct medal (third award), National Defense Service medal, Vietnam Service medal, Vietnam Campaign medal (Vietnamese) Combat Infantryman badge, Parachutist badge (Vietnamese).

Bryant and his wife Lizzie had five children.

On March 24, 1969, Sergeant Bryant displayed unusual bravery and leadership while serving in Long Khanh Province, Republic of Vietnam. He was posthumously awarded the nation's highest

*Sergeant First Class William M. Bryant*

military honor, the Medal of Honor on February 16, 1971. His citation reads as follows:

*Sergeant First Class William M. Bryant, assigned to Company A, Fifth Special Forces Group,*

First Special Forces, distinguished himself on 24 March, 1969 while serving as commanding officer of Civilian Irregular Defense Group Company 321, Second Battalion, Third Mobile Strike Force Command, during combat operations in Long Khanh Province, Republic of Vietnam. The battalion came under heavy fire and became surrounded by the elements of three enemy regiments. Sergeant Bryant displayed extraordinary heroism throughout the succeeding thirty-four hours of incessant attack as he moved throughout the company position heedless of the intense hostile fire while establishing and improving the defensive perimeter, directing fire during critical phases of the battle, distributing ammunition, assisting the wounded, and providing leadership and inspirational example of courage to his men. When a helicopter drop of ammunition was made to resupply the beleaguered force, Sergeant Bryant with complete disregard for his own safety ran through the heavy enemy fire to retrieve the scattered ammunition boxes and distributed needed ammunition to his men. During a lull in the intense fighting, Sergeant Bryant led a patrol outside the perimeter to obtain information of the enemy. The patrol came under intense automatic weapons fire and was pinned down. Sergeant Bryant single-handedly repulsed one enemy attack on his small force and by his heroic action inspired his men to fight off other assaults. Seeing a wounded enemy soldier some distance from the patrol location, Sergeant Bryant crawled forward alone under heavy fire to retrieve the soldier for intelligence purposes. Finding that the enemy soldier had expired, Sergeant Bryant crawled back to his patrol and led his men back to the company position where he again took command of the defense. As the siege continued, Sergeant Bryant organized and led a patrol in a daring attempt to break through the enemy encirclement. The patrol had advanced some two hundred meters by heavy fighting when it was pinned down by the intense automatic weapons fire from heavily fortified bunkers and Sergeant Bryant was severely wounded. Despite his wounds he rallied his men, called for helicopter gunship support, and directed heavy suppressive fire upon the enemy positions. Following the last gunship attack, Sergeant Bryant fearlessly charged an enemy automatic weapons position, overrunning it and single-handedly destroying its three defenders. Inspired by his heroic example, his men renewed their attack on the entrenched enemy. While regrouping his small force for the final assault against the enemy, Sergeant Bryant fell mortally wounded by an enemy rocket. Sergeant Bryant's conspicuous gallantry, selfless concern for his comrades, and intrepidity at the cost of his own life and beyond the call of duty are in keeping with the highest traditions of the military service and reflect great credit upon himself, his unit, and the United States Army.[16]

*Colonel Alfred J. Cade*

## Alfred J. Cade

Colonel, Headquarters, Two Hundred and Tenth Artillery Group

Alfred J. Cade was born in Fayetteville, North Carolina on February 4, 1931. He attended elementary and secondary schools in Emporia, Virginia. Cade graduated from Virginia State College,

Petersburg, Virginia in 1952; he has a bachelor of science degree and a regular Army commission as a second lieutenant from the Reserve Officers Training Corps (ROTC).

Colonel Cade's military assignments have been quite varied. He has performed duties as a battery commander in Korea, Germany and New Jersey. In the Republic of Vietnam, he served as an assistant sector advisor, sector advisor, deputy province senior advisor and later as commander of the First Battalion, Ninety-Second Field Artillery. Upon his return from Vietnam, Colonel Cade served in comptrollership positions with the Headquarters, Department of the Army and Army Material Command.

Colonel Cade's advance civilian and military education include a master's degree in business administration from Syracuse University in 1965,

and successful completion of the Command and General Staff College (regular course) in 1966 and the Industrial College of the Armed Forces (resident course) in 1970.

Cade's awards and decorations include: Legion of Merit with two oak leaf clusters, Bronze Star medal, Meritorious Service medal, Air medal with oak leaf clusters, Army Commendation medal, Vietnamese Armed Forces Honor medal, Vietnamese Gallantry Cross with two Silver Stars, Combat Infantry Badge, National Defense Service medal, Korean Service medal, Vietnam Service medal, United Nations Service medal and the Republic of Vietnam Campaign Ribbon.

Colonel Cade is married and the father of four sons and one daughter. His current assignment, in U.S. Army Europe, Germany, is commander of Two Hundred Tenth Artillery Group.[17]

*Captain Wayman G. Caliman Jr.*

## Wayman G. Caliman Jr.

Captain, U.S. Navy.

Wayman Caliman was born in New York City and enlisted in the U.S. Navy in October, 1950, as a seaman recruit. His first shipboard duty was on the USS *Cascade,* a destroyer tender, and his last tour of sea duty before reporting in 1972 as ma-

terial department director of the Oakland, California, Naval Supply Center, was as supply officer of the *Cascade.* Caliman was commissioned in 1952 after attending Officer Candidate School and is the sixth known black American to attain the rank of captain in the U.S. Navy.[18]

*Brigadier General Roscoe C. Cartwright*

### Roscoe C. Cartwright

Brigadier General, U.S. Army.

Roscoe Cartwright was born on May 27, 1919, in Kansas City, Kansas. He has a B.A. in social science from San Francisco State College and an M.B.A. in business administration from the University of Missouri. He also attended the Artillery School, U.S. Army, Command and General Staff College, and the Industrial College of the Armed Forces and is a distinguished military graduate of the Industrial College of the Armed Forces.

After completing over thirty-one years of active military service, Roscoe Conklin Cartwright was promoted brigadier general on August 1, 1971. During the period November, 1971 to January, 1972, General Cartwright was assigned as director of management, Review and Analysis, Office Comptroller of the Army, Washington. Other major duty assignments have been: comptroller, Seventh Army Training Center, U.S. Army, Europe; commanding officer, Second Howitzer Battalion, Fifth Artillery, U.S. Army, Europe; comptroller, U.S. Army Garrison, Fort Leavenworth, Kansas; chief, Management Systems Research and Development Division, Directorate of Management (additional duty; deputy project management), office of the Director of Management, Comptroller of the Army, Washington, D.C.; commanding officer, One Hundred and Eighth Artillery Group, U.S. Army, Pacific-Vietnam; deputy commanding officer, U.S. Army Support Command, U.S. Army, Pacific-Vietnam; chief, Budget and Five-Year Defense Program, Coordinating Division, Manpower and Forces Directorate Office of the Assistant Chief of Staff for Force Development, U.S. Army, Washington, D.C., and assistant division commander, Third Infantry Division, Headquarters, U.S. Army Europe. His current (1973) assignment is Comptroller, Headquarters, U.S. Army Europe.

General Cartwright has received the following medals and awards: Legion of Merit (with oak leaf clusters), Bronze Star medal (with two oak leaf clusters), Air medal (with oak leaf clusters), Army Commendation medal (with two oak leaf clusters), and the Meritorious Service medal.[19]

### Thomas E. Clifford
Brigadier General, U.S. Air Force

Thomas K. Clifford was born on March 9, 1929 in Washington, D.C. In 1949 he graduated from Howard University in Washington, D.C. with a bachelor of arts degree. General Clifford was commissioned a second lieutenant through the ROTC. He began active duty in September 1949. In November, 1950, Clifford entered student officers' pilot training. He completed pilot training and was assigned in April, 1952 as an all-weather jet pilot with the Fifth Fighter Interceptor Squadron, McGuire Air Force Base, New Jersey.

General Clifford's military assignments include: fighter pilot, Four Hundred and Forty-Ninth Fighter Interceptor Squadron, Alaska, 1953; fighter pilot, Four Hundred and Thirty-Seventh Fighter Interceptor Squadron, Oxnard Air Force Base, 1956; weapons training officer and flight commander, Three Hundred and Twenty-Ninth Fighter Interceptor Squadron, George Air Force Base, 1959; management analyst, Headquarters, U.S. Air Forces, Europe, 1963; staff officer, Office of the Deputy Chief of Staff; Programs and Resources, Headquarters, U.S. Air Forces, Europe, 1966; assistant for continuity of operations planning in the Office of the Secretary of Defense, 1967 and deputy commander of operations and later vice commander, Three Hundred and Sixty-Sixth Tactical Fighter Wing, Republic of Vietnam, 1971

In December, 1971 General Clifford was assigned to Germany as commander, Fifty-Second Tactical Fighter Wing. He was assigned as vice commander, Seventeenth Air Force, U.S. Air Forces, Europe in July, 1973.

Brigadier General Clifford has a master's degree in business administration from George Washington University and is also a graduate of the Industrial College of the Armed Forces. His awards and decorations include: Legion of Merit, Distinguished Flying Cross, Air medal (with one oak leaf cluster), and the Air Force Commendation medal (with one oak leaf cluster).[20]

*Brigadier General Thomas Clifford*

240

### Vernon C. Coffey

Lieutenant Colonel, U.S. Army.

Vernon Coffey is the second Negro to be assigned as an army aide to the President of the United States. He is a graduate of St. Benedict's College, Atchinson, Kansas and the U.S. Army Command and General Staff College. Lieutenant Colonel Coffey served as a battalion commander in Vietnam and was awarded the Silver Star while serving there with the First Infantry Division. He is responsible for coordinating all army supervised logistics required to support the president. He is also concerned with the planning of specific official functions, including medal of honor presentations and wreath-laying ceremonies; briefing the president in times of emergency, assisting him at honor ceremonies and being available to the president at official functions and journeys. Lieutenant Colonel Coffey's assignment as a presidential aide is an example of the opportunities that are becoming available to Negro officers as they progress toward attaining a more equitable share of the prestigious assignments that were not available to them in the past.[21]

*Lieutenant Colonel Vernon C. Coffey*

*Major Jerome Cooper*

### Jerome Cooper

Major, U.S. Marine Corps.

Jerome Cooper was born on October 2, 1936 in Lafayette, Louisiana, the son of Mr. and Mrs. Algernon J. Cooper, of Mobile, Alabama. He attended public schools in Lafayette, graduated from the University of Notre Dame in 1958 with a B.S. in commerce and was commissioned a U.S. Marine Corps Reserve second lieutenant. He was a member of the Naval ROTC unit at the University of Notre Dame. In March, 1959, he completed the Basic School, Marine Corps Schools, Quantico, Virginia.

During his military career, he has been assigned as rifle platoon leader, company executive officer, Company E, Second Battalion, Fourth Marine (Reinforced) First Marine Brigade, FMF, San Francisco, California; Training Officer, G3, First Marine Brigade (Second Battalion); Assistant Provost Marshal Officer, commanding officer, Security Company, and special services officer, Marine Corps Supply Center, Barstow, California. He was integrated into the regular marine corps in April, 1960.

Major Cooper served a two-year tour of sea

duty as commanding officer, Marine Detachment, on the *USS Chicago*. In April, 1966, he reported to Vietnam, where he served as commanding officer, Company M, Third Battalion and subsequently as civil affairs and psychological warfare officer of the Ninth Marines, Third Marine Division. In August, 1967, he was assigned as commanding officer, Company A, at Headquarters Marine Corps.

Military honors awarded to Major Cooper are the Bronze Star medal with combat "V", Purple Heart with gold star in lieu of a second award, the Presidential Unit Citation, National Defense Service medal, Vietnam Service medal with two bronze stars, the Vietnamese Gallantry Cross with silver star and the Republic of Vietnam Campaign medal.

Major Cooper and his wife, Charlotte, have three children. He resigned his active duty commission in 1969 and is currently commanding officer, Thirteenth Reconnaissance Company, Reserve Force Unit, Mobile, Alabama.[22]

*Lieutenant Colonel Woodrow W. Crockett*

### Woodrow W. Crockett

Lieutenant Colonel, U.S. Air Force.

Woodrow Crockett is the former deputy director of the F-106 Joint Test Force, McGuire Air Force Base, New Jersey. He was one of the first Negro officers to be assigned to the National Guard Bureau (Air Force), Washington, D.C.[23]

### Russell W. Curtis

Gunnery Sergeant, Supply Battalion, First Force Service Regiment, U.S. Marine Corps.

Russell Curtis was in Vietnam on August 21, 1967 when he was called on to help in the removal of a large mine which was located on a vital trail network. After assessing the situation, it was determined that the only feasible way of removing the mine was by hand. When the small force at the scene came under vicious sniper fire from a nearby tree line, Sergeant Curtis immediately dispersed his men to give covering fire and proceeded to remove the fuse and check the mine for additional booby traps. While the mine was being removed, Gunnery Sergeant Curtis noticed a M-26A1 hand grenade fixed to the mine. With complete disregard for his own safety, he shoved his comrade aside and shouted a warning. Unable to throw the grenade because of the close proximity of the friendly troops, he elected to absorb the impact of the explosion with his own body, thereby saving his comrades from death or injury. By his bold initiative, dauntless courage, and unselfish concern for his fellow marines, Gunnery Sergeant Curtis reflected great credit upon himself and the Marine Corps and upheld the highest traditions of the United States Naval Service. He was awarded the Navy Cross for his heroic performance beyond the call of duty.[24]

## Benjamin Oliver Davis Jr.

Lieutenant General, U.S. Air Force.

Benjamin O. Davis Jr. was born in Washington, D.C. on December 18, 1912. He graduated from Central High School, Cleveland, Ohio in 1929, attended Western Reserve University at Cleveland and later the University of Chicago. He entered the U.S. Military Academy at West Point, New York in July, 1932 and graduated in June, 1936 with a commission of second lieutenant of infantry.

In June, 1937 he was appointed commander of an infantry company at Fort Benning, Georgia, where he later attended the Infantry School, graduated and assumed duties as professor of military science at Tuskegee Institute, Tuskegee, Alabama. In May, 1941, he entered Advanced Flying School at nearby Tuskegee Army Air Base and received his pilot's wings in March, 1942.

General Davis transferred to the Army Air Corps in May, 1942. As commander of the Ninety-Ninth Fighter Squadron, he moved with his unit from Tuskegee Army Air Base to North Africa in April, 1943 and later to Sicily. He returned to the United States in October, 1943, assumed command of the Three Hundred and Thirty-Second Fighter Group at Selfridge Field, Michigan, and returned with the group to Italy two months later.

He returned to the United States in June, 1945 to command the Four Hundred and Seventy-Seventh Composite Group at Godman Field, Kentucky, and later assumed command. In March, 1946 he went to Lockbourne Army Air Base, Ohio, as commander of the base and in July, 1947 became commander of the Three Hundred and Thirty-Second Fighter Wing there.

In 1949, General Davis went to the Air War College, Maxwell Air Force Base, Alabama, and after graduation was assigned to the deputy chief of staff for operations, Headquarters U.S. Air Force, Washington, D.C. He served in various capacities with Headquarters until July, 1953, when he went to the advanced jet fighter gunnery school at Nellis Air Force Base, Nevada.

In November, 1953 he assumed duties as commander of the Fifty-First Fighter-Interceptor Wing, Far East Air Forces (FEAF), Korea. He served as director of operations and training at FEAF Headquarters, Tokyo, from 1954 until 1955, when he assumed the position of vice commander, Thirteenth Air Force, with additional duty as commander, Air Task Force 13 (Provisional), Taipei, Formosa.

In April, 1957 General Davis arrived at Ramstein, Germany, as chief of staff, Twelfth Air Force, United States Air Forces in Europe (USAFE). When the Twelfth Air Force was transferred to Waco, Texas, in December, 1957, he assumed new duties as deputy chief of staff for operations, Headquarters USAFE, Wiesbaden, Germany.

In July, 1961 he returned to the United States and Headquarters U.S. Air Force where he served as the director of manpower and organization, deputy chief of staff for programs and requirements; and in February, 1965 was assigned as assistant deputy chief of staff, programs and requirements. He remained in that position until his assignment as chief of staff for the United Nations Command and U.S. Forces in Korea in April, 1965. He assumed command of the Thirteenth Air Force at Clark Air Base in the Republic of the Philippines in August, 1967.

General Davis was assigned as deputy commander in chief, U.S. Strike Command, with headquarters at MacDill Air Force Base, Florida, in August, 1968, and also had additional duty as commander in chief, Middle-East, Southern Asia and Africa.

His military decorations include the Air Force Distinguished Service medal, Army Distinguished Service medal, Silver Star, Legion of Merit with two oak leaf clusters, Distinguished Flying Cross, Air medal with four oak leaf clusters, Air Force Commendation medal with two oak leaf clusters and the Philippine Legion of Honor. He is a command pilot. General Davis retired from active service on 1 February 1970.[25]

*Lieutenant Colonel Clarence L. Davis*

## Clarence L. Davis

Lieutenant Colonel, U.S. Marine Corps.

Clarence Davis was born on May 9, 1933, in Ville Platt, Louisiana. He attended Central High School in Galveston, Texas and Texas Southern University. In December, 1953, he enlisted in the U.S. Naval Reserve as an aviation cadet and received flight training at Pensacola, Florida and Kingsville, Texas. He was designated a naval aviator and commissioned a Marine Corps Reserve second lieutenant on June 28, 1955. He was integrated into the regular Marine Corps in August, 1967.

During his military career he has served as a pilot, VMF-232m MAG-k3m Air FMF, Pacific Hawaii; instrument flight instructor, Kingsville, Texas; pilot, VMF-451, MAG 15, Third Marine Aircraft Wing, Air FMF Pacific, Marine Corps Air Station El Toro, Santa Ana, California, and later with VMF-451, MAG 11, First Marine Wing, Air FMF Pacific in Taiwan and at Atsugi, Japan. He has also served as data processing officer, Marine Corps Air Station, El Toro (Santa Ana) California; air liaison officer, administrative officer, and executive officer, VMF 232, MAG 13, First Marine Brigade, First Anglico, FMF, Hawaii.

In July, 1965, Lieutenant Colonel Davis was assigned as officer in charge of Sub Unit No. 2 and officer in charge of a section, First Marine Aircraft Wing, DaNang, Republic of Vietnam. He has also received UMIE transition helicopter training at Camp Pendleton, California and earned a B.S. in chemistry from Chapman College, Orange, California, in June, 1967.

Lieutenant Colonel Davis has been awarded the National Defense Service medal, the Vietnam Service medal and the Republic of Vietnam Campaign medal.[26]

## Rodney M. Davis

Sergeant, Second Platoon, Company B, First Battalion, Fifth Marines, First Marine Division, U.S. Marine Corps.

Rodney Davis was born on April 7, 1942, at Macon, Georgia, the son of Gordon N. and Ruth A. Davis. He and his wife, Judy, have two children. On August 31, 1961, at Macon, Georgia, he enlisted in the U.S. Marine Corps. He received his recruit training at Parris Island, South Carolina, and completed additional training at Camp Lejeune, North Carolina. In June, 1964, he was assigned as a guard, U.S. Marine Detachment, Naval Activities, London, England. In August, 1967, he was assigned as a platoon guard, Company B, First Battalion, Fifth Marines, First Marine Division, Republic of Vietnam. During his military career, Davis received the following awards and decorations: Purple Heart, Good Conduct medal, National Defense Service medal, Armed Forces Expeditionary medal, Vietnam Service medal, Gal-

*Sergeant Rodney M. Davis*

lantry Cross with Palm and Republic of Vietnam Campaign medal.

On September 6, 1967, Sergeant Davis saved his fellow marines from injury and possible loss of life by throwing himself upon a grenade. He was awarded the Medal of Honor posthumously for his gallant deeds. His citation read as follows:

*For conspicuous gallantry and intrepidity at the risk of his life above and beyond the call of duty while serving as the right guide of the Second Platoon, Company B, First Battalion, Fifth Marines, First Marine Division, in action against enemy forces in Quang Nam Province, Republic of Vietnam, on 6 September 1967. Elements of the Second Platoon were pinned down by a numerically superior force of attacking North Vietnamese Army Regulars. Remnants of the platoon were located in a trenchline where Sergeant Davis was directing the fire of his men in an attempt to repel the enemy attack. Disregarding the enemy hand grenades and high volume of small arms and mortar fire, Sergeant Davis moved from man to man shouting words of encouragement to each of them while firing and throwing grenades at the onrushing enemy. When an enemy grenade landed in the trench in the midst of his men, Sergeant Davis, realizing the gravity of the situation, and in a final valiant act of complete self-sacrifice, instantly threw himself upon the grenade, absorbing with his own body the full and terrific force of the explosion. Through his extraordinary initiative and inspiring valor in the face of almost certain death, Sergeant Davis saved his comrades from injury and possible loss of life, enabled his platoon to hold its vital position, and upheld the highest traditions of the Marine Corps and the United States Naval Service. He gallantly gave his life for his country.*[27]

**Frederic Ellis Davison**

Major General, U.S. Army.

Frederic Davison was born in Washington, D.C. on September 28, 1917. He attended public schools in the District of Columbia and graduated from Dunbar High School in 1934. He entered Howard University in September, 1934 and was awarded a B.S. degree (cum laude) in 1938. Upon graduation he completed ROTC training and was commissioned a second lieutenant in the Infantry Reserve on March 17, 1939. He received an M.S. degree in 1940 from Howard University and in 1962 earned a second graduate degree, an M.A. in international affairs, from George Washington University.

On March 3, 1941, Davison was ordered to active duty with the Three Hundred and Sixty-Sixth Infantry Regiment at Fort Devens, Massachusetts. He was promoted to first lieutenant and later, captain, while serving as a machine gun platoon leader, executive officer and company commander of a heavy weapons company.

In 1946, Davison was separated from the army, enrolled in the Howard University College of Medicine and completed one year of study. After his initial year at medical school, he was offered an appointment in the regular army, which he accepted. He reported for duty at Fort Dix, New Jersey, as a training company commander. Other successful assignments have been: assistant PMS&T ROTC, South Carolina Agricultural and Mechanical College, Orangeburg, South Carolina; battalion operations officer, Three Hundred and Seventieth Armored Infantry Battalion, Munich, Germany; staff officer, Personnel Services Division, G-1 Section, Eighth United States Army, Korea; G-1 staff officer, HQ Eighth U.S. Army; Fort George C. Meade, Maryland; commander, Third Training Brigade (BCT), U.S. Army Training Center (AD), Fort Bliss, Texas.

General Davison has also been assigned to the Pentagon as chief, Reserve Components Division, Office of the Undersecretary of the Army; interim executive officer to the deputy undersecretary for manpower and reserve forces.

One of the most notable achievements of General Davison's illustrious career was his appointment as deputy brigade commander and later brigade commender, One Hundred and Ninety-Ninth Light Infantry Brigade, Republic of Vietnam.

General Davison has been a member of the Williams Board, Office of Personnel Operations, U.S. Army, Washington, and director of Enlisted Personnel Directorate, Office of Personnel Operations, U.S. Army, Washington.

In September, 1971, General Davison was assigned as Deputy Chief of Staff, Personnel Headquarters, U.S. Army, Europe and Seventh U.S. Army.

General Frederic Davison became the first black American officer to command a U.S. Army Division when he assumed command in the spring, 1972 of the Eighth Infantry Division at Bad Kreuznach, Germany.

The general has graduated from the U.S. Army Command and General Staff College, Regular Course, and U.S. Army War College. His decorations include the Distinguished Service medal, Legion of Merit, Bronze Star medal, Air medal (with eighteen oak leaf clusters), Army Commendation medal (with two oak leaf clusters) and Combat Infantryman badge (second award).

General Davison and his wife, Jean, have three daughters.[28]

*Major General Frederic E. Davison and (right)*
*Brigadier General Oliver W. Dillard*

## Oliver William Dillard

Brigadier General, U.S. Army.

Oliver Dillard was born on September 28, 1926, in Margaret, Alabama. He graduated from the University of Omaha, Nebraska (B.G.E., general education) and George Washington University (M.S., international affairs). He has also attended the Infantry School, U.S. Army, Europe, Signal School; U.S. Army Command and General Staff College (regular course), the National War College (regular course), and Foreign Service Institute Vietnam Province Advisor Course.

General Dillard's major military assignments have included: deputy chief of mission, Operations and Intelligence Section, U.S. Military Mission to Liberia, Monrovia, Liberia; chief, Europe, Africa and Middle East Section, Special Warfare and Foreign Assistance Branch CI/P Division Office; assistant chief of staff for intelligence, Department of Army; staff officer, U.S. Army Combat Developments Command, Institute of Special Studies, Fort Belvoir, Virginia; commanding officer, Fifth Combat Support Training Brigade, Fort Dix, New Jersey, and province senior advisor, Advisor Team No. 41, U.S. Military Assistance Command, Vietnam, and assistant chief of staff, Intelligence Department of the Army, Washington, Office of the Deputy Assistant Chief of Staff for Intelligence. His awards and medals include the Silver Star, Legion of Merit (with oak leaf cluster), Army Commendation medal (with oak leaf cluster), Purple Heart and Combat Infantryman Badge.

On February 1, 1972, Dillard was promoted to brigadier general. He has completed more than twenty-three years of military service.[29]

*Judge Robert M. Duncan being sworn in at the U.S. Court of Military Appeals*

## Robert M. Duncan

Judge, U.S. Court of Military Appeals.

Robert M. Duncan was born in Urbana, Ohio, on August 24, 1927. He attended secondary school in Urbana, Ohio and Ohio State University (B.Sc., 1948). He was president of the 1952 class, Ohio State University College of Law, where he received a J.D. degree. He has also completed the appellate judge's seminar, School of Law, New York University and attended the National College of State Trial Judges, University of Nevada.

Judge Robert M. Duncan's professional experience has included: assistant attorney general; attorney examiner, Bureau of Workmen's Compensation; assistant city attorney, City of Columbus, Ohio; chief counsel to the attorney general of Ohio; judge, Franklin County Municipal Court, Ohio; justice of the Supreme Court of Ohio.

On September 21, 1971, President Nixon appointed Robert M. Duncan to the U.S. Court of Military Appeals and the Senate confirmed his appointment on October 6, 1971. Judge Duncan's professional memberships include: Ohio State and Columbus Bar Association; Ohio Judicial Conference Executive Committee; Ohio Criminal Rules Advisory Committee; American Bar Association, and National Bar Association. His other memberships include Kappa Alpha Psi and Sigma Pi Phi fraternities, Franklin County and Buckeye Republican Clubs, Ohio Republican Council, United Community Council Community Relations Committee, Ohio Crime Commission, Executives Club, National Legal Committee of the NAACP, and Presidents' Development Council of Wilberforce University. Duncan is also a member of the Board of Trustees of Defiance College, Franklin University, Columbus, Ohio; Ohio Law Opportunity Fund, Columbus International Program and Central District Boy Scouts of America. Judge Duncan served in the U.S. Army from 1952 to 1954. He and his wife, Shirley, have three children.[30]

*Captain Edward J. Dwight Jr.,
the first black astronaut trainee.*

*James C. Evans*

### James Carmichael Evans

Civilian Counselor to Assistant Secretary of Defense for Manpower and Resources.

James Evans was born in Gallatin, Tennessee, on July 1, 1900. He is the son of James Royal and Lillie (Carmichael) Evans. He attended Roger Williams University, Memphis, Tennessee (B.S., 1921; M.S., electrical and construction engineering, 1925). He also has LL.D. degrees from Virginia State College (1955) and Central State College (1956), and an L.H.D., Agriculture and Technical College, North Carolina (1961). Mr. Evans married the former Rosaline McGoodwin on August 18, 1928. They have two children.

Mr. Evans served as a military instructor during World War I. He has received the following honors; Dorie Miller Memorial Foundation Award, 1953; Career Service Award, National Civil Service League, 1959; Harman Award in Science for research in electronics, 1926. He is the author of monographs on training and placement in technical fields and the holder of a patent on utilization of exhaust gases to prevent icing on aircraft.

During the period 1921 to 1941, Mr. Evans held the following positions: teacher, Booker T. Washington High School, Miami, Florida; professor of technical industries and director of trade and technical division, West Virginia State College, Institute, West Virginia; administrative assistant to Council of National Defense, War Manpower Commission. In 1941, Mr. Evans was appointed assistant civilian aide to the Secretary of War. He served in that capacity until July, 1947, at which time he was appointed civilian aide to the secretary of the army. Upon the reorganization of the armed forces he was designated civilian aide counselor to the assistant secretary of defense. James C. Evans is a member of the Institute of Radio Engineers, American Institute of Electrical Engineers, American Association of University Professors, Adelphian (Miami, Florida) Club, Alpha Phi Alpha Social Fraternity, Sigma Pi Phi and Beta Kappa Chi (scientific) fraternities. He has held office in the National Technical Association. Mr. Evans has also served as a visiting professor of engineering at Howard University, Washington, D.C.

Midshipman from Prairie View A & M
College aboard the USS Lexington (above);
First Lieutenant Francis R. Lentz conducts
a class at the Race Relations School
in Oberammergau, Germany.

Members of the Task Force on the
Administration of Military Justice in the
Armed Forces at a meeting in
Washington, D.C. (above, left); Captain
Ken Schaefer with three members of his
Race Relations Class (below, left).

The appointment of Mr. Evans as an assistant to the secretary of defense was a milestone in the continuing progress of race relations in America's armed forces. This was evident in the increasing authority and latitude accorded Mr. Evans in advising the secretary in racial matters in the integrating services. He worked closely with the Personnel Policy Board of the Military for uniform procedures and practices to assure equality of treatment and opportunity for all personnel. He has constantly appraised the Negro officer's promotion and assignment progress in the three services. In 1960 and 1962, he published a pamphlet, a representative listing of Negro personnel selected for range of assignments in the various services and historical notes of their progress through the Korean conflict.

An illustration of Mr. Evans' behind-the-scenes legitimate interest and advice can best be seen from the following incident quoted from an article in NATO's Fifteen Nations Act, November 1968, "The Role of the Negro in the US Armed Forces":

*Although all Negro units did not rate well in Korea there was indication some of this failure was due to poor white leadership. I recall a regimental commander complaining that his Negro troops ran to the rear under moderate fire. He related this story to the staff in Washington. Present for this meeting was the Negro advisor to the Secretary of Defense. This gentleman cornered the Commander prior to his leaving the room and said: "Colonel, I understand you outdistanced your troops in leading them to the rear."*

James C. Evans has been an inspiration and a guiding light to many Negro personnel in the armed forces during his career. Many of the current achievements of Negro military personnel in promotions and assignments can be attributed to his advice and to the devotion to duty that Mr. Evans has maintained through the years.[31]

*Colonel Hampson H. Fields*

## Hampson H. Fields

Colonel, U.S. Army.

Hampson Fields was born in Cleveland, Ohio and graduated from East Tech High School in June, 1938. He attended Western Reserve University for one year and enlisted in the army in March, 1941. After serving three years with an engineer regiment and reaching the grade of technical sergeant E-7, he attended Officer Candidate School in Brisbane, Australia, and was commissioned a second lieutenant, infantry, on April 1, 1943. From October, 1945 to June, 1948 he was on inactive duty with the U.S. Army Reserve; he attended Fenn College in Cleveland for one year during this period.

He returned to active duty on June 21, 1948, as a first lieutenant, Transportation Corps and was assigned to the Forty-Eighth Transportation Company, Fort Eustis, Virginia, where he attended the Transportation Officers Basic Course. Later assignments included Camp Kilmer, N.J., Fort Dix, N.J. and Oakland Army Base, California. In February, 1950, he returned to Fort Eustis to take the Transportation Advanced Course, and in January, 1951 he was promoted to captain. He was next assigned to Korea for duty with the Three Hundred and Fifty-First Transportation Group and was later transferred to Japan as post transportation officer.

Colonel Fields returned from Japan to command the Sixteenth Transportation Company at Fort Eustis and later served as S-3, Forty-Eighth Transportation Group. He attended Command and General Staff College, and was assigned to Europe as S-3 of the Fourth Transportation Battalion.

Colonel Fields returned to CONUS in 1959 for assignment as advisor to the New Jersey Army National Guard. In 1963 he attended the University of Maryland under the Bootstrap Program and received a B.S. degree. He attended the Vietnamese Language School in California in preparation for a tour of duty in Vietnam where he was senior advisor to the Vietnamese Transportation Officer. He was promoted to lieutenant colonel while serving in Vietnam.

Completion of his Vietnam tour brought Colonel Fields to his first assignment in Washington, D.C., where he was assigned to the DA staff. In 1965, he attended the transportation management program of Stanford University and in January, 1967, he was transferred to Europe to command the One Hundred and Eighty-First Transportation Battalion. On June 17, 1968, he was promoted to colonel and assigned as deputy commander, Rhineland Pfalz district. During the last two years of his European tour of duty he served as CO, Support Activity, EUCOM and Post Commander, Patch Barracks.

Colonel Fields has served as pentagon commandant and commanding officer, Headquarters, U.S. Army Service Center for the Armed Forces since September, 1970. He has been awarded the Legion of Merit, the Bronze Star medal with oak leaf cluster, Meritorious Service medal, Joint Service Commendation medal, and Army Commendation medal with two oak leaf clusters.[32]

*Deputy Assistant Secretary of Defense
H. Minton Francis*

## H. Minton Francis

Deputy Assistant Secretary of Defense
(Equal Opportunity)

H. Minton Francis is a native of Washington, D.C. He is a graduate of Paul Lawrence Dunbar High School, Washington, D.C. and is a 1944 graduate of the U.S. Military Academy at West Point, New York. Francis has a master of business administration degree from Syracuse University. He has held positions as vice president and general manager of AVCO Printing and Publishing Division of AVCO Corporation in Boston, Massachusetts.

On July 6, 1973, Secretary of Defense James R. Schlesinger announced the appointment of H. Minton Francis as Deputy Assistant Secretary of Defense (Equal Opportunity) in the Office of the Assistant Secretary of Defense (Manpower and Reserve Affairs). He replaced Donald L. Miller who resigned in January, 1973.

Francis is married to the former Doris E. Hull of Washington, D.C. They have five children: Mrs. Marsha Jones, Henry M. Jr., Peter M., Marya K. and John H. Prior to his appointment Francis resided in Roxbury, Massachusetts. He was sworn into office on August 3, 1973 during a Pentagon ceremony.[33]

**Samuel L. Gravely**

Admiral, U.S. Navy.

Samuel Gravely was born on June 4, 1922, in Richmond, Virginia, the son of Samuel L. and Mary George (Simon) Gravely. He attended Armstrong High School in Richmond and Virginia Union University and enlisted in the U.S. Naval Reserve on September 15, 1942. Later he was commissioned ensign in the USNR, the first Negro to graduate from a Midshipman School. He has served in various assignments including assistant battalion commander, Naval Training Center; communications officer, electronics officer, and personnel officer, Sub-Chaser Training Center, Miami, Florida. He was released from active duty in April, 1946. In August, 1949, Admiral Gravely returned to active duty in the navy. He was assigned as assistant to the officer in charge for recruiting at the Naval Recruiting Station, Washington, D.C. In June, 1953, he served aboard the USS Toledo as communications officer and assistant operations officer. In July, 1955, Gravely was assigned to Headquarters, Third Naval District, New York, as assistant district security officer. He became executive officer of the USS Theodore E. Chandler and on February 15, 1961 he was made commanding officer of the Chandler. On January 31, 1962, Gravely assumed command of the radar picket destroyer escort USS Falgout, based at Pearl Harbor, Hawaii. He was the first Negro to command two United States warships, the USS Falgout and the USS Taussig.

From August, 1963 to June, 1964, he attended a course in naval warfare at the Naval War College, Newport, Rhode Island. He was the first black line officer to attain the rank of navy captain. During the period, June, 1968 to 1970, Captain Gravely was assigned to coordinator, Navy Satellite Communications Program, Office of the Assistant Chief, Naval Operations. On May 22, 1970, he assumed command of one of the navy's most modern guided missile Frigates, USS Jouett.

The U.S. Navy made an announcement on June 2, 1971 that the first black American navy officer had been promoted to the rank of rear admiral. Admiral Gravely then assumed duties as director, Naval Communications and commander, Naval Communications Command. His current assignment is commander, cruiser destroyer flotilla TWO.

Admiral Gravely's decorations include: Meritorious Service medal, Korean Presidential Unit Citation Ribbon, Naval Reserve medal, American Campaign medal, World War II Victory medal, National Defense Service medal with bronze star, China Service medal, Korean Service medal with two bronze stars, United Nations Service medal, Armed Forces Expeditionary medal and Vietnam Service medal.

The Admiral is married to the former Alma Bernice Clark of Christiansburg, Virginia and they have three children.[34]

## Edward L. Green

Major, U.S. Marine Corps.

Edward Green was born on September 9, 1937 in Henderson, North Carolina. He later moved to Bryn Mawr, Pennsylvania and attended junior and senior high schools in Haverford, Pennsylvania. In May, 1959, he obtained a bachelor of science degree from State Teachers College, Westchester, Pennsylvania, where his record was impressive; he earned athletic awards in cross country track meets and as a senior was selected for *Who's Who in American Colleges and Universities.*

He enrolled in the platoon leader's class in 1955 and was commissioned a U.S. Marine Corps Reserve second lieutenant on June 3, 1959. He completed the Basic School, Marine Corps Schools, Quantico, Virginia, in April, 1960 and the Communications Officer Orientation Course at the Marine Corps Schools in May, 1960.

During his military career, Major Green has been assigned as watch officer, First Marine Division (Reinforced) FMF, radio platoon commander, executive officer and commanding officer, First Communication Company (Provisional), Third Marine Division, Okinawa.

On August 5, 1964, he was assigned to the Republic of Vietnam. He deployed with advance elements of the Ninth Marine Expeditionary Brigade and was commanding officer with the Fifth Communication Battalion, Third Marine Division, FMF. In October, 1964, he was assigned duty as communications officer at the Marine Corps Air Facility, New River, Jacksonville, North Carolina. In November, 1966, he was transferred to Twenty-nine Paline, California and was assigned as company officer, Radio Relay and Construction Company, Ninth Communication Battalion, Force Troops, FMF, Pacific. He has also served on the staff J-6, Military Assistance Command, Republic of Vietnam. He has been awarded the National Defense Service medal and the Armed Forces Expeditionary medal.

Major Green is married to the former Lilian Miles of Philadelphia, Pennsylvania. They have three children.[35]

## John S. Green

Gunnery Sergeant, U.S. Marine Corps.

John Green was awarded the Navy Cross for unusual heroism while serving in Vietnam. His citation read as follows:

*For extraordinary heroism in action against enemy forces while serving as Company Gunnery Sergeant, Company F, Second Battalion, Fifth Marines, First Marine Division (Reinforced) in the Republic of Vietnam on June 2, 1967. During Operation UNION II, Company F came under intense enemy small arms, automatic weapons and mortar fire from a well-entrenched enemy force and was temporarily halted. Gunnery Sergeant Green, with complete disregard for his own safety, led a frontal assault against the enemy positions. Leading his men across 800 meters of open, fire-swept rice paddy, he quickly overran the Viet Cong machine gun position and personally accounted for ten enemy killed. After seizing the objective, he immediately established a hasty defense and began redistributing ammunition to his men. He fearlessly braved the intense enemy fire by exposing himself in carrying wounded to positions of relative safety. By his daring initiative, valiant fighting spirit and selfless devotion to duty in the face of danger and insurmountable odds, Gunnery Sergeant Green was responsible in great measure for saving many of his comrades and thereby upheld the highest traditions of the Marine Corps and the United States Naval Service.[36]*

## Paul Green

Captain, U.S. Navy.

Paul Green was born on December 25, 1919, in Manson, North Carolina. He graduated from Shaw University, Raleigh, North Carolina and the Howard University College of Medicine. He was commissioned a lieutenant in the Medical Corps of the U.S. Naval Reserve on October 15, 1949, and in November, 1949, was ordered into active naval service assigned to the Naval Hospital Portsmouth, Virginia. Later, he was assigned to the Naval Gun Factory, Washington, D.C.; the Naval Hospital, San Diego, California, and the Naval Hospital, Long Beach, California. He was promoted captain in August, 1968, the first Negro physician to achieve this rank in the U.S. Navy Medical Corps and one of the few Negro captains in the U.S. Navy. His recent assignment has been at the U.S. Naval Hospital in LeMoore, California as executive officer and chief of professional services. He is married and he and his wife, Virginia, have one son.[37]

*Captain Paul Greene*

# THE VIETNAM WAR

An integrated group from the Women's Air Force, photographed near the Pentagon (left); Members of the 2045th Communications group prepare to use a UNIVAC machine (below, left); U.S. Coast Guard SPARS receive assignments (above) and mess together (below).

260

*Brigadier General Edward Greer*

**Edward Greer**

Brigadier General, U.S. Army.

Edward Greer was born on March 8, 1924, in Gary, West Virginia. He has a B.S. in biological science from West Virginia State University, and an M.S. in international affairs from George Washington University. He has also attended the Ground General School, Artillery School, the U.S. Army Command and General Staff College, and the National War College. His major duty assignments have been: personnel management officer, Assignment Branch, Artillery Officers Division, Washington, personnel management officer, Artillery Branch, Combined Arms Division, Office of Personnel Operations, U.S. Army, Washington; commanding officer, First Battalion, Seventeenth Artillery, U.S. Army, Korea; author-instructor, Command Section, Department of Command, U.S. Army, Command and General Staff College, Fort Leavenworth, Kansas; member, General Operations Division, J-3, Organization of the Joint Chiefs of Staff, Washington; deputy commander, XXIV Corps Artillery, U.S. Army, Vietnam, and assistant director, Directorate for Reserve Forces, Plans Programs and Budgets, Office of the Assistant Secretary of Defense (Manpower and Reserve Affairs), Washington.

General Greer has received the following military honors: Silver Star, Legion of Merit, Bronze Star medal (with oak leaf cluster), Air medal, Joint Service Commendation medal, and Army Commendation medal (with oak leaf cluster).

After the completion of more than twenty-six years of military service, Edward Greer was promoted to brigadier general in 1972.[38]

*Brigadier General Arthur James Gregg*

### Arthur James Gregg

Brigadier General, U.S. Army.

Arthur Gregg was born on May 11, 1928 in Florence, South Carolina. He received a B.S. degree in Business Administration from St. Benedict College and also attended the Quartermaster School, U.S. Army Command and General Staff College, and U.S. Army War College. His major duty assignments have been: operations officer Ninety-Fifth Quartermaster Battalion, U.S. Army, Europe; logistical plans officer, Concepts Branch, Plans Division, later assistant secretary, U.S. Army Materiel Command, Washington; commanding officer, Ninety-Sixth Quartermaster Battalion, later Supply and Service Battalion, Fort Riley, Kansas, later Vietnam; logistics officer, J-4, U.S. European Command, U.S. Army, Europe; deputy director of troop support, Office, Deputy Chief of Staff for Logistics, U.S. Army, Washington; commanding officer, Nahbollenbach Army Depot, U.S. Army, Europe. He is currently commander, European Exchange System (EES).

General Gregg has received the following medals and awards: Legion of Merit (with oak leaf cluster), Joint Service Commendation medal, and Army Commission medal (with two oak leaf clusters). After the completion of over twenty-six years of military service, Arthur James Gregg was promoted brigadier general in 1972.[39]

*Chief Warrant Officer Annie L. Grimes*

**Annie L. Grimes**
Chief Warrant Officer, U.S. Marine Corps.

Annie Grimes was born in Arlington, Tennessee, the daughter of Mr. and Mrs. Horace K. Grimes, and attended high school in Summerville, Tennessee and the Ray Vogue Trade School in Chicago, Illinois. On February 2, 1950, she enlisted in the Marine Corps, in Chicago, and was assigned to Parris Island, South Carolina, where she completed recruit training and was promoted to private first class. In April, 1951, she was promoted to corporal; in November, 1951, to sergeant; in June, 1952, to staff sergeant, and in June, 1953 to gunnery sergeant. From 1950 to 1953 she served with the supply branch, Headquarters, Marine Corps. Continuing to advance in rank, Sergeant Grimes became a master sergeant in January, 1961 and a warrant officer in July, 1966. In August, 1968, she attained the rank of chief warrant officer.

Chief Warrant Officer Grimes' assignments have included: procurement chief, Marine Corps Depot of Supplies (Supply Forwarding Annex), San Francisco, California; procurement chief, Marine Corps Base Camp, Pendleton, California, and procurement chief, Marine Corps Supply School, Marine Corps Base, Camp LeJeune, North Carolina. In 1967, she was assigned to the Marine Corps Supply Center, Barstow, California, as project officer, Woman Marine Company.

She has been awarded the Good Conduct medal with two bronze stars, the National Defense Service medal with one bronze star, and a meritorious mast. Chief Warrant Officer Grimes retired from the Marine Corps in 1971.[40]

*General Ralph E. Haines Jr., CG CONARC, congratulates Sergeant First Class Larry J. Hamilton on his Meritorious Service Medal.*

### Larry J. Hamilton

Sergeant First Class, Equal Opportunity and Race Relations Division, Office of the Deputy Chief of Staff for Personnel, U.S. Army, Europe.

Larry J. Hamilton, a native of Birmingham, Alabama, was born on August 17, 1945. He has served as an administrative assistant and stenographer for several general officers at high level staff positions throughout his army career. Sergeant Hamilton has also been assigned in the area of Equal Opportunity and Race Relations as the first Chief NCO of the U.S. Army, Europe Equal Opportunity Staff.

On February 8, 1972, Sergeant Hamilton was awarded the Meritorious Service medal for outstanding performance of duty as administrative assistant/stenographer for the former commanding general, Continental U.S. Army Command, General Ralph E. Haines. He is the first known black enlisted man to serve as an administrative assistant/stenographer for a four-star general at a high level staff position. He has traveled to every army installation throughout CONUS with the general. This is significant because military history reveals that many black enlisted personnel have served faithfully and efficiently as enlisted aides, cooks and chauffeurs for high ranking general officers. His administrative knowledge has given him several high level assignments as stenographer for the commander, U.S. Army Transportation Command (Vietnam) (1967–68), stenographer for the commander, Sixth Artillery Group, Fort Bliss, Texas (1966–67), and as chief, Administrative NCO, Deputy Chief of Staff, Personnel, HQ, U.S. Continental Army Command, prior to joining General Haines' staff in 1970. Sergeant Hamilton's awards and decorations include the Meritorious Service medal, Bronze Star medal and Army Commendation medal.[41]

*Brigadier General James F. Hamlet*

## James Frank Hamlet

Major General, U.S. Army.

James Hamlet was born on December 13, 1921, in Alliance, Ohio. He is a graduate of St. Benedict's College, and has also attended the U.S. Army Infantry School, Artillery School, Army Aviation School, Command and General Staff College (regular course), and Army War College (regular course).

General Hamlet's major military assignments have included: staff officer, Budget Section Program and Budget Branch, Requirements Division, Office of Chief of Staff for Logistics, Washington, D.C.; action officer, Materiel, Programs and Review and Facilities Division, Aviation Directorate, Office Deputy Chief of Staff for Force Development, Washington; project officer, U.S. Army Combat Developments Command Combined Arms Agency, Fort Leavenworth, Kansas; operations officer, Eleventh Aviation Group, First Cavalry Division, U.S. Army, Pacific-Vietnam; commanding officer, Two Hundred and Twenty-Seventh Aviation Battalion; executive officer, Eleventh Aviation Group, First Cavalry Division, U.S. Army Pacific-Vietnam; chief, Air Mobility Branch, Doctrine and Systems Division, U.S. Army Combat Developments, Command Combat Arms Group, Fort Leavenworth, Kansas, and commanding officer, Eleventh Aviation Group (Airmobile) U.S. Army, Vietnam. His current assignment is commanding general, Fourth Infantry Division (Mech) and Fort Carson, Colorado.

General Hamlet's medals and awards include: Legion of Merit (with two oak leaf clusters); Distinguished Flying Cross, Soldiers' medal, Bronze Star medal (with oak leaf clusters), Army Commendation medal (with three oak leaf clusters) and Combat Infantryman Badge.

On September 1, 1971, James Frank Hamlet was promoted to brigadier general. In June, 1971, he was assigned as the assistant division commander, One Hundred First Airborne Division (Airmobile), U.S. Army, Vietnam. General Hamlet has completed over twenty-seven years of military service.[42]

## Benjamin Lacy Hunton

Brigadier General, U.S. Army Reserves.

Benjamin Hunton was born on November 29, 1919 in Washington, D.C. He graduated from Dunbar High School in 1936 and attended Howard University, graduating in 1940. He has an M.A. in history (1942) from Howard University and a Ph.D in public administration (1954) from American University.

General Hunton's civilian job experience has included employment in District of Columbia Public Schools from 1941 to 1966. He has served as a teacher, supervisor and administrator at junior and senior high school levels and as an assistant superintendent in charge of junior and senior high schools. He has also taught classes at Catholic and Howard Universities. Since 1966, he has worked for the federal government as an area director, Equal Educational Opportunities Program, U.S. Office of Education; civil rights specialist, Office for Civil Rights, Department of Health, Education and Welfare, and as a Job Corps program officer in the U.S. Department of Information. Currently, he is assigned as an assistant director for Education and Training, Bureau of Mines, U.S. Department of the Interior.

General Hunton has had a broad and varied military career. Upon graduation from Howard University in 1942, he received a commission as second lieutenant, attaining the rank of captain in January, 1945. During World War II, the general also served as an assistant professor of military science and tactics at Howard University.

General Hunton's other military assignments have included: battalion commander, Four Hundred and Twenty-Eighth Infantry Regiment, battalion executive officer, Three Hundred and Seventeenth Glider Infantry Regiment; battalion commander, Three Hundred and Seventeenth Infantry; regimental commander, Three Hundred and Seventeeth Regiment (Basic Combat Training) Eightieth Division (Training), and brigade commander, First Brigade, Eightieth Division (Training).

Brigadier General Hunton has attended the Army Command and General Staff College, Fort Leavenworth, Kansas. His military decorations are the American Campaign Ribbon, World War

*Brigadier General Benjamin L. Hunton*

II Victory Ribbon and Armed Forces Reserve medal with clasp.

After his thirty years of commissioned service, the U.S. Senate confirmed Benjamin L. Hunton as brigadier general, Army Reserve, effective June 4, 1971. General Hunton became the first known black reserve general officer in the history of U.S. Armed Forces Reserves. His present military reserve mobilization assignment is Minority Affairs Office, Office of the Chief of Reserve Components, Department of the Army. He was named commander of the Ninety-Seventh Army Reserve Command at Fort Meade, Maryland in 1972.

The general is second vice chairman of AMVETS Post 15; member of the Health and Welfare Council, District of Columbia; the School Club of Washington and Ardwick Civic Association. General Hunton and his wife Jean have one son and presently reside in Hyattsville, Maryland.[43]

## Al C. Irby

Command Sergeant Major, U.S. Army Field Artillery School, Fort Sill, Oklahoma.

Al Irby is from Montgomery, Alabama and graduated from Lovelace High School, Montgomery. He is married, and has two daughters and two sons. Irby has traveled extensively during his thirty years of service. He served in the Pacific Theater during World War II, and completed assignments in England, France, Turkey, Germany, Vietnam, and various posts in the United States. He was selected on the first increment for the command sergeant's program in 1968. His major assignments have included battalion supply sergeant, regimental supply sergeant, combat team transportation NCO, first sergeant, service training and operations NCO for a Military Museum Advisory Team, battalion sergeant major, U.S. Army Training Center, field artillery sergeant major, first field forces artillery command sergeant major, and artillery group command sergeant major.

*Command Sergeant Major Al C. Irby*

Sergeant Irby was chosen in 1946 to be the senior color (flag) sergeant of a combat team color guard, Armed Forces Day Parade in Washington, D.C., and in 1965 selected to be a member of the cordon participating in the inauguration day ceremony for the president of the United States. During his outstanding career, Irby has been awarded the Legion of Merit with oak leaf cluster, the Bronze Star, the Air medal, and the Commendation medal with oak leaf cluster. Command Sergeant Major Irby is one of the select group of top senior non-commissioned officers in the United States Army.[44]

## Daniel (Chappie) James Jr.

Lieutenant General, U.S. Air Force, Deputy Assistant Secretary of Denfense for Public Affairs.

General James was born in Pensacola, Florida on February 11, 1920. He graduated from Washington High School, Pensacola, Florida in June 1937, and studied at Tuskegee Institute, Tuskegee, Alabama, from September, 1937 to March, 1942, majoring in physical education; he also received his pilot training while at Tuskegee. James became a civilian instructor pilot and taught Army Air Corps cadets until January, 1943. He entered the Aviation Cadet Program and was commissioned in July, 1943. He received fighter overseas combat training at Selfridge Field, Michigan. Upon completion of his training he was assigned to the Three Hundred and Thirty-Second Composite Group as squadron operations officer, flying model plane P-47's. In September, 1949, James was assigned as a flight leader in the Twelfth Fighter Bomber Squadron, Eighteenth Fighter Wing, Clark Field, Philippines. In July, 1950, he was transferred to Korea, where he successfully flew one hundred and one combat missions in F-51 and F-80 model planes. He became an all-weather jet pilot assigned to Otis Air Force Base, Massachusetts in July, 1951. Later he was assigned as the operations officer, Fifty-Eighth Fighter Squadron. In August, 1955, he assumed command of the Sixtieth Fighter Interceptor Squadron. During his assignment in Massachusetts he was quite active in community relations programs. He was selected by the Massachusetts Junior of Commerce as Outstanding Man of the Year for 1955. General James has attended senior air force service schools. Some unique assignments during his career have been: staff officer, Office of the Deputy Chief of Staff for Operations, Air Defense Division, Pentagon; assistant director of Operations Eighty-First Fighter Wing Royal Air Force Station, Bentwaters, England, and commander Ninety-Second Tactical Fighter Squadron at the Royal Air Force station in Woodbridge, England. In September, 1964, General James was assigned to Davis Monthan Air Force Base as director of operational training and later as deputy commander for operations, 4453 Combat Crew Training Wing, flying F-4C model

*Lieutenant General Daniel (Chappie) James Jr.*

planes. He has served in Thailand where he flew F-105 model planes on seventy-eight combat missions. He was appointed vice commander of the Eighth Tactical Fighter Wing. Prior to his assignment to the Pentagon, General James was assigned commander of the Seventy-Two Hundred and Seventy-Second Flying Training Wing, Wheelus Air Base, Libya, and commander, Wheelus Air Force Base.

General James has been awarded the Distinguished Flying Cross, Air medal with seven clusters, Distinguished Unit Citations, Presidential Unit Citation and the Air Force Outstanding Unit Award. He is married to the former Dorothy Watkins of Tuskegee Ala. and they are the parents of three children.[45]

*Private First Class Robert H. Jenkins*

## Robert H. Jenkins

Private First Class, Company C, Third Reconnaissance Battalion, Third Marine Division.

Robert Jenkins was born on June 1, 1948, in Interlachen, Florida, the son of Robert and Willie Mae Jenkins. He was educated in public schools in Palatka, Florida, and on February 2, 1968, enlisted in the U.S. Marines at Jacksonville. He received his recruit training at Parris Island, South Carolina, with additional training at Camp Le-Jeune, North Carolina.

Jenkins was assigned in July, 1968 to the (Reinforced) HQ and Service Company, Republic of Vietnam. Later he was reassigned to Company C, of the Third Reconnaissance Battalion as a scout and driver. During his military career, Jenkins was awarded the Purple Heart, the National Defense Service medal, the Vietnam Service medal

with two bronze stars and the Republic of Vietnam Campaign medal. On March 5, 1969, while serving as a machine gunner with Company C at Fire Support Base Argonne, south of the Demilitarized Zone. Jenkins was killed in action. PFC Jenkins was awarded the Medal of Honor posthumously. His citation read as follows:

*For conspicuous gallantry and intrepidity at the risk of his life above and beyond the call of duty while serving as a Machine Gunner with Company C, Third Reconnaissance Battalion, Third Marine Division, in connection with operations against enemy forces in the Republic of Vietnam. Early on the morning of 5 March 1969, Private First Class Jenkins' twelve-man reconnaissance team was occupying a defensive position at Fire Support Base Argonne, south of the Demilitarized Zone. Suddenly, the marines were assaulted by a North Vietnamese Army platoon employing mortars, automatic weapons, and hand grenades. Reacting instantly, Private First Class Jenkins and another marine quickly moved into a two-man fighting emplacement, and as they boldly delivered accurate machine-gun fire against the enemy, a North Vietnamese soldier threw a hand grenade into the friendly emplacement. Fully realizing the inevitable results of his actions, Private First Class Jenkins quickly seized his comrade, and pushing the man to the ground, he leaped on top of the marine to shield him from the explosion. Absorbing the full impact of detonation, Private First Class Jenkins was seriously injured and subsequently succumbed to his wounds. His courage, inspiring valor and selfless devotion to duty saved a fellow marine from serious injury or possible death and upheld the highest traditions of the Marine Corps and the United States Naval Service. He gallantly gave his life for his country.*[46]

## Lawrence Joel

Specialist Six, Aidman, First Battalion (Airborne), Five Hundred and Third Infantry.

Lawrence Joel was born on February 22, 1928, at Winston-Salem, North Carolina, the son of Mr. and Mrs. Trenton Joel. His foster parents are Mr. and Mrs. Clayton Samuel of Winston-Salem. He and his wife have two children.

Joel attended school in Winston-Salem and entered the military service in 1946. He served at various posts in the United States and in Germany, Italy, Okinawa and Vietnam. He has been awarded the Purple Heart Medal, Good Conduct medal (three awards), World War II Victory medal, Army of Occupation medal (Germany), National Defense Service medal (with oak leaf clusters), Armed Forces Expeditionary medal, Vietnam Service medal and Combat Medical Badge.

While assigned as a medical aidman in Vietnam, Joel displayed heroic courage and sustained performance of duty in treating the wounded while being exposed to hostile fire. He received the Medal of Honor on March 9, 1967, for his gallant action. The citation read as follows:

*Specialist Five Lawrence Joel distinguished himself by gallantry and intrepidity at the risk of his life above and beyond the call of duty on November 8, 1965 while serving as a medical aidman, Headquarters and Headquarters Company, First Battalion (Airborne), Five Hundred Third Infantry on a battlefield in the Republic of Vietnam. Specialist Joel demonstrated indomitable courage, determination, and professional skill when a numerically superior and well-concealed Viet Cong element launched a vicious attack which wounded or killed nearly every man in the lead squad of the Company. After treating the men wounded by the initial burst of gunfire, he bravely moved forward to assist others who were wounded while proceeding to their objective. While moving from man to man, he was struck in the right leg by machine gun fire. Although painfully wounded his desire to aid his fellow soldiers transcended all personal feeling. He bandaged his own wound and self administered morphine to deaden the pain, enabling him to continue his dangerous undertaking. Throughout this period of time, he constantly shouted words of encouragement to all around him. Then completely ignoring the warning of others, and his own pain, he continued his search for wounded, exposing himself to hostile fire; and, as bullets dug up the dirt around him, he held plasma bottles high while kneeling, completely engrossed in his life-saving*

*mission. Then, after being struck a second time and with a bullet lodged in his thigh, he dragged himself over the battlefield and succeeded in treating thirteen more men before his medical supplies ran out. Displaying resourcefulness, he saved the life of one man by placing a plastic bag over a severe chest wound to congeal the blood. As one of the platoons pursued the Viet Cong, an insurgent force in concealed positions opened fire on the platoon and wounded many more soldiers. With a new stock of medical supplies, Specialist Joel again shouted words of encouragement as he crawled through an intense hail of gun fire to the wounded men. After the twenty-four-hour battle subsided and the Viet Cong dead numbered 410, snipers continued to harass the Company. Throughout the long battle, Specialist Joel never lost sight of his mission as a medical aidman and continued to comfort and treat the wounded until his own evacuation was ordered. His meticulous attention to duty saved a large number of lives and his unselfish, daring example under most adverse conditions was an inspiration to all. Specialist Joel's profound concern for his fellow soldiers, his conspicuous gallantry, and his intrepidity at the risk of his life above and beyond the call of duty are in the highest traditions of the United States Army and reflect great credit upon himself and the armed forces of his country.*[47]

*Specialist Lawrence Joel*

**Dwight Hal Johnson**

Specialist Five, Company B, First Battalion, Sixty-Ninth Armor, Fourth Infantry Division.

Dwight Johnson was born on May 7, 1947, at Detroit, Michigan, the son of Mrs. Joyce Johnson Alves. He attended public schools in Detroit, and entered the service on July 28, 1966, at Detroit. During his career he has been assigned to Fort Knox, Kentucky; the Republic of Vietnam; and Fort Carson, Colorado. He has received the following awards and decorations: the Medal of Honor, National Defense Service medal, Vietnam Service medal, Vietnam Campaign medal (Vietnamese). Johnson was awarded the Medal of Honor for distinguishing himself heroically during combat operations in Vietnam. His citation read as follows:

*Specialist Five Dwight H. Johnson distinguished himself by gallantry and intrepidity at the risk of his life above and beyond the call of duty on January 15, 1968 near Dak To, Kontum Province, Republic of Vietnam. On that date, Specialist Johnson, a tank driver with Company B, First Battalion, Sixty-Ninth Armor, Fourth Infantry Division, was a member of a reaction force moving to aid other elements of his platoon, which was in heavy combat with a battalion-size North Vietnamese force. Specialist Johnson's tank, upon reaching the point of contact threw a track and became immobilized. Realizing that he could do no more as a driver, he climbed out of the vehicle armed only with a .45 caliber pistol. Despite intense hostile fire, Specialist Johnson killed several enemy soldiers before he had expended his ammunition. Returning to his tank through a heavy volume of anti-tank rockets, small arms and automatic weapons fire, he obtained a submarine gun with which to continue his fight against the advancing enemy. Armed with this weapon, Specialist Johnson again braved deadly enemy fire to return to the center of the ambush site where he courageously eliminated more of the determined foe. Engaged in extremely close combat when the last of his ammunition was expended, he killed an enemy soldier with the stock of his submarine gun. Now weaponless, Specialist Johnson ignored the enemy fire around him, climbed into*

*Specialist Dwight H. Johnson*

*his platoon sergeant's tank, extricated a wounded crew member and carried him to an armored personnel carrier. He then returned to the same tank and assisted in firing the main gun until it jammed. In a magnificent display of courage, Specialist Johnson exited the tank and again armed with only a .45 caliber pistol, engaged several North Vietnames troops in close proximity to the vehicle. Fighting his way through devastating fire and remounting his own immobilized tank, he remained fully exposed to the enemy as he bravely and skillfully engaged them with the tank's externally-mounted .50 caliber machine gun, where he remained until the situation was brought under control. Specialist Johnson's profound concern for his fellow soldiers, his conspicuous gallantry, and his intrepidity at the risk of his life above and beyond the call of duty are in keeping with the highest traditions of the military service and reflect great credit upon himself and the United States Army.*[48]

*Private First Class Ralph H. Johnson*

## Ralph H. Johnson

Private First Class, Company A, First Reconnaissance Battalion, First Marine Division (Reinforced), FMF.

Ralph Johnson was born on January 11, 1949, in Charleston, South Carolina, the son of Mrs. Rebecca Johnson. He attended public schools in Charleston, enlisted in the Marine Corps Reserve on March 23, 1967 and in the regular Marine Corps in July, 1967. He completed basic recruit training at San Diego, California and additional training at Camp Pendleton, California.

On January 1, 1968, Johnson arrived in Vietnam for duty with the First Reconnaissance Battalion. He was assigned as a reconnaissance scout with Company A. During his military career he was awarded the Purple Heart, the National Defense Service medal, the Vietnam Service medal with two bronze stars, the Vietnam Cross of Gallantry with Palm, the Vietnamese Military Merit medal and the Republic of Vietnam Campaign medal. On March 5, 1968, while participating in operation "ROCK" near Quan Duc Valley, Johnson was killed in action. He was awarded the Medal of Honor for his intrepid actions at the cost of his own life. His citation read as follows:

*For conspicuous gallantry and intrepidity at the risk of his life above and beyond the call of duty while serving as a Reconnaissance Scout with Company A, First Reconnaissance Battalion, First Marine Division in action against the North Vietnamese Army and Viet Cong Forces in the Republic of Vietnam. In the early morning hours of 5 March 1968, during Operation ROCK, Private First Class Johnson was a member of a fifteen-man reconnaissance patrol manning an observation post on Hill 146 overlooking the Quan Duc Cuc Valley deep in enemy controlled territory. They were attacked by a platoon-size hostile force employing automatic weapons, satchel charges and hand grenades. Suddenly, a hand grenade landed in the three-man fighting hole occupied by Private Johnson and two fellow marines. Realizing the inherent danger to his two comrades, he shouted a warning and unhesitatingly hurled himself upon the explosive device. When the grenade exploded, Private Johnson absorbed the tremendous impact of the blast and was killed instantly. His prompt and heroic act saved the life of one marine at the cost of his own and undoubtedly prevented the enemy from penetrating his sector of the patrol's perimeter. Private Johnson's courage, inspiring valor and selfless devotion to duty were in keeping with the highest traditions of the Marine Corps and the United States Naval Service. He gallantly gave his life for his country.*[49]

## Edgar J. Jones

Warrant Officer, U.S. Navy.

Edgar Jones has been assigned as a member of the U.S. Navy's Seal team. He is one of the few Negro navy personnel to be used in this unique team.[50]

## Albert B. Kilby

Colonel, Director of Instruction, Defense Race Relations Institute.

Albert Kilby was born on October 14, 1918 in Covington, Kentucky, where he attended public schools. He graduated from West Virginia State College in 1940, with a B.A. in sociology, and later earned a master's degree in social work from the Georgia University School of Social Work, Atlanta, in 1942.

During World War II, Kilby was drafted into the U.S. Army in April, 1942. He attended officer's candidate school at Camp Davis, North Carolina and was commissioned a second lieutenant in the anti-aircraft branch, July, 1943. He served in New Guinea and the Philippines. Kilby was discharged from the army in April, 1946 with the rank of captain.

Albert Kilby returned to Kentucky after his military discharge and taught in the Covington public school system. Later he was employed in Philadelphia, Pennsylvania, as a psychiatric social worker for the Veterans Administration Mental Hygiene Clinic and also a parole agent for the state.

In June, 1951, Kilby was recalled to active military duty as an anti-aircraft officer. During the Korean conflict he was transferred to the Medical Service Corps. His assignments since 1951 have been primarily as a social work officer. He has been chief of social work services at various army general hospitals and mental hygiene consultation services. He has been active with the Urban League, Family Service, Plays for Living, and the Gestalt Institute in San Francisco, California in race relations seminars.

Albert B. Kilby was promoted to the rank of colonel, U.S. Army in 1968, becoming the first black full colonel in the Medical Service Corps Branch. He also was the first director of instruction at the Defense Race Relations Institute, Patrick Air Force Base, Florida.

Kilby's military decorations include the Legion of Merit (with oak leaf cluster) and the AMC (with oak leaf cluster).

Colonel Kilby is the father of two sons, Kraig and Bruce Kilby.[51]

## Garfield M. Langhorn

Private First Class, Troop C, Seventh Squadron (Airmobile), Seventeenth Cavalry, First Aviation Brigade.

Garfield Langhorn was born on September 10, 1948, at Cumberland, Virginia. He attended Riverhead High School, Riverhead, New York, and on May 6, 1968, was inducted into the U.S. Army at Fort Hamilton, Brooklyn, New York. He served at Fort Jackson, South Carolina and Fort Leonard Wood, Missouri before his transfer to Vietnam in October, 1968. He has been awarded the Purple Heart, Good Conduct medal, National Defense Service medal, Vietnam Service medal and Vietnam Campaign medal (Vietnamese).

On April 7, 1970, Langhorn's family accepted the Medal of Honor, awarded posthumously, from the president of the United States. Private First Class Garfield M. Langhorn was honored for conspicuous gallantry and intrepidity in action at the risk of his life above and beyond the call of duty. His citation read as follows:

*Private First Class Garfield M. Langhorn distinguished himself at the cost of his life above and beyond the call of duty on 15 January 1969, while serving as a radio operator with Troop C, Seventh Squadron (Airmobile), Seventeenth Cavalry, First Aviation Brigade, near Plei Djereng in Pleiku Province, Republic of Vietnam. Private Langhorn's platoon was inserted into a landing zone to rescue two pilots of a Cobra helicopter shot down by enemy fire on a heavily timbered slope. He provided radio coordination with the command-and-control aircraft overhead while the troops hacked their way through dense undergrowth to the wreckage, where both aviators were found dead. As the men were taking the bodies to a pickup site, they suddenly came under intense fire from North Vietnamese soldiers in camouflaged bunkers to the front and right flank, and within minutes they were surrounded. Private Langhorn immediately radioed for help from the orbiting gunships, which began to place mini-gun and rocket fire on the aggressors. He then lay between the platoon leader and another man, operating the radio and providing covering fire for the wounded who had been moved to the center of*

*Private First Class Garfield M. Langhorn*

## Matthew Leonard

Platoon Sergeant, Company B, First Battalion, Sixteenth Infantry Division.

Matthew Leonard was born on November 26, 1929, in Eutaw, Alabama. He and his wife Lois had three children. He went to school at A.H. Parker High School in Birmingham, Alabama and on August 29, 1947, he entered the army at Fort Benning, Georgia. During his military career he served at Fort Dix, New Jersey; Japan; Fort Devens, Massachusetts; Korea; Camp Breckenridge, Kentucky; Fort Jackson, Kentucky; Germany; Fort Riley, Kansas; Fort Leonard Wood, Missouri; and the Republic of Vietnam. Sergeant Leonard received the following awards while serving in the active U.S. Army: Purple Heart, Combat Infantry Badge, second award, Good Conduct medal, third award, Army of Occupation medal with Japan and Germany clasps, Korean Service medal with four bronze service stars, National Defense Service medal, Vietnam Service medal, Military Merit

*Platoon Sergeant Matthew Leonard*

the small perimeter. Darkness soon fell, making it impossible for the gunships to give accurate support, and the aggressors began to probe the perimeter. An enemy hand grenade landed in front of Private Langhorn and a few feet from the personnel who had become casualties. Choosing to protect those wounded, he unhesitatingly threw himself on the grenade, scooped it beneath his body and absorbed the blast. By sacrificing himself, he saved the lives of his comrades. Private Langhorn's conspicuous gallantry and extraordinary heroism at the cost of his own life were in keeping with the highest traditions of the military service and reflect great credit on himself, his unit and the United States Army.[55]

medal (Vietnamese), Victoria Campaign medal (Vietnamese) and United Nations Service medal.

In February, 1967, Sergeant Leonard succumbed to multiple wounds received while engaging in combat operations with his company. The secretary of the army awarded the Medal of Honor posthumously to Sergeant Leonard for his profound courage and unusual gallantry, resulting in his death. His citation read as follows:

*Platoon Sergeant Leonard distinguished himself during combat operations with Company B, First Battalion, Sixteenth Infantry, near Suoi Da, Republic of Vietnam, on 28 February 1967. His platoon was suddenly attacked by a large enemy force employing small arms, automatic weapons, and hand grenades. Although the platoon leader and several other key leaders were among the first wounded, Sergeant Leonard quickly rallied his men to throw back the initial enemy assaults. During the short pause that followed, he organized a defensive perimeter, redistributed ammunition, and inspired his comrades through his forceful leadership and words of encouragement. Noticing a wounded companion outside the perimeter, he dragged the man to safety but was struck by a sniper's bullet which shattered his left hand. Refusing medical attention and continuously exposing himself to the increasing fire as the enemy again assaulted the perimeter, Sergeant Leonard moved from position to position to direct the fire of his men against the well-camouflaged force. Under the cover of the main attack, the enemy moved a machine gun into a location where it could sweep the entire perimeter. This threat was magnified when the platoon machine gun in this area malfunctioned. Sergeant Leonard quickly crawled to the gun position and was helping to clear the malfunction when the gunner and other men in the vicinity were wounded by fire from the enemy machine gun. Sergeant Leonard rose to his feet, charged the enemy gun, and destroyed the hostile crew despite being hit several times by enemy fire. He moved to a tree, propped himself against it, and continued to engage the enemy until he succumbed to his many wounds. His fighting spirit, heroic leadership, and valiant acts inspired the remaining members of his platoon to hold back the enemy until assistance arrived. Sergeant Leonard's profound courage and devotion to his men are in keeping with the highest traditions of the military service, and his gallant actions reflect great credit upon himself and the United States Army.[53]*

*Specialist Robert Lewis III, on his way home after five years as a prisoner of war.*

*Sergeant Donald R. Long*

## Donald Russell Long

Sergeant, Troop C, First Squadron, Fourth Cavalry Regiment, First Infantry Division.

Donald Long was born on August 27, 1939, at Blackfork, Ohio, the son of Mr. and Mrs. Herman Long. He attended public schools in Blackfork and on April 16, 1963, was inducted into the army at Ashland, Kentucky. He was assigned to the following installations during his military career: Fort Knox, Kentucky; Fort Jackson, South Carolina; Fort Riley, Kansas, and Hawaii. In September, 1965, he was assigned to Troop C, First Squadron, Fourth Cavalry at Fort Riley, Kansas. He received the following awards and decorations: Purple Heart, Good Conduct medal, National Defense Service.medal, Vietnam Service medal with the bronze service star, Vietnam Campaign medal and Combat Infantryman's Badge.

While serving in Vietnam as an assistant to the platoon leader, Troop C, First Squadron, Fourth Cavalry, his unit was attacked by a Viet Cong

force. During this attack Long exhibited unusual gallantry, risking his life to save his comrades. His Medal of Honor citation read, in part, as follows:

*He inspired his comrades by repeatedly exposing himself to enemy fire while assisting the wounded and by fearlessly standing unprotected to repel the attackers with rifle fire and grenades. When an enemy grenade was hurled onto the deck of his Armored Personnel Carrier he immediately shouted a warning and pushed to safety a man who had not heard. Realizing that these actions would not fully protect the exposed crewmen, Sergeant Long threw himself over the grenade to absorb the blast and thereby saved the lives of eight of his comrades at the expense of his own life.*[54]

*Major Norman McDaniel*

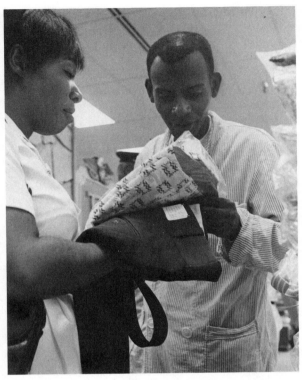

*Sergeant Cordine McMurray looks over the new styles after his release as a prisoner of war (above); Colonel John T. Martin (right).*

## John Thomas Martin

Colonel (Retired) U.S. Army.

John Martin was born on April 29, 1920, in New York City. He has a B.A. from Howard University (1940), and was awarded an academic scholarship to attend Howard University Law School from 1940–1941, but started active military duty with the U.S. Army on March 3, 1941. During his military career, he attended the following schools: the Infantry School, Fort Benning, Georgia; the Army Information School, Carlisle Barracks, U.S.A. Command General Staff College, Fort Leavenworth, Kansas; the School of Journalism, University of Wisconsin (received public relations course certificate), and Session II, Federal Executive Institute course for federal employees in super grades GS-16 (or equivalent) and above.

Colonel Martin's military assignments have included: chief, Public Information Division, News Branch, Headquarters, U.S. Army Europe; deputy G-4. Headquarters First Infantry Division, Wurzburg, Germany; executive to the civilian assistant, Office, Assistant Secretary of Defense (Manpower), Washington; deputy chief, Organization and Industry Branch, Office, Chief of Information, Department of the Army, Washington; information officer, Headquarters, I Corps (Group) Korea; staff officer, Office of the Deputy Assistant Secretary of Defense (Industrial Relations and Civil Rights). Colonel Martin retired as a colonel in the U.S. Army after more than twenty-seven years of active service. He is experienced in management and staff functions in logistic operation and information activities. He was instrumental in the preparation of a DOD pamphlet, *Integration of the Negro Officer in the Armed Forces of the United States of America.* Presently, Colonel Martin is director of selective service, District of Columbia, 441 G Street, NW, Washington, D.C. Colonel Martin is married and the father of five children.[55]

*Lieutenant Colonel Hurdle L. Maxwell*

## Hurdle L. Maxwell

Lieutenant Colonel, U.S. Marine Corps.

Hurdle Maxwell was born on April 1, 1930, in St. Louis, Missouri. He graduated from high school in Terre Haute, Indiana, and attended Indiana State Teachers college for three years, later receiving his B.S. from that institution. On August 9, 1951, he enlisted in the Marine Corps Reserve. He accepted a commission as a reserve second lieutenant on March 14, 1953, and in September, 1953 received a regular commission. Lieutenant Colonel Maxwell has attended service schools at Quantico, Virginia, and the Armor School, Fort Knox, Kentucky. His unique duty assignments have included: company officer, Fourth Replacement Battalion, Camp Pendleton, California; Third Marine Division, Japan; First Marine Division, Korea; Aviation Detachment, Naval Air Station, Pensacola, Florida; Marine Corps Air Station, Kaneoke

Bay, Hawaii; Marine Corps Landing Force Development Center, Marine Corps School, Quantico, Virginia; Republic of Vietnam, and Okinawa.

Lieutenant Colonel Maxwell is the first Negro marine officer to command an infantry battalion. In January, 1969, he was assigned commanding officer, First Battalion, Sixth Marines, Second Marine Division, Camp Lejeune, North Carolina.

He has been awarded the Navy Commendation medal with combat "V," the National Defense Service medal, the Korean Service medal, the Vietnam Service medal and the United Nations Service medal. He is married to a navy nurse, Hattie Elam Maxwell, and is the father of one son.[56]

## Noel A. Merrick

Lieutenant (Junior Grade), U.S. Navy.

Noel Merrick is one of the Negro navy personnel who have been assigned to the U.S. Navy's Aerospace Recovery Facility.[57]

## Clarence A. Miller Jr.

Colonel, U.S. Army, Defense Race Relations Institute, Patrick Air Force Base, Florida.

Colonel Miller was born on July 21, 1931, at Chatfield, Texas. Miller attended high school in Corsicana, Texas and Dallas, Texas. In 1951 he graduated from Prairie View A & M College in Texas with a major in biology. Colonel Miller was commissioned as a second lieutenant, Infantry, U.S. Army Reserves through the ROTC. He began active duty at Fort Benning, Georgia in August, 1951, and attended the Infantry Associate Company Officer Course. Miller's military assignments include: Platoon Leader, Seventh Cavalry Regiment, First Cavalry Division, Japan; Platoon Leader, Twenty-Third Infantry Regiment, Second Division, Korea. He was wounded in action (Korea) in September, 1952. After the Korean conflict, he was assigned to Fort Bliss, Texas as company commander of a basic training company. In 1956 Miller transferred to the artillery branch of the army and attended the Anti-Aircraft Artillery Battery Officer Course. Later he was assigned to the Anti-Aircraft Artillery and Guided Missile School as an instructor. In 1957 he was sworn into the regular U.S. Army.

During the period 1958 to 1959 Miller attended the Advanced Artillery Officer Course and Airborne Training. Upon completion of training he was assigned to Germany as a battery commander and later battalion operations officer.

In 1962 Colonel Miller was appointed an assistant professor of military science at Indiana University. While there he received a master's degree in higher education. Miller has attended the Army Command and General Staff College, and also completed a one-year course in the Arabic language. Later Colonel Miller was assigned to the U.S. Military Training Mission in Saudi Arabia as the senior army air defense advisor.

Colonel Miller has commanded a Hawk missile battalion at Fort Bliss, Texas and during the Vietnam conflict served as deputy brigade commander of the Second Brigade, One Hundred and First Airborne Division and Deputy Installation Coordinator of the Phu Bai Combat Base. Upon his return from Vietnam, he completed a year's study at the Army War College, Carlisle Barracks, Pennsylvania. His recent assignment has been deputy director for instruction, Defense Race Relations Institute (DRRI).

Colonel Miller's awards and decorations include: Legion of Merit, Bronze Star medal with oak leaf cluster, Meritorious Service medal, Army Commendation medal with two oak leaf clusters and the Purple Heart. He also qualifies for a Combat Infantry Badge and Parachutist Badge.

Colonel Miller is married to Margaret Yvonne Clerkley and is the father of two children.[58]

*Donald L. Miller*

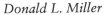

### Donald L. Miller

Deputy Assistant Secretary of Defense (Equal Opportunity)

Donald Miller was born in New York City on January 10, 1932. He attended elementary and secondary schools in New York, and in 1948 volunteered for the U.S. Army. Miller served in Korea as a battalion sergeant major from 1952 to 1953. Upon his return from Korea, he was assigned as an army recruiter in New York City. He was a distinguished graduate of the U.S. Army's Infantry Officer Candidate school in September, 1956. After receiving his commission as a second lieutenant, he attended airborne school. Miller was later assigned to the Tenth and Twenty-Fourth Infantry divisions, and also served with the Eleventh Airborne Division. Other major military assignments were: staff officer, John F. Kennedy Special Warfare Center, Fort Bragg, North Carolina; faculty member, Adjutant General's School, Fort Harrison, Indiana; and chief, Inspections Branch, Army Postal Service, Adjutant General's office, Department of the Army, Washington.

Donald Miller retired in 1969 as a major and upon his retirement was awarded the Legion of Merit for exceptionally meritorious service. His other decorations include the Army Commendation medal, and Expert Infantryman and Parachutist badges.

Mr. Miller worked as a vice president for industrial relations, Seatrain Ship Building Corporation, Brooklyn, New York upon his retirement from the military service. He has a B.S. degree from the University of Maryland, and has pursued graduate studies in government, politics and public administration. He has also completed the Harvard Graduate School of Business Administration's program for management development.

Mr. Miller is a member of Alpha Sigma Lambda, Pi Sigma Alpha and Phi Kappa Phi honor societies and Alpha Phi Alpha fraternity. He is the author of *An Album of Black Americans in the Armed Forces*. He is married to the former Ann Davis of Augusta, Georgia and they have two children.

Donald Miller was appointed deputy assistant

*Private First Class Milton L. Olive III*

secretary of defense (equal opportunity) on December 1, 1971.[59]

## Milton L. Olive III

Private First Class, Company B, Second Battalion (Airborne), Five Hundred and Third Infantry Regiment, One Hundred and Seventy-Third Airborne Brigade.

Milton Olive was born on November 7, 1946, in Chicago, Illinois, the son of Milton L. Olive Jr. and Clare Lee Olive. He attended public schools and Saints Junior College High School in Chicago. He enlisted in the regular army on August 17, 1964, and was assigned to U.S. Army Training Center, Fort Knox, Kentucky. His other assignments were to U.S. Army Artillery and Missile School, Fort Sill, Oklahoma; U.S. Army Training Center, Fort Polk, Louisiana; U.S. Army

Infantry School, Fort Benning, Georgia. In May, 1969, Olive was assigned to the One Hundred and Seventy-Third Airborne Brigade in Vietnam. During his career he received the Purple Heart with oak leaf cluster, Armed Forces Expeditionary medal, Combat Infantryman's Badge, Parachutist Badge and Marksman Badge with qualification bar for Rifle (M-14).

On October 22, 1965, Private Olive was killed in Vietnam on a search and destroy mission. His heroism during this operation was recognized by the posthumous award of the Medal of Honor. He was the first black American to receive the nation's highest military honor since the Korean War, and the first to receive the medal in the Vietnam War. His citation read as follows:

*Private First Class Milton L. Olive III distinguished himself by conspicuous gallantry and intrepidity at the risk of his own life above and beyond the call of duty while participating in a search and destroy operation in the vicinity of Phu Cuong, Republic of Vietnam, on 22 October 1965. Private Olive was a member of the Third Platoon of Company B, Second Battalion (Airborne), Five Hundred and Third Infantry, as it moved through the jungle to find the Viet Cong operating in the area. Although the platoon was subjected to a heavy volume of enemy gun fire and pinned down temporarily, it retaliated by assaulting the Viet Cong positions, causing the enemy to flee. As the platoon pursued the insurgents, Private Olive and four other soldiers were moving through the jungle together when a grenade was thrown into their midst. Private Olive saw the grenade, and then saved the lives of his fellow soldiers at the sacrifice of his own by grabbing the grenade in his hand and falling on it to absorb the blast with his body. Through his bravery, unhesitating actions, and complete disregard for his own safety, he prevented additional loss of life or injury to the members of his platoon. Private Olive's conspicuous gallantry, extraordinary heroism, and intrepidity at the risk of his own life above and beyond the call of duty are in the highest traditions of the United States Army and reflect great credit upon himself and the Armed Forces of his country.*[60]

*Captain Thomas D. Parham Jr.*

**Thomas D. Parham Jr.**

Captain, Chaplain Corps, U.S. Navy.

Thomas Parham was born on March 21, 1920, in Newport News, Virginia, the son of Thomas David and Edith R. (Seabrook) Parham. He attended Hillside High School in Durham, North Carolina, and has a B.A. degree (1941) from North Carolina State College in Durham and bachelor's and master's degrees in sacred theology from the Western Theological Seminary in Pittsburgh, Pennsylvania. In 1944, he was ordained in the Presbytery of Mahoning, Youngstown, Ohio and in the same year, on September 24, was commissioned a lieutenant in the Chaplain Corps, U.S. Naval Reserve. He transferred to the regular U.S. Navy on August 1, 1955 and was promoted captain on February 1, 1966. Chaplain Parham's unique assignments have been: assistant chaplain, Naval Training Center, Great Lakes, Illinois; Manana Barracks, Oahu, Hawaii; and chaplain, First Marine Division, Fleet Marine Force. In June, 1967, he was assigned to the Bureau of Naval Personnel, Navy Department, Washington, where he now serves as assistant chief of chaplains

for plans. Captain Perham has the Naval Reserve medal, American Campaign medal, Asiatic-Pacific Campaign medal, World War II Victory medal, Navy Occupation medal, Asia clasp, National Defense Service medal with bronze star, Korean Service medal, United Nations Service medal and the Armed Forces Expeditionary medal (Vietnam).

Thomas Parham was commissioned in the first class of Negro staff officers in 1944, and was the first Negro to attain the rank of captain.[61]

*Lieutenant Colonel Frank E. Peterson*

**Frank E. Peterson Jr.**

Lieutenant Colonel, U.S. Marine Corps.

Frank Peterson was born on March 2, 1932, in Topeka, Kansas, and attended public schools there. He was a student at Washington University, St. Louis, Missouri and George Washington University in Washington, D.C. On April 20, 1951, he enlisted in the U.S. Navy Reserve as an aviation cadet. He was commissioned a U.S. Marine Corps Reserve second lieutenant and designated a naval aviator after completing flight training at the U.S. Naval Air Station, Pensacola, Florida and Corpus

Christie, Texas, on October 22, 1952. He received further training at the Marine Corps Air Station, El Toro (Santa Ana), California. Peterson was promoted to first lieutenant in April, 1954, and was transferred to the regular Marine Corps in February, 1955. He flew thirty-one missions against the enemy in Korea. He was assigned to the First Marine Aircraft Wing (Reinforced) FMF and was liaison officer, Second Battalion, First Marine Division (Reinforced) FMF from November, 1953 until April, 1954. Later he became embarkation officer, MAES-17, Marine Wing Service Group 17, First Marine Aircraft Wing, until May, 1954.

During the period July, 1954 to January, 1960, Lieutenant Colonel Peterson was stationed at El Toro (Santa Ana), California. He was a student pilot with MAG-15 Air FMF Pacific, then served as pilot and assistant aircraft maintenance officer with VMF (N)-542. He was promoted to captain in June, 1956. In June, 1968 he assumed command of VMF-314, Marine Aircraft Group 13, Republic of Vietnam. He became the first Negro officer to command a squadron in the U.S. Navy or Marine Corps. He has also been assigned to Hawaii, the Naval Air Station, Willow Grove, Pennsylvania, and Cherry Point, North Carolina.

His medals and decorations include the Distinguished Flying Cross, the Air medal (with one silver star), Korean Service medal, the Korean Presidential Unit Citation, the National Defense Service medal (with one bronze star), and the United Nations Service medal. Lieutenant Colonel Peterson and his wife Eleanor have four children. He is currently assigned in the Washington, D.C. area.[62]

### John E. Peterson

Master Sergeant, U.S. Air Force; First Sergeant, Three Hundred and Fifty-Fifth Security Police Squadron, Takhli RTAFB, Thailand.

John Peterson wears the Thai parachutist's badge and is also an honorary Green Beret. He was cited by the Forty-Sixth Special Forces Unit for making several jumps with the Thailand paratroops. Sergeant Peterson is one of many senior black non-commissioned officers of the U.S. Air Force who have attained responsible positions.[63]

*Master Sergeant John E. Peterson*

### Riley Leroy Pitts

Captain, Company C, Second Battalion, Twenty-Seventh Infantry, Twenty-Fifth Infantry Division.

Riley Pitts was born on October 15, 1937 at Fallis, Oklahoma, the son of Mr. and Mrs. Theodore H. Pitts of Oklahoma City. He attended public schools in Oklahoma City and the University of Wichita in Kansas. He was married and he and his wife, Eula, had two childern.

On June 5, 1960, Pitts entered the army at Wichita, Kansas and was assigned to the Infantry School, Fort Benning, Georgia. Later he served at Fort Sill, Oklahoma and in France. In December, 1966, he was assigned to the Twenty-Fifth Infantry Division in Vietnam. He was later assigned to Company C, Second Battalion, Twenty-Fifth Infantry of the Twenty-Fifth Division.

282

Top Sergeant Julie Barrows prepares a pressure suit for presidential inspection (below); Ensign Jesse W. Arbor, one of the first black officers to serve in the U.S. Naval Reserve with SLC James Austin (below far right); Savannah State College Naval Officers visiting a reading room in the Pentagon (right); Lady Officer Candidate students receiving instruction in how to sit properly (below right).

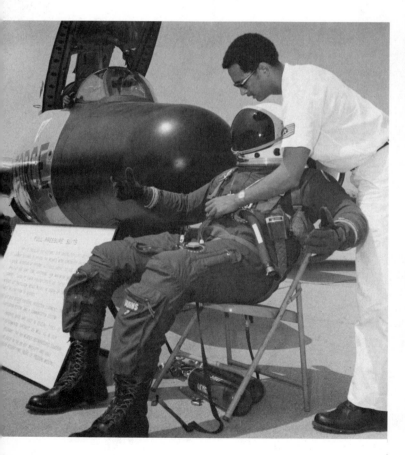

Captain Pitts was awarded the following military honors: Silver Star medal, Bronze Star medal, Purple Heart, Combat Infantryman Badge, National Defense Service medal, Meritorious Unit Citation, Parachutist Badge, Expert Infantryman Badge, National Order of Vietnam, Fifth Class (Vietnamese), Gallantry Cross with Palm (Vietnamese) and Vietnam Campaign medal (Vietnamese).

While serving as Company Commander of Company "C", 2nd Battalion, Twenty-Seventh Infantry, Captain Pitts gave his life in heroic action beyond the call of duty. He was posthumously awarded the nation's highest military honor, the Medal of Honor. His citation read:

*Captain Riley L. Pitts, Infantry, United States Army, distinguished himself by exceptional heroism while serving as Company Commander of Company C, Second Battalion, Twenty-Seventh Infantry, during an airmobile assault in the vicinity of Ap Dong, Republic of Vietnam, on 31 October 1967. Immediately after his company landed in the area, several Viet Cong opened fire with automatic weapons. Despite the enemy fire, Captain Pitts*

*Captain Riley L. Pitts*

*forcefully led an assault which overran the enemy positions. Shortly thereafter, Captain Pitts was ordered to move his unit to the north to reinforce another company heavily engaged against a strong enemy force. As Captain Pitts' company moved forward to engage the enemy, intense fire was received from three directions, including fire from four enemy bunkers, two of which were within fifteen meters of Captain Pitts' position. The severity of the incoming fire prevented Captain Pitts from maneuvering his company. His rifle fire proving ineffective against the enemy due to the dense jungle foliage, he picked up an M-79 grenade launcher and began pinpointing the targets. Seizing a Chinese Communist grenade which had been taken from a captured Viet Cong's web gear, Captain Pitts lobbed the grenade at a bunker to his front, but it hit the dense jungle foliage and rebounded. Without hesitation, Captain Pitts threw himself on top of the grenade which, fortunately, failed to explode. Captain Pitts then directed the repositioning of the company to permit friendly artillery to be fired. Upon completion of the artillery fire mission, Captain Pitts again led his men toward the enemy positions, personally killing at least one more Viet Cong. The jungle growth still prevented effective fire to be placed on the enemy bunkers. Captain Pitts, displaying complete disregard for his life and personal safety, quickly moved to a position which permitted him to place effective fire on the enemy. He maintained a continuous fire, pinpointing the enemy's fortified positions, while at the same time directing and urging his men forward, until he was mortally wounded. Captain Pitts' conspicuous gallantry, extraordinary heroism, and intrepidity at the cost of his own life, above and beyond the call of duty, are in the highest traditions of the United States Army and reflect great credit upon himself, his unit, and the armed forces of his country.*

Captain Riley Leroy Pitts was the first known Negro officer to receive the Medal of Honor since the award has been established, although Negro noncommissioned officers who were later commissioned as second lieutenants for bravery or received National Guard Commissions, received the award.[64]

## Henry B. Richardson

Command Sergeant Major, U.S. Army.

Henry Richardson was born in Berea, Ohio and has lived in Greenville, New Hampshire. He is married and has three children. He has studied at the Conservatory of Music, Baldwin College, in Berea and has degrees from Wilberforce University and Wharton American School in Blackpool, England.

Richardson enlisted in the army in 1942 and served at Fort Sill, Oklahoma, and in France, Belgium and Germany as well as Korea and Vietnam. In 1951, he was an instructor/writer at the Ordnance School, Aberdeen Proving Grounds, and in 1954 he was assigned as an ROTC instructor at Hampton Institute, Hampton, Virginia. He served with Headquarters Supreme Allied Powers Europe and Seine Area Command Paris in 1956 and in Vietnam from 1966 to 1967.

Command Sergeant Major Richardson has seventeen decorations and service medals, among them the Bronze Star medal, Meritorious Service medal, Army Commendation medal and Good Conduct medal. He is an active member of various organizations, including the Alpha Phi Alpha fraternity, Masonic Lodge, Protestant Men of the Chapel and the American Legion.[65]

## Jettie Rivers Jr.

Second Lieutenant, Company D, First Battalion, Ninth Marines.

Jettie Rivers was presented the Navy Cross posthumously for extraordinary heroism as company first sergeant serving with the Ninth Marines in Vietnam. His citation read:

*For extraordinary heroism as Company First Sergeant while serving with Company D, First Battalion, Ninth Marines in the Republic of Vietnam on 14 and 15 May 1967. While engaged in search-and-destroy operations against units of the North Vietnamese Army, Company D became engaged with an estimated reinforced enemy company and Second Lieutenant (then First Sergeant) Rivers, a member of the company command group, was wounded. Realizing that the enemy had forced a gap between the command group and one platoon and the two rear platoons, he immediately informed the company commander. At dusk the enemy fire and mortar barrages intensified, and as casualties mounted, the two separate elements set up a hasty perimeter defense. Second Lieutenant Rivers expertly directed his men's fire, placed personnel in strategic positions, and personally participated in repelling the enemy assault. Observing a number of enemy soldiers maneuvering toward the perimeter he mustered a small force of Marines and personally led them to meet the enemy, killing several of the enemy soldiers. When evacuation of the wounded was completed, Second Lieutenant Rivers requested permission to take the point in an attempt to link up the smaller element with the other two platoons. A short distance from the perimeter, the group encountered withering machine-gun fire which instantly killed the platoon sergeant and seriously wounded the platoon leader. Second Lieutenant Rivers immediately took command of the situation, aiding the wounded and personally pinning down the enemy machine gun while the casualties were removed. Now under crossfire and sporadic mortar barrages, Second Lieutenant Rivers assisted in joining the two units. Discovering that all of the platoon leaders had become casualties, he assisted the company commander in setting up an effective perimeter and personally supervised the medical evacuation preparations. Presently a deadly mortar barrage precipitated an all-out enemy assault on the company. Second Lieutenant Rivers was everywhere—encouraging the men, directing the fire, assisting the wounded and distributing ammunition to critical positions. Wounded himself, he continued that pace until late in the afternoon when relief arrived. By his initiative, devotion to duty, and aggressive leadership, he served to inspire all who observed him and was instrumental in saving the lives of many Marines. His great personal valor reflected great credit upon himself, the Marine Corps and the United States Naval Service.[66]*

*Brigadier General Roscoe Robinson*

## Roscoe Robinson Jr.

Brigadier General, United States Army.

Roscoe Robinson Jr .was born on October 28, 1928 in St. Louis, Missouri where he received his elementary and secondary education. After graduating from Charles Sumner High School, Robinson was appointed to the U.S. Military Academy, and on graduation was commissioned a second lieutenant in the U.S. Army. He has a B.S. in military engineering from the U.S. Military Academy. Later he received a MPIA degree in international affairs from the University of Pittsburgh.

Robinson has attended the Infantry School, U.S. Army Command and General Staff College and the National War College.

General Robinson's major military assignments include: author/instructor, Department of Command, U.S. Army Command and General Staff College, Fort Leavenworth, Kansas; personnel management officer, Infantry Branch, Officer Personnel Directorate, Office of Personnel Operations, U.S. Army, Washington, D.C.; G-4, First Cavalry Division (Airmobile), U.S. Army Pacific, Vietnam; commanding officer, Second Battalion, Seventh Cavalry, First Cavalry Division (Airmobile), (The Second Battalion, Seventh Cavalry was constituted on 28 July, 1866 in the Regular Army as Company B, Seventh Cavalry at Fort Riley, Kansas, later redesignated the Second Battalion, Seventh Cavalry, on June 5, 1963. The campaign participation of this unit includes the Indian Wars, Mexican Expedition, World War II and Korean War. During the days of the Indian Wars the U.S. Seventh Cavalry did not have one black member assigned for actual physical duty. It was not until 1963 that this unit was able to have its colors and streamers beside a black commander, its first in combat confrontations, then LTC Roscoe Robinson Jr.) General Robinson was plans officer, later Southeast Asia special actions officer, J-5, U.S. Pacific Command and Executive to the Chief of Staff, U.S. Pacific Command, and Commanding Officer, Second Brigade, Eighty-Second Airborne Division, Fort Bragg, North Carolina.[67]

*Brigadier General Charles C. Rogers*

worth, Kansas for attendance at the U.S.A. Command and General Staff College. His overseas assignments have been in Germany, Korea, and Vietnam. Rogers has received the following awards and decorations: Medal of Honor, Legion of Merit, Distinguished Flying Cross, Bronze Star medal with "V" device (with three oak leaf clusters), Air medal (with nine oak leaf clusters), Joint Service Commendation medal, Army Commendation medal (with two oak leaf clusters), Purple Heart, National Defense Service medal (with one oak leaf cluster), Army of Occuption medal (Germany), Parachutist Badge, Vietnam Service medal, Vietnam Campaign medal (Vietnamese).

On May 14, 1970, the Medal of Honor was presented to Lieutenant Colonel Charles C. Rogers by the president of the United States in recognition of his gallantry and intrepidity in action in Vietnam. Rogers is the highest-ranking Negro officer to have received the Medal of Honor. His citation reads as follows:

*Lieutenant Colonel Charles C. Rogers, Field Artillery, distinguished himself by conspicuous gallantry and intrepidity in action on November 1, 1968, while serving as Commanding Officer, First Battalion, Fifth Artillery, First Infantry Division during the defense of a forward fire support base in the Republic of Vietnam. In the early morning hours, the fire support was subjected to a concentrated bombardment of heavy mortar, rocket and rocket-propelled grenade fire. Simultaneously the position was struck by a human wave ground assault, led by sappers who breached the defense barriers with bangalore torpedoes and penetrated the defense perimeter. Colonel Rogers, with complete disregard for his own safety, moved through the hail of fragments from bursting enemy rounds to the embattled area. He aggressively rallied the dazed artillery crewmen to man their howitzers and he directed their fire on the assaulting enemy. Although knocked to the ground and wounded by an exploding round. Colonel Rogers sprang to his feet and led a small counterattack force against an enemy element that had penetrated the howitzer positions. Although painfully wounded a second time during the assault, Colonel Rogers pressed the attack killing several of the enemy and driving*

## Charles Calvin Rogers

Brigadier General, U.S. Army.

Charles Rogers was born on September 6, 1929, at Claremont, West Virginia, the son of Mr. and Mrs. Clyde Rogers Sr., of Indianapolis, Indiana. He attended Fayetteville Consolidated High School, Fayetteville, Dubois High School, Mount Hope, West Virginia and West Virginia State College. He entered the military service at Institute, West Virginia on May 27, 1951. During his colorful military career he has been assigned to Fort Sill, Oklahoma; Fort Hood, Texas, Fort Campbell, Kentucky; Fort Devans, Massachusetts; Fort Lewis, Washington; Fort Bliss, Texas, and Leaven-

*the remainder from their positions. Refusing medical treatment, Colonel Rogers reestablished and reinforced the defensive positions. As a second human wave attack was launched against another sector of the perimeter, Colonel Rogers directed artillery fire on the assaulting enemy and led a second counterattack aganist the charging forces. His valorous example rallied the beleaguered defenders to repulse and defeat the enemy onslaught. Colonel Rogers moved from position to position through the heavy enemy fire, giving encouragement and direction to his men. At dawn the determined enemy launched a third assault against the fire base in an attempt to overrun the position. Colonel Rogers moved to the threatened area and directed lethal fire on the enemy forces. Seeing a howitzer inoperative due to casualties, Colonel Rogers joined the surviving member of the crew to return the howitzer to action. While directing the position defense, Colonel Rogers was seriously wounded by fragments from a heavy mortar round which exploded on the parapet of the gun position. Although too severely wounded to physically lead the defenders, Colonel Rogers continued to give encouragement and direction to his men in the defeating and repelling of the enemy attack. Colonel Rogers' dauntless courage and heroism inspired the defenders of the fire support to the heights of valor to defeat a determined and numerically superior enemy force. His relentless spirit of aggressiveness, conspicuous gallantry and intrepidity in action at the risk of his own life above and beyond the call of duty are in the highest traditions of the military service and reflect great credit upon himself, his unit and the United States Army.*[68]

## Thomas Sanders

Corporal, U.S. Marine Corps.

Thomas Sanders was posthumously awarded the Navy Cross for outstanding heroism while assigned as a machine-gun squad leader in Vietnam. His citation read as follows:

*For extraordinary heroism as a Machine Gun Squad Leader with Company C, Battalion Landing Team One Three, in the Republic of Vietnam on May 10, 1967. While participating in Operation BEAVER CAGE, in Tinh Quang Nam Province, Corporal Sanders enabled his platoon to move from positions exposed to heavy automatic and small arms fire, to a protected trench line, by advancing himself to an exposed position with his squad's machine gun when all other members of the squad became casualties. He then placed a heavy volume of accurate fire on the Viet Cong and North Vietnamese Army troops causing them to cease fire. When the enemy troops advanced to the cover of the trench line, in which other members of his platoon were located, he placed himself between the enemy and friendly troops. As the enemy approached to within six meters in front of him, Corporal Sanders delivered machine gun fire down the long axis of the trench line killing approximately two of them and wounding three others before he was killed by enemy fire. As a result of his heroic conduct and fearless devotion to duty, his actions enabled nine marines, some of whom were wounded, to gain cover in the trench line and to gain positions where grenades and M-79 fire could be delivered on the enemy. By his outstanding courage, exceptional fortitude and valiant fighting spirit, Corporal Sanders served to inspire all who observed him and upheld the highest traditions of the Marine Corps and the United States Naval Service. He gallantly gave his life for his country.*[69]

## Ruppert Leon Sargent

First Lieutenant, Company B, Fourth Battalion, Ninth Infantry, Twenty-Fifth Infantry Division.

Ruppert Sargent was born on January 6, 1938, in Hampton, Virginia. He was educated at public schools in Hampton and at Virginia State College and the Hampton Institute. On January 8, 1959, he enlisted in the regular army at Richmond, Virginia, for a three-year period. He completed basic and advanced training at Fort Jackson, South Carolina, and was later assigned to Fort Sill, Oklahoma and Fort Benning, Georgia. From 1960 to 1962 he served as a machine gunner and team leader with Company A, Second Battle Group, Tenth Infantry, Fort Davis, Canal Zone. On his return to the United States on March 7, 1962, he was released from active duty and transferred to the U.S. Army Reserve from March 13, 1962.

Sargent reenlisted in the regular army on May 14, 1962 at Richmond, Virginia for a period of six years. He was assigned to Fort Knox, Kentucky, where he attended the Noncommissioned Officers Academy and upon graduation was designated Distinguished Graduate of the Leadership Course, Class 64–4. In October, 1965, Sargent was assigned to the Fiftieth Company, Fifth Student Battalion, The Student Brigade, Fort Benning, Georgia. Upon graduation from this school he was designated a distinguished graduate, standing Number 8 in competition with 157 other officer candidates of class number 9–65. On October 13, 1965, he was appointed second lieutenant, Infantry, U.S. Army Reserve. His first assignment as an officer was at Fort Benning, Georgia, where he served as tactical officer of an Infantry Officer Candidate Platoon. In 1966 he was assigned to Vietnam for duty with the Ninth Infantry.

On March 15, 1961, while serving as a platoon leader in Vietnam, Lieutenant Sargent died as the result of a metal fragment wound. He was awarded the nation's highest military honor, the Medal of Honor, for his gallantry and heroic deeds. His citation read as follows:

*While leading a platoon of Company B, Fourth Battalion, Ninth Infantry, Twenty-Fifth Infantry Division, on 15 March 1967, Lieutenant Sargent was investigating a reported Viet Cong meeting house and weapons cache located in Hau Nghia Province, Republic of Vietnam. A former Viet Cong led the search party through the deserted village to a well-concealed tunnel entrance which Lieutenant Sargent observed was booby trapped. He tried to destroy the booby trap and blow the cover from the tunnel using hand grenades, but this attempt was not successful. He and his demolition man moved in to destroy the booby trap and cover which flushed a Viet Cong soldier from the tunnel, who was immediately killed by the nearby platoon sergeant. Lieutenant Sargent, the platoon sergeant, and a forward observer moved toward the tunnel entrance. As they approached, another Viet Cong emerged and threw two hand grenades that landed in the midst of the group. Lieutenant Sargent fired three shots at the enemy then turned and unhesitatingly threw himself over the two grenades. He was mortally wounded, and his two companions were lightly wounded when the grenades exploded. By this courageous and selfless act of exceptional heroism, he saved the lives of the platoon sergeant and forward observer and prevented the injury or death of several other nearby comrades. Lieutenant Sargent's actions were in keeping with the highest traditions of the military service and reflect great credit upon himself and the United States Army.*

During his military career Lieutenant Sargent also received the following decorations and awards: Purple Heart (posthumous), Good Conduct medal, Good Conduct medal clasp (bronze) with two loops, National Defense Service medal with one bronze oak leaf cluster, Vietnam Service medal with one bronze service star, Republic of Vietnam Campaign medal with device (1960), Combat Infantry Badge, Sharpshooter Badge with Rifle, Machine Gun and Flamethrower bars, National Order medal, Fifth Class (Vietnam), Gallantry Cross with Palm (Vietnam).

He was married and he and his wife, Mary Jo, had two children.[70]

*Specialist Clarence E. Sasser*

**Clarence E. Sasser**

Specialist Five, Headquarters and Headquarters Company, Third Battalion, Sixtieth Infantry, Ninth Infantry Division.

Clarence Sasser was born on September 12, 1947, at Chenango, Texas. He went to high school at Angleton, Texas and was a student at the University of Houston. He entered military service at Houston, Texas, on June 15, 1967. During his military career he has been assigned to Fort Polk, Louisiana; U.S. Army Medical Training Center, Fort Sam Houston, Texas; Headquarters and Headquarters Company, Third Battalion, Sixtieth Infantry Division, Republic of Vietnam, and U.S. Army Hospital, Camp Zama, Japan. He entered the U.S. Military Academy Preparatory School, Fort Belvoir, Virginia, in January, 1969. Specialist Sasser has received the following awards: Medal of Honor, Purple Heart, Combat Medical Badge, National Defense Service medal, Vietnam Campaign medal (Vietnamese).

On January 10, 1969, Sasser was serving as a medical aidman on a reconnaissance mission in Vietnam. His courage and self-sacrifice under fire earned him the Medal of Honor, the citation reading:

*Specialist Five Clarence E. Sasser (then Private First Class) distinguished himself by conspicuous gallantry and intrepidity on 10 January 1968 while assigned to Headquarters and Headquarters Company, Third Battalion, Sixtieth Infantry, Ninth Infantry Division in the Republic of Vietnam. On this date he was serving as a medical aidman with Company A, Third Battalion, on a reconnaissance in force operation in Ding Tuong Province. His company was making an air assault when suddenly it was taken under heavy small arms, recoilless rifle, machine gun and rocket fire from well-fortified enemy positions on three sides of the landing zone. During the first few minutes, over thirty casualties were sustained. Without hesitation, Specialist Sasser ran across an open rice paddy through a hail of fire to assist the wounded. After helping one man to safety, he was painfully wounded in the left shoulder by fragments of an exploding rocket. Refusing medical attention, he ran through a barrage of rocket and automatic weapons fire to aid casualties of the initial attack and, after giving them urgently needed treatment, continued to search for other wounded. Despite two additional wounds immobilizing his legs, he dragged himself through the mud toward another soldier one hundred meters away. Although in agonizing pain and faint from loss of blood, Specialist Sasser reached the man, treated him, and proceeded on to encourage another group of soldiers to crawl two hundred meters to relative safety. There he attended their wounds for five hours until they were evacuated. Specialist Sasser's conspicuous gallantry, extraordinary heroism and intrepidity at the risk of his own life, above and beyond the call of duty, are in keeping with the highest traditions of the military service and reflect great credit upon himself, his unit and the United States Army.[71]*

*Brigadier General Fred C. Sheffey*

## Fred Clifton Sheffey

Brigadier General, U.S. Army.

Fred Clifton Sheffey was born on August 27, 1928 in McKeesport, Pennsylvania. Sheffey received a bachelor of science degree in economics and business from Wilberforce University. He also has master's degrees in business administration from Ohio State University and in international affairs from George Washington University.

General Sheffey has completed courses at the Quartermaster School, U.S. Army Command and General Staff College and the National War College.

He entered on active military service in July, 1950. His military assignments include: chief, Clothing and Textile Material Section, Supply Branch, Quartermaster Division, Third Logistical

Command, U.S. Army Europe; assistant division supply officer, Fourth Infantry Division; executive officer, Fourth Supply and Transport Battalion, Fourth Infantry Division; executive officer and commanding officer, Two Hundred and Sixty-Sixth Quartermaster Battalion, Fort Lewis, Washington; logistical plans officer and chief, Plans and Policy Branch, G-4 Section, U.S. Army, Vietnam; chief, Facilities Branch, Operations Research Management Office, Office of the Deputy Chief of Staff for Logistics, U.S. Army, Washington, D.C.; logistical plans officer and later chief, Logistical Plans Section, J-4, U.S. Pacific Command, Hawaii and commanding officer, Fifty-Fourth General Support Group, U.S. Army, Pacific, Vietnam. His most recent assignment is chief, Financial Resources Division, Supply and Material Directorate, Office, Deputy Chief of Staff for Logistics, U.S. Army, Washington, D.C.

Brigadier General Sheffey's awards and decorations include the Legion of Merit (with two oak leaf clusters), Bronze Star medal, Army Commendation medal, Purple Heart and Combat Infantryman Badge. General Sheffey received his commission as a reserve officer training Corps military graduate.[72]

*Brigadier General George M. Shuffer*

**George Macon Shuffer Jr.**

Brigadier General, U.S. Army.

George Shuffer Jr. was born on September 27, 1923, in Palestine, Texas. He has a B.S. in military science and an M.A. in European history from the University of Maryland, and also attended the Infantry School, U.S. Army Command and General Staff College, and U.S. Army War College. His major duty assignments have been: training advisor, Army Section, U.S. Military Assistant Advisory Group, China; commanding officer, Second Battalion, Second Infantry, Fort Devens, Massachusetts; assistant G-2, II Field Force, Vietnam Staff Officer, Troop Operations Division, Operations U.S. Army, Washington; assistant for continuity of operations plans, Office, Assistant Secretary of Defense (administration), Washington; commanding officer, One Hundred Ninety-Third Infantry Brigade, U.S. Army Forces, Southern Command, Fort Kobbe, Canal Zone, and assistant director of individual training office, Deputy Chief of Staff for Personnel, U.S. Army, Washington; assistant deputy chief of staff, personnel, U.S. Army, Europe, and his most recent assignment is assistant division commander, Third Infantry Division U.S. Army, Europe.

General Shuffer has received the following medals and awards: Silver Star (with two oak leaf clusters) Legion of Merit (with oak leaf cluster), Bronze Star medal with "V" device (with two oak leaf clusters) Air medal (fifth award), Purple Heart, Combat Infantryman Badge (third award) and Parachutist Badge.

After the completion of over thirty-one years of military service, George Macon Shuffer was promoted to brigadier general in September, 1972.[73]

*Brigadier General Clifford C. Sims*

**Clifford Chester Sims**

Staff Sergeant, Company D, Second Battalion (Airborne), Five Hundred and First Infantry, One Hundred and First Airborne Division.

Clifford Sims was born on June 18, 1942, the son of Mr. and Mrs. James Sims of Port Saint Joe, Florida, where he attended high school. He was married and he and his wife Mary had one daughter. He enlisted in the army at Jacksonville, Florida, on October 16, 1961, and reenlisted on October 16, 1964. He served at Fort Jackson, South Carolina; Fort Benning, Georgia, Fort Campbell, Kentucky, and Fort Bragg, North Carolina. From May to September, 1966 he was assigned to Company B, Second Battalion, Five Hundred and Eighth Infantry, Eighty-Second Airborne Division in the Dominican Republic. In December, 1967, he was assigned to the One Hundred and First Airborne Division, Republic of Vietnam.

Sergeant Sims received the following awards during his military career: Silver Star, Bronze Star medal, Purple Heart, National Defense Service medal, Armed Forces Expeditionary medal, Vietnam Service medal, Gallantry Cross with Palm, Military Merit medal, Combat Infantryman Badge, Parachutist Badge and Vietnam Campaign medal (Vietnamese).

Staff Sergeant Sims was killed in Vietnam in a gallant action in which he sacrificed his own life to protect his comrades. His citation read as follows:

*Staff Sergeant Clifford C. Sims distinguished himself on 21 February 1968, while serving as a squad leader with Company D, Second Battalion (Airborne), Five Hundred and First Infantry, One Hundred and First Airborne Division, near Hue, in the Republic of Vietnam. Company D was assaulting a heavily fortified enemy position concealed within a dense wooded area when it encountered strong enemy defensive fire. Once within the woodline, Sergeant Sims led his squad in a furious attack against an enemy force which had pinned down the First Platoon and threatened to overrun it. His skillful leadership provided the platoon with freedom of movement and enabled it to regain the initiative. Sergeant Sims was then ordered to move his squad to a position where he could provide covering fire for the company command group and to link up with the Third Platoon, which was under heavy enemy pressure. After moving no more than thirty meters Sergeant Sims noticed that a brick structure in which ammunition was stocked was on fire. Realizing the danger, Sergeant Sims took immediate action to move his squad from this position. Though in the process of leaving the area two members of his squad were injured by the subsequent explosion of the ammunition. Sergeant Sims' prompt actions undoubtedly prevented more serious casualties from occurring. While continuing through the dense woods amidst heavy enemy fire, Sergeant Sims and his squad were approaching a bunker when they heard the unmistakable noise of a concealed booby trap being triggered immediately to their front. Sergeant Sims warned his comrades of the danger and unhesitatingly hurled himself upon the device as it exploded, taking the full impact of the blast. In so protecting his fellow soldiers, he willingly sacrificed his own life. Staff Sergeant Sims' conspicuous gallantry, extraordinary heroism and intrepidity at the cost of his own life, above and beyond the call of duty, are in keeping with the highest traditions of the military service and reflect great credit upon himself and the United States Army.[74]*

*Lieutenant Gloria A. Smith*

## Gloria A. Smith
Lieutenant, U.S. Marine Corps.

Gloria Smith was born in Rockville, Maryland, the daughter of George and Ella Smith. She attended public school in Rockville and in 1961 enrolled at Central State College, Wilberforce, Ohio, where she earned a degree in physical education. After graduation she taught at Montgomery County's Damascus Junior High School in Maryland. She has been a judo competitor, and has a white belt in judo.

In 1967 Gloria Smith was selected for Officers' Candidate School at Quantico, Virginia, and after completion of the course was commissioned a second lieutenant. She has attended the woman officer basic course at Quantico, and the woman officer personnel administration school at Parris Island, South Carolina. In December, 1967, Lieutenant Smith was assigned administrative officer of the Woman Marine Company, Camp Pendleton, California.

Lieutenant Gloria Smith is one of the few Negro women marine officers who are currently serving on active duty with the U.S. Marine Corps.[75]

## Merle J. Smith Jr.

Lieutenant, U.S. Coast Guard.

Merle J. Smith Jr. was born on August 11, 1944 in Greenville, South Carolina. He is the son of Colonel Merle J. Smith Sr., USA (Ret.), and Mrs. Jacqueline T. Smith of Baltimore, Maryland. Smith received his elementary and secondary education in Washington, D.C.; Tokyo, Japan; Albuquerque, New Mexico; Kaiserlautern, Germany and Aberdeen, Maryland.

On 9 July 1962, he became the first known black graduate of the U.S. Coast Guard Academy at New London, Connecticut.

Smith was promoted to an ensign on June 8, 1966. He was granted a B.S. degree from the USCG Academy and then assigned as communications officer, *USCGC Minnetonka* (WHEC-67), Long Beach, California (1967). His other assignments have included: commanding officer, USCG Cape Washington (WPB-95310), Monterey, California (1968), commanding officer, *USCGC PT Mast* (WPB-82316), CGRONONE, Republic of Vietnam and commanding officer, *USCGC PT Ellis* (WPB-82330), CGRONONE, Republic of Vietnam (1969). In 1970 Smith was assigned to the International Affairs Division, Coast Guard Headquarters, Washington, D.C.

Smith's decorations and awards include: Combat Action Ribbon, Expert Pistol, Vietnam Service Ribbon, Vietnam Campaign, National Defense medal, and the Vietnam Training medal (First Class).

Smith is married to the former Jo Ann Henry of Carson, California. He entered George Washington Law School in September, 1972.[76]

*Lieutenant Merle J. Smith*

*Curtis R. Smothers (left) and Donald L. Miller.*

## Curtis R. Smothers

Director, Equal Opportunity (Military).

Curtis Smothers was born in Baltimore, Maryland, on August 26, 1943. He attended public schools in Baltimore, and graduated from Morgan State College in 1964 in political science, cum laude. He received a commission in the regular army on June 1, 1964 and, as a distinguished military graduate, he was selected as one of thirty-five army officers to participate in the Judge Advocate General's Excess Leave Program. Smothers enrolled at the Georgetown University Law Center in September, 1964, and received his J.D. degree in 1967. He served as chief, Military Justice, Eighth Infantry Division in Germany from December, 1967 to April, 1968. He had gained valuable experience in military law while serving as claims adjudicator at Fort Holabird, Maryland and as a staff member of the Judge Advocate General's Office in Washington during vacation periods from Georgetown Law School.

In May, 1968, Curtis Smothers assumed duties as chief, Special Action Branch, Military Justice Division at Army European Headquarters at Heidelberg, Germany. He also served as an attorney advisor and prosecutor, and defense counsel before special and general courts-martial.

On August 1, 1969, Smothers was certified as a military judge under the provision of 10. U.S.C. 826 (1969). He was the army's youngest full-time trial judge at the age of twenty-six and he was one of six magistrates assigned to the European Command.

During his tour in Europe, Judge Smothers served on the faculty of the Dolmetscher Institut, University of Heidelberg as an instructor in American political science and history. He has testified before German courts as an expert on American criminal and administrative law. He has been admitted to the practice of law before the highest courts in Maryland and the District of Columbia and the U.S. Court of Military Appeals.

His honors and awards include the John Hay Whitney Fellowship, the American Jurisprudence Prize for Excellence (local government law), the Army Commendation medal and numerous academic scholarships and awards.

In April, 1971, Judge Smothers returned to Washington to assume duties as an attorney advisor with the general counsel, Office of the Secretary of Defense. Later he resigned his commission to accept the position of director, Equal Opportunity (Military). On December 1, 1971, he was appointed to his current position.[77]

*Brigadier General Lucius Theus*

### Lucius Theus

Brigadier General, U.S. Air Force.

Lucius Theus was born in Madison County, Tennessee, on October 11, 1922. He attended elementary schools in Robbins, Illinois and high school in Blue Island, Illinois.

In 1942, he entered the army air force from Chicago and during World War II was assigned as an administrative clerk, chief clerk, and first sergeant of pre-aviation and basic squadrons at Kessler Field, Mississippi.

General Theus started his commissioned service when he graduated in 1946 from Officer Candidate School. His major assignments have been: base statistical control officer, Lockbourne Air Force Base, Ohio; analysis and presentation control officer, Ending Air Depot, Germany; chief, Material Logistic Statistics Branch, Headquarters, U.S. Air Force, Washington; statistical services

staff officer, Headquarters Control Air Material Forces, Europe, Chateauroux Air Base, France, and technical statistical advisor to comptroller, Headquarters Air Material Forces, Europe. From January, 1959 to July, 1971, General Theus was responsible for the following important assignments: base comptroller, Kinksley Field, Oregon; base comptroller and acting deputy base commander, Cam Ranch Bay Air Base, Vietnam (five months), and director of management analysis, Office of the Comptroller, Air Force.

General Theus has a B.S. from the University of Maryland, an M.B.S. in business administration from George Washington University, and has pursued postgraduate studies in French at the University of Maryland. He is also a graduate of the Harvard Advanced Management Program at the Harvard Graduate School of Business Administration. His decorations include the Bronze Star medal, Air Force Commendation medal with one oak leaf cluster, Air Force Outstanding Unit award, Good Conduct medal and Republic of Vietnam Commendation medal. The general is married to the former Gladys Marie Davis of Chicago, Illinois.[78]

*Specialist Cynthia J. Walker*

## Cynthia Jean Walker

Specialist-Five, Women's Army Corps, Alcohol and Drug Control Office, Fort Hamilton, New York.

Cynthia Jean Walker, a black WAC, is the army's first WAC certified alcoholism counselor. One of her duties is to monitor messages left by clients on a telephone answering service at the Alcohol and Drug Control Office.[79]

## John E. Warren Jr.

First Lieutenant, Company C, Second Battalion (Mechanized), Twenty-Second Infantry, Twenty-Fifth Infantry Division.

John Warren was born on November 16, 1946 in Brooklyn, New York, the son of John E. and Lillian Warren. He attended Brooklyn High School and Brooklyn College. He was inducted into the army at Brooklyn on October 19, 1966. After completing officer candidate course at the U.S. Army Infantry School, Fort Benning, Georgia, he was commissioned a second lieutenant on September 21, 1967. From 1966 to 1968 he was stationed at Fort Jackson, South Carolina; Fort McClellan, Alabama; Fort Benning, Georgia, and Fort Eustis, Virginia. He was assigned to the Republic of Vietnam in 1968, serving with the Twenty-Fifth Infantry Division.

Lieutenant Warren received numerous awards and decorations, including the Bronze Star, Silver Star, Purple Heart, National Defense medal, Vietnam Service medal, Vietnam Campaign medal (Vietnamese) and the Combat Infantryman's Badge.

On January 14, 1969, while serving in Vietnam, Lieutenant Warren lost his life in an attempt to save his men. He was posthumously awarded the nation's highest military honor, The Medal of Honor, at the White House on August 6, 1970. His citation read as follows:

*First Lieutenant John E. Warren Jr., Infantry, distinguished himself at the cost of his life above and beyond the call of duty on 14 January 1969, while serving as a platoon leader with Company C, Second Battalion (Mechanized), Twenty-Second Infantry, Twenty-Fifth Infantry Division in* *Tay Ninh Province, Republic of Vietnam. On this date while moving through a rubber plantation to reinforce another friendly unit, Company C came under intense fire from a well-fortified enemy force. Disregarding his own safety, Lieutenant Warren with several of his men began maneuvering through the hail of enemy fire toward the hostile positions. When he had come to within six feet of one of the enemy bunkers and was preparing to toss a hand grenade into it, an enemy grenade was suddenly thrown into the middle of his small group. Thinking only of his men, Lieutenant Warren fell in the direction of the grenade, thus shielding those around him from the blast. His action, performed at the cost of his own life, saved three men from serious or mortal injury. First Lieutenant Warren's ultimate action of sacrifice to save the lives of his men was in keeping with the highest traditions of the military service and reflects great credit on him, his unit, and the United States Army.*[80]

## Bobby Charles Wilks

Commander, U.S. Coast Guard.

Bobby Wilks was born on May 12, 1931, in St. Louis, Missouri, the son of Mr. and Mrs. W. R. Booker. He is married to the former Aida R. Agores of Danvers, Massachusetts. Wilks attended school in St. Louis and has an M.A. (1955) from St. Louis University. He entered the Coast Guard Academy in 1955 and in 1956 was appointed an ensign. He has served in the following capacities during his coast guard career: student, flight training, Pensacola, Florida and Corpus Christi, Texas, 1956–1957; pilot, Coast Guard Air Station, Sangley Point, Philippines, 1960–1961; recruiting officer, Coast Guard Headquarters, Washington, D.C., 1961–1962; pilot, Coast Guard Air Station, New York, 1962–1965; executive officer, Coast Guard Air Station, Italy, 1965–1968; pilot, Coast Guard Air Station, Salem, Massachusetts, 1968–

Commander Bobby Charles Wilks is one of the senior Negro U.S. Coast Guard officers presently on active duty and since his graduation from the Coast Guard Academy in 1956 he has accumulated an outstanding record as a pilot and in administrative assignments.[81]

*Captain Francis Koval inspects Watts Locke
High School Naval ROTC (above, far left);
Prairie View ROTC Cadets learn the use of a
sextant (beow, left); U.S. Coast Guard SPARS;
and (above) a Navy Seabee in action*

### John E. Wise

Command Sergeant Major, Third Squadron, Sixth Armored Cavalry Regiment.

John Wise was born in New Jersey and entered the army at Fort Dix, in 1942. During his tour of duty he has served at Fort Lee, Virginia; Fort McClellan, Alabama; Fort Riley, Kansas; Fort Huachuca, Arizona, and Fort Meade, Maryland. He has served in the European Theater, including France, Italy and Germany, and with the Third Infantry Division in Korea. Command Sergeant Major Wise has completed a total of twenty-eight years of active military service. He has been decorated with three Silver stars, three Bronze stars, four Army Commendation medals (with "V" device), the Combat Infantryman Badge (with two stars), the Air medal (with one oak leaf cluster) and the Purple Heart. Wise has served through three conflicts and was on active duty in the Vietnam War. He has attained the highest position open to an enlisted man, and has a remarkable record of military service.[82]

### Lloyd Woods

Corporal, Company F, U.S. Marine Corps.

Lloyd Woods received the Navy Cross for heroism while serving in Quang Tin province, Republic of Vietnam, on June 2, 1967. His citation read as follows:

*During Operation UNION II, Corporal Woods' company came under intense enemy automatic weapons, small arms and mortar fire which temporarily pinned down the first platoon in an exposed rice paddy. In the initial burst of fire, the platoon sustained numerous casualties, including the platoon commander. Upon observing his wounded commander lying exposed to the intense enemy fire, he unhesitatingly ran through the heavy volume of fire to his side, placed him on his shoulder and carried him to a position of relative safety. Then, rallying four companions, he again moved across the open rice paddy to evacuate another wounded marine who was lying in close proximity to an enemy machine-gun position. Upon reaching the wounded man and realizing it was impossible to move him because of the enemy machine-gun fire, he boldly maneuvered into the tree line toward the enemy position, and single-handedly assaulted the gun, killing the gunner, and capturing his weapon. He then boldly leaped into the adjacent emplacement and in fierce hand-to-hand combat, killed that gunner and commenced to fire the enemy machine gun against other hostile positions, providing cover while his companions evacuated the wounded man. As a result of Corporal Woods' courageous actions his unit was able to regroup and succeeded in evacuating its casualties to positions of safety. By his intrepid fighting spirit, exceptional fortitude and gallant initiative, Corporal Woods inspired all who observed him and upheld the highest traditions of the Marine Corps and the United States Naval Service.[83]*

## Notes to Chapter Ten

1. Martin R. Delaney, *The Condition of the Colored People* (Philadelphia: 1852).
2. Office of the Assistant Secretary of Defense (Public Affairs), Washington, D.C.
3. *Ibid.*
4. *Ibid.*
5. Department of the Navy, Bureau of Naval Personnel, Public Affairs Office, Washington, D.C.
6. Technical Liaison Office, Office of the Surgeon-General, Washington, D.C.
7. Office of the Assistant Secretary of Defense (Public Affairs).

8. *Ibid.*

9. Public Information Office, Department of Transportation, U.S. Coast Guard, Washington, D.C.
Ruth D. Wilson, *Jim Crow Joins Up* (New York: J. Clark Press, 1944), p. 60.
Personal Interview with Lieutenant Maxie Berry Jr., U.S.C.G.

10. Information Services Office, Marine Corps Development and Education Command, Quantico, Virginia.

11. Office of the Assistant Secretary of Defense (Public affairs).

12. Information Services Office, Quantico.

13. Office of Assistant Secretary of Defense (Public Affairs).

14. *The Negro History Bulletin* 18 (February, 1955), p. 107.

15. Office of Assistant Secretary of Defense (Public Affairs).

16. *Ibid.*

17. *Ibid.*

18. Department of the Navy, Office of Information, Washington, D.C.

19. Office of Assistant Secretary of Defense (Public Affairs).

20. *Ibid.*

21. *Army Digest,* January, 1970.

22. Information Services Office, Quantico.

23. Office of the Assistant Secretary of Defense Manpower, *Integration and the Negro Officer in the Armed Forces of the United States of America* (Washington, D.C.: U.S. Government Printing Office, March, 1962).

24. Information Services Office, Quantico.

25. Biography, Office of the Secretary, U.S. Air Force, Washington, D.C.

26. Information Services Office, Quantico.

27. Office of the Assistant Secretary of Defense (Public Affairs).

28. *Ibid.*

29. *Ibid.*

30. *Ibid.*

31. *Who's Who in America* 33 (1964–1965) (Chicago: Marquis Who's Who Inc.).

32. Office of the Assistant Secretary of Defense (Public Affairs).

33. *Ibid.*

34. Department of the Navy, Office of Information, Washington, D.C.

35. Information Services Office, Quantico.

36. *Ibid.*

37. Navy Office of Information, Internal Relations Division, Washington, D.C.

38. Office of Assistant Secretary of Defense (Public Affairs).

39. *Ibid.*

40. Information Services Office, Quantico.

41. Personal interviews with SFC Larry J. Hamilton, July 5, 1973.

42. Office of the Secretary of Defense (Public Affairs).

43. Information Office, Department of the Army, Office of the Chief Army Reserve, Washington, D.C.

44. Office of the Information Officer, U.S. Army, Fort Sill, Oklahoma.

45. Biography, Office of the Secretary, U.S. Air Force, Washington, D.C.

46. Office of the Assistant Secretary of Defense (Public Affairs).

47. *Ibid.*

48. *Ibid.*

49. *Ibid.*

50. Minority Affairs Division, Office of Information, Navy Department, Washington, D.C.

51. Office of the Assistant Secretary of Defense (Public Affairs).

52. Public Information Division, Office of the Chief of Information, Department of the Army, Washington, D.C.

53. Office of the Assistant Secretary of Defense (Public Affairs).

54. *Ibid.*

55. Director of Selective Service, Office for the District of Columbia, Washington, D.C.

56. Information Services Office, Quantico.

57. Public Information Office, U.S. Navy, Washington, D.C.

58. Office of Assistant Secretary of Defense (Public Affairs).

59. *Ibid.*

60. *Ibid.*

61. Navy Office of Information, Internal Relations Division, Washington, D.C.

62. Information Services Office, Quantico.

63. *Air Force Times* (Washington, D.C.), May 21, 1969.

64. Office of the Assistant Secretary of Defense (Public Affairs).

65. Personal Interview with CSM Richardson, Seoul, Korea, July, 1970.

66. U.S. Marine Corps, Office of Information, Washington, D.C.

67. Office of the Assistant Secretary of Defense (Public Affairs).
68. *Ibid.*
69. Information Services Office, Quantico.
70. Office of Assistant Secretary of Defense (Public Affairs).
71. *Ibid.*
72. *Ibid.*
73. *Ibid.*
74. Public Information Division, Office of the Chief of Information, Department of the Army.
75. Information Services Office, Quantico.
76. Department of Transportation, U.S. Coast Guard.
77. Office of the Assistant Secretary of Defense (Public Affairs).
78. *Ibid.*
79. Public Information Division, Office of the Chief of Transportation, Department of the Army.
80. Office of the Assistant Secretary of Defense (Public Affairs).
81. Public Information Office, Department of Transportation, U.S. Coast Guard, Washington, D.C.
82. Public Information Office, U.S. Army, Fort George G. Meade, Maryland.
83. U.S. Marine Corps, Information Office, Washington, D.C.

# Appendix I

## Black Commissioned and Non-Commissioned Officers

Colonel Joseph L. Bailey

Colonel Spencer M. Bracey

Colonel Arthur H. Booth

Colonel William D. Brooks

Colonel DeWitt Cook

Colonel Martha D. Cleveland (Retired)

Colonel Lee A. Cousin (Retired)

Colonel Charles P. Cox

Colonel Clarence M. Davenport Jr.

Colonel Terrence A. Debeal

Colonel Harvey G. Dickerson Jr.

Chaplain (Colonel) John A. Deveaux

Colonel Claude M. Dixon

*Colonel Grover A. Dubose*

*Colonel Luther Evans Jr.*

*Colonel Charles Finch*

Colonel Foster F. Fountain

Colonel Earl N. Franklin

Colonel Ernest R. Frazier

Colonel Leonce E. Gaiter

Colonel Pola L. Garrett

Colonel Edward C. Gleed

*Colonel George B. Hamilton*

*Colonel Harris*

*Colonel John W. Handy Jr.*

Colonel S. Hicks

Colonel Alexander H. Hunt

Colonel Ernest L. Hunter

Colonel C. C. Johnson

*Colonel Elmer D. Jones Jr.*

*Colonel Harry T. Jones*

*Colonel Albert B. Kilby (see also p. 272)*

*Colonel William C. Kilpatrick*

*Colonel John C. Littlejohn*

*Colonel Ruth A. Lucas*

*Colonel John E. McDaniels*

*Colonel Thomas J. Money*

*Colonel Ronald W. Mordecai*

*Colonel William B. Neal*

*Colonel Fitzroy Newsum*

*Colonel Melvin W. Ormes*

*Colonel Herbert C. Parker*

*Colonel Robert L. Peters*

*Colonel Manuel S. Pina*

Colonel Oscar Randall

Colonel George S. Roberts

Colonel James H. Robinson

*Colonel Felix Salvador*

*Colonel Harry A. Shephard*

*Colonel Dudley W. Stevenson*

*Colonel Herbert F. Smith*

Colonel Willard C. Stewart

Colonel Samuel D. Stroman

Colonel John A. Strambler

Colonel Horace E. Thompson

Colonel Raymond E. Tinsley

Colonel G. Turner

*Private First Class James Anderson, posthumously awarded the Medal of Honor.*

ANDERSON HALL

NAMED IN HONOR OF

PRIVATE FIRST CLASS
JAMES ANDERSON, JR.

2241921, U.S. MARINE CORPS RIFLEMAN
CO. F. 2ND BN., 3RD MAR., 3RD MAR. DIV.

AWARDED THE MEDAL OF HONOR
(POSTHUMOUSLY) FOR ACTION AGAINST
ENEMY FORCES IN REPUBLIC OF VIETNAM
ON 28 FEB. 1967 HE GALLANTLY GAVE
HIS LIFE FOR HIS COUNTRY

*Lieutenant Colonel Thomas J. Bembry*

*Captain (Doctor) Frank W. Berry*

*Sergeant Major Cornelius Boykin, member of the
Information Service of the US Army reserve, poses
with Sergeant Major Chester Webb (left), Major
General William J. Sutton, and the Silver Anvil
Award, presented for outstanding achievements in
community relations throughout the United States.*

*Major Sharon Cadonia*

*Lieutenant Colonel William A. Campbell*

*Third Lieutenant Michael Calhoun, an Air Force Academy cadet, reviews a manual with Top Sergeant Joseph L. Hinton.*

*Captain William H. Cobb is presented with the Air*
*medal by Major General Nils O. Olman*

Gunnery Sergeant Greene

Major Felton

*Twin sisters serving in the U.S. Navy: Edith and Ada Haynes.*

*Lieutenant Colonel Albert C. Johnson*

*Major George J. Iles*

*Major Ribert H. Lawrence Jr.*

*Major Maurice C. Lane*

*Major Norval Lee*

*Sergeant M. H. Long*

*Lieutenant Colonel Thomas M. Madison is welcomed by Colonel Emil J. Wengel following his release as a prisoner of war.*

*Lieutenant Colonel Dean B. Mohr*

Ensign Harold Moses and Yeoman Bill Riegert of the U.S. Coast Guard at Washington University, St. Louis, where they attend classes during off-duty hours.

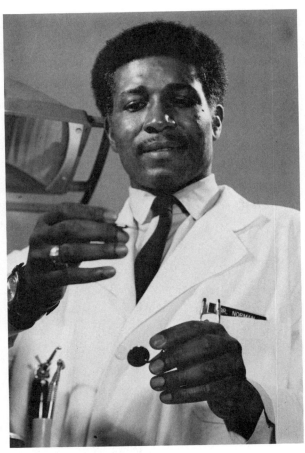

Dental Surgeon Major Philip R. Norman

Major Joyce C. Nurse

*Second Lieutenant Geraldine E. Peeler*

*Yeoman Second Class Marjorie Powell*

*Lieutenant (JG) Phyllis Prue OK's medication*

*Major Barbara Robinson*

*Major John M. Scott*

*Lieutenant Colonel Travis J. L. Stephens*

Commander Gerald Thomas, commanding officer
NROTC unit, Prairie View A & M College, Texas

Lieutenant Colonel Emma L. Vaiton

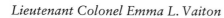

Sergeant Joseph E. Telfair

*Lieutenant Colonel Craig T. Wiesley*

*Sergeant First Class Elizabeth Williams is awarded the Meritorious Service medal*

# Appendix II

## Black Military Milestones

The ordeals, frustrations, experiences and accomplishments of the American Negro are an important part of the history of America. The significant contributions that blacks have made are milestones of black military history. In the following pages some incidents are sketched—humorous, serious and, in some cases, pathetic—events that illustrate the Negro's long and arduous struggle toward equal status and recognition in the U.S. military services.

### Pre-Revolutionary Conflicts

The American Negro's contribution to the defense of his country's freedom can be traced back to pre-revolutionary times. The birth of this nation was assisted by the sweat and toil of black men who fought for their masters' freedom, though they themselves were still in servitude. The following paragraphs depict black participation in colonial and pre-revolutionary conflicts.

*In 1641, settlers of the Dutch West Indian Company armed their slaves with a tomahawk and a half pike to assist in fighting the Indians. The Hollanders used slaves to construct breastworks in order to defend the city against the English sent to America by Charles II. In 1643, a list was prepared in Plymouth, Massachusetts stating the names of men capable of bearing arms. The list contained the name of Abraham Pearse and described him as a Blackmoor (a dark skinned-person, especially Negro). In 1652, an act was passed in the Plymouth Colony requiring that: "All Negroes and Indians from sixteen to sixty years of age, inhabitants or servants to the English be listed and hereby enjoined to attend training as well as the English. In 1707, free Negroes and mulattoes of Massachusetts were required to perform services equivalent to that of the militia, under the command of the officers in charge of the military district in which they lived. Virginia planters moving southward in 1658 carried their slaves into North Carolina. Every master was offered fifty acres of land for each slave over fifteen years of age who could be armed in time of need. In 1706, all free men of a North Carolina Colony from sixteen to sixty, unless exempted by law, were required to organize and keep a supply of ammunition and whenever an outbreak occurred, slaves as well as free men were called upon to render military services. The area of Roanoke, North Carolina was the scene of Indian hostilities in 1711. Thirty-seven settlers were killed. This was the beginning of the Tuscarara War which lasted for two years. Free men of color, by an act of 1706, participated in this conflict.*

*Around the year of 1671, Negroes were employed on the breastworks of Charleston, South Carolina. They were furnished tools, carts, and horses. Entrenchments, flankers, and parapets were constructed by the Negroes. In 1704, a law was enacted which called upon slaves to render military aid in time of alarm. In some cases, the colonial lords granted the slaves their freedom for faithful service rendered.*

*In 1715, the Colony of South Carolina was threatened when a tribe of Indians called the Yemasees joined by their neighbors, the Muskogees, the Appalachians, Catawbas, Congarees and Cherokees decided to band together and destroy the settlement on the Ashley River. The governor of the colony placed an embargo on all ships, and proclaimed martial law and armed a band of trusty Negroes to assist in military operations. A fortification on Goose Creek was defended by forty blacks and seventy whites. Many slaves were killed during this three-year conflict.*

*Some of the slaves who rendered military service were given their freedom. The blacks were integrated with the whites in the battle.*

*The colony of Rhode Island utilized the services of Negroes during the Queen Anne's War*

*The first recorded act calling Negroes into service in Virginia was in 1723. An act required that "Free Negroes, Mulattoes, or Indians shall be obliged to attend and march with the Militia and do the duty of pioneers, or any such other servile duty as they may be directed to perform." Later in 1723, another act was enacted that required that "Every free Negro, Mulatto, or Indian being a housekeeper shall be enlisted in the militia and may be permitted to keep and use guns, powder and shot or other weapons offensive or defensive, having first obtained a license for the same from some justice of the peace of the county wherein such plantations lie." The services of the Free Negroes were retained in the army through an act of the General Assembly passed in 1738. They were employed only as pioneers, drummers, or trumpeteers.*

*In 1740, the fortification of Saint Augustine was defended by seven hundred regulars, two troops of horse and four companies of armed Negroes. This offensive force precluded the capture of the fortification by the English under Oglethorpe.*

*In 1742, the Spanish sent an expedition from Havana to proceed against Oglethorpe. In this expedition there was a regiment of Negroes, with officers of the same race, bearing the same rank as the Spanish officers.*

In 1690 conflicts occurred in which the French and and the English were aided by friendly Indians and sometimes by Negroes. The French were more favored by the Indians than the English

In 1702 all of New England was involved in the bloody struggle known as Queen Anne's War. In 1711 the English of New Jersey and New York, with their dark-skinned allies, marched against the French in Montreal.

By 1716 the English had opened a road across the Blue Ridge Mountains and had made settlements on the Oswego River by 1721. This made them neighbors of Five Nations, living in the region about the Great Lakes. The French, fearing the friendliness which they saw growing between the Indians and the English in this section might result unfavorably to them, planned to break up the latter's strength. To that end they made stronger their own holdings by erecting defenses on Lake Champlain and by inviting the French of Newfoundland and Arcadia to leave those settlements and go to Louisburg. Both of these places had formerly been ceded to Great Britain. The English objected to the exodus that resulted and did what they could to prevent it. This was followed by more outbreaks and there was serious trouble in Maine. At this time Negroes of Massachusetts gave assistance. There was Nero Benson, from Framingham. He was a trumpeteer in the company of Captain Isaac Clark. He entered His Majesty's service August 27, 1723. Black men were called to duty not only on land but also on sea at this time, for record is made of Caesar ————, a Negro, in a list of officers and men on board the transport sloop George. He was registered in March, 1722.

In 1755, England sent General Braddock with three thousand picked veterans to take charge of military affairs and to direct an expedition against Fort Duquesne. Braddock reached Hampton Roads in February of the same year, and proceeding up the Potomac River, landed in Alexandria, Virginia. The commander-in-chief traveled in a stately and very cumbersome coach which he had purchased in Alexandria. Many of the wagoners at this time were Negroes. Among them were Sandy Jenkins, of Fairfax County, Virginia. This man lived to the great age of one hundred and fifteen, dying in Lancaster, Ohio, in February, 1849.

In the ranks led by Braddock were several companies of Independents from South Carolina and New York. Black men were among their number and were with them when a halt was made at Fort Fredericktown, now Frederick, Maryland, on May 13, 1755. Black men helped to clear ground and took part in a parade at two o'clock on the evening of that day. It is evident that Braddock picked up black recruits in several places on his line of march to Fort Duquesne. In Pennsylvania there was Captain Jack, called "Black Jack" and sometimes "Susquehanna Jack." He was a well-known scout and a fearless Indian hunter of mixed blood, Caucasian and African. This man lived on the Juanita River, and his hatred for Indians was very great because his whole family had been murdered by them. He dressed as they did, and often with a band of followers made war upon them. He offered his services to Braddock with those of his men, who were all familiar with the woods, if they might go as free lances in the expedition. Although Jack had already rendered personal service to no small degree as a guide to the general, his offer was not accepted. Pennsylvania sent another of her darker sons in the person of Billy Brown, of Frankfort, to help in the attack on the French fortification. He was born in Africa and was brought to this country as a slave. He was alive in 1826 at the age of ninety. From Bucks County in the same state came another Negro, Jack Miner, who went as a recruit in the company of Captain Walker. There, too, were Abraham Lawrence, and Archibald Kelso.

When within eight miles of the fort the English were attacked by the French and Indians. Unnecessarily exposing himself to the foe, the leader had four horses shot under him. On the fifth he received a wound that ended his life. As he lay dying on the ground he bequeathed to George Washington, Bishop, a very dignified black man, who is described as being the general's bodyguard. Others of the same race as Bishop at this time with Washington were Gilbert and John Alton.

In August of the same year (1758) thirteen colored men were in camp at Raystown, eight of whom were with the Royal American Regiment. In September three black men were reported as being connected with the Sixty-Seventh Regiment, First Highlanders, in camp at Fort Cumberland at Raystown. All of the points mentioned were not far from Fort Duquesne. Raystown, however, not proving near enough to the coveted point for satisfactory military operation, another post was established at Loyal Hanna (Ligionier) with Colonel Bouquet as commander. He had here a force of two thousand men. A list, capulated "Effective Rank and File," reports that thirty-six Negroes were with these men under Colonel Washington on October 21, 1758. It was on the 24th of November that these black and white men of arms began their march to assail Fort Duquesne. When in sight of the place they discovered *it in flames. Its magazine had been blown up by the French commander who, knowing the strength of the force proceeding against him, realized that there was nothing for him but defeat.*

*On one occasion to punish the Indians, a band of volunteers under Colonel Creasap marched as far as what is now known as Negro Mountain. With them was a black man of gigantic stature, who was killed on the mountain in the fierce fight that followed after they met the Indians. It is this event that immortalized the name Negro on the ridge near the headwaters of the Potomac, for the high land has been called Negro Mountain ever since.*

*In the year 1758, new expeditions were also sent against Crown Point and Ticonderoga, both in the hands of the enemy, in northern New York. The first of these fortifications was built by the French in 1741. During the conflict the English had made several previous efforts to secure it, always to fail. This time, however, they outnumbered the enemy, whose commander, realizing his inability to hold out against such a force, set the fort afire and then abandoned it. About the same time an advance was made upon Ticonderoga in much the same way and it was secured by the English. In their ranks on the occasion of both of these attacks were a number of Negroes from the northern colonies, especially Massachusetts. One of these is recorded as Caesar ————, of Westfield, a private under Jedediah Preeble, and another of the same race, from Hingham, bearing a similar name. Black militiamen were also present at Fort Williams, a stockade on the road to Oswego, New York. This place was at the southwestern end of Lake George and was built in 1735.*

*Until 1759, Canada was unreduced. That year eight thousand men, under Wolfe, fought the terrible battle of the Plains of Abraham, not far from the city of Quebec. Negroes were in this battle in more than one capacity. Among those who served as body servants was Tony Proctor. He was only sixteen years of age at the time of the conflict. He lived to be a very old man, and died in Florida in 1855. Some of the privates were Pompey ————, a native of Guinea, who was sworn in in Captain Maynard's company; Cuff ————, of Warren, who served His Majesty under Jeffery Amherst, and Cuff ————, of the Second Massachusetts Regiment of Provincials.*

*The next year France made an unsuccessful effort to regain her lost territory in America, and New Jersey sent her black men into the ranks. By an act of the legislature they were in 1790 enlisted with their masters' consent. The same year an act of Parliament provided for the enlistment of servants as soldiers. For the services of such persons the masters were paid by the recruiting officers out of the public funds.*

*The war continued until 1763, but the English were then too strong to lose what had fallen into their hands. A treaty of peace, signed that same year, made Great Britain the mistress of all of the land east of the Mississippi River and north to the Iberville in Louisiana. As has been said, there were many Negroes in this war. They came especially from the northern colonies to help the English win their victory. Many were enrolled in the colony of Massachusetts simply as Caesar, Caezer, Cesar, Cezar, Sarser, Seazon, Eunta, Ceser, Ceezer, Seasar, Ceasar, Sarser, Seazon, and Augustus.[1]*

### The American Revolution

#### Mistaken Identity at King's Mountain

During the American Revolution there was a battle underway at King's Mountain, North Carolina. On October 7, 1780, the following incident occurred and this provides documentation that blacks were present at the battle.

*In the beginning of the action, Colonel Campbell's famous Bald Face, a black horse, proving skittish, he exchanged him with his namesake, Mr. Campbell, of his own corps, for a bay animal; and Bald Face was sent to the rear, and placed in charge of the colonel's servant, John Broddy, who was a tall, well proportioned mulatto, and in the distance very much resembled his master. Broddy's curiosity prompted him to ride up within two hundred yards of the raging battle, saying he had come to see what his master and the rest were doing. Broddy, with his coat off, and sitting upon Bald Face, unwittingly deceived Colonels Shelby and Sevier, Captain Moses Shelby and perhaps others into the belief that it was Colonel Campbell himself intently watching at a respectful distance, the progress of the engagement. But Campbell was all this time in the thickest of the fight, riding his bay horse till he became exhausted, when he abandoned him and was the remainder of the battle at the head of his men on foot, with his coat off, and shirt collar open.*

According to Draper, it is believed that other Negroes besides Broddy aided in menial occupations on the campaign. "Colonel J. R. Logan stated that there is a tradition in the King's Mountain region that something more than a dozen Negroes were under arms in the battle, in behalf of liberty, and demeaned themselves bravely."[2]

## Maryland Blacks and the Revolution

A visit to the Maryland Hall of Records revealed the following documents mentioning the presence of Negroes in the military services during the American Revolution either as slaves or on loan for labor, serving for their masters or as enlisted free men. The Maryland legislature passed an act in October, 1780 allowing the recruitment of slaves with permission of their masters. During this time, a proposal was introduced into the General Assembly to raise a regiment of blacks. It was, however, defeated.

Revolutionary Papers Box 2—Folder I
*No. 18, 1777 January 29. John Grant and Black Yankee to Elizabeth Wilson to one week, Board each at 15 shillings."*

Revolutionary Papers Box 15—Folder II
*A list of drafts and substitutes who did not serve cover states relative to drafts—substitutes who did not render their personal service.*
*Page 11—Box 15, Folder II Negro George was naughted and appointed though having made his naught in by name of George Pombston, naught Hartford, May 1781.*
*Negro Ned—did not appear naught, Montgomery County, May 1781, delinquent excused.*
*Negro Jesse, Naught Somerset County, October 1780, delinquent.*

Revolutionary Papers, Box 6—Folder 6
*Payrolls for fort at Whetstone Point, 1776. Shows Negro Beth, servants and Negroes: Asgenaths Eleck, Pames London, Cho Orricks, Sam Orricks, Plowman Joe, Stinson Cateo.*

*Free Men: Daniel Weaver, Frances Luke, Charles Marmer, Tho Kelly, Cornelius Murphy, George Robeson, William Pool, William Johnson, Michael Jones, Elias Button, William Tomlin, John Heans, Richard Brown.*[3]

## The Marshpee Indians

During the American Revolution, the County of Barnstable, Mass., was required to raise a regiment of four hundred men in the Continental Army. The Indian district of Marshpee (presently called the town of Mashpee) located in Barnstable County provided twenty-seven black soldiers who fought in the battles, and all but one of them were killed. Among these Marshpee volunteers were: Church Ashur, Joseph Ashur, Amos Babcock, Castel Barnet, Tern Caesar, David Hatch, Abel Hoswitt, Elisha Keeter, James Keeter, Joseph Keeter, John Manix, Samuel Moses, Mark Negro, James Nocake, John Pearce, Daniel Pocknit, Hosea Pognit, Joshua Pognit, James Rimmon, Job Rimmon, George Shaun, Demos Squibs, Gideon Tumpum, Francis Websquish.[4]

## The Black Regiment of Rhode Island

In 1778, the state of Rhode Island and Providence Plantations voted and resolved at the February General Assembly session that a regiment of slaves would be enlisted into the Continental service and the regiment would be commanded by a Colonel Greene. Each slave that enlisted was made a free man. The black regiment displayed outstanding valor in the defense of Red Bank. A great devotion to their officers was exhibited by members of Greene's regiment. In the attack made upon the American lines near Croton River on May 13, 1781, Colonel Greene, regimental commander, was mortally wounded; however, the faithful and valiant blacks of his regiment continued to protect him and drive back the charging enemy.

The following names were listed on the muster roll of the Second Company of the First Battalion of Rhode Island Forces in the service of the United States, commanded by Colonel Christopher Greene. They were present for duty or on furlough on May 22, 1777—Drummer: Scipio Brown; fifers: Richard Cozzens, Cuff Gardner; privates: Richard Allen, Prince Bucklin, Africa Burk, Frank Brown, Newport Champlin, Gudjo Champlin, Jack Covington, William Greene, Cato Greene, Prince Ingraham, Mingo Robinson, John Dunbar.[5]

## Humphrey's Black Militia

The Colony of Connecticut organized a battalion of blacks during the American Revolution. A company of these blacks was commanded by a Captain David Humphreys, a confidant of General Washington, later promoted to the rank of General Officer. The following names are extracted from the payroll of the Second Company, Fourth Regiment of the Connecticut line of the Revolutionary Army: Jack Arabus, John Cleveland, Phineas Strong, Ned Fields, Isaac Higgins, Juba Freeman, Cato Robinson, Prince George, Prince Crosbee, Shubael Johnson, Tim Caesar, Jack Little, Bill Sowers, Dick Violet, Buster Baker, Caesar Baydon, Gamaliel Terry, Lent Munson, Herman Rogers, Job Caesar, John Rogers, Ned Freedom, Ezekiel Tupham, Tom Freeman, Congo Zado, Peter Gibbs, Prince Johnson, Alex Judd, Leevis Martin, Caesar Chapman, Peter Mix, Philo Freeman, Hector Williams, Pomp Liberty, Cuff Liberty, Pomp Cyrus, Harry Williams, Sharo Rogers, John Ball, John McLean, Jessee Vase, Daniel Bradley, Sharp Camp, Jo Otis, James Dinah, Solomon Sowtice, Peter Freeman, Huba Dyer, Andrew Jack, Peter Morando, Peter Lion, Sampson Cuff, Dick Freedom, Pomp McCuff.[6]

## Pension for French War Veteran

*To the Great and General Court now sitting in Boston. We, Your Honors' Petitioners, humbly show that whereas one George Gire, a Negro man living in Grafton became infirm by reason of the hard service in the French War, the General Court settled a pension on him of forty shillings per year during said Court's pleasure and he hath drawn that sum or near the value thereof to June 1779. Said George still remains infirm. Therefore we, your Honors' Petitioners, humbly pray to have said George circumstances taken into your wise consideration and allow George for one year from June, 1779 which is now behind such sum as this we humbly submit.*

*Grafton, December 14th, 1780.*

*John Stow, Joel Brooke, Moses Holbrook, Elijah Drury, Jos. Bruce, Selectmen for Grafton. George [(x) his mark] Gire.*[7]

## Black Veterans of New Hampshire

During the American Revolutionary War, the state of New Hampshire welcomed the services of many blacks. The following names appeared on the New Hampshire State Papers Revolutionary Roll, compiled by Hammond (Volume 3 Pages 242–245—"Cesar Wood, negro, Ceser Wingate, negro, Cato Hale, negro, Prince Clemmons, black, Tumbrel Pickering, black, Mickel Sudrek, black, John Webb, mulato; page 709—Peter, a black fellow, servant of Josiah Bartlett; page 845—Fortunatus, a mulato."[8]

## Black Bravery

A story related to William C. Nell, historian, concerned a "black artillerist who, while having charge of a cannon with a white fellow soldier, was wounded in one arm. He immediately turned to his comrade, and proposed changing his position, exclaiming that he had yet one arm left with which he could render some service to his country. The change proved fatal to the soldier for another shot killed him upon the spot."

Nell's story is one of the many incidents of the heroic stamina of blacks during the American Revolution.[9]

## Black Rhode Island Troops Excel

*On August 29, 1778, it was the newly raised black regiment, under Colonel Greene that distinguished it-self by deeds of desperate valor. Posted behind a thicket in the valley, they three times drove back the Hessians who charged repeatedly down the hill to dislodge them. The Hessians attempted to rush up the hill under a heavy fire in order to take the redoubt. Here they experienced a more obstinate resistance than they had expected. They found large bodies of troops behind the works and at its sides chiefly wild-looking men in their shirt sleeves among them many Negroes.*[10]

## Blacks on Early Casualty Report

The Massachusetts Manuscript, National Archives, Volume 35, page 15, states the following: "Casualty Report 7–25–1689 Men slain in a fight at Falmouth an Indian an Negro Negro Colo Tyngs."[11]

## Deborah Gannet, Mistaken Identity

In 1855, William C. Nell, noted Negro historian, published a book entitled *The Colored Patriots of the American Revolution*. On page 23 of this book, Nell wrote, "Lemuel Burr (grandson of Seymour) a resident of Boston often speaks of their reminiscences of Deborah Gannet." He quoted extracts from the Resolves of the General Court of Massachusetts during the session of 1791 which awarded Deborah Gannet 34 pounds with interest from October, 1783 in compensation for her services during the American Revolution. Nell did not give any indication of her complexion, or racial description. Through the years some authors have categorized the heroine of the American Revolution as an American Negro. A careful literature search and a visit to Massachusetts were undertaken by the author to ascertain the most plausible identity of Deborah Gannet. The following summary of her life and family background should satisfy the reader that Deborah Gannet was a Caucasian and through the years she was inadvertently accepted by some as being a black heroine. This information is being presented, as a digression from the general theme of the manuscript in order to clarify any doubts about her identity.

Deborah Gannet was born on December 17, 1760 in Plympton, Plymouth County, Massachusetts. It is alleged that she was a descendant of Governor Bradford of Plymouth County. Her father was Jonathan Sampson born April 3, 1729 at Plympton. He married Deborah's mother, Deborah, October 27, 1751. She was the daughter of Elisha Bradford of Massachusetts. It has also been stated that Deborah was a descendant of Captain Miles Standish of the *Mayflower*. There is a legend that Deborah was in love with David Potter of Holden, Massachusetts, where she taught school and when he departed for the war, she decided to enlist. She left home and enlisted as a Continental soldier for a term of three years at Worcester. After being mustered in she left for West Point with a group of soldiers. Deborah Gannet endured many hardships while disguised as a male. She experienced long marches, excessive heat and actual warfare. Stories relate that while near the area of West Point, she was twice wounded, once in the thigh. She extracted the musket ball herself with a penknife and needle before medical aid arrived. Once she served as an orderly for General Patterson.

In October 1781, during the Yorktown Campaign, Deborah suddenly became ill and was sent to a hospital. There the attending physician discovered her sex but did not immediately make it known. Later the proper authorities were informed and she was released from military service.

Deborah Gannet disguised herself so perfectly that often female admirers were attracted to her, believing that she was a male. However, after she was released from the service and returned to Sharm, she married Benjamin Gannet, a farmer from Bridgewater. They had a family of three children. After the war, Deborah Gannet was considered a gallant soldier and many honors were bestowed upon her. A street was named for her and several societies have revered her memory.

A review of Deborah Gannet's brother's pension file has revealed various statements claiming that he had a sister who fought in the American Revolution disguised as a man. Deborah's brother was Ephriam Sampson, a Caucasian, who served as a private in the companies of Captain James Harlow (Colonel Simeon Cary's Regiment); Captain Thomas Turner (Colonel Thomas Marshall's Regiment); Captain Stutivants (Colonel Titcomb's Regiment); and Lieutenant Wood's Company (Colonel Thomas Lothrop's Regiment). The following statements were made by officials and citizens who knew Ephriam Sampson and reveal that he had a sister known as Deborah Gannet who had served in the American Revolution.

Benjamin Besse Bumpus of Wareham, Massachusetts, County of Plymouth, 9 August 1854: *He had a sister named Deborah Gannet who dressed as a man and served several years as a soldier in the War of the Revolution.*

William C. Folger, Nantucket, Massachusetts, December 15, 1854: *Dispositions taken in the towns of Halifax and Middleboro correspond with several former ones now on file in the pension office stating that Ephraim Sampson was brother to Deborah Gannet who*

*fought in the revolution dressed in male attire—this was stated to me by Theodore (son of Ephraim Sampson) last spring and I saw in Wareham a little wooden keg which was calculated to be slung to the person, which was said to have been carried by her in the war to carry water in.*

Irene Soule (daughter of a sister of Ephraim Sampson), Middleboro, County of Plymouth, December 4, 1854: *I well remember Deborah Sampson, my mother's sister, her visiting us and I and my brothers visiting her when she lived in Sharm, then the wife of Benjamin Gannet. I well remember hearing my mother and others talking about Deborah, being a soldier in the revolution.*

William Soule, Town Clerk of Plympton County, Commonwealth of Massachusetts: *I have the records of said town in my custody and I find in Book 2, page 576, the death of Sylvia Cushman, wife of Jacob Cushman, that mention is made of her being the daughter of a Jonathan Sampson and Deborah his wife of Plymouth, said Deborah was a daughter of Elisha Bradford of Kingston and the mother of Deborah Sampson who served in the War of the Revolution as a soldier in men's apparel and after the war married Benjamin Gannett of Bridgewater.*

In consideration of the above information concerning the heroine, Deborah Gannet, it is unlikely with her background family heritage, a direct lineage, and constant identification by individuals of her past, that she was a free Negro or of known Negro ancestry, although she could possibly have been an indentured servant.

A sketch of Deborah Gannet has been reproduced and reveals no indications of any outward evidence of Negro ancestry. Deborah Sampson Gannet was a soldier in the American Revolution, but it is believed, based on documented reports, that though a heroine she was not black.[12]

### Free Negro Requests Pay for His Revolutionary Service

*To His Excellency John Rutledge, President of the Colony of South Carolina.*

*The Memorial of John Featherston, a free Negro man most humbly—*

*That your memorialist served on Board the Schooner Defence [under] Capt. Simon Tuffy for the space of Seven months, and never rece'd more than two months pay. Tho often applyd to said Capt. for the balance of my wages and obtained for answers to apply to your Excellency.*

*Your said petitioner is in the Public Service for this two months under the command of Capt. Gimball, most humbly prays your Excellency will be pleased to take into consideration and order such relief as and he in his wisdom shall deem meet—And in thy bound will ever pray—John Featherston, Charlestown, Aug. 21, 1776.[13]*

## Virginian Justice in 1683 and 1834

During the American Revolution, some free citizens of the state of Virginia, both slave owners and ordinary citizens, were obligated to satisfy the recruitment quota for Virginia's enlistments for regiments and corps. Some free persons chose to have their slaves or free blacks substitute for them as soldiers in the Virginia Militia.

The General Assembly of the State of Virginia enacted on Monday, October 20, 1783, in the eighth year of the Commonwealth an act that directed the emancipation of certain slaves who had served as soldiers in the state of Virginia during the Revolutionary War.

In October, 1834, a John T. Kilby, clerk of the County Court of Nansemond County, Virginia, certified an extract of the act passed by the General Assembly of Virginia in 1783. The following is a true copy of the Extract Act:

*Extract Chap. 3*

*An act directing the emancipation of certain slaves who have served as soldiers in this state.*

*Whereas it hath been represented to the present general assembly, that during the course of the war, many persons in the state had caused their slaves to enlist in certain regiments or corps raised within the same, have tendered such slaves to the officers appointed to recruit forces within the state, as substitutes for free persons, whose lot or duty it was to serve in such regiments or corps, at the same time representing to such recruiting officers that the slaves so enlisted by their direction and concurrence were free men; and it appearing further to this assembly, that on the expiration of the term of enlistment of such slaves that the former owners have attempted again to force them to return to a state of servitude, contrary to the principles of justice, and to their own solemn promise.*

*And whereas it appears just and reasonable that all persons enlisted as aforesaid, who have faithfully served agreeable to the terms of their enlistment, and have thereby of course contributed towards the establishment of American liberty and independence, should enjoy the blessings of freedom as a reward for their toils and labours; Be it therefore enacted, that each and*

*every slave, who by the appointment and direction of his owner, hath enlisted in any regiment or corps raised within this state, either on continental or state establishment, and hath been received as a substitute for any free person whose duty or lot it was to serve in such regiments or corps, and hath served faithfully during the term of such enlistment, or hath been discharged . . . service by some officer duly authorized to grant such discharge, shall from and after the passing of this act, be fully and completely emancipated, and shall be held and deemed free in as full and ample a manner as if each and every of them were specially named in this act; and the attorney general for the commonwealth, is hereby required to commence an action, in forma pauperis, in behalf of any of the persons above described who shall after the passing of this act be detained in servitude by any person whatsoever; and if upon such prosecution it shall appear that the pauper is entitled to his freedom in consequence of this act, a jury shall be empanelled to assess the damages for his detention.*

*State of Virginia County of Nansemond Scilicet.*

*I, John T. Kilby, Clerk of the County Court of Nansemond in the state aforesaid, do hereby certify that the foregoing is an extract from an act of assembly passed by the General Assembly of Virginia at the session which was begun and held at the Public Buildings in the City of Richmond on Monday the twentieth day of October, in the year of our Lord one thousand seven hundred and eighty-three and in the eighth year of the commonwealth; and which may be found in Henning's Statutes at Large volume eleventh (thus vol. 11) page 308 and which act of assembly is still applicable to any slave or slaves coming within the purview of the same.*

*In Testimony whereof I hereunto subscribe my name and cause the seal of my County to be affixed this 31st day of October A.D. 1834. John T. Kilby.[14]*

## Louisiana's Black Militia 1729–1815

The American Negro has responded to the citizen's call to arms since pre-colonial days. The state of Louisiana is an example of the Negro's military service of state and nation through the years. The following is a brief account of these men of color who all were dedicated to the cause of fighting for freedom in Louisiana during the period of 1729–1815. Free men of color were used to assist in military skirmishes as early as 1729, during the Natchez Massacre and military assistance was rendered by blacks during Governor Perier's term of office. In April, 1736, when the governor and military commandant of Louisiana, Sieur de Bienville, organized his militia, free Negroes and slaves comprised the muster rolls. These 140 Negroes were commanded by a captain whose dedication, courage, and gallantry were a catalyst in developing confidence among his troops. These troops were loyal to the French settlers and assisted them in their numerous conflicts. Governor DeVaudrevil included Negroes in his military forces in 1746.

In the year of 1762, the black troops of Louisiana were utilized by the Spanish regime to defend their ground and alleged rights to the territory. The governor and regiment commandant of New Orleans, Bernardo de Galvez, had among his military forces an estimated eighty blacks. Some of the sub-lieutenants had black names such as Francisco Drovuill, Noel Carrière, Bacus Nichols, and Luis la Nuit. These colored troops experienced combat action along the Mississippi river, during the Gulf expedition and the Cimanen War. The Negro militia was also utilized at various times for construction projects such as repairing levees. When Don Francisco, Luis Hector and Baron Carondelet developed a defense plan for the colony, the Negro militia was considered to be included in the plan.

Two companies of free men of color participated in the parade celebrating the transfer of Louisiana from France to the United States in 1803. Members of these units petitioned Governor Claiborne in 1804, to be continued as part of the state militia. There was considerable debate by the governor and the secretary of State for several years concerning whether to consider the Negro unit as part of the militia. On Monday, September 7, 1812, Governor Claiborne approved an act to organize in a corps of militia for the service of the new state of Louisiana a certain portion to include free men of color. There was the nucleus for Claiborne to organize his colored militia. The official reactivation of the colored militia commenced when the battalion became known as the Battalion of Free Men of Color. Robert McConnell stated in his text that the commission issued for Isidore Honore, a free man of color, appointed second lieutenant in the battalion as of October 12, 1812, represented the first example of a state of the union commissioning a colored officer.

Prior to its legal activation, the free men of color were used to quell a slave insurrection in the parish of St. John the Baptist on January 8, 1811.

The most celebrated military engagement that involved the black militia was the Battle of New Orleans on December 23. Major D'Aquin's Battalion of Free Men of Color and mulatto drummer boy Jordan Noble, participated in the battle. One adjutant and six privates among the black troops were wounded during the battle of December 23, 1814. Companies of the colored battalion were displayed at various locations during the campaign. Captain Ferdinand Liotean's Company was dispatched to Fort St. Philip to defend the area against a British Naval attack. On December 26, 1814, Major Lacoste's Free Men of Color were sent to Chalmette and stationed next to D'Aquin's battalion of free men of color. The British troops centered their main strength January 8, 1815, on the line defended by American troops under Generals Carroll, Coffee, and Adam. It was at this main part of the line where the majority of the action occurred. The two colored battalions were located approximately between the main portion of the battle and the British near the river. As the fighting ceased, sniper fire, sporadic firing, and personnel attempting to capture prisoners and recover the wounded presented problems for the American troops. Captain Joseph Savary of D'Aquin's Second Battalion of Free Men of Colour obtained permission to lead a company into the field to assist in quelling the sporadic skirmishes by the British. He performed his mission heroically and eliminated the snipers. Grenadier Vincent Nolte of Major Jean Baptiste Plauche's Uniformed Battalion of Orlean Volunteers wrote a letter after the battle to the *Baltimore Niles Weekly Register,* which was published in the February 11, 1815, edition. It stated that, "D'Aquin's so called mulatto corps was next to us and the New Orleans colored regiment were so anxious for glory that they could not be prevented from advancing over our breast works and exposing themselves. They fought like desperadoes and deserved distinguished praise." Savary's company suffered the following casualties, his brother, Sergeant Belton Savary and George Mors were killed, and Alexis Audry wounded. Major Savary commanded the Second Battalion of Free Men of Color, which had colored line officers.

On the 23rd of December 1814, a separate company was organized and was under the command of a Negro captain, Charles Forneret. The company was part of the Louisiana Militia. The company performed various tasks as garrison troops during the early phases of the Battle of New Orleans. The defense of Fort St. Leon was assisted by Farreret garrison troops.

In addition to the two famed battalions of Free Men of Colour, records included a Captain Alexandre Lemelle's Company of Free Men of Colour. This unit of fifty men was mustered out of service in St. Martin's Parish on March 13, 1815. It appears to have been a part of the Fifteenth Regiment of Louisiana Militia although Captain Lemelle was mentioned as being under the command of Colonel Baker. There was a notation on a muster roll of a company of the Fourth Regiment of Louisiana Militia indicating that its first sergeant had been appointed captain of the Free Men of Colour. This could not be verified. General Jackson praised the black troops for their heroic service during the War of 1812. The General Assembly of Louisiana by joint resolution on February 1, 1815, acknowledged the patriotism and bravery of the black militia during the conflict. On March 19 and 25, 1815, the two Negro battalions respectively were mustered out of service and relieved to the jurisdiction of the state of Louisiana. After 1815, the interest in the black militia declined and the strength of personnel was quite low. The veterans of the black militia returned to their civilian occupations. The black militia was gradually declining in personnel and support, but its past gallant record of bravery was history.[15]

## War of 1812

### Black Labor Preferred to Militia

The Commissioner Governor of Washington, D.C., during the War of 1812 realized that the utilization of one hundred Negroes would be more practical to complete a labor task than to use the services of three hundred men of a division of militia. The following letter written by Commissioner Governor John P. VanNess indicates his preference of the use of Negro labor.

*Washington, July 22, 1813.*

*Sir: According to your orders, after a consultation with Col. Wadsworth, I detached upwards of three hundred men of my Division of Militia who are now employed, as a fatigue party, at Greenleaf's Point. But considering the materials of which the party is composed, and from what I have actually seen myself, I am satisfied that One Hundred Negroes or common laborers do fully as much work as the whole party—and I am informed they can be had without any difficulty, principally from one person in the neighborhood whose usual business, owing to the present state of things here, is suspended. —I am, your obedt. Servant John P. Van Ness (signed), Commander and Governor at Washington. John Armstrong.[16]*

### Black Bravery at Sea

The *Pittsburgh Mercury* dated March 9, 1814, included an article concerning the only known persons killed on board the *General Tompkins*. Captain Sholer mentioned their bravery.

*The name of my poor fellow who was killed ought to be registered in the books of Fame and remembered with reverence as long as bravery is considered a virtue. He was a black man by the name of John Johnson. A twenty-four-pound shot struck him in the hip, and took away all the lower part of his body. In this state, the poor, brave fellow lay on the deck, and several times exclaimed to his shipmates, "Fire away my boys! No haul a color down!"*

*The other was also a black man by the name of John Davis, and was struck in much the same way. He fell near me, and several times requested to be thrown overboard, saying he was only in the way of others. While America has such tars [sailors], she has little to fear from the tyrants of Europe.[17]*

### The Negro and the Battle of Lake Erie

During the War of 1812, the United States decided to defend its water approaches along Lake Erie.

*To secure those waters Captain O. H. Perry, a young naval officer, was appointed to create a squadron in addition to superintending it. Boats for the brigs, schooners and gunboats were all built under his eye and direction at Presque Island, now Erie, Pennsylvania during the winter of 1813–1814. By the tenth of July there were ten vessels manned by a force of four hundred men, "one-fourth of whom were Negroes." Perry was much dissatisfied with the latter class of seamen sent to him by Commodore Chauncey, so much that on July 26th he wrote to his superior officer saying, "The men that came by Mr. Chaplin were a motley set, blacks, soldiers and boys. I cannot think that you saw them after they were selected. I am however pleased to see anything in the shape of a man." To this letter the gallant Chauncey replied, "I regret you were not pleased with the men sent you by Messrs. Chaplin and Forrest, for to my knowledge a part of them are not surpassed by any seamen in the fleet, and I have yet to learn that the color of the skin or the cut and trimmings of the coat can affect a man's qualifications or usefulness. I have nearly fifty blacks on this boat, many of them are among the best of my men, and those people you call soldiers have been to sea from two to seventeen years." Chauncey was engaged in the capture of Fort George, in New York. Many blacks saw service with him in the engagement.*

*Perry's fleet began the preparations for training of guns and the like. The winter had been a hard one and many of the men had been sick. On September 13th the enemy was sighted in Put In Bay with boats manned by sixty-five guns. The engagement began a few min-*

*utes before twelve on the same day, the British firing as soon as the Americans were half a mile away. The guns of three or four of the largest belonging to the foe were centered upon the* Lawrence, *Perry's largest flagship. This caused her to lose many of her spars, save one on the starboard side. So fierce was the attack upon this boat that she was finally forced to drop out of the fight, and Perry's flag was transferred to the* Niagara. *The passage was made in a small sailboat, in which rode the commander, his young brother, and several of the crew. Included in the latter was a black man, Cyrus Tiffany. It is he whose likeness is seen in the painting representing the Battle of Lake Erie hanging in the Capitol in Washington, D.C. This man was a resident of Taunton, Massachusetts. He was a noted musician, having fifed with the drummer, Simeon Crossman, for the Revolutionary soldiers of his native town, and served on the warship, the* Alliance, *in 1797. When passing from the frigate* Lawrence *to the* Niagara *through a storm of bullets and shot, Tiffany acting on impulse tried to pull Perry down into a seat out of danger. The painting above referred to shows him in this act, of which he was very proud, and concerning which he often spoke on his return home after the war was over. Through Perry he was pensioned. He later lived in Newport, Rhode Island, with that officer, and at last died in the service on board the* Java *at the age of eighty, in 1815.*

*The battle on Lake Erie made it possible for American troops to invade Canada, and the brilliant campaign which followed was due to the removal of the hostile fleet. The result of this momentous event was the Battle of the Thames, through which the British lost the territory of Michigan. It also came about that the Indian tribes, allies to the English, were separated, and Tecumseh, their great leader, lost his life. On his report of this battle Perry spoke most highly of the conduct of the black men to whose presence he had formerly objected, saying in a letter to the secretary of the Navy: "They seemed to be absolutely insensible to danger." Among the Negroes who played a large part in this victory were Jessie Wall, a fifer on the* Niagara, *and Abraham Chase. The latter was alive in 1860. He was ninety years of age at that time and sat down to a dinner given in Cleveland to the survivors of the battle when the statue to Perry was unveiled in that city. Abraham Williams, of Pennsylvania, also took a very active part in this engagement. He entered the navy in 1812, under Captain Elliott, and held a position at one of the guns on the flagship* Lawrence. *He was born in Salem, Massachusetts, and died in Readville, Pennsylvania, in 1834.*[18]

## The Civil War

### The Unsung Black Regiment

The daring feats of bravery and accomplishment of the Massachusetts Fifty-Fourth Regiment during the Civil War are widely known. The Fifty-Fifth, however, has enjoyed less mention and its limited combat participation has given it a background role. It is the intent of this author to describe and relate some of the interesting experiences and heroic exploits of this famous but seldom mentioned black Civil War Regiment from Massachusetts.

*The Fifty-Fifth Regiment of Massachusetts Volunteer Infantry was on 12 May 1863 at Readville. Lieutenant Colonel N. P. Hallowell and Captain A. S. Hartwell were designated as commanders of the regiment attaining the ranks of colonel and lieutenant colonel. While stationed at Readville, the regiment was recruiting personnel, receiving instructions in various tactics and military subjects. On 18 July 1863, the Governor of Massachusetts John A. Andrew presented the regiment the Massachusetts state colors and the Ohio colors.*

*The regiment departed on July 21, 1863 for the area of Folly Island, South Carolina where they would experience isolated incidents in skirmishes and contact with enemy troops. Upon arriving in the area of Folly Island, the regiment established camp and prepared the necessary defensive fortifications. . . .*

*During the month of February, 1864, Company F of the Fifty-Fifth was serving with Rockwell's battery that took part in an expedition to John's Island under Brigadier General Schimmelfenning of Gordon's Division. They were under artillery fire and were reported as having performed their duty faithfully. Companies D, E, G, H, and some men from Companies B and I were sent on an expedition on 21 May to James Island. There they were confronted with the enemy and engaged in several skirmishes prior to reaching their objective.*

*On July 1, 1864, Company D of the regiment was deployed near James Island and was engaged in skirmishes. They deployed into a line and advanced under severe enemy fire. They charged ahead and captured twelve-pounder Napoleon guns. Several of the shells were found and they used them against the retreating enemy.*

*While the regiment was attempting to perform its assigned duty mission, there existed among the troops some unrest due to a discrepancy concerning the payment of the troops. The regiment had enlisted as the*

*Massachusetts Volunteers under the same [conditions] as other regiments of her quota. The fifty-fourth and Fifty-Fifth volunteer regiments were provided the same pay rations and clothes as the other troops received. The Governor of Massachusetts had authorized the officers of both regiments to promise their men the same pay and treatment as white troops. After considerable debate, the government agreed to pay the regiment as originally promised. On October 7, 1864, the payment of the regiment to August 3 was completed. It is interesting to state that the enlisted men of the Fifty-Fifth regiment had sent a total of 60,000 dollars home to their families upon receipt of their pay. The post sutler or post exchange officer had sold items to the men on credit. He had also lent money to the men without security. It was not known according to a regimental officer of a single case where a man present with the regiment refused to repay his debts. The men of the Fifty-Fifth also raised eleven hundred dollars without the aid and suggestions from the officers to supply their band and drum corps with new instruments.*

Credit must be given to Governor John A. Andrew for his unusual interest and untiring efforts to secure equal pay and treatment for his black troops. This copy of a telegram he sent illustrated his earnest intention at that time.

*Commonwealth of Massachusetts*
*Executive Department*
*Boston, Feb. 7, 1864.*

*Hon. Charles Sumner, U.S. Senator*
*Hon. Henry Wilson, U.S. Senator*

*Washington, D.C.*

*The order under which the Fifty-Fourth and Fifty-Fifth Massachusetts is in the following words, viz:— [as stated in a letter dated March 24]*

*Therefore, even if men employed under the $10 section of the act of July 1862 are soldiers; or if any soldiers mustered and sworn as such, can be turned off with less than soldier's pay (which I deny as a lawyer), still our two regiments are not under such disabilities.*

*They were raised, enlisted, mustered, sworn in, and used, under the laws for raising and accepting volunteers, in every respect as the foregoing orders show, standing on the same foundation of law which supports the rights of white soldiers. To deny them those rights, I declare as a lawyer, would not rise to the dignity of a respectable blunder.*

*At all events, Secretary Stanton's order, my pub-*

*lished promise thereunder, the written contracts of enlistment by the men, with their subsequent muster-in pursuant thereto, by the United States regular mustering officer, are conclusive on the government. I will never give up the rights of these men while I live whether in this world, or the next. John A. Andrew*

The Fifty-Fifth Regiment was continuing to experience contact with the enemy on November 30, 1864. The regiment was now in the vicinity of Honey Hill, South Carolina and was in formation advancing toward the village of Grahamville. Around noon, the regiment encountered enemy skirmishes. When the firing commenced, the Fifty-Fifth was ordered to form a line in the field and then proceed in a double column forward. Some of the companies moved ahead in a desperate charge and during the last charge the regiment experienced several casualties. Captain Crane and Colonel Hartwell were wounded. Several non-commissioned officers sustained injuries.

On the morning of December 1, the regiment again marched toward the front line. Six companies of the regiment engaged the enemy on December 5 and located several Confederate troops in a church, when an exchange of fire occurred.

The Fifty-Fifth regiment remained at Boyd's landing until January 1, 1865. On January 11, the regiment departed for Savannah by way of Hilton Head and arrived at Fort Thunderbolt near Savannah on January 12.

During February the Fifty-Fifth regiment moved toward Folly Island and on February 9 they moved toward the Stono Inlet on an expedition to James Island. A line was formed in old entrenchments that had been dug previously. On the morning of February 10, the regiment advanced toward the enemy which was composed of the Charleston battalion under Major Manigault. As the regiment advanced, they captured seven prisoners.

On February 19, 1865, news was received of the evacuation of Charleston. Provost Guards were detailed from the regiment and later the regiment was assigned garrison and defensive duty.

The Fifty-Fifth Massachusetts Volunteer Regiment was mustered out of service on August 29, 1865. On September 23 the regiment was paid and all troops formally discharged. Thirty-two officers and 822 enlisted men were mustered out.

Some interesting statistics of the regiment revealed that 247 had been slaves; 550 were pure blacks; 430 were of mixed blood; 477 could read; 319 could not read; 52 were church members and 219 were married;

the average age was twenty-three years; 30 deserted. The majority of recruits were born in Ohio, Pennsylvania, Virginia, Indiana, Kentucky or Missouri. Only one was born in Africa. There were 596 farmers and 76 were laborers.[19]

## Southern Memorial to Slaves

On May 21, 1896, Captain S. E. White, Fort Mills, South Carolina, unveiled a monument that he had erected in memory of the slaves that were faithful to the South during the Civil War. Wills, a former Confederate soldier and slave owner, had the following inscription placed on the front of the monument:

*1860, Dedicated to the faithful slaves who, loyal to a sacred trust, toiled for the support of the army with matchless devotion and with sterling fidelity, guarded our defenders' homes, women and children during the struggle for the principles of our Confederate States of America, 1865.*[20]

## Black Manpower in the Civil War

## General Order No. 154

*Headquarters Army of the Peninsula*
*Assistant Adjutant's Office*
*Yorktown, March, 1862.*

*The order stated that Negro attendants will be substituted for hospital nurses when the latter are enlisted men. Substitute Negro teamsters as far as possible for enlistment men in hospitals. Negro mechanic substitute. J. B. Magruder, M.G. Commanding.*

*Jackson, Mississippi*
*November 21, 1862.*

*Major General Earl Van Dorn, Abbeville, Mississippi.*

*Send cavalry out in the adjoining country and seize as many Negroes as may be necessary for the work on Pontotoc. J. C. Pemperton, Lieutenant General Commanding.*[21]

## Commendable Performance of Burnside's Colored Troops

Captain James H. Rickard, a former commander in the Nineteenth U.S. Colored Troops, in 1894 made some laudatory comments concerning Negro soldiers' heroism in combat:

*The world's standard of heroism is the Spartan Greeks at Thermopylae, but the assault of Colored Troops at the Crater and the assault and capture of Fort Harrison at New Market Heights without firing a gun (the caps having been taken from the guns) using bayonets only, where General Butler says he counted 543 black heroes dead in a space not 300 yards long, challenge Greek, Roman, or any other heroism. These regiments of blacks fighting with bayonets on the ramparts of Fort Millikens Bend and successfully bayonetting back General Henry McCullough's rebel division is a record that cannot be smirched with sneers or prejudiced injustices.*

*The charge of Ferrer's Division at the Crater at Petersburg, Va. through a broken and demoralizing divison of white troops then forming line inside enemy walls, and temporary capture of the interior works with awful losses, killed, wounded and murdered is a record to win back the previously prejudiced judgement of the President, cabinet, Generals, and officers of the Army of the Potomac who up to this time thought Negroes all right for service in a menial capacity, but from henceforth to take responsible places like the right flank of the army at Deep Bottom, Va. and the storming of strong works.*

*The last charge at Appomatox was by the black brigade of Generals Doubleday and William Birney.*[22]

## Black Loyalty to the Confederacy

There have been numerous accounts of the Southern Negroes' loyalty to master and the Confederate cause during the war years. Many reasons can be cited for the black man's devotion and desire to support his master in time of need. As mentioned previously, the black man's bondage and environment of ignorance and oppression were vital determining factors in his choice between flight to freedom or a life of slavery. The following newspaper account illustrates some instances of Negroes' loyalty to master and the Confederate cause.

*Patriotic Negroes—We yesterday took occasion to allude to the fact that a company of Negroes had been offered to Gov. Moore to assist in defending the South against her Black Republican enemies. Since that time other evidences of the loyalty and patriotism of the slave population have been given, Albert, a slave, belonging to Gen. Hardaway, and Alfred, another slave, belonging to Col. W. C. Bibb, having subscribed to the authorized loan of the Confederate States. The former took coupon bonds to the amount of $300, and the latter to the amount of $100. They are perfectly satisfied with their investment.*

*And perhaps we had as well mention, in this connection, that on yesterday, when the intelligence of the secession of Virginia reached the city, an old Negro acquaintance of ours, who wears a secession medal, remarked, after indulging in an ejaculatory chuckle, 'Bress God, my old State am all right!*[23]

### Lone Black Staff Member

A free military school for applicants who would command colored troops during the Civil War. The roster listed one Negro as part of the school's staff. He was listed as: James Buchanan, a messenger (colored).[24]

### Chaplain Assists the Illiterates

During the Civil War, a great majority of the Negro Union soldiers were not able to read or write. The chaplains were instrumental in establishing regimental schools to teach the illiterate troops. A monthly journal of the National Freedman's Relief Association, *The National Freedman Advocate*, relates the progress of a chaplain's learning program in Vicksburg, Mississippi. A letter from a chaplain to the journal read as follows:

*Headquarters, Fiftieth U.S. Colored Infantry*
*Vicksburg, Mississippi, February 7, 1865.*

*Rev. C. C. Leigh*

*I have repeatedly been requested by several of the agents of the National Freedmen's Relief Association to write again, for publication in the* Advocate, *some facts in regard to the educational enterprise of the Fiftieth Colored Regiment U.S. Infantry, of which I am Chaplain, but have not done so, from the fact that I have so much to do that I can not find the time to tell of it.*

*The regiment has been on garrison duty at this post most of the time since it was organized, but we are now ordered to New Orleans to go into "Field Service," as we suppose.*

*During the year 1864, we had school in the regiment under a great variety of discouraging circumstances, equivalent to about ten months teaching, at six hours per day for one teacher.*

*A soldier's attendance at school is necessarily very irregular, averaging, probably, not more than two hours out of a whole week that he can be in the presence of his teacher, often coming in only to recite and then retire; but by constantly carrying his book with him and studying every leisure moment he can get, with such aid as his more advanced comrades may give him he advances with an astonishing rapidity; so that when he comes into the school again the teacher finds it necessary to re-classify him. Some who at the beginning of last year did not know the alphabet, can now read readily and write legibly. Geography and*

*arithmetic has also been taught orally to the man with good success.*

*Our schoolroom accommodations have been change-able and various—a school tent; a cane brush bower, the regimental guard-house, the Chaplain's private tent, the shade of a tree, and a room in the barracks, just to suit circumstances. Sometimes with seats and sometimes without. Sessions of school have been held in* A.M., *in the* P.M., *and evening. Some of the time only one teacher engaged one hour per day, and at other times several at a time for six hours a day, and some weeks no school at all.*

*The demand for school books has been much greater than the Chaplain has been able to supply; consequently the more zealous and less scrupulous have stolen spelling books in order to get one to study.*

*Results: As to the result of the year's labor, under all sorts of inconveniences and discouragements, the following figures will give an idea of the progress and standing of the men at the close of the year 1864:*

*Whole number of men in the Regiment 646*
*Whole number who can read readily 48*
*Whole number who can read easy sentences 165*
*Whole number who know the alphabet only 242*
*Whole number who know the alphabet or more 455*
*Whole number who are ignorant of the alphabet 191*
*Whole number who can write readily 17*
*Whole number who can write his own name 37*
*Number who have since enlisting learned the alphabet 252*
*Number who have since enlisting learned to write 97*
*Number who have since enlisting learned to read 35*

*Those who are ignorant of the alphabet are mostly new recruits. During the month of January, 1865, increased facilities were afforded for school, especially for the non-commissioned officers. A class for teaching reading and writing one hour per day was well attended, and promised large success, but as we are now ordered into the field, probably our formal schools are broken up permanently.*

*I write this on my knee, and if you can make anything out of what I have written above, in the midst of camp confusion, you are welcome to publish such part of it as you may think will be of public interest, or throw the whole into your basket of scraps and waste paper.*

*Yours in haste, without time to correct the slips of my pen, James Peet.*[25]

### The Confrontation

*During the capture of the outer lines of forts around*

*Petersburg in the Virginia Campaign of 1864, it is related that a colored lieutenant who was the senior officer in command at the time, demanded the surrender of a fort from the rebel commander. The latter replied that he would not surrender as a prisoner to a Nigger. The lieutenant remonstrated, and urged his surrender but the Virginian probably hoping that a white officer would be summoned to receive the surrender still refused. "Very well," said the Negro officer, "I have offered you your life and you won't have it. You may stay here." And seizing a musket from the hands of one of his men, he pinned the Confederate officer to the earth with the bayonet.*[26]

### The Admirable Soldier

An officer of the Ninth Corps stated the following in 1863:

*If you should ask me for the type of an admirable soldier, I would present you with the mulatto. It seems that he unites in himself physically speaking the perfection of both races.*[27]

### Blacks Among the Confederate Gray

Throughout the years, there has been considerable doubt as to whether Negroes actually served in combat with Confederate forces. The following is an account of an official report submitted by scouts who cited the presence of Negroes manning a howitzer battery in 1861.

*Camp Butler, Newport News, Virginia.*
*August 11, 1861.*

*Sir: Scouts from this post represent the enemy as having retired. They came to New Market Bridge on Wednesday and left the next day. They said the enemy talked of having nine thousand men. They were recalled by dispatches from Richmond. They had twenty pieces of artillery among which was the Richmond howitzer battery manned by Negroes.*

*I am, respectfully, your obedient servant, J. W. Phelps, Colonel Commanding.*

*Lieutenant Charles C. Churchill, Acting Assistant Adjutant General, Fort Monroe, Virginia.*[28]

### The Blacks Held the Line

*During the Civil War in a disastrous fight near Guntown, Mississippi, when the irresolution and mismanagement of the Union Commander, generally attributed to intoxication, resulted in one of the most disgraceful defeats and retreats in the annals of the war, it was the half-drilled Colored troops, most of them under fire for the first time, who when the white*

*troops were completely demoralized and panic stricken by the failure of their commander, fought with the utmost desperation, and kept back the Confederate troops until their white comrades and a portion of the train could make good their escape. One of the ammunition wagons was near them, and the brave fellows, with the intention of maintaining their resistance to the last, filled the breast of their shirts with cartridges and fired away till the cartridges had become so moist with perspiration that they could not be fired. But they accomplished their objective and having held the Confederates at bay for some hours they finally retreated bringing up the rear of the Union Forces.*[29]

### Negro Troops Assist in Defense of Richmond

Through the years historians have stated that there is sparse evidence concerning the presence of Negro troops engaging in combat or being utilized by the Confederate Forces other than as body servants or cooks. Brewer's *The Confederate Negro* (Duke University Press, 1969) mentions the presence of Negro soldiers from Winder and Jackson hospitals engaging in combat during the defense of Richmond in March, 1865. His facts were based on Winder's Hospital records and existing Confederate records. This author made a thorough check of the National Archives Records and was successful in finding a microfilm true copy of a letter from assistant surgeon and major, Commanding, Jackson Battalion, reporting on the use of Negro troops on the front. The letter read as follows:

*Richmond, Va., HQ Qrs. Jackson Battalion*
*March 16, 1865*

*Sir: I have the honor to report that in obedience to your order, received through Surg. Hancock, I ordered my battalion from the 1st, 2nd, 3rd, and 4th Div'ns of Jackson Hospital to the front on Saturday night at 12 o'clock and reported by order of Maj. Pegram to Col. Ship., Provisional Army Confederate States, Comdg. Cadet Corps. I have great pleasure in stating that my men acted with the utmost promptness and good will.*

*I had the pleasure of turning over to Major Chambliss a portion of my Negro company to be attached to his Negro command. Allow me to state that they behaved in an extraordinary creditable manner. I would respectfully ask that Major Chambliss be particularly noticed for the manner [in] which he handled that very important element about to be inaugurated in our service. Resp'y your Obdt Servt. H. C. Scott, Asst. Surg. & Major Comdg., Jackson Battalion.*[30]

## A Hero's Reasons for Leaving the Military

The black American has been struggling for a long time for equality in job opportunities and rank in the U.S. military. His struggles have been arduous but the progress has been remarkable and quite rewarding. However, in 1865, black American soldiers realized the problems that they must face in order to gain equal status in the armed forces. One of America's black Medal of Honor men, Christian Fleetwood, wrote on June 8, 1865 to a former employer and friend his earnest desire to gain equal status for the black soldier:

Dr. James Hall.

*Dear Sir: I much regret that you disapprove or rather do not approve of my leaving the service at the expiration of my term of enlistment.*

*Be assured that in this matter I am actuated by the same motives which induced me to leave your office, and light and agreeable employment and take to the arduous and adventurous duties of the camp—some personal ambition to be sure but mainly from a desire to benefit my race.*

*From representations made by Col. Birney and from the position assumed by our friends in Congress, you remember we were induced to believe or hope that on evidence of merit and ability to do our duty we should receive promotion, at least to the rank of company and regimental officers. That I have well performed the duties of the office which I have held the past two years, it becomes me not to say, although I bear a medal conferred for some special acts as a soldier, yet am bold to say that no regiment has performed more active, arduous dangerous service than the Fourth U.S. Col'd. Troops.*

*Leaving Baltimore in September 1863, we reported at Yorktown, Va., and in less than a week were ordered on a raid, making thirty (30) miles per day, with no stragglers. We remained at Yorktown until April, engaging in similar expeditions once or twice in every month.*

*In April we were ordered to Point Lookout, Md. to guard the rebel prisoners there, and remained until the organization of the first division of colored troops in the U.S. service with the 3rd Division, 18th Army Troops.*

*Leaving Fortress Monroe with the James River Expedition in May we were the first ashore at City Point, and built works, held them and made reconnaissances from then to June 15th when the first serious demonstration was made upon Petersburg, losing on that day about two hundred and fifty (250) out of less than six hundred (600) men. Assisted in the siege of Petersburg*

*until August when we were transferred to Dutch Gap, working in the canal under the shelling of the rebel batteries until the latter part of September when we were ordered to Deep Bottom and under Major Gen. Birney on the 29th Sept. at the taking of new Market Heights and Fort Homison lost two-thirds of our available force. Entrenching on the lines before Richmond we remained until Gen. Butler's Expedition to Fort Fisher returned to our old camp and in a few days again embarked under Gen. Terry upon his successful expedition and have taken part in all of the marches and fighting encountered by "Terry's Command" until the surrender of Johnson's army in April last. Upon all our record there is not a single blot, and yet no member of this regiment is considered deserving of a commission or if so cannot receive one. I trust you will understand that I speak not of and for myself individually or that the lack of the pay or honor of a commission induces me to quit the service. Not so by any means, but I see no good that will result to our people by continuing to serve. On the contrary it seems to me that our continuing to act in a subordinate capacity with no hope of advancement or promotion is an absolute injury to our cause. It is a tacit but telling acknowledgement—on our part that we are not fit for promotion, and that we are satisfied to remain in a state of marked and acknowledged subservincy.*

*A double purpose induced me and most others to enlist, to assist in abolishing slavery and to save the country from ruin. Something in furtherance of both objects we have certainly done and now it strikes me that more could be done for our welfare in the pursuits of civil life. I think that a camp life would be decidedly an injury to our people. No matter how well and faithfully they may perform the duties they will shortly be considered as "lazy niggers or as drones in the great hive."*

*I have trespassed upon your time to a much greater extent than I intended but I wished you correctly to appreciate my motives for leaving the service.*

*Very truly and respectfully Yours, Christian A. Fleetwood, Sergt. Major, U.S. Col'd. Troops.*[31]

## The Negro as a Soldier

A former commander of black troops during the Civil War wrote in 1913 his personal observations concerning the Negro's performance during the conflict. The following excerpts from his remarks are indicative of the abundant praise that was rendered to the black troops by their leaders:

*We once saw a white regiment its ammunition ex-*

*hausted just as the Confederates charged with their famous yell break ranks in confusion and flee in disorder through the Union lines. We saw the Seventh Regiment of United States Colored Troops (USCT) sent to the relief of fleeing whites. We saw them advance in perfect order with the steadiness of Veterans without charging a musket until the order was given and they then met the rushing charge of the foe.*[32]

## Heroism at Port Hudson

The following story relates an act of unusual heroism by Negro troops during the Civil War. This is one of the many stories that have been told concerning the black man's bravery, but have not been documented.

*On June 14, 1863, General H. E. Paine, leading his troops was severely wounded in the leg while far in advance and left upon the ground while his troops were driven back several hundred yards by the constant and deadly fire of the enemy who swept the whole field with their artillery. The general's adjutant general called for volunteers to go to the general's relief and bring him off the field if possible. The men looked upon the wide plain, swept with a constant artillery fire under which nothing could live, and though the adjutant general offered large rewards, not a man could be found willing to risk the almost inevitable death which would follow the attempt. In vain the adjutant general pleaded and urged. The men could not be induced to take the risk. But now stepped forward a little squad of Colored Men from the "Corps d'Afrique" and one of them acting as spokesman for the rest said to the adjutant, "We's been thinking Sar, dat dere's got to be a good many killed in this war, fore our people can get deir freedom and p'raps it may as well be we as anybody else; so if you please sar, we'll go after the general." The adjutant general accepted their offer and there being sixteen of the volunteers, they formed into fours, and the first squad with a stretcher and supplies of water, etc. moved off towards the fire-swept plain. The first fifty yards were hardly passed when one of the four were struck down; his companion didn't stop, but pressed forward, when another and another and finally the fourth fell. Without uttering a word or hesitating a moment, the second squad of four stepped out and similarly equipped, moved forward and they too were struck down. Instantly and without a moment's delay, a third squad of four went forward. Two of these fell wounded but the other two reached the general, and though unable to bring him off, gave him water and remained with him till the evening when he was carried to the bivouac of the troops.*[33]

## A Tale of the Confederacy

Munroe, a faithful old servant accompanied his master, James F. Steward when he enlisted in the Confederate Army in 1862. Later Munroe was separated from Steward. Being a mulatto and wearing his master's cadet uniform, Munroe was taken prisoner and mistaken for a Confederate officer. The Union authorities exchanged Munroe for two Yankee Dutchmen.[34]

## Blacks Participate in Occupation of a Louisiana Town

An extract from a Return of the District of Natchez, Mississippi, commanded by Brigadier General J. W. Davidson, for the month of March, 1865, revealed the following:

*March 25th, an expedition consisting of detachments of the Sixth U.S. Colored Artillery (heavy) and the Tenth Tennessee Cavalry, (in all about five hundred men), accompanied by thirty men from the steamer Benton U.S. Navy, sent out under Brevet Brigadier General Farrar. On March 27, they occupied the town of Trinity, Louisiana, without loss, capturing two captains, one lieutenant, and twenty-two privates; also forty horses, twenty-five stands of arms, and a quantity of commissary stores.*[35]

## A Civil War Spy

The pages of history concerning the American Revolution reveal various cases where Negroes served as scouts, spys or informers. During the Civil War a Negro citizen was used to convey valuable information to General Philip Henry Sheridan prior to the battle of Winchester, in 1864. General Sheridan related in his personal memoirs the bravery and loyalty of a Negro man.

*While stationed near Harper's Ferry, Sheridan decided to employ additional scouts to gain information concerning the enemy. These scouts provided him with a plan to gain information from a young Caucasian lady named Rebecca Wright; however she would use the services of an old Negro man who had a permit from the Confederate commander to come into Winchester three time a week and depart. The purpose of his visit was to sell vegetables. The scouts had determined that this man was trustworthy and suggested that he be used to transfer information. After the general was convinced of the old man's fidelity, a message was to be given to him to carry on his next visit to Winchester. The message was prepared by writing it on tissue paper, which was then compressed into a small pellet and protected by wrapping it in tin-foil so that it could be safely carried in the man's mouth. The letter appealed to Miss Wright's patriotism and re-*

quested her to furnish information regarding the strength of Early's Army. The note was delivered to Miss Wright and she answered the note, giving it to the old man later, who successfully returned it to General Sheridan. The information provided by Miss Wright was instrumental in the final success of General Sheridan's plan to defeat General Early's troops.

The success of this general's battle was documented with tribute to the woman who provided valuable information, but history did not record the name of the humble, loyal and faithful Negro man who answered to the call of the Union to give his services as an unofficial spy. Some soldiers whose courage and deeds will always be revered are classified unknown; the memory of this unknown old man deserves a similar place in history.[36]

### Robert Smalls—Ship's Pilot and Master

The identification of Robert Smalls, legislator and militia general as a captain, possibly in the naval service, has been somewhat confused because of his relationship with the Civil War vessel *Planter*. The following letters should clarify Robert Smalls' status as far as his nautical service was concerned. On December 26, 1882, Robert Smalls wrote a letter to the quartermaster general to request information concerning his record in that department.

*Washington, D.C., December 26, 1882*
*Genl. Rufus Quartermaster General, Washington, D.C.*

*General: I have the honor to request that you will furnish me with a transcription of my record in your department.*

*On the first of December, 1863, I was detailed as a pilot in the Army and in carrying the* Planter *through Folly Island she was fired upon by the Rebel Battery and was abandoned by Capt. Nicholson. I took charge of and carried this boat safely through and Genl. Q. A. Gillmore then commanding the Department of the South with headquarters on Morris Island made an order to Capt. Dutton of the Quartermaster Department that I should be put in charge of the steamer* Planter *and on the first of Dec. 1863 I was placed in charge of the boat by an order of Col. J. S. Ellsworth, Chief Quartermaster of the Department, which position I held until September, 1866 when the boat was out of commission at Baltimore. I particularly desire copies of any letters from Genl. Gillmore and other officers in relation to this matter.*

*I have General, the Union to be Robert Smalls (signed) Late Capt. U.S. Steamer* Planter.

On January 3, 1883 the Quartermaster General's office replied to Robert Small's letter of December 26, 1882.

*War Department, Quartermaster General's Office, Washington, D.C.*
*January 3, 1883*

*Hon. Robert Smalls, Member of Congress, Washington, D.C.*

*Sir: Your communication of the 26th ult. in relation to your services on the steamer* Planter *during the rebellion, and requesting copies of any letters from General Gillmore and other officers on the subject, has been received.*

*The records of this office show that the name of Robert Smalls is reported by Lt. Col. J. J. Elwell, Hilton Head, S.C. as a Pilot at $50 per month, from March 1, 1863, to September 30, 1863, and from October 1, 1863, to November 20, 1863, at $75. per month.*

*He was then transferred to Capt. J. L. Kelly, A.Q.M., November 20, 1863, by whom he was reported as Pilot from November 21 to November 30, 1863. He is reported by that officer in the same capacity from December 1, 1863, until February 29, 1864, at $150. per month.*

*Office of the Chief Quartermaster, Hilton Head, S.C. September 10, 1862.*

*General: I have this day taken a transfer of the small steamer* Planter, *of the Navy. This is the Confederate steamer which Robert Smalls, a contraband, brought out of Charleston on the 13th day of May last. The Navy Department, through Rear Admiral Dupont, transfers her, and I receipt for her, just as she was received from Charleston. Her machinery is not in any good order, and will require some repairs, etc.; but this I can have done here. She will be of much service to us, as we have comparatively no vessels of light-draft. I shall have her employed at Fort Pulaski, where I am obliged to keep a steamer.*

*Please find enclosed a copy of the letter of Rear Admiral Dupont to Gen. Brannan in regard to this matter. I am, Genl., very respectfully Your most obed't. serv't. J. J. Elwell (signed), Capt. A.Q.M.*

*The name of Robert Smalls is then reported by Capt. Kelly as Captain of the Steamer* Planter, *at $150. per month from March 1, 1864, until May 15, 1864, when transferred to the Quartermaster in Philadelphia.*

*He is reported by Captains C. D. Sheridan, G. R. Orue, W. W. Vawitess, and John R. Jennings, Asst. Quartermasters at Philadelphia, as Captain of the*

Planter, at $150. per month from June 20, 1864, to December 16, 1864, when transferred to Capt. J. L. Kelly, A.Q.M., Hilton Head, S.C., by whom he is reported to January 31, 1865.

From February 1, 1865, he is reported as a "contractor, victualling and manning the steamer Planter."

I respectfully enclose, herewith, copy of a letter, dated September 10, 1862, from Capt. J. J. Elwell, Chief Quartermaster, Department of the South, in relation to the capture of the steamer Planter, which is the only one found on file in this office on the subject. Very respectfully, Your obedient servant, (signed) Dep'ty Quartermaster Gen'l, U.S.A. Act'y Quartermaster General

Contract

A contract for victualling and manning the U.S. Steamer Planter was signed by Captain John L. Kelly, Assistant Quartermaster for the United States and Robert Smalls, Master. The price wa s agreed as $1,603 per month, the contract to take effect at 12 M. July 19, 1865. (Contract Book y 133, Approved (signature—3), rec'd July 31, 1865).

ARTICLES OF AGREEMENT, made this fifteenth day of July in the year one thousand eight hundred and sixty-five, between Robert Smalls, Master of the U.S. Transport Steamer called the Planter, of the first part, and Capt. John L. Kelly. A.Q.M. U.S.A., for the United States, of the second part, WITNESSETH: That the said Robert Smalls, Master of the U.S. Transport Steamer Planter for himself, his heirs, executors, and administrators, and the said Capt. John L. Kelly, A.Q.M for and in behalf of the U.S. Quartermaster's Department, have mutually agreed, and by these presents do mutually covenant and agree, to and with each other, in manner following, to wit:

The said Robert Smalls, Master of the U.S. Transport Steamer Planter, for the purpose of manning, victualing, and running said Transport Steamer Planter, shall furnish the following officers and crew, and pay to each the rates following, viz:

| | |
|---|---|
| 1 Captain, at $ One hundred and twenty-five per month. | 125.00 |
| 1 First Mate, at $ Seventy-five per month. | 75.00 |
| 1 Second Mate, at $ Fifty per month. | 50.00 |
| 1 Steward, at $ Fifty per month. | 50.00 |
| 1 Cook, at $ Thirty each per month. | 30.00 |
| 1 Waiter, at $ Fifteen each per month. | 15.00 |
| 6 Seamen, at $ Twenty-five each per month. | 150.00 |
| 2 Quartermasters, at $ Forty each per month. | 80.00 |
| 1 Engineer, at $ One hundred and twenty-five per month. | 125.00 |
| 1 First Assistant Engineer at $ Eighty-five per month. | 85.00 |
| 1 Second Assistant Engineer, at $ Fifty per month. | 50.00 |
| 1 Third Assistant Engineer, at $ Fifty per month. | 50.00 |
| 4 Firemen, at $ Forty each per month. | 160.00 |
| 3 Coal Passers, at $ Thirty each per month. | 90.00 |
| For victualling 25 men and one pilot at 60¢ per month. | 468.00 |
| | 1603.00 |

It being further agreed that none but experienced and competent officers and engineers shall, under any circumstances, be employed under this contract.

And the said Robert Smalls, agrees further to subsist the foregoing officers and crew on good and wholesome food, allowing to each one ration daily, equal in quality to that issued to troops in the service of the United States by the Subsistance Department of the U.S. Army.

And it is further understood, that should a vacancy occur for any period during the month, and remain unfilled, in the foregoing lists of officers and crew of said vessel, such vacancy shall be reported to the said Captain John L. Kelly, Assistant Quartermaster U.S. Army, in order that a corresponding deduction may be made in the compensation allowed. This period, as well as that of the service of officers and crew, to be verified by the affidavit of said Robert Smalls, Master of the U.S. Transport Planter.

In consideration whereof, the said party of the second part, for and in behalf of the Quartermaster's Department, U.S. Army, agrees to pay, or cause to be paid, to said Robert Smalls Master of the U.S. Transport Steamer Planter, for and in consideration of the foregoing services, the sum of Sixteen hundred and three dollars per month, being [payment] in full for officering, manning, victualling, and running said U.S. Transport Steamer Planter.

THIS AGREEMENT shall go into effect at 12 o'clock M. of the fifteenth day of July, 1865, and shall continue in force during the pleasure of the Quartermaster's Department.

Subject to approval or revision by the Quartermaster General U.S. Army.

R. S., July 14, 1865 (stamped).

No member of Congress shall be admitted to any share of this Contract, or any benefit to arise therefrom.

IN WITNESS WHEREOF, the said parties to these presents have hereunto, interchangeably, set their *hands and affixed their seals, on the* Sixteenth *day of* July, 1865.

*(signed) Robert Smalls (seal)*
*(signed) John L. Kelly (seal)*
*(signed) Capt. of AQM KAQM*
*(Executed in Quintuplicate.)*
*Signed, sealed, and delivered in presence of—*
*(signed) Ellis*
*(signed) Y. J. P. Owens.*[37]

## A Confederate Negro Regiment

Records and official documents of the Civil War period reveal very little information concerning organized Negro companies or regiments officially mustered into the Confederate service. A search of archives materal concerning this subject has revealed the following. A citizen of New Orleans wrote General Ainsworth, Chief of Records and Pensions, War Department, on March 17, 1903, requesting that the War Department include the names of colored men who had volunteered and served under the name of "Native Guards." This citizen mentioned that the two regiments established after Farragut had captured New Orleans and that some of the colored officers were still living in the city in 1903. He also said that the French newspaper *New Orleans Bee* contained notice of the regiment's drills during 1861 and 1862. General Ainsworth replied on March 24, 1903 that the War Department had only the roll of a Captain Louis Lainer's or Lainez's Company of Infantry called the Louisiana Native Guards, "Endorsed report of Louisiana Native Guards on parade November 23, 1861."

A New Orleans newspaper dated May 10, 1903, published an article concerning the first Negro Regiment raised in New Orleans for the Confederacy. The following excerpts will explain the background of this controversial unit that was prepared to support the Confederate course in 1861.

*In 1861, New Orleans had a Negro population of 26,000 of whom nearly half, or 12,000 were free and 14,000 slaves. The free Negro population had been as high as 25,000 at one time, but the growing excitement over the Negro question had driven many of them to France, for they were mainly mulattoes or quadroons, speaking French and with a considerable proportion of French blood. Those who remained in New Orleans were generally men of property or mechanics. Some of them had received a good education abroad; and a number of them owned slaves of their own.*

*Their position was curious in the Civil War, where slavery played so large a part. The attack on Sumter aroused a strong military sentiment in New Orleans and Louisiana, and in March and April, military companies sprang up by the dozen.*

*Among those who caught the fever were the free people of color of New Orleans. A number of them were sons and grandsons of the Negroes who distinguished themselves at the battle of New Orleans and won the praise of Jackson.*

*The most prominent of them issued a call for a meeting to express their views on the situation, and to organize a regiment for the protection of the South, and New Orleans in particular, against the "enemy."*

*The meeting was held April 21, 1861. There were 1,500 free Negroes present, two-thirds of the free men of color in New Orleans. This resolution was passed:*

*Resolved, That the population to which we belong, as soon as a call is made on them by the Governor of the State, will be ready to take up arms and form ourselves into companies for the defense of their homes, together with the other inhabitants of the city, against any enemy who may aim ot disturb its tranquility.*

*The necessary call was made by Governor Moore and the free men of color began to organize themselves into a regiment of eight companies, under the name of the Native Guards of Louisiana. They were under Negro officers who were commissioned by the Governor. Jordan Noble, the Negro drummer boy of Chalmette, who died here only the other day, undertook to raise a Negro company in Jefferson parrish.*

*There is no reason to doubt that the men who organized the Native Guards were in earnest in their offers of service to the State of Louisiana and the Confederacy. All their interests lay in the South. Many of them were slave owners. The defeat of the South could only injure them; and, as they were already free, no emancipation could be of any benefit to them, while the ballot for Negroes was not dreamed of by Mr. Lincoln at that time.*

*If the Native Guards did not figure conspicuously in the Confederate service, as the Choctaw Indians did, it was due to conditions that arose soon after they were organized. A number of free Negroes were found masquerading as slaves and traveling on slave passes. As these Negroes were mainly from the West, the conclusion was reached—and in all probability, correctly—that they were being employed to learn the military preparation of the South. Some of these free Negroes were arrested; and while the threat of selling them into slavery was not carried out, as nothing could be proved against them, it produced a suspicion and distrust of all free Negroes, from which the Native Guards suffered.*

The Native Guards were sworn in as a part of the First Division of the Louisiana Volunteers. They turned out in the big military review of Nov. 23, 1861, and it was then that a roll was made of Captain Lainez's company, the only record the War Department has been able to get of the regiment of Negroes who enlisted to perpetuate slavery.

They were out again in the big parade of January 27, 1862, when 24,818 soldiers were in line. The parade was given for the benefit of Farragut and Butler, it being desired to show the Union spies, of whom there were many in New Orleans, how strong the Confederates were in troops.

The Federal fleet off the passes increased the distrust of the Negro regiment and the Militia law passed by the Louisiana Legislature, which went in effect Feb. 15, 1862, practically abolished the Native Guards by restricting the militia to white men. Barely a month afterwards, however, all this was reversed. The white regiments had been hurried out of New Orleans to join the Army of Tennessee and take part in the campaign of which Shiloh was the central figure.

The free people of color were invited to join the Confederate service again and on March 24 Governor Moore issued the following order:

The Governor and Commander-in-Chief, relying hopefully upon the loyalty of the free colored people in the city and state, for the protection of their homes and believing that the military organization which existed during the War, called upon them to maintain their organization and be prepared for such orders as may be transmitted to them.

They did maintain their organization, but that is all. In another month New Orleans had fallen into the hands of the Union army. During the short interval which prevailed between the evacuation of the city and the occupation by the Union forces, the Foreign Leigon, consisting of the French, Spanish and British subjects in New Orleans, was called out by Mayor Moore to preserve order, but the Native Guards were ignored. They did not leave New Orleans with the new Confederate troops but remained behind, practically disbanded.

The Native Guards were treated with a scant courtesy that killed any enthusiasm they might have felt for the Confederate cause. They were sworn in and mustered out of the service and called back again only in the last few desperate days before the capture of the city by Farragut's fleet.

Four months after his occupation of the city General Butler took up the work where the Confederates dropped it. He saw the possibility of utilizing the free men of color who had had some military education and discipline and on August 22, 1862, he issued an order calling upon all members of the Native Guards to enlist in the service of the United States.

Joseph T. Wilson's *Black Phalanx* contains a roster of some of the members of the Louisiana Native Guards. The following are some of the black officers who were part of the Louisiana Native Guards in 1861. Wilson lists three regiments.

*First Regiment Louisiana Native Guards. Captains:* Andrew Cailloux, Louis A. Snaer, John Depass, Henry L. Rey, Adeide Lewis, James Lewis, Edward Carter, James H. Ingraham; *Lieutenants:* Ernest Sougpne, William Harding, J. G. Parker, John Hardman, J. D. Paddlick, V. Lesner, Louis D. Lucien, F. Kimball.

*Second Regiment Louisiana Native Guards. Major F. E. Dumas; Captains:* E. A. Bertonneau, E. P. Chase, P. B. S. Pinchback, Joseph Villeverde, W. P. Barett, William Beelez, Hannibal Carter, S. W. Ringold, M. Menllim, R. H. Isabellu; *Lieutenants:* J. P. Lewis, Calvin Glover, George T. Watson, Rufus Kinsley, Soloman Hays, Louis Degray, Alphonso Fleury, Peter O. Depremont, Jasper Thompson, J. Wellington, Joseph Jones, Ernest Hubian, Alfred Arnes.

*Third Regiment Louisiana Native Guards. Captains:* Jacques Gla, Joseph C. Oliver, John J. Holland, Peter A. Gardner, Charles W. Gibbons, Leon G. Forstall, Samuel Lawrence. *Lieutenants:* Paul Paree, Eugene Rapp, E. Moss, G. W. Talmon, E. Detredge, G. B. Miller, Charles Butler, Chester W. Converse, Morris W Morris, E. T. Nash, Octave Foy.[38]

## A Senior Citizen of Vienna, Virginia Tells War Stories

On June 24, 1970, this author had the unusual pleasure of visiting Mr. William West, a respected, intelligent and outstanding citizen of Vienna, Virginia and, at ninety-six, its oldest inhabitant. In listening to Mr. West tell stories of his father in the Civil War, of Colonel Charles Young in the Spanish-American War, and of General George Patton the years seemed to drop away and I felt I was hearing a man of fifty to sixty talking about the recent past.

William Alexander West was born in Vienna in 1874. He attended Howard University for three years and taught school for fourteen years in Cartersville, Odruck Corner and Vienna. In 1908 he began working for the U.S. Government and in 1917 transferred to the Army War College where he remained until his retirement in 1942. During his years at the War College he received a meritorious promotion recommended by the Chief of Staff, Army Ground Forces. Mr. West has interested himself in the advancement and improvement of Negroes in Virginia: he was secretary of the NAACP in his community from 1944 to 1964, and was awarded a life membership in the NAACP for his services. He has been active in religious affairs and he is knowledgeable in local church history, as well as in the history of the Negro in Virginia. The following stories were told me by this remarkable Vienna citizen.

### A Separate Call to Arms

In 1861 the family of Daniel West, father of William Alexander West, lived five miles from Fairfax Court House as slaves on the estate of Major Chichester. There were five boys and two girls in the West family. Just before the Civil War, Major Chichester decided to send three of the boys and one girl to Mississippi, keeping Daniel, who was the youngest and had been trained as a house servant, and one of his sisters. Whenever Major Chichester had boots made, he would have two pairs, giving one to Henry, who had very small feet, to wear in order to break them in. Henry decided that he was not going to Mississippi so one day he put some clothes and two pairs of the major's boots into a sack, saddled a horse and at nightfall rode away. The horse returned the next day, but without Henry, who had succeeded in reaching an underground railroad station and made his way to Connecticut. This did not deter Major Chichester from sending the other children to Mississippi however.

In 1861, when the Civil War commenced, Daniel West, then sixteen, went with his master, Major Chichester, to serve as bodyguard. He served with the major throughout the war from Bull Run to Appomattox and Gettysburg. Ironically, Henry had joined the Union Army in Connecticut and was also at the battle of Gettysburg and must have faced his Confederate brother Daniel from the Union line.

Daniel West often told his son William about his war experiences. He spoke of the musket that he carried to protect his master and of a fierce three-day battle when men were shot in the saddle and were dragged along by their horses, their feet caught in the stirrups.

### A Servant's Loyalty

One day in 1863, when the Confederates were firing on a train carrying Union soldiers from Alexandria, a Union officer was killed. It was believed that a Captain Franklin Williams of the Mosby Raiders had killed the officer and every day Union troops went to the Williams estate looking for the captain. If he was at home, he would be hidden. The third day the Union troops

came Simon Alexander (William West's grandfather) hid his master Franklin Williams in the horse's manger which was fielled with hay. The horse was standing close by, eating, and the troops did not suspect that their quarry was there, The Union soldiers burned the house down, but without unearthing Captain Williams.[39]

### Slave Displays Heroism for Confederates

A report of Major General James E. B. Stuart, Confederate States Army, Headquarters Cavalry Corps, February 13, 1864, stated that "While the Second Virginia Cavalry (Colonel T. T. Munford) was pursuing a party of marauders under Means, near the areas of Point Rock Road, Edwards Ferry and Waterford, during the skirmish Edmund, a slave of one of the men, charged with the regiment and shot Everhart, one of the most notorious ruffians of Means' party."[40]

### Black Cadets at U.S. Military Academy Before 1875

Appointments of black qualified men to the U.S. Military Academy were made as early as 1870. Unfortunately during this period the Negro cadet was not openly received by the other cadets and an atmosphere of hostility was constantly present. The young black cadets faced the traditional strict military discipline and a tedious curriculum. Besides this, they also experienced oppressive attitudes and acts by those persons who resented their presence. The following men were appointed to the academy based on their qualifications and selected traits, and attempted to pursue the challenging goals of the academy. Some were reported deficient in their studies, and several had personality problems. None the less these men established the climate for the eventual acceptance of other Negro candidates: Thomas Van Renslaer Gibbs, Florida; Michael Howard, Mississippi; Henry Alonzo Napier, Tennessee; James Elias Rector, Arkansas; John Washington Williams, Virginia.[41]

## The Indian Campaigns

### The Black Indian Fighter

In America's conquest and defense of her western and southwestern frontiers black men with Indian blood, the Seminole Negro Indian Scouts, played an integral role. During the days of slavery, free Negroes and runaway slaves needed havens of freedom and tranquility. Some went to far northern states and Canada and small groups found their way into Indian camps where some became slaves again and others intermarried and cohabited with the Indian tribes. The

Seminole Indians of Florida saw the Negro come and go, but while Negroes lived with the Indians they miscegenated and the two races became mixed. American Negroes can claim an Indian genetic heritage which in some cases is physically dominant.

In Texas today there are descendants of a small group of Negroes who joined the Seminole Indians some 120 years ago. Many stories have been told concerning their ancestors, but little has been written. The following paragraphs attempt a brief description of this group of black defenders whose achievements, although they include four Medal of Honor awards to Seminole Negro Indian scouts, are not widely known.

The Seminole Negro Indian spoke both an Indian language and English. They were mostly Baptists, but in many cases observed Indian ritual and custom. Their homes were in separate villages where they tended their own fields and cattle. A chief, Negro Chief John Horse, had been chosen among the group and in 1849, with Chief Wild Cat, he led a group of dissenting Seminole Indians who departed for Mexico. They eventually settled in the area of Laguna de Parras, southwestern Coahuila, around 1870. Other Negro-Indian groups had settled at Nacimiento, Coahuila, Matamoras and on the Nueces River. According to official correspondence between the post at Fort Clark, Texas, and the adjutant general, Department of Texas, San Antonio, Texas, dated August 26, 1884:

*Captain Perry of the Twenty-Fourth Infantry Regiment went to Mexico and asked the Seminole Negro Indians to come on the Texas side of the Rio Grande and the government would give them a reservation. It was also stated that General McKenzie told the group that had arrived on the Texas side and become scouts not to return in 1879 because they would later be provided with a reservation. Those scouts that had departed Mexico were supplied with arms, ammunition and rations. They provided their own horses and received compensation. Their dress was similar to Indian style.*

Over a period of thirteen to fifteen years the Negro Indian scouts performed their missions in a superb manner. Their contributions to the regular army units were commendable and essential. The part they played, though it may have appeared insignificant, was instrumental in achieving many victories and successes for the regular army units they were assisting. Some examples of their heroic action follow.

*In 1874, Colonel MacKenzie was on an expedition against the Cheyenne, Comanche and Kiowa Indians in Palo Duro Canyon. During this expedition twenty-one*

*Seminole Negro Scouts accompanied him and displayed unusual bravery. . . . The scouts searched for horse thieves in Mexico and hunted Indian raiders. In many cases they were utilized to seek out the location of hostile enemy camps.*

The Seminole Negro Indian Scouts and their families resided at Forts Duncan and Clark. In 1873, the Indian Scouts realized that they could not forever exist on government reservations, therefore they began to demand the responsive action to the alleged promises they had received. There was considerable discussion as to the disposition of the Scouts and their families. Correspondence between the Executive Office, Seminole Nation and the U.S. Indian agent, dated September 17, 1883, stated that the Seminole Nation cannot recognize the Negro Scouts' claim to return to Seminole reservations and that because of their flight to Mexico, they have no claim. The Principal Chief [of the] Seminoles, John Jumper was quite adamant in his refusal to accept the Negro Indian Scouts. Official correspondence during the period revealed that the government was indecisive as to where the Negro Indian Scouts and their families should be located.

In consideration of their devotion to duty and country, their earnest fidelity and loyalty as Scouts, it was believed by some supporters that they should be given adequate land to satisfy their existing problems.

Excerpts from correspondence written by two officers of the United States Army who knew the Indian Scouts and were aware of their tribulations should best illustrate the urgency and importance of their request during that time.

*They have undoubtedly lost all claim to their lands given them by the Mexican government, and it is not known whether that Government will see fit to renew the grant, but in any event, I believe it would be cheaper to place them on a United States Reservation. They have done good service as scouts during the last thirteen years, and are entitled to consideration. I think if a reservation was given them, nearly all would go to it, if not at once, within a very short period. Some of them ask permission to occupy the houses they have built on the reservation until the spring of 1885, when they hope if not otherwise provided for to be able to obtain work in Texas, and support their families, some of them I think will return to Mexico in any event.*

*Z. R. Bliss, Lieutenant Colonel, Nineteenth Infantry, Commanding Post, Fort Clark, Texas, 26 August, 1884.*

*I now forward the enclosed correspondence to*

*show how hopeless it is to expect any relief from the Indian Bureau. Thirty-four men all with wives and children who have served as soldiers for the average of thirteen years, without any trades or property and with habits essentially Indian, are thrown upon a community itself poor and hostile to these harmless vagabonds.*

*The thirty-four enlisted scouts to be discharged represent at the least one hundred and fifty souls, and how they are to live, or what is to become of them, I cannot imagine.*

*To turn them loose upon the people of Kinney County, wherein they now are, is hardly a right thing to do and will probably lead to trouble. My impression is that they should be sent to the Indian Territory and settled in the manner of the Modoes and Nez Perces.*

*D. H. Stanley, Brigadier General, Commanding, Headquarters Department of Texas, San Antonio, August 27, 1884.*

The proud and loyal Negro Seminole Indian Scouts were disbanded around 1914. These dedicated soldiers and their families were not granted all their requests for land and security, but they have attained a place of distinction and honor in the history of America's black defenders.[42]

### The Spanish-American War

#### Black Volunteers in the Spanish-American War

The history of America's National Guards and their service to the country during various conflicts would be incomplete without the inclusion of the Negro volunteer units that served in Cuba and the States during the Spanish-American War. The following is a brief résumé of these units' contribution.

#### Ninth Battalion, Ohio Volunteer Infantry

The battalion was ordered into camp at Columbus, Ohio on April 25, 1898. On May 14, 1898 the battalion was mustered into volunteer service with Colonel Charles Young, U.S.A., commanding the Ninth Battalion OVI. He was granted an indefinite leave of absence from the regular army to accept his volunteer commission of major.

The Ninth Battalion did not experience combat action in Cuba, however. It was located in Virginia, Pennsylvania and South Carolina during the war, performing garrison guard duty. The battalion was mustered out of service January 29, 1899.

#### Sixth Virginia Regiment

The regiment was composed of eight companies and was under the command of Lieutenant Colonel Richard C. Croxton, regular army, and two Negro majors, J. B. Johnson and W. H. Johnson. The unit was mustered into service near Knoxville, Tennessee. The unit experienced garrison duty in the states during the war.

An incident occurred wherein the regiment's officers, including one major, were to appear before a board of examiners in order to give evidence of their fitness to command. The officers concerned resented this order and resigned. The vacancies were filled by the governor and the appointees were Caucasian.

#### Third North Carolina Volunteer Infantry

The officers of the North Carolina Infantry Regiment were all Negroes. The commanding officer was Colonel Young, a North Carolina statesman. This unit also served in the states during the Spanish-American War.

#### Third Alabama Volunteer Infantry

This unit consisted of all Negro enlisted personnel and Caucasian officers. The regiment experienced no service and was confined to its immediate locality.

#### Indiana's Two Negro Companies

Two companies of Negro men with Negro captains were mustered into service from Indiana and later attached to a Colonel Huggins Eighth. . . . The companies were stationed at Fort Thomas, Kentucky and at Chickamauga. The units were designated companies A and B. The commanders were Captains Porter and Buckner and Lieutenant Thomas was the quartermaster. These units were mustered out of service at an early date.

#### Twenty-Third Kansas Volunteers

The Twenty-Third Kansas was organized in Kansas and its officers were Negroes. The unit arrived in Cuba on August 30, 1898 and was stationed near San Luis. This unit experienced mostly garrison and guard duty while stationed in Cuba.

The Twenty-Third Kansas Volunteers returned to the states in March 1899 and were mustered out of service.

#### The Eighth Illinois Volunteer Infantry Regiment

The Eighth Illinois was organized from the Ninth Battalion, Illinois National Guard. The governor of Illinois was approached in 1898 by some Negro leaders and asked to accept the services of a Negro regiment commanded by Negro officers. The governor concurred in their request and recruitment for the Eighth Illinois began with a muster roll of 1,195 enlisted men and 46 officers in July, 1898. Of these 46 officers, 10 had received college educations, 6 were lawyers and others were educated in the public schools or had served in the regular army as non-commissioned officers. On August 15, 1898, the Eighth Illinois landed in Cuba, the first all-Negro military unit, including officers, to land on foreign soil in defense of America. The regiment's commanding officer was Colonel Marshall who served as commander of the post and also governor of the Province of San Luis, Cuba. A detachment of the regiment under the command of Major Jackson was dispatched to Palma Soriana.

The Eighth Illinois returned to the states in March, 1899 and was mustered out of the service.[43]

### The San Juan Tragedy

Corporal John Walker, Troop D. 10th U.S. Cavalry, wrote the following account of his unit's part in the San Juan tragedy and the death of Lieutenant Jules G. Ord.

*Upon the 1st day of July, as the Tenth Cavalry went into battle at San Juan Hill against the Spanish Forces, Troop D deployed to the left and joined Hawkins' brigade in the charge, the Sixth Infantry becoming excited and retreating. They stampeded the entire line, making the charge. Lieutenant Jules G. Ord, of the Sixteenth Infantry and Captain Bigelow of the Tenth Cavalry endeavored to rally the American forces and succeeded by their timely and brave assurances that by standing their ground and continuing the charge up the hill, victory was in store for them. Immediately after which Lieutenant Ord walked down the line toward the road leading to the city of Santiago. Upon seeing the gatling gun detachment selecting a more advantageous position from which to play upon the Spanish lines, and becoming greatly encouraged at this, he hastily retraced his steps down the line saying: "Men, for God's sake raise up and move forward, for our gatling guns are going to open up now." As the gatling gun opened fire upon the enemy's trenches, the Tenth Cavalry and the Sixteenth Infantry arose from their reclining position and charged forward, commanded by Captain Bigelow and Lieutenant Ord respectively.*

*In the charge Captain Bigelow fell pierced by four bullets from the enemy's guns. Upon falling he implored the men thus: "Men, don't stop to bother with me, just keep up the charge until you get to the top of the hill." Captain Bigelow's fall left Lieutenant Ord in command of the front forces in the charge as they* *ascended San Juan Hill. As we reached the Spanish trenches at the top of the hill, Lieutenant Ord with two privates of the Sixteenth Infantry and I being the first to reach the crest, and at that time the only ones there captured four Spaniards in their entrenchments, one of whom was armed with a side arm [revolver] which I took from him. Lieutenant Ord said: "Give it to me as I have lost mine, and we will proceed to this blockhouse and capture the rest of the Spanish soldiers." Taking the revolver from my hand, he and I walked toward the blockhouse. Lieutenant Ord stopped near a large tree, directing his attention to the firing which was coming from the Spaniards who had previously occupied the blockhouse fortification. Just as he tip-toed to see over the high grass, Lieutenant Ord was shot through the throat by a Spanish soldier who lay concealed in the heavy underbrush at the foot of the tree by the side of which he paused to watch the Spanish firing. As Lieutenant Ord fell upon the spot, the Spaniard jumped up and ran toward the already retreating Spanish line.*

*As he started to run, I shot him twice in the small of the back, killing him, one bullet entering close to the other. I was by Lieutenant Ord's side when he received the mortal wound and he fell at my feet. Without moving out of my tracks, I fired twice at the fleeing Spaniard while standing directly over Lieutenant Ord, and just before he gasped his last, he muttered: "If the rest of the Tenth Cavalry were here, we could capture this whole Spanish Command." Corporal John Walker, Troop D.[44]*

### Henry Ossian Flipper Court-Martial Controversy

Second Lieutenant Henry Ossian Flipper was the first black graduate of the U.S. Military Academy in 1877. On August 13, 1881, Flipper was accused of failing to mail $3,791.77 in public funds to the Chief Commissary. The court ruled that Henry Ossian Flipper was not guilty of the charge of embezzlement but guilty of the charge of conduct unbecoming an officer and gentleman.

Liberal and concerned congressmen in later years attempted to have Flipper's sentence remitted, restore his military title and grant him official retirement. A Senator Wadsworth and a former secretary of interior displayed unusual interest in Flipper's case. The following letters reveal the personal interests, sincerity and opinions related to Flippers court martial case:

On September 9, 1922, the secretary of the interior, Albert B. Fall, wrote Senator James W. Wadsworth

Jr., chairman, Senate Committee on Military Affairs of the U.S. Senate the following letter:

*September 9, 1922*
*Hon. James W. Wadsworth Jr., Chairman, Senate Committee on Military Affairs, United States Senate.*

*My Dear Senator Wadsworth: I was very much disappointed to learn a few days since, that a bill pending before your Committee for the restoration and retirement of Lieutenant H. O. Flipper, had been postponed indefinitely.*

*I have had this matter up with the Secretary of War personally, within the last month, and had arranged for him to meet Mr. Flipper and discuss this bill fully and then inform you as to his feeling in the matter.*

*I am very deeply concerned in Mr. Flipper's behalf. I have known him now thirty years. Without any hesitancy or qualification whatsoever, I can say to you that he is one of, if not the highest class colored men whom I have ever met in my life. He graduated from West Point where he went through, as I have been informed by his classmates, with the respect of the white boys with whom he was associated. Of course he had a most difficult and trying time. He was assigned to a company and, as I know personally, he commanded white troops.*

*One of his company happens to live in my county and has worked for me from time to time as a carpenter for many years. He has told us that every soldier in the company respected and loved Flipper.*

*In the old days I talked with ex-District Attorney John Dean, with ex-Judge Falvey, and lawyers of the Western District and I think without exception those civilians who knew of the Flipper case sympathize most fully with him in his trouble, and this is in a district where the Negro has no voice in affairs and receives but scant courtesy or consideration, as practically all the old time white residents were southern born and life-long Democrats.*

*I knew Flipper during his connection with the Court of Private Land Claims, as special agent of the Department of Justice, in 1895 to 1901; he served with Hon. Matt Reynolds, one of the most eminent lawyers in the country, who was the United States attorney for this court. I knew every individual member of the court and certainly there was never organized in this country or any other, a court composed of more eminent lawyers and high class gentlemen fitted for and performing their duty in the important matters entrusted to their care with the extreme of ability and with results satisfactory to private claimants and to the public.*

*Mr. Flipper is a master of the Spanish language*

*without a superior; he is thoroughly and fully acquainted with the civil law of Spain and of Mexico, and was the person on whom principal reliance was placed in the investigation of land grant frauds, securing witnesses and testimony, as assisting in the preparation of all the cases before the court for trial.*

*Flipper graduated from West Point in the engineering class with General Goethals. After his retirement from the service with the Court of Private Land Claims, he became associated with companies and individuals with whom I was working in the Republic of Mexico.*

*I had charge of all legal matters of several corporations and companies engaged in mining, building and operating railroads, in installing large modern lumber mills, etc., etc. I was also the attorney-in-fact for these companies and my associates. I represented all their business before the Mexican authorities, state and national, as well as the Mexican courts. Mr. Flipper was my right hand man and adviser.*

*I had him out for something like eight months on one engineering expedition in charge of other competent engineers and a field force and in charge of finances, consisting generally of sums of cash amounting to thousands of dollars for meeting payrolls in the field, where no bank facilities were available. His accounts have always been kept with the most scrupulous care and under the audit of as competent men as could be employed in any enterprise, never one question was raised as to any account rendered by Flipper.*

*His life is a most pathetic one. By education, by experience and because of his natural high intellectual characteristics, he can find no pleasure in association with many of his own race, and because of his color he was and is precluded in this country from enjoying the society of those whom he would be mentally and otherwise best fitted to associate with. I have never known a more honorable man in my somewhat varied experience.*

*He has now been associated with me, in one way or another, since about 1905, and at times intimately. He has never presumed. He has always been assiduous in attention to his duties and performs every task willingly, cheerfully and efficiently.*

*Aside from his other duties here in my Department, he does all my Spanish translating and, in addition thereto, translates from the French technical oil articles, books, pamphlets, etc., which I am accustomed to having examined and placed before me in considering matters of oil production, costs, etc., as well as general mineral production in all countries of the world. He is the most reliable interpreter and translator whom*

*I have come in contact with in my office in the public
service.*

*The enactment of the bill would simply result in his
restoration and immediate retirement on account of
age.*

*Of course I am aware that some of our officers are
opposed to the passage of this bill. I had hoped, however, that a thorough consideration by the Committee,
after the Secretary of War had also personally considered the matter, would have resulted favorably.*

*Is there anything which can be don in this matter?*

*Very sincerely yours, (Signed) Albert B. Fall, Secre-
tary of the Interior.*

The secretary of war, John W. Weeks, replied to
Secretary Albert B. Fall's letter on October 6, 1922, as
follows:

*Honorable Albert B. Fall, Secretary of the Interior,
Washington, D.C.*

*My dear Mr. Secretary: I acknowledge receipt of
your letter of September 9th, enclosing a copy of the
letter written by you to Senator Wadsworth with
reference to the bill for the relief of Mr. H. O. Flipper,
an employee of the Interior Department, who, as an
officer of the Tenth Cavalry, was dismissed from the
military service on June 30, 1882.*

*I find that before a Court-Martial which convened
in November, 1881, Second Lieutenant Henry O. Flipper, Tenth Cavalry, was tried under two charges, the
first being "Embezzlement, in violation of the Sixtieth
Article of War" of the sum of $3,791.77 public funds;
the second "Conduct unbecoming an officer and a
gentleman," with five specifications which respectively
were, false official statements made to his commanding
officer on four different occasions to the effect that he
had transmitted to the Chief Commissary at San Antonio, Texas, on July 9, 1881, $3,791.77, which funds
"were not so in transit but had been retained by him
or applied to his own use or benefit." The fifth speci-
fication under this charge was that when required officially to make an exhibit of the public funds in his
personal possession he showed to his commanding
officer as part of the funds for which he was accountable a check for $1,440.43 "which check was fraudu-
lent and intended to deceive the said commanding
officer, as he, Lieutenant Flipper, neither had nor never
had had, personal funds in said bank, and had no
authority to draw said check."*

*The action of the court was to acquit Lieutenant
Flipper on the charge of embezzlement, which was undoubtedly due to some technical construction of the*

*term embezzlement, for the court proceeded to find
him guilty of all the specifications under the other
charge, which involved the retention by him of public
funds to be applied to his own use or benefit. Under
the charge of conduct unbecoming an officer and a
gentleman, supported by the five specifications which
I have explained, the finding of the court was guilty
and the sentence was dismissal, which was carried into
effect June 30, 1882.*

*It is proposed to restore this man to the grade, rank
and status in his arm to which he would have attained
had he remained continuously in the service until the
date of the approval of this Act, which would make
him the senior colonel in the army, and place him on
the retired list. The best that this government can do
for the most valuable officer in the service, the one
with the longest service, of the most gallant conduct,
and of the most unblemished and irreproachable record is to place him on the retired list at the end of his
continuous and faithful service. Officers are only
placed on the retired list when stricken with permanent illness or disabled by wounds, or after at least
thirty years of service. This reward your request would
give to an officer educated by the government, who
within five years of his graduation was disgracefully
dismissed from the service, and in the intervening forty
years has rendered no service whatever to the army.
I believe if you will consider the matter, you will agree
that I can not with any propriety concur in this proposi-
tion. To place a man of this record on the retired list
of the army would be a reflection on every honorable
officer on it and would give him, unearned, all that
comes to other officers after the devoted service of a
life-time.*

*Sincerely yours, (Signed) John W. Weeks, Secretary
of War.*

Evidently Henry O. Flipper had an opportunity to
refute some of the statements that were written by
Secretary Weeks to Secretary Fall. The following is
excerpted from Flipper's remarks. He wrote:

*The statement "which was undoubtedly due to
some technical construction of the term embezzlement" IS GRATUITOUS.*

*The record shows that the charge of embezzlement
under the Sixtieth article of War was abandoned and
an effort made to convict for constructive embezzlement under sections 5488, 5489, 5490, 5491, 5492 and
5493 of the Revised Statutes. UNDER neither of which
sections was there charge, indictment, or arraignment
for trial, hence the ACQUITTAL. See Original Record,*

*pp. 153 to 169 and pp. 7 to 10 of Argument of Counsel for Defense.*

As to the check, the commanding officer himself testified:

*"The only time I can swear positively to observing the check was on the 8th day of July, when I spoke to him in reference to it." Record, Certified Copy, pp. 93, 94.*

*"Q.-Then, on the 26th or 27th of June, on the occasion which you speak of, he had ALL THE FUNDS with which he was responsible?"*

*"A.—Undoubtedly. I did not inspect him on the 26th of June as the papers show, but I did inspect him on the 8th of July up to that date and he had ALL THE MONEY that he was accountable for. It was public money and I considered it correct,"*

WHERE IS THE GUILT?

*The commanding officer had previously testified the check had been submitted to him sometime "in May and thereafter weekly until the 6th of July." Recorded, Certified Copy, Part 1, p. 46.*

*As a matter of fact the check was first submitted in May, was made and submitted to commanding officer by his orders to make such check and forward funds to some bank as personal funds. The check was never forwarded because of his order to hold it till further orders.*

*The Secretary of War is in error as to retirements. The most inconspicuous officer of the lowest or any other grade in the army is entitled to retirement after 40 years' service or at sixty-two years of age or after thirty years' service at his own request, as well as for disability incurred in the service. See Revised Statutes, sections 1243 et seq.*

*As to "reflection on every honorable officer," did the restoral of Captain George A. Armes, Paymaster Major Reese, Judge Advocate General D. G. Swain and others mentioned in my Brief as precedents impose any less reflection on these gentlemen? Henry O. Flipper.*[45]

## Black Gallantry in the Philippine Islands

When the United States dispatched military forces during the Philippine Insurrection, there were blacks among the troops. Here again the black soldier was on the scene, making gallant contributions that in some cases were not reported in the pages of history. A speech in the House of Representatives on Monday, June 8, 1914 by the Honorable Martin B. Madden (Illinois) relates an episode from the outstanding record of Negro troops in the Philippines. Some of the historical data for his speech was researched by a Mr. Daniel Murray, a former assistant librarian, Library of Congress for more than fifty years.

The following account depicts the bravery of American Negro soldiers under the leadership of a capable and heroic commander.

*During the Philippine trouble it is related by Dr. Joseph M. Heller, late major and surgeon, United States Army, that during the campaign Captain Batchelor, a North Carolinian by birth and a hero if ever there was one, with 350 colored troopers, a brave and splendidly disciplined little band, marched and fought their way over a distance of 310 miles in one month. The route selected was over roads so difficult as to be almost impossible to travel. In fact, the route did not really deserve the name of roads, but was simply trails, through which the men plodded along, sinking at times to their knees in mud.*

*The expedition at the time was chasing Aguinaldo through the northern and central portions of Luzon and toward the China Sea. Dr. Heller stated that he never saw men show truer courage than those troops with Captain Batchelor. They were insufficiently clothed for the long march, and without guides in a strange region, but through chilling nights and sweltering days they forded 123 streams and crossed precipices and mountains where the daily average of ascent and descent was not less than 8,000 feet. For three weeks these troops lived on unaccustomed and insufficient foodstuffs and drove the enemy twice from strong position. They captured many of the natives and set free more than four hundred prisoners. They finally forced the surrender of the commander of the insurrecting forces and made the people of Luzon enthusiastic advocates of American supremacy. No other single command during the Philippine trouble stood as many hardships or accomplished so much as these Negro soldiers under Captain Batchelor. Such was the report made at the time; and although General Lawton was killed, Captain Batchelor carried out his verbal orders, and died of cholera in the Philippines, thus going to his grave without any further reward or recognition for one of the bravest expeditions ever attempted by soldiers in modern times.*[46]

## New Bedford Newspaper Cites Black Troopers' Valor

A New Bedford Massachusetts newspaper in August 22, 1915, presented an article that described the famed Twenty-Fifth U.S. Infantry Regiment's response for assistance to the residents of a burned area in Spokane, Washington. The article read as follows:

*Thirty Fire-Fighters Believed Lost*

*Spokane, Wash. Aug. 22-Thirty men out of a crew of forty-seven fire-fighters, in charge of Forest Ranger Holingshead, are missing and are believed to have perished Saturday night when their camp on Big Creek, a tributary to the St. Joe river, sixteen miles from Avery, Idaho, was swept with flames.*

*At least five farmers are dead near Newport, Wash. Several persons were rendered temporarily insane. Mrs. Ernest Reinhardt broke away from her rescuers after they had borne her away from her burning home and madly rushed into the flames. Fire is still threatening Newport.*

*Soldiers of the Twenty-Fifth United States Infantry, colored, who are patrolling Wallace, Idaho, under the direction of Major Hensen, have been ordered to shoot vandals whose depredations have become serious. Chicago, Milwaukee and Puget Sound refugee trains through the burned region are furnished with guards of Negro soldiers. The discipline, valor and general efficiency of the Negro troops are eliciting the highest praise from residents of the burned area.*

*A westbound train of the Northern Pacific reached Spokane today after an exciting run through the flames. Every car was scorched.*[47]

## The Brownsville Affair, 1906 and 1972

Until September 1972, official and public accounts of the Brownsville Affair had been summarized as follows:

On August 13, 1906, three companies of the all-black companies (except officers) were involved in a riot in Brownsville, Texas. The white citizens of the town had alleged that the blacks had shot up the town and that Negroes had murdered and maimed the (white) citizens of Brownsville. One citizen was killed, one wounded and the Chief of Police was injured. Based on official military reports and other investigations, the president of the United States in 1906, Theodore Roosevelt, of Spanish-American War fame, dismissed the entire battalion from federal military service without honor and disqualified the members from future enlistment and loss of benefits.

Many Americans both black and white protested. John Milholland, of the Constitution League rallied in the support of the dismissed soldiers. Senator Joseph B. Foraker, Ohio, demanded a full and fair trial for the soldiers. The Senate responded to his request by authorizing a general investigation. After several months, the majority members of the Senate committee upheld the president's decision.

September 28, 1972. Secretary of the Army Robert F. Froehlke announced that an Army Review Board had reviewed the 1906 discharges of 167 black soldiers of the First Battalion, Twenty-Fifth Infantry (Colored) who were discharged in 1906 without honor as a result of a shooting incident which occurred in Brownsville, Texas.

The army's summary of the incident was: "Around midnight on August 13, 1906, some sixteen to twenty individuals on horseback rode through the streets of Brownsville firing their weapons into homes and stores. As a result of the shooting, one man was killed and two were injured. Witnesses alleged that the riders were colored soldiers. At this time the First Battalion, Twenty-Fifth Infantry (Colored) was stationed outside of the town of Brownsville.

A series of military inquiries and a county grand jury failed to establish the identity of the riders involved. Finally all members of companies B, C, D of the First Battalion were assembled and the guilty told to step forward and identify themselves or all would be discharged without honor. None stepped forward; all maintained their innocence. Their discharge without honor followed. Subsequent courts of inquiry failed to recommend remedial action and relief legislation introduced on behalf of various individuals was never enacted. An internal army review of administrative and judicial policies brought this instance of mass punishment to the secretary. Although the practice was occasionally invoked under extreme circumstances during frontier times, the concept of mass punishment has for decades been contrary to army policy and is considered gross injustice.

The results of the military review of the Brownsville Affair enabled Dorsie Willis, eighty-seven years of age, Minneapolis, Minnesota, and Edward Warfield of Los Angeles, possibly the only survivors of the group of the Twenty-Fifth Infantry unit that received dishonorable discharges, to be exonerated.

Even though the military news release stated that "the practice (decision concerning 167 black soldiers in 1906) was occasionally invoked under extreme circumstances during frontier times," the known facts today, 1973, and those of 1906 pose two questions. Was it a normal practice in an area not actually a frontier, Brownsville, Texas, to dismiss 167 men from the military service dishonorably, with the final decision executed by the president of the United States? Could the Brownsville affair's decision of mass punishment have been politically oriented? A noted black historian, Professor Rayford W. Logan stated "One must conjecture whether Roosevelt's [Theodore Roosevelt] abrupt order for the dishonorable discharge of three companies of the Twenty-Fifth Infantry after the Brownsville Riot stemmed from a further desire to propitiate the South."[48]

### The Truth About Carrizal

On June 21, 1916, newspapers throughout America carried the tragic news concerning a small-scale American massacre at Carrizal, Mexico. Though the only participants were three American white army cavalry officers and black troopers of Troops C and K, Tenth U.S. Cavalry, the nation was stunned and concerned. The black press and community was saddened by the incident and for some time were not made aware of the actual facts. The following account of the Carrizal incident has been summarized from official correspondence between the investigating officer of the incident, commanding general, punitive expedition, U.S. Army, Mexico, and commanding general, Southern Department, Fort Sam Houston, Texas during the period June to September, 1916.

A Lieutenant Colonel George O. Cress, Inspector General's Department stated the following in his report to General Pershing, Commanding General, Punitive Expedition, U.S. Army, Bublan, Mexico:

*Captain Charles T. Boyd, Troop C, Tenth Cavalry, and Captain L. S. Morey, Troop K, Tenth Cavalry were each ordered by the commanding general, punitive expedition, to make reconnaissances, from their respective stations, in the direction of Ahumada. There was no cooperation between these troops ordered by the Commanding General, Punitive Expedition [Cooperation by Commanders].*

When Captain Boyd arrived at Santo Domingo ranch on June 20, 1916, he decided to assume responsibility for both troops, with Captain Morey as his subordinate. Carrizal was approximately eight miles from Santo Domingo ranch. Ahumada was some twenty miles away. Boyd decided to pass through Carrizal on the way to his destination.

Captain Boyd arrived at an irrigation ditch near Carrizal and sent a messenger into town to request permission from the Mexican militia to pass through the town. After several conferences with Mexican officers (Lieutenant Colonel Rivas, and General Gomez), he was informed that American troops could not pass east, west or south of the area. During these conferences, the American troops had advanced east across an open flat toward the southwest edge of Carrizal, where Mexican troops were formed. As the American troops decided to advance forward in a line of platoon

column, he ordered Captain Morey and a Lieutenant Adair to defend their flanks. The Tenth Cavalry were facing 315 Mexican soldiers, mounted and dismounted.

The inspecting officer of the incident stated:

*Captain Boyd appeared to be of the opinion that his orders required him to pass through the town of Carrizal . . . Lieutenant Adair appeared to hold the same view. Captain Morey differed with Captain Boyd . . .*

Finally Captain Boyd decided to go through the town according to a sworn statement by Quartermaster Sergeant Dalley Farrior, Troop C, Tenth Cavalry. Farrior said:

*When we arrived near Carrizal, the captain had us load our rifles and pistols. We halted and sent a messenger in to ask permission to pass through the town. When the messenger returned, several Mexicans came with him and they halted at our point. The captain went forward and talked to them. He returned to us and said that it looked favorable but we could only go north. He said his orders were to go east and he meant to go that way. By this time the general of the Carrizal Troops had come out and the captain went forward to talk to him. When he returned he said the general had given us permission to go through the town, but we would go through as foragers. As we formed lines of foragers the general called him back again. When he returned he said he would execute fight on foot and advance in that formation. We did this and ordered no man to fire until fired upon. As we moved forward Troop K was on the right and Troop C on the left. The captain cautioned Sergeant Winrow, who commanded the right of C troop to keep his men on a zig zag line.*

*The Mexicans during this time had formed a line to our front about 200 yards away and opened fire on us. We laid down and fired back . . . Then we advanced by rushes. On the second rush I was wounded in the right arm and stood where I was. The line had been moving forward. On their third rush they reached the Mexican's first line of defense, where there were two machine guns. By this time Captain Boyd had been shot in the hand and shoulder . . . The captain tried to get troop K, which was in our rear to move up to us. He was shot and killed at that time. Lieutenant Adair had gone with his men and was out of sight. Captain Morey said to assemble K troop on him and we would all surrender. But several men of C troop remonstrated with Captain Morey and induced him to make towards an adobe house in our left rear, where we could make a stand. Captain Morey was very weak from loss of blood and fainted once. From here I finally made my way to the Santo Domingo ranch.*

Lieutenant Colonel Cress's conclusions of his investigation were:

*That in carrying out his mission Captain Charles T. Boyd, Tenth Cavalry, did not obey the instructions given him by the Commanding General, Punitive Expedition, and that in failing to do so and in assuming command of troop K, Tenth Cavalry, he became responsible for the encounter between the American troops and the forces of the de facto government at Carrizal, June 21, 1916.*

There was no further action recommended due to the peculiar conditions at the time.

General Pershing stated in his endorsement that:

*Under the circumstances, unfortunate as they were, it is not believed that any disciplinary action is indicated as adviseable. There is no reliable evidence obtainable to sustain charges against any individual or group of these men for their conduct. Notwithstanding the disaster resulting from this encounter, it must be said to the credit of this little body of men that they fought well as long as their officers remained alive to lead them and for some time after. . .*

The Mexicans sustained a loss of forty-two killed and fifty-one wounded. The following Tenth Cavalry soldiers gave their lives in the line of active combat duty at Carrizal.

Captain Charles T. Boyd, Tenth Cavalry; Lieutenant Henry R. Adair, Tenth Cavalry; Private De Witt Rucker, Troop K, Tenth Cavalry; *Private Charles Mathews, Troop K, Tenth Cavalry; *Sergeant Will Hines, Troop C, Tenth Cavalry; *Lance Corporal William Roberts, Troop C, Tenth Cavalry;* Private James E. Day, Troop K, Tenth Cavalry; *Private Walter Gleeton, Troop C, Tenth Cavalry.[49]

## World War I

### Black Exploits During World War I

In October 1919, J. E. Sadler delivered an address at an Afro-American Convention in Asbury Park, New Jersey. His subject was "The Negro From Jamestown to the Rhine." The following excerpts are his recollections of the Negro's contribution during World War I.

*Leo Patterson of Joplin, Missouri won the Lightweight Championship of the American Expeditionary Forces. He toured France and the occupied area of German territory defending his title against all comers.*

*Frank Turner of Tyler, Texas, won the Light Heavyweight Championship of the First Army Area.*

*Sol Butler won the world's championship for the*

_____
*Remains were interred in Arlington National Cemetery.

*broad jump in the allied games at Pershing Stadium.*

*Colored engineers and pioneer infantrymen built the great Pershing Stadium where the inter-allied games were held.*

*Harvey Butler of Montclair and Corporal Philander Clark of East Orange, New Jersey were among the successful athletes at the Dijon meet and they qualified to enter the inter-allied games.*

*Colored Engineers, the Five Hundred and Fifth and Five Hundred and Sixth regiments, built over two hundred miles of railroad in the vicinity of Bordeaux, erected two immense steel warehouses and built up a Camp at San Sulpice to accommodate thirty thousand soldiers and twenty thousand German prisoners.*

*Colored stevedores handled freight shipped into France.*

*Colored labor battalions cut millions of French cords of wood, thousands of railroad ties and lumber.*

*Colored soldiers prepared the National Cemetery at Romagne and reburied twenty-three thousand American dead.*

*Colored soldiers contributed three hundred thousand Francs for the French poor and destitute Belgian orphans.*

*Colored soldiers contributed an estimated $1,200 for the redemption of the home of Frederick Douglass.*

*The Ninety-Third Division claimed the record of being the only division which never lost one single foot of territory or a single prisoner. Their total casualties were estimated at 1,640. The Ninety-Second Division suffered 1,478 casualties.*[50]

### Brief History of the Third Battalion, Three Hundred and Seventy-Second Infantry (Rifle, Colored)

The Third Battalion, Three Hundred Seventy-Second Infantry was an unattached company of infantry from 1863–1865, and during the period 1866–1876, an unattached company of infantry, first brigade. In 1878, the unit was designated as L Company, Sixth Infantry; in 1919, L Company, Sixth Infantry, Massachusetts Volunteer Militia. In 1920, the unit was redesignated as Second Separate battalion infantry MNG (Cos A-B). The third battalion Three Hundred Seventy-Second Infantry (rifle, colored) minus one company designation was given in 1925. In 1940, the unit was designated as third battalion, Three Hundred Seventy-Second Infantry (rifle, colored) and was ordered into federal service in March 1941. The unit was inactivated January 31, 1946. The U.S. Service has included the Spanish-American War, Guanica, Puerto Rico, World War I, Argonne Sector, Meuse Argonne Offensive and the Vosges sector.[51]

## World War II

### Generals Praise the Black Tankers of World War II

During World War II, the employment of American Negro Troops in combat operations was slight and when they were committed there was constant controversy concerning their performance of duty. The Negro press during this period took the lead in attempting to report the truth concerning the Negro's abilities as a soldier and his performances at the front. Even today many persons question the validity of the news coverage during this period, however the following quotes from two heroic World War II generals should satisfy and dubious reader's impression of Negro press coverage during World War II.

*The Ninety-Second jumped into La Spezia and with other Fifth Army Units took Bologna. Then they moved into Genoa and took it, much to the surprise of the enemy and Headquarters. I needed the Ninety-Second and if anyone had tried to take it from me, I would have protested loudly.... they were glorious—General Mark Clark. Commander, Fifth United States Army.*

*The Negro tank battalion attached to my command fought bravely in the critical battle of Bastogne.... the Negro soldiers were damn good soldiers, of which the nation could be mighty proud.—General George S. Patton. Commander Third U.S. Army on the Western front.*[52]

### Army Nurse Corps, Black Angels of Mercy

The American Negro female has played an outstanding role in the military services of this country. During World War I, Negro women assisted in the war effort as members of the Red Cross Society, Women's Auxiliaries of Military Units, Loan Drives, Young Women's Christian Association Hostesses' Program, and Red Cross Registered Nursing Service and Canteen war workers.

The advent of World War II saw the introduction of the Negro female into the Armed Services Nurse Corps. After considerable debate and requests by Negro leaders, the Negro woman was accepted into the Army Nurse Corps. Because of the military policies at that time, Negro doctors and nurses were not integrated with white professional personnel in the operation of hospitals treating white patients. Therefore, all-Negro hospitals and wards were established. In 1942, an all-Negro station hospital was organized at Fort Huachuca, Arizona, at a post at which Negro troops were being treated. Negro nurses on duty with the army increased from 218 in December 1943, to 512

by July, 1945. Some of the nurses continued to serve with all-Negro hospitals in this country and others were used on a nonsegregated basis in four general hospitals, three regional hospitals, and at least nine station hospitals in the United States.

In May, 1944, the surgeon general appealed personally to the chief surgeon of the European Theater to use Negro nurses in at least one hospital. The chief surgeon agreed and in July, 1944, sixty-three Negro nurses among whom were some who had formerly served with the Twenty-Fifth Station Hospital in Africa and had been returned to the United States at the end of 1943, arrived in the European Theater. After a period of training, these nurses were assigned on September 16, 1944, to replace white nurses in the One Hundred and Sixty-Eighth Station Hospital located in England. Until December 4, 1944, the station hospital was used as a prisoner of war hospital. A plea was made by the present One Hundred and Sixty-Eighth Station Hospital staff, to put the new nurses under white supervision and the chief nurse, the operating room supervisor and two section supervisors were mentioned. The chief nurse and the operating room supervisor were permitted to remain. Since the Korean War and integration in the military services, the army Negro nurse has benefited professionally from the equal opportunities that are offered. The Negro nurse performed outstandingly during the segregated period and today in an integrated society, she is continuing to pursue a path to success.

The following is a list of some of the Negro nurses presently on active duty in the Army Nurse Corps: Colonel Margaret Bailey, Health Manpower Training Specialist, Job Corps, Department of Labor; Lieutenant Colonel Geraldine Felton, Anesthesiology Nursing University of Hawaii; Lieutenant Colonel Martha Cleveland, Chief Nurse, Kenner Army Hospital, Fort Lee, Virginia; Lieutenant Colonel Leona Moseley, Chief Nurse, Raymond W. Bliss Army Hospital, Fort Huachuca, Arizona; Major Clara Leich Adams, Staff, WRAMC Student Nurse Program; Lieutenant Colonel Hazel Johnson, Key Project Office Surgical Directorate, U.S. Army Research and Development Command Surgeon's Office; Lieutenant Colonel Essie Wilson, Student Health Care Administration, Brooke Army Medical Center; Major Joyce Nurse, Faculty Walter Reed Army Institute of Nursing.[53]

### The Negro and the Marine Corps Prior to 1942

A thorough search of existing literature and personal communications with military historians challenges the belief that no Negroes were enlisted in the

U.S. Marine Corps before 1942. A statement found in correspondence of the Office of Naval Records and Library, Navy Department, dated December 29, 1924, however, alleges the nonexistence of Negro marines before that year.

An excerpt from instructions to a lieutenant of marines on the U.S. Frigate *Constellation,* dated 16 March, 1798, enclosed with letter from War Department to Captain Truxton of the *Constellation* repreparation of the vessel for immediate duty.

*3. No Negro, mulatto or Indian to be enlisted nor any description of men except natives of fair conduct or foreigners of unequivocal characters for sobriety and fidelity. (Any recruiting officer enlisting a vagrant transient person, who shall desert, shall reimburse (from) his pay the loss sustained by such desertion.)*

*Memorandum for Commander Townsend (Lloyd W., U.S.N.), Army War College. The above shows the policy as to the Marines from the earliest days. J. H. Sypher, Commander, U.S.N., Superintendent.*

Contrary to the above, this author has been successful in locating the names of five black men who were officially listed on the Size Roll of the marines during the period 1813–1863. In consideration of possible discrepancies, extreme caution was caused in the extraction of this information. Twelve volumes of the actual Size Rolls of Marines during the period 1798–1900 were carefully reviewed page by page, checking general and descriptive information. Selection included the names only of those whose complexion was written "marine-*black*." The birthplace of each of the five was the United States. A second person was called to verify the fact that the column read "black" so that no error was possible.

While the finding of these five marines listed as black and the two names listed on a roster dated 1776 is not a major historical discovery, it does support the theme of this work that if one black was present, there must have been more.[54]

## Black Navy Seabees

Throughout the military services the Negro-American has used his skills and labors in the construction of fortifications, buildings, roads, air fields and housing. Although to some these tasks may seem menial, the commander knows that they must be accomplished and their completion will determine the potentials of planned combat operations and successes in many instances. During World War II the Negroes were extensively employed on construction projects; however the navy's experienced Seabees also used Negroes,

who made a commendable contribution in the Pacific Theater. The following extracts depict the black Seabees' accomplishments during World War II.

*The Thirty-fourth Construction Battalion, organized at Camp Allen in Virginia, sailed outside the continental limits of the United States on January 7, 1943.*

*Their first job was the construction of the Halavo Sea-plane Base at Halavo in the Florida Islands. Brigaded there with the Acorn (Red) Four, an air unit, the Thirty-fourth Battalion helped carve its camp out of a deep jungle. During February and March, 1943, the two outfits experienced two direct enemy bombings and were under almost nightly enemy raids in the area for a period of five months. Casualties from these raids resulted in two killed and twenty-eight wounded.*

*A detachment of approximately 350 men were transferred on March 19, 1943 to Guadalcanal to assist other battalions in constructing fuel and gas storage facilities. This detachment remained on Guadalcanal until November, 1943, constructing all types of air field facilities and housing. They were under frequent enemy air raids for the first six months of their duty there and then less frequent raids, the last of which occurred in October 1943. No casualties resulted.*

*On April 20, 1943, another detachment of approximately two hundred men with 75 percent of the battalion's heavest equipment was transported by LCT's to Russell Island where, together with the Thirty-fifth Construction Battalion, they laid out and constructed the second fighter strip north of Renard Sound on Banika Island. This detachment was a part of what was essentially a regimental command consisting of the entire Forty-seventh Battalion and one-half of the Twentieth Battalion. It was assigned the task of constructing a 6,000-foot bomber strip and a 4,500 fighter strip on the Russells in time for the New Georgia campaign. These Seabee units completed their assigned tasks on time and the first three units later enlarged the bomber facilities south of Renard, completing this assignment by August, 1943. At Russells the detachment was subjected to constant enemy bombing until the completion of the New Georgia campaign in July. The Negro detachment experienced five casualties, consisting of three killed and two injured with minor burns in the operation of the fighter strip, caused during the crash of a navy plane on the field.*

*The entire battalion was reunited in November, 1943, in the Tulagi area: with approximately one-half of the battalion quartered at Halavo, and the other half scattered over the adjacent islands of Tulagi, Savo, and Phillips Peninsula on Purvis Bay. The construction tasks at Halavo varied from marine railways, fueling docks, and coastal defense gun mounts, to harbor boat nests, dolphins, piers, and considerable jungle and mountain roads for the army defense. A unit at Tulagi took over and performed naval base maintenance, relieving the Twenty-Seventh Seabees until the arrival of the two CBMU's to release the battalion for assignment to Guadalcanal in March, 1944.*

*The battalion was re-equipped with new housing facilities and a small quantity of new equipment and supplies early in 1944. The movement of the entire battalion personnel and equipment from the Tulagi area to Guadalcanal was completed in approximately six days aboard three LTS's.*[55]

### The Seven Hundred and Sixty-First Battalion, World War II

The Seven Hundred and Sixty-First Tank Battalion was activated on April 1, 1942. The battalion received its early training at Camp Hood, Texas (later Fort Hood, Texas). They had received praise from the Second Army Commander, Lieutenant General Ben Lear and Lieutenant General Lesley J. McNair.

The morale of the unit was quite high. Brigadier General Ernest J. Dawley addressed the men of the Seven Hundred Sixty-First on three occasions. On one occasion he told the men that some things will happen during a war for which there would be no obvious explanation but which must be laid to the "fog of war." He concluded: "When you get in there put an extra round of ammunition and fire it for General Dawley!" This speech made a lasting impression on the men of the Seven Hundred Sixty-First. When the unit entered combat in Europe during World War II one of their tanks was named "The Fog of War" and to top it off several rounds of ammunition were put into it and fired for General Dawley according to the unit's historian.

The reputation of this unit was so high that when men of the battalion who were hospitalized subsequently transferred, they attempted to return to the Seven Hundred Sixty-First Tank Battalion.

Military historian U. S. Lee stated that "The Negro armored units, by virtue of their use in task forces and the attachment of their companies and platoons to infantry, had closer continuing contacts with the main stream of battle than most other small supporting black units."

The Seven Hundred Sixty-First Tank Battalion was the first black Negro armored unit to be committed to combat. The unit landed at Omaha Beach on October 10, 1944 after brief garrison duty in England. The unit had 6 white and 30 black officers and 676 enlisted men.

The men of the Seven Hundred Sixty-First received praise from General George S. Patton Jr. on November 2, 1944. Patton remarked: "Men, you are the first Negro tankers to ever fight in the American army. I would have never asked for you if you were not good. I have nothing but the best in my army. I don't care what color you are, so long as you go up there and kill those Kraut sonsabitches. Everyone has their eyes on you and is expecting great things from you. Most of all, your race is looking forward to you. Don't let them down; don't let me down."

The unit spent 183 days in action. While fighting with the Third U.S. Army, the Seven Hundred Sixty-First Tank Battalion was attached to the Twenty-Sixth, Seventy-First and Eighty-Seventh Divisions, Seventeenth Airborne Division, Seventeenth Armored Group. They were also assigned to the Ninth Army, Ninety-Fifth and Seventy-Ninth Divisions and XVI Corps, Seventh Army, One Hundred and Third and Seventy-First Divisions. The unit fought with larger units in Belgium, Holland, Luxembourg, Germany and Austria.

On November 8, 1944, the Seven Hundred Sixty-First Tank Battalion was attached to elements of the Twenty-Sixth Division and placed in special task forces at Athainville east of Nancy. Company A of the Seven Hundred and Sixty-First was attached to the Three Hundred and Twenty-Eighth Infantry Provisional Task Force. A contained Company K of the One Hundred and First Infantry Engineers, the Six Hundred and Second Tank Destroyer Battalion and the remainder of the Seven Hundred and Sixty-First Tank Battalion (excepting its mortar, assault gun and reconnaissance platoons in reserve). All of these units were under the command of a Lieutenant Colonel Peter J. Kopcsak, Commander of the Six Hundred and Second Tank Destroyer Battalion.

Later a Lieutenant Colonel Hollis E. Hunt, Seventeenth Armored Group, was assigned to assist Lieutenant Colonel Kopcsak. Both commanders were wounded by shell fire. After Colonel Kopcsak was evacuated, Colonel Hunt, though wounded, assumed command of the task force.

The heroic exploits of this outstanding black tank battalion during World War II have not been properly credited in the current military literature. This is attested by *the fact* that a motion picture company within the last several years produced a movie highlighting the life of General George S. Patton Jr. and his triumphant military tactics and achievements in Europe during World War II. The script of the movie did not concern itself with black tank participation with Patton's Third Army. Some concerned black citizens questioned why the producers and directors mentioned only General Patton's black enlisted military aide. Unfortunately there was a negative response. Were blacks really there as tankers? The American military newspaper, *The Stars and Stripes* of November 14, 1944 answered the question positively with the following headline and news coverage:

### NEGRO TANKERS CUT DEEP INTO GERMAN LINES

*With U.S. Third Army Forces east of Chateau-Silins, Nov. 13.—Negro tank forces, making their combat debut with Gen. Patton's troops sweeping northward across the Seille River and toward the Siegfried defenses, have figured in the successful U.S. breakthrough launched in this sector.*

*Early last Wednesday (Nov. 8) two companies of a Negro tank battalion started fighting in the vicinity of Bezange and Moncourt as H-hour of the first round of the offensive struck.*

*But the main and sternest mission of the tankers began early Thursday morning when the unit spearheaded an important task force whose objective lay deep in German-held territory.*

*Commanded by Lt. Col. Peter J. Kopcsak, a TD battalion C.O. from Pittsburgh, the task force included tanks, TDs, combat engineers and assault infantrymen, who rode the Sherman [tanks].*

*Crossing the rain-swollen Seille, just north of the recently taken town of Myonvic, the column was subjected to enemy artillery emplaced on the hills northeast of the river. Shellbursts threw up huge geysers all around the bridge.*

*At the little village of Salival it was stopped again by German artillery ranged in on the road. Tanks deployed in and around the little cluster of buildings housing German troops, rooting them out with direct HE fire while doughboys mopped up.*

*But the battle for the town of Morville-les-Vic was the real testing of the tankers. Furious shelling met them at the crossroads, six hundred yards from the town. Tank-infantry teams moved down on the town from three directions and the battle was joined at once.*

*Within ninety minutes of the start of the push, Nazi prisoners were being sent rearwards by the first Negro tank troops ever committed to combat operations.*

*... tankers suffered their heaviest losses in a running three-hour fight with German AT guns concealed in woods capping a high hill northeast of Morville.*[56]

## The Negro and the U.S. Coast Guard

The presence of Negroes in the coast guard has been minimal compared to their participation with the U.S. Army, Navy, Marines and Air Force in recent years. The progress of the few Negro coast guard personnel has, however, been outstanding, and it is felt that the following summary is appropriate for separate coverage.

The coast guard lifted restrictions to officer ranks and general service ratings to Negroes early in World War II, and the program met with remarkable success. Negro officers and enlisted men served aboard all U.S. Coast Guard craft, and there were instances of Negro officers serving as commanding officers. These men were indoctrinated and commissioned in mixed units at the Coast Guard Academy.

In 1941, the status of the Negro in the coast guard was almost identical to his position in the navy. Aside from the personnel of an all-Negro coast guard station at Pea Island, North Carolina, all Negro guardsmen were in the steward's branch.

Following Secretary of the Navy Knox's announcement, in April, 1942, that Negroes would be accepted in the coast guard as well as in the navy in capacities other than messmen, the coast guard started to enlist Negroes for general service. From the spring of 1942 until the end of the war, a few Negro general service recruits entered the coast guard each month until in August, 1945, there were more than 3,560 Negro guardsmen. This constituted only 2 percent of the entire U.S. Coast Guard personnel; the low percentage, however, was not due to an effort to limit the number of Negro recruits, but rather to the small number of Negroes who sought to enter this service.

The coast guard never attempted to establish a separate training camp for Negroes, the small size of the organization precluding any such possibility. Negro recruits were trained at various coast guard stations, but most of them received their training at the chief station at Manhattan Beach, Brooklyn, New York. These men were trained to become coxswains and electricians, boatswains and pharmacists, carpenters and radarmen.

Separate housing facilities constituted the only form of segregation at Manhattan Beach, where sailors of all colors ate together, trained together and played together. Among the instructors at Manhattan Beach were a number of Negro non-commissioned officers; these men taught all recruits, regardless of color. One of these instructors was Clarence Samuels, a warrant officer and boatswain and veteran of over twenty years in the navy and the coast guard. To ensure the enforcement of coast guard policy at Manhattan Beach, Samuels also served as a racial advisor for coast guard headquarters.

Improvements in the coast guard policy came rapidly during the war years. In 1943, the coast guard became the first branch of the naval services to commission colored personnel. Joseph C. Jenkins, a Negro, graduated as an ensign in the coast guard reserves, April, 1943, almost a year before the first Negro was commissioned in the navy. Two other Negroes were commissioned in the coast guard during this time. Clarence Samuels was promoted from warrant officer to lieutenant (junior grade), in October, 1943, and in 1944, Ensign Harvey C. Russell graduated from the OCS School at the Coast Guard Academy.[57]

### Negro Troops in Combat and Support Operations in Theaters of War, World War II

The following excerpts from the War and Navy Department files are a brief summary of the Negro troops' courageous and outstanding accomplishments in the European and Pacific Theaters of War during World War II. Although an increase in the Negro soldiers' participation in combat wasn't until the VE-Day Operations in May, 1945, his service, though short, was commendable and the record he assessed is notable history.

#### European Theater

Combat Troops: Twenty-two Negro combat units participated in the operations of the American Expeditionary Forces against the Wehrmacht. These were; the Three Hundred and Thirty-Third, Three Hundred and Forty-Ninth, Three Hundred and Fiftieth, Three Hundred and Fifty-First, Five Hundred and Seventy-Eighth, Six Hundred and Eighty-Sixth, Seven Hundred and Seventy-Seventh, Nine Hundred and Sixty-Ninth, and Nine Hundred and Ninety-Ninth Field Artillery Battalions; Four Hundred and Fifty-Second Anti-Aircraft Artillery Battalion; Seven Hundred and Sixty-First and Seven Hundred and Eighty-Fourth Tank Battalions; Six Hundred and Fourteenth and Eight Hundred and Twenty-Seventh Tank Destroyer Battalions; One Hundred and Eighty-Third, One Hundred and Eighty-Fourth, Sixteen Hundred and Ninety-Fifth, Sixteen Hundred and Ninety-Sixth, Sixteen Hundred and Ninety-Seventh, Sixteen Hundred and Ninety-Eighth, Sixteen Hundred and Ninety-Ninth, and Seventeen Hundredth Engineer Combat Battalions.

The Three Hundred and Twentieth Barrage Balloon Battalion was the only Negro combat unit to take part in the initial landings on the Normandy coast on June 6, 1944.

Negro artillerymen of the Three Hundred and Thirty-Third Field Artillery Battalion landed their 155-millimeter howitzers in Normandy on D-Day plus 10 and went into action shortly afterward as a unit of the Eighth Corps. Their first mission was to fire in support of the Ninetieth Infantry Division and take part in the bloody battles at St. Jores, Lessay, Hill 95, and Hill 122 in the Forêt de Monte Castret.

The Seven Hundred and Seventy-Seventh Field Artillery Battalion was the only Negro 4.5-inch gun unit in the ETO and fought with the Ninth Army. One distinction claimed by the Seven Hundred and Seventy-Seventh is that it fired the first American artillery round across the Rhine River near München-Gladbach.

Other veteran ETO Negro artillery units were the Nine Hundred and Ninety-Ninth Field Artillery Battalion, which fired its 8-inch howitzers from lower Normandy to central Germany, and the Five Hundred and Seventy-Eighth, another 8-inch howitzer unit that helped to stem the Nazi tide in the Ardennes in December and January (1944–1945).

The Seven Hundred and Sixty-First Tank Battalion, was committed as attached armor of the Twenty-Sixth Infantry Division in the Third United States Army, becoming the first Negro tank unit to go into action.

For "outstanding performance of duty in action against the enemy" at Climbach, France, on December 14, 1944, the third platoon of company C of the Six Hundred and Fourteenth Tank Destroyer Battalion received a distinguished unit citation.

Infantry: In December, 1944, several thousand Negro soldiers answered a general appeal for volunteers for training as infantry riflemen. Some 2,500 volunteers from Negro units of the Communications Zone were trained at a ground force reinforcement command depot at Noyons, France, and committed to action with infantry and armored divisions of the First and Seventh Armies as assigned platoons and companies.

Negro rifle platoons fought with the First, Second, Eighth, Ninth, Sixty-Ninth, Seventy-Eighth, Ninety-Ninth, and One Hundred and Fourth Infantry Divisions of the First Army, and Negro companies joined armored infantry battalions of the Twelfth and Fourteenth Armored Division.

In its first action the Negro platoon of the K Company of the Three Hundred and Ninety-Fourth Infantry Regiment of the Ninety-Ninth Division, led an attack on the town of Honningen across the Rhine River, cleared one-fourth of it and captured over 250 prisoners.

Another platoon with E Company of the Three Hundred and Ninety-Third Regiment of the same division got its baptism of fire on March 25 when it attacked German positions near Jahrfeld, Germany. Employing marching fire they advanced, routing the Germans, knocking out a Mark IV tank and a flak wagon, killing forty-eight of the enemy and capturing sixty. These men gained their objective, Hill 373.

The Negro platoon of Company G of the Two Hundred and Seventy-Third Infantry Regiment helped the Sixty-Ninth Infantry Division to become the first American unit to make contact with the Russian forces. During the platoon's first combat action at Hann Numden, Staff Sergeant Ames Shipper, of Philadelphia, Pa., took 118 prisoners from a barn.

Signal Corps: During the campaign against the German Army in Europe, 5,500 Negro Signal Corps troops belonging to twenty signal units participated in the vital battle of communications.

These Negro troops worked in two main types of Signal Corps units—light and heavy signal construction battalions and companies.

Negro units that participated in various campaigns were the Twenty-Fifth, Twenty-Ninth, Thirty-Seventh, Fortieth, Forty-First, Forty-Second, Forty-Third, and Forty-Fourth Signal Construction Battalions, and the Two Hundred and Fifty-Eighth, Two Hundred and Fifty-Ninth, Two Hundred and Sixty-First, Two Hundred and Sixty-Seventh, Two Hundred and Sixty-Eighth, Two Hundred and Sixty-Ninth, Two Hundred and Seventieth, Two Hundred and Seventy-Fifth, Five Hundred and Thirty-Fourth, Five Hundred and Thirty-Fifth, Five Hundred and Thirty-Seventh, and Four Hundred and Ninety-Sixth Signal Construction Companies.

Negroes comprised 7.5 percent of the total Signal Corps personnel in the European theater.

A recent estimate of communications wire put in by Negro troops released by Communications Zone Headquarters included these figures: over 10,000 miles of open wire set up, over 500 miles of field wire, and over 500 miles of rubber, and 4 cables of lead spiral.

The Twenty-Ninth Signal Construction Battalion arrived in France on D-day plus 9 and 10. Its first major mission—rehabilitation of the Chef du Pont-Valognes railroad pole line, was accomplished in the face of enemy snipers, mines, and artillery fire.

Chemical Warfare: Chemical Warfare Service headquarters in the European theater of operations disclosed that of the 9,500 Chemical Warfare Service troops in the theater on VE-day, 2,442 of these were Negro enlisted men and officers. Other Negro Chemical Warfare Service units were the three chemical decontamination companies, the Twenty-Fifth, Thirty-Second, and Thirty-Fourth.

The record shows that the smoke-generator companies which saw action performed excellently, often under heavy enemy fire, winning praise from infantry commanders and chemical officers.

The Eighty-Fourth Chemical Smoke Generator Company arrived in France on D-day-plus-1. Its first important combat test came when it was attached to the Fifth Infantry Division in the latter part of September, 1944.

The Eighty-Fourth provided smoke for the screening of bridge-building operations across the river  and materially assisted in the winning of the first major United States bridgehead east of the Moselle in that part of the valley.

One of the greatest artificial fogs in military history was created in December, 1944 by the all-Negro One Hundred and Sixty-First Smoke Generator Company when it shrouded the upper Saar River Valley with a dense cloud of fog that completely obscured the movements of one entire division, the Nineteenth Infantry Division. During this operation the One Hundred and Sixty-First fed 146,000 gallons of oil into their M2 smoke generators.

The One Hundred and Sixty-Third Chemical Smoke Generator Company was assigned to the job of screening the crossing of the Neckar River at Heilbronn, Germany, by the One Hundredth Infantry Division of the Seventh Army. The mission was successfully accomplished.

Negro chemical smoke generator companies that operated on the Continent between D-day and VE-day were: The Eighty-First, Eighty-Second, Eighty-Third, Eighty-Fourth, Eighty-Fifth, Eighty-Sixth, Eighty-Seventh, Seventy-Fourth, One Hundred and Sixty-First, One Hundred and Sixty-Second, One Hundred and Sixty-Third, One Hundred and Sixty-Fourth, One Hundred and Sixty-Fifth, One Hundred and Sixty-Seventh, and One Hundred and Seventy-First Chemical Smoke Generator Companies.

Ordnance: Of the 6,000,000 tons of ammunition handled by ordnance ammunition companies on the Continent between D-day and VE-day, more than 4,500,000 tons passed through the hands of Negro ordnancemen.

A noncombat Negro ordnance ammunition company earned the title of the "Fighting Fifty-Sixth" when its members engaged fifty-one German SS troops near the Belgian border early in September. When the shooting was over, thirty-six Nazis were killed, three wounded, and the rest taken prisoner.

Of the twenty ordnance motor-vehicle distributing companies in the European Theater of Operations, two were manned by 480 Negro ordnancemen. These distribution companies furnished the combat troops with armored vehicles and service troops with the trucks necessary to keep the front-lines supplied.

The remainder of the Negro personnel, 165 in number, were active in the administrative divisions of battalion headquarters.

Medical Corps: Negro personnel formed 2.2 percent of the total European Theater of Operations medical service strength or 5,482, a statement released by the office of the chief surgeon of the ETA disclosed.

Negro officers were distributed as follows: medical officers, fifty-one; Dental Corps, twenty-eight; Medical Administrative Corps, seventeen; and Nurse Corps, sixty-seven. Sixty-five of the Negro nurses were attached to the One Hundred and Sixty-Eighth Station Hospital in England.

Working with divisions at the front the performance of Negro medics was particularly outstanding.

The Four Hundred and Twenty-Eighth Medical Battalion operating with the First Army, carried more than 1,200,000 patients in their ambulances in evacuating wounded to rear areas.

Of the 230,000 patients hauled by the Five Hundred and Ninety-Second Ambulance Company, only two were lost, those being caused by enemy action when an ambulance was strafed by enemy aircraft at Malmedy during the German counteroffensive of December 1944.

Corps of Engineers: Of the 259,172 Negro troops in the European Theater of Operations as of May 15, [1945], a little more than one in every five was an engineer soldier, according to information released by the office of the chief engineer of the European Theater of Operations.

On May 31 [1945], there were 54,600 Negro engineer enlisted men, 320 officers, and 54 warrant officers, of a total of 337,000 in the theater's engineer command. This total included personnel of general service regiments, engineer dump-truck companies, engineer fire fighting units, aviation engineer battalions, and separate battalions. There were 165 engineer units of all types.

A survey of Negro engineer units showed that Negro engineers participated in all of the main operations by United States forces on the continent which required engineering, from D-day landings and beachhead op-

erations of June, 1944, to the conquest of the Rhineland.

One unit, the Five Hundred and Eighty-Second Engineer Dump Truck Company landed on Omaha Beach shortly after H-hour on June 6, 1944 and worked continuously up until and after the crossing and bridging of the Rhine.

Silver and Bronze Stars were awarded to several men of the unit for bravery under fire, First Sergeant Norman Day of Danville, Ill., received the Silver Star for heroism on the beach where he directed U.S. Army traffic under heavy shelling. Day also received the Purple Heart for wounds and the British Distinguished Service Medal.

During the Rhine crossing operations the Five Hundred and Eighty-Second was significantly well up forward working as a XVI Corps unit, hauling crushed rock for bridge building operations.

The Four Hundred and Thirty-Fourth, another Negro dump truck company, assisted the One Thousand and Fifty-Sixth Port Construction and Repair Group in rehabilitating the port of Cherbourg in July, 1944. They worked day and night on a double shift basis, removing thousands of tons of debris that had accumulated from bombing and demolition work.

The following excerpt from the unit history of the Five Hundred and Seventy-Second Engineer Dump Truck Company, a Negro unit, describes a front-line incident; "July 3, 1944, Private William Wright Jr. wounded by enemy shell fire while on operations delivering engineer supplies to a bridge site which was under fire."

By VE-day 60 percent of all engineer general service regiments assigned or attached to Communications Zone were Negro units, thirty out of fifty reported on May 31 [1945].

Another Negro general service regiment, the Ninety-Fifth, arrived in France on July 8 [1944]. It had worked on the Alcan Highway to Alaska and in Wales. Its first operational mission said; "Road construction and maintenance, debris clearing and street reconstruction in the Valognes and Cherbourg areas."

During this assignment mines and booby traps were encountered in hundreds. They had to be removed and defused. The regiment also built during this period a very important traffic circle in the heart of shattered Valognes. Through that circle passed a vast and vital flow of traffic between Cherbourg and the beaches, toward the front.

Transportation Corps: Of a total of 157,327 troops in the Transportation Corps in the ETO reported on

May 3, 1944, 69,914 were in Negro units—or 44.4 percent.

Thirty-two of the forty-one port battalions reported were Negro, while out of fifty separate port companies in the theater thirty-eight were Negro, making a personnel total of 31,763 in all-Negro port units.

In the quartermaster truck field, 316 of the 453 quartermaster truck companies operating under Transportation Corps control were Negro companies. Ten of the nineteen quartermaster groups were Negro, and there were thirty-one Negro battalions among the eighty-six quartermaster battalions listed. There was one Negro quartermaster car company, the Five Hundred and Twenty-Fourth, and four Negro chemical smoke generator companies under Transportation Corps command.

Negro troops of the Transportation Corps were in the initial waves on D-day, came ashore with the engineer brigades and helped start what eventually became the greatest supply operation in military history.

The Normandy supply battle was won by units like the Four Hundred and Ninetieth Port Battalion, which came in with the second tide on D-day and unloaded crucial supplies of ammunition, food, and equipment to be used by the assault troops.

Six Negro companies, the Four Hundred and Sixty-Seventh, Four Hundred and Sixty-Eighth, Four Hundred and Sixty-Ninth, Four Hundred and Seventieth, Eight Hundred and Nineteenth and Eight Hundred and Twenty-First Amphibian Truck Companies, had been attached to the Eleventh Port for "Plan Neptune," in the invasion operation.

On May 30, [1944] there were sixteen amphibian truck companies in the ETO, ten of them Negro units with a total personnel of 1,730. One Negro unit, the Four Hundred and Sixty-Ninth, ferried supplies and personnel across the Rhine River during the attack that placed American forces on the east bank of the river. As of May 30, 1944, 69 percent of all truck drivers in Transportation Corps motor transport branch in the ETO were Negro. This percentage remained much the same following the beachhead phase of the battle of Europe.

Some of these units operated continuously after D-day. Negro cargo truck units landed vehicles and personnel on Omaha Beach on June 6. The Thirty-Six Hundred and Eighty-Third Quartermaster Truck Company had vehicles ashore on D-day. The Three Hundred and Seventieth Quartermaster Truck Company, a transportation unit, was scheduled to land 55 vehicles and 115 men on the beach on D-plus-1. Instead, it got 24 men and 12 trucks ashore as early as the morning of D-day.

The first motor express line—the famous Red Ball Express—was started on August 25, 1944. It was built on the one-way traffic principle. Trucks were kept operating twenty-two hours out of twenty-four with only two hours reserved for maintenance. Drivers worked an average of thirty-six hours on the road without sleep.

At its peak Red Ball contained 67 percent Negro personnel. Its initial target was to haul 4,850 tons daily from the ports and beaches to army or forward destinations. The peak reached by the system was 6,000 tons daily.

One impressive testimony to the work of the drivers of the Transportation Corps, including the 35,839 members of Negro Transportation Corps truck units, is the tremendous total tonnage forwarded by Motor Transport service in Europe between June 17, 1944, and May 31, 1945. It was 22,644,609 tons.

### Pacific Theater

The Ninety-Sixth Engineer Regiment landed—in Port Moresby, New Guinea, on April 29, 1942, the first American troops in New Guinea and probably the first American troops to face the enemy after Bataan.

In Alaska, the South, Southwest, and Central Pacific Areas, and in the China-Burma-India theater, Negro troops played an important role in engineering activity. This included the construction of roads, airfields, ports, camps, and storage facilities and their maintenance.

Three of the seven army engineer regiments—the Ninety-Third, the Ninety-Fifth, and the Ninety-Seventh, which helped to build the Alcan Highway, were Negro. The highway, 1,671 miles long, runs from Dawson Creek, Northwest of Edmonton, Alberta, to Fairbanks, Alaska. Although most of the Negro soldiers in these regiments had never before been out of the South, only 140 men were incapacitated by the cold, and all except four recovered completely with no ill effects. The four suffered minor amputations.

After helping to blast through the brutal terrain of Alaska, building the Alcan Highway, the Ninety-Seventh was transferred to New Guinea.

A Negro aviation engineer battalion participated in the victory of the Battle of the Coral Sea, which was fought on May 7 and 8, 1942. It worked twenty-four hours a day to construct an airfield in New Caledonia, which was effectively used by army and navy aircraft engaged in battle.

One of the most amazing construction feats of the war was the Ledo Road. Negro soldiers christened it

"The Road to Tokyo." This highway from India to China via Burma was begun on December 12, 1942. Although they had originally been brought in to construct U.S. airfields in Assam, a battalion of Negro aviation engineers were pressed into service as road builders after they had finished their initial assignment of building runways and dispersal areas.

On March 21, 1944 the Ninety-Third Infantry Division moved its Twenty-Fifth Combat Team to Empress Augusta Bay Perimeter on Bougainville Island with the least practicable delay. The combat team was composed of the Twenty-Fifth Infantry Regiment, Five Hundred and Ninety-Third Field Artillery Battalion, Five Hundred and Ninety-Sixth Field Artillery, Company A of the Three Hundred and Eighteenth Combat Engineer Battalion, Company A of the Three Hundred and Eighteenth Medical Battalion, Ninety-Third Reconnaissance Troop, a detachment of the Ninety-Third Signal Company, a detachment of the Ninety-Third MP Platoon.

By March 31, the Combat Team was in position and at 2:30 P.M. on April 2, PFC Issac Moore of Brooklyn, New York, pulled the lanyard on the No. 2 gun of Battery A of the Five Hundred and Ninety-Third Field Artillery which sent the first round fired by the Ninety-Third Division into enemy positions. The Ninety-Third Division was in combat.

On April 4, the Second Battalion of the Ninety-Third Division which had been detached from the American Division and passed to operational control of the Commanding General of the Thirty-Seventh Infantry Division closed with the enemy and killed approximately twenty-five Japanese soldiers.[58]

### First Black Casualties, Pacific, World World II

During World War II, when the First Battalion, Twenty-Fourth Infantry Regiment was attached to the One Hundred and Forty-Eighth Infantry, Thirty-Seventh Division, Company B of the First Battalion moved forward on March 11 to reinforce the main line of resistance between the First and Third Battalions of the One Hundred Forty-Eighth. That night this position was attacked and two men were killed. It is believed that Private First Class Leonard Brooks, and Private Annias Jolly were probably the first Negro infantrymen to be killed by the enemy grenade and rifle fire in the Pacific, World War II.[59]

### Ft. Leavenworth Honors Tenth Cavalry

In 1969 the first eight stained glass windows were installed inside Fort Leavenworth's James Franklin Bell Hall, academic building of the U.S. Army Command and General Staff College. The windows bear the coats of arms of the Third, Sixth, Seventeenth and Twentieth infantries, Fourth artillery and the First, Seventh and Tenth Cavalries. The Tenth Cavalry was organized at Leavenworth in 1866 and was one of two Negro Cavalry regiments. The Tenth's participation in the frontier's defense was historical and commendable.[60]

### Black General Officers, National Guard and Active Service, 1870–1973

1. Major General Robert B. Elliott, Commanding General, National Guard of the State of South Carolina (1870).
2. Brigadier General Samuel J. Lee, Chief of Staff, National Guard of the State of South Carolina (1872).
3. Brevet Brigadier General William Beverly Nash, National Guard of the State of South Carolina (1873).
4. Brigadier General H. W. Purvis, Adjutant and Inspector General, National Guard of the State of South Carolina (1873).
5. Brigadier General Joseph Hayne Rainey, Judge Advocate General, National Guard of the State of South Carolina (1873).
6. Major General Prince R. Rivers, Commanding General, Third Division, National Guard of the State of South Carolina (1873).
7. Major General Robert Smalls, National Guard of the State of South Carolina (1873).
8. Major General Stephens Atkin Swails, Commanding General, First Division, National Guard of the State of South Carolina (1873).
9. Brigadier General William J. Whipper, Second Brigade, Second Division, National Guard of the State of South Carolina (1873).
10. Brigadier General T. Morris Chester, Fourth Brigade, National Guard of the State of Louisiana (1873–1874).
11. Brigadier General Benjamin O. Davis Sr., United States Army (1940).
12. Brigadier General Edward O. Gourdin, National Guard of the State of Massachusetts (1945–1950).
13. Brigadier General Chauncey M. Hooper, National Guard of the State of New York (1945–1950).
14. Brigadier General Richard Lee Jones, National Guard of the State of Illinois (1945–1950).
15. Brigadier General Raymond Watkins, National Guard of the State of Illinois (1945–1950).
16. Lieutenant General Benjamin O. Davis Jr., United States Air Force (1970).

17. Major General Frederic Davison, United States Army (1972).
18. Major General James Frank Hamlet, United States Army (1972).
19. Lieutenant General Daniel J. (Chappie) James, United States Air Force (1972).
20. Brigadier General Lucius Theus, United States Air Force (1972).
21. Brigadier General Oliver W. Dillard, United States Army (1972).
22. Brigadier General Edward Greer, United States Army (1972.
23. Brigadier General Roscoe C. Cartwright, United States Army (1972).
24. Brigadier General Arthur James Gregg, United States Army (1972).
25. Brigadier General Harry W. Brooks Jr., United States Army (1972).
26. Brigadier General George M. Shuffer Jr., United States Army (1972).
27. Brigadier General Julius W. Becton Jr., United States Army (1972).
28. Brigadier General Fred Clinton Sheffey, United States Army (1973).
29. Brigadier General Roscoe Robinson Jr., United States Army (1973).
30. Brigadier General Charles C. Rogers, United States Army (1973).
31. Brigadier General Thomas E. Clifford, United States Air Force (1973).
32. Brigadier General Cunningham C. Bryant, National Guard of the District of Columbia (1972).
33. Brigadier General Benjamin L. Hunton, United States Army Reserves (1972).

## United States Military Services, Black Medal of Honor Winners, 1863–1971

1. Landsman Aaron Anderson, U.S. Navy, Civil War
2. Private First Class James C. Anderson, U.S. Marine Corps, Vietnam War.
3. Sergeant First Class Webster Anderson, U.S. Army, Vietnam War.
4. Sergeant First Class Eugene Ashley Jr., U.S. Army, Vietnam War.
5. Ships Cook First Class Daniel Atkins, U.S. Navy, Spanish-American War.
6. Private First Class Oscar P. Austin, U.S. Marine Corps, Vietnam War.
7. Sergeant Major (later Second Lieutenant) Edward L. Baker, Tenth U.S. Cavalry, Spanish-American War.

8. Private William H. Barnes, U.S. Colored Troops, Civil War.
9. First Sergeant Powhatan Beaty, U.S. Colored Troops, Civil War.
10. Private Dennis Bell, Tenth U.S. Cavalry, Spanish-American War.
11. Contraband Robert Blake, U.S. Navy, Civil War.
12. Sergeant Thomas Boyne, Ninth U.S. Cavalry, Indian Campaigns.
13. First Sergeant James H. Bronson, U.S. Colored Troops, Civil War.
14. Sergeant Benjamin Brown, Twenty-Fourth U.S. Infantry Regiment, Indian Campaigns.
15. Landsman William H. Brown, U.S. Navy, Civil War.
16. Boy Wilson Brown, U.S. Navy, Civil War.
17. Sergeant First Class William Maud Bryant, U.S. Army, Vietnam War.
18. Sergeant William H. Carney, Fifty-Fourth Massachusetts Colored Infantry, Civil War.
19. Sergeant Cornelius H. Charlton, U.S. Army, Korean War.
20. Ordinary Seaman John Davis, War of 1812.
21. Sergeant Rodney M. Davis, U.S. Marine Corps, Vietnam War.
22. Seaman Clement Dees, U.S. Navy, Civil War.
23. Sergeant John Denny, Ninth U.S. Cavalry, Indian Campaigns.
24. Sergeant Decatur Dorsey, U.S. Colored Troops, Civil War.
25. Private Pompey Factor, U.S. Army Detachment, Seminole Indian Scouts, Indian Campaigns.
26. Private Lee Fitz, Tenth U.S. Cavalry, Spanish-American War.
27. Sergeant Major Christian A. Fleetwood, U.S. Colored Troops, Civil War.
28. Private James Gardiner, U.S. Colored Troops, Civil War.
29. Corporal Clinton Greaves, Ninth U.S. Cavalry, Indian Campaigns.
30. Sergeant James H. Harris, U.S. Colored Troops, Civil War.
31. Sergeant Major Thomas Hawkins, U.S. Colored Troops, Civil War.
32. Sergeant Major Alfred B. Hilton, U.S. Colored Troops, Civil War.
33. Sergeant Major Milton M. Holland, U.S. Colored Troops, Civil War.
34. Private First Class Robert H. Jenkins, Jr., U.S. Marine Corps, Vietnam War.
35. Specialist Six Laurence Joel, U.S. Army, Vietnam War.

36. Specialist Five Dwight Hal Johnson, U.S. Army, Vietnam War.
37. Sergeant Henry Johnson, Ninth U.S. Cavalry, Indian Campaigns.
38. Seaman John Johnson.
39. Private First Class Ralph H. Johnson, U.S. Marine Corps, Vietnam War.
40. Cooper William Johnson.
41. Sergeant George Jordan, Ninth U.S. Cavalry, Indian Campaigns.
42. First Sergeant Alexander Kelly, U.S. Colored Troops, Civil War.
43. Private First Class Garfield M. Langhorn, U.S. Army, Vietnam War.
44. Landsman John Lawson, U.S. Navy, Civil War.
45. Platoon Sergeant Matthew Leonard, U.S. Army, Vietnam War.
46. Sergeant Donald Russell Long, U.S. Army, Vietnam War.
47. Sergeant William McBryar, Tenth U.S. Cavalry, Indian Campaigns.
48. Corporal Isaiah Mays, Twenty-Fourth U.S. Infantry Regiment, Indian Campaigns.
49. Engineer's Cook James Mifflin, U.S. Navy, Civil War.
50. Corporal James Miles, U.S. Army, Civil War.
51. Seaman Joseph B. Noil, U.S. Navy, 1872 Era.
52. Private First Class Milton L. Olive, U.S. Army, Vietnam War.
53. Private Adam Paine, U.S. Army Detachment, Seminole Indian Scouts, Indian Campaigns.
54. Private Isaac Payne, U.S. Army Detachment, Seminole Indian Scouts, Indian Campaigns.
55. Seaman Joachim Pease, U.S. Navy, Civil War.
56. Fireman First Class Robert Penn, U.S. Navy, Spanish-American War.
57. First Sergeant Robert Pinn, U.S. Colored Troops, Civil War.
58. Captain Leroy Riley Pitts, U.S. Army, Vietnam War.
59. First Sergeant Edward Ratcliff, U.S. Colored Troops, Civil War.
60. Brigadier General Charles Calvin Rogers, U.S. Army, Vietnam War.
61. First Lieutenant Ruppert Leon Sargent, U.S. Army, Vietnam War.
62. Specialist Five Clarence E. Sasser, U.S. Army, Vietnam War.
63. Sergeant Thomas Shaw, Ninth U.S. Cavalry, Indian Campaigns.
64. Sergeant Clifford Chester Sims, U.S. Army, Vietnam War.
65. Seaman John Smith.
66. Sergeant Emanuel Stance, Ninth U.S. Cavalry, Indian Campaigns.
67. Ordinary Seaman John A. Sweeney.
68. Private First Class William Thompson, U.S. Army, Korean War.
69. Private William H. Tompkins, U.S. Colored Troops, Civil War.
70. Private Charles Veal, U.S. Colored Troops, Civil War.
71. Private Augustus Walley, Ninth U.S. Cavalry, Indian Campaigns.
72. Private George H. Wanton, Tenth U.S. Cavalry, Indian Campaigns.
73. Sergeant John Ward, U.S. Army Detachment, Seminole Indian Scouts, Indian Campaigns.
74. Lieutenant John E. Warren Jr., U.S. Army, Vietnam War.
75. First Sergeant Moses Williams, Ninth U.S. Cavalry, Indian Campaigns.
76. Corporal William O. Wilson, Ninth U.S. Cavalry, Indian Campaigns.
77. Sergeant Brent Wood, Ninth U.S. Cavalry, Indian Campaigns.

## Notes to Appendix I

1. Laura E. Wilkes, *Missing Pages in American History, 1641–1815* (Washington: 1919).
2. Lyman C. Draper, *King's Mountain and Its Heroes: History of the Battle of King's Mountain* (Cincinnatti: Peter G. Thompson, 1881), pp. 267–268.
3. Miscellaneous Manuscript Papers, Hall of Records, Maryland Archives, Annapolis, Maryland.
4. William C. Nell, *The Colored Patriots of the American Revolution* (Boston: Robert F. Walcut, 1855).
5. *Ibid.*
6. Wilkes, *Missing Pages.*
7. *The Negro in the Military Service of the United States 1639–1886,* Microcopy T-823, Vol. 1, Roll I, National Archives, Washington, D.C.
8. Hammond,—compiler, *New Hampshire State Papers, Revolutionary Rolls* 3, XVI, pp. 242–245, 709, 845.
9. Nell, *The Colored Patriots.*
10. *The Negro in the Military Service of the U.S.*
11. *Ibid.*
12. Military Pension Files of Ephraim Sampson, No. 15, Records of the Adjutant General's Office, National Archives.

Military Pension Files of Deborah Sampson Gannet, *loc. cit.*

Nell, *The Colored Patriots*, p. 23.

Edward Snow, *True Tales and Curious Legends* (New York: Dodd, Mead, 1969), pp. 101–109.

John Laffin, *Women in Battle* (New York: Abelard-Achuman, 1969), pp. 31–33.

13. Record of Revolutionary War Service of John Featherston, Folder AA 2567, South Carolina Department of Archives and History, Columbus, S.C.

14. Military Pension Files of Abram Read, *loc. cit.*

15. Christian Marcus, *The Battle of New Orleans, Negro Soldiers in the Battle of New Orleans* (New Orleans: Louisiana Landmarks Society, 1965).

Roland C. McConnell, *Negro Troops of Antebellum Louisiana* (Baton Rouge, La.: Louisiana State University Press, 1968)

Powell A. Casey, *Louisiana in the War of 1812* (Baton Rouge: 1963).

16. RG 94, Record of the Adjutant General's Office, October 21, 1896, National Archives.

17. Nell, *The Colored Patriots.*

18. Wilkes, *Missing Pages.*

19. *Record of the Service of the Fifty-Fifth Regiment of Massachusetts* (Cambridge: Printed for the Regimental Association, Press of John Wilson, 1968).

20. "Notes and Queries," *Southern History Association Journal*, 1 (1897), 157.

21. *The Negro in the Military Service of the U.S.*

22. James H. Richard (late Captain, 19th U.S. Colored Troops), *Personal Narratives, Services in the Colored Troops in Burnside's Corps* (Providence: Soldiers and Sailors Historical Society of Rhode Island, 1894).

23. Military Records Division, Department of Archives and History, Montgomery, Alabama.

24. John H. Taggart (late Colonel, 12th Regiment, Pennsylvania Reserves, Chief Preceptor), *Free Military School for Applicants for Command of Colored Troops*, 2d edition (King & Baird, 1864).

25. Paul Lawrence Dunbar's Miscellaneous Papers, Carter G. Woodson Papers, Manuscript Division, Library of Congress.

26. L. P. Brockett, *The Camp, The Battle Field, and the Hospital, or Lights and Shadows of the Great Rebellion* (St. Louis: National Publishing Co., 1866), p. 509.

27. *Notes on Colored Troops and Military Colonies of Southern Soil by an Officer of the 9th Corps* (New York: 1863).

28. *The Negro in the Military Service of the U.S.*

29. Brockett, *The Camp, The Battle Field.*

30. *The National Freedman* (a monthly journal of the National Freedman's Relief Association) 1 (April 1, 1863).

31. *The Negro in the Military Service of the U.S.*

32. George R. Sherman (Captain of the U.S. Colored Infantry and Brevet Lieutenant, Colored United States Volunteers), *The Negro as Soldier* (Providence: Soldiers and Sailors Historical Society of Rhode Island, 1913).

33. Brockett, *The Camp, The Battlefield.*

34. Military Records Division, Department of Archives and History, Montgomery, Alabama.

35. *The Negro in the Military Service of the U.S.*

36. P. H. Sheridan, *Personal Memoirs of P. H. Sheridan, General United States Army*, 2 (New York; Charles L. Webster, 1888), pp. 2–4.

37. Miscellaneous Navy Records (Robert Smalls), R. G. 1b, National Archives, Washington, D.C.

38. Letter dated March 17, 1903 received Chief of Record and Pension Office, War Department, RG 94, National Archives, Washington, D.C. Letter dated March 24, 1903 despatched from Chief of Records and Pension Office, *loc. cit.*

*New Orleans Newspaper*, May 10, 1903, R.G. 94, National Archives.

39. Personal interview with William Alexander West, Vienna, Virginia, June 24, 1970.

40. *The Negro in the Military Service of the U.S.*

41. *Henry Ossian Flipper: The Colored Cadet at West Point* (notes by Sarah Dunlap Jackson, National Archives), (New York: Arno Press and The New York Times, 1969).

42. Correspondence related to Seminole Negro Indian Scout Files, RG 75, National Archives.

Kenneth Wiggins Porter, "The Seminole Negro Indian Scouts, 1870–1881," *The Southwestern Historical Quarterly* 55 (July, 1951-April, 1952).

43. Chaplain Steward, *The Colored Regulars in the U.S. Army* (Philadelphia: AME Book Concern, 1904), pp. 282–290.

44. H. V. F. Cashin and Neely Tennyson, *Under Fire with the 10th U.S. Cavalry* (New York: 1899).

45. Miscellaneous Papers, Manuscript Division, Library of Congress.

46. Hon. Martin B. Madden (Ill.), Speech. June 8, 1914, *Congressional Record*, June 9, 1914, pp. 10930–10931.

47. Beverly Perea Papers, Manuscript Division, Library of Congress.

48. John Hope Franklin, *From Slavery to Freedom* (New York: Random House, 1969), p. 442.

News Release, September 28, 1972 (Washington, D.C.: Office of the Assistant Secretary of Defense [Public Affairs], 1972).

Rayford W. Logan, *The Betrayal of the Negro* (London: Collier-Macmillan, 1970), p. 347.

49. Commanding General, Punitive Expedition, U.S. Army, Mexico, to Commanding General, Southern Department, Fort Sam Houston, Texas, September 2, 1916, Punitive Expedition, Mexico, 1916–1917, RG 395, National Archives.

Sworn statement, Quartermaster Sergeant Dalley Farrior, Troop C, 10th Cavalry, Dublin, Mexico, June 27, 1916, Punitive Expedition, U.S. Army Mexico, 1916–1917, *loc. cit.*

50. J. E. Sadler, "The Negro Press from Jamestown to the Rhine" (Address to the Afro-American Convention of New Jersey, Asbury Park, N.J.), October, 1919.

51. Military Division, War Records Section, State House, Boston, Mass.

52. *Pittsburgh Courier* (Washington edition), July 7, 1945.

53. Clarence McKettrick Smith, *The Medical Department, Hospitalization and Evaculation, Zone of the Interior* (Washington: Office of the Chief of Military History, 1956.

Annual Report, Headquarters, 168th Station Hospital, January 3, 1945 (Courtesy of the Historical Unit, U.S. Army Medical Department, Forest Glen section).

Technical Information Office, Surgeon's Office, Department of the Army, Washington, D.C.

54. RG 127 (15), National Archives.

55. Helen G. Douglas, *The Negro Soldier*, Congressional Reprint (Washington, D.C.: U.S. Government Printing Office, 1946).

56. T. W. Anderson, *Come Out Fighting: The Epic Tale of the 761st Tank Battalion, 1942–1945* (Salsburger Druckerci, 1945), pp. 15–21.

Ulysses S. Lee. *The Employment of Negro Troops in World War II* (Washington, D.C.: U.S. Government Printing Office, 1966), pp. 660, 661–662, 663. *Stars and Stripes,* November 14, 1944.

57. Public Information Office, Department of Transportation, U.S. Coast Guard, Washington, D.C.

58. Douglas, *The Negro Soldier.*

59. Lee, *The Employment of Negro Troops,* p. 538.

60. *Pentagram News* (Washington, D.C.: U.S. Army Military District, May 7, 1770).

# Appendix III

## Documents

Ship's muster rolls, unit muster rolls, letters and official papers are the kind of documentation that can bring the reader a little closer to the events of history. The Negro's participation in the military through the years has been documented in many official state and government administrative papers, and in the news media. The following documents have been selected because of their significance, validity, and their testimony to the facts of the black man's experiences in America's armed services.

## Black Labor and the Confederate Army

During the Civil War, the Confederate Congress passed an act to increase the efficiency of the army by the employment of free Negroes and slaves in certain capacities. The act was approved on February 17, 1864. Slaves and free Negroes were used in war factories, in erecting defensive works, and in military hospitals. The following is a copy of an enrolling office paper for receipt of two Negro men for impressment.

*Enrolling Office, Choctaw County, Mt. Sterling, Ala. 27th day of November, 1864.*
*Received of Jesse Taylor the following negro men named Solomon and Mack and described below, contracted for or impressed under Par. IV, Special Orders No. 85, Headquarters Major General WITHERS, made in pursuance of an Act of Congress entitled "An Act to Increase the efficiency of the army by the employment of free negroes and slaves in certain capacities," approved February 17th, 1864.*

| Name of Owner | Name of Slave | Age | Height Feet | Height In. | Weight | Color | Value | Post Office of Owner |
|---|---|---|---|---|---|---|---|---|
| Jesse Taylor | Solomon | 23 | 5 | 6 | 157 | Copper | Five Thousand dollars ($5,000) | Tompkinsville Choctaw Co. Ala. |
| Jesse Taylor | Mack | 25 | 5 | 9 | 201 | Black | Fifty-Five Hundred Dollars ($5,500) | Tompkinsville Choctaw Co. Ala. |

*WDT Evington, Enrolling Officer, Choctaw County, Ala.*
*Mt. Sterling, Alabama, November 27th, 1864*
*WE, the undersigned, a Board of Appraisers, appointed under the provision of the Act of Congress regulating impressments, for the purpose of valuing negroes contracted for or impressed under the provisions of the Act of February 17th, 1864, do hereby certify that the amount stated in writing, opposite each name in the above Descriptive Roll, is the just valuation of such above.*

*Marion E. Farvin, Jesse Jackson, Board of Appraisers*[1]

## Service to the Union is Freedom to the Slave

During the Civil War Congress passed an Act on March 1, 1865, awarding freedom to wives and children of all black men who enlisted in the military service of the government.

*Headquarters Department of Kentucky, Louisville, Kentucky*

*General Orders No. 10*

*The General commanding announces to the colored men of Kentucky that by an Act of Congress passed on the 3rd day of March, 1865, the wives and children of all colored men who have heretofore enlisted, or who may hereafter enlist, in the military service of the Government, are made free.*

*This act of justice to the soldiers claims from them renewed efforts, by courage, fortitude, and discipline, to win a good name, to be shared by a free wife and free children. To colored men not in the army it offers an opportunity to coin [earn] freedom for themselves and posterity.*

*The rights secured to colored soldiers under this law will, if necessary, be enforced by the military authorities of this Department, and it is expected that the loyal men and women of Kentucky will encourage colored men to enlist in the army: and, after they have done so, recognize them as upholders of their Government and defenders of their homes, and exercise toward the helpless women and children made free by the law that benevolence and charity which has always characterized the people of the State.*
*BY COMMAND OF MAJOR GENERAL PALMER:*
*J. P. Watson, Captain and A.A.A.G. OFFICIAL.*[13]

# BLACK CREW MEMBERS, U.S. NAVY

## USS Powhatan, Philadelphia, 21 Aug., 1860.[2]

| Name | Rank or Rating | Date of Enlistment | Where Born | Age | Occupation | Description | | |
|---|---|---|---|---|---|---|---|---|
| | | | | | | Hair | Eyes | Complexion |
| Kelly, Dennis | Ship's Cook | Sept. 8, 1857 | Conn. | 42 | | Black | Black | Black |
| Williams, Walter | Landsman | Nov. 24, 1857 | Norfolk, Va. | 28 | | Black | Hazel | Mulatto |
| Stephens, James | Landsman | Nov. 15, 1857 | Va. | 23 | | Black | Black | Negro |
| Mears, John | Steward | Nov. 19, 1857 | Norfolk, Va. | 23 | | Black | Black | Negro |
| Newson, Isaiah | Landsman | Nov. 23, 1857 | Norfolk, Va. | 24 | | Black | Black | Black |
| Rodgers, William | Cook | Nov. 18, 1857 | Norfolk, Va. | 21 | | Black | Black | Negro |
| Brown, Charles | Landsman | Nov. 14, 1857 | Maryland | 33 | | Dark | Dark | Mulatto |
| Bell, George | Landsman | Nov. 19, 1857 | Norfolk, Va. | 19 | | Black | Black | Negro |

## U.S. Steamer Sloop Powhatan, Jan., 1863[3]

| Name | Rank or Rating | Date of Enlistment | Where Born | Age | Occupation | Description | | |
|---|---|---|---|---|---|---|---|---|
| | | | | | | Hair | Eyes | Complexion |
| Brister, Charles | Landsman | July 19, 1862 | Phil, Pa. | 28 | Cook | Wooly | Black | Black |
| Booth, James A. | Landsman | July 19, 1862 | Phil, Pa. | 31 | Barber | Wooly | Black | Black |
| Cropper, Isaac | Landsman | Aug. 6, 1862 | Chester, Pa. | 35 | Cook | Wooly | Black | Black |
| Dant, Benjamin | Landsman | July 30, 1862 | Fredericksburg, Pa. | 19 | Waiter | Wooly | Black | Black |
| Davis, Jon | Landsman | Aug. 12, 1862 | Salsburg, Md. | 25 | | Wooly | Black | Black |

## U.S. Steamer Black Hawk, Jan. 1, 1863[4]

| Name | Rank or Rating | Date of Enlistment | Where Born | Age | Occupation | Description | | |
|---|---|---|---|---|---|---|---|---|
| | | | | | | Hair | Eyes | Complexion |
| Gray, George | 1st class Boy | July 21, 1862 | Penn. | 18 | Barber | | | Mulatto |
| Brown, John | 3rd class Boy | July 1, 1862 | Fayette, Tenn. | 20 | Cook | Black | | Black |
| Peterson, F. B. | 1st class Boy | Aug. 6, 1862 | New Haven, Conn. | 16 | Farmer | | | Mulatto |
| Wilson, George | Landsman | Dec. 11, 1862 | Evansville, Ind. | 29 | Waiter | | | Negro |
| Bell, William | 1st class Boy | Aug. 10, 1863 | Washington, D.C. | 46 | Field hand | | | Negro |
| Brown, Louis | 1st class Boy | Jan. 10, 1863 | Spring Hall, Tenn. | 13 | Field hand | | | Negro |
| White, Bob | 1st class Boy | Nov. 17, 1862 | Tenn. | 28 | None | | | Negro |
| Alexander, Richard | Ordinary Seaman | March 14, 1863 | Kentucky | 26 | Field hand | | | Mulatto |
| Claeborne, Isaac | 1st class Boy | Jan. 7, 1863 | Springfield, Ill. | 22 | Boatman | | | Negro |
| Douglas, John | 1st class Boy | March 15, 1863 | Prince Geo. Co., Md. | 45 | Field hand | | | Negro |

U.S. Steamer Glenville, Feb. 28, 1863[5]

| Name | Rank or Rating | Date of Enlistment | Where Born | Age | Occupation | Description | | |
| --- | --- | --- | --- | --- | --- | --- | --- | --- |
| | | | | | | Hair | Eyes | Complexion |
| Butler, Francis | Landsman | Oct. 21, 1861 | New York | 22 | | | | Mulatto |
| Hall, Charles | Ordinary Seaman | Feb. 6, 1863 | Boston, Mass. | 23 | | | | Colored |
| Price, William A. | Ordinary Seaman | Feb. 6, 1863 | Jamaica, W. Indies | 24 | Carpenter | | | Negro |
| Thompson, Nicholas | Ordinary Seaman | Feb. 11, 1863 | New York | 38 | | | | Negro |
| Williams, Alonso P. | Ordinary Seaman | Feb. 6, 1863 | Boston, Mass. | 20 | | | | Negro |
| Davis, Frank | Ordinary Seaman | Feb. 7, 1863 | Glanchester, Mass. | 23 | Seaman | | | Mulatto |
| Jackson, Melville | Landsman | Feb. 23, 1863 | New York | | Porter | | | Mulatto |
| Smith, John IV | Nurse | Feb. 18, 1863 | Baltimore, Md. | | Cabin Boy | | | Negro |
| Stevens, Samuel | Ordinary Seaman | Jan. 30, 1863 | Mt. Holly, N.Y. | | Seaman | | | Mulatto |
| Johnson, Henry | Landsman | Oct. 25, 1861 | New York | | Waiter | | | Mulatto |

USS Sloop of War Hartford, March 31, 1863[6]

| Name | Rank or Rating | Date of Enlistment | Where Born | Age | Occupation | Description | | |
| --- | --- | --- | --- | --- | --- | --- | --- | --- |
| | | | | | | Hair | Eyes | Complexion |
| Allison, William | Seaman | Dec. 9, 1861 | Nova Scotia | 23 | None | Wooly | Black | Mulatto |
| Banks, Charles II | Landsman | Jan. 7, 1862 | Phila., Pa. | 23 | Porter | Wooly | Black | Mulatto |
| Brown, Charles F. | Landsman | Dec. 24, 1862 | Va. | 21 | None | Wooly | Dark | Mulatto |
| Claxton, Bobb | Landsman | Nov. 22, 1861 | New Jersey | 18 | None | Wooly | Black | Negro |
| Cloud, Ottwis | Landsman | Jan. 1, 1862 | New Orleans, La. | 19 | None | Wooly | Black | Black |
| Edwards, George | Landsman | May 21, 1861 | New York | 25 | None | Wooly | Black | Mulatto |
| Hughes, Benjamin | Landsman | Jan. 20, 1862 | Pa. | 19 | Waiter | Wooly | Black | Mulatto |
| Jackson, Samuel S. | Landsman | Jan. 17, 1862 | Phila., Pa. | 36 | Cook | Wooly | Black | Black |
| Pilot, Thomas | Landsman | Aug. 15, 1862 | Newburn, N.C. | 30 | Cook | Wooly | Black | Black |
| Percy, Alphonse | 1st Boy | Aug. 11, 1862 | Donaldsville, La. | 27 | None | Black | Black | Mulatto |
| Pierson, Gustavo | 1st class Boy | Aug. 11, 1862 | New Orleans, La. | 23 | None | Wooly | Dark | Negro |
| Landy, George W. | 3rd Class Boy | Aug. 11, 1862 | Charleston, S.C. | 24 | None | Wooly | Black | Negro |
| Lyons, A. | Landsman | Feb. 20, 1863 | La. | 18 | None | Black | Black | Mulatto |
| Mathew, James | Steward | Jan. 19, 1862 | Mich. | 27 | None | Black | Black | Black |
| Manning, Harry | Seaman | Dec. 9, 1861 | West Indies | 31 | Shoemaker | Wooly | Black | Mulatto |

U.S. Coast Survey Steamer Bebb, 13 July, 1866[7]

| | | | | | | Description | | |
| Name | Rank or Rating | Date of Enlistment | Where Born | Age | Occupation | Hair | Eyes | Complexion |
|---|---|---|---|---|---|---|---|---|
| Lee, Joseph | Landsman | Dec. 8, 1865 | Charleston, S.C. | 17 | None | | | Mulatto |
| Mathews, Oglivie | Landsman | Apr. 1, 1865 | Charleston, S.C. | 20 | Brick Mason | | | Mulatto |
| McKenzie, Alex | Landsman | Dec. 6, 1865 | Charleston, S.C. | 21 | None | | | Negro |
| Rivers, Pinckney | Cook | Apr. 1, 1865 | Charleston, S.C. | 44 | None | | | Negro |
| Patterson, William | Seaman | Aug. 12, 1867 | Portland, Me. | 19 | None | | | Negro |
| Robinson, James H. | Ship's Cook | Aug. 20, 1867 | Bristol, Me. | 21 | Mariner | | | Negro |
| Robinson, John W. | Cabin Cook | Nov. 2, 1867 | Norfolk, Va. | 26 | Mariner | | | Negro |

USS Patterson, March 31, 1886[8]

| | | | | | Description | | |
| Name | Rank or Rating | Date of Enlistment | Where Born | Occupation | Hair | Eyes | Complexion |
|---|---|---|---|---|---|---|---|
| Cornicks, Lewis | 2nd Class Fireman | April 9, 1884 | Norfolk, Va. | Laborer | | | Negro |

USS Jamestown[9]

| | | | | | Description | | |
| Name | Rank or Rating | Date of Enlistment | Where Born | Occupation | Hair | Eyes | Complexion |
|---|---|---|---|---|---|---|---|
| Perkins, W. C. | Ordinary Seaman | May 12, 1886 | Fluvanna, Va. | Mariner | | | Negro |
| Coates, W. H. | 3rd Class Apprentice | June 1, 1886 | Oxenville, N.M. | | Dark | Black | Negro |
| West, L. D. | 3rd Class Apprentice | Feb. 20, 1886 | Washington, D.C. | | Brown | | Mulatto |

USS Wyandank, March 31, 1865[10]

| | | | | | Description | | |
| Name | Rank of Rating | Date of Enlistment | Where Born | Age | Occupation | Hair | Eyes | Complexion |
|---|---|---|---|---|---|---|---|---|
| Cummings, John H. | Ordinary Seaman | Dec. 29, 1863 | Wilmington, Del. | 21 | Farmer | | | Colored |
| Dorsey, David | Ordinary Seaman | July 18, 1863 | Virginia | 22 | Butcher | | | Colored |

Muster Roll of 2nd Lieut. E. H. Rubottom, Detachment Seminole Negro Indian Scouts, Thirty-first October[11]

| Names | Rank | Enlisted | | |
| | | When | Where | By Whom |
|---|---|---|---|---|
| Rubottom, E. H. | 2nd Lieut. 9th Cavalry | | | |
| July, Ben | 1st Sergt. | Jan. 19, 1898 | Fort Ringgold, Texas | Lt. Hall |
| July, John | Lance Corpl. | Jan. 20, 1898 | Fort Ringgold, Texas | Lt. Hall |
| Clayton, Sie | Private | Mar. 1, 1898 | Fort Ringgold, Texas | Lt. Wade |
| Daniels, Charles | Private | Feb. 17, 1898 | Fort Ringgold, Texas | Lt. Wade |
| Daniels, Thomas | Private | Oct. 4, 1898 | Fort Ringgold, Texas | Lt. Dapray |
| Fay, Sandy | Private | Jan. 1, 1898 | Fort Ringgold, Texas | Lt. Lazelle |
| July, Billy | Private | Jan. 10, 1898 | Fort Ringgold, Texas | Lt. Hall |
| July, Fay | Private | Apr. 5, 1898 | Fort Ringgold, Texas | Lt. Hall |
| McClain, Adam | Private | Feb. 26, 1898 | Fort Clark, Texas | Lt. Dapray |
| Payne, Charles | Private | Feb. 26, 1898 | Fort Clark, Texas | Lt. Dapray |
| Payne, Isaac | Private | Jan. 22, 1898 | Fort Ringgold, Texas | Lt. Hall |
| Shields, William | Private | Feb. 17, 1898 | Fort Ringgold, Texas | Lt. Wade |
| Washington, Sam | Private | Jan. 16, 1898 | Fort Ringgold, Texas | Lt. Hall |
| Williams, Bill | Private | Jan. 17, 1898 | Fort Ringgold, Texas | Lt. Hall |

Muster Roll of a detachment of the Seminole Negro Indian Scouts from the 31st day of December, 1910[12]

| Names | Rank | Enlisted | | |
| | | When | Where | By Whom |
|---|---|---|---|---|
| July, Fay | 1st Sergt. | Apr. 5, 1910 | Fort Clark, Texas | Lt. Barney |
| Remo, Joe | Sergt. | July 28, 1908 | Fort Clark, Texas | Lt. Haydur |
| Carlino, Warrior | Corpl. | March 9, 1910 | Fort Clark, Texas | Lt. Barney |
| Daniel, Caesar | Private | March 8, 1910 | Fort Clark, Texas | Lt. Barney |
| Daniels, John | Private | June 29, 1910 | Fort Clark, Texas | Lt. Barney |
| Jefferson, Curley | Private | Aug. 13, 1908 | Fort Clark, Texas | Maj. Page |
| Jefferson, John | Private | May 16, 1908 | Fort Clark, Texas | Cpt. Page |
| July, Billy | Private | Jan. 10, 1910 | Fort Clark, Texas | Lt. Barney |
| July, Charles J. | Private | Oct. 12, 1908 | Fort Clark, Texas | Lt. Archer |
| Kibbetts, George | Private | June 25, 1908 | Fort Clark, Texas | Capt. Guiney |
| Perryman, Ignacio | Private | March 12, 1910 | Fort Clark, Texas | Lt. Barney |
| Sanchez, Antonio | Private | Apr. 1, 1910 | Fort Clark, Texas | Lt. Barney |
| Shields, John | Private | Feb. 26, 1910 | Fort Clark, Texas | Lt. Barney |
| Washington, Larn | Private | Jan. 17, 1910 | Fort Clark, Texas | Lt. Barney |
| Wilson, Billy | Private | March 9, 1910 | Fort Clark, Texas | Lt. Barney |
| Wilson, Isaac | Private | March 15, 1910 | Fort Clark, Texas | Lt. Barney |
| Wilson, William | Private | March 9, 1910 | Fort Clark, Texas | Lt. Barney |

### A Handbill Requesting Black Volunteers During the Civil War

MEETING FOR THE ORGANIZATION OF A COL-ORED REGIMENT FOR THE DISTRICT OF COLUMBIA.

The President has authorized Col. J. B. Turner, late Chaplain in the Army and Lieut. W. G. Raymond, late Chaplain, Trinity Hospital of this city to raise a regiment of colored troops in the District of Columbia. A meeting will be held in Asbury Chapel, Corner of 11th and R Streets on Monday evening next, May 4, 7:30 o'clock to organize and make arrangements to visit the President and receive his orders. All who desire to enlist in the 1st Regiment of District of Columbia Colored Volunteers, and there demonstrate their manhood are earnestly invited to be present and hear consult and decide.

By order of J. D. Turner, W. G. Raymond.[14]

### Black Troop Recruitment in the Civil War, 1861–1865

The states in which forces were recruited or drafted during the Civil War are as follows:

| | |
|---|---:|
| Alabama | 4,969 |
| Arkansas | 5,526 |
| Colorado Territory | 95 |
| Connecticut | 1,764 |
| Delaware | 954 |
| District of Columbia | 3,269 |
| Florida | 1,044 |
| Georgia | 3,486 |
| Illinois | 1,811 |
| Indiana | 1,537 |
| Iowa | 440 |
| Kansas | 2,080 |
| Kentucky | 23,703 |
| Louisiana | 24,052 |
| Maine | 104 |
| Massachusetts | 3,966 |
| Maryland | 8,718 |
| Michigan | 1,367 |
| Minnesota | 104 |
| Mississippi | 17,869 |
| New Hampshire | 125 |
| New Jersey | 1,185 |
| New York | 4,125 |
| North Carolina | 5,035 |
| Ohio | 5,099 |
| Pennsylvania | 8,612 |
| Rhode Island | 1,837 |
| South Carolina | 5,462 |
| Tennessee | 20,133 |
| Texas | 47 |
| Virginia | 5,723 |
| Vermont | 120 |
| West Virginia | 196 |
| Wisconsin | 165 |

Total: 178,975[15]

### True Copy

*Chapter No. 129, Senate Bill No. 1,342*
*(By Mr. Graham).*

*An Act to be entitled an Act to provide pensions for those colored men who served as servants and cooks in the Confederate Army in the war between the states —1861–1865.*

SECTION 1. *Be it enacted by the General Assembly of the State of Tennessee, that the colored men who acted as servants or cooks in the Confederate Army in the War Between the States, are hereby permitted to make application to the Pension Board for a pension and* when they make proper proof of their service, acceptable to said board, that their names be placed on the Pension List and that they be paid out of the pension fund, the sum of ten ($10.00) dollars per month or thirty dollars per quarter.

*SECTION 2. Be it further enacted, that this act take effect from and after its passage, the public welfare requiring it.*

*Passed April 9, 1921.*
*W. W. Bond, Speaker of the Senate*
*Andrew L. Todd,*
*Speaker of the House of Representatives.*

*Approved April 9, 1921.*
*A. A. Taylor, Governor.*[16]

### Black Medal of Honor Winner Defends Integrity of Fourth U.S. Colored Troops

On June 2, 1864, Sergeant Major Christian A. Fleetwood, Fourth U.S. Colored Troops, wrote a letter to the editor, *Anglo-African Newspaper,* to correct a misstatement in a news account concerning the Fourth U.S.C.T. during a battle skirmish.

*Before Petersburg, Va., June 28, '64.*
*Robert Hamilton Esq., Ed., Anglo-African.*

*Dear Sir: Permit me to occupy a small space in your paper to correct a* misstatement *made in your paper by someone writing from 5th Mass. Cav. over the nom de plume of "Africano." I will do so in as few words as possible. He states that the 4th Regt. being deployed as skirmishers were unable to sustain themselves and fell back upon them (the 5th Cav.) in confusion. Our Regt. advanced through the woods in the line of battle, its front covered by skirmishers, two companies deployed, the 22d U.S.T.C. on our right, the 6th on our left, the 5th Mass. Cav. and 5th U.S.C.T. forming the reserve.*

*Our regiment was the first to clear the woods and receive the concentrated fire from the rebel works completely enfilading our lines, notwithstanding this we charged the works at a double quick until the 5th Mass. Cavalry, our reserve, who were not yet out of the woods nor in sight of the enemy fired a volley which took effect upon our [troops] throwing our entire left wing into confusion.*

*The shot from the rebel battery still moving down we were ordered back into the woods to form and fell back accordingly, reformed again, advanced in time to lose several more men killed and wounded.*

*A better and braver regiment than the 5th U.S.C.T. is not in the service. Yet "Honor to whom honor is due" it was the 22nd U.S.C.T. and not the 5th which carried the works after we had fallen back.*

*One thing more and I close, "Africano" wondered why the casualties were so small in his Regt. perhaps the fact that they did not come out of the friendly shelter of the woods until the action was over may partly account for their loss being so small while ours summed up to one hundred and sixty killed and wounded out of less than sixty in the short time of ten minutes.*

*In justice to our boys, I trust you will give this [sic] an insertion.*

*Yours respectfully, C. A. Fleetwood, Sergt. Major, 4th U.S.C.T.*[17]

## World War I Statistics

At the beginning of the war there were 10,000 Negroes in the regular army and 10,000 in the National Guards. Between June 5, 1917 and September 12, 1918, 2,290,529 Negro men registered for service: 400,000 served in the U.S. Army; 200,000 served in France; 42,000 were combatant troops; 10,000 volunteered for the U.S. Navy; 2,000 served in the American Transport Force. The Ninety-Second Division was the largest group of Negroes, who also served in the infantry, field artillery, machine gun battalion and signal corps.

The following decorations were awarded to 194 officers and men: Congressional Medal of Honor, Distinguished Service Cross, Croix de Guerre, Legion of Honor.

Some noted heroes were Henry Johnson and Needham Roberts (who were the first Americans to receive the French Croix de Guerre, for wiping out a German raiding party of 20 men), and Sergeant William Butler. At the Battle of Argonne, the Three Hundred and Sixty-Eighth Negro Infantry did noble service. Lieutenant Robert L. Campbell was decorated for rescuing Private Edward Sanders who was carrying a message.

Twelve Hundred Negro officers served in every branch of the armed forces except the Air Corps.

The Fifteenth Regiment of New York was under fire for 191 days.[18]

## Negro Members of WAAC Graduating Class at Fort Des Moines, Iowa, World War II

| | |
|---|---|
| E. Adams<br>Columbia, S.C. | Violet W. Askens<br>Chicago, Ill. |
| Frances C. Alexander<br>Toledo, Ohio | Veraneal M. Austin<br>New York City, N.Y. |
| Myrtle E. Anderson<br>Everett, Mass. | Mary A. Bordeaux<br>Louisville, Kentucky |
| Geraldine G. Bright<br>Pittsburg, Texas | Alice M. Jones<br>Nacogdoches, Texas |
| Annie L. Brown<br>Brenham, Texas | Mary F. Kearney<br>Baptist, Conn. |
| Harriet Buhile<br>Los Angeles, Calif.[19] | Mary K. Lewis<br>Orlando, Florida |
| A. N. Campbell<br>Tuskegee Institute, Ala. | Ruth A. Lucas<br>Stamford, Conn. |
| V. G. Campbell<br>New York City, N.Y. | Charline J. Mary<br>Falls Church, Nebraska |
| Mildred E. Carter<br>Boston, Mass. | Ina M. McFadden<br>St. Louis, Missouri |
| Irma J. Cayton<br>Chicago, Ill. | Mary I. Miller<br>St. Augusta, Georgia |
| Natalie F. Donaldson<br>New York City, N.Y. | Glendora Moore<br>Washington, D.C. |
| Sarah R. Emmert<br>Chicago, Illinois | Sarah E. Murphy<br>Atlanta, Georgia |
| Geneva V. Ferguson<br>Camp Dennison, Ohio | Doris M. Norrel<br>Indianapolis, Ind. |
| Ruth L. Freeman<br>Liberty, Texas | Mildred Osby<br>Everett, Mass. |
| Evelyn F. Green<br>Washington, D.C. | Gertrude J. Peebles<br>Omaha, Nebraska |
| Elizabeth G. Hampton<br>Los Angeles, California | Corris S. Sherard<br>Atlanta, Georgia |
| Vera A. Harrison<br>Hamilton, Ohio | Jessie L. Ward<br>New York City, N.Y. |
| Dovey M. Johnson<br>Charlotte, N.C. | Harriet M. West<br>Washington, D.C. |

## U.S. Navy Stresses Black Naval ROTC Units

Throughout the history of America's Reserve Officer Training Corps, both on a high school and college level, a choice selection by many students has been the elite U.S. Navy's "NROTC." Unfortunately in the past, this opportunity was denied the black youths eager to pursue future careers at sea or with the navy's aviation program.

During the past few years the U.S. Navy has implemented a very enlightened and successful program to establish NROTC's at predominantly black high schools and colleges. Prairie View A. & M. College in Texas was the first predominantly black university or college to obtain such a unit.

Additional NROTC units were activated at Southern University, Baton Rouge, Louisiana and Savannah State College, Georgia.

The first all-black Naval Junior Reserve Officers Training Corps (NJROTC) unit in any high school in the nation was officially activated recently at Locke High School in Watts, California.[20]

## Colored Troops Urged to Volunteer for Front-Line Assignment

*Declassified-DOD Directive No. 5200.9.27, September, 1958*

*AG 322 X 353 XSGS, Headquarters, Communications Zone, European Theater of Operations, APO 887, 26 December, 1944.*

*Subject: Volunteers for Training and Assignment as Reinforcements*

*To: Commander of Colored Troops, Com Z.*

*1. The Supreme Commander desires to destroy the enemy forces and end hostilities in this theater without delay. Every available weapon at our disposal must be brought to bear upon the enemy. To this end the Commanding General, Com Z, is happy to offer to a limited number of colored troops who have had infantry training, the privilege of joining our veteran units at the front to deliver the knockout blow. The men selected are to be in the grades of Private First Class and Private. Non-commissioned officers may accept reduction in order to take advantage of this opportunity. The men selected are to be given a refresher course with emphasis on weapon training.*

*2. The Commanding General makes a special appeal to you. It is planned to assign you without regard to color or race to the units where assistance is most needed, and give you the opportunity of fighting shoulder to shoulder to bring about victory. Your comrades at the front are anxious to share the glory of victory with you. Your relatives and friends everywhere have been urging that you be granted this privilege. The Supreme Commander, your Commanding General, and other veteran officers who have served with you are confident that many of you will take advantage of this opportunity and carry on in keeping with the glorious record of our colored troops in our former wars.*

*3. This letter is to be read confidentially to the troops immediately upon its receipt and made available in Orderly Rooms. Every assistance must be promptly given qualified men to volunteer for this service.*

*John C. H. Lee*
*Lieutenant General, U.S.A., Commanding*

*Distribution: A plus*
*\*CG, Southern L/C 5*
*\*CG, U.K. Base 5*

*\*Ea Sec Cmdr 5*

*AG 322 X 353 XSGS GA 1st Ind HJL/rm*

*Headquarters Normandy Base Section, Com Z, European Theater of Operations*
*APO 562, U.S. Army*

*To: Commanding Officers, All Colored Units*
*For information and compliance*
*By command of Major General Aurand*

*Frank Cumiskey*
*Lt. Colonel, AGD*
*Adjutant General*

*Distribution: Special*
*Commanding Officers, All Colored Units, MBS*
*Utah District (2), Omaha District (2), AG Enlisted Per (1), G-1 (10), G-3 (1), C/S (1), AG Files (1).[21]*

## Negro Troops

(Commentary: J. Raymond Walsh, WMCA, 7:30 P.M., March 15, 1945.)

*A dispatch came from Rome this morning from Truman K. Gibson Jr., Civilian Aide to Secretary of War Stimson. He is a Negro. He was sent to Italy two weeks ago to investigate on the ground the menacing charges that the Negro troops cannot fight. The charge has been current among the worst elements in the army. It has been picked up too by high officers of unquestioned integrity, although often by men whose knowledge of the Negro Ninety-Second Division in Italy is not first hand. And it has been commented upon increasingly in the Negro press at home.*

*Mr. Gibson denies the generalization on the basis of his inspection. "If the division proves anything," he states, "It does not prove that Negroes cannot fight. There is no question in my mind about the courage of Negro officers or soldiers. Any generalization based on race is entirely unfounded. "He went on to state that certain units of the Ninety-Second Division had engaged in "more or less panicky retreats, particularly at night." These retreats have not been confined to Negroes. In other divisions it happens too, except that with the whites it is apt to be individuals, whereas with the Negroes, it is likely to be disintegration of a patrol or platoon as a unit.*

*One can imagine what a Representative Rankin or Senator O'Daniel will do with this subject. Any one can*

*\*Each of these commanders will take necessary action, within twenty-four hours after the receipt hereof, to reproduce and disseminate to the commanders of all colored units, down to and including companies under their respective commands.*

*imagine too how easily others may be taken in by superficial thought on the matter. It is important—all important—to attend to Mr. Gibson's further observations; namely, that the very high illiteracy rate among Negroes is at the bottom of the trouble, and makes any comparisons between whites and Negroes unfair. The Ninety-Second Division, for example, shows 17 percent of its personnel in class V of the Army Literacy Tests. Class V is the lowest class there is. Seventy-five percent of the division is in Class IV, which is very low too. General army figures show 64 percent of Negroes in Class V and 35 percent in Class IV. As he concludes: "You can't apply the same training schedules where that many men are illiterate as where only 4 percent are." He is right of course.*

*And here is where chickens come home to roost. For why is the illiteracy rate among Negroes so high? The answer is the same as to the question why their maternity death rate is so high, their rate of children dying at birth so high, their incomes so low. The answer is that we have imposed these conditions on our Negro fellow citizens, and in all conscience we had better recognize it.*

*It's pretty appalling to face facts like the following: The pre-war income of the Negro farm families averaged $480 a year, of whites $1,100. The pre-war income of northern City Negroes was $1,095, of whites $1,720. In 1940, 33 Negro mothers out of 1000 died in childbirth against 11.3 white mothers. In 1939–40 in Alabama the investment in education was $14.63 a year for Negro youngsters, for white children $47.59. In Mississippi the figures were $7.36 for Negroes and $52.01 for whites. Before the war, there wasn't a year when unemployment was not twice as high proportionally among Negroes as among whites. Even during the war, the Negroes are only slightly represented in the best paying industries and best paying jobs. In all the nation, there are only 245,000 Negroes working as skilled workers or foremen. Not because there aren't plenty of them who are capable, but because we simply keep them out. Even a number of the labor unions discriminate openly or covertly, but always cruelly, against their fellow workers of the Negro race.*

*But the Negroes for the most part have accepted the war as their war, and have entered into it willingly, heroically, and up to the limit of the opportunities afforded them and the abilities we have permitted them to develop. It is good that Secretary Stimson sent Mr. Gibson to Italy to spike those rumors, and pin them down with the facts. It is good to have those facts put into context that gives them meaning. Every instance of a retreat by a Negro boy or man from the firing line is a stab at the conscience of every white citizen of our country. For in fact, we are partly responsible, and there is plenty we can do about it now.*[22]

## Excerpt from General Eisenhower's interview on "High Spots of His Road to Victory"

Supreme Headquarters, Allied Expeditionary Force, Paris, June 15, 1945.

(Taken from the *New York Times*, June 16, 1945).

Q. Would you be good enough to comment on the contribution Negro soldiers made to the European Theatre of operations?

A. To start with, I would like to say this: That I do not differentiate among soldiers. I do not say white soldiers or Negro soldiers, and I do not say American or British soldiers. To my mind I have had a task in this war that makes me look upon soldiers as soldiers. Now I have seen Negro soldiers in this way and I have many reports on their work where they have rendered very valuable contributions and some of them with the greatest enthusiasm.

In late November, when we were getting short of reinforcements, replacements, some 2,600 Negro soldiers volunteered for front-line service and they did good work. All my commanders reported that those volunteers did excellent work.

But their major job has been in services of supply, engineer units, quartermaster units, ordnance units. There, so far as I know and certainly as far as any official reports, they have performed equally with every kind of ordnance battalion, quartermaster battalion and engineer battalion. They have done their job and they have done the job given them.[23]

## Call for Combat Volunteers

*Declassified-DOD Directive No. 5200.9.27
September, 1958*

*AG 322 X 353 XSGS, Headquarters, Communications Zone, European Theater of Operations, APO 887, 26 December 1944*

*Subject: Volunteers for Training and Assignment as Reinforcements*

*To: Commanding General, Southern Line of Communications; Commanding General, United Kingdom Base; Section Commanders, Communications Zone.*

*1. The Supreme Commander desires to destroy the enemy forces and end hostilities in this theatre without delay. Every available weapon at our disposal must be brought to bear upon the enemy. To this end the Theater Commander has directed the Communications*

*Zone Commander to make the greatest possible use of limited service men within service units and to survey our entire organization in an effort to produce able bodied men for the front line. This process of selection has been going on for some time but it is entirely possible that many men themselves, desiring to volunteer for front line service, may be able to point out methods in which they can be replaced in their present jobs. Consequently, Commanders of all grades will receive voluntary applications for transfer to the infantry and forward them to higher authority with recommendations for appropriate type of replacement.* This opportunity to volunteer will be extended to all soldiers without regard to color or race, but preference will normally be given to individuals who have had some basic training in infantry. Normally, also, transfers will be limited to the grade of private and private first class unless a noncommissioned officer requests a reduction.

2. In the event that the number of suitable Negro volunteers exceeds the replacement needs of Negro combat units, these men will be suitably incorporated in other organizations so that their service and their fighting spirit may be efficiently utilized.

3. This letter may be read confidentially to the troops and made available in Orderly Rooms. Every assistance must be promptly given qualified men who volunteer for this service.

*John C. H. Lee*
*Lieutenant General, U.S. Army, Commanding*[24]

**Postwar Use of Negroes**

*Circular No. 124, War Department, Washington 25, D.C.*

*27 April, 1946 (Effective until October, 1947 unless sooner rescinded or superseded.)*
*Utilization of Negro Manpower in the Postwar Army Policy.*

To effect the maximum efficient utilization of the authorized Negro manpower in the postwar period, the War Department has adopted the following policy:

Negro manpower in the postwar Army will be utilized on a broader professional scale than has obtained heretofore. The development of leaders and specialists based on individual merit and ability, to meet effectively the requirements of an expanded war Army will be accomplished through the medium of installations and organizations. Groupings of Negro units with white units in composite organizations will be accepted policy.

*Implementation of Policy*

In order to develop the means required for maximum utilization of the authorized manpower of the nation in the event of a national emergency the following will obtain:

1. The troop basis for the postwar Army will include Negro troops approximately in the 1 to 10 ratio of the Negro civilian population to the total population of the nation.

2. To meet the requirements of training and expansion, combat and service units will be organized and activated from the available Negro manpower. Employment will be in Negro regiments or groups, separate battalions or squadrons, and separate companies, troops or batteries, which will conform in general to other units of the postwar Army. A proportionate number of these units will be organized . . . by Negro officers who prove qualified to fill the assignment. In addition, Negro manpower with special skills or qualifications will be employed as individuals in appropriate overhead and special units.

3. Additional officer supervision will be supplied to units which have a greater than normal percentage of personnel within the AGCT classification of IV and V: 50 percent or more Class IV and V, 25 percent increase of officers; 70 percent or more Class IV and V, 50 percent increase of officers. Increased officer personnel will be of company grade.

4. The planning, promulgation, implementation, and revision of this policy will be coordinated by the Assistant for Planning and Policy Coordination, Office of the Assistant Chief of Staff, G-1, War Department General Staff.

5. Officers will be accepted in the Regular Army through the operation of the present integration policy without regard to race.

6. The present policy of according all officers, regardless of race, equal opportunities for appointment, advancement, professional improvement, promotion, and retention in all components of the Army will be continued.

7. Negro Reserve officers will be eligible for active duty training and service in accordance with any program established for other officers of like components and status. All officer requirements for expansion of the Regular establishment as distinguished from the Regular Army and for replacement, regardless of race, will be procured in the existing manner from current sources; namely: ROTC honor students, Officer's Reserve Corps, direct appointments, graduates of officer candidate schools, Regular Army appointments from

the Army of the United States and graduates of the United States Military Academy.

8. All enlisted men whether volunteers or selectees will be accorded the same processing through appropriate installations to insure proper classification and assignment of individuals.

9. Surveys of manpower requirements conducted by

the War Department will include recommendations covering the positions in each installation of the Army which could be filled by Negro military personnel.

10. At posts, camps, and stations where both Negro and white troops are assigned for duty, the War Department policies regarding use of recreational facilities will be observed.[25]

## Notes to Appendix II

1. Military Records Division, Department of Archives and History, Montgomery, Alabama.
2. Ship Muster Rolls, RG 45, National Archives, Washington, D.C.
3. *Ibid.*
4. *Ibid.*
5. *Ibid.*
6. *Ibid.*
7. *Ibid.*
8. *Ibid.*
9. *Ibid.*
10. *Ibid.*
11. *The Negro in the Military Service of the United States 1639–1886*, Microcopy T-823, Vol. 1, National Archives.
12. Muster Rolls, Seminole Negro Indian Scout Files, RG 75, National Archives.
13. *The Negro in the Military Service of the U.S., loc. cit.*
14. *Ibid.*
15. *Ibid.*
16. Tennessee State Library and Archives, Nashville, Tennessee.
17. Christian A. Fleetwood Papers, Manuscript Division, Library of Congress.
18. James C. Evans, Counsellor to the Secretary of Defense, Washington, D.C.
19. Colonel Campbell C. Johnson Manuscript Collection, Moorland Room, Founders Library, Howard University, Washington, D.C.
20. Department of the Navy, Office of Information, Washington, D.C.
21. James C. Evans, *loc. cit.*
22. *Ibid.*
23. *Ibid.*
24. *Ibid.*
25. *Ibid.*

# Bibliography

The following Bibliography is based on an exhaustive literature search of available published material, manuscripts, and official records relating to the history of the American black in the military service of the United States from 1775 to 1972. The fullest available information has been given, but where a reference is incomplete, it has been included in the hope that it will still be of use.

Abbott, Abial E. "The Negro in the War of the Rebellion" in *Military Essays and Recollections* 3. Chicago: The Dial Press, 1899.

Adams, J. W. *Letter to the Honorable Secretary of War on the Examination of Field Officers for Colored Troops.* New York: n.p., 1863.

Addeman, J. M. "Reminiscences of Two Years with the Colored Troops." *Personal Narratives of Events in the War of the Rebellion.* Providence, R.I.: N. Bangs Williams & Co., 1880.

Alexander, Charles. *Battles and Victories of Allen Allensworth.* Boston: Sherman, French & Co., 1914.

Alexander, Lawrence A. *A Storm Over Atlanta. The Story of Count D'Estaing and the Siege of the Town in 1779.* Athens, Ga.: University of Georgia Press, 1951.

Allen, Henry T. *The Rhineland Occupation.* Indianapolis: Bobbs-Merrill, 1927.

Allen, M. P. *Battle Lanterns.* New York: Longmans, 1949.

American Battle Monuments Commission. *92nd Division Summary of Operations in the World War.* Washington, D.C.: U.S. Government Printing Office, 1944.

————. *93rd Division Summary of Operations in the World War.* Washington, D.C.: U. S. Government Printing Office, 1944.

Anderson, Osbourne P. *A Voice from Harper's Ferry.* Boston: n.p., 1861.

Anderson, T. W. *Come Out Fighting. The Epic Tale of the 761st Tank Battalion, 1942–45.* Salzburg; Austria: Salzburger Druckerei und Verlag, 1945.

Appleman, Ray E. *United States Army in the Korean War. South to the Natong, North to the Yalu. June–November, 1950.* Washington, D.C.: U.S. Government Printing Office, 1966.

Aptheker, Herbert. *The Negro in the American Revolution.* New York: International Publishers, 1940.

————. *The Negro in the Civil War.* New York: International Publishers, 1938.

Armstrong, William H. "The Negro as a Soldier" in *War Papers.* Indianapolis: Military Order of the Loyal Legion, Indiana Commandery, 1898.

*Army Services Manual M5. Leadership and the Negro Soldier.* Headquarters, Army Service Forces, October, 1944.

Arthur, Stanley C. *The Story of the Battle of New Orleans.* New Orleans: Louisiana Historical Society, 1915.

Baird, George W. *The 32nd Regiment U.S.C.T. at the Battle of Honey Hill.* n.p., 1889.

Baird, Henry C. (Ed.). *George Washington and General Jackson on Negro Soldiers.* Philadelphia: Henry C. Baird, 1863.

Bancroft, George. *History of the Battle of Lake Erie, and Miscellaneous Papers.* New York: Robert Benner's Sons, 1891.

Bangs, T. S. *The Ullman Brigade (In Military Order) of the Loyal Legion of the U.S. Marine Commandery War Papers 2,* pp. 290–310. Portland: n.p., 1902.

Battle, Charles A. *Negroes on the Island of Rhode Island.* Newport: n.p., 1932.

Beatty, John. *The Citizen-Soldier, or Memoirs of a Volunteer.* Cincinnati: Wilstach, Baldwin & Co., 1897.

Bennett, Lerone Jr. *Before the Mayflower: A History of Black America.* Chicago: Johnson Publishing Co., 1961, 1969.

Beyer, Walter F. and Keydel, O. F. *Deeds of Valor.* Perrien Keydel Co., 1903.

Bigalow, John. *Reminiscences of the Santiago Campaign.* New York: Harper Bros., 1899.

*Biographical Directory of the American Congress 1774–1949.* Washington, D.C.: U.S. Government Printing Office, 1950.

Black, Robert C. *Railroads of the Confederacy.* Chapel Hill, N.C.: University of North Carolina Press, 1952.

Bliss, Paul S. *Victory: History of the 805th Pioneer Infantry* . . . St. Paul, Minn.: Augsburg Publishing House, 1919.

Blocksom, Augustus P., et al. *Affray at Brownsville, Texas, August 13 and 14, 1900. Investigation of the Conduct of U.S. Troops* . . . Washington, D.C.: U.S. Government Printing Office, 1906.

Boatner, Mark M. *Encyclopedia of the American Revolution.* New York: D. McKay Co., 1961.

Bogart, Leo, et al. *Social Research and the Desegregation of the U.S. Army.* Chicago: Markham, 1969.

Botken, N. A. *A Civil War Treasury of Tales, Legends, and Folklore.* New York: Random House, 1960.

Bouton, Edward. *Events of the Civil War.* Los Angeles: Kingsley, Moles & Collins, n.d.

Bradfort, J. H. *A Tribute to Tom, or the Servant Question Among the Volunteers.* Washington, D.C.: Military Order of the Loyal Legion of the U.S. Commandery of the District of Columbia, 1895.

Braithwaite, William S. *Story of the Great War (World War II).* Worcester, Mass.: Commonwealth Press, 1928.

Brawley, Benjamin. *Negro Builders and Heroes.* Chapel Hill, N.C.: University of North Carolina Press, 1937.

———. *A Short History of the American Negro.* New York: Macmillan Co., 1931.

Brewer, James H. *The Confederate Negro: Virginia's Craftsmen and Military Laborers, 1861–1865.* Durham, N.C.: Duke University Press, 1969.

Brown, Letitia. *The Negro in the District of Columbia.* New York: Oxford University Press, 1972.

———. *Washington in the New Era, 1870–1970.* Washington, D.C.: Smithsonian Institution, 1972.

———and Lewis, Elsie M. *Washington from Banneker to Douglass, 1791–1870.* Washington, D.C.: Smithsonian Institution, 1972.

Brown, William Wells. *The Negro in the American Rebellion.* Boston: Lee & Shepard, 1867.

———. *The Rising Sun or The History of the Colored Race.* Boston: Little, Brown, 1874.

Browne, Frederick W. *My Services in the U.S. Colored Cavalry.* Cincinnati: Commandery of the Loyal Legion, 1908. (Located in the Library of Congress, Washington, D.C.)

Bryant, Lawrence C. *Negro Senators and Representatives in the South Carolina Legislature, 1868–1902.* Bryant, 1968. (Located in the Library of Congress, Washington, D.C.).

Buck, Irving A. *A Captain Cleburne and his Command.* Jackson, Tenn.: McCowat Press, 1959.

Bullard, Robert Lee. *Personalities and Reminiscences of the War.* Garden City, N.Y.: Doubleday, 1925.

Burchard, Peter. *The Gallant Rush. Robert Gould Shaw and his Brave Black Regiment.* New York: St. Martins Press, 1865.

Burdolph, Richard. *The Negro Vanguard.* New York: Rinehart, 1959.

Burt, Olive W. *Negroes in the Early West.* New York: Julian Messner, 1969.

Butler, Benjamin. *Major General Butler at Home,* n.p., n.d.

———. *Butler's Book.* Boston: A. M. Thayer, 1892.

Cade, John B. *Twenty-Two Months With Uncle Sam.* Atlanta: n.p., 1929.

Califf, J. M. *Record of the Services of the 7th Regiment,* *U.S. Colored Troops from September, 1863 to November, 1866.* Providence: E. L. Freeman, 1878.

Carroll, John M. *The Black Military Experience in the American West.* New York: Liveright, 1971.

Carter, Solon A. "Fourteen Months' Service with Colored Troops" in *Civil War Papers* 1. Boston: Military Order of the Loyal Legion, Massachusetts Commandery, 1900.

Casey, Powell A. *Louisiana in the War of 1812.* Baton Rouge: Powell A. Casey, 1963.

Cashin, Herschel V. *Under Fire With the Tenth U.S. Cavalry.* New York: F. Tennyson Niele, 1899.

Chenery, William H. *The 14th Regiment, Rhode Island, Heavy Artillery (Colored) in the War to Preserve the Union, 1861–1865.* Providence: Snow & Farnham, 1898.

Chew, Abraham and Washington, R. L. *A Biography of Colonel Charles Young.* Washington, D.C.: R. L. Pendleton, 1923.

Christmas, Walter. *Negro Heritage Library.* Yonkers, N.Y.: Educational Heritage, 1966.

Christopher, Maurine. *America's Black Congressmen.* New York: Thomas Y. Crowell, 1971.

*Civil War Official Records of the Union and Confederate Navies in the War of the Rebellion, 1894–1927.* 34 vols. 1927. (Located in National Archives, Washington, D.C.)

*Civil War Papers Read Before the Commandery of the State of Massachusetts Military Order of the Loyal Legion . . .* Boston: n.p., 1900.

Clark, Mark W. *Calculated Risk.* New York: Harper & Bros., 1950.

Clark, Peter H. *The Black Brigade of Cincinnati: Being a Record of Its Labors and a Muster Roll of Its Members . . .* New York: Arno Press, 1970 (first published, 1874).

Clayton, R. *The Aftermath of the Civil War in Arkansas.* New York: n.p., 1915.

Cochrane, John. *Arming the Slaves in the War for the Union.* New York: Rogers & Sherwood, 1875.

Coffin, Charles Carlton. *Four Years of Fighting.* Boston: n.p., 1866.

Commission of the Constitutional League of the U.S. *Preliminary Report of the Commission . . . on the Affray at Brownsville, Texas, August 13 and 14, 1906.* Washington, D.C.: U.S. Government Printing Office, 1906.

*Complete History of the Colored Soldier in the World War.* New York: Bennett & Churchill, n.d.

Cornish, Dudley Taylor: *The Sable Arm, Negro Troops in the Union Army, 1861–1865.* New York: Longmans Green, 1966.

Coston, W. Hilary. *The Spanish-American War Volunteer: 9th U.S. Volunteer Infantry*. Camp Mead, Pa.: W. H. Coston, 1899.

Cowden, Robert. *A Brief Sketch of the Organization and Services of the 59th Regiment of the U.S. Colored Infantry*. Dayton, Ohio: United Brethren Publishing Co., 1883.

Crane, Charles J. *The Experiences of a Colonel of Infantry*. New York: Knickerbocker Press, 1923.

Crowell, Benjamin. *The Spirit of '76 in Rhode Island*. Boston: 1850.

Cullen, Joseph P. *The Concise Illustrated History of the American Revolution*. Gettysburg, Pa.: American History Illustrated, 1972.

Curtis, Mary. *The Black Soldier*. Washington, D.C.: Murray Bros., 1915.

Dalfiume, Richard M. *Desegregation of the U.S. Armed Forces, 1939–1953*. Columbia, Mo.: University of Missouri Press, 1969.

Daniel, John W. *The Power of the President Under the Articles of War. He Has the Right to Discharge a Soldier at Any Time*. Washington, D.C.: n.p., 1907.

David, Jay and Crane, Elaine. *The Black Soldier: From the American Revolution to Vietnam*. New York: William Morrow, 1971.

Davis, John P. (Ed.). *The American Negro Reference Book*. Englewood Cliffs, N.J.: Prentice-Hall, 1966.

Deckard, Percy E. *List of Officers Who Served with the 371st Infantry and Headquarters 186th Infantry Brigade During the World War*. Allegany, N.Y.: The Allegany Citizen, 1929.

Delsante, Walter W. *Negro Democracy and the War*. Detroit: Wolverine Printing Co., 1919.

Dennett, George M. *History of the 9th U.S.C. Troops . . .* Philadelphia: King & Baird, 1866.

Director of Selective Service. *Selective Service in Wartime. 2nd Report, 1941–1952*. Washington, D.C.: U.S. Government Printing Office, 1943.

———. *As the Tide of the War Turns, 3rd Report, 1943–1944*. Washington, D.C.: U.S. Government Printing Office, 1945.

———. *Selective Service and Victory, 4th Report, 1944–45*. Washington, D.C.: U.S. Government Printing Office, 1948.

Dobler, Lavinia and Toppin, Edgar A. *Pioneers and Patriots*. Garden City, N.Y.: Doubleday, 1965.

Downey, Fairfax. *Buffalo Soldiers in the Indian Wars*. New York: McGraw-Hill, 1969.

Drimmer, Melvin (Ed.). *Black History. A Reappraisal*. Garden City, N.Y.: Doubleday, 1968.

Drum, Richard C. and Stafford, Frederick A. (Compilers). *Adjutant's Department Medals of Honor Awarded for Distinguished Service During the War of the Rebellion*. Washington, D.C.: n.p., n.d.

Du Bois, W. E. B. *Black Folk, Then and Now: An Essay in the History and Sociology of the Negro Race*. New York: Henry Holt & Co., 1939.

———. *Black Reconstruction, 1860–1880*. New York: Harcourt, Brace, 1935.

———. *A Select Bibliography of the Negro American*. Atlanta, Ga.: n.p., 1915.

Ebony, Editors of *The Negro Handbook*. Chicago: Johnson Publishing Co., 1966.

Edwards, Frank E. *The '98 Campaign of the Sixth Massachusetts U.S.V.* Boston: Little, Brown, 1899.

Emilio, Luis F. *History of the 54th Regiment of Massachusetts Volunteer Infantry, 1863–1865*. Boston: The Boston Book Co., 1894.

———. *The Assault on Fort Wagner, July 18, 1863. The Memorable Charge of the 54th Regiment of Massachusetts Volunteers, 1863–1865*. Boston: Rand Avery Co., 1887.

Esposito, Vincent J. (Ed.). *West Point Atlas of American Wars, 1689–1900*. New York: Praeger, n.d.

Evans, James C. *Integration in the Armed Services*. Washington, D.C.: U.S. Government Printing Office, 1955.

———. *The Negro in the Army: Policy and Practice. Special Report No. 1–495*. Washington, D.C.: U.S. Government Printing Office, 1948.

Fahy Committee Report. *Freedom to Serve*. Washington, D.C.: U.S. Government Printing Office, 1950.

Fishel, Leslie H. Jr. and Quarles, Benjamin (Eds.). *The Negro American: A Documentary History*. New York: William Morrow, 1967, rev. ed., 1970.

Fleetwood, Christian A. *The Negro as a Soldier*. Washington, D.C.: Howard University Print, 1895.

Fleming, Walter L. *Civil War Reconstruction in Alabama*. New York: Columbia University Press, 1905.

Flipper, Henry O. *Colored Cadet at West Point*. New York: Homer Lee & Co., 1878.

Foley, Albert S. *Beloved Outcasts*. New York: Farrar, Straus, 1954.

———. *God's Men of Color*. New York: Farrar, Straus, 1955.

Foner, Jack D. *The U.S. Soldier Between Two Wars: Army Life and Reforms, 1865–1898*. New York: Humanities Press, 1970.

Fowler, Arlen L. *The Negro Infantry in the West, 1869–1891.* Westport, Conn.: Greenwood, 1971.

*Forty-Fourth Regiment U.S. Colored Troops.* Gettysburg, Pa.: J. E. Wible, 1866.

Fox, William F. *Regimental Losses in the American Civil War.* Albany, N.Y.: n.p., 1889.

Francis, Charles E. *Tuskegee Airmen: The Story of the Negro in the U.S. Air Force.* Boston: Bruce Humphries, 1955.

Frank, E. Edward. *Campaign of the Sixth Massachusetts.* Boston: Little Brown, 1899.

Franklin, John Hope. *From Slavery to Freedom.* 2d rev. ed. New York: Alfred A. Knopf, 1965.

Frazier, E. Franklin, *The Negro in the United States.* New York: The Macmillan Co., 1957.

Freeman, Henry V. "A Colored Brigade in the Campaign and Battle of Nashville" in *Military Essays and Recollections 2.* Chicago: A. McClurg & Co., 1894.

Fuller, T. O. *Pictorial History of the American Negro.* Memphis: Pictorial, 1933.

Funston, Frederick. *Memories of Two Wars.* New York: Scribners, 1914.

Furnas, J. C. *Goodbye to Uncle Tom.* New York: William Sloane, 1956.

Furness, William Elliott. "The Negro as a Soldier" in *Military Essays and Recollections.* Chicago: A. C. McClurg, 1894.

Furr, Arthur. *Democracy's Negroes.* Boston: The House of Edinboro, 1947.

Ganoe, William A. *The History of the U.S. Army.* New York: D. Appleton & Co., 1926.

Garrison, William Lloyd. *The Loyalty and Devotion of Colored Americans in the Revolution and War of 1812.* Boston: n.p., 1851.

Ginzburg, Eli. *The Negro Potential.* New York: Columbia University Press, 1956.

Glass, Edward. *History of the Tenth Cavalry.* Tucson: Acme Printing Co., 1921.

Goode, W. T. *The 8th Illinois.* Blakeley Printing Co., 1899.

Grant, Ulysses S. *Use of the Army in Certain of the Southern States.* Message . . . Ex. Doc. No. 30, 44th Cong., 2d. Sess. New York: Arno Press, 1909 (originally published 1877).

Greene, Lorenzo J. *The Negro in Colonial New England, 1620–1776.* New York: Columbia University Press, 1942.

Guthrie, James M. *Campfires of the Afro-American or Colored Man as Patriot.* Philadelphia: Afro-American Publishing Co., 1899.

Guzman, Jessie Parkhurst. *Negro Year Book: A Review of Events Affecting Negro Life, 1941–1946.* Tuskegee, Ala.: Department of Records and Research, Tuskegee Institute, 1947.

Hallowell, Norwood. *The Negro as a Soldier in the War of the Rebellion.* Boston: Little, Brown, 1897.

Harris, Theodore (Ed.). *Henry O. Flipper, Negro Frontiersmen.* El Paso: Texas Western College Press, 1963.

Harrison, William Henry Jr. *Colored Girls and Boys. Inspiring U.S. History and a Heart to Heart Talk About White Folks.* n.p., 1922.

Hastie, William H. *On Clipped Wings: The Story of Jim Crow in the Army Air Corps.* New York: NAACP, 1943.

Hayes, D. H. *The Colored Man's Part in the War.* Atlanta, Ga.: D. H. Hayes, 1919.

Healy, M. A. *Report of the Cruise of the Revenue Steamer "Corwin" in the Arctic Ocean in the Year of 1884.* Washington, D.C.: U.S. Government Printing Office, 1887.

Henri, Florette. *Bitter Victory: A History of Black Soldiers in World War II.* Garden City, New York: Doubleday, 1970.

Heywood, Chester D. *Negro Combat Troops in the World War: The Story of the 371st Infantry.* Worcester, Mass., Commonwealth Press, 1928.

Higginson, Thomas Wentworth. *Army Life in a Black Regiment.* Boston: n.p., 1870.

Hill, Jim Dan. *The Minute Man in Peace and War. A History of the National Guard.* Harrisburg, Pa.: The Stackpole Co., 1964.

*Historical and Pictorial Review 76th Coast Artillery (AA).* Baton Rouge, La.: Army & Navy Publishing Co., 1941.

*Historical and Pictorial Review 77th Coast Artillery (AA).* Baton Rouge: Army & Navy Publishing Co., 1941.

*Historical and Pictorial Review, 10th Cavalry of the U.S. Army.* Fort Riley, Kans.: n.p., 1941.

*History of the American Negro.* South Carolina Edition, Atlanta, Ga.: A. B. Caldwell, 1919.

Hughes, Langston. *Famous Negro Heroes of America.* New York: Dodd, Nead & Co., 1958.

———— and Meltzer, Milton. *A Pictorial History of the Negro in America.* New York: Crown Publishers, 1956.

Ingraham, Edyth H. *Negroes in the Military Service.* Washington, D.C.: Association for the Study of Negro Life and History, n.d.

Jamison, J. A. *Complete History of the Colored Soldiers in the World War.* New York: Bennett & Churchill, 1919.

Janowitz, Morris. *The Professional Soldier. A Social and Political Portrait.* Glencoe, Ill.: The Free Press, 1960.

Johnson, Edward A. *A School History of the Negro Race in America from 1619 to 1893,* n.p., n.d.

———. *History of Negro Soldiers in the Spanish-American War.* Raleigh, N.C.: Capital Printers & Binders, 1899.

Johnson, Henry H. *The Black Man's Part in the War.* London: Simpkin Marshall, Hamilton, Kent & Co., 1917.

Johnson, Jesse J. (Ed.). *The Black Soldier Documented (1619–1815). Missing Pages in U.S. History.* Hampton, Va.: Jesse J. Johnson, 1969.

———. *Ebony Brass.* New York: William Frederick Press, 1967.

———. *A Pictorial History of Black Soldiers in the United States (1619–1969) in Peace and War.* Hampton, Va.: Jesse J. Johnson, 1970.

Johnson, Kathryn and Hunter, Addie W. *Two Colored Women with the American Expeditionary Forces.* New York: Brooklyn Eagle Press, 1920.

Johnson, Walker H. *With Old Eph in the Army.* By a Soldier from France. Baltimore: R. E. Houck & Co., 1919.

Johnson, William H. *History of the Colored Volunteer Infantry of Virginia, 1871–99.* Richmond: n.p., 1923.

Katz, William L. *Eyewitness: The Negro in American History.* New York: Pitman Publishing Co., 1971.

Kidder, Frederic. *History of the Boston Massacre.* Albany, N.Y.: n.p., 1870.

Killens, John O. *And Then We Heard the Thunder.* New York: Alfred A. Knopf, 1963.

Kindell, Warren F. *Dissertations in History, 1873–1890.* Louisville: University of Kentucky Press, 1965.

Klingberg, Frank J. *An Appraisal of the Negro in Colonial South Carolina.* n.d.

Koger, Bruce A. *The Maryland Negroes in Our Wars.* Maryland: pamphlet, 1942.

Laffin, John. *Women in Battle.* New York: Abelard Schuman, 1967.

Langley, Harold D. *Social Reform in the U.S. Navy, 1798–1967.* Urbana, Ill.: University of Illinois Press, 1967.

Leckie, William H. *The Buffalo Soldiers. A Narrative of the Negro Cavalry in the West.* Norman, Okla.: University of Oklahoma Press, 1967.

Lee, Irvin H. *Negro Medal of Honor Men.* New York: Dodd, Mead & Co., 1967.

Lindenmeyer, Otto. *Black and Brave. The Black Soldier in America.* New York: McGraw-Hill, 1969.

Littler, Arthur W. *From Harlem to the Rhine. The Story of New York's Colored Volunteers.* New York: Orvici Friede, 1936.

Livermore, George. *An Historical Research.* Boston: John Wilson & Sons, 1882.

Logan, Rayford W. *The Negro in the United States.* Princeton: Van Nostrand, 1957.

———. *Howard University. The First Hundred Years, 1867–1967.* New York: New York University Press, 1969.

Lossing, Benson J. *The American Revolution and the War of 1812.* New York: Book Concern, 1875.

———. *The Pictorial Book of the Revolution 2.* New York: n.p., 1860.

Lowell, Louise L. *Israel Angell. Colonel of the 2nd Rhode Island Regiment.* New York: Knickerbocker Press-G. P. Putnam's Sons, 1921.

Lyman, Olin L. *Commodore Oliver Hazard Perry and the War on the Lakes.* New York: New Amsterdam Book Co., 1905.

Lynk, Miles V. *The Black Troopers.* Jackson, Miss.: M. V. Lynk Publishing Co., 1899.

———. *Negro Pictorial History of the Great War.* Memphis, Tenn.: 20th Century Art Co., n.d.

McCarthy, Agnes and and Reddick, Lawrence. *Worth Fighting For. A History of the Negro During the Civil War.* Garden City: Doubleday, 1965.

McConnell, Roland C. *Negro Troops of Antebellum Louisiana.* Baton Rouge: Louisiana State University Press, 1968.

McIntyre, Irwin W. *Colored Soldiers.* Macon, Ga.: Burke, 1923.

Mackenzie, Alex S. *The Life of Commodore Oliver Hazard Perry.* 2 vols. New York: Harper & Bros., 1840.

McPherson, James M. *Marching Toward Freedom. The Negro in the Civil War, 1861–1865.* New York: Alfred A. Knopf, 1968.

———. *The Negroes' Civil War.* New York: Pantheon, 1965.

———. *The Struggle for Equality.* Princeton: Princeton University Press, 1964.

McWilliams, Carey. *Brothers Under the Skin.* Rev. ed. Boston: Little, Brown, 1951.

Madden, Samuel H. *A Brief Consideration of the American Negro Soldiers.* W.P.A. Public Archives Programs, Washington, D.C.: U.S. Government Printing Office, 1942.

Main, E. M. *The Story of the Marches, Battles, and Incidents of the Third U.S. Colored Cavalry, 1861–65.* Louisville, Ky.: Globe Printing Co., 1908.

Mandelbaum, David G. *Soldier Groups and Negro Soldiers.* Berkeley: University of California Press, 1952.

Marshall, S. L. A. *The River and the Gauntlet.* New York: William Morrow, 1953.

Marshall, Thurgood. *Report on Korea.* New York: NAACP, 1951.

Martin, John T. *The Negro in the Armed Forces of the U.S.A.* Washington, D.C.: U.S. Government Printing Office, 1960.

Mason, Monroe and Furr, Arthur. *The American Negro Soldier with the Red Hand of France.* Boston: The Cornhill Co., 1920.

Matson, D. "The Colored Man in the Civil War" in *War Sketches and Incidents* 2. Des Moines: The Kenyon Press, 1898.

Mazyck, Walter B. *George Washington and the Negro.* Washington, D.C.: Associated Publishers, 1932.

*Medal of Honor Record. Issued to the Blue Jackets and Marines of the U.S. Navy, 1862–1888.* Washington, D.C.: U.S. Government Printing Office, 1888.

Meyer, Howard N. *Colonel of the Black Regiment: The Life of Thomas Wentworth Higginson.* New York: W. W. Norton & Co., 1967.

Michigan Adjutant General's Office. *Record of Service of Michigan Volunteers in the Civil War, 1861–1865: First Colored Infantry.* Kalamazoo, Mich.: Michigan Legislature, n.d.

Middleton, Harry J. *The Compact History of the Korean War.* New York: Hawthorn Books, 1966.

*Military Essays and Recollections Read Before the Commandery of the State of Illinois, Military Order of the U.S.* Chicago: n.p., 1894.

Miller, Kelly. *New Pictorial History of the World War for Human Rights . . .* Washington, D.C.: Austin Jenkins, 1919.

Mitchell, Joseph B. *The Badge of Gallantry. Recollections of Civil War Congressional Medal of Honor Winners.* New York: Macmillan Co., 1968.

Moore, Frank. *Diary of the American Revolution.* 2 vols. New York: Charles Scribner's Sons, 1860.

——— (Ed.). *The Rebellion Record. A Diary of American Events.* 11 vols. New York: D. Van Nostrand, 1861–1868.

Moore, George H. *Historical Notes on the Employment of Negroes in the American Army of the Revolution.* New York: Charles T. Evans Co., 1862.

———. *Notes on the History of Slavery in Massachusetts.* New York: Negro Universities Press, 1968. (Originally published, 1866.)

Morgan, Thomas J. "Reminiscences of Services with Colored Troops in the Navy Cumberland, 1863–1865." *Personal Narratives.* . . . Providence: Soldiers & Sailors Historical Society of Rhode Island, 1885.

Mosley, Mrs. Charles C. *The Negro in Mississippi History.* Jackson, Miss.: n.p., 1950.

Moss, James A. *Memories of the Campaign of Santiago.* San Francisco: Mysell-Rollins Co., 1899.

Muller, William G. *The 24th Infantry Past and Present.* n.p., 1923.

NAACP. *Black Heroes of the American Revolution, 1775–1783.* New York: NAACP, n.d.

Nankivell, John H. *History of the 25th Regiment, U.S. Infantry, 1869–1926.* Denver: Smith-Brooks Printing Co., 1927.

National Analysts, Inc. *A Study of Military Athletes Among Negro Males . . .* Washington, D.C.: National Guard Bureau, 1968.

"Negroes in Our Army" in *Southern Historical Society Papers* 31. Richmond, Va.: The Society, 1903.

Nell, William C. *Services of Colored Americans in the Wars of 1776 and 1812.* Boston: Robert F. Wallcut, 1852.

Nelson, Dennis D. *The Integration of the Negro in the U.S. Navy, 1776–1947.* New York: Farrar Straus, 1951.

Newton, A. H. *Out of the Briars. Personal Experiences and Reflections of the Negro 29th Regiment of Connecticut Volunteers.* Philadelphia: AME Book Co., 1910.

Nichols, Lee. *Breakthrough on the Color Front.* N.Y.: Random House, 1954.

*Ninety-Third Division. Summary of Operations.* Washington, D.C.: U.S. Government Printing Office, 1944.

Norton, Henry Allyn. "Colored Troops in the War of the Rebellion" in *Glimpses of the Nation's Struggle* 5. St. Paul, Minn.: Review Publishing Co. 1903.

O'Connor, Thomas H. *Massachusetts in the Civil War.* 3, 5. Boston: Massachusetts Civil War Centennial Commission, 1965.

Office of the Assistant Secretary of Defense. *Integration and the Negro Officer in the Armed Forces of the U.S.A.* Washington, D.C.: U.S. Government Printing Office, 1962.

Officer of the Ninth Corps. *Notes on Colored Troops and Military Colonies on Southern Soil.* New York: n.p., 1863.

O'Reilly. *First Organization of Colored Troops in the State of New York.* n.p., 1864.

**P**almer, Robert R. *et. al. The Procurement and Training of Ground Combat Troops in the Official History of the U.S. Army in World War II.* Washington, D.C.: U.S. Government Printing Office, 1948.

Paynter, John. *Joining the Army.* Hartford, Conn.: American, 1895.

*Personal Narratives of Events in the War of the Rebellion.* Providence, R.I.: Soldiers and Sailors Historical Society of Rhode Island, 1913.

*A Pictorial History of Black America.* Washington, D.C.: United Publishing, 1971.

Pipkin, J. J. *The Negro in Revelation in History and in Citizenship.* St. Louis, Mo.: A. D. Thompson Publishing Co., 1902.

Ploski, Henry and Brown, Roscoe C. *Negro Almanac.* New York: Bellwether Publishing Co., 1967.

Porter, Dorothy B. *The Negro in the U.S.: A Selected Bibliography.* Washington, D.C.: Library of Congress, 1970.

Porter, Kenneth Wiggins. *The Negro on the American Frontier.* New York: Arno Press, 1971.

President's Committee on Equal Opportunity in the Armed Forces. *Freedom to Serve.* Washington, D.C.: U.S. Government Printing Office, 1950.

Purdy, Milton D. and Blockson, Augustus P. *Additional Testimony Relating to the Brownsville Affray . . .* Washington, D.C.: U.S. Government Printing Office, 1907.

**Q**uarles, Benjamin T. *The Negro in the American Revolution.* Durham: University of North Carolina Press, 1967.

———. *The Negro in the Civil War.* Boston: Little, Brown, 1953.

———. *The Negro in the Making of America.* New York: Collier, 1964.

**R**amsberger, Jack F. (Ed.). *Battle History 473rd U.S. Infantry.* n.p., 1945.

Randall, J. G. and Donald, David. *The Civil War and Reconstruction.* Boston: D. C. Heath, 1961.

Raymond, Marcius D. *Colonel Christopher Greene: A Paper Read Before the Sons of the Revolution of New York.* New York: Tarrytown Argus Print, 1902.

*Record of the Service of the 55th Regiment of Massachusetts Volunteer Infantry.* Cambridge: John Wilson, 1968.

*Record of the Service of the 7th Regiment, U.S. Colored Troops.* Providence: E. L. Freeman & Co., 1878.

Redding, Saunders. *The Lonesome Road.* New York: Doubleday, 1958.

Rhodes, James Ford. *History of the United States from the Compromise of 1850.* New York: Macmillan, 1900.

Richard, James H. "Services with the Colored Troops in Burnside's Corps," in *Personal Narratives of Events in the War of the Rebellion.* Providence: Soldiers & Sailors Historical Society of Rhode Island, 1894.

Richardson, Clement. *The National Encyclopedia of the Colored Race.* Montgomery, Ala.: National Publishing Co., 1919.

Rider, Sidney Smith. *An Historical Enquiry Concerning the Attempt to Raise a Regiment of Slaves by Rhode Island During the War of the Revolution.* Providence: Providence Press, 1880.

Roche, John P. *The Quest for the Dream; The Development of Civil Rights and Human Relations in Modern America.* New York: Macmillan, 1963.

Rodenbough, Theodore and Haskin, William L. (Eds.). *The Army of the United States. Historical Sketches of the 9th and 10th Regiments of Cavalry and the 24th and 25th Regiments of Infantry.* New York: Maynard, Merrill & Co., 1896.

Rogers, Helga M. *Africa's Gift to America.* New York: Helga M. Rogers, 1961.

Rollins, Frank A. *The Life of Martin Delaney.* Boston: n.p., 1868.

Romeyer, Henry. *With Colored Troops in the Army of the Cumberland.* Washington, D.C.: Commandery of the District of Columbia, 1904.

Ross, Warner A. *My Colored Battalion.* Chicago: n.p., 1920.

Russell J. H. *The Free Negro in Virginia.* Baltimore: Johns Hopkins Press, 1913.

Russell, L. Adams. *Great Negroes Past and Present.* Chicago: Afro-American, 1963.

**S**choenfeld, Seymour J. *The Negro in the Armed Forces.* Washington, D.C.: Associated Publishers, 1945.

Schofield, John M. *Forty-Six Years in the Army.* New York: The Century Co., 1897.

Scott, Emmet J. *Official History of the American Negro in the World War.*

Sefton, James E. *The U.S. Army and Reconstruction, 1865–1877.* Baton Rouge, La.: Louisiana State University Press, 1967.

Sexton, William T. *Soldiers in the Sun: An Adventure in Imperialism.* Harrisburg Pa.: Military Service Publishing Co., 1939.

Sher, Ronald. *Integration of the Negro in the U.S. Army, Europe. 1952–1954.* Historical Division, HQ, USAREUR, 1950.

Sherman, George. "The Negro As a Soldier," *Personal Narratives.* . . . 7th ser. Providence: Soldiers & Sailors Historical Society of Rhode Island, 1913.

Silvera, John D. *The Negro in World War II.* New York: Arno Press, 1969.

Singletary, Otis A. *Negro Militia and Reconstruction.* New York: McGraw-Hill, 1957.

Smith, Clarence M. *The Technical Services: The Medical Department, Hospitalization and Evacuation Zone of Interior.* Washington, D.C.: U.S. Government Printing Office, 1956.

*"Smoked Yankees" and the Struggle for Empire: Letters from Negro Soldiers, 1898–1902.* Urbana: University of Illinois Press, 1971.

Snow, Edward R. *True Tales and Curious Legends.* New York: Dodd, Mead & Co., 1969.

Spooner, John C. *Dismissal of Three Companies of 25th Infantry.* Washington, D.C.: U.S. Government Printing Office, 1907.

Staples, Thomas S. *Reconstruction in America.* Gloucester Press, 1964.

Starr, Chester G. *et al. Salerno to the Alpa. A History of the Fifth Army.* 9 vols. Washington, D.C., n.p., n.d.

Stauffer, S. A. *The American Soldier.* Princeton: Princeton University Press, 1949.

Steward, T. G. *The Colored Regulars in the U.S. Army.* Philadelphia: A.M.E. Church Press, 1904.

Stewart, Robert Armstead. *The History of Virginia's Navy of the Revolution.* Richmond, Va.: n.p., n.d.

Stillman, Richard J. II. *Integration of the Negro in the U.S. Armed Forces.* New York: Praeger, 1968.

Stouffer, Samuel A. *et al. The American Soldier.* 4 vols. Princeton: N.J., 1949.

*Summary Discharge or Mustering Out of Regiments or Companies. Message from the President of the U.S. Transmitting a Report from the Secretary of War.* Doc. No. 155, 59th Cong., 2d Session. Washington D.C.: U.S. Government Printing Office, 1907.

Sutherland, G. E. *Negro in the Late War. In Military*

*Order of the Loyal Legion of the U.S.* Milwaukee: Wisconsin Commission War Papers, 1891.

Sweeney, W. *History of the American Negro in the Great World War.* G. G. Sapp, 1919.

Taggart, John H. *Free Military School for Applicants for Command of Colored Troops.* Philadelphia: King & Baird, 1864.

Taylor, A. *The Negro in South Carolina During the Reconstruction.* New York: Russell & Russell, 1969.

Taylor, C. M. *Memorials of Lieutenant George W. Walcott.* Boston: Sabbath School Society, 1865.

Taylor, Susie King. *Reminiscences of My Life in Camp.* Boston: 1902.

Theus, Lucius. *Education Program in Race Relations.* Washington, D.C.: U.S. Government Printing Office July, 1970.

Thompson, Charles. "The American Negro in World War I and II" in *The Journal of Negro Education Yearbook* 3, no. 12. Washington, D.C.: Howard University Press, 1943.

*Three Hundred and Seventy-Second Infantry Regiment U.S. Army, Fort Huachuca, Arizona.* Baton Rouge: Army & Navy Publishing Co., 1945.

Tindall, George Brown. *South Carolina Negroes, 1877–1900.* Columbia, S.C.: University of South Carolina Press, 1952.

Tompkins, Frank. *Chasing Villa.* Harrisburg, Pa.: n.p., 1934.

Toppin, Edgar A. *Blacks in America Then and Now.* Christian Science Monitor Reprints, 1969.

Trudeau, Arthur G. "Army Experiences and Problems of Negro Education" in *Education for Victory* 3 (April 20, 1845).

Tucker, Roger. *The Negro in World War II.* n.p., 1945.

Turner, Edward R. *The Negro in Pennsylvania.* n.p., n.d.

*Twenty-Fourth Infantry Organization Day Exercises, 71st Aniversary.* Fort Benning, Ga.: 24th U.S. Infantry, 1940.

Ulman, Daniel A. *The Organization of Colored Troops* (Before the Soldiers and Sailors Union of the State of New York). Washington, D.C.: 1868.

U.S. Army Court of Enquiry. *Companies B, C and D 25th U.S. Infantry: Report of the Proceedings of the Court of Enquiry . . .* 12 vols. Sen. Doc. No. 701, 61st Cong., 3rd Sess. Washington, D.C.: n.p., 1911.

U.S. Army, Department of Texas. *Affray at Brownsville, Texas, August 13 and 14, 1906. Proceedings of a General Court-Martial . . . April 15, 1906 in the Case of Captain Edgar A. Macklin* . . . Washington, D.C. U.S. Government Printing Office, 1907.

———. *Affray at Brownsville, Texas, August 13 and 14, 1906. Proceedings of a General Court-Martial . . . February 4, 1907 in the Case of Major Charles W. Penrose* . . . Washington, D.C.: U.S. Government Printing Office, 1907.

———, Inspector-General. *The Brownsville Affray: Report of the Inspector-General.* Sen. Doc. No. 389 60th Cong., 1st sess. Washington, D.C.: U.S. Government Printing Office, 1908.

———, Historical Division. *U.S. Army in the World (War), 1917–1919.* 17 vols. Washington, D.C.: U.S. Government Printing Office, 1948.

———, Service Forces. *Leadership and the Negro Soldier: Army Service Forces Manual M5.* Washington, D.C.: U.S. Government Printing Office, 1944.

U.S. Bureau of Naval Personnel. *The Negro in the Navy, U.S. Naval Administration in World War II.* Washington, D.C.: U.S. Government Printing Office, 1947.

U.S. Commission on Civil Rights, South Dakota. *Advisory Committee Report.* Washington, D.C.: U.S. Government Printing Office, 1963.

U.S. Congress Senate Committee on Military Affairs. *Affray of Brownsville Texas. Hearings* . . . 3 vols. Washington, D.C.: U.S. Government Printing Office, 1907.

———. *The Brownsville Affray. Report* Sen. Doc. No. 355. 60th Cong. 1st Sess. Washington, D.C.: U.S. Government Printing Office, 1907.

U.S. Department of Defense. *The Black Man in America. A Working Bibliography for Armed Forces Personnel.* Washington, D.C.: Phototype, n.d.

U.S. Naval History Division. *Naval Documents of the American Revolution.* Washington, D.C.: U.S. Government Printing Office, 1964.

U.S. Office of Naval Records. *Official Records of the Union and the Confederate Navies in the War of the Rebellion.* Washington, D.C.: U.S. Government Printing Office, 1894–1922.

———. *Naval Documents Related to the U.S. Wars with the Barbary Power.* Washington, D.C.: U.S. Government Printing Office, 1939–44.

U.S. War Department. *Command of Negro Troops.* Pamphlet No. 20–6. Washington, D.C.: U.S. Government Printing Office, 1944.

———. *Names of Enlisted Men Discharged on Account of Brownsville Affray with Application for Reenlistment: Letter from Acting Secretary of War* . . . Sen. Doc. No. 430, 60th Cong. 1st Sess.

Washington, D.C.: U.S. Government Printing Office, 1908.

———. *The War of the Rebellion, a Compilation of the Official Records of the Union and Confederate Armies.* 128 vols. Washington, D.C.: U.S. Government Printing Office, 1880–1901.

———. Second Military District Military Commission. *Proceedings in the Case of the U.S. Against Duncan G. McRae . . . for the Murder of Archibald Beebee at Fayetteville, N.C., on the 11th Day of February, 1867.* Raleigh, N.C.: Robert Avery, 1867.

———. *Infantry Tactics . . . for the Use of Colored Troops.* New York: D. Van Nostrand, 1863.

*Utilization of Negro Manpower in the Post-War Army Policy.* Army Circular No. 24. Washington, D.C. U.S. Government Printing Office, April 27, 1946.

Utley, Robert M. *Fort Davis, National Historic Site, Texas.* Washington, D.C.: National Park Service, 1965.

**V**andercook, John W. *Black Majesty: The Life of Christophe.* New York: Harper, 1928.

Voegeli, V. Jacques. *Free But Not Equal: The Midwest and the Negro During the Civil War.* Chicago: University of Chicago Press, 1967.

**W**akin, Edward. *Black Fighting Men vs. History.* New York: Lothrop, Lee and Shepard, 1970.

Wallace, Lew *et al. The Story of American Heroism . . . During the Great Civil War as Told by the Medal Winners and Roll of Honor Men.* New Haven: Butler & Alger, 1896.

Washington, Booker T. *The Colored Soldier in the Spanish-American War.* Chicago: Chicago Library and Publications Commission, 1899.

Weaver, William G. *Yankee Doodle Dandy.* Ann Arbor, Mich.: Edwards Bros., 1958.

Wesley, Charles H. *Collapse of the Confederacy.* Russell, 1968.

———. *Ohio Negroes in the Civil War.* Columbus, Ohio: Ohio State University Press, 1962.

——— and Romero, Patricia W. *Negro Americans in the Civil War.* Washington, D.C.: Russell, 1967.

Wharfield, H. B. *Tenth Cavalry and Border Fights.* El Cajon, Calif.: H. B. Wharfield, 1965.

White, Walter. *A Rising Wind. Report on Negro Troops in World War II.* Garden City, N.Y.: Doubleday, 1945.

Whitman, S. E. *The Troopers, An Informal History of the Plains Cavalry, 1865–1890.* New York: n.p., 1962.

Wiley, Bell Irvin. *Southern Negroes, 1861–1865*. New Haven: Yale University Press, 1965 (originally published 1938).

Williams, Charles H. *Sidelights on Negro Soldiers*. Boston: B. J. Brimmer Co., 1923.

Williams, George W. *History of the Negro Race in America*. 1 and 2. New York: G. P. Putnam & Sons, 1883.

——. *History of the Negro Troops in the War of the Rebellion, 1861–1865*. New York: Harper & Bros., 1888.

Wilson, Joseph T. *The Black Phalanx*. Hartford, Conn.: American Publishing Co., 1890.

Wilson, Ruth D. *Jim Crow Joins Up*. New York: William J. Clark, 1944.

Woodson, Carter G. *Negro Makers of History*. Washington, D.C.: Associated Publishers, 1927.

—— and Wesley, Charles H. *The Negro in Our History*. Washington, D.C.: Associated Publishers, 1966.

Woodward, C. Vann. *Strange Career of Jim Crow*. New York: Oxford University Press, 1966.

Woodward, Elon A. *The Negro in the Military Service of the U.S. 1639–1886*. 8 vols. Washington, D.C.: Adjutant General's Office, 1888. (National Archives Microcopy T0823.)

Work, Monroe (Ed.) *Negro Year Book: An Annual Encyclopedia of the Negro, 1937–1938*. Tuskegee: Negro Year Book Publishing Co., 1937.

Wright, James M. *The Free Negro in Maryland*. New York: Columbia University Press, 1921.

Yancey, Francis. *This Is Our War*, Chicago: Afro-American Company, 1945.

### Periodicals and Newspapers

*Afro-American Newspaper,* September 3, 1968, article on Medal of Honor Winner PFC William Thompson.

*Air Force and Space Digest,* February, 1969, "Filling the Military's 'Heritage Gap'" by George W. Boyd.

*Airman* 15, August, 1971, "Brotherhood is the Name of the Game" by Robert P. Everett.

*American History Illustrated* 4, January, 1970, "A Black Man in the Long Gray Line" by Ezra J. Warner.

*American West* 9. January, 1972, "Court Martial of Henry O. Flipper" by Bruce J. Dinges.

*Armed Forces Journal,* November 30, 1968, "It Boils Down to Management of Resources" by John W. Carpenter III.

——, August 10, 1968, "Negro Progress in the Armed Forces."

——, November 30, 1968, "Moskowitz Cites Negro Progress, Problems."

*Armed Forces Management,* June, 1970, "Black vs. White" by C. V. Glines.

*Army Digest,* January, 1969, "War Heroes and Captain Leroy Pitts, U.S. Medal of Honor (posthumous)."

——, July, 1968, "Negro Army Heritage."

——, August, 1966, "Racial Integration in the Army."

*Army Magazine* 18, November 22, 1968, "Meeting the Challenge of a Changing World" by Stanley R. Resor.

——, December, 1969, "Attracting and Keeping the Black Career Officer."

*Atlantic* 91, June, 1903, "The Negro in the Regular Army" by Oswald Garrison Villard.

*Canadian Military Gazette* 46, October 27, 1931, "Crossing the Color Line" by Caleb Johnson.

*Cavalry Journal* 6, December, 1906, "Some Indian Experiences," by Richard A. Pratt.

*Century Magazine,* April, 1889, "A Scout with the Buffalo Soldiers" by Frederic Remington.

—— 34 (1887), "The Colored Troops at St. Petersburg."

*Chicago History,* Summer, 1961, "Blacks in Blue."

*Chronicles of Oklahoma* 47, Spring, 1969, "Negro Troop Activity in Indian Territory" by Larry C. Rampp.

*Civil War History,* 17, December, 1971, "The 'Father of Black Nationalism': Another Contender" by Floyd J. Miller.

*Coast Artillery Journal* 88, May-June, 1945, "Service with Colored AAA Troops in New Guinea" by John H. Jemison and James A. Taylor Jr.

*Colliers Weekly,* April 27, 1918, "Making Soldiers in Dixie."

*Colored American Magazine* 1, May, 1900, "Company 'L' in the Spanish-American War" by George H. Braxton.

—— 1, June, 1900, "The Eighth Illinois, U.S.V." by Charles W. Hall.

———— 5, May, 1902, "The Enlisted Man in Action or the Colored American Soldier in the Philippines" by Rienzi B. Lemus.

*Commanders Digest* 11, January 20, 1972, "Solving Racial Problems is Challenge to Armed Services" by John H. Chafee.

*Congressional Record* 56, part 12, 1918, appendix, 65th Congress, 2nd session, "A Tribute for the Negro Soldier" by John E. Bruce.

*Cornet,* June, 1960, "What the Armed Forces Taught Us About Integration" by Morton Puner.

*Cosmopolitan,* February, 1897, "Vagabonding with the Tenth Horse" by Frederic Remington.

*Crisis,* August, 1918, "The Looking Glass; Over There."

————, March, 1919, "The Black Man in the Revolution of 1914–1918."

————, June, 1919, "An Essay Toward a History of the Black Man in the Great War," by W. E. B. Du Bois.

*Current History,* December, 1919, "The Negro in the War: How French and American Black Troops Performed Deeds of Valor on Many Battlefields."

*Ebony,* October, 1946, "Germany Meets the Negro Soldier."

————, January, 1965, "Guardian of Western Coastline, Lt. Cdr. George I. Thompson."

————, June, 1966, "Bugle Call for Negro Cadets."

———— Special Issue, August, 1968, "The Black Soldier."

————, October, 1969, "Master of Sir Defense: J. J. Kelly."

*Education for Victory* 3, April 20, 1945, "Army Experiences and Problems of Negro Education" by Arthur G. Trudeau.

*Field Artillery Journal* 36, April, 1946, "Negro Artillery in World War II."

*Florida Historical Quarterly* 49, July, 1970, "Negro Troops in Florida, 1898" by Willard B. Gatewood Jr.

*Freedomways,* Summer, 1961, "Negroes in the American Revolution."

*The Freeman* (Indianapolis), October 13, 1900.

*Frontier Times* 4, April, 1927, "A Trooper of the Ninth Cavalry."

*Harpers Magazine,* April, 1946, "Report on the Negro Soldier" by Warman Welliver."

*Harpers Weekly,* March 28, 1885, "Oklahoma."

————, August 21, 1886, "Our Soldiers in the Southwest."

————, December 22, 1889, "Practice Maneuvers in Arizona."

*Harvard Crimson* (1970), "Integration in the Armed Forces" by Stephen A. Sylvester.

*The Historian* 29, August, 1967, "The Recruitment of Colored Troops in Kentucky, Maryland and Missouri" by John W. Blassingame.

*Historical Society Quarterly Bulletin* 8, 1930, "Negroes in the Revolutionary War, West Chester County" by William S. Hadaway.

*Illustrated Review,* n.d., "Ninth Cavalry USA, Fort D. A. Russell, Wyoming."

*The Independent* 54, February 13, 1902, "Race Discrimination in the Philippines."

*The Independent and Harpers Weekly,* March 15, 1919, "With This Black Man's Army."

*Infantry Journal,* December, 1946, "Report on the Negro Soldier" by Robert F. Cocklin.

————, (1947), "Negro Soldiers in Combat" by Charles B. McDonald.

*International Military Digest,* March, 1919, "The Negro Officer."

*International Review* 9, November, 1880, "West Point and the Colored Cadet" by George L. Andrews.

*Journal of American History* 143, 1911, "Negroes in the American Revolution."

*Journal of Cavalrymen,* January, 197?, "The Cavalry Fight at Carrizal," by Lewis S. Morey.

*Journal of the Military Service Institutions of the U.S.* 13, January, 1892, "10th Regiment of Cavalry" by John Bigelow Jr.

———— 29, July, 1901, "The Negro Volunteer: Some Characteristics" by R. L. Bullard.

*Journal of Negro Education* 12, Summer, 1943, "The Negro in the Armed Forces of the U.S. Prior to World War I" by Horace Mann Bond.

*Journal of Negro History,* April, 1916, "The Negro Soldiers in the American Revolution" by W. B. Hartgrove.

————, July, 1919, "Negro Soldiers in the Confederate Army."

————, 1940, "The Negro in the Westward Movement" by W. Sherman Savage.

———— July, 1942, "Virginia Negro Soldiers and Seamen in the American Revolution" by Luther P. Jackson.

———— 31, January, 1946, "George Washington Williams, Historian" by John Hope Franklin.

—— 32, April, 1947, "The Negro in the Union Navy" by Herbert Aptheker.

—— 32, April, 1947, "The Negro in the U.S. Navy During World War II."

—— 33, July, 1948, "Isaiah Dorman and the Punitive Expedition."

—— 35, January, 1949, "The Negro Policy of the U.S. Army, 1775–1945" by L. D. Reddick.

——, July, 1951, "Negroes and the Seminole War, 1817–1818" by Kenneth W. Porter.

——, April, 1952, "Some Observations in the Black Regiment of Rhode Island in the American Revolution" by Lorenzo J. Greene.

——, October, 1952, "Pennsylvania Negro Regiments in the Civil War" by Frederick M. Binder.

—— 38, October, 1953, "Emigres and Militiamen: Free Persons of Color in New Orleans, 1803–1815" by Donald E. Everett.

—— 22, October, 1956, "The Role of Negro Soldiers in Protecting the Indian Frontier from Intruders" by W. Sherman.

——, July, 1960, "The Significance of Milliken's Bend in the Civil War" by Martha M. Begelow.

*Journal of the West* 7, April, 1968, "The Negro Soldiers on the Frontier: A Fort Davis Case Study" by Erwin N. Thompson.

*Literary Digest,* January 18, 1919, "Croix de Guerre and Rare Praise for American Negro Troops."

*Magazine of History* 5, August-November, 1909 and January-March, 1910, "Negro Soldiers in the U.S. Army" by Paul T. Arnold.

—— 18, Autumn, 1968, "The Affair at Carrizal" by H. B. Wharfield.

*Maryland Historical Magazine* 67 (1963), "The Recruitment of Negro Troops in Maryland" by John W. Blassingame.

*The Messenger,* September, 1919, "The Failure of the Ninety-Second Division."

*Midwest Journal* 4, Winter 1951–1952, "Opposition of Negro Newspapers to American Philippine Policy, 1899–1900" by George P. Marks.

*Military Affairs* 35, October, 1971, "West Point and the First Negro Cadet" by William P. Vaughn.

*Military Review* 50, July, 1970, "Race Relations in the Army" by James S. White.

*Mississippi Valley Historical Review* 45, March, 1959, "The Colonial Militia and Negro Manpower" by Benjamin Quarles.

*The Nation* 112, March 9, 1921, "The Black Troops on the Rhine."

*Naval War College Review* 22, January, 1970, "Constraints of the Negro Civil Rights Movement on American Military Effectiveness: A Survey" by George L. Jackson.

*Negro History Bulletin* (1949), "Forgotten Abolishment" by R. A. Burlington and James Forten.

—— (1958), "Social Status of the Free Negro in Antebellum Georgia."

——, March, 1951, "The Negro in the Armed Forces of the U.S., 1619–1783" by Lorenze Greene.

*New Republic,* January 18, 1969, "Whites Against Blacks in Vietnam" by Z. B. Grant.

*North American Review* 186, June, 1907, "The Negro Soldier in War and Peace" by Stephen Bonsal.

*North Carolina Historical Review* 48, October, 1971, North Carolina's Negro Regiment in the Spanish-American War" by Willard B. Gatewood Jr.

*Ordnance Notes No. 232,* November 20, 1882, "Some Considerations Respecting Desertion in the Army." (UF7a15).

*Outlook,* February 26, 1919, "Honor to Whom Honor Is Due."

*Science and Society,* December, 1961, "The Negro and the American Civil War" by W. E. B. Du Bois.

*Scribners Magazine,* April, 1899, "Roosevelt."

*Southern Bivouac,* February, 1886, "The Defense of Fort Wagner" by Paul Hamilton Hayne.

*Survey Graphic,* January, 1947, "The Negro in the Armed Forces" by Charles Dollars and Donald Young.

*Time Magazine,* 89, May 26, 1967, "Democracy in the Foxhole."

—— 44, October 2, 1944, "Mutiny on Mare Island."

*Tuesday Magazine,* July and August, 1970, "The Buffalo Soldiers" by Philip St. Laurent.

*U.S. Cavalry Journal,* December, 1897, "Tenth Cavalry, 1867–1897."

——, December, 1906, "Some Indian Experiences" by Richard H. Pratt.

——, October, 1916, "The Tenth Cavalry in Mexico" by O. C. Troxel.

U.S. Naval Institute Proceedings 97, April, 1971, "Command Leadership and the Black Serviceman" by Howard L. Bennett.

*Washington Post,* May 26, 1928, "One Out of the Twelve Million" by E. H. Lawson.

*Wilson Bulletin for Librarians,* June, 1932, "The Negro Veteran and His Books" by S. P. Delaney.

*World Today* 12, March, 1907, "The Negro as an American Soldier" by William H. Head.

*Yank, The Army Weekly* 3, September 29, 1944, "Negro Strength."

## Documents and Unpublished Manuscripts

Columbia University. Conservation of Human Resources Division Research Project. "Family Life and Military Desegregation" by Quentin B. Ridgley.

Falls Church, Virginia. "Negro Regulars in the American Army: An Indian Wars Combat Record.

Georgetown University. "The Early Career of General John J. Pershing, 1860–1903."

George Washington University. "Negro in U.S. History: The Revolt of the Evil Forces" by Victor Kavy.

Howard University, Founders Library, Moorland Room.

"The Organization and Use of Troops in the Union Army, 1861" by John W. Blassingame.

"History of the 75th U.S. Colored Infantry Regiment" by Mary Francis Berry.

"A Defence of Colored Soldiers in France" by John E. Bruce.

"Opinions of Early Presidents Upon Negroes as Men and Soldiers" by W. C. Bryant & Co.

"Colonel Charles Young, Soldier and Diplomat" by Robert E. Greene, M.A. thesis.

"The Light and the Dark of the Negro Reflection" by Charles E. Lester.

"Sketch of the Discharges from Companies B and D, 25th Infantry Regiment" by Henry Cabot Lodge.

"The Negro in the Confederacy, 1861–1865," a dissertation by Bernard H. Nelson, May 15, 1935.

"The Colonial Militia and Negro Manpower" by Benjamin Quarles.

"Pictures of the Civil War" by William Russell.

"Colored Soldiers in France" by Edward L. Sayler.

Lehigh University. "Negroes in the U.S. Navy, 1861–1865" by Donald L. Valuska.

Louisiana State University. "The Afro-American in the Civil War" by C. Peter Ripley.

Maxwell Air Force Base, Alabama, Air University. "The Segregation of Negroes in the Army Air Forces" by Noel F. Parrish, May, 1947.

"The Other War" by Charles W. Kinney, April, 1970.

Morgan State College. "ROTC and the Negro College Student" ROTC Staff Study.

National Archives, Washington, D.C. Adjutant General's Muster and Pay Roll Volunteers of Louisiana, 1814–1815.

"Historical Sketch, Tenth U.S. Cavalry, 1868–1892," U.S. Army Commander, R.G. 98.

New Britain High School, New Britain, Conn. "Desegregation of the Negro in the Military from World War III Forward" Student Project by Richard Pinkerton *et al.*

Notre Dame University. "Stratification and Minority Group Ideology: Black Soldiers' Belief About Military Opportunities" by Kathlein M. Weigert, Ph.D. dissertation.

Rice University. "Behind the Sheltering Bomb: Military Indecision from Almagordo to Korea" by Noel F. Parrish.

Shippenburg State College. "The Negro Soldier in the Spanish-American War" by Gerald H. Early, M.A. thesis, August, 1970.

Tufts University. "Integration Transition in the U.S. Armed Services, 1948–54" by Alan L. Gropman, Ph.D. dissertation, 1971.

U.S. Army Military Information Division. "Handbook of Creole as Spoken in Hayti" by Charles Young, July 27, 1905.

U.S. Army War College Files, Washington, D.C. "Social Attitudes of American Generals, 1898–1940" by Richard Carl Brown, Ph.D. thesis, Microfilm D-13 nr. 6.

U.S. Army War College, Carlisle Barracks, Pa.

"Books of Help in the Leadership of Negro Troops."

"Review of the Present Status of Armed Forces Integration" by Harry W. Brooks.

"The Gathering Storm: An Analysis of Racial Instability Within the Army" by Harry W. Brooks and James Miller" March 9, 1970.

Class of 1919–1920, Intelligence Course, Committee 31. "Summary of the Estimate on the U.S., Part 3, Military Situation" October 21, 1919.

Class of 1920–1921, Training Course, Committee 7. "Organization, Training and Military Use of Negroes" May 2, 1921.

Class of 1924–25, G-1 Course, Committee 1. "Estimate of the Military Manpower of the U.S." October 15, 1924.

Class of 1924–25, G-1 Course, Committee 7. "Investigation and Formulation of Basic Principles on The Employment of Negro Manpower in War" December 20, 1924.

Class of 1931–1932. G-1 Course. Committee 3, Subcommittee 1. "The Use of Negro Manpower in War and Recommendations for its Use in a Future War" October 20, 1931.

Class of 1932–1933. G-1 Course. Committee 3. "Manpower" October 20, 1932.

Class of 1933–1934, G-1 Course, Committee 2, Subcommittee 3. "Use of Negro Manpower" October 18, 1933.

Class of 1934–1935, G-1 Course, Committee 2, Subcommittee 2. "Study and Report on the War Department Plans and Policies for the Use of Negro Manpower in War" October 27, 1934.

Class of 1935–1936, G-1 Course, Committee 2, Subcommittee 2 "Negro Manpower in War" October 15, 1935.

Class of 1937–1938, G-1 Course, Committee 1. "Manpower" November 12, 1937.

Class of 1938–1939, G-1 Course. Committee 1, Subcommittee 3. "Manpower in Continental U.S." October 28, 1938.

Class of 1939–1940, G-1 Course, Committee 1, Subcommittee 2. "Utilization of Manpower" October 31, 1939.

"Combat Experience of Negro Troop Units" Memo for Chief of Staff, Army Ground Forces. March 9, 1944.

"National Survival—Racial Imperative" by Louis O. Giuffrida.

"The Colored Soldier in the U.S. Army" 1942.

"The Ninth Regiment of Cavalry" by Grote Hutchenson."

"Negro Combat Potential Past and Future in the U.S. Army" by Rucgard H. Maeder, March 1, 1965.

"The Use in Battle of Allies, Auxiliaries, Colored Troops, and Troops Raised in the Insular Possessions" by S. C. Vestal, April 30, 1924.

U.S. Navy, Bureau of Naval Personnel, Historical Section. "The Negro in the Navy," Office of Naval Records and Library. "Navy Services of Negroes, U.S. Navy" December 10, 1924.

University of Georgia. "The Negro-American and World War I" by Vincent L. Sexton.

University of Illinois. "The Military Reenlistment Incentives Among Black Americans" by Frederik J. Horne, 1970.

University of Maryland. "The Negro Soldier in the Spanish-American War" by Ted Samuelson.

"Generals and Negroes: Education of Negroes by the Union Army, 1861–1865" by Robert Stanley, 1965.

University of Michigan. "The Negro Soldier Movement and the Adoption of National Conscription 1652–1865" by Mary Frances Berry, Ph.D. dissertation, 1966.

"The Civilian Conservation Corps: The Role of the Army" by Charles W. Johnson, Ph.D. dissertation.

University of North Carolina. "Federal Troops in the South Atlantic States During Reconstruction 1865–1877" by John Robert Kirkland, 1967.

University of Virginia. "The First World War and the American Negro" by Carl S. Mathews.

University of Wisconsin. "Social Attitudes of American Generals, 1898–1940" by Richard Carl Brown, Ph.D. thesis, 1961.

"The Negro Soldier and the U.S. Army, 1891–1917" by Marvin E. Fletcher, Ph.D. thesis, 1969.

"The Military and the Melting Pot: The American Army and Minority Groups, 1865–1924" by William Bruce White, Ph.D. dissertation, 1968.

Washington State University. "The Negro Infantry in the West, 1869–1891" by Arlen Lowery Fowler, dissertation, 1968.

Western Reserve University. "American Negro Combat Soldiers in World War I" by William F. Fleming.

# INDEX OF NAMES*

*Since the purpose of this book has been to identify and authenticate black Americans who have served their country since pre-Revolutionary times, this is a name index only. The events covered are summarized at the beginning of each chapter